CEYLON

AN ACCOUNT OF THE ISLAND

PHYSICAL, HISTORICAL, AND TOPOGRAPHICAL

WITH NOTICES OF ITS
NATURAL HISTORY, ANTIQUITIES, AND PRODUCTION

CEYLON

AN ACCOUNT OF THE ISLAND

PHYSICAL, HISTORICAL, AND TOPOGRAPHICAL

WITH NOTICES OF ITS
NATURAL HISTORY, ANTIQUITIES, AND PRODUCTION

JAMES EMERSON TENNENT

ILLUSTRATED BY MAPS, PLANS, AND DRAWINGS

IN 2 VOLUMES
VOLUME TWO

ISBN : 978-93-5324-389-0 (Set)

ISBN : 978-93-5324-391-3 Vol. 2 (HB)

First Published, London, 1859

Published, 2020

Published by

Facsimile Publisher
12 Pragati Market
Ashok Vihar, Ph-2
Delhi-110052
E-mail: books@facsimilepublisher.com

Printed at: G. Print Process, Delhi.

CEYLON

An Account of the Island
Physical, Historical, and Topographical
With Notices of Its
Natural History, Antiquities, and Production

Author: James Emerson Tennent

CEYLON

AN ACCOUNT OF THE ISLAND

PHYSICAL, HISTORICAL, AND TOPOGRAPHICAL

WITH

NOTICES OF ITS NATURAL HISTORY, ANTIQUITIES AND PRODUCTIONS

BY

SIR JAMES EMERSON TENNENT, K.C.S. LL.D. &c.

ILLUSTRATED BY MAPS, PLANS, AND DRAWINGS

SECOND EDITION

VOLUME II.

LONDON

LONGMAN, GREEN, LONGMAN, AND ROBERTS

1859

ELEPHANTS CAPTURED IN A CORRAL.—Vol. 2 p. 37[illegible].

Frontispiece for Vol. 2

CONTENTS

OF

THE SECOND VOLUME.

PART VI.

MODERN HISTORY.

CHAPTER I.

THE PORTUGUESE IN CEYLON.

CHAP. II.

THE DUTCH IN CEYLON.

CHAP. III.

ENGLISH PERIOD.

PART VII.

SOUTHERN AND CENTRAL PROVINCES.

CHAPTER I.

POINT DE GALLE.

CHAP. V.

KANDY — PAREDENIA.

CHAP. VI.

GAMPOLA AND THE COFFEE DISTRICTS.

CHAP. VII.

PUSILAWA AND NEUERA-ELLIA.

PART VIII.

THE ELEPHANT.

CHAPTER I.

STRUCTURE.

CHAP. II.

HABITS.

CHAP. III.

ELEPHANT SHOOTING.

CHAP. IV.

AN ELEPHANT CORRAL.

CHAP. V.

THE CAPTIVES.

CHAP. VI.

CONDUCT IN CAPTIVITY.

PART IX.

THE NORTHERN FORESTS.

CHAPTER I.

FOREST TRAVELLING IN CEYLON.

CHAP. II.

BINTENNE — THE MAHAWELLI-GANGA — THE ANCIENT TANKS.

PART X.

THE RUINED CITIES.

CHAPTER I.

SIGIRI AND POLLANARUA.

CHAP. II.

THE TANK OF MINERY.—ANARAJAPOORA, AND THE WEST COAST.

ILLUSTRATIONS IN THE SECOND VOLUME.

MAPS.

PLANS AND CHARTS.

WOOD ENGRAVINGS.

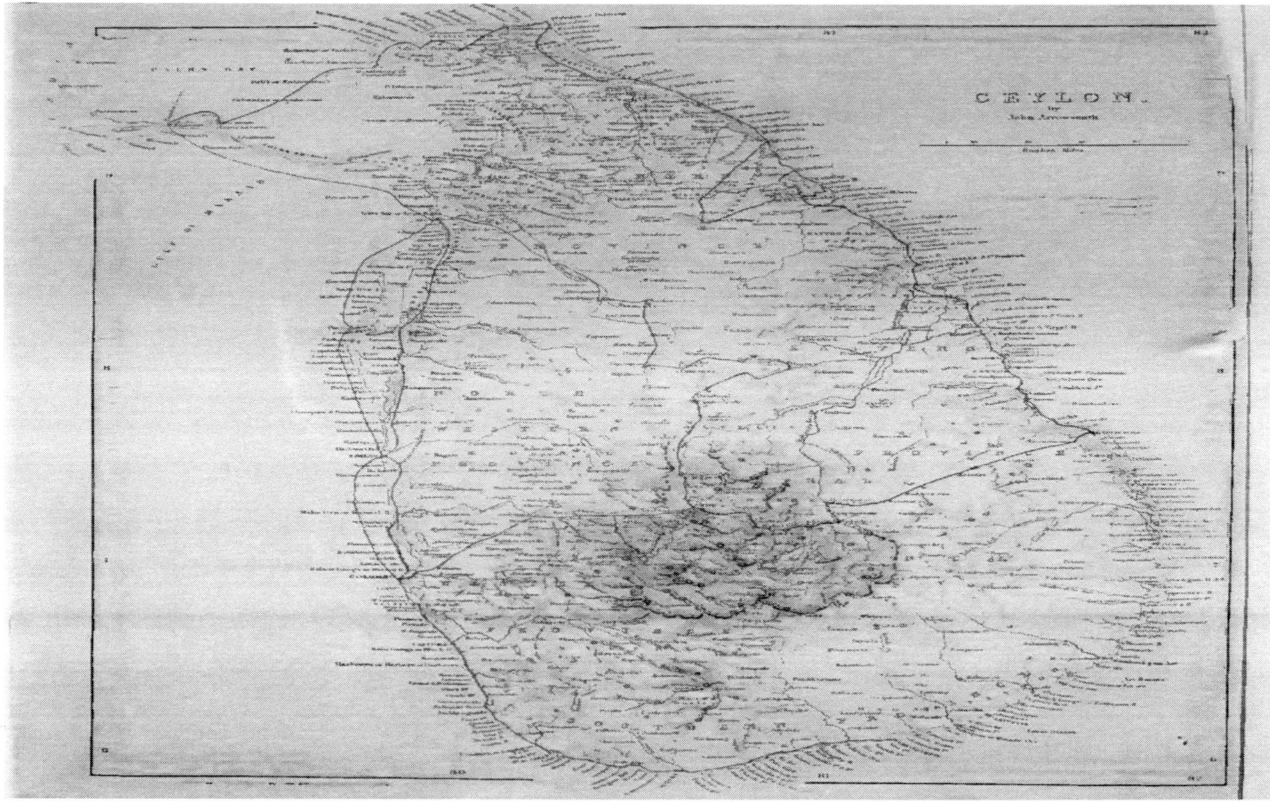
CEYLON.
by
John Arrowsmith
English Miles

PART VI.

MODERN HISTORY.

CHAPTER I.

THE PORTUGUESE IN CEYLON.

THERE is no page in the story of European coloni- A.D.
sation more gloomy and repulsive than that which re- 1505.
counts the proceedings of the Portuguese in Ceylon. Astonished at the magnitude of their enterprises, and the glory of their discoveries and conquests in India, the rapidity and success [1] of which secured for Portugal an unprecedented renown, we are ill-prepared to hear of the rapacity, bigotry, and cruelty which characterised every stage of their progress in the East. They appeared in the Indian Seas in the threefold character of merchants, missionaries, and pirates. Their ostensible motto was, "amity, commerce, and religion." [2] Their expeditions consisted of soldiers as well as adventurers, and included friars and a chaplain-major. Their instructions were, "to begin by preaching, but, that failing, to proceed to the decision of the sword." [3] At once aggressive and timid, they combined the profession of arms with that of trade; and thus their factories became fortresses, from under

[1] The annexed sketch of a Portuguese Discovery Ship of the fifteenth century is copied from a drawing in LA PLACE's *Circumnavigation de l'Artemise*, tom. i. p. 54.

[2] FARIA Y SOUZA, *Asia Portuguesa*, Lisbon, 1666—75: translated by Stevens, London, 1695, vol. i. pt. i. ch. v. p. 54. DE COUTO says: "Os Reys Portugal sempre per tendêram nesta conquista do Oriente unir tanto os dous poderes espiritual e temporal, que em nenhum tempo se exercitasse hum sem o outro."—Dec. vi. lib. iv. ch. vii. p. 323.

[3] *Ibid.*, p. 53.

PORTUGUESE DISCOVERY SHIP.

A.D. 1505. whose guns their formidable galleons carried war and desolation against all weaker commercial rivals. The remarkable fact is, that the picture of their policy has been drawn by friendly hands, and the most faithful records of their mis-government are contained in the decades of their own historians. The atrocities attributed to the Portuguese in the *Tohfut-ul-mujahideen* [1], might be ascribed to the resentment of its Mahometan author, on witnessing the havoc inflicted on his co-religionists in wars undertaken by Europeans, in order to annihilate the commerce of the Moors in Hindustan; but no similar suspicion can attach to the narratives of MAFFEUS [2], DE BARROS and DE COUTO [3], CASTANHEDA [4], FARIA Y SOUZA [5], and RIBEYRO [6], each descriptive of actions that consign their authors to infamy.

---

[1] The *Tohfut-ul-mujahideen*, written by Sheikh Zeen-ud-deen, gives an account of the proceedings of the Portuguese against the Mahometans from the year 1498 to 1583 A.D.

[2] MAFFEI, *Historia Indicarum*, A.D. 1570, written under royal authority.

[3] *Da Asia dos Feitos que os Portuguezes fizeram no descubrimento e conquista das terras e mares do Oriente.* Por JOÃO DE BARROS e DIOGO DE COUTO. Lisboa, 1778—88. De Barros, who is preeminently the historian of Portuguese India, never visited the East, but held at Lisbon the office of Custodian of the Records of India, "Feitor da Casa da India," in which capacity he had access to all official documents and despatches, from the contents of which he compiled his great work, of which he lived to publish only the first three Decades, the fourth being posthumous. He died in 1570; so that he was cotemporary with Albuquerque, whose achievements he celebrates, and to whom, as CRAWFURD observes in his *Dictionary of the Indian Islands*, he stood "in the same relation that Orme the historian of India does to the English conqueror Clive." His unfinished labours were taken up by numerous Portuguese authors; but his ablest continuator was DIEGO DE COUTO, (or more properly DIOGO DO COUTO,) who died at Goa, in 1616. He brings down the narrative of DE BARROS to the viceroyalty of the Count Admiral Don Francisco de Gama, A.D. 1596.

[4] FERNANDO LOPES DE CASTANHEDA, *Historia do Descubrimento e Conquista da India pelos Portugueses.* Coimbra, 1551—61. It has been translated into English by Litchfield, London, 1582.

[5] MANUEL DE FARIA Y SOUZA, *Asia Portuguesa, &c.* Lisbon, 1666. This was a posthumous publication, written in Spanish, but inferior, both in authenticity and ability, to the works of DE BARROS and DE COUTO. It has been translated into English by Captain John Stevens; 3 vols., London, 1695.

[6] RIBEYRO, *Hist. de l'Isle de Ceilan.* It is doubtful if this work was ever published in the Original Portuguese, in which it was written and "presented to the King of Portugal in 1685." But from it the French version was prepared by the Abbé Le Grand, and printed at Trevoux in 1701. There is an English translation by Lee, Colombo, 1847. To the above list may be added the *Historia de la India Oriental*, written in

The Portuguese were nearly twenty years in India before they took steps to obtain a footing in Cey- A.D. 1505.

Spanish by SAN ROMANO Y RIVADENEYRA, a Benedictine of Valladolid, A.D. 1603, which describes the proceedings of the Portuguese in India down to the death of John III., A.D. 1557.

Note to 2nd Edition.—Since the publication of the first edition, I have

PORTUGUESE MAP OF CEYLON, A.D. 1685.

1. Columbo.
2. Cotta.
3. Calituré.
4. Alicam.
5. Galle.
6. Beligam.
7. Maturé.
8. Tanavaré.
9. Grevayas.
10. Balavé.
11. Batecalou.
12. Capello de Frade.
13. Marinhas do Sal.
14. Trinquimalé.
15. Terra dos Bêdas.
16. Ovany.
17. Ponta das Petras.
18. Jafanapatão.
19. Ilha de Cardiva.
20. Ilha das Cabras.
21. Ilha dos Forcados.
22. Ilha das Vacas.
23. Rio Salgado.
24. Ilha de Manaar.
25. Mantota.
26. Praya de Aripo.
27. Serra de Grudumalé.
28. Patalam.
29. Ilha de Cardiga.
30. Chilão.
31. Negumbo.
32. Verganpenin.
33. Malvana.
34. Grubebe.
35. Ruanella.
36. Manicavaré.
37. Ceitavacia.
38. Safregam.
39. Dinavaca.
40. Uva.
41. Candia.
42. Matalé.
43. Serra de Balané.
44. Praya de Moroto.
45. Beletote.
46. Curaca.
47. Mapolegama.
48. Enceada dos Arcos.
49. Panaturé.
50. Acumena.
51. Picco de Adam.
52. Vilacem.
53. Pasdun Corla.
54. Reygan Corla.
55. Salpiti Corla.
56. Quatro Corlas.
57. Sele Corlas.
58. Cotiar.

ascertained that the work of RIBEYRO (or, as he writes his name, RIBEIRO) has been printed in the original Portuguese, by the Academia Real das Sciencias. It forms the fifth vol. of a series entitled, *Collecção de Noticias para a Historia e Geografia das Nações Ultramarinas, que vivem nos Dominios*

A.D. 1505. lon.[1] Vasco de Gama, after rounding the Cape, anchored at Calicut A.D. 1498, and Lorenzo de Almeyda visited Galle A.D. 1505; but it was not till A.D. 1517, that Lopez Soarez, the third viceroy of the Indies, bethought himself of sending an expedition to form a permanent trading settlement at Colombo[2]; and so little importance did the Portuguese attach to the acquisition, that within a very few years, an order (which was not acted upon) was issued from Goa to abandon the fort, as not worth the cost of retention.[3]

Portuguezas ou lhes são visinhas; and was published at Lisbon in 1836, from the identical MS. presented by the author to King Pedro II. In this, RIBEYRO entitles his work, *Fatalidade Historica da Ilha de Ceilão*; and the editor, after alluding in strong terms to the discreditable neglect in which it had so long been permitted to remain in Portugal, points out that its French translator, Le Grand, had not only committed gross errors, but had omitted whole chapters from the 2nd and 3rd Books, and altered the sense of numerous passages, owing to his imperfect acquaintance with the Portuguese language. Ribeyro illustrated his narrative by a map of Ceylon, which is a remarkable evidence of the very slight knowledge of geography possessed by his countrymen in the seventeenth century. A *fac simile* of it is given above.

[1] DE BARROS, dec. iii. lib. ii. ch. 2. vol. iii. pt. i. p. 119.

[2] This fact is not without significance in relation to the claim of Ceylon to a "natural monopoly," of the finest qualities of cinnamon. Its existence as a production of the island had been made known to Europe by DI CONTI, seventy years before; and IBN BATUTA asserts that Malabar had been supplied with cinnamon from Ceylon at a still earlier period. It may therefore be inferred, that there can have been nothing very remarkable in the quality or repute of the spice at the beginning of the sixteenth century; else the Portuguese, who had been mainly attracted to the East by the fame of its spices, would have made their earliest visit to the country which afterwards acquired its renown by producing the rarest of them.

> "canella
> Com que Cellaõ he rica, illustre, e bella."
> CAMOENS, canto ix. st. 14.

On the contrary, their first inquiries were for *pepper*, and their chief resort was to the Dekkan, north of Cape Comorin, which was celebrated for producing it. (*Tohfut-ul-Mujahideen*, ch. iv. s. i. p. 77.) It was not till 1516 that BARBOSA proclaimed the superiority of Ceylon cinnamon over all others, and there is reason to believe, whatever doubt there may be as to its early introduction into the island, that its high reputation is comparatively modern, and attributable to the attention bestowed upon its preparation for market by the Portuguese, and afterwards in its cultivation by the Dutch. DE BARROS, however, goes so far as to describe Ceylon as *the Mother of Cinnamon*, "canella de que ella he madre como dissemos."—Dec. iii. lib. ii. ch. i.

[3] FARIA Y SOUZA, vol. i. ch. ix. p. 281. VALENTYN says the order was actually carried into force, and the fort of Colombo demolished by the Portuguese in 1524, but shortly afterwards reconstructed. (*Oud en nieuw Oost-Indien, &c.*, vol. v. pt. i. ch. vii. p. 91.)

The political condition of Ceylon at the time was deplorable. The seaports on all parts of the coast were virtually in the hands of the Moors; the North was in the possession of the Malabars, whose seat of government was at Jaffna-patam; and the great central region (since known as the Wanny), and Neuerakalawa, were formed into petty fiefs, each governed by a *Wanniya*, calling himself a vassal, but virtually uncontrolled by any paramount authority. In the south, the nominal sovereign, Dharma Prakrama Bahu IX., had his capital at Cotta, near Colombo, whilst minor kings held mimic courts at Badulla, Gampola, Peradenia, Kandy, and Mahagam, and caused repeated commotions by their intrigues and insurrections. They ceased to busy themselves with the endowment of temples, and the construction of works for irrigation, so that already in the fourteenth century, Ceylon had become dependent upon India for supplies of food, and annually imported rice from the Dekkan.[1] A.D. 1505.

The first appearance of the Portuguese flag in the waters of Ceylon, in the year 1505, was the result of an accident. The profitable trade previously conducted by the Moors, in carrying the spices of Malacca and Sumatra to Cambay and Bassora, having been effectually cut off by the Portuguese cruisers, the Moorish ships were compelled to take a wide course through the Maldives, and pass south of Ceylon, to escape capture. Don Francisco de Almeyda, the Viceroy of India, despatched his son, Lorenzo, with a fleet from Goa to intercept the Moors on their route, and wandering over unknown seas, he was unexpectedly carried by the current to the harbour of Galle[2]; where he found Moorish ships loading with cin-

[1] BARTHEMA, Itinerario, &c., p. xxvii.

[2] DE BARROS, dec. i. lib. i. ch. v.; FARIA Y SOUZA, vol. i. pt. i. ch. x.; RIBEYRO, b. i. ch. v.; DE COUTO, dec. v. lib. i. ch. iii. DE BARROS and SAN ROMANO describe this as "the discovery of Ceylon,"—an expression which must have been merely conventional, as in addition to all earlier travellers, Ceylon had been described by a Portuguese, THOMÉ LOPEZ, in A.D. 1502. See RAMUSIO, vol. i. p. 333.

A.D. 1505. namon and elephants. Their owners, alarmed for their own safety, attempted to deceive him by the assertion that Galle was the residence of Dharma Prakrama IX., the king of Ceylon, under whose protection they professed to be trading; and by whom, they further assured him, they were authorised to propose a treaty of peace and commerce with the Portuguese, and to compliment their Commander, by a royal gift of four hundred bahars of cinnamon. They even conducted Payo de Souza, the lieutenant of Almeyda, to an interview with a native who personated the Singhalese monarch, and who promised him permission to erect a factory at Colombo. Don Lorenzo, though aware of the deception, found it prudent to dissemble; and again put to sea after erecting a stone-cross at Point de Galle, to record the event of his arrival.[1]

A.D. 1517. Twelve years elapsed before the Portuguese again visited Ceylon. In the interim, their ascendancy in India had been secured by the capture of Ormuz, the fortification of Goa, the erection of forts at various places in Malabar, and the conquest of the spice country of Malacca. Midway between their extreme settlements, the harbours of Ceylon rendered the island a place of importance[2]; and at length, in 1517, Lopo Soarez de Albergaria appeared in person before Colombo, with a flotilla of seventeen sail, and with materials and workmen for the erection of a factory in conformity with the promise alleged to have been made by the king to Don Lorenzo de Almeyda, in 1505, and afterwards

---

[1] DE BARROS, dec. i. lib. x. ch. v. vol. i. pt. ii. p. 425; DE COUTO, dec. v. lib. i. ch. v. vol. ii. pt. i. p. 58; SAN ROMANO, lib. i. ch. xviii. p. 106. CAMOENS, in a passage in the *Lusiad*, implies that the Portuguese came provided with these columns, "padraõs," to be erected in commemoration of their expected discoveries.

"Hum padraõ nesta terra alevantámos
Que para assignalar lugares taes
Trazia alguns, &c." Canto v. st. 78.

[2] The importance of Ceylon, both for the facility and security of Portuguese commerce in India, has been ably discussed by RAYNAL in his *Histoire des Etablissements et du Commerce des Européens dans les Indes*, v. i. ch. xv. vol. i. p. 166.

repeated by letter to the Viceroy Alfonzo de Albuquerque.[1] But the apprehensions of the Singhalese court were aroused by the discovery that seven hundred soldiers were carried in the merchant ships of the Viceroy, and that the proposed factory was to be mounted with cannon. In justification of this proceeding, Soarez pleaded the open hostility of the Moors, and the insecurity of the new traders when exposed to their violence; — but the arguments by which he succeeded in removing the king's scruples were proffers of the military services upon which the latter might rely, in case of assault from his aspiring relatives, and assurances of the riches to be derived from the trade which the Portuguese proposed to establish. Dazzled by such promises and prospects, the king gave a reluctant assent, and the first European stronghold in Ceylon began to rise on the rocky beach at Colombo.[2] A.D. 1517.

The Moors, instinctively alive to the dangers which threatened their trade, soon succeeded in re-kindling the alarms of the king at the consequences of his precipitancy. He made another attempt to draw back from his recent engagements; he encouraged the Moors to resistance, and the Portuguese were closely besieged for several months. But the effort was ineffectual; the garrison was relieved by the arrival of succour from India, and the only result of the demonstration was to render the Singhalese king more helplessly dependent upon the power of the Viceroy. He submitted to acknowledge himself a vassal of Portugal, and to pay an annual tribute of cinnamon, rubies, sapphires, and elephants, and with this important convention inscribed on plates of gold, Lopo Soarez took his departure from Ceylon, leaving Juan de Silveira in command of the new settlement.[3]

---

[1] FARIA Y SOUZA, vol. i. pt. iii. 2; DE BARROS, dec. iii. lib. ii. ch. ii. vol. iii. pt. i. p. 118.

[2] DE BARROS, dec. iii. lib. ii. ch. ii. vol. iii. pt. ii. p. 121. BALDÆUS, ch. xl.

[3] DE BARROS, dec. iii. vol. iii. p. 132. DE COUTO, dec. v. vol. iii. p.

A.D. 1517. Owing to the difficulty of finding lime or even suitable stone on the spot, the first entrenchment of the Portuguese consisted of earth-work and stockades; and it was A.D. 1520. not till A.D. 1520, that Lopo de Brito was despatched with 400 soldiers, besides masons and carpenters, with orders to transport the shells of the pearl-oyster, which still form vast mounds along the sea-shore of Aripo, and to burn them for cement to complete the fortifications of Colombo.[1] The Moors availed themselves of this undisguised attempt to convert a factory into a fortress, as an argument to rouse the indignation of the Singhalese; and an army of 20,000 men was collected, which for upwards of five months held the Portuguese in utmost peril within the area of their entrenchments[2], till the besiegers, alarmed by the arrival of reinforcements from India, suddenly dispersed, and left the garrison at liberty to complete their fortifications.

But hostilities were merely suspended, not abandoned, and a war now commenced which endured almost without intermission during the entire period the Portuguese held possession of the maritime provinces; a war which, as DE COUTO observes, rendered Ceylon to Portugal what Carthage had proved to Rome — a source of unceasing and anxious expenditure, "gradually consuming her Indian revenues, wasting her forces and her artillery, and causing a greater outlay for the government of that single island than for all her other conquests in the East."[3]

---

445. CAMOENS, in the *Lusiad*, celebrates this incident of the *tribute of Cinnamon* as the crowning triumph which signalized the planting of the "Lusitanian standard on the towers of Colombo."

> "Della darà tributo à Lusitana
> Bandeira, quando excelsa e gloriosa
> Vencendo se erguerá na torre erguida
> Em Columbo, dos proprios taõ temida."
> Canto x. st. 51.

[1] DE BARROS, dec. iii. lib. iv. ch. vol. iii. pt. i. p. 445; FARIA Y SOUZA, vol. i. pt. iii. ch. iv. p. 238; RIBEYRO, book i. ch. v.; SAN ROMANO, lib. ii. ch. xxvi. p. 348.

[2] SAN ROMANO, lib. ii. ch. xxvi. p. 349.

[3] DE COUTO, dec. v. pt. i. ch. v. RODRIGUES DE SAA, in his narrative of the rebellion in Ceylon, in which his father perished in 1630, records a similar opinion:—"Varios y estraños casos succedidos en una conquista, que siendo a los Estados de la India como otro Cartago a Roma en la horribel y prolixo de la guerra, igualó sin duda a los más formidables de Europa; porque ha ciento y veinte siete años que dura con igual obstinacion

The king, Dharma Prakrama IX., the first with whom the Portuguese came in contact, is correctly described by RIBEYRO, as a weak and irresolute prince, who lacked the courage to refuse any request.[1] The same may be said of his brother, Wijayo Bahu VII., and of Bhuwaneka VII., son and successor of the latter. Though nominally the paramount sovereign of Ceylon, such was the minute subdivision of the island into petty fiefs, that the territory under the direct government of the king was not only insignificant in extent, but from its position, insusceptible of defence. On one side Cotta, his capital, lay almost within range of the Portuguese guns; and on all others he was overawed by his own vassals, who, from their strongholds in the hills, threatened him with revolt and invasion. The kings of Cotta thus exposed to demands from arrogant strangers which they were powerless to resist, and alarmed by the resentment of their own people, called forth by their concessions, were compelled, for security, to draw closer the ill-omened alliance with Portugal, in order to protect themselves from the indignation of their nominal subjects.

A.D. 1520.

A.D. 1527.

The first to organise an armed resistance to the encroachments of the new settlers, were the mountaineers of Kandy and the surrounding regions. From the earliest ages the inhabitants of these lofty ranges have been distinguished by their patriotism and ardent resistance to every foreign invader. The same impatient spirit, which had stimulated their forefathers fifteen hundred years before, to avenge the first aggressions of the Malabars, now animated their descendants to repel the intrusion of European adventurers, whose mingled arrogance and duplicity served to inflame a

---

de Zingalas y Portuguesas, pugnando, estos por el Imperio y la exaltacion de nuestra santa Fe Catolica; y aquellos por la libertad de los cuerpos."—RODRIGUES DE SAA, *Rebelion de Ceylon*, &c., p. 2.

[1] RIBEYRO, book i. chap. v.

A.D. 1527. resistance which no blandishments could divert and no reverses allay, and which served to keep alive an internecine war, never relaxed nor suspended till the Portuguese were expelled from Ceylon, one hundred and fifty years after their first landing.

The effects of this long-sustained struggle left strongly marked impressions upon the national character of the Kandyans. It not only called forth their patriotism and daring, but taught them the profession of arms; and, as an illustration of the maxim of Scipio, that a continual war against a single people teaches the aggressors in time to strengthen themselves by adopting the tactics of their enemies, DE COUTO instances the remarkable fact, that whereas on the arrival of Almeyda, in 1505, the Singhalese were ignorant of the use of gunpowder, and there was not a single firelock in the island, they soon excelled the Portuguese in the manufacture of muskets, and before the war was concluded, they could bring twenty thousand stand of arms into the field.[1]

---

[1] The astonishment of the natives at the first discharge of a cannon by the Portuguese at Colombo, is forcibly described in the *Rajavali*: "making a noise like thunder when it breaks upon Jungara Parwata—and a ball from one of them, after flying some leagues, will break a castle of marble." (p. 278). The passage in DE COUTO is as follows:—"neste tempo nem huma só espingarda havia em toda a Ilha; e depois que nós entrámos nella, com o continuo uso da guerra que lhe fizemos, se fizeram tão déstros como hoje estam; e a fundirem a melhor, e mais formosa artilheria do mundo, e a fazeram as mais formosas espingardas, e melhores que as nossas, de que hoje ha na Ilha de vantagem de vinte mil."—Dec. v. lib. i. ch. v.

FARIA Y SOUZA mentions that the Singhalese at the close of the Portuguese dominion "made the best firelocks of all the East." (Vol. ii. pt. iv. ch. xix. p. 510.) See also RODRIGUES DE SAA, *Rebelion*, &c., ch. i. p. 29. LINSCHOTEN, the Dutch traveller, who visited Ceylon in 1805, says, "the natural born people or *Chingalas*, make the fairest barrels for pieces that may be found in any place, which shine as bright as if they were silver." Lond. 1598. And PYRARD, the French traveller, who landed at Galle after having been wrecked on the Maldives, in 1605, expresses unqualified admiration of the Singhalese workmanship on metals; and especially in the fabrication and ornamenting of arms, which he says were esteemed the finest in India, and even superior to those of France. "Ie n'eusse iamais pensé q'ils eussent esté si excellens à bien faire des arquebuses et autres armes ouuragées et façonnées, qui sont plus belles que celles que l'on fait icy."—PYRARD DE LAVAL, *Voyages*, &c., Paris, 1679, ch. x. tom. ii. p. 88.

The original leader of the insurgent Singhalese was Maaya Dunnai[1], youngest son of Wijayo Bahu VII., and grandson of the king by whom the Portuguese had been originally suffered to establish themselves at Colombo. This prince, exasperated by the degrading policy of his family towards the Europeans, and alarmed by an attempt of his father to set aside his brothers and himself from the succession in favour of children by a second marriage, levied war against the king, procured his assassination, and succeeded in placing the heir apparent, Bhuwaneka Bahu VII.[2], on the throne; reserving the fief of Sitawacca for himself, and that of Rayagam for his second brother.

A.D. 1527.

A.D. 1534.

The new king, however, outvied his predecessor in

---

[1] Called by the Portuguese historians *Madune*;—his son and successor, Raja Singha I., is the *Raju* of De Barros and De Couto. I have prepared the genealogical table which is subjoined with a view to facilitate reference to the complicated alliances of the sovereigns of Ceylon at this period.

I. Dharma Prakrama Bahu IX. 1505. Died 1527. — Raja Singha. Dead. — II. Wijayo Bahu VII. 1527. Murdered by his sons, 1531. — Raygam Banda. Dead.

(Sons of II.:) III. Bhuwaneka Bahu VII. 1534. Killed accidentally, 1542. — Rayagam Banda. — Maaya Dunnai, murdered by his son, Raja Singha. — Dewa Raja Kumara. Son by a 2nd marriage.

(Of III.:) A daughter, m. Tribula Banda.

(Of her:) IV. Don Juan Dharmapala, 1542. A Christian. His authority was confined to Colombo, his grand-uncles having possession of the rest of his dominions. He died, A.D. 1581; and by will left the King of Portugal heir to his kingdom.

(Of Maaya Dunnai:) 2 sons, d. — A daughter, Died. — V. Raja Singha I. 1581, d. 1592.

Suriya Comara, 1592. deposed by

VI. Wimala Dharma. 1592. King of Kandy, m. Donna Catharina.

VII. Senerat. 1604. Brother of late king, m. Donna Catharina, his widow.

VIII. Raja Singha II. 1635.

IX. Wimala Dharma Suriya II. 1689.

X. Sri Wira Prakrama. 1707. Son. At his death, in 1736, the Singhalese line extinct.

XI. Sri Wijaya Raja Singha. 1739. A Malabar.

XII. Kirti Sri. 1747. Brother-in-law.

XIII. Rajadhi Raja Singha. 1781.

XIV. Sri Wikrema Raja Singha. 1798, nephew. Deposed by the English, 1815.

[2] A.D. 1534, "This king is the *Banoega Bao* of De Couto, and *Boe Negaba Pandar* of Ribeyro.

A.D. 1536. faithlessness to his country and his religion, and in subserviency to the rising power of the Portuguese; and before two years, Maaya Dunnai, assisted by the Moors, "the greatest enemies of the Portuguese in India,"[1] and supported by two thousand troops sent by the Zamorin of Calicut, invested Cotta, which, after a siege of three months, was relieved by the timely arrival of Portu-
A.D. 1538. guese reinforcements from India.[2] In 1538 he renewed the war with the co-operation of Paichi Marcar, a powerful Moor of Cochin[3]; but the forces sent by the latter having been intercepted and destroyed by the Portuguese fleet, Maaya Dunnai again found it prudent to temporise. The death of his brother, the chief of Rayagam, and the acquisition of his territory, having greatly enhanced his strength, he renewed his solicitations to the Zamorin and Paichi Marcar, and again laid
A.D. 1540. siege to Cotta in 1540.[4] Again the viceroy of India was forced to interpose, and a third time Maaya Dunnai was obliged to sue for peace, which he purchased by a treacherous surrender of Paichi Marcar, and the chiefs of his Moorish allies, whose heads raised on spears he presented to the Portuguese general.[5]

The king of Cotta, Bhuwaneka VII., was now so utterly estranged from the sympathies of his own countrymen, and so entirely at the mercy of his foreign allies, that he appealed to the Portuguese to ensure the succession to his grandchild, the only male representative of his family. To give solemnity to their acquiescence, he adopted the strange expedient of despatching to Europe a statue of the boy cast in gold, together with a

[1] FARIA Y SOUZA, vol. i. pt. iv. ch. 8. SAN ROMANO, lib. iv. ch. xx. p. 734.

[2] DE COUTO, dec. v. lib. i. ch. vi.; ib. lib. ii. ch. iv.; FARIA Y SOUZA, vol. i. pt. iv. ch. xvii.

[3] A.D. 1538, FARIA Y SOUZA, vol. i. pt. iv. ch. viii.; DE COUTO, dec. v. lib. ii. ch. iv.-v.

[4] DE COUTO, dec. v. lib. i. ch. x.; lib. v. ch. vi.

[5] DE COUTO, dec. v. lib. ii. ch. viii.; FARIA Y SOUZA, vol. ii. pt. i. ch. ii. TURNOUR says he was *christened* in effigy at Lisbon (*Epitome, &c.*, p. 49), but DE COUTO, with more probability, says the ceremony was a coronation. (Dec. v. lib. vii. ch. iv.; dec. vi. lib. iv. ch. vii.)

crown ornamented with jewels;—his ambassadors were A.D.
received with signal honours by John III., and the form 1541.
of a coronation in effigy was performed at Lisbon in A.D. 1541[1], the name of *Don Juan* being conferred on the young prince in addition to his previous patronymic of Dharmapala[2] Bahu.

In return for this condescension, the king of Portugal, true to the policy of extending religion conterminously with his dominions[3], exacted a further concession from the Singhalese sovereign. A party of Franciscans were directed to accompany the ambassadors on their return from Lisbon to Ceylon; licence was claimed to preach the gospel of Christ in all parts of the island, and the first Christian communities were organised at various parts of the coast between Colombo and Galle.[4]

Fresh outbursts of hostility and rebellion ensued on this attempt to overturn the national faith. Maaya Dunnai and his followers again took up arms, and in
1542 the pusillanimous king, whilst preparing to en- A.D.
counter him, was accidentally shot by a Portuguese 1542.
gentleman on the banks of the Kalany-ganga.[5] His memory in the annals of the Singhalese occupies a place similar to that of Count Julian in the chronicles of Spain, as a traitor alike to his country and his God; and the circumstances of his death are pointed to as a judgment to mark the indignation of heaven at the calamities which he entailed on his country.[6]

On his death, the young prince, his grandson, nominally succeeded to the throne; but throughout the entire period of his rule, his dominions can scarcely be

---

[1] VALENTYN, *Oud en Nieuw Oost-Indien, &c.*, ch. vii. p. 92.

[2] Called *Drama Bolla Bao* by DE COUTO.

[3] DE COUTO, dec. vi. lib. ii. ch. vii.; FARIA Y SOUZA, vol. ii. pt. ii. ch. vi. p. 121.

[4] For an account of the proceedings of the Portuguese missions, see Sir J. EMERSON TENNENT's *Christianity in Ceylon*, ch. i. DE COUTO says, the first Roman Catholic converts were made, A.D. 1542, at Pantura, Macu (Malwane ?) Berberin, Galle, and Belligam.—Dec. vi. lib. iv. ch. vii.

[5] DE COUTO, dec. vi. lib. ix. ch. xvi. tom. iii. pt. iii. p. 339—341.

[6] *Rajavali*, p. 290—293; FARIA Y SOUZA, vol. ii. pt. iii. p. 364; BALDÆUS, ch. xl.

A.D. 1542. said to have extended beyond the fortifications of Colombo. To conciliate his protectors, he eventually abjured the Buddhist religion and professed himself a convert to Christianity; many nobles of his court being baptized on the occasion, and, according to the *Rajavali*, the lower castes, as well as the higher, hastened to profess Christianity, "for the sake of the Portuguese gold."[1]

His accession served to revive the animosity and energies of Maaya Dunnai and the national party, whilst his helplessness placed the Portuguese in the position of principals rather than auxiliaries in the long war which ensued. In this new relation, relieved from even the former semblance of restraint, their rapacity betrayed itself by wanton excesses. They put to the torture the subjects of the king they professed to succour, in order to extort the disclosure of the buried treasures of his family; and after the first conflict with Maaya Dunnai, in which the Portuguese were victorious, they not only exacted the full charges of the expedition from their young ally, but in violation of their compact, appropriated to themselves the entire of the plunder of Sitawacca, "the wants of India," as FARIA Y SOUZA observes, "not permitting the performance of promises."[2]

For many years the maritime provinces were devastated by civil war in its most revolting form. Cotta was so frequently threatened as to be kept in a state of almost incessant siege. Every town on the coast where the Portuguese had formed trading establishments, Pan-

[1] *Rajavali*, p. 291. Hence the frequent occurrence at the present day, of Portuguese names, in addition to the Singhalese patronymics in families of the highest rank in the maritime provinces. They were assumed at baptism three centuries back, and are still retained even where the bearers have abandoned Christianity.

[2] FARIA Y SOUZA, vol. ii. pt. ii. ch. ix. p. 159; DE COUTO, dec. vi. lib. ix. ch. xviii. tom. iii. pt. ii. p. 350; *Rajavali*, p. 292. Restitution was made at a later period, John III. having ordered the restoration of all the plunder; and this order came to Ceylon, says FARIA Y SOUZA, in the same ship which carried the poet CAMOENS, A.D. 1553, "to try if he could advance by his sword that fortune which he had failed to win by his pen." (Vol. iii. p. 169.)

tura, Caltura, Barberin, Galle, and Belligam were ravaged by the partisans of Maaya Dunnai, their churches and buildings destroyed, and their Christian inhabitants butchered by the Singhalese.[1] A.D. 1542.

In these sanguinary forays, the renown of Maaya Dunnai himself was eclipsed by that of his youngest son; who, beginning his military career whilst yet a child, had accompanied the army of his father in an expedition against one of the refractory chieftains of the south, on which occasion the boy won the title of Raja Singha, "the Lion King."[2]

This fiery leader had the audacity to besiege Colombo in 1563; and afterwards attacked Cotta with such vigour and perseverance, that the Portuguese officer, Ataide, alarmed at the failure of provisions during a protracted defence, caused the flesh of those killed in the assault to be salted as a resource against famine.[3] Warned by this critical emergency of the impossibility of maintaining Cotta as a fortress, it was judged expedient, in 1564, to dismantle it[4], and the humiliated king thenceforth resided within the walls of Colombo; where, says FARIA Y SOUZA, "he was no less tormented by the covetousness of the Portuguese Commander than he had been before by the tyranny of Raja Singha."[5] A.D. 1563. A.D. 1564.

During this wretched struggle, it was the policy of Portugal to induce the minor chiefs of Ceylon to detach themselves from the national party, by inflaming their apprehensions, and exciting their jealousy of the ascendency and pretensions of Maaya Dunnai and his son; and the more firmly to consolidate an alliance, the strongest inducements were held out to them to profess Christianity; but

[1] A.D. 1555. FARIA Y SOUZA, vol. ii. pt. ii. ch. xii. p. 181; DE COUTO, dec. vi. lib. x. ch. xii. tom. iii. p. 479.

[2] *Rajavali*, p. 29; RIBEYRO, b. i. ch. v.

[3] FARIA Y SOUZA, vol. ii. pt. iii. ch. ii. p. 249.

[4] DE COUTO, dec. viii. lib. vii. ch. vii. tom. i. pt. i. p. 57.

[5] *Portuguese Asia*, vol. ii. pt. iii. ch. ii. p. 248.

A.D. 1546. too feeble to contribute any effectual aid to their new allies, their treason and apostacy drew down on them the indignation of their rightful sovereign, and served only to furnish pretexts for their overthrow and his further aggrandisement.

It was thus that the territory of Kandy was seized by
A.D. 1547. Raja Singha, in 1582. Jaya-weira, its king, in 1547, invited the Roman Catholic fathers to his dominions, permitted a church to be erected at his capital, and intimated a wish, which was promptly complied with, that a military party should be stationed at Kandy, with the double object of extending the faith and protecting the sovereign from the resentment of his own people, should he openly embrace Christianity.[1] An officer, with one hundred and twenty men, was despatched on this service, in 1548, and landed at Batticaloa, whence his party crossed the island westward to Kandy; but a sudden change in the king's intentions led him to place an ambush to cut off the militant mission, which, with difficulty, effected its escape to Colombo.[2]

So intent were the Portuguese upon the extension of the faith that, untaught by this act of treachery, they subjected themselves to a still more disastrous repetition of it in A.D. 1550, when Kumara Banda, the son of Jaya-weira[3], renewed the application of his father for spiritual and military assistance. A force despatched at his request was permitted to march to within three miles of Kandy, when they were surrounded by the followers of the prince, and lost upwards of seven hundred men (of whom one-half were Europeans) in a headlong retreat to the coast.[4]

---

[1] The soldiers were despatched, according to DE COUTO, at once to confirm him in "the faith and in his possessions," *pera invenar e assistar com aquelle Rey até ó segurarem na Fe e no reyno.*" DE COUTO, dec. vi. liv. iv. ch. vii. p. 324.

[2] DE COUTO, dec. vi. lib. iii. ch. vii. viii. vol. iii. pt. i. p. 320.

[3] He resided, according to the *Rajavali*, at Coral Taddea, and is called by the Portuguese writers, Caralea Pandur. DE COUTO, dec. vi. lib. viii. ch. 4. tom. iii. pt. ii. p. 155. c. vi. p. 165.

[4] DE COUTO, dec. vi. lib. viii. ch. vii. vol. iii. pt. ii. p. 178; FARIA Y SOUZA, vol. ii. pt. ii. ch. viii. p. 148.

Meanwhile Raja Singha who, though the youngest of his family, succeeded to the territories of his father on the death of Maaya Dunnai in 1571, proceeded to develope his designs for concentrating in his person supreme authority over the other petty kingdoms of Ceylon. He put to death every troublesome aspirant of the royal line[1], and directed his arms against every chief who had been hostile or neutral during his struggles with the king of Cotta. In the course of a very few years he made himself virtually master of the interior, and drove into exile the King of Kandy, who, with his queen and children, fled for safety to the Portuguese fort at Manaar, where he and his daughter became Christians, and were baptized, she as Donna Catharina, and he under the name of Don Philip, in honour of Philip II., who had just acquired the crown of Portugal with that of Spain. On her father's decease, Donna Catharina was left a ward of the Portuguese, and through their instrumentality was afterwards made queen of her ancestral dominions. A.D. 1586.

Unable, from the extent of the military operations in which he was engaged, to retain possession of the Kandyan country, Raja Singha adopted the precaution of disarming the Kandyans, and was thus enabled to concentrate his attention on preparations for the siege of Colombo, which he at length invested with a formidable force. To this memorable assault he brought, according to the account of the Portuguese, fifty thousand fighting men, and an equal number of pioneers and camp followers, with upwards of two thousand elephants and innumerable baggage oxen.[2] He even collected a naval force with which to threaten the fleet of the Viceroy. He took up his position before the fort in August, A.D. 1586, and con-

[1] A.D. 1581. The Portuguese assert, that Raja Singha I., to clear his own way to the throne, murdered not only his brothers, but his aged father, Maaya Dunnai. DE COUTO, dec. x. ch. xiii. vol. vi. pt. ii. p. 215; FARIA Y SOUZA, vol. iii. pt. i. ch. iv.

[2] FARIA Y SOUZA, vol. iii. pt. i. ch. vi; DE COUTO, dec. x. ch. iv. vol. vi. pt. ii. p. 419.

A.D. 1586. tinued to harass it by repeated assaults till the end of May in the following year. The barbarities practised by the garrison are related without emotion by the Portuguese historians of the siege — the tortures inflicted on the living, and the orgies perpetrated over the remains of the dead[1] — and as the entire country beyond the walls of Colombo was in possession of the enemy, Portuguese galleons were despatched to destroy the villages along the southern coast. The expedition, according to the complacent narrative of De Couto, achieved its mission with circumstances of signal atrocity, especially towards the women and their little ones, whose hands and arms the soldiers hacked off in their eagerness to secure their pendants and bangles; and returned to Colombo in triumph, with their spoils and captives.[2]

In a second expedition these outrages were repeated on a still greater scale. Thomé de Sousa d'Arronches, in February, 1587, sacked and burned the villages of Cosgodde, Madampé, and Gindura, surprised and ravaged Galle, Belligam, and Matura, and utterly destroyed the great temple of Tanaveram or Dondera, then the most sumptuous in Ceylon, built on vaulted arches on a promontory overlooking the sea, with towers elaborately carved and covered with plates of gilded brass. De Sousa gave it up to the plunder of his soldiers; overthrew more than a thousand statues and idols of stone and bronze, and slaughtered cows within its precincts in order indelibly to defile the sacred places. Carrying away quantities of ivory, precious ornaments, jewelry, and gems, he committed the

---

[1] DE COUTO relates, that an arachy of singular bravery, who on a former occasion had killed with his own hand twenty-nine Singhalese lascarins, having been brought prisoner into Colombo, a Portuguese soldier cut open his heart and drank the blood out of his hands, "hum delles chamado Maroto, a quem devia deter bem escandalizado, lhe deo huma cutilada sobre o coração, que abrio todo, e por tres vezes lhe tomou o sangue com os mãos, e bebeo por fartar a sede do odio que lhe tinha." —Dec. x. ch. v. vol. vi. pt. ii. p. 562.

[2] *Rajavali*, p. 308; FARIA Y SOUZA, vol. iii. pt. i. ch. vi.

ruins of the pagoda and the surrounding buildings to the flames.[1] A.D. 1587.

Raja Singha, stunned by the intelligence of these disasters, disheartened by the utter failure of his repeated assaults on Colombo, and alarmed by the intelligence of the arrival of large reinforcements to the garrison from Goa, suddenly abandoned the siege, and drew off his forces to the interior.

He survived his discomfiture at Colombo but a very few years, and died at Sita-wacca, in 1592, at an extremely advanced age.[2] Authority and success seem equally to have deserted him towards the close of his career; the Portuguese taking advantage of his involvements and anxieties during the siege, contrived to excite a formidable diversion by rousing the Kandyans to revolt; and Kunappoo Bandar of Peradenia, a Singhalese of royal blood who had embraced Christianity taking at his baptism the name of Don Juan[3], was despatched with an armed force to prepare the way for enthroning Donna Catharina, the daughter of the late fugitive king Jaya-weira, who had been educated at Manaar. The expedition was signally successful; the Kandyans not only asserted their own independence, but descending to the territories of Raja Singha, laid waste his country to the walls of his palace at Sita-wacca.[4] Don Juan, intoxicated by his victories, and indignant that the Portuguese, whilst continuing him in his military command, should have conferred the sovereignty of the interior on Don Philip, a rival on whom they intended also to bestow the hand of Queen Catharina, turned his arms against his allies, and drove the Portuguese from Kandy, removed Don Philip by poison, and conducted on his own account hostilities

[1] DE COUTO, dec. x. ch. xv. vol. vi. pt. ii. p. 665.

[2] The Portuguese say Raja Singha was upwards of 120 years old when he died; but this is an obvious exaggeration.

[3] *Rajavali*, p. 310; RIBEYRO, b. i. ch. v. VALENTYN says he was christened Don Juan, to compliment Don John of Austria, the hero of Lepanto.

[4] RIBEYRO, ch. v.

A.D. 1592. against Raja Singha.[1] A few years were wasted in desultory warfare in the Kandyan highlands, and then followed a decisive action at Kukul-bittra-welle, near the pass of Kadaganauwa[2], in which Raja Singha was unsuccessful, and died in 1592, refusing surgical assistance for a wound, and murmuring at the departure in his old age of that good fortune which had signalised his career in his boyhood.[3]

Thus left undisputed master of the interior of Kandy, Don Juan seized on the supreme power, and assumed the Kandyan crown under the title of Wimala Dharma. To secure the support of the priesthood, he abjured Christianity, and, availing himself of the faith of the nation in the *dalada*, "the sacred tooth of Buddha," as a palladium, the possession of which was inseparable from royalty, he produced the tooth which is still preserved in the temple at Kandy as the original one; and, notwithstanding the destruction of the latter at Goa in 1560[4], he had no difficulty in persuading the Kandyans that the counterfeit was the genuine relic, which he assured them had been removed from Cotta on the arrival of the Portuguese, and preserved at Delgammoa in Saffragam.

The Portuguese attempted to depose Don Juan, and despatched a force to the mountains under the command of Pedro Lopez de Souza, to escort the young Queen Catharina to the capital, and to restore the crown to its legitimate possessor. Don Pedro succeeded in expelling the usurper; but, after a very short interval, Wimala Dharma returned, effectually detached the Kandyan forces from their alliance, utterly routed the Portuguese gar-

---

[1] The events of this period are given with particularity in the *Description of Ceylon*, by PHILIP BALDÆUS, "Minister of the word of God in Ceylon;" printed at Amsterdam, 1672, and of which an English translation will be found in CHURCHILL'S *Collection*, vol. iii. p. 501.

[2] *Rajavali*, p. 312.

[3] "Since my eleventh year, no king has made way against me till now; but my might is diminished; this king is more powerful than me."—*Rajavali*, p. 313.

[4] For an account of the Sacred Tooth and its destruction, see Vol. II. p. 29. 199.

rison, slew their leader, possessed himself of the person of the queen, and seized the Kandyan throne, of which he held undisturbed possession till his decease, twelve years afterwards.[1] A.D. 1592.

Wimala Dharma thus succeeded to the rank and position of Raja Singha as the paramount sovereign of the whole island, and chief of the national party opposed to the Portuguese. The latter, resenting at once his treason and their own defeat, resorted to violent measures of retaliation, and a war of extermination ensued, unsurpassed in atrocity and bloodshed.[2] Jerome Azavedo, a soldier less distinguished by his prowess than infamous for his cruelties, was despatched to Ceylon in 1594, to avenge the indignities endured by his fellow-countrymen at the hands of the Kandyan usurper. Faria y Souza, in a review of the career of this commander, which ended in a dungeon at Lisbon, says his reverses were a judgment from the Almighty for his barbarities in Ceylon. In the height of his success there, he beheaded mothers, after forcing them to cast their babes betwixt mill-stones. Punning on the name of the tribe of Gallas or Chalias, and its resemblance to the Portuguese word for cocks, *gallos*, "he caused his soldiers to take up children on the points of their spears, and bade them hark *how the young cocks crow!*" "He caused many men to be cast off the bridge at Malwané for the troops to see the crocodiles devour them, and these creatures grew so used to the food, that at a whistle they would lift their heads above the water."[3] A.D. 1594.

---

[1] BALDÆUS, ch. vi. p. 608. RIBEYRO tells a story of a Singhalese moodliar (whom BALDÆUS calls Janiere) who joined Lopo de Souza in this expedition, bringing a large force to his aid; but whom Don Juan contrived to get rid of, by addressing to him fictitious letters with allusions to a pretended plot to betray the Portuguese. De Souza, without giving the moodliar an opportunity for explanation, passed his sword through his heart.—RIBEYRO, ch. vii. p. 47.

[2] VALENTYN, who describes the savage conduct of the Portuguese during this war (*Oud en Nieuw Oost-Indien*, ch. vi. p. 82), says his information was chiefly obtained from the reports of the Singhalese, who had a vivid recollection of these horrors.

[3] FARIA Y SOUZA, *Stevens' Translation*, vol. iii. pt. iii. ch. xv. p. 279.

A.D. 1594. An internecine war now raged for years in Ceylon, the Portuguese in successive forays penetrating to Kandy, and even to Oovah and Saffragam, burning towns, uprooting fruit trees, driving away cattle, and making captives to be enslaved in the lowlands.

These conflicts were, however, of uncertain success. On some occasions the invaders, overpowered by the energy of the Kandyans, were defeated and put to flight, followed by the exasperated mountaineers to the gates of Colombo.[1] The frontier which separates the maritime districts from the hill country, was the scene of sanguinary conflicts, and at length the low-country Singhalese, roused to desperation by the miseries drawn down on them in never-ending hostilities, and by the atrocities perpetrated by the Portuguese soldiery[2], manifested a determined resistance to the common oppressors, who, alarmed in turn for their own safety, mutinously resisted the orders of their officers, and the Viceroy at Goa was appealed to to arrest the disorganisation and utter ruin of the new settlement.[3]

In the midst of these scenes of blood and disaster,

---

[1] FARIA Y SOUZA, vol. iii. pt. iii. ch. viii. ix. xii. &c.

[2] "We had not grown odious to the Chingalas (Singhalese), had we not provoked them by our infamous proceedings. Not only the poor soldiers went out to rob, but those Portuguese who were lords of villages added rapes and adulteries, which obliged the people to seek the company of beasts in the mountains rather than be subject to the more beastly villanies of men."—FARIA Y SOUZA, vol. iii. pt. iii. ch. iii. p. 203. A thrill of horror has been imparted to all who have read the story of the atrocities perpetrated on the wife of Eheylapola, the minister of the king of Kandy, who, on the occasion of her husband's revolt in 1815, compelled her to kill her own children by pounding them in a rice-mortar. But it ought to be known that this inhuman practice *was taught to the Kandyans by the Portuguese;* according to the truthful Robert Knox, Simon Correa, "when he got any victory over the Chingulays, he did exercise great cruelty. He would make the women beat their own children in their mortars wherein they used to beat their corn."—KNOX, *Hist. Relat.*, pt. iv. ch. xiii. p. 177.

It is a curious illustration of the conviction left on the minds of the Kandyans of the cruelty of Europeans, that in 1664, when Raja Singha wished to inflict the utmost possible punishment on one of his ministers, he sent him to Colombo to be executed, thinking that the Dutch, like the Portuguese, were ingenious in the invention of tortures. They, however, restored him to liberty.—VALENTYN, ch. xiv. p. 199; ch. xv. p. 249.

[3] DE COUTO, dec. xi. ch. xxxiii. tom. vii. p. 178; FARIA Y SOUZA, vol. iii. pt. i. ch. ix. p. 73.

died the last legitimate emperor of Ceylon, Don Juan Dharmapala. He expired at Colombo in May, 1597, bequeathing his dominions by will to Philip II. By this deed the Portuguese acquired their title to the sovereignty of the island[1], with the exception of Jaffna, the nominal king of which they still recognised, and Kandy, to the throne of which they had themselves asserted the right of Donna Catharina the Queen.

A.D. 1597.

Ribeyro gives a remarkable account of the mutual arrangement under which the Singhalese chiefs now took the oath of allegiance to the new dynasty. It was at first proposed that the laws of Portugal should be introduced for all races alike, reserving to the native chiefs their ranks and privileges; but after an interval asked for deliberation by the deputies, they returned a reply to the effect that, being by birth and education Singhalese, and earnestly attached to their own religion and customs, it would be difficult, if not perilous, to require them to abandon them on the instant for others which were utterly unknown to them. Such changes, they said, were often the precursors of revolutions, that swept away both institutions, the new as well as the old, to the injury alike of the people and the king. On all other points they were ready to recognise Philip II. as their legitimate sovereign; and so long as his majesty and his ministers respected the rights and usages of the nation, they would meet with the same loyalty and fidelity which the Singhalese had been accustomed to show to their own princes. On these conditions they were ready to take the oath, the officers of the king being at the same time prepared to swear in the name of their master to respect and maintain the ancient privileges and laws of Ceylon.

The covenant was concluded and proclaimed, together with a solemn declaration that the priests and religious orders were to have full liberty to preach Christianity,

[1] DE COUTO, dec. xii. ch. v. tom. viii. p. 39; RIBEYRO, bk. i. ch. ix.

A.D. 1597. neither parents restraining their children, nor children opposing the conformity of their parents, and that all offences against religion were to be punishable by the legal authorities.

The territory now under the direct government of the Portuguese embraced the maritime circuit of the island, with the exception of the peninsula of Jaffna, and a portion of the country to the south of it (which was not annexed till 1617), and extended inland to the base of the lofty zone which encircles the kingdom of Kandy.

It was from their strongholds in these mountains, protected on all sides by naturally fortified passes, that the Kandyans, who had become the scourge and terror of the Portuguese, were enabled to direct their forays into the low lands. To watch them, and to protect their own territory in the plains, the Portuguese were obliged to keep up two camps, one at Manicavare in the Four Corles, and a second at Saffragam, on the confines of Oovah. To garrison these and their forts at various points on the coast they were compelled to maintain an army of upwards of 20,000 men, of whom less than one thousand were Europeans.

The value of the trade carried on under such circumstances was incommensurate with the expenditure essential for its protection[1]; the products of the island were collected, it may almost be said, sword in hand, and shipped under the guns of the fortresses. Still tranquillity was so far preserved throughout the districts bordering on the coast from Matura to Chilaw, that the low country husbandmen pursued their ordinary avocations, and the patriarchal village system still regulated the organisation of agriculture. The military forces were recruited by the feudal service of the peasantry; and the revenues in the same form in which they had been raised by the kings of Cotta, were collected

[1] VALENTYN, *Oud en Nieuw Oost-Indien, &c.*, ch. xv. p. 282.

by the captain-general of Colombo, who governed with A.D. 1597.
the local title of "King of Malwane."[1] Trade was prohibited to all other nations, and even to the native Singhalese. Besides the royal monopolies of cinnamon, pepper, and musk, the chief articles of export were cardamoms, sapan-wood, areca-nuts[2], ebony, elephants, ivory, gems, and pearls, and along with these there were annually shipped small quantities of tobacco, silk, and tree-cotton.

In quest of these commodities, vessels came to Colombo and Galle from Persia, Arabia, the Red Sea, China, Bengal, and Europe; and according to Ribeyro, the surplus of cinnamon beyond that required by these traders was annually burned, lest any accumulation might occasion the price to be reduced, or the Chalias to relax their toil in searching the forests for the spice.[3] The taxes were paid in kind. Trade was altogether conducted by barter, and money was almost unused in the island, except in the seaports and their immediate vicinity.

Colombo, as the seat of government and commerce, became a place of importance; and its palisades and earthworks[4] were replaced by fortifications of stone mounting upwards of two hundred guns. Convents, churches, monasteries, and hospitals were erected within the walls, and at the period of its capture by the Dutch, in 1656, upwards of 900 noble families were residing within the town, besides 1500 families of those con-

---

[1] A very minute detail of the military and revenue system of the Portuguese will be found in the First Book of RIBEYRO, ch. x. xi.

[2] A passage in RIBEYRO's account of the productions of Ceylon has puzzled both his translators and readers, as it describes the island as despatching "tous les ans, plus de mille bateaux, chacun de soixante tonneaux, *d'un certain sable*, dont on fait un très-grand débit dans toutes les Indes."—ch. iii. Lee naively says that "he cannot discover what this *sand* is." But as Le Grand made his French translation from the Portuguese MS. of the author, it is probable that by a clerical error the word *arena* may have been substituted for *areca*, the restoration of which solves the mystery.

[3] RIBEYRO, b. i. ch. x.

[4] "Les murailles n'ont été long-tems que de *taipa singella*," &c.—RIBEYRO, pt. i. ch. xii. p. 80.

A.D. 1597. nected with the Courts of Justice, merchants, and traders.

The value of Galle consisted chiefly in the facilities which its harbour afforded for commercial operations, and the Portuguese did not think it necessary to increase its natural strength by any considerable military defences. Caltura and Negombo were maintained chiefly as stations for the collection of cinnamon, and the ports on the opposite side of the island, Batticaloa and Trincomalie, were neither occupied nor fortified till shortly before the expulsion of the Portuguese from Ceylon.

A.D. 1617. It was not till the year 1617, that they took forcible possession of Jaffna, and having deposed the last sovereign of the Malabar dynasty, assumed the direct government of the country. Jaffna had long been coveted by them, less from any capabilities which it presented for extending their commerce than for the security it gave to their settlements in the richer districts of the south; and apparently for the opportunity which it presented of displaying their missionary zeal in a region insusceptible of political resistance. Their first attempts to reduce this part of the island had been made in 1544, when an expedition, fitted out to plunder the Hindu temples on the south coast of the Dekkan, summoned the chief of the Peninsula either to submit and become tributary to Portugal, or to prepare to encounter the marauding fleet. He chose the former alternative, and agreed to pay 4000 ducats yearly.[1] In the same year such numbers of the inhabitants of Manaar embraced Christianity at the hands of the Roman Catholic missionaries under the direction of St. Francis Xavier, that the Raja of Jaffnapatam sought to exterminate apostacy by the slaughter of six hundred of the new converts. The heresy, however, reached his own palace; his eldest son embraced the new faith, and was put to death in

[1] FARIA Y SOUZA, vol. ii. pt. i. ch. xiii. p. 83.

consequence; and the second fled to Goa to escape his father's resentment. A.D. 1617.

John III. directed the Viceroy of India "to take a slow and secure but severe revenge" for these excesses.[1] In 1560, the Viceroy of India, Don Constantine de Braganza, fitted out another armament against Jaffna on the double plea that the persecution of the Christians had been renewed at Manaar and that the reigning sovereign had usurped the rights of his elder brother the fugitive at Goa. De Couto has devoted the Seventh Decade of his History of India, to a pompous description of this sacred war, in which the bishop of Cochin accompanied the fleet along with the Viceroy, erected an altar on the shore, and in the presence of the invading army inaugurated the assault on the city by the celebration of a mass, the announcement of a plenary indulgence for all who should fight, and of a general absolution for all who might fall in the cause of the Cross.[2] The assault was successful but disastrous; many fidalgos were slain by the cannon of the enemy, the city was taken, the palace consumed, and the king in his extremity, being forced to make terms with the conquerors, was permitted to retain his sovereignty on condition of his disclosing the place of concealment of the treasures taken from Kandy and Cotta by Tribula Banda, son-in-law of Bhuwaneka VII. and father of Don Juan Dharma Pala.[3] He was to pay in addition a sum of 80,000 cruzadoes[4], and surrender the island of Manaar to the Portuguese, who forthwith occupied and fortified it.

Amongst the incidents of the victory De Couto dwells on the seizure, by the viceroy, of the *dalada*, the "celebrated tooth of Buddha," which had been carried

---

[1] BALDÆUS, in CHURCHILL'S *Voyages*, vol. iii. p. 647.

[2] DE COUTO, dec. vii. lib. iv. ch. ii. vol. iv. pt. ii. p. 309.

[3] DE COUTO, dec. vii. lib. iii. ch. v. vol. iv. pt. i. p. 210.

[4] A "cruzado," so called because bearing a cross on the reverse, was worth two shillings and ninepence.

A.D. 1617. to Jaffna during the commotions in the Buddhist states. The Portuguese insist that it was the tooth of an ape[1], and worshipped in honour of Hanuman. It was mounted in gold, and had been deposited for security in one of the pagodas. On the intelligence of its capture by Don Constantine, the King of Pegu sent an embassy to Goa to tender as a ransom three or even four hundred thousand cruzadoes, with offers of his alliance and services in many capacities, and an engagement to provision the Portuguese fort at Malacca as often as it should be required of him.[2] The fidalgos and commanders were unanimous in their wish, to accept the offer as a means of replenishing the exhausted treasury of India. But the archbishop, Don Gaspar, was of a different mind. He firmly resisted the offer, as an encouragement to idolatry, and was supported in his opposition by the inquisitors and clergy. The Viceroy, in consequence, rejected the proposal of the infidel king, the tooth was placed in a mortar by the archbishop, in presence of the court, and reduced to powder and burned, its ashes being scattered over the sea."[3] "All men," says Faria y Souza, "then applauded the act; but not long after, *two teeth being set up instead of that one, they as loudly condemned and railed at it.*"[4]

In 1591 and 1604, fresh expeditions were sent out from Goa, to punish the King of Jaffna for assisting the Singhalese chiefs in their opposition to the Portuguese, but on each occasion a ready submission on the part of the weaker power sufficed to avert the threatened danger.[5] The determination, however, had been already

---

[1] DE COUTO, dec. v. lib. ix. ch. ii. vol. iv. pt. ii. p. 316.

[2] DE COUTO, dec. vii. lib. ix. ch. xvii. vol. iv. pt. ii. p. 428; FARIA Y SOUZA, vol. ii. pt. ii. ch. xvi. p. 209.

[3] DE COUTO, dec. vii. lib. ix. ch. xvii.

[4] FARIA Y SOUZA, vol. ii. pt. iii. ch. ii. p. 251. A detailed account of the destruction of the Sacred Tooth, as narrated by DE COUTO, will be found appended to the account of Kandy in the present work, Vol. II. Pt. VII. ch. v.

[5] FARIA Y SOUZA, vol. iii. pt. i. ch. viii. p. 65; pt. ii. ch. v. p. 125.

taken to assert the claim of Portugal to the Jaffna territories, and the consummation was only postponed as a matter of convenience.[1] In 1617, under the vice-royalty of Constantine de Saa y Noroña, an expedition was directed against Jaffna; the city was captured with circumstances of singular barbarity. The king was carried captive to Goa, and there executed; his nephew, the last of the Malabar princes, having resigned his claim to the crown, and entered a convent of Franciscans, his inheritance was formally incorporated with the dominions of Portugal.[2] True to their hereditary instincts, the Malabars, in 1622, fitted out an expedition to recover their ancient possession of Jaffna and the Peninsula; but the vigour of the Portuguese governor, Oliveira, defeated the attempt.[3]

A.D. 1617.

But a new and formidable rival now appeared to contend with Portugal for the possession of Ceylon. The Dutch had obtained a footing at the Kandyan court, and formed an alliance with the king, alike disastrous to the missionary zeal and the commercial enterprise of the Portuguese, who, after a struggle of nearly fifty years' duration, were finally expelled from the island, which their kings had magniloquently declared that "*they would rather lose all India than imperil.*"[4]

---

[1] FARIA Y SOUZA, vol. iii. pt. iii. ch. xii. p. 259.

[2] *Ibid.*, ch. xvi. p. 289, &c.

[3] BALDÆUS, ch. xvii. p. 630.

[4] Van Goens, the Dutch governor of Ceylon in 1663, says that he had seen amongst the Portuguese records at Colombo, the royal orders to the viceroys of India, containing this expression: "*Dat men liever, geheel India zoude laten verloren gaan, dan Ceylon in prykel van verlies brengen.*" —VALENTYN, *Oud en Nieuw Oost-Indien, &c.*, ch. xiii. p. 174.

CHAP. II.

DUTCH PERIOD.

A.D. 1617. ABOUT the same time — A. D. 1580, — that Philip II. acquired the kingdom of Portugal in addition to his hereditary possessions, the United Provinces of the Netherlands, exasperated to revolt by his unendurable tyranny, consummated their revolt by abjuring their allegiance to the Spanish Crown.[1]

During their struggles for independence, the Dutch organised with surprising rapidity not only a mercantile marine, but also a navy of surpassing gallantry for its protection; and engaging with energy in a branch of

[1] The principal authorities for the history of the Dutch administration in Ceylon are the *Beschryving der Oostindischen Landscapen, Malabar, Coromandel, Ceylon, &c.*, by BALDÆUS, an English version of which will be found in CHURCHILL'S *Collection*, vol. iii. p. 500; under the title of *A true and exact Description of Malabar, Coromandel, and also of the island of Ceylon, &c.*, by PHILIP BALDÆUS, Minister of the Word of God in Ceylon, Amsterdam, 1672; and VALENTYN'S *Beschryving van Oud en Nieuw Oost-Indien*, 5 vols, fol. Dordrecht and Amsterdam, 1726. The great work of VALENTYN has never, I believe, been published in any other language than Dutch, in which it was written; so that it is comparatively unknown in Europe, and is aptly described by PINKERTON as "a treasure locked up in a chest, of which few have the key." Sir ALEXANDER JOHNSTON, when Chief Justice of Ceylon, caused a very incorrect and imperfect translation to be made of the part which refers to that island; but it still remains in MS. amongst the collections of the Royal Asiatic Society. Of the volumes which relate to continental India and the Eastern Archipelago, I am not competent to judge; but the portion which treats of Ceylon seems to be scarcely worthy of the high reputation of the work. The official documents of which it is mainly composed are of unquestionable value, although it is more than doubtful that their statistics are falsified to conceal the frauds of the Dutch officials (see LORD VALENTIA'S *Travels*, vol. i. ch. vi. p. 310). As to the general information supplied by Valentyn himself, it is both meagre and incorrect. Some of the materials of his later chapters are taken from Knox's narrative of his own captivity.

commerce peculiarly suited to their position, their merchant ships successfully competed, as the carriers of Europe, with those of the Hanse Towns and Italy. In this department the Dutch maintained an intimate intercourse with Portugal, and their vessels resorted to Lisbon in search of the rich productions of India, which they transported to all the countries of the North.[1] For some years a lucrative and prosperous trade, mutually advantageous to both countries, was permitted to flourish, uninterrupted even by the rupture between the Low Countries and Spain; the Portuguese as an independent people having no other interest in the quarrel between Philip II. and his Dutch subjects, than that which arose from the accident of the two peninsular kingdoms being ruled by the same sovereign. A.D. 1617.

At length in 1694, Philip, impatient to strike a blow at the commerce of the Dutch, and regardless of the consequent injury to the trade of the Portuguese which the contemplated prohibition involved, forbade his new subjects to hold intercourse with his enemies, laid an embargo on the Dutch ships in the Tagus, imprisoned their supercargoes and masters, and, professing to treat them as heretics, subjected them to the discipline of the Inquisition.[2]

It admits of no question that this despotic effort to annihilate the commerce of Holland, acted as an immediate stimulus to its expansion; and suggested to the Dutch those enterprising expeditions to India, which led to the acquirement of large territory, the establishment of their own trade and the subversion of the Portuguese monopoly in the East.[3]

Within a year from the issue of the tyrannous veto to

[1] RAYNAL, *Commerce des Indes, &c.*, liv. ii. ch. i. vol. i. p. 305.

[2] *Recueil des Voiages de la Compagnie des Indes Orientales, &c.*, vol. i. p. 195.

[3] "Il sembloit que ces tirannies devoient ruiner le pais et faire périr la nation : mais au-contraire elles ont causé le salut et la prospérité de l'un et de l'autre!"—*Recueil, &c.*, vol. i. p. 9; VALENTYN, ch. xv. p. 282.

A.D. 1617. trade with Portugal, the Dutch had despatched their first convoy to India.[1] A "Company for distant Lands" was speedily organised, and, in 1595, Cornelius Houtman, who shortly before had been released from a prison, conducted the first fleet of free merchantmen round the Cape of Good Hope.[2]

As the Dutch acquired a practical knowledge of the route, other expeditions followed in rapid succession. Java, the Moluccas, and China were first explored as being the most distant, and least likely to bring them into premature conflict with the Portuguese; and at length on the 30th May, 1602, the first Dutch ship seen in Ceylon, "La Brebis," commanded by Admiral Spilberg, cast anchor in the Port of Batticaloa.[3] So imperfectly were the Dutch informed regarding the island, that they expected to find cinnamon as abundant on the east coast as at Colombo, and announced that its purchase was the object of their visit.[4]

Wimala Dharma, the successful usurper and the husband of Donna Catharina, was, at that time, the sovereign of Kandy, where he had assumed the style of Emperor of Ceylon, in order to mark his supremacy over the subordinate princes, who took the title of kings in their several localities.[5] One of these, the petty prince of Batticaloa,

[1] It is a curious evidence of the prudence of the Dutch in taking this bold step in defiance of the inhibitions of Charles V. and Philip II., by which the rest of Europe was formally excluded from any share in the trade with India, that in forming their first navigation company for the East, they suppressed the name of India, and called it "*La Compagnie des Païs Lointains.*"—"Het Maatschappy van verre landes." It is also observable that, to avoid if possible any conflict with the Spanish cruisers, their earliest attempts to reach India were directed to the Arctic Ocean, in the hope to find a north-eastern passage to China.

[2] Raynal, *Commerce des Indes, &c.*, liv. ii. ch. i. vol. i. p. 308.

[3] *Recueil, &c.*, vol. ii. p. 417.

[4] Valentyn, ch. xv. p. 223, 224, says that in 1675 cinnamon was still found near Batticaloa, and must have been exported thence prior to the arrival of the Dutch. The latter point admits of doubt, but Mr. Thwaites of the Royal Botanical Garden at Paradenia, writes to me that in 1857 he found cinnamon growing in that locality, and under circumstances which led him to doubt whether it had not at some former period been systematically cultivated there.

[5] The style adopted was "Emperor of Ceylon,—King of Cotta, Kandy, Sitavacca and Jaffnapatam—Prince of Oovah, Bintenne, and Trincomalie —Grand Duke of Matelle and Ma-

though nominally tributary to Portugal, was attached by loyal sympathies to the cause of his native sovereign, between whom and the Portuguese hostilities were still actively carried on. A.D. 1617.

Suspecting the Dutch to be Portuguese in disguise, the chief of Batticaloa accorded to the strangers a jealous and reluctant reception[1]; but, after detaining Spilberg a month, on pretence of delivering cinnamon, he eventually facilitated his journey to Kandy, to enable him to present to the king in person his credentials from the Prince of Orange, which contained the offer of an alliance offensive and defensive.[2]

The king received him with a guard of honour of a thousand men, who bore arms and standards that had been captured from the Portuguese, and his cortége on the occasion was swelled by numbers of Portuguese prisoners, many of them deprived of their ears, "to denote that they had been permitted to enter the royal service."[3] Spilberg, besides the banner of the United Provinces, caused a standard-bearer to lay at the feet of the king the flag of Portugal *with the blazon reversed.*

Wimala Dharma, accustomed to be importuned for cinnamon, and eager to discourage the trade in that article, anticipated the expected demand by an offer of a small quantity at an extravagant cost; but on being assured in reply that the object of the mission was to seek not commerce but an alliance, and to offer his majesty the assistance of Holland against his enemies, the king folded the admiral in his arms, raised him from the ground in the ardour of his embrace, and accepted the proposal with

---

naar, Marquis of Toompane and Yatteneura—Earl of Cottiar and Batticaloa—Count of Matura and Galle, Lord of the ports of Colombo, Chilaw and Madampe, and Master of the Fisheries of pearl." The places enumerated were occasionally varied. VALENTYN, ch. xiv. p. 200.

[1] *Recueil, &c.*, tom. ii. "Relation du Voyage de George Spilberg en qualité d'Amiral aux Indes Orientales," p. 417; VALENTYN, *Oud en Nieuw Oost-Indien*, vol. v. pt. i. ch. viii. p. 101.

[2] "D'être ami de ses amis et ennemi de ses ennemis."—SPILBERG, *Relation, &c.*, p. 423.

[3] SPILBERG, *Relation, &c.*, vol. ii. p. 428; VALENTYN, vol. v. p. i. ch. viii. p. 104.

A.D. 1617. alacrity. As to cinnamon, he said all in his dominions was at the service of the Prince of Orange without purchase, his only regret being that the quantity was small, as he had ordered the destruction of the trees, to put an end to the Portuguese trade.

The king detained Spilberg at Kandy till the approach of the monsoon warned him to return to his ship: and having presented him to Donna Catharina and her children, and given unsolicited permission to the Dutch to erect a fort in any part of his domains, he added that, if necessary, the queen and her children would assist to collect the materials for its construction.[1]

The admiral, at the request of the king, left behind him his secretary, with two musicians of his band, and returned to Batticaloa loaded with honours and gifts.[2] Here he captured, and presented to Wimala Dharma, a Portuguese galliot, laden with spices and manned by a crew of forty men; thus testifying at once his obligations to the Kandyans, and the hostility with which he regarded their enemies.

Pursuant to the agreement with the Dutch envoy, one of Spilberg's officers, Sibalt de Weert, left Batticaloa in 1603, with three ships, to cruise against the Portuguese, and undertake the siege of Galle; but the prizes which he took he set at liberty, contrary to the expectations of the emperor, who required one moiety to be given up to himself. An altercation ensued, in which the Dutch commander, excited by wine, repudiated his engagement to bombard Galle, and forgot himself so far as to make an insulting allusion to the empress. Wimala Dharma resented it by directing his instant arrest; but

---

[1] "Ziet, ik, myn keizerin, Prins, Prinszes, zullen de steenen, kalk, en andre bouwstoffen, zoo de Heeren algemeene Staaten en den Prins een vesting in myn lande begeeren te bouwen, op onze schouderen dragen." —VALENTYN, ch. viii. p. 105; see also SPILBERG, *Relation, &c.*, vol. ii. p. 433.

[2] One luxury highly praised by the admiral in his narrative was the *wine*, made from grapes grown at Kandy, which he pronounces excellent. — SPILBERG, *Relation, &c.*, vol. ii. p. 451.

the attendants of the king, exceeding their orders, clove his head in the ante-room, and massacred his boat's crew on the beach.[1] The emperor returned to Kandy, and anticipating a breach with the Dutch, sent a pithy message to the ships of De Weert. "*He who drinks wine, comes to mischief. God is just. If you seek peace, let it be peace; if war, war be it.*"[2] The Government of the Netherlands was too prudent to make even the murder of their officer the ground of a rupture with Kandy; no formal notice was taken of the event, and the decease of the emperor, in the following year, did away with the pretext for war. A.D. 1617.

On the death of Wimala Dharma, in 1604, Donna Catharina, as Queen in her own right, assumed the sovereignty of Ceylon, her sons being children. But a contest ensued between the Prince of Oovah and a brother of the late king[3], then a priest in a temple at Adam's Peak, relative to the guardianship of the minors, which ended in the murder of the prince and the marriage of the widowed empress with the assassin, who, on his coronation in 1604, assumed the title of Senaratena, or Senerat.

For a brief interval Ceylon enjoyed comparative tranquillity; and although Donna Catharina declined to enter into any formal treaty of peace with the Portuguese, she formed an alliance offensive and defensive with the Dutch in 1609. The opportunity for this convention arose out

[1] VALENTYN and BALDÆUS extenuate the conduct of Wimala Dharma, by saying that the order which he gave, was to "bind that dog," *mara isto can!* But "*mara*" is not Portuguese;—and it is possible that the king's order was *atar*, "to bind," which may have been mistaken by the bystanders for *matar* "to kill." VALENTYN, ch. ix. p. 108, ch. xii. p. 141. BALDÆUS, ch. vii. p. 611. PYRARD, the French traveller, who visited Ceylon shortly after, says the Portuguese avowed to him that De Weert was killed at their instigation; but this seems untrue.—*Voyage, &c.* Paris, 1679, pt. ii. ch. ii. p. 90.

[2] The emperor, from his early education at Goa, spoke a little Portuguese. His words on the occasion were "*Que bebem Vinho naõ he bon. Deos ha faze justicia. Se quesieres pas, pas; se guerra, guerra.*"—BALDÆUS, ch. vii. p. 612; VALENTYN, ch. ix. 109.

[3] Called by the Dutch historians, "Cenewierat."

A.D. 1617. of the conclusion of a truce for twelve years between the Low Countries and Spain[1], one of the articles of which recognised the right of Holland to share in the commerce with India. But as this armistice did not extend to the hostilities still active in the East between the Dutch and the Portuguese, the States General, prompt to avail themselves of the interval to re-establish their influence in Ceylon, despatched Marcellus de Boschouwer with overtures to Kandy. He was also the bearer of a letter from Prince Maurice of Nassau addressed to the emperor, tendering the friendship of the United Provinces, and offering, in the event of a renewal of Portuguese aggression by land or sea, to assist his majesty with ships, forces, and munitions of war.[2] The result was a treaty, by which the Singhalese sovereign, in return for the promised military aid, gave permission to the Dutch to erect a fort at Cottiar, on the southern side of the bay of Trincomalie, and secured to them a monopoly of the trade in cinnamon, gems, and pearls. So eager was he to mature the alliance, that he prevailed upon Boschouwer to remain behind at Kandy, in the double capacity of representative of Holland and adviser of the emperor, who created him Prince of Migone[3] and Anarajapoora, Knight of the Sun, and President of his Military Council, and High Admiral of the Fleet.[4]

Immediately on the erection of the new fort at Cottiar by the Dutch in 1612, it was surprised and destroyed by a Portuguese force, which was secretly marched across the island; and Senerat, in turn, made preparations for a simultaneous attack on the forts of Galle and Colombo; with the resolution to give no quarter to any subject of Portugal, save women and

---

[1] DAVIES, *History of Holland*, vol. iii. p. 436.

[2] BALDÆUS, ch. ix. p. 614.

[3] Migone was the Mangel Corle, north of the Deddroo oya.

[4] VALENTYN, ch. ix. p. 112; BALDÆUS, ch. xi. p. 617.

children.[1] The plan was, however, disconcerted by the Portuguese taking the field, and compelling an engagement in the Seven Corles, in which the Kandyans were worsted, and his new principality of Migone wrested from Boschouwer. A.D. 1617.

At the same time, the eldest son of Donna Catharina was taken off by poison, administered by his stepfather the Emperor, and the broken-hearted mother died within a few months of this calamity. Disasters quickly followed: the Portuguese troops on two occasions marched to within a few miles of Kandy, and were with difficulty repulsed, and in 1615 Boschouwer was despatched to Holland by Senerat to solicit reinforcements, pursuant to the recent convention. But, at the moment of his arrival, he found the people of Holland impressed with dislike to the character of the Kandyans[2], and disinclined to active proceedings in Ceylon; whilst the States General, dissatisfied with the conduct and demeanour of the envoy, who approached them not as a subject of Holland but as a prince and ambassador from the sovereign of Kandy, declined to send the required forces. Boschouwer, thus repulsed, addressed himself to the Danes, who were eager to obtain a footing in India, and persuaded Christian IV. to fit out a squadron of five
ships, with which he sailed from Copenhagen, in 1618. A.D. 1618.
Boschouwer died upon the voyage, and, on the arrival of
the Danish commander at Cottiar in 1620, Senerat repudiated the acts of his deceased agent, declined to receive the proffered assistance, and the vessels were sent back to Denmark.[3] A.D. 1620.

The Portuguese availed themselves of the perplexity of the Emperor, occasioned by these occurrences, to

---

[1] BALDÆUS, ch. xi. p. 618; VALENTYN, ch. x. p. 112.

[2] VALENTYN, ch. xii. p. 142.

[3] VALENTYN, ch. x. p. 116, ch. xii. p. 142; BALDÆUS, ch. xvii. p. 629. "Being in want of refreshments, they put into Tranquebar, on the Coromandel coast; and this circumstance gave rise to the first settlement of the Danish colony, which has continued there ever since."—PERCIVAL'S *Ceylon, &c.*, p. 28.

A.D. 1624. renew their solicitations for a truce, which they succeeded in obtaining, in 1624; but, in violation of its conditions, they commenced, in 1627, to fortify Batticaloa, having previously, in 1622, erected a fort at Trincomalie.[1]

A.D. 1627. The Emperor, alarmed by these proceedings, apparently deserted by his Dutch allies, and seeing his kingdom encircled on all sides by Portuguese garrisons[2], made a vigorous and successful effort to rouse the native Singhalese, and organise a national movement for the expulsion of the perfidious Europeans. The flame of war was simultaneously kindled at opposite points of the island; the most influential moodliars of the low country entered earnestly into the conspiracy with the Kandyans, and the people of Colombo, exasperated by the treatment which they had experienced at the hands of the common enemy, expressed their readiness to revolt. The Governor, Don Constantine de Saa y Noroña, already stung by sarcastic despatches from the Viceroy of Goa, which insinuated inactivity and indifference to the interests of Portugal, was induced, by delusive representations from the chiefs of the high country, to concentrate all his forces for an expedition against Oovah, where he was falsely assured that the population were prepared to join his standard against their native dynasty.

A.D. 1630. In August, 1630, he advanced with fifteen hundred Europeans, about the same number of half-castes, and eight or ten thousand low-country Singhalese, and was allowed without resistance to enter by the mountain passes and penetrate to the city of Badulla, which he plundered and burned. But on his return his Singhalese troops, at a point previously arranged with the Kandyans, deserted in a body to the enemy, and the Portuguese, thus caught in the toils, were mercilessly

---

[1] RIBEYRO, lib. ii. ch. i. p. 189.

[2] The Portuguese had now eight fortified places around the coast: Jaffna, Manaar, Negombo, Colombo, Cultura, Galle, Belligam, Batticaloa, and Trincomalie.

slaughtered, and the head of their commander carried on a drum, and presented to Raja Singha, the son of the emperor, who was bathing in a neighbouring brook.[1] The Kandyans, flushed by their signal victory, followed it up by an immediate march on Colombo, which was only saved from their hands by the timely arrival of assistance from Goa.[2] A.D. 1630.

"There was no native of Portugal in the island," says RIBEYRO, "who was unmoved to tears on hearing of the fate of the general; and the memory of Don Constantine de Saa will be venerated by posterity so long as men shall honour valour and worth, and the day of his death was the beginning of sorrows to my fellow-countrymen in Ceylon."[3] Both nations were, however, temporarily exhausted by the effort of the war, and a truce was agreed to, at the solicitation of the emperor[4], who even agreed to pay a tribute of two elephants yearly, conformably to the former treaty with the Kings of Cotta.

Senerat died shortly after[5], leaving his son, Raja Singha II., heir to his Kandyan dominions; the young king's brothers being at the same time invested with the principalities of Matelle and Oovah. A.D. 1632.

---

[1] VALENTYN, ch. xi. p. 116, ch. xii. p. 142. The *Rajavali* says this massacre took place at the foot of the mountain of Welle-wawey, in the field called Rat-daneyia-welle, p. 323. KNOX says that Constantine de Saa, rather than fall by the enemy, "called his black boy to give him water to drink, and snatching the knife from his side, stabbed himself."—*Relation, &c.*, pt. iv. ch. xiii. p. 177.

[2] FARIA Y SOUZA, pt. ii. ch. viii. p. 377. The Portuguese were so unprepared for this assault, that during the siege FARIA Y SOUZA says that they ate the dead, and mothers their own children.—ch. ii. p. 396. BALDÆUS, ch. vii. p. 631, mentions that amongst the forces sent at this time to the relief of Colombo were a company of Caffres. This is probably their first appearance in Ceylon.

[3] RIBEYRO, lib. ii. ch. ii. p. 207. The filial affection of Don Rodrigues de Saa, son to the ill-fated Don Constantine, has left a touching vindication of his memory in a narrative of the expedition entitled "*Rebelion de Ceylan y los Progressos de su conquista en el gobierno de Constantino de Saa y Noroña. Escribela su Hijo Juan Rodrigues de Saa y Menezes y dedicala a la Virgen Nuestra Senora Madre de Miserecordias.*" Lisbon, 1681.

[4] FARIA Y SOUZA, pt. xiv. ch. ii. p. 401.

[5] TURNOUR, *Epitome, &c.*, p. 52, says that Senerat died in 1635; but Baldæus and Valentyn fix the date in 1632.

A.D. 1632. It was in the reign of this gloomy tyrant, that the Portuguese were eventually driven from Ceylon, and his Dutch allies installed in all their conquests. With their wonted bad faith, the Portuguese seized the opportunity of the emperor's death to renew their forays into the possessions of his successor, and Raja Singha, forced to the conclusion that their presence in the island was incompatible with the hope of any permanent peace, addressed himself to the Dutch at Batavia, and solicited their active co-operation for the utter expulsion of the Portuguese.[1]

A.D. 1638. The invitation was promptly accepted, and Commodore Koster was despatched to Ceylon in 1638, to concert the plan of a campaign preparatory to the arrival of the Admiral with the squadron designed for service against the Portuguese forts. In the meantime, the Portuguese Governor of Colombo, alarmed by the intelligence of this new alliance, and eager to defeat it, directed a sudden attack upon Kandy, which his troops entered and burned; but on retiring they were surrounded in the mountains, at Gonnarua, and with the exception of a few prisoners, the entire army was exterminated, and the skulls built in a pyramid by the Kandyans.[2]

A.D. 1638. At length, in May 1638, Admiral Westerwold appeared with his promised fleet in the waters of Ceylon, and the conflict was commenced between the Dutch and the Portuguese, which terminated twenty years after in the retirement of the latter from the island. The story of this conflict has been told by two historians who from opposite sides were eye-witnesses of the strife; —by Ribeyro, who served as a soldier in the armies

[1] The letters of Raja Singha II., enumerating the repeated acts of aggression and breaches of treaties by the Portuguese, will be seen in BALDÆUS, ch. xix. p. 632, 636.

[2] *Rajavali*, p. 324; BALDÆUS, ch. xx. p. 641; VALENTYN, ch. xi. p. 118; ch. xii. p. 142; Ribeyro ascribes the immediate cause of this ill-starred expedition to an act of perfidy and meanness on the part of the Portuguese Governor of Colombo, which led to a personal altercation with Raja Singha II. It is amusingly told in the 4th chap. of his 2nd book, p. 220.

of Portugal, and by Baldæus, who at a later period served as a chaplain to the forces of Holland[1]; but little interest comparatively attaches to the narrative of the strategy of the two European rivals, except so far as it involves the fortunes, or developes the character, of the Singhalese. A.D. 1638.

In 1638 the fort of Batticaloa was taken by Westerwold from the Portuguese after a very brief resistance, and a fresh treaty with the Emperor of Kandy was forthwith concluded under its walls, by which the contracting parties bound themselves to carry on the war, the Dutch finding ammunition and forces, the emperor defraying all other charges, and both sharing the spoil.[2]

In 1639 Trincomalie was occupied and garrisoned by the Dutch, but they afterwards retired from the city. In 1640 they were equally successful at Negombo, Matura, and Galle[3]; and Colombo, which was invested by the army of Raja Singha, might have been captured with facility, but the Kandyan sovereign, apparently alarmed by the rising power of the Dutch, not only permitted the fortress to be retained by the Portuguese, but afforded them the opportunity of recapturing Negombo[4] in 1640. A.D. 1639.

This policy paralysed the proceedings of the Dutch; further operations were suspended; and at length, on the

---

[1] Ribeyro landed in Ceylon in 1640 in the suite of the Count d'Aveiras, and remained till the capture of Colombo in 1658. Baldæus arrived in 1656, and remained till 1665. VALENTYN, ch. xvii. p. 413. Another writer who was present at the final struggle between the Dutch and Portuguese, JOHAN JACOB SAARS, has given, in his *Ost-Indianische Funfzehn Jahrige Kriegs-dienst*, or *Fifteen Years' Military Service, between* 1644 *and* 1659, Nuremburg, 1662, an account of the campaign in which Colombo was captured, p. 122—128.

[2] See a copy of the treaty in BALDÆUS, ch. xxii. p. 641.

[3] Galle was reduced by Commodore Koster, who acted as envoy to the Court of Kandy. But the Dutch were singularly unfortunate in the selection of agents on these occasions. Koster, a rude sailor, insulted Raja Singha II., as De Weert had previously outraged Wimala Dharma; he was dismissed without the usual diplomatic courtesies, and murdered on his return to Batticaloa.—BALDÆUS, ch. xlii. p. 710; VALENTYN, ch. xii. p. 143.

[4] RIBEYRO, pt. ii. ch. viii. p. 102. The expressions of VALENTYN are very curious on the point of the duplicity of Raja Singha:—"toen al considererende dat 't beter was van twee natien gecaresseerd, als van een stoute wydberoemde overheerd te werden, liet hy de Portugeesen weer adem scheppen."—ch. xii. p. 143.

A.D. 1640. arrival of intelligence in India, that Portugal had finally emancipated herself from the dominion of the Kings of Spain, and had expelled Philip IV. to enthrone John of Braganza in his stead; peaceful overtures were made to the States General, and in 1646, an armistice was arranged between Portugal and Holland for ten years from 1640, the two countries retaining their respective conquests in Ceylon.[1]

A.D. 1646. During the pause, the emperor, whose confidence in the Dutch had by no means been confirmed by personal intercourse with their authorities, hopeless of ever liberating his country from both combatants, and seeing his best chance of safety in their mutual rivalry, not only persevered in infesting the territories of each by desultory attacks, but contrived with success to embroil them in hostilities by passing through the possessions of the one to attack the subjects of the other. Conformably to these tactics, he marched through the Portuguese territory to reach the fort of Negombo, made prisoners of the garrison, and sent the heads of their officers rolled in silk to the Dutch commandant at Galle.[2]

The patient endurance of these and similar outrages is one of the remarkable features of the policy of the Dutch. They contented themselves with supplications to be permitted to trade in cinnamon, and with offers to surrender some of the strong places in their keeping on being reimbursed the costs of the war; acquitting the emperor of deliberate bad faith and imputing his alienated feelings to the machinations of their rivals, who were irritated at the Westerwold treaty. Thus by blandishments and presents[3], the Dutch governor succeeded

[1] Holland had previously regained Negombo from the Portuguese in 1644. RIBEYRO, p. ii. ch. xiv. p. 123; VALENTYN, ch. xii. p. 143.

[2] VALENTYN, ch. xii. p. 121, 142.

[3] In the midst of this sullen correspondence, the Dutch Governor alludes to the arrival at Galle of "*a Persian horse worthy to be bestrode by a king*," and asks permission to forward it to Kandy together with a saddle from Holland. (VALENTYN, ch. xi. p. 125.) Red cloth, gold and silver lace, Spanish wine, and Dutch liqueurs, were also employed to heal the breaches between Kandy and Holland. (VALENTYN, ch. xi. p. 125, ch. xii. p. 136.) One injunction of Raja Singha, however, the Dutch firmly resisted; they declined either

in allaying irritation, recovered the prisoners of war, and retained possession of the two important stations of Negombo and Galle, on the confines of the cinnamon country, till the expiration of the truce with Portugal in 1650, and the declaration of war by the Netherlands two years afterwards. A.D. 1646. A.D. 1650.

At that moment the Portuguese in Colombo were in a state of mutiny against the Governor Mascarenhas Homem; and Raja Singha, no doubt influenced by this circumstance, signified his readiness to take the field along with the Dutch. Some time was spent in skirmishes whilst the latter were waiting for reinforcements from Batavia; but at length in October 1655, on the arrival of the Director-General Gerard Hulst, an advance was made from Galle which led to the surrender of Caltura[1], and Colombo, which was forthwith invested, capitulated on the 12th May, 1656.[2] A.D. 1656.

No sooner was the victory achieved, than hostilities broke out between the Kandyans and their new allies; the Dutch persisting in retaining their conquests, which Raja Singha contended they were bound to deliver over to him, by the terms of the Westerwold treaty.[3] In an attempt to wrest Colombo from them, the emperor

---

to recognise or address him by the title of "God."—*Ibid.* p. 136. ch. xiii. p. 178. The Kandyans literally attach the idea of divinity to royalty; they style the King, Kumara Devyo, which means "*the Prince God.*" The palace had the same decorations as a temple, including the emblem of the sacred goose (see *ante*, Vol. I. P. IV. ch. vii. p. 148), and the homage to the sovereign was called *pinkama* "worship." See KNOX, pt. ii. ch. ii. p. 38. Nor were the Dutch themselves consistent in their resistance to this profanity; for in 1665 they received in Colombo a fanatic who, under the name of "*the Unknown God,*" was engaged in fomenting revolt against Raja Singha.—VALENTYN, *Oud en Nieuw Oost-Indien*, ch. XV. p. 261.

[1] BALDÆUS, ch. xxiii. p. 647; VALENTYN, ch. xii. p. 143, 146.

[2] Copious details of the long siege of Colombo are given by BALDÆUS, ch. xxiv. to xxix.

[3] BALDÆUS, ch. xxv. p. 633, 650. This alleged breach of the treaty is constantly referred to, by all the recent historians of Ceylon, but certainly, on looking to the letter of the Westerwold convention as it is given in BALDÆUS, ch. xxii. p. 641, there is nothing in the text which binds the Dutch to give up the captured fortresses to the King of Kandy. That such was the expectation of Raja Singha scarcely admits of a doubt, but in all probability the treaty was so worded by the Dutch, as to bear the construction which they afterwards gave it.

A.D. 1656. was defeated [1], but being enabled to occupy the surrounding districts with his army, he cut off supplies from the fortress, and renewed friendly relations with the Portuguese.[2] These occurrences necessarily retarded A.D. 1658. the further progress of the Dutch, but in 1658 they were enabled, by means of their fleet, to possess themselves of the island of Manaar, and marching through the country of the Wanny [3], they invested the fort of Jaffnapatam, which capitulated on terms; the garrison being transported to Europe, and the ecclesiastics to Coromandel.

Thus virtual masters of the whole seaboard and low lands of Ceylon, their European rivals extruded, and their dangerous ally at Kandy enclosed within the zone of his own impenetrable mountains, the Dutch applied themselves deliberately to extract the utmost possible amount of profit from their victory. Their career throughout the period of their dominion in the island, exhibits a marked contrast to that of the Portuguese; it was characterised by no lust for conquest, and unstained by acts of remorseless cruelty to the Singhalese.[4]

The fanatical zeal of the Roman Catholic sovereigns for the propagation of the faith, was replaced by the earnest toil of the Dutch traders to entrench their trading monopolies; and the almost chivalrous energy with

---

[1] VALENTYN, ch. xii. p. 146.

[2] RIBEYRO says that Raja Singha, to mark his quarrel with the Dutch, invited the Portuguese who remained in the island to establish themselves within his dominions, and they availed themselves of this encouragement to such an extent, that upwards of seven hundred families settled at Ruanwelle with their priests and secular clergy.—Liv. iii. ch. ii. p. 351.

[3] BALDÆUS, who accompanied the Dutch army to the assault on Jaffna, gives a personal narrative of this interesting march. (ch. xliv. p. 710.)

[4] When the English took Colombo in 1796, they found a rack and wheel, and other implements of torture; but these, it was explained, had been used only for criminals and slaves. (PERCIVAL'S *Ceylon*, p. 124.) WOLF, in his account of his residence in Ceylon, says, that "criminals were not broken on the wheel by the Dutch as in Germany; but instead of that, the practice was to break their thighs with an iron club. The generality of criminals were hanged on gallows, but sometimes they were put into a sack and thrown into the sea."—*Life, &c.*, p. 272.

which the soldiers of Portugal resented and resisted the attacks of the native princes, was exchanged for the subdued humbleness with which the merchants of Holland endured the insults and outrages perpetrated by the tyrants of Kandy upon their envoys and officers. The maintenance of peace was so essential to the extension of commerce, that no provocation, however gross, was sufficient to rouse them to retaliation, provided the offence was individual or local, and did not interrupt the routine of business at their factories on the coast.[1]

A.D. 1658.

The unworthiness of such a policy was perceptible even to the instincts of the barbarians with whom they had to deal; and Raja Singha II., by the arrogance and contempt of his demeanour and intercourse, attested the scorn with which he endured the presence of the faithless intruders, whom he was powerless to expel.

He disregarded all engagements, violated all treaties, laid waste the Dutch territory, and put their subjects

---

[1] VALENTYN, ch. xvii. p. 177. In the instructions which Herr Von Goens left for his successor on retiring from the Government of Ceylon in 1661, the leading injunction was to humour Raja Singha to the utmost, to do him all honour, and rather to endure offences committed by him than to resort to retaliation; at the same time to watch and distrust him. "Men moet ook in alle manieren betragten om Raga Singha geen redenen van misnoegen te geven; maar veel liever hem caresseeren hem veel eerbied bewyzen, en liever wat ongelyk van hem lyden dan hem dat aandoen; dog ondertusschen hem ook nergens in betrouwen en op hem wel naeuw letten." (Ch. ix. p. 148.) See also ROGGENWEIN'S *Voyage*, Harris's Coll., vol. i. p. 290.

It is to be regretted that the postponement of national honour to commercial advantages was not confined to the subjects of Holland in the East, and the observance of the same humiliating policy is to be found, on a still greater scale, in the early intercourse of the British East India Company with the Emperor of Delhi.

There is nothing in the records of the Dutch more disgraceful than these official documents of the English in India, at the beginning of the last century, who, in the name of "God," laid at the feet of the Great Mogul "*the supplication of the Governor of Bengal, whose forehead is his footstool;*" setting out that "*the Englishmen trading to Bengal are his Majesty's slaves, always intent on doing his commands, and having readily obeyed his most sacred orders, have thereby found favour*"—and they "crave as his servants a firman for trade and protection to follow their business without molestation."—*Letter of Governor Russell*, 15th September, 1712.

A.D. 1658. to the sword; yet, in spite of these atrocities, they addressed him with adulation [1], whilst he replied with studied contumely; and they persisted in sending him embassies and presents, although he repelled their advances, and imprisoned, and even executed, their ambassadors.[2]

---

[1] "The Dutch knowing his proud spirit, make their advantage of it by flattering him with their ambassadors, telling him that they are his majesties humble subjects and servants, and that it is out of their loyalty to him that they build forts and keep watches round about his country to prevent foreign nations and enemies from coming; and that as they are thus employed in his majesties service, so it is for sustenance which they want that occasioned their coming up into his majesties country. And thus by flattering him and ascribing to him high and honorable titles, which are things he greatly delights in, sometimes they prevail to have the country and he to have the honor."—KNOX, pt. ii. ch. ii. p. 39. See also pt. iv. ch. xiii. p. 179.

[2] VALENTYN, ch. xiii. p. 178, ch. xiv. p. 200, ch. xv. p. 283. The presents usually selected included some rather curious articles. Besides horses and their caparison of velvet and gold, the Dutch sent, in 1679, ten hawks, each attended by a Malabar slave, six civets carried in cages, six game-cocks from Tuttocoryn, two Persian sheep, a stem of sandal wood, and a case of wine. The escort which delivered these with great pomp at Ruanwelle, were so beaten by the king's messengers who received them, that they barely escaped with their lives. (VALENTYN, ch. xv. p. 302.) Two years before, the Dutch Governor had sent a present of a lion to Raja Singha, with some canting compliment on so suitable an offering; but the king refused the gift, and put the messenger under restraint. The officer, maddened by his long detention, attempted to approach the king to entreat his dismissal, but the guards were ordered to detain him *where he stood*, and he was compelled to remain for three days upon the spot, "and what became of him afterwards," says VALENTYN, "we never learned." (Ch. xv. p. 246.) He was still alive at Kandy when Knox fled in 1697. Raja Singha had a passion for hawking, and turned the subserviency of the Hollanders to account in gratifying his taste. I have a curious MS. letter written by him in Portuguese from Badulla, 6th August, 1652, and addressed *To the Governor Jacob Von Kittenstein, residing in my Fortress of Galle as my loyal vassal.* It alludes to the arrival of presents which he had not yet deigned to look at, and continues thus: "I brought up a hawk with great love and tenderness, and taking him with me one day to the chase I gave him wing, and he disappeared for ever. I think it reasonable that I should write to you about these things that are to my taste, and when you are informed of them you are bound to give effect to my wishes. If it should be, therefore, in your power to procure for me some good hawks, as well as other birds of prey that hunt well, and other matters pertaining to the chase, please to send them as presents to me." Another of the king's weaknesses, was an extraordinary style of dress quite peculiar to himself, including mosquito drawers, and a cap with a quantity of feathers. These caps were amongst the presents sent by the Dutch, and so decorated, VALENTYN says, that he looked rather like a buffoon than a king: "en zoo wonderlyk van kleederen en toetakeling in zyn leven, dat hy veel beter een ouden Portuguees met zyn

When, after twenty years of captivity, Knox made his escape from Kandy in 1679, Raja Singha held in detention or imprisonment upwards of fifty subjects of the Netherlands; including five with the rank of ambassador, besides a number of French and English, whose liberation Sir Edward Winter had in vain solicited by a mission from Madras fifteen years before.[1] A.D. 1658.

Unable, from his defective military resources, to direct any decisive measures against his enemies in the low country, the fury of the tyrant expended itself in savage excesses against his own subjects in the hills, — putting to death with remorseless cruelty the families and connections of all whom he suspected of disaffection or of intercourse with the Dutch.[2] At length, the limit of endurance being passed, the Kandyans attempted a revolt in 1664. Having forced the emperor to fly to the mountains, they proclaimed his son, a boy of twelve years old, his successor. But the child fled in terror to A.D. 1664.

---

miskiten-of muggen-broek, en een hof-nar, met zyn muts vol pluymen

RAJA SINGHA.—FROM KNOX.

dan wel een keizer geleek."—Ch. xv. p. 200, ch. iii. p. 45. It is another coincidence (if anything were wanting) to attest the truthfulness of KNOX'S *Relation of Ceylon*, that the portrait which he gives of the king, includes the feathered cap spoken of by the Dutch Governor.

[1] KNOX'S *Relation, &c.*, pt. iv. ch. xiii. p. 180. In 1680, two English sailors reached Colombo, who twenty-two years before had been seized at Calpentyn, where they had landed for fresh water. (VALENTYN, ch. xv. p. 302.)

[2] "His cruelty appears both in the tortures and painful deaths he inflicts, and in the extent of his punishments, viz., upon whole families for the miscarriage of one of them. And this is done by cutting and pulling away their flesh by pincers, burning them with hot irons; sometimes he commands to hang their two hands about their necks, and to make them eat their own flesh, and mothers to eat of their own children; and so to lead them through the city in public view, to terrify all, unto the place of execution, the dogs following to eat them. For the dogs are so accustomed to it, that they seeing a prisoner led away, follow after."—KNOX, pt. ii. ch. ii. p. 39.

A.D. 1664. his father; and the rebels, unprepared for such a result, dispersed in confusion. Raja Singha, to prevent a recurrence of the treason, caused his son to be poisoned[1], and for some years after this abortive rebellion, the Dutch in the low country were comparatively free from his assaults and excesses.

During the period which followed their capture of Colombo,—a period neither of war nor of absolute peace, but involving the expenditure of the one without purchasing the security of the other,—the military policy of the Dutch had been purely precautionary and defensive. Ceylon was guarded as the gem of the country, "*een kostelyk juweel van compagnies*,"[2] every maritime position was strengthened, and fortifications were either constructed or enlarged at Matura, Galle, Colombo, Negombo, Chilaw, and Jaffna. Batticaloa and Trincomalie were abandoned, not only from the want of troops to protect the east coast of the island, but from the equally prudential consideration that cinnamon was only to be had on the west. There every preparation was made for defence; ammunition was largely stored, each garrison was provisioned for a year, and, in addition to the command of the sea, the inland waters were rendered navigable at various points on the west coast between Bentotte and Negombo, and boats were placed on the Kalany Ganga to maintain a communication by the river from the confines of the Kandyan kingdom.

Thus prepared for any sudden attack, trade at Galle and Colombo was carried on with confidence; and, in addition to shipments to Europe, vessels from all parts of the East, from Mocha, Persia, India, and the Moluccas, were laden with the produce of Ceylon; but only at the government stores; trade in private hands, either in exports or imports, being rigidly prohibited.[3]

---

[1] KNOX, pt. ii. ch. vi. p. 58; VALENTYN, ch. xiv. p. 198.

[2] VALENTYN, ch. xii. p. 148.

[3] Towards the close of the Dutch Government in Ceylon, this monopoly of trade was partially opened,

The kings of Cotta, in order to procure supplies of cinnamon for the Portuguese, had organised the great establishment of the *Mahabadde*, under which the tribe of Chalias were bound, in consideration of their location in villages, and the protection of their lands, to go into the forest to cut and deliver at certain prices a given quantity of cinnamon, properly peeled and ready for exportation.[1] This system remained unaltered so long as Portugal was master of the country; and the Dutch, on obtaining possession of the ports, not only continued the collection in the hills by special permission of the Emperor of Kandy, but sought earnestly to encourage the growth of the spice in the lowlands surrounding their fortresses from Matura to Chilaw. In the latter district especially, the quality proved to be so fine, that in 1663, the cinnamon of Negombo was esteemed "*the very best in the universe, as well as the most abundant.*"[2] But the woods in which it was found were exposed to perpetual incursions from the Kandyans, and the obstruction of the Chalias and peelers was a favourite device of the emperors to annoy and harass the Dutch. Hence the cost of maintaining an army to guard the cinnamon country was so great as to render it doubtful whether the trade so conducted was worth the expense of its protection. Towards the close of their career, the company were compelled to form enclosed plantations of their own, within range of their fortresses; and here, so jealous and despotic was their policy, that the peeling

A.D. 1664.

and foreign ships were allowed to import rice and a few other unimportant articles.

[1] The term *Mahabadde*, "the great trade or industry," which was first applied in the time of the Portuguese, is expressive of the high value which they attached to the object. The "*Captain of the Mahabadde*," a title invented by them, was originally a high caste Headman placed over the whole department, the officers and component body of which were low caste. The code of instructions under which the whole was managed in the time of the Dutch, will be found in VALENTYN, ch. xv. p. 316.

[2] "Alwaar de allerbeste caneel groeid van den geheelen bekenden aardbodem; ook en zeer groote quantiteit." — *Memoir of Van Goens.* VALENTYN, ch. xiii. p. 166.

A.D. 1664. of cinnamon, the selling or exporting of a single stick, except by the servants of the government, or even the wilful injury of a cinnamon plant, were crimes punishable with death.[1]

Elephants.—Next to cinnamon, elephants were, in the estimation of the Dutch, the most important of their exports. The chief hunting grounds were the Wanny in the north, and the forests around Matura, in the south of the island. Those captured in the latter were shipped at Galle for the east coast of India, and those taken in the Wanny were embarked at Manaar for the west. But the trade in these animals does not appear to have been ever productive of any considerable gain, and latterly it involved an annual loss.[2]

Areca Nuts.—A third article of export which the Dutch guarded with marked attention was the fruit of the Areca palm, the nuts of which were shipped in large quantities to India, to be used by the natives in conjunction with the leaf of the betel vine; and the story of the trade in this commodity is singularly illustrative of the policy adopted by the Dutch to crush their commercial rivals. On the capture of Ceylon a large portion of the active trade of the island was in the hands of the energetic Moors, who not only maintained a brisk intercourse by sea with the ports on the opposite coast, but also, by virtue of their neutrality, were enabled to

---

[1] By the Dutch laws every tree of cinnamon which grew by chance in the ground of an individual became "immediately the property of the state, and was put under the law of the Chalias, who may enter the garden to peel it. If the proprietor destroys the tree or otherwise disposes of it, the punishment is, I believe, capital."—Private letter of Mr. NORTH *to the Earl of Mornington*, 22nd Oct. 1798; *Wellesley MSS.* Brit. Mus. No. 13,865, p. 57.

[2] VALENTYN, ch. xv. p. 272. This was owing chiefly to the scarcity of ivory. The headmen of Matura were under obligation to produce annually thirty-four elephants, of which four were to have tusks—*Ibid.*, ch. xii. p. 133: and at a later period, A.D. 1707, one of the instructions of the Dissaves was to bribe the people of the emperor secretly to drive down tusked elephants across the Kandyan frontiers towards the company's hunting grounds. (*Ibid.*, ch. xv. p. 310.) The total number exported in 1740 was about 100 elephants. (See the *Report of Baron Imhoff* in the Appendix to LEE's *Ribeyro*, p. 170; BURNAND's *Memoir*, *Asiat. Journ.*, vol. xii. p. 5.)

penetrate to the dominions of the emperor, carrying A.D. 1664.
up commodities from the low country for the supply of the Kandyans. The Portuguese offered no opposition to this proceeding, and when freed from apprehension of the Moors as military allies of the enemy, they were utterly indifferent to their operations as dealers. Not so the Dutch, with whom commerce was more an object than conquest; and not content with having secured to themselves a rigid monopoly of all the great branches of trade, they evinced a narrow-minded impatience of the humble industry carried on by the enterprising Moors.

Among the principal articles protected, were the nuts of the areca, which, at the time when the Dutch took possession of Galle, the Moors were in the habit of collecting in the interior of the island, to be exchanged on the coast for cotton cloths, to be sold at a profit to the Kandyans and Singhalese. This traffic the Dutch resolved to stop, not from any design to profit by it themselves, but with the determination, even with the anticipation of a loss, to extinguish the commerce of the Moors, whose name is seldom introduced into their official documents without epithets of abhorrence.[1]

[1] Ryklof Van Goens, the Governor of Ceylon, in the Memoir which he left in 1675 for the guidance of his successor, describes the Moors as a detested race, the offspring of Malabar outcasts converted to Islam by the Mahometans of Bassora and Mocha, and whose appearance in the Ceylon seas was first as pirates, and then as pedlars. (VALENTYN, ch. xv. p. 146.) Every expedient was adopted to crush them; their trade was discouraged—they were forbidden to hold land in the country (*Ibid.* ch. xii. p. 148), and prohibited from establishing themselves in the fortified towns (*Ibid.*, ch. xiii. p. 160), a small number only being permitted to reside at Colombo as tailors. (*Ibid.*, ch. xiii. p. 174.) The celebration of their worship was interdicted (*Ibid.*, p. 128); they were subjected to a poll tax; they were obliged once a year to sue out a licence for permission to live in the villages (*Ibid.*, p. 174); and, at death, one third of their property was forfeited to the Government. (*Ibid.*, p. 174.) But all these devices of tyranny were unsuccessful; the endurance and enterprise of the Moors were not to be exhausted, and at length the Dutch were compelled to admit that every effort to "extirpate these weeds," "onkruid te zuiveren," had only tended to increase their numbers and energy.—VALENTYN, ch. xvi. p. 409.

A.D. 1664. To effect their object the Dutch conceived the plan of purchasing arrack, on Government account, sending it to Surat and Coromandel, and there exchanging it for cloth with which to under-sell the Moors.[1] But the scheme was not successful, and they adopted the bolder course of taking the arecas into their own hands as a Government monopoly, and prohibiting the import of cloths by the Moors except on condition that they disposed of them wholesale to the burghers, by whom alone they were to be afterwards retailed to the natives.[2] Further to ensure their discouragement, the Government resorted to the singular expedient of imposing differential custom duties upon goods according to the *religion of the importer.* The tax on cloth entered by Mahometans was raised to double that imposed upon cloth imported by Christians, and other articles which Christians imported free, were taxed five per cent. if brought in by Moors.[3] But, notwithstanding every device, this patient and intelligent class persevered in their pursuit, and continue to the present day, as they did throughout the entire period of the Dutch ascendancy, to engross a large share of the internal trade of the island; bringing down to the coast the produce of the hills in exchange for manufactured articles, introduced from the Indian continent. At first, the areca monopoly, under the management of the Government, was comparatively unprofitable, but by degrees it became lucrative, and, in 1664, it was described as "extremely productive."[4]

The other productions which constituted the exports of the island were sapan-wood[5], to Persia; and choya-roots[6], a substitute for madder, collected at Manaar and

[1] VALENTYN, ch. xii. p. 134.
[2] *Ibid.*, ch. xiii. p. 173.
[3] *Ibid.*, ch. xiii. p. 174.
[4] *Ibid.*, ch. xiv. p. 195.
[5] *Cæsalpinia Sappan.* This dye-wood was chiefly obtained in the woods around Colombo and Galle; but in 1664, so recklessly had the trees been cut, that there was none to be procured at the latter place.—VALENTYN, ch. xiv. p. 194.
[6] *Oldenlandia umbellata*, Lin.

other places on the north-west coast of the island, for transmission to Surat.[1] A.D. 1664.

Cinnamon-oil, pepper, and cardamoms were sent to Amsterdam; timber and arrack to Batavia; and jaggery (the *black sugar* extracted from the Palmyra and Kitool palm trees) to Malabar and Coromandel.[2] The cultivation of indigo was unsuccessfully attempted in the Seven Corles, in 1646[3]; and some years later silk was tried, but with no satisfactory result, at Jaffnapatam.[4]

Very few of the articles which form at the present day the staple exports of Ceylon appear in the commercial reports of the Dutch Governors. As to coffee, although the plant had existed from time immemorial on the island (having probably been introduced from Mocha by the Arabs), the natives were ignorant of the value of its berries, and only used its leaves to flavour their curries, and its flowers to decorate their temples. It was not till nearly a century after the arrival of the Dutch that one of their Governors attempted to cultivate it as a commercial speculation; but, at the point when success was demonstrable, the project was discountenanced by the Government of Holland, with a view to sustain the monopoly of Java;—as the growth of pepper had been discouraged some years before, to avoid interference with its collection in Malabar.[5] Cotton grew well in the Wanny, but as the

---

[1] Choya has long since ceased to be collected in Ceylon. It is too bulky an article to be carried profitably to Europe, and there is no purpose to which it is applicable that cannot be more cheaply accomplished by madder. (BANCROFT *on Permanent Colours*, vol. ii. p. 282.) The Dutch required the delivery of a given quantity of choya as a tribute from the Singhalese of the coast.

[2] VALENTYN, ch. xiii. p. 174.

[3] *Ibid.*, ch. xii. p. 134.

[4] In 1664, VALENTYN, ch. xiii. p. 173, ch. xiv. p. 194.

[5] See the *Report* of *Governor Schreuder*, Appendix to LEE'S *Ribeyro*, p. 192–3. M. BURNAND, in his *Memoir*, says, "Coffee succeeded very well in the western parts of the island. It was superior in quality to the coffee of Java, and approached near to that of Arabia, whence the first coffee plants came."—*Asiat. Journ.* vol. xii. p. 444.

A.D. 1664. people did not know how to spin it, the crop was neglected.[1]

In addition to their ordinary trading operations, the Dutch had certain monopolies which served to realise a revenue. They farmed the collection of salt at the leways and lagoons on both sides of the island; the fishery of chank shells[2] was conducted for them at a profit in the Gulf of Manaar; but the pearl-fishery at Aripo, though perseveringly tended, was seldom productive of remunerative results.[3] Gems being procurable only within the territories of the Kandyan emperor, contributed nothing to the trade or resources of Holland. Besides these sources of income, there were taxes suited to the habits of the native population: a poll tax payable in articles of various kinds, such as iron ore and jaggery; a land tax assessed on produce; a tithe on coco-nut gardens; a licence for fishermen's boats, besides a fish tax on the capture; the proceeds of ferries; and an infinity of minor items collected by the native headmen and their subordinates.

The intervention of the latter officers was indispensable in a state of things under which no European could live securely beyond the limits of the garrisoned towns. The policy of conciliating the native chiefs was therefore transmitted by each Governor to his successor, with injunctions to encourage and caress the headmen; they were to be "nourished with hopes," and their attachment secured by gratifying their ambition for titles

[1] VALENTYN, ch. xiii. p. 173; BURNAND'S *Mem., Asiat. Journ.*, vol. xii. p. 445.

There is a very succinct but very unfavourable account of the Dutch system of trade and finance as it existed in Ceylon, given by Lord VALENTIA in his *Travels*, vol. i. ch. vi. p. 309. It may be regarded as pretty correct, as the information conveyed in it was furnished by Mr. North, the British Governor, in 1804; who had previously examined the Dutch records with close attention.

[2] *Turbinella rapa.*

[3] "It is a matter for reflection," says Baron IMHOFF in 1740, "whether the Company derives any advantage whatever from the fishery of pearls, and whether the whole affair is not rather *glitter than gold*."—*Appendix* to LEE'S *Ribeyro*, p. 247. VALENTYN tries to account for this by saying, that the pearls of the Gulf of Manaar were inferior both in lustre and whiteness to those of Ormus and Bahrein.—*Oud en Nieuw Oost-Indien*, ch. ii. p. 34.

and rank.[1] The "Instructions" extant in 1661, defining the functions and the powers of the Dissave of the western province, include every function of Government, and show the absolute dependency of the Dutch on the personal influence of these exalted chiefs. To them was entrusted the charge of the *thombo*, or registry of crown lands, their sale and management; the assessment and levy of taxes; the superintendence of education; the decision of civil cases, the arrest and punishment of criminals; and, in short, the detailed executive of the Civil government in peace, and the commissariat and clothing of the army in time of war.[2] A.D. 1664.

Throughout all the records which the Dutch have left us of their policy in Ceylon, it is painfully observable that no disinterested concern is manifested, and no measures directed for the elevation and happiness of the native population[3]; and even where care is shown to have been bestowed upon the spread of education and religion, motives are apparent, either latent or avowed, which detract from the grace and generosity of the act. Thus schools were freely established, but the avowed object was to wean the young Singhalese from their allegiance to the emperor, and the better to impress them with the power and ascendancy of Holland.[4] Churches were built because the extension of the Protestant faith was likely to counteract the influence of the Portuguese Roman Catholics[5], and the spread of

---

[1] VALENTYN, ch. xv. p. 151.

[2] See the Code of Instructions for the Dissaves, A.D. 1661. VALENTYN, ch. xi. p. 151. A succinct account of the native headmen and their functions, civil and military, will be found in CORDINER'S *Ceylon*, ch. i. p. 18.

[3] An able memoir, on the policy of the Dutch in Ceylon, will be found in the *Asiatic Journal* for 1821, p. 444, written by M. BURNAND, a Swiss who had been member of the last Land-raad or Provincial Council, and who remained in the island after the Dutch had been expelled by the English. The great feature of their rule, he says, was the "utter neglect of the country and its interests, owing to the selfishness, egotism, folly, and want of energy, of the general government."—Vol. xi. p. 442.

[4] VALENTYN, ch. xii. p. 130. Dutch soldiers were allowed to marry Singhalese women, but only on the condition of their wives becoming Christians. — *Ibid.*, ch. xiv. p. 195.

[5] *Ibid.*, p. 175.

A.D. 1664. Christianity to discourage the Moors and Mahometan traders.[1]

In the promotion of agriculture the interests of the Government were identified with those of the peasants, and the time was eagerly expected, but never arrived, when the necessity would cease for the importation of rice for the troops from Batavia and the coast of Canara.[2] But notwithstanding these partial efforts for the advancement of the people, successive governors were obliged to admit the fact of habitual oppression, by the headmen and officials[3]; and to record their conviction that as the condition of the Singhalese was no better under the Dutch than it had been under the Portuguese, so would they one day turn on them, as they had before shaken themselves free of their predecessors.[4]

Nor was the discontent confined to the Singhalese alone; disappointment was felt in Holland at the failure of those brilliant estimates which had been formed of the wealth to be drawn from Ceylon; the hopes of the emigrants who had rushed to the island were crushed by the reality; and the Company's officers and servants were loud in their complaints of the impossibility of subsisting on their salaries and perquisites. The former were absurdly small, the permission to trade formed the great supplementary inducement, and as trade was unproductive, discontent was inevitable.[5] To this the condition of the Governors formed an exception; for although their nominal income was but 30*l.* per month[6] besides rations and allowances, yet, according to Valentyn, such were the secret opportunities for personal

[1] VALENTYN, ch. xii. p. 134. For a narrative of the exertions made by the Dutch for the extension of education and religion, see Sir J. EMERSON TENNENT'S *History of Christianity in Ceylon*, ch. xi. p. 37. A detailed account of the churches and schools will be found in the seventeenth chapter of VALENTYN, p. 409.

[2] VALENTYN, ch. xii. p. 148.

[3] *Ibid.*, ch. xiii. p. 176.

[4] This account will be found in the *Report of* HENDRIC ADRIAN VAN RHEEDE, 1677; VALENTYN, ch. xv. p. 273.

[5] VALENTYN, ch. xv. p. 252.

[6] BERTOLACCI, p. 56.

gain, that in two or three years they became rich; a circumstance observable also in the case of the commandants of Jaffna and Galle, provided they maintained a good private understanding with the governors of Colombo, and knew how to take and give.[1] A.D. 1664.

In fact, from the commencement to the conclusion of the Dutch dominion in Ceylon, their possession of the island was a military tenure, not a civil colonisation in the ordinary sense of the term. Strategetically its occupation was of infinite moment for the defence of their factories on the continent of India; and for the interests of their commerce, its position (intermediate between Java and Malabar) rendered it of value as an entrepôt. But all attempts to make it productive as a settlement were neutralised by the cost of its defence and establishments. For a series of years, previous to its final abandonment, the excess of expenditure over income from all sources, involved an annual deficiency in the revenue[2]; and Baron Imhoff, in 1740, contrasting the renown of the conquest, and the magnitude of the anticipations with which it had been heralded, with the littleness of the

---

[1] The passage in Valentyn is so curious that I give it in the original. "De onbekende en geheime voordeelen zyn niet wel na te rekenen, hoewel't zeker is, dat zy in twee of drie jaaren schat-ryk zyn, hoedanig het mede (hoewel met eenig onderscheid, en na dat zy zich in de gunst van den Landvoogd weten te houden en met een ryp oordeel to geven en to nemen) met de Commandeurs van Galle en Jaffnapatam gelegen is."—*Oud en Nieuw Oost-Indien, &c.*, ch. i. p. 26.

[2] An exposure of this result is given in the official *Report of* Van Rheede, A.D. 1677, which is printed *in extenso* by Valentyn, *Oud en Nieuw Oost-Indien*, ch. xv. p. 247.

Mr. Lee has appended to his Translation of Ribeyro a Table prepared from the records in the chamber of Archives at Amsterdam which shows that between the years 1739 and 1761 the annual deficit for the administration, after deducting the necessary expenses from the profits of trade and the income from taxes, was 172,042 florins, equal to 14,410*l.* sterling. (*Appendix*, p. 201.) See also the *Memoir of* M. Burnand, *Asiat. Journ.*, vol. xi. p. 442. But it must be borne in mind that the civil servants of the Dutch had no interest in the collection and disposal of the revenues, and that their peculation and corruption were matters of notoriety. To such an excess was this carried that it became necessary to vitiate the public documents for the concealment of frauds. Hence Lord Valentia, in accounting for the little value attaching to the Dutch Records, says, "they cannot be relied on; they appear to have falsified all the accounts of Ceylon to deceive their masters at home, a measure necessary to cover their own peculations."—*Travels*, vol. i. ch. vi. p. 310.

A.D. 1664. ascertained result, compared Ceylon to one of the costly tulips of Holland, which bore a fabulous nominal price, without any intrinsic value.[1]

To such lengths did misgovernment prevail, that Holland was at last threatened with the loss of the "jewel" altogether, by the treason of her own officers, and the rebellion of the Singhalese. Vuyst, the governor of Ceylon, in 1626 aspired to become sovereign of the island, and visited with forfeiture, torture, and death every chief who opposed him. For this he was broken on the wheel at Batavia, and his body burned and scattered on the sea.[2] Versluys, who was sent to supersede him, was removed for extortion and cruelty; and in the midst of the discontent and anarchy which ensued, a change in the reigning dynasty at Kandy gave encouragement to the lowlanders to attempt their own deliverance by revolt.

The forced tranquillity of Raja Singha II., after the ominous insurrection of his own subjects in 1664, A.D. 1672. remained unbroken till 1672, when on the outbreak of war between Louis XIV. and the United Provinces, a French squadron made its appearance at Trincomalie, commanded by Admiral De la Haye. They were eagerly welcomed by the emperor as unexpected allies, likely to aid him in the expulsion of the pestilent Hollanders. The French took instant possession of Trincomalie, and the Dutch in their panic abandoned the forts of Cottiar and Batticaloa, but the inability of the former to maintain their position in Ceylon, and their sudden disappearance, sufficed to allay the apprehensions of the Dutch.[3]

---

[1] *Appendix to* LEE'S *Ribeyro*, p. 182.

[2] Narrative of ROGGEWEIN'S *Voyage*, Harris's Coll., vol. i. p. 288.

[3] VALENTYN, ch. xv. p. 256. On this occasion the French Admiral De la Haye sent M. Nanclars de Lanerolle as ambassador to Kandy. But this gentleman having violated the imperial etiquette by approaching the palace on horseback, and manifested disrespectful impatience on being kept too long waiting for an audience, Raja Singha *ordered him and his suite to be flogged;* a sentence which was executed on all but the envoy,

Raja Singha II. died in 1687[1]; his son, Wimala Dharma II., and his grandson Koondasala, followed as successors to the throne; but being indifferent to everything except the revival of Buddhism, which had fallen into decay during the prevalence of war, they gladly accorded peace to the Dutch, who in return placed ships at their disposal to bring from Arracan priests of sufficiently high rank to restore the *upasampada* order in Ceylon.[2]

A.D. 1687.

A.D. 1707.

On the decease of Koondasala in 1739, the Royal Singhalese line became extinct, and a Malabar Prince[3], brother of the late queen, was accepted as emperor under the title of Sri Wijayo Raja or Hanguranketta. Two other sovereigns of the same foreign lineage followed, and during their reigns the utmost encouragement was given to the lowlanders to combine with the Kandyans for the deliverance of their country from the despotism of Holland.[4]

A.D. 1739.

The alliance was, however, powerless from the decay of the native forces, and the want of munitions of war; the Dutch, by an exertion of unwonted vigour, conducted an army to Kandy[5], which they held for some months; and a protracted struggle terminated in 1766, under the judicious management of M. Falck, by a treaty which secured to the Dutch a considerable accession of territory, and the adjustment of more favourable conditions for the conduct of the Company's trade.

A.D. 1766.

The story of the dominion of Holland in Ceylon is

---

whom he detained in captivity for a number of years.—VALENTYN, c. xiv. p. 202.

[1] TURNOUR, in his *Epitome*, fixes the date of his death 1685, but the Dutch, who were not likely to be mistaken, record, with minute particularity, that it occurred on the 6th December, 1687.—VALENTYN, ch. xv. p. 343.

[2] VALENTYN, ch. xv. p. 344.

[3] Although the new dynasty are spoken of under the generic name of Malabars, it is necessary to observe that they were not of the Tamil race, who had been the ancient invaders and enemies of Ceylon, but *Telugus*, of the royal family of Madura, with whom the Singhalese kings had intermarried.

[4] BERTOLACCI, p. 28; *Memoir of* M. BURNAND, *Asiat. Journ.* vol xi. p. 442.

[5] A.D. 1763.

A.D. 1766. not altogether unrelieved by passages indicative of more generous impulses, but these were so transient and so uniformly succeeded by reversions to the former pusillanimous system, that the general character of their administration is unredeemed from the charge of meanness and tyranny. The presence of such Governors as Imhoff and Falck were but episodes in the wearisome tale of extortion and selfishness; and when at length towards the close of the last century the British troops made their appearance before Colombo, after occupying the other strongholds in the island, the surrender of the fortress without a struggle for its defence may be regarded as an evidence that the Dutch had become as indifferent to its retention as the Singhalese were rejoiced at its capture.

CHAP. III.

BRITISH PERIOD.

THE first Englishman who ever visited Ceylon landed at Colombo on the 5th March, 1589. This was Ralph Fitch[1], one of those pioneers of commerce, who, excited by the successes of the Portuguese in Asia, longed to secure for Great Britain a participation in the gorgeous trade of the East. Twenty years prior to the granting of the royal charter, that gave its first organisation to the germ which afterwards expanded to the imperial dimensions of the East India Company, four adventurous merchants, — Leedes, Newberry, Storey, and Fitch, — were commissioned by the Turkey Company to visit India and ascertain what openings for British enterprise existed there. They traversed Syria, descended the Tigris to Bassora, and thence took shipping to Ormus and Hindustan. One entered the service of the Emperor Akbar, another died in the Punjab, a third became a monk at Goa, and the fourth, after wandering to Siam and Malacca, halted at Ceylon on his return and was probably the first of his nation who ever beheld the island.[2] A.D. 1766.

[1] PURCHAS, in his *Pilgrims*, calls him Ralph Fitz (vol. ii. p. 110).

[2] FITCH's account of his voyage will be found in HAKLUYT, vol. ii. p. 263. Raja Singha I. was then in the midst of hostilities against the Portuguese, and FITCH describes the energy of his character and the strength of his army "with their pieces which be muskets." — MILL's *Hist. of British India*, b. i. ch. i. p. 19. I take no account of Sir John Mandeville, "the author," as COOLEY says, "of the most unblushing volume of lies ever offered to the world," who professed to have visited Ceylon between 1332, when he set out for St. Albans, and 1366, when he returned to Liege, where he died. He professes to have visited India and China, but his book bears internal evidence that he had never wandered further east than Jerusalem. His pretended description of Ceylon is borrowed from Marco Polo and Odoric of Portenau.

A.D. 1766. Although the passage by the Cape of Good Hope had been in use for more than two hundred years, no vessel bearing the flag of England had yet been seen on the Indian Ocean. Portugal, in virtue of her priority of discovery and under pretext of a Bull granted by Martin V.[1], claimed the exclusive navigation of those seas,—a right which she asserted by force of arms[2], and in which the other powers of Europe at that time were not sufficiently interested to contest it with her; and it was not till after the return of Drake from his circumnavigation of the globe in 1579, that Queen Elizabeth proclaimed the right of her own subjects to navigate the Indian Seas on an equality with those of Spain.[3] In pursuance of this bold declaration, the first vessels that ever sailed direct from England to India were despatched in 1591, not, however, to trade with the natives, facilities for which had not yet been ascertained, but to "cruize upon the Portuguese."[4] The expedition was unfortunate, the admiral perished, and Lancaster, the surviving officer, on his way home from Malacca touched at Ceylon, and "ankered at a place called *Punta del Galle*, about the 3rd of December 1592."[5] Thus the "Edward Bonaventure" was the first British ship, as Ralph Fitch had been the first British subject, that had visited Ceylon.

Nearly two centuries elapsed after the appearance of the English on the continent of India before their

[1] The Bull of Martin V. was renewed by the succeeding Popes Nicholas and Sextus.—PURCHAS, vol. i. p. 6.

[2] MILL'S *Hist. Brit. India*, b. i. ch. i. p. 6.

[3] MACPHERSON'S *Annals of Commerce*, vol. ii. p. 166. Long after the power of the Portuguese had declined, the Dutch, as their successors, maintained the same indefensible doctrine of the monopoly of Indian trade; and in Ceylon, next to the duty enjoined on successive governors to secure peace with the King of Kandy, was the injunction to exclude all other European nations from the trade of the island, "*weeren van alle andere Europianen van Ceylon.*"—VALENTYN, ch. xv. p. 343. It was only at the conclusion of the war with Holland in 1784 that Great Britain insisted on a formal declaration of the free navigation of the Indian seas.

[4] HARRIS, vol. i. p. 875. PREVOST, *Hist. Gén. des Voy.*, t. i. p. 337.

[5] HAKLUYT, vol. ii. p. 107.

attention was turned to the acquisition of Ceylon.[1] A.D. 1766.
The vast seaborde of Hindustan afforded so wide a field for enterprise that it was unnecessary to contend with two European states for the trade of an island off its coast. Fully occupied in the establishment of their successive settlements at Surat, Madras, Bombay, and Bengal, and with the quarrels regarding them, which arose with the Portuguese, the Dutch, and French, as well as in their conflicts with the native princes, the attention of the English was not directed to Ceylon till late in the eighteenth century, when the seizure of the Dutch possessions became essential to the protection of their own, as well as for the humiliation of the only formidable rival who then competed with Great Britain for the commerce of the Indian seas.

The only intercourse which the English had previously attempted with the Singhalese Emperor, arose out of the unaccountable passion of Raja Singha II. for the detention of "white men" as prisoners in his dominions.[2] Hence Sir Edward Winter was led, in 1664,

---

[1] From the necessities of their position, the Dutch saw nothing of the interior of Ceylon themselves, and discouraged the travellers of other nations from visiting or describing it. Hence accounts of the island during their presence there are rare. The most curious is contained in the *Life of Jo. Christian Wolf*, who was one of their officials at Jaffna. Tavernier, the French traveller, touched at Galle in 1648; and Thunberg, the Swedish naturalist, landed on the island in 1777, but his journeys extended no further than from Matura to Colombo, and his information is confined to the collection of gems at the one place and the preparation of cinnamon at the other. (THUNBERG, *Voyages*, vol. iv.) Amongst the few English travellers who visited Ceylon during the Dutch period, was Sir Thomas Herbert, a cadet of the Pembroke family, who has given an erudite account of the island in his *Travels into Africa, the Great Asia, and some parts of the Oriental Indies and Isles adjacent*, Lond. MDCXXXIV. He, however, records it as "the tradition of this place that Melec Perimal, king of that island (Ceylon), was one of the Magi that offered gold, frankincense, and myrrh unto our Blessed Saviour; and also that at his return he made known the history of God's incarnation, and made many proselytes, of which some to this very day retain the faith." "Candace's Eunuch," he says, "baptized by Philip, preached Christ in Taprobane, if Dorotheus, Bishop of Tyre, who lived in the days of the great Constantine, had good authority for reporting it." Sir Thomas mentions that "infamous *ape's tooth* which Constantine, a late Goau viceroy, forcibly took away, and upon their proffering a ransom burned it to ashes," p. 358.

[2] KNOX himself, one of these *dé-*

A.D. 1766. to make an attempt, though an ineffectual one, by means of a special mission to the king, to effect the deliverance of the English seamen held in captivity in Kandy.[1]

The first evidence of any desire to obtain a footing in Ceylon is to be traced to the act of the governor of Madras, who, in 1763, sent an envoy to Kandy to propose to the king Kirti Sri an amicable treaty. The overture was favourably received; but, owing to the subsequent indifference of the English Government, no steps were taken to mature an alliance.[2]

A.D. 1782. Twenty years later, when war was levied against Holland by Great Britain in 1782, and Trincomalie occupied by a British force under Sir Hector Munro[3]; Hugh Boyd was commissioned by Lord Macartney to proceed to the court of Kandy, and solicit the active co-operation of Rajadhi Raja Singha against the Dutch. But the recollection was still fresh in the minds of the

---

tenus from 1659 to 1679, states his inability to assign any adequate motive in explanation of this strange propensity of Raja Singha. His English captives all appear to have been kidnapped sailors, whom shipwrecks or other disasters had forced to land on his shores (*Hist. Relation*, pt. iv. ch. xiv.). Besides Knox's own companions, there were at the same time sixteen other Englishmen confined at Kandy, the crew of a merchantman, which had been wrecked on the Maldives in 1656 (*Ib.* ch. iv.); Valentyn states that in 1672, two Englishmen made their escape to Colombo after twenty-two years' detention at Kandy, having been seized at Calpentyn when landing from a ship in search of fresh water. (VALENTYN, ch. xv. p. 302.) We have no evidence of this seizure and detention of strangers being a national custom of the Singhalese kings, but it is curious that in the tract of Palladius *De Moribus Brachmanorum*, erroneously ascribed to St. Ambrose (see *ante*, Vol. I. Pt. v. ch. i. p. 530), the Theban scholar who describes Ceylon, says that he was seized and detained there by the king, for no other reason than that he had dared to set foot upon the island: ὥς τολμήσας εἰσελθεῖν ἐις τὴν χώραν την ἐκεῖ, &c. Knox says that it was the practice of Raja Singha II. to feed his European prisoners with rice and provisions sent daily for their use (pt. iv. ch. ii.); and in the same way the Theban throughout the six years of his forced residence in Taprobane received regularly a supply of grain at the expense of the king, κατασχεθεὶς οὖν παρ᾽ αὐτοῖς ἑξαετίαν ὑπηρετησα τῷ ἀρτοκόπῳ παραδοθεὶς ἐις εργασίαν. (PSEUDO-CALLISTHENES, iii. ch. ix.) De Foe has availed himself of this habit of the Singhalese to seize the persons of foreigners, to introduce an incident in his story of the *Adventures and Piracies of Captain Singleton*, ch. xvii. The same propensity has been exhibited at times by the people of Japan and other portions of the East.

[1] VALENTYN, ch. xiv. p. 200. The Dutch historian calls him *Lord* Winter.

[2] Lord VALENTIA's *Travels*, vol. i. ch. vi. p. 278.

[3] MILL, *Hist. Brit. India*, book v. ch. v. vol. iv. p. 225. PERCIVAL's *Ceylon, &c.*, p. 50.

Kandyans of the slight endured in 1763, and the Emperor declined to negotiate with the East India Company, or to enter into any treaty, except with the King of Great Britain direct.[1] Mr. Boyd, on his return to Trincomalie, had the mortification to discover that, during his absence, the fort had been surprised by a French fleet under Admiral Suffrein, and the British garrison transported to Madras. Trincomalie, on the occurrence of peace in the year following, was restored to the Dutch. A.D. 1782.

At length, in 1795, Holland, after being overrun and revolutionised by the armies of the French Republic, found herself helplessly involved in the great war which then agitated Europe — and the time at last arrived when Ceylon was to be absorbed into the Eastern dominions of the British Crown. A.D. 1795.

This consummation was facilitated by the renewal of hostilities between the Dutch and the court of Kandy, the sovereign being now as willing to avail himself of the aid of the English to expel the forces of Holland, as his predecessor, one hundred and fifty years before, had been eager to accept the assistance of the Dutch to rid his country of the Portuguese.

On the 1st August, 1795, an expedition fitted out by Lord Hobart, the governor of Madras, and commanded by Colonel James Stuart, landed at Trincomalie, which capitulated, after a siege of three weeks; Jaffna surrendered within the following month, and Calpentyn was occupied on the 5th November. A Singhalese envoy[2], with the high rank of Adigar, was now despatched to Madras by king Rajadhi Raja Singha, to negotiate a treaty between Great Britain and Kandy; but before his return, Colonel Stuart, early in 1796,

[1] An interesting account of Mr. Boyd's Embassy to Kandy will be found in his *Miscellaneous Works*, vol. ii. p. 107, and in the volume of the *Asiatic Annual Register* for 1799.

[2] Migasthene, Dissave of the Seven Corles, who died in 1806.

A.D. 1796. took possession of Negombo, and summoned the garrison of Colombo, which, on the 16th February, marched out without striking a blow. Van Angelbeck, the governor, had previously signed a convention by which Caltura, Point de Galle, Matura, and all the other fortified places, were simultaneously ceded to Great Britain.[1]

By this capitulation Ceylon, with all its fortresses, ammunition and artillery, its archives, and the contents of its treasury and stores, was ceded to the victorious English. Private property was declared inviolable, the funds of charitable foundations were held sacred, the garrison marched out with the honours of war, piled arms on the esplanade, and returned again to their barracks. Night closed on the descending standard of Holland, and at sunrise the British flag waved on the walls of Colombo.[2]

---

[1] *Annual Register*, 1796, p. 194. *Ibid.* Appendix, p. 75.

[2] Percival, who served in this campaign, gives a remarkable picture in his *Account of the Island of Ceylon*, of the degraded state to which the Dutch military establishments were reduced at this crisis. The march of the British from Negombo to Colombo was entirely unimpeded, although it lay through thick woods and jungle, from behind which an enemy might have been destroyed whilst the assailants were unseen. The English were allowed to cross the Kalany river at Mutwal without molestation, upon rafts of bamboo; a battery erected at Grand Pass was abandoned by the Dutch, who fled on the appearance of the British. A few shots were aimed at them as they approached Colombo, but the firing party were repulsed, and fled within the fortifications, whence, without waiting to be attacked, they instantly sent to propose terms of surrender. Van Angelbeck, the governor, afterwards confessed, such was the demoralisation and mutiny of the garrison, that he lived in perpetual dread of assassination, and although eager to defend the fortress to the last, he was unable to prevail on his officers to encounter the enemy. This state of things Percival ascribes to the thirst for gain and private emolument, which had overcome every other feeling, and produced a total extinction of every sentiment of public spirit and national honour. When the English entered the gates the Dutch "were found by us in a state of the most infamous disorder and drunkenness, in no discipline, no obedience, no spirit. The soldiers then awoke to a sense of their degradation, but it was too late; they accused Van Angelbeck of betraying them, vented loud reproaches against their commanders, and recklessly insulted the British as they filed into the fortress, even spitting on them as they passed."—Percival, p. 118, 150, 180.

The Dutch tell a different story. They openly assert the treason of Van Angelbeck, and imply that as the Stadtholder in 1795 had thrown himself on the protection of the English, the Governor of Ceylon had

The dominion of the Netherlands in Ceylon was nearly equal in duration with that of Portugal, about one hundred and forty years; but the policies of the two countries have left a very different impress on the character and institutions of the people amongst whom they lived. The most important bequest left by the utilitarian genius of Holland is the code of Roman Dutch law, which still prevails in the supreme courts of justice, whilst the fanatical propagandism of the Portuguese has reared for itself a monument in the abiding and expanding influence of the Roman Catholic faith. This flourishes in every hamlet and province where it was implanted by the Franciscans, whilst the doctrines of the reformed church of Holland, never preached beyond the walls of the fortresses, are already

A.D. 1796.

---

contrived the surrender of the island to gratify his new allies. M. THOMBE, an officer who had served in Batavia, published in 1811 his *Voyage aux Indes Orientales*, in the second volume of which he has inserted an apology for the capture of Colombo, from data supplied to him by individuals at Java, who had served during the brief assault. He specifies vigorous and earnest preparations for the siege for months before it actually took place, which were ostensibly continued up to the approach of the English. But he recalls many suspicious acts of the Governor prior to and during the advance of the British (vol. ii. p. 186, &c.). At length on their approach to Colombo, and the appearance of the English squadron in the roads, the Governor's conduct became unequivocal. He held frequent conferences with Major Agnew, an English envoy, who landed from a frigate in the offing; and immediately after his departure, the Swiss regiment of De Meuron announced their intention to transfer their services to the British. Van Angelbeck then commenced to conceal his plate and valuables; and awaited the enemy with a composure that, coupled with a multitude of minor circumstances, awoke the garrison to consciousness that they had been betrayed: "Le 16 Fevrier toutes les troupes, pensant avec raison qu'elles étaient trahies, voulurent se révolter et plusieurs coups de fusils étaient dirigés sur la maison du Gouverneur Van Angelbeck."—Vol. ii. p. 214. Under these circumstances the doomed fortress surrendered; and such was the indignation of the soldiers, that nothing but the presence of the English saved the Governor from their vengeance.

It is certainly a remarkable circumstance that Van Angelbeck should have remained in Ceylon after the capture of Colombo. He lived there some years, and according to M. THOMBE, he eventually committed suicide under the influence of remorse for his treason. The English have made no mention of the latter fact, but CORDINER describes his funeral by torchlight in September 1799, when "the body was deposited in the family vault by the side of that of his wife, whose skeleton was seen through a glass in the cover of the coffin."—CORDINER, p. 36.

A.D. 1796. almost forgotten throughout the island, with the exception of an expiring community at Colombo. Already the language of the Dutch, which they sought to extend by penal enactments [1], has ceased to be spoken even by their direct descendants, whilst a corrupted Portuguese is to the present day the vernacular of the middle classes in every town of importance.[2] As the practical and sordid government of the Netherlands only recognised the interests of the native population in so far as they were essential to uphold their trading monopolies, their memory was recalled by no agreeable associations; whilst the Portuguese, who, in spite of their cruelties, were identified with the people by the bond of a common faith [3], excited a feeling of admiration by the boldness of their conflicts with the Kandyans, and the chivalrous though ineffectual defence of their beleaguered fortresses. The Dutch and their proceedings have almost ceased to be remembered by the lowland Singhalese; but the chiefs of the south and west perpetuate with

---

[1] In order that the children of the Singhalese might be taught Dutch by their attendants, the heads of all slaves who could not speak it were ordered to be shaved, and a fine for neglect was imposed upon their masters. Thus, as avowed in the proclamation, it was hoped "to destroy the language of the Portuguese, in order that the name of our enemies may perish, and our own flourish in its stead."—VALENTYN, ch. xvii. p. 414.

[2] Even amongst the English, the number of Portuguese terms in daily use is remarkable. The grounds attached to a house are its "compound," *campinho;* a wardrobe is called an "almirah," *almarinho;* a tradesman is shown a "muster," *mostra,* or pattern; the official register of lands is the *tombo;* and elephants are captured in a "corral," or *curral,* "an enclosed field."

[3] The different effects of the Dutch and Portuguese policy in matters of religion is very forcibly put in an able minute by Colonel de Meuron, a Swiss who commanded a regiment of mercenaries in the pay of Holland, and who, on the expulsion of the Dutch, entered the service of the British East India Company: "When the Portuguese established themselves in Ceylon," he says, "commerce was not their only object; they wished to convert the natives to Christianity. Persons of the highest rank became sponsors when Singhalese families were to be baptized, and gave their names to the converts. This is the origin of the numerous Portuguese names amongst the Singhalese. The Dutch occupied themselves less with conversion, but employed the more speedy means of making nominal Christians by giving certain offices to men of that religion only. But the instruction given to *these official converts* was too superficial to root out their prejudices in favour of the idolatry of their ancestors."—*Wellesley MSS.,* Brit. Mus., No. 13,864, p. 96.

pride the honorific title of *Don*, accorded to them by their first European conquerors, and still prefix to their ancient patronymics the sonorous Christian names of the Portuguese.[1] A.D. 1796.

On the surrender of Colombo, such of the civil inhabitants of the place as had means to establish themselves elsewhere took their departure from Ceylon; persons with capital transferred themselves to Batavia; the clergy, and the judicial officers, continued in their position (the latter for a given time to decide pending suits), whilst the bulk of those employed in the public departments retained their occupations and emoluments. Their industry and abilities secured to them a continuance in the career to which they had attached themselves. Under the British dominion they became writers and practitioners in the Courts of Law; and in every public office in the colony, at the present time, the establishment of clerks is composed almost exclusively of burghers and gentlemen who trace their ancestry to Holland.

Ceylon having thus become an English possession by right of conquest, its future administration was a question of embarrassment. Mr. Pitt and Lord Melville were anxious to retain it under the direct control of the crown; but it had been formally ceded to the East India Company after being captured by their forces, and the Court of Directors were naturally eager to retain the government and patronage of so valuable an acquisition. Besides it was still doubtful whether, in the event of a general peace, the island might not be

[1] WOLF, in his autobiography, says the title of "Don" was sold by the Portuguese for a "few hundred dollars," on the receipt of which, "the Governor took a thin silver plate, on which the name of the individual was written with the title of *Don* prefixed, and bound it with his own hand on the forehead of the individual, he kneeling at the same time; and ordered him to "rise Don So and so!" By this contrivance the Portuguese got an enormous sum, as every one that could scrape together the amount required, got himself ennobled. The Dutch afterwards made still sorrier work of it, and sold the title of Don for fifty, twenty-five, and even so low as ten dollars."—*Life and Adventures, &c.*, p. 255.

A.D. 1797. wholly or in part restored to the Batavian Republic[1]; and in the meantime its management was confided to the Governor and Council of Madras.

No arrangement could have proved more unfortunate. Mr. Andrews, a Madras civilian, who, in response to the overtures of the king of Kandy, in 1796, was sent to negotiate a treaty of alliance, was entrusted, in addition to his mission as ambassador, with extraordinary powers as superintendent of the Ceylon revenues, a capacity in which he was empowered to revise and re-adjust the financial system of the new colony. He was a rash and indolent man, utterly uninformed as to the character and customs of the Singhalese, and seemingly unconscious that great changes amongst a rude and semi-civilised people can only be effected, if suddenly, by force — if gradually, by persuasion and kindness. Ignorant of any fiscal arrangements, except those which prevailed in the Madras Presidency, Mr. Andrews, by a rude exertion of power, swept away the previously existing imposts and agencies for their collection in Ceylon; and substituted, in all its severity, the revenue system of the Carnatic, introducing simultaneously a host of Malabar subordinates to enforce it. The service tenures by which the people held their otherwise untaxed lands were abolished, and a proportion of the estimated produce demanded in substitution, together with a tax upon their coco-nut gardens. The customs duties, and other sources of income, were farmed out to Moors, Parsees, and Chetties from the coast; and the Moodliars and native officers who had formerly managed matters involving taxation, were superseded by Malabar dubashes, men aptly described "as enemies to the religion of the Singhalese, strangers to their habits, and animated by no impulse but extortion."[2] Unhap-

---

[1] Ceylon was not finally incorporated with the British possessions till the Peace of Amiens, 27th March, 1802.

[2] Letter of the Hon. F. North to the Earl of Mornington, 27th October, 1798. (*Wellesley MSS.*, Brit. Mus., No. 13,685, p. 52.)

pily, under the belief that their functions were but temporary, and that Ceylon would shortly be given back to the Dutch [1], Mr. Andrews and his European colleagues exerted no adequate influence to control the excesses of these men, and the atrocities and cruelties perpetrated by them were such as almost defy belief.[2] The result may be anticipated; the Singhalese population were exasperated beyond endurance, their chiefs and headmen, insulted by the supercession of their authority, and outraged by the rapacity of low caste dubashes, encouraged the resistance of the people; the Dutch civilians inspired them with the assurance of assistance from the French [3]; and under these combined influences the population, in 1797, rose in violent revolt, and occupied intrenched positions on the line leading from the low country towards the Kandyan hills. The moment was in every respect critical; three military governors of Colombo had died within the five months that the English had been in possession of the island [4]; a force of Sepoys was sent against the rebels, severe conflicts ensued, but it was not till after considerable loss on both sides that the insurgents were subdued. In the meantime, Colonel de Meuron [5] was despatched by Lord Hobart from Madras, and placed at the head of a commission directed to inquire into the causes of discontent, and the means of allaying it.

A.D. 1797.

This calamity in Ceylon had the instant effect of deciding the policy of Mr. Pitt, and of the Government at home, as to the future disposal of the island. It was

[1] During the abortive negotiations of the Earl of Malmesbury with the French Directory for peace in 1797, the restoration of Ceylon to the Batavian Republic was one of the conditions required and refused.—MALMESBURY's *Diary, &c.*, vol. iii.

[2] Facts regarding the proceedings of the Madras officials will be found in a passage in the *Travels of* Lord VALENTIA, vol. i. ch. vi. p. 315. The statement bears internal evidence of having been supplied by Mr. North.

[3] *Minute* of Lord HOBART, 15th March, 1798.

[4] PERCIVAL's *Ceylon, &c.*, p. 132; BURNAND's *Mémoire, Asiat. Journ.*, vol. xi. p. 444.

[5] See Note 2, p. 68.

A.D. 1798. resolved to administer the colony direct from the crown, and in October, 1798, the Honourable Frederick North, afterwards Earl of Guildford, landed as the first British governor. His appointment, and that of all the civil officers, were made by the king; but in the conduct of affairs, he was placed under the orders of the Governor-General of India [1], an arrangement which endured till Ceylon was incorporated with the British dominions by the treaty of Amiens, in 1802.

Mr. North arrived in time to carry into effect the recommendations of De Meuron, that the Carnatic revenue system should be forthwith suspended, and the Malabar dubashes sent back to the continent; that the native Moodliars should be re-instated in their offices and dignities; the obnoxious taxes abolished, and till a preferable arrangement could be introduced by degrees, that the Dutch system should be resorted to for the moment. "I have no scruple," said Mr. North, in his first executive minute, "in declaring that as it was established and administered under the Dutch and their predecessors, no system could be imagined more directly hostile to property, to the industrial improvement, and felicity of the people. But the inveteracy of habit prohibits all but gradual change, and the experience of what has passed since our conquest of the island must have convinced every one, that abrupt and total revolutions in laws and civil polity are not the means by which an enlightened government can improve the understanding, stimulate the industry, and encourage the prosperity of

[1] In describing the administration of Mr. North, I have had the advantage of access to a collection of his private letters addressed, during the period of his government, to the Marquis of Wellesley, and deposited, after the death of the latter, by his representatives in the British Museum, where they form Nos. 13,864, 5, 6, 7 in the Catalogue of Additional MSS. These important documents throw a light altogether new over the leading events of the period, especially upon the excesses and corruptions of the Madras officials, and the more than questionable negotiations between Mr. North and the prime minister of the King of Kandy, which were the prelude to the lamentable massacre of the British troops in 1803.

a people long accustomed to poverty, and slothful submission to vexatious and undefined authority."[1] A.D. 1798.

The Augean task of reforming such a state of fiscal affairs was rendered infinitely more difficult by the intrigues, inefficiency, and corruption of the Madras civil servants, the majority of whom he was compelled to get rid of by suspension, dismissal, and forced resignations.[2]

Another source of annoyance was the lapse of the period allowed by the capitulation of Colombo for the duration of the Dutch tribunals, whilst there still remained suits to be decided; and although the island was thus left without any legal courts, the Dutch officials, who were still subjects of Holland, and looked forward to an early restoration of her authority, firmly refused to take the oath of allegiance, and accept judicial appointments under the British crown. This embarrassment Mr. North met by obtaining legal assistance from Bengal, and organising circuits round the island for the administration of justice.[3]

The attention of the governor was now attracted to the strange occurrences which were passing at Kandy. The king, Rajadhi Raja Singha, was deposed, and died in 1798, two years after the arrival of the British[4], and, leaving no issue, the Adigar or prime minister, Pilámé

[1] Mr. NORTH to the Earl of MORNINGTON (afterwards Marquis of WELLESLEY), Nov. 1798. (*Wellesley MSS.*, Brit. Mus., No. 13,865, p. 212.)

[2] Mr. North writes to the Earl of Mornington, of "the infamous faction of Madras civilians," and his letters contain the details of the plunder of the Government to the extent of 60,000 pagodas by one gentleman who had charge of the Pearl Fishery; and of another, under whose corrupt judicial management in the Eastern Province, "more than 4000 inhabitants from the single district of the Wanny had been driven away since our occupation of the island."—*Wellesley MSS.*, No. 13,866, p. 173; No. 13,867, p. 28. See also Mr. North's Letter to the Secret Committee, 5th October, 1799 (*Ibid.*, p. 35).

[3] Mr. NORTH to the Earl of MORNINGTON, 27th October, 1798 (*Wellesley MSS.*, No. 13,866, p. 52; 3rd November). *Ibid.*, p. 161; 30th October, 1799, No. 13,867, p. 60. The first head of the judicial establishment was Sir Edmund Carrington, a friend and fellow-student of Sir William Jones.

[4] TURNOUR, in his *Epitome*, gives no particulars of his fate; but Mr. North, writing to Lord Mornington the same year in which he died, 1798, says "the *deposition* of the late king, and the elevation of the boy

A.D. 1798. Taláwé, in virtue of a Kandyan usage, proceeded to nominate, as his successor, a nephew of the queen, a boy eighteen years old, who ascended the throne as Wikrema Raja Singha; the last in the long list of kings who reigned over Ceylon.

Although the late king had died without ratifying the treaty negotiated in 1796, the most amicable relations subsisted between his successor and the English, and Mr. North was preparing to do honour to the new sovereign by an embassy of unusual magnificence, when communications of a most confidential nature were opened with him by the Adigar. In the course of numerous interviews with the governor, and his secretary, Pilámé Taláwé avowed unreservedly his hatred of the reigning Malabar family, his desire to procure the death or dethronement of the king, and his ambition to restore in his own person a national dynasty to the kingdom.[1] Mr. North, while he disclaimed participation in projects so treasonable, discerned in the designs of the Adigar an opportunity for establishing a military protectorate at Kandy with a subsidised British force, on the model of the mediatised provinces of India; and it must be regretted that in the too eager pursuit of this object, Mr. North not only forbore to denounce the treason of the minister, but lent himself to intrigues inconsistent with the dignity and honour of his high office.

A.D. 1799. In the development of the Governor's plans the Adigar was encouraged to disclose his designs for the ruin of the young king, whom it was his intention to stimulate to acts of atrocity such as would make him at once odious to his own nation and hostile to the English, thus provoking a war in which the Adigar was to profit by his overthrow.[2] Mr. North did not consider it unbecom-

who now reigns, was the work of Pilámé, first minister,—a great friend of ours."—Letter, 27th Oct. 1798, *Wellesley MSS.*, No. 13,866, p. 55.

[1] Pilámé Taláwé boasted his descent from the royal line of Ceylon.

[2] There are two works which may be regarded as containing Mr. North's

ing his high position to discuss with him the terms of a compromise in a matter so revolting; and stipulating only for the personal safety and nominal rank of the king, he came to an agreement by which the Kandyan sovereign was to be reduced to a nonentity, and the Adigar to be virtually invested with regal authority. It was even contemplated that the king should be induced to retire altogether from the capital, to take up his residence at Jaffna within the British dominions, and that Pilámé Taláwé was to become regent of the kingdom, within which a British force was to be maintained at the cost of the Kandyan people.[1]

A.D. 1799.

The project was to be carried into execution by means of an embassy, which was forthwith to be despatched, ostensibly to negotiate a treaty with the king, but it was privately arranged that the ambassador was to be the General commanding in the island; and the intended subsidiary force was to be introduced under the name and guise of his "escort."

It is impossible to read without pain the letters in which Mr. North communicates confidentially, for the information and approval of the Governor-General of India, the progress of this discreditable intrigue. He labours to persuade himself that in taking a disingenuous course he was adopting the only line open to him at

apology for his share in these transactions, and his defence of his general administration. Viscount VALENTIA, in 1804, spent three weeks in Ceylon as the guest of the Governor, and in the *Travels* which he afterwards published, he has embodied an elaborate review of Mr. North's policy. But being, as he says, confined by indisposition, the particulars which he supplies concerning the island were "*derived from the most authentic sources*"—and, in fact, on comparing his statement with the private letters of Mr. North to the Marquis of Wellesley, we find that they exhibit internal evidence of being, in part at least, the work of one hand (*Travels*, vol. i. p. 277-279). About the same time, the Rev. J. CORDINER, who had been chaplain in the island from 1799 to 1804, wrote his *Description of Ceylon*, and in pt. ii. ch. i. vol. ii. p. 155, he gives a narrative of the Kandyan campaign in 1803, and the causes which led to it; and this, too, evidently emanated from the same source as the account given by Lord Valentia. Reading these two manifestoes by the light of Mr. North's confidential correspondence with the Governor-General, the events they record assume an aspect greatly to be regretted.

[1] Lord VALENTIA, ch. vi. p. 282.

A.D. 1799. once to save the life of the king of Kandy[1], and to promote the political interest of Great Britain.

The reception of an "armed British force in the central capital" he regards as so "highly essential to British interests, that he will not endanger the success of the negotiation by any over-strictness in the terms on which it is to be obtained."[2] His principal object now is, he says, to collect such a military force in the island, as would enable him to despatch to Kandy "a body of troops capable of effectuating all the objects of the intended treaty, and of subduing by its own strength any opposition which it may experience."[3] "As to the king's dignity," he adds, "I shall never conspire to take it away, but if he loses it I shall give myself as little concern as when he usurped it—and should the Adigar succeed without any concurrence of mine in dethroning him, I suppose you would make no objection to having the said Adigar as a vassal." It is obvious that the sentiments thus privately expressed to the Marquis of Wellesley are at variance with the simultaneous declarations of Mr. North to the Adigar, as stated on his authority by Lord Valentia.[4]

In 1800 the programme already sketched out was agreed on, and the Adigar took his departure for Kandy, to obtain the formal assent of the king to the entrance of so unprecedented a body of troops in the suite of an ambassador.[5] He was to be asked to allow 1000 men

---

[1] "I am certain that if the troops are not sent, and if they are not put into possession of the capital, the poor king would be deposed, if not murdered, or that he would be driven into aggression against us, which I hope will excuse me in your eyes and in those of the world for not being so delicate as I otherwise should about forcing his inclination or abridging his power."—Mr. NORTH to the Earl of MORNINGTON, 4th Feb. 1800.—*Wellesley MSS.*, No. 13,867, p. 75.

[2] Mr. NORTH to the Earl of MORNINGTON, 25th Dec. 1799.—*Wellesley MSS.*, No. 13,867, p. 65.

[3] *Ibid.*

[4] See Lord VALENTIA'S *Travels*, ch. vi. p. 294.

[5] Writing to Lord Mornington, 3rd February, 1800, Mr. North avows that one object he had in view for despatching the Adigar on this errand was *to test his influence* over the king. "If he has it," he continues, "I own I shall have little scruple in taking this the only measure which can preserve the king's life and prevent a

to "escort" General MacDowall, but Mr. North intimates that there would in reality be 1,800, and that they might eventually be raised to 2,500.[1] A.D. 1800.

Still anxious for self-justification on the plea that the presence of the English army would save the life of the king, Mr. North persuaded himself that the step he had resolved on was the only one to avert an invasion of the British territory by the Kandyans. So frank had the Adigar been in discussing this step, as an expedient to precipitate hostilities, that he had asked, "*What would be considered as a sufficient aggression?* and with how many men he was to invade the low country, to compel the British governor to take up arms? I therefore cannot but think," says Mr. North, "that a very minute attention to diplomatic forms would be sacrificing the reality of justice for sake of its appearance; and as the troops will only interfere for securing the government established by the existing power, I do not imagine that the most rigid publicist could find fault with what I am about to do. It is, however, impossible that I should not feel anxious and uneasy in conducting so singular a business."[2]

The influence of the Adigar was sufficiently powerful to overcome the scruples of the king, and permission was granted for the advance of the ambassador with his formidable escort.[3] But the scheme so elaborately con-

---

civil war, as well as an aggression against us, into which it is the intention of this *Lord Sunderland* to hurry his poor master, that he may overturn him."—*Wellesley MSS.*, No. 13,867, p. 72.

[1] Lord VALENTIA, ch. vi. p. 286.

[2] Mr. NORTH to the Earl of MORNINGTON, 7th Feb. 1800 (*Ibid.*, p. 76).

[3] This was announced to the Marquis of Wellesley in the following terms by Mr. North, 16th March, 1800:—"The decision is made, and General MacDowall set out with his escort on Wednesday last. The Adigar, *Rogorum longe turpissimus!* is to meet him at Sitavaca. Only fancy if one of *our* ministers were to behave so about King George, and oblige the Abbé Siéyes to stipulate for his life! I hope that I have not done wrong, but I am not yet certain whether I have acted like a good politician or like a great nincompoop."—*Wellesley MSS.*, No. 13,867. The march of this embassy has been described with great minuteness by PERCIVAL, p. 376, and by CORDINER, vol. ii. ch. vi. p. 287. There is also an interesting account of it in the *MSS.* of M. JOINVILLE, who accompanied the expedition in the capacity

A.D. 1800. cocted, and launched with so much enterprise, was doomed to an early failure. The alarm of the king was at length excited by the nobles; a large portion of the English troops was ordered to remain at the frontier, the march of the others was impeded by leading them through impracticable passes, where the heavy guns were left behind, and on his arrival at Kandy the General was received with only a small part of his intended "army." Here the patience of the embassy was exhausted by long delays, the reception of a subsidised British force was firmly declined, even the negotiation of a treaty was indefinitely postponed, and the General returned to Colombo with his diminished escort, unsuccessful and disappointed.

But the abortive attempt was speedily productive of disastrous results. Mr. North had sown the teeth of

---

of Naturalist and Draughtsman; and in it he has introduced the following characteristic sketch of the Ambassador and the Adigar.

INTERVIEW BETWEEN GENERAL MACDOWALL AND THE ADIGAR.

1. General MacDowall. 2. Pilâmé Talâwé. 3. The Moodliar Interpreter.

the dragon, and they germinated into an early and fearful harvest of blood. A.D. 1801.

The Adigar, foiled in his endeavours to reduce his sovereign to a pageant, turned to his remaining device of provoking a war by aggression on British territory and subjects. Nearly two years were spent in efforts to this end; first his agents excited insurrections, which were speedily quelled, at Negombo and Manaar[1], and next he himself sought alternately to embroil the governor by secret charges against the king, and to infuriate the king by insinuations against the governor.[2] Overtures for a treaty were made from Kandy, but on conditions so inadmissible as to ensure their rejection. At length, in April 1802, armed parties began to disturb the frontier; and a rich tavalam or caravan of Moors, British subjects, returning from Kandy to Putlam, were forcibly deprived of their property by officers of the king. A.D. 1802.

This was the "sufficient aggression" which the Adigar had so long meditated. Compensation was evaded, war ensued, and in February, 1803, a British force of 3000 men under General MacDowall took possession of Kandy, which they found evacuated by the inhabitants. A.D. 1803.

The king fled to Hanguran-ketty, after firing the palace and temples; and the English general, in concert with the perfidious Adigar, placed Mootoo Saamy, a compliant member of the royal family, on the throne. The first act of the new sovereign was to realise the desired policy

---

[1] Mr. NORTH to the Earl of MORNINGTON, 15th June, 1800 (*Wellesley MSS.*, p. 125). The pretext was the imposition of a tax on the wearing of jewels. Mr. NORTH says, he "had evidence on oath that the Adigar had at the same time attempted to organise a revolt at Colombo, with assurances of co-operation from Kandy."

[2] Amongst other imputations by which he alarmed the king, was the insinuation that the 5000 British troops assembled at Trincomalie in 1801, under the command of Colonel Wellesley, afterwards Duke of Wellington, and intended for the reduction of Batavia, were in reality designed for the invasion of Kandy. —Mr. NORTH to the M. of WELLESLEY, 13th June, 1801. This force was subsequently conducted to Egypt by Sir David Baird.

A.D. 1803. of Mr. North, by accepting a subsidiary force, and conceding extensive territory to the British Crown. The Adigar who, in the midst of the turmoil, contrived to retain his influence with all parties, entered into a separate convention with the general, by which the grand object of his ambition was at last to be realised:—The fugitive king was to be delivered up to the English, the king *de facto* was to be relegated with a suitable appanage to Jaffna, and "the illustrious Lord Pilámé Taláwé," with the title of Grand Prince (*Ootoon Kumarayen*), was to wield the supreme authority at Kandy. On the faith of this convention with an undisguised traitor, the British general retired to Colombo on an ominous anniversary, the 1st April, 1803; leaving behind him 300 English and 700 Malays as the subsidised British contingent.

But it was soon ascertained that the new king was despised by his own countrymen; he had undergone public punishment at a former period for convicted fraud,—"he met with no adherents, and remained in the palace surrounded only by domestics, and supported by no other power than the British army,"[1] who were speedily decimated by disease.

The Adigar, apparently hurried beyond his usual discretion by the rapid success of his treason, saw but another step between him and the throne. Of the two kings, one was an outlaw, the other an imbecile *fainéant;* the British troops were prostrated by sickness, and the moment appeared propitious to grasp the crown he had so long coveted. He formed the bold design to seize the person of the English governor; to exterminate the attenuated English garrison; to destroy the rival sovereigns, and found a new dynasty in Kandy. The first plot was defeated by an accident[2], but the massacre of the forces was fearfully realised.

The hospitals at the moment were surcharged with

---

[1] Lord Valentia, ch. vi. vol. i. p. 298; Cordiner, vol. ii. p. 188.

[2] The person of Mr. North was to have been seized during an inter-

sick, and the available strength of the British was reduced to a handful of European convalescents and about four hundred Malays and gun-lascars, under an incompetent and inexperienced commandant, Major Davie. A.D. 1803.

On the morning of the 24th June, Kandy was surrounded by thousands of armed natives; who assailed the British garrison from the hills which overhang the ancient palace; numbers were killed, and the residue, exhausted and helpless, were compelled to capitulate. The Adigar guaranteed their safety and that of the royal *protégé*, Mootoo Saamy, with whom they were permitted to march about three miles, to the banks of the Mahawelli-ganga, on their way to Trincomalie. But they were detained for two days, unable to pass the river, which was swollen by the recent rains; and here they were forced to surrender the person of the prince, who was instantly slain. Major Davie was led back to Kandy, his soldiers were persuaded to give up their arms, the Malays were made prisoners, and the British officers and men, led two by two into a hollow out of sight of their comrades, were felled by blows from behind, inflicted by the Caffres, and despatched by the knives of the Kandyans.

One soldier alone escaped from the carnage and survived to tell the fate of his companions.[1] An officer[2] who commanded at Fort MacDowall, about eighteen miles eastward of Kandy, spiked his guns, abandoned his

view which the Adigar solicited at Dambedenia, in the Seven Corles, but the attempt was rendered abortive by the unforeseen arrival of an officer with a detachment of 300 Malays, who came to pay their respects to the Governor.—CORDINER, vol. ii. p. 201.

[1] This was Corporal Barnsley, whose singular story will be found in the *Historical Sketch of the Conquest of Ceylon by the British*, written by HENRY MARSHALL, Deputy Inspector-General of Hospitals, a book which contains by far the best account of the military operations of the British from 1803 to 1804. Dr. DAVY, in his work on the *Interior of Ceylon* (ch. x. p. 313), has given a number of curious particulars of these occurrences, gleaned by personal inquiry from the Kandyans—from which it would appear that the actual massacre was the work of the king, and not of the Adigar. CORDINER'S Narrative of the same events will be found in his 2nd vol. ch. iii. p. 203.

[2] Captain Madge.

A.D. 1803. sick, and with difficulty succeeded in bringing off his men to Trincomalie — another held his position at Dambedenia till brought off by a relief from Colombo; but within the briefest possible space, not one British soldier was left within the dominions of Kandy.[1]

Years were allowed to elapse before any adequate retribution was inflicted on the authors of this massacre. CORDINER, who was at Colombo when the intelligence arrived, describes the effect as "universal consternation; it was like a burst of thunder portended by a dark and gloomy sky and followed by an awful and overpowering calm."[2] The first impulse of the English was for general and indiscriminate vengeance on the Kandyan people; but death and disease had so reduced the British force, that even this was impracticable for want of troops, and the few that remained serviceable had soon ample occupation in defending their own territory from the dangers with which it was threatened from Kandy.

The bloody triumph he had achieved seemed to have suddenly inflamed the savage king with a sense of his own strength and a consciousness of the impregnability of his natural defences. By a strenuous exertion of his authority and influence over the low-country Singhalese, he succeeded in exciting a spirit of revolt, and in a very few weeks there was not a point throughout the entire circuit of the island, from Hambangtotte and Tangalle to Jaffna and Trincomalie, at which the native population were not preparing to take up arms for the expulsion of the British; whilst the Kandyans themselves, descending in hordes from the hills, made simultaneous attacks upon Matura on the south, Chilaw and Putlam on the west, Moeletivoe and

---

[1] Major Davie was detained in captivity at Kandy till 1810, when he died without having any opportunity to communicate with his country, or to leave a defence of his memory from the serious imputations that rest upon it.

[2] CORDINER, ch. iii. vol. ii. p. 219.

Jaffna on the north, and Batticaloa and Cottiar on the eastern coast. The king in person led an army to lay siege to Colombo, and advanced to Hangwelle within eighteen miles of the Fort; but he was driven back by the garrison, who recovered from his discomfited followers a number of the guns and muskets which had belonged to the ill-fated force of Major Davie. Equally foiled at all other points, the king went up into his mountain fastnesses, leaving the English in the low country so exhausted by the campaign that the last available soldiers were withdrawn from Colombo, and the duty of the garrison entrusted to pensioners and invalids.[1] A.D. 1803.

Mr. North applied to the Governor-General of India for at least 3000 troops[2], to enable him to take vengeance on the Kandyans; but the renewal of hostilities between England and France in 1803 rendered it impossible to send such reinforcements to Ceylon as would have enabled the Governor to take effectual measures for the recapture of Kandy[3];—and for the two following years he was forced to confine his operations to the chastisement of the Singhalese districts which had

[1] CORDINER, vol. ii. ch. iii. p. 236.

[2] Mr. NORTH to the Marquis of WELLESLEY, 29th July, 1804 (*Wellesley MSS.*, p. 264).

[3] One effort was contemplated in 1804 for an assault upon Kandy by a simultaneous advance of British troops from six different points of the coast, all concentrating at the capital. Orders were issued to some of the intended commanders, but on further inquiry the attempt was found impracticable, and abandoned. Amongst others, Captain Johnston had been directed to march from Batticaloa, and make his appearance at Kandy on a given day—and this order, by some strange accident, *it was omitted to countermand.* Captain Johnston, in consequence, advanced with about 300 men, of whom 82 were Europeans, on the 20th September—fought his way to Kandy, which he occupied for three days, and retracing his perilous course, brought off his men to Trincomalie on the 20th October, 1804, with only the loss of 10 British soldiers, and 6 wounded. This heroic adventure came opportunely to retrieve the character of the British army from the disgrace into which it had sunk in the minds of the Kandyans. Forbes was informed by one of the chiefs who had harassed Captain Johnston's retreat, that an impression left on the natives was that he "must have been in alliance with supernatural powers, as his judgment and energy, superior as they were, were insufficient to account for his escape through one continued ambush.—FORBES' *Eleven Years in Ceylon*, vol. i. p. 41. Captain Johnston has left an account of his *Expedition to Kandy*, London, 1810, which is one of the most thrilling military narratives on record.

A.D. 1803. displayed disaffection, and to laying waste the outlying territories of Kandy, burning the villages and temples, and destroying the harvests and fruit trees. The private correspondence of Mr. North at this period with the Governor-General of India evinces the intensity of his anxiety for peace. Messages were sent secretly to the king, through the high priest of Kandy, to entreat him to ask for pardon, as all the Governor required was not treasure or territories, "but satisfaction for the horrid crime he had perpetrated;" but the only reply was a refusal on the ground that the butchery had been committed without his orders by the Adigar, from whom he had since withdrawn his confidence.[1] A sullen peace ensued from the exhaustion of the enemy; and the long-deferred retribution for the atrocities of 1803 was not exacted till 1815, when a renewal of similar aggressions and cruelties by the Kandyan sovereign led to the final and effectual overthrow of his authority.

The administration of Mr. North, although dimmed by these diplomatic errors and the sanguinary results by which they were followed, was characterised by signal success in the organisation of the civil government; the promotion of religion, education, and commerce; the establishment of courts of justice; the reform of the revenue; and the advancement of native agriculture and industry. The three military governors who succeeded him between 1805 and 1820[2], devoted to the civil improvement of the colony all the attention compatible with the inadequate income of the settlement, and the vigilance and precautions indispensable for its protection from foreign, as well as internal enemies.

During this interval, the career of the Kandyan king

[1] Mr. NORTH to the Marquis of WELLESLEY, 17th January, 1804 (*Wellesley MSS.*, p. 287). CORDINER states (ch. iii. vol. ii. p. 259), that these advances for peace were "made by the Kandyans," but the letter quoted above shows that they emanated from the Governor.

[2] 1805, Lieutenant General the Right Honourable Sir Thomas Maitland, G.C.B. 1811, Major-General Wilson, Lieutenant-Governor. 1812, General Sir Robert Brownrigg, Bart., G.C.B.

presents a picture of tyrannous atrocity unsurpassed, A.D. 1803.
if it be even paralleled, in its savage excesses, by any recorded example of human depravity. Distracted between the sense of possessing regal power and the consciousness of inability to wield it, he was at once tyrannous and timid, suspicious and revengeful. Insurrections were excited by his cruelties, and the chiefs who remained loyal became odious from possessing the influence to suppress them. The forced labour of the people was expended on works of caprice and inutility[1]; and the courtiers who ventured to remonstrate were dismissed and exiled to their estates. At length, the often-baffled traitor, Pilámé Taláwé, was detected in an attempt to assassinate the king, and beheaded in 1812, A.D. 1812.
and his nephew, Eheylapola, raised to the office of Adigar.

But Eheylapola inherited with the power all the ambitious duplicity of his predecessor; and availing A.D. 1814.
himself of the universal horror with which the king was regarded, he secretly solicited the connivance of the Governor, Sir Robert Brownrigg, to the organisation of a general revolt. The conspiracy was discovered and extinguished with indiscriminate bloodshed; whilst the discomfited Adigar was forced to fly to Colombo, and supplicate the protection of the British.[2] And now followed an awful tragedy, which cannot be more vividly described than in the language of Davy, who collected the particulars from eye-witnesses of the scene. "Hurried along by the flood of his revenge, the tyrant, lost to every tender feeling, resolved to punish Eheylapola who had escaped, through his family, who still remained in his power: he sentenced his wife and children, and his brother and his wife, to death; the brother and children to be beheaded, and the females to be drowned. In front of the queen's palace, and between the Nata and Maha

[1] The ornamental lake at Kandy was formed about the year 1809, by order of the king.

[2] In May, 1814.

A.D. 1814. Vishnu Dewales, as if to shock and insult the gods as well as the sex, the wife of Eheylapola and his children were brought from prison, where they had been in charge of female gaolers, and delivered over to their executioners. The lady, with great resolution, maintained hers and her children's innocence and her lord's; at the same time, submitting to the king's pleasure, and offering up her own and her offsprings' lives, with the fervent hope that her husband would be benefited by the sacrifice. Having uttered these sentiments aloud, she desired her eldest child to submit to his fate; the poor boy, who was eleven years old, clung to his mother terrified and crying; her second son, of nine years, heroically stepped forward: and bade his brother not to be afraid—he would show him the way to die! By the blow of a sword the head of this noble child was severed from his body; streaming with blood, and hardly inanimate, it was thrown into a rice mortar, the pestle was put into the mother's hands, and she was ordered to pound it, or be disgracefully tortured. To avoid the infamy, the wretched woman did lift up the pestle and let it fall. One by one the heads of her children were cut off; and one by one the poor mother . . . but the circumstance is too dreadful to be dwelt on. One of the children was an infant, and it was plucked from its mother's breast to be beheaded: when the head was severed from the body, the milk it had just drawn ran out mingled with its blood. During this tragical scene, the crowd who had assembled to witness it wept and sobbed aloud, unable to suppress their feelings of grief and horror. Palihapanè Dissave was so affected that he fainted, and was expelled his office for showing such sensibility. During two days, the whole of Kandy, with the exception of the tyrant's court, was as one house of mourning and lamentation, and so deep was the grief that not a fire, it is said, was kindled, no food was dressed, and a general fast was held. After the execution of her children, the sufferings of the mother were speedily relieved. She and her sister-in-law were led to the little tank in the immediate neighbourhood of Kandy, called Bogambara, and drowned."[1] A.D. 1814.

This awful occurrence in all its hideous particulars, I have had verified by individuals still living, who were spectators of a scene that, after the lapse of forty years, is still spoken of with a shudder.

But the limit of human endurance had been passed: revolt became rife throughout the kingdom: promiscuous executions followed, and the terrified nation anxiously watched for the approach of a British force to rescue them from the monster on the throne. At length, the insensate savage ventured to challenge the descent of the vengeance that awaited him. A party of native merchants, British subjects, who had gone up to Kandy to trade, were seized and mutilated by the tyrant; they were deprived of their ears, their noses, and hands, and those who survived were driven towards Colombo, with the severed members tied to their necks.[2]

An avenging army was instantly on its march. War was declared in January 1815[3], and within a few weeks the Kandyan capital was once more in possession of the English[4], and the despot a captive at Colombo, whence he was eventually transferred to the Indian A.D. 1815.

---

[1] DAVY, ch. x. p. 321.

[2] It cannot extenuate so wanton an atrocity to mention that in the *Mahawanso*, the exploit is related with complacency of Mogallana, who, on the deposition of his parricidal brother, Kaasyapa, A.D. 495, "*cut off the ears and noses* of the late king's ministers before driving them into exile."—*Mahawanso*, ch. xxxix.

[3] The declaration of war sets out that it was undertaken in compliance with "the prayers of more than one half the Kandyan kingdom," and with the sympathies of the rest, for the vindication of British subjects outraged by the king, and the security of his majesty's possessions, which had already been violated by the irruptions and depredations of Kandyan forces across the border. "War," it announced, "was not directed against the people but their tyrant, who had become an object of abhorrence to mankind," and protection was offered to every Kandyan subject who was prepared to welcome their deliverers.

[4] 14th February, 1815. "From this day we date the extinction of Singhalese independence—an independence which had continued without material interruption for 2,357 years." — KNIGHTON, ch. xvii. p. 325.

A.D. 1815. fortress of Vellore.[1] The proclamation of the Viceroy recalled the massacre of 1803 as one of the many causes of the war, and on the 2nd March, 1815, a solemn convention of the chiefs assembled in the audience hall of the palace of Kandy, at which a treaty was concluded formally deposing the king and vesting his dominions in the British Crown; on condition that the national religion should be maintained and protected, justice impartially administered to the people, and the chiefs guaranteed in their ancient privileges and powers. Eheylapola, who had cherished the expectation that the crown would have descended to his own head, bore the disappointment with dignity, declined the offers of high office, and retired with the declaration that his ambition was satisfied by being recognised as "the Friend of the British Government."

A.D. 1816. Happy as this consummation appeared, the tranquillity which ensued was but transient; before two years the same people who had invited the English as deliverers rose in rebellion to expel them as intruders. Nor is this anomaly, strange as it may seem, without explanation. With the mass of the population the king was less odious than the chiefs who were "the real tyrants of the country;"[2] and as these were still to be maintained in all their dangerous powers, the people, even whilst the cannon were thundering salutes in honour of the victory, exhi-

---

[1] A curious account of the capture of the king, and his demeanour after his deposition, is contained in a pamphlet published in 1815, under the title of "*A Narrative of Events which have recently occurred in Ceylon*, written by a Gentleman on the spot; London, Egerton, 1815." From the identity of the materials with those in the xxvth ch. of the *History of Ceylon*, by PHILALETHES, the two statements appear to have been written by the same person, and evidently by one who was present in Colombo whilst the occurrences he describes were in progress. One remark which the king made is worth recording: "Your English governors," he said, "have one advantage over us kings of Kandy—they have councillors near them who never allow them to do anything in a passion; but, unfortunately for us, the offender is dead before our resentment has subsided."—P. 180. The king died at Vellore, 30th January, 1832.

[2] SAWYER'S *MS. Notes on the Conquest of Kandy;* MARSHALL, p. 70.

bited a sullen indifference to the change.[1] The remoteness of Britain rendered its abstract authority unintelligible, and the Kandyans were unable to realise the myth for which they had exchanged a visible king. The chiefs themselves soon discovered that their rank failed to command its accustomed homage and obedience; the nice distinctions of caste were unappreciable by the English soldiers, and its prejudices and peculiarities were unconsciously subjected to incessant violations.[2] Two years of the experiment were sufficient to ripen the universal disappointment into an appetite for change.[3] So impatient had all classes become, that uniformity of feeling supplied the place of organisation[4]; and without combination or concert, nearly the whole kingdom rose simultaneously in arms in the autumn of 1817. An aspirant to the crown was duly adopted and obeyed; the dissave of Oovah, who had been sent to tranquillise the disturbed districts, placed himself at the head of the insurgents, and Eheylapola, the ardent "friend of the British Government," was seized and expatriated for fomenting the rebellion.[5] A guerilla war ensued, in which regular troops, traversing damp forests by jungle tracks and mountain passes, were less distressed by the enemy than by exposure, privations, and disease. For more than ten months discomfiture seemed imminent, and so universal was the conspiracy of the inhabitants, that not a Kandyan leader of any

A.D. 1816.

A.D. 1817.

[1] MARSHALL, who was present during the conference in Kandy, says, "they did not leave their ordinary occupations even to look at the troops which were assembled in review order in the great square before the Audience Hall. Apparently, they regarded the transfer of the Government from an Oriental to a European dynasty with perfect unconcern."—P. 163.

[2] DAVY, ch. x. p. 326; MARSHALL, p. 174.

[3] The Kandyans used to inquire when the English meant to leave the maritime provinces? "You have deposed the king," said one, "and nothing more is required, you may leave us now." "They showed no dislike to us individually, but as a nation, they abhorred us; they made no complaint of oppression or misrule, simply wishing that we should leave the country."—MARSHALL, p. 175.

[4] MARSHALL, p. 179.

[5] Eheylapola was transported to the Mauritius, where he died in exile in 1829.

A.D. 1817. consequence was taken, and not a district was either pacified or subdued.[1] So great was the apprehension of the Government, and such the horrors of the species of warfare in which they were involved, that the expediency had already been discussed of abandoning the contest and withdrawing the British forces to the coast[2], when towards the close of 1818, the Kandyans, harassed by the destruction of their villages and cattle, rendered destitute by the devastation of their country, and disheartened by the loss of upwards of ten thousand persons, either fallen in the field or destroyed by famine and fever[3], began to throw out signals of submission. The rebellious chiefs were captured; the pretender fled; the great palladium, "the sacred tooth" of Buddha, which had been stolen and paraded to arouse the fanatical enthusiasm of the people, was recovered and restored to its depository in Kandy; and before the close of the year, the whole country returned to tranquillity and order.

The rebellion of 1817 was the last great occasion on which the English forces were arrayed in hostility against the natives of any portion of Ceylon. Amongst the Singhalese of the maritime districts, there has never prevailed any long-sustained feeling of discontent with the British rule, and the insurrectionary disturbances around the coast, which followed the massacre of 1803, were excited by the influence, and carried on by the direct instrumentality, of the Adigar and the King of Kandy. But a very few years' experience of the beneficence of English government sufficed to eradicate any tendency to disaffection, and in our subsequent struggles with the people of the hill country, the inhabitants of the lowlands exhibited neither sympathy nor co-operation with the enemy.

The case was, however, different with the Kandyan

---

[1] DAVY, ch. x. p. 327.
[2] MARSHALL, p. 191.
[3] DAVY, *Ibid.*, p. 331.

chiefs, and the measures essential to conciliate the mass of the population were calculated to increase the irritation of their feudal masters. A.D. 1817.

The relation of clans-men to a Kandyan chief had always been one of stolid bondage; their lands, their labour, and almost their lives, they held dependent on his will; and their priests, although the doctrines of the Buddhist faith repudiate distinctions of caste, taught them to yield a superstitious homage to the exaltation of rank.[1] Sir Robert Brownrigg, on the suppression of the revolt, availed himself of the rupture of the previous treaty by the chiefs to commence the emancipation of the people from their thraldom, by limiting the application of compulsory labour to the construction of works of public utility; imposing a tithe on cultivated lands, in lieu of personal services; transferring the administration of justice from the native headmen to European civilians, reserving to the governor the appointment of the headmen employed in collecting revenue; and substituting official salaries, instead of local assessment, for the remuneration of the chiefs. This was the commencement of a policy, afterwards consistently developed by further changes, all tending to narrow the range of feudal power, and expand the influence and protection of law. The resentment provoked by these salutary measures, led to frequent displays of impotent disloyalty: treasonable plots were

---

[1] See the Report of the Committee of the House of Commons on the Affairs of Ceylon in 1850. Evidence of Sir J. EMERSON TENNENT, No. 2,786, 2,787, &c. As the priests of Buddha had been from the first opposed to the substitution of British rule for a native sovereignty, and as they were the main instigators and abettors of the last rebellion, Sir Robert Brownrigg took this opportunity to alter very materially the terms of the obligations contracted in 1815, as regards the Buddhist worship. "By the Convention of 1815, the religion of Buddha is declared *inviolable*, and its rites and places of worship were to be *maintained* and *protected*." But by the proclamation issued in 1818, the only engagement undertaken by the English Government was, that "the priests as well as the ceremonies of the Buddhist religion, shall *receive the respect* which in former times was shown to them;" but by the same document equal protection was "to be given to all other religions."

A.D. 1817. concocted by the chiefs, and rebellion again threatened to disturb the ancient Kandyan kingdom. But civil authority had become consolidated and supreme; the pretenders and conspirators were in every instance arrested and punished, and the island was saved the calamity of renewed civil war.[1]

One event, in the meantime, had for ever altered the aspect of Kandyan warfare. The indomitable mountains which encircled their dominions, had long inspired the kings of Kandy with an audacious confidence in their own security.[2] From the summits of these towering bulwarks they had been accustomed to look down with scorn and defiance on their enemies in the lowlands. The power that crouched behind them was regarded by the Europeans on the coast with a feeling of mystery and alarm; and mindful of the many calamities that had overtaken those who had made the attempt, the undertaking to scale them, should it ever become unavoidable, was regarded with gloomy apprehension. The captor of Kandy in 1815 conceived the bold idea of giving permanence to his conquest, by breaching this gigantic rampart, and forming a highway from the lofty fastness in the hills to the level plains below. The realisation of the project was impeded by the outburst of rebellion in 1817; but no sooner was it quelled than Sir Edward Barnes, who A.D. 1820. succeeded Sir Robert Brownrigg as Governor in 1820, applied with energy all the resources of the Govern-

[1] Such was the impatience of the Kandyan chiefs and the Buddhist priests to restore the Kandyan monarchy that, in addition to the formidable rebellion of 1817, a pretender agitated Welasse in 1820; a Buddhist priest made a similar attempt at Matelle in 1823; a plot was discovered at Bintenne in 1824; arrests for treason took place in 1830; and in 1835 six chiefs of the highest rank were tried for a conspiracy to levy war against the king, and seduce the army from its allegiance in support of a native aspirant to the crown. In 1843, Chandrayotte, a priest, was convicted of high treason at Badulla, and in 1848, the most formidable rising of the Kandyans since 1817 was crushed and defeated by the promptness and vigour of Viscount Torrington.

[2] "He (Raja Singha) hath no forts or castles, but nature hath supplied the want of them. For his whole country standing upon such high hills, and these so difficult to pass, is all an impregnable fort."—KNOX, *Relation, &c.*, pt. ii. ch. vi. p. 44.

ment, and succeeded in carrying a military road, unsurpassed in excellence, into the heart of the Kandyan country, reaching an altitude of more than six thousand feet above the sea. Rocks were pierced, precipices scarped, and torrents bridged, to effect the passage; and the Kandyans, when the task was accomplished, recalled the warning of ancient prophecy, and felt that now the conquest of their country was complete.[1] A.D. 1820.

When the English landed in Ceylon in 1796, there was not in the whole island a single practicable road, and troops, on their toilsome marches between the fortresses on the coast, dragged their cannon through deep sands along the shore.[2] Before Sir Edward Barnes resigned his government, every town of importance was approached by a carriage road; and the long desired highway from sea to sea, to connect Colombo and Trincomalie, was commenced. Civil organisation has since been matured with equal success, domestic slavery has been abolished, religious disqualifications removed, compulsory labour abandoned, a charter of justice promulgated, a legislative council established, trading monopolies extinguished, commerce encouraged in its utmost freedom, and the mountain forests felled to make way for plantations of coffee, whose exuberant produce is already more than sufficient for the consumption of the British empire.

By the Singhalese of the maritime provinces, long familiar with the energy and enterprise of Europeans, these results are regarded with satisfaction. But the Kandyans, brought into more recent contact with civilisation, look on with uneasy surprise at the effect it is producing. The silence of their mountain solitudes has been broken by the din of industry, and the seclusion of their villages invaded by bands of hired labourers from the Indian coast. Their ancient habits have been interrupted and their prejudices startled; A.D. 1850.

[1] See the description of this road and its passes, Vol. II. P. VII. ch. iv.

[2] CORDINER, ch. i. p. 15.

A.D. 1850. and a generation may pass away before the people become familiar or their headmen reconciled to the change. But the blessings of peaceful order, the mild influence of education, and the gradual influx of wealth, will not fail to produce their accustomed results; and the mountaineers of Ceylon will, at no distant day, share with the lowlanders in the consciousness of repose and prosperity under the protection of the British Crown.

PART VII.

SOUTHERN AND CENTRAL PROVINCES.

CHAPTER I.

POINT DE GALLE.

We landed at Galle on Saturday the 29th of November 1845. No traveller fresh from Europe will ever part with the impression left by his first gaze upon tropical scenery, as it is displayed in the bay and the wooded hills that encircle it; for, although Galle is surpassed both in grandeur and beauty by places afterwards seen in the island, still the feeling of admiration and wonder called forth by its loveliness remains vivid and unimpaired. If, as is frequently the case, the ship approaches the land at daybreak, the view recalls, but in an intensified degree, the emotions excited in childhood by the slow rising of the curtain in a darkened theatre to disclose some magical triumph of the painter's fancy, in all the luxury of colouring and all the glory of light. The sea, blue as sapphire, breaks upon the fortified rocks which form the entrance to the harbour; the headlands are bright with verdure; and the yellow strand is shaded by palm-trees that incline towards the sea, and bend their crowns above the water. The shore is gemmed with flowers, the hills behind are draped with forests of perennial green; and far in the distance rises the zone of purple hills, above which towers the sacred mountain of Adam's Peak, with its summit enveloped in clouds.

But the interest of the place is not confined to the mere loveliness of its scenery. Galle is by far the most venerable emporium of foreign trade, now existing in the universe; it was the resort of merchant ships at the earliest dawn of commerce[1], and it is destined to be the

[1] For more copious details of the early commerce of Galle, see *ante*, Vol. I. Pt. v. ch. ii. p. 565. A condensed view of the trade of Ceylon

centre to which will hereafter converge all the rays of navigation, intersecting the Indian Ocean, and connecting the races of Europe and Asia.

In modern times, Galle was the mart of Portugal, and afterwards of Holland; and long before the flags of either nation had appeared in its waters, it was one of the entrepôts whence the Moorish traders of Malabar drew the productions of the remoter East, with which they supplied the Genoese and Venetians, who distributed them over the countries of the West.[1] Galle was the "Kalah" at which the Arabians in the reign of Haroun Alraschid met the junks of the Chinese[2], and brought back gems, silks, and spices from Serendib to Bassora.[3] The Sabæans, centuries before, included Ceylon in the rich trade which they prosecuted with India, and Galle was probably the furthest point eastward ever reached by the Persians[4], by the Greeks of the Lower Empire, by the Romans[5], and by the Egyptian mariners of Berenice, under the Ptolemies.[6] But an interest, deeper still, attaches to this portion of Ceylon, inasmuch as it seems more than probable that *the long-sought locality of Tarshish may be found to be identical with that of Point de Galle.*

---

in the early ages, and its importance as the great emporium between the Eastern and Western World, will be found in the Essay of HEEREN, *De Ceylone Insula per Virginiti fere sæcula communi Terrarum Marumque Australium Emporio: Gottingen*, 1831.

[1] DE BARROS, *Asia, &c.*, tom. i. pt. ii. p. 428; BARBOSA *in Ramusio*, vol. i. p. 313; VARTHEMA, *Itinerario, &c.*, p. xxvii.

[2] FA HIAN, *Foë-Kouë Ki*, ch. xl. p. 357; EDRISI, *Trad. Jaubert.* tom. i. p. 73.

[3] REINAUD, *Voyages Arabes et Persans, &c.*, tom. i. p. xxxix. lxii.

[4] Robertson in his Disquisition on India, thinks the Persians took no part in this trade, but Cosmas Indico-pleustes found them established in Ceylon early in the sixth century. *Christ. Topogr.* Montfaucon, Coll. vol. ii. p.178; and Hamza of Ispahan says, Cosroes-Nushirvan, who reigned at that period, conquered the cities of Ceylon. *Annal.* p. 43.

[5] Pliny expressly says that he learned from the embassy sent to the Emperor Claudius from Ceylon, that the great port of the island *fronted the south*, "ex iis cognitum portum contra meridiem;" lib. vi. ch. xxiv.; a description which applies only to the harbour of Galle.

[6] *Periplus Mar. Erythr.*, HUDSON, vol. i. p. 35; VINCENT, *Commerce of India, &c.*, vol. ii. p. 22: "Ceylan fut depuis un temps immémorial l'entrepôt où les Phéniciens, les peuples de l'Arabie méridionale, les Grecs, les Romains, et les Arabes devenus Musulmans venaient s'approvisionner des denrées de l'Inde, de l'Archipel d'Asie, de la Chine et de celles non moins riches que le sol y fait naitre." —DULAURIER, *Asiat. Journ.*, tom. xlix. p. 174.

A careful perusal of the Scripture narrative suggests the conclusion, that there were two places at least to which the Phœnicians traded, each of which bore the name of Tarshish: one to the north-west, whence they brought tin, iron, and lead; and another to the east, which supplied them with ivory and gold. Bochart was not the first who rejected the idea of the *latter* being situated at the mouth of the Guadalquiver; and intimated that it must be sought for in the direction of India; but he was the first who conjectured that Ophir was Koudramalie, on the north-west of Ceylon, and that the Eastern Tarshish must have been somewhere in the vicinity of Cape Comorin.[1] His general inference was correct and irresistible from the tenor of the sacred writings; but from want of topographical knowledge, Bochart was in error as to the actual localities. Gold is not to be found at Koudramalie[2]; and Comorin being neither an island nor a place of trade, does not correspond to the requirements of Tarshish. Subsequent investigation has served to establish the claim of Malacca to be the golden land of Solomon[3], and Tarshish, which lay in the track between the Arabian Gulf and Ophir, is recognisable in the great emporium of Ceylon.

The ships intended for the voyage were built by Solomon at "Ezion-geber on the shores of the Red Sea,"[4] the rowers[5] coasted along the shores of Arabia and the Persian Gulf[6], headed by an east wind.[7] Tarshish, the

---

[1] BOCHART, *Géogr. Sacr. Phaleg.* lib. ii. ch. 27, "forte ad promontorium Cory." *Ibid. Canaan,* lib. i. ch. xlvi.

[2] No inference bearing on this inquiry is to be drawn from the circumstance that the Tamil names for Ceylon are "Ilam" which signifies *gold*, and "Ila-nadu" *the island of Ilam*, which the Portuguese corrupted into "Ilanare." (*De Couto,* dec. v. ch. v. tom. i. pt. ii. p. 49.) It was called *Ilam* in conformity with a legend, which says that the island was formed by three peaks, from the mythical mountain of the golden Meru, which were flung into the sea in a conflict between Sesha, the great serpent which encompasses the earth, and Vasu Deva, the god of the winds. See CASIE CHITTY's *Gazetteer*, vol. i. p. 59.

[3] Malacca is the Aurea Chersonesus of the later Greek Geographers, and "*ophir*" in the language of the Malays, is the generic term for any "gold mine."—1 Kings x. 11, and 2 Chron. ix. 21.

[4] 1 Kings ix. 26.

[5] Ezekiel xxvii. 26.

[6] By Sheba in Arabia Felix and Dedan at the entrance of the Persian Gulf.—Ezekiel xxxviii. 13.

[7] Ezekiel xxvii. 26; Psl. xlviii. 7.

port for which they were bound, would appear to have been situated in an island[1], governed by kings[2], and carrying on an extensive foreign trade.[3] The voyage occupied three years in going and returning from the Red Sea[4], and the cargoes brought home to Ezion-geber consisted of gold and silver, ivory, apes, and peacocks.[5] *Gold* could have been shipped at Galle from the vessels which brought it from Ophir[6], "*silver* spread into plates," which is particularised by Jeremiah[7] as an export of Tarshish, is one of the substances on which the sacred books of the Singhalese are even now inscribed; *ivory* is found in Ceylon, and must have been both abundant and full grown there before the discovery of gunpowder led to the wanton destruction of elephants; *apes* are indigenous to the island, and *peafowl* are found there in numbers. It is very remarkable too, that the terms by which these articles are designated in the Hebrew Scriptures, are identical with the Tamil names, by which some of them are called in Ceylon to the present day: thus *tukeyim*, which is rendered "peacocks" in one version, may be recognised in *tokei*, the modern name for these birds; "*kapi*" apes is the same in both languages, and the Sanskrit "*ibha*" ivory, is identical with the Tamil "*ibam.*"[8]

Thus by geographical position, by indigenous productions, and by the fact of its having been from time immemorial the resort of merchant ships from Egypt,

---

[1] Isaiah xxiii. 1, 3, 6. It must be observed, however, that the early geographers did not sufficiently discriminate between a *peninsula* and an *island:* Tyre itself was termed an *island* by them.

[2] Psl. lxxii. 10; Isaiah associates Tarshish with "Pul and Lud *that draw the bow,*" lxvi. 19; a characteristic which is maintained by the Veddahs (the remnant of the aboriginal inhabitants) to the present day.

[3] Isaiah xxiii. 2; Ezekiel xxvii. 10, 25.

[4] 1 Kings x. 22. It is curious that in the *Garshasp Nameh*, a Persian poem of the tenth century which professes to describe an expedition from Jerusalem for the conquest of Ceylon, the time occupied in the outward voyage was *eighteen months*, being one half the "three years" occupied by the ships of Solomon in going to and returning from Tarshish.

[5] *Ibid.*

[6] 1 Kings x. 11.

[7] Jerem. x. 9.

[8] Note on the Tamil Language by the Rev. Mr. Hoisington.

Arabia, and Persia on the one side, and India, Java, and China on the other, Galle seems to present a combination of every particular essential to determine the problem so long undecided in biblical dialectics, and thus to present data for inferring its identity with the Tarshish of the sacred historians, the great eastern mart so long frequented by the ships of Tyre and Judea.[1]

Every object that meets the eye on entering the bay is new and strange. Amongst the vessels at anchor lie the dows of the Arabs, the petamars of Malabar, the dhoneys of Coromandel, and the grotesque seaboats of the Maldive and Laccadive islanders. But the most remarkable of all are the double canoes of the Singhalese, which dart with surprising velocity amongst the shipping, managed by half-clad natives, who offer for sale beautiful but unfamiliar fruits, and fishes of extraordinary colours and fantastic forms.

These canoes are dissimilar in build, some consisting of two trees lashed together, but the most common and by

DOUBLE CANOE OF CEYLON.

far the most graceful are hollowed out of a single stem from eighteen to thirty feet long, and about two feet in depth, exclusive of the wash-board, which adds about a

[1] The articles brought by the navies of Hiram and Solomon to Ezion-geber, were carried across the isthmus of Suez to Rhinocolura, the modern El-Arish, and thence transferred into Mediterranean vessels to be carried to Joppa (Jaffa) and Tyre. — ROBERTSON'S *India*, sec. 1.

foot to the height. This is sewed to the gunwale by coir yarn, so that no iron or any other metal enters into the construction of a canoe. But their characteristic peculiarity is the balance-log, of very buoyant wood, upwards of twenty feet in length, carried at the extremity of two elastic outriggers each eighteen feet long. By this arrangement not only is the boat steadied, but mast, yard and sail are bound securely together.[1]

The outrigger must of necessity be always kept to windward, and as it would not be possible to remove it from side to side, the canoe is so constructed as to proceed with either end foremost, thus elucidating an observation made by Pliny eighteen hundred years ago, that the ships which navigated the seas to the west of Taprobane *had prows at either end*, to avoid the necessity of tacking.[2]

These peculiar craft venture twenty miles to sea in a strong wind; they sail upwards of ten miles an hour, and nothing can be more picturesque than the sight at daybreak, of the numerous fleets of fishing boats, which cruise along the coast whilst the morning is still misty and cool, and hasten to shore after sunrise with their captures, consisting not only of ordinary fish, whose scales are flaked with silver or "bedropped with gold," but also including those of unusual shapes, displaying the brightest colours of the rainbow.

Passing the grim old Portuguese batteries[3], and

---

[1] It is remarkable that this form of canoe is found only where the Malays have extended themselves throughout Polynesia and the coral islands of the Pacific; and it seems so peculiar to that race that it is to be traced in Madagascar and the Comoros, where a Malayan colony was settled at some remote period of antiquity. The outrigger is unknown amongst the Arabs, and is little seen on the coast of India.

[2] "Ob id *navibus utrinque proræ* ne per angustias alvei circumagi sit necesse."—PLINY, *Nat. Hist.*, lib. vi. ch. xxiv. Strabo mentions the same fact; lib. xv. ch. xv.

[3] The most conspicuous outwork bears the name of the "Portuguese battery," but the Portuguese, not anticipating the approach of an enemy from sea, never effectually fortified Galle, except on the land side; and the batteries which now command the harbour were constructed by the Dutch in 1663.—VALENTYN, ch. xiv. p. 177.

landing at the pier constructed to replace the one erected by the Dutch for embarking their cinnamon[1], we passed under the gateway of the fortress, and ascended by a steep and shady street to the Queen's House, the official residence of the Governor, which Sir Colin Campbell had placed at our disposal.[2] The mansion, like all those built by the Dutch in Ceylon, is adapted to the heat, and other peculiarities of the climate; with spacious rooms, latticed windows, tiled floors, and lofty roofs, imperfectly concealed by ceilings, which are generally left unclosed lest the white ants should destroy the timbers undetected. The neglected garden, with its decaying terraces and ruined "lusthof," contains Indian fruit trees and plants almost returned to their primitive wildness. Oranges, custard apples, bread-fruits, bilimbis, and bananas are mingled with the crimson hibiscus and innumerable other flowering shrubs, whose branches were covered with exquisite climbing plants, clitoriæ and convolvuli; and beneath their moist shade grew innumerable balsams in all their endless varieties of colour.

The groups collected about the landing place, and lounging in the streets and bazaars of Galle, exhibit the most picturesque combinations of costumes and races; Europeans in their white morning undress, shaded by japanned umbrellas; Moors, Malabars, and Malays, Chinese, Caffres, Parsees, and Chetties from the Coromandel coast, the latter with their singular head-dresses and prodigious earrings, Buddhist priests in yellow robes, and

---

[1] The landing wharf, with its covered way, is described by VALENTYN as the favourite promenade in 1663. It was called the *Wambays*, ch. i. p. 22.

[2] Above the entrance of this building, there is a stone let into the wall bearing the date A. D. 1687, under the carved figure of a cock. If it was a mistake of the Dutch to believe that the name of Galle was derived, not from the Singhalese word *galla*, "a rock," but from *gallus*, they inherited the misconception from the Portuguese, one of whose generals, Azevedo, Faria y Souza describes as hoisting the children of the *Chalia* or *Galla* caste on the spears of his soldiers, and shouting, "How these young cocks (*gallos*) crow!"—*Portuguese Asia, &c.*, vol. iii. ch. xiv. p. 277 (See *ante*, Vol. II. Pt. VI. ch. i. p. 23.

Moodliars, Mohandirams, and other native chiefs, in their rich official uniforms, with jewelled buttons, embroidered belts, and swords of ceremony.

One peculiar custom of the Singhalese in this district not only attracts the eye of every stranger by its singularity, but presents the most remarkable instance, with which I am acquainted, of the unchanging habits of an eastern race. Seventeen hundred years ago, Ptolemy, speaking of the people of Taprobane, alluded to the length of their hair; and Agathemerus, who, if not a contemporary, lived immediately after Ptolemy, describes with minuteness their mode of dressing it. "The men," he says, "who inhabit Ceylon, allow their hair an unlimited growth, and *bind it on the crown of their heads, after the manner of women*."[1] Agathemerus had doubtless been told of the custom by some Grecian seamen returning from Galle, for this fashion of dressing the hair is confined to the south-west coast of the island, and prevails neither in the interior nor amongst the people of the north and east. So closely do the low-country Singhalese follow the manners of women in their toilet that their back-hair is first rolled into a coil, called a *kondé;* this is fixed at the top of the head by a large tortoise-shell comb, whilst the hair is drawn back from the forehead, *à l'impératrice*, and secured by another circular comb.

A SINGHALESE WITH HIS COMBS.

[1] "*Τοὺς κατοικουντας αὐτὴν ἄνδρας μαλλοῖς γυναικίας ἀναδεῖσθαι τὰς κεφαλάς.*"—Agathemerus, *Geogr.*, lib. i. ch. vi; Hudson, vol. ii. p. 45. It is strange that among the multitude of ancient writers who have treated of Ceylon, Agathemerus and Ptolemy should be the only two who have told of this peculiarity of the low-country Singhalese. I have found it noticed nowhere else except in the *Epitome of Geography*, compiled in the fifth century by Moses of Chorene, who evidently copied it from Agathemerus, "viri regionis istius capillis, muliebribus sua capita redimunt."—Mosis Chorenensis, *Hist. Armeniæ et Epit. Geogr.*, edit. Whiston, 1726; p. 367.

Albyrouni is doubtless correct, when he says that the practice of the Indian natives, before the birth of Mahomet, to wear their hair unshorn, was an intuitive precaution against the excessive heat of the sun [1], but that the fashion in Ceylon should have assumed an essentially feminine form, and have preserved it through so many centuries, presents one of the most remarkable evidences with which I am acquainted, of the enduring tenacity of oriental habit.

With their delicate features and slender limbs, their frequent want of beards [2], their use of earrings and their practice of wearing a cloth round the waist called a *comboy* [3], which has all the appearance of a petticoat, the men have an air of effeminacy very striking to the eye of a stranger. [4]

The Singhalese women dress with less grace than simplicity, their principal garment being a white muslin jacket, which loosely covers the figure, and a comboy or waist cloth, similar to that worn by the men. But their aim is the display of their jewelry, necklaces, bangles and rings, the gems of which are often of intrinsic value, though defective both in cutting and mounting. The children are beautiful, their hair

---

[1] "Ce qui convient au corps c'est une température à peu près constante; et rien n'est plus propre à produire cet effet, qu'une espèce d'envelope naturelle qu'on est libre de rendre plus ou moins puissante." —REINAUD, *Mém. sur l'Inde*, p. 238.

[2] Their slender limbs and the absence of beards among the Singhalese is noticed in the story of Jambulus as recorded by DIODORUS, lib. ii. ch. xxxvi. The Chinese in the seventh century, accustomed to the flat features of the Mogul races, were surprised at the prominent noses of the Singhalese; and HIOUEN THSANG describes the natives of Ceylon, as having the "beak of a bird with the body of a man," —*un corps d'homme et un bec d'oiseau;* tom. ii. p. 140.

[3] For the origin of this word, see the chapter on the intercourse of the Chinese with Ceylon, Vol. I. p. 588. So tenaciously do the Singhalese cling to ancient habits, that even when a man has partially adopted European costumes, he will still wear a comboy over his trousers.

[4] It is said that the Spaniards gave the name of "Amazon" to the river of South America, from finding on it a tribe of Indians of delicate configuration, the men of which parted their hair in front, and winding it round their head, secured it with a comb made from the horny fibres of a palm tree, and surmounted by feathers. —WALLACE'S *Travels on the Amazon*, p. 277, 493; KIDDER and FLETCHER'S *Brazil*, Philad. 1857, p. 458, 507.

wavy and shining, and as they wear no covering of any kind till four or five years old, a group of these little creatures at play suggests the idea of living bronzes.

Galle has a large population of Moors, who are mostly lapidaries, or dealers in gems[1], and one of the earliest visits received by a stranger on his arrival, is from these persevering jewellers, with whom it requires both experience and judgment to negotiate with safety. It ought to be borne in mind, that it is the custom among Oriental races for the buyer, and not the seller, to place the value on any article he requires. An Eastern in the bazaar, makes an offer for what he wants, and waits for the owner to take or refuse it. Long contact with Europeans has so far modified this practice in Ceylon, that a buyer expects the seller to name a price for his commodities; and when a traveller adduces, as an evidence of fraud or rapacity, that a dealer may have asked double what he has eventually accepted, it would be well to remember, that it is contrary to custom for the owner to be the appraiser, and that "*caveat emptor*" is the rule amongst Orientals, from whom the Romans borrowed the maxim.[2]

Tortoise-shell is another article in which the workmen of Galle have employed themselves since the time of the Romans[3], and of which they still make bracelets, hair pins, and ornaments of great taste and beauty. But the principal handicrafts-men are cabinet-makers, carpenters, and carvers in Calamander-wood, ebony, and ivory. Their skill in this work is quite remarkable, considering the simplicity of their implements and tools; but owing to their deficiency in design, and the want of

---

[1] An account of the pursuits of these people will be found *ante*, Vol. I. Pt. v. ch iv. p. 605.

[2] "Ubi enim judicium emptoris est ibi fraus venditoris quæ potest esse?" —CICERO *De Off.*, iii. 14.

[3] STRABO, ii. i. 14. Ceylon formerly exported tortoise-shell, but the demand has become so great for home manufacture, that it is now imported from Penang and the Maldive Islands.

proper models, their unaided productions are by no means in accordance with European tastes.[1]

The share of the commerce of Ceylon which at present belongs to the port of Galle is small compared with that of Colombo. The latter, from its nearer vicinity to the coffee estates and the cinnamon districts, exports the largest proportion of these, as well as of other articles, from the interior and the north, whilst the chief trade of Galle consists in the productions of the coco-nut tree with which the southern province is so densely covered that the country in every direction for some distance from the sea, appears a continuous forest of palms.[2] The oil expressed from the nut; coir and cordage manufactured from its fibre; and arrack distilled from the sap of the tree, are shipped in large quantities for Europe and India.

But the local prosperity of Galle is mainly dependent on the merchant vessels and steam packets which make it their rendezvous; and on the travellers from all parts of the East who are carried there in consequence. These are sufficient to support its numerous hotels, lodging houses, and bazaars; but private residents complain, and with justice, of the increase of prices, and the excessive cost of living, which has been entailed upon them in consequence.

The Dutch carried to their Eastern settlements two of their home propensities, which distinguish and embellish the towns of the Low Countries; they indulged in the excavation of canals, and they planted long lines of trees to diffuse shade over the sultry passages in their Indian fortresses. For the latter purpose they

---

[1] At Galle and elsewhere, I found the cabinet makers and carvers using as a substitute for sand-paper to polish their work, the rough leaves of a species of figtree, called by them *sewana mediya*, and of a creeper known as the *korossa-mael*. I am unable to identify them scientifically.

[2] It is a curious illustration of the innumerable uses of the coco-nut palm, that some years ago a ship from the Maldive Islands touched at Galle, which was entirely built, rigged, provisioned, and laden with the produce of that tree.—PERCIVAL, p. 326.

employed the Suriya (*Hibiscus populneus*), whose broad umbrageous leaves and delicate yellow flowers impart a delicious coolness, and give to the streets of Galle and Colombo the fresh and enlivening aspect of walks in a garden.

In the towns, however, the suriya is productive of one serious inconvenience. It is the resort of a hairy greenish caterpillar[1], longitudinally striped, which frequents it in great numbers, and at a certain stage of its growth descends by a silken thread to the ground and hurries away, probably in search of a suitable spot in which to pass through its metamorphosis. Should it happen to alight, as it often does, upon some lounger below, and find its way to his unprotected skin, it inflicts, if molested, a sting as pungent, but far more lasting, than that of a nettle or a star fish.

Attention being thus directed to the quarter whence the assailant has lowered himself down, the caterpillars above will be found in clusters, sometimes amounting to hundreds clinging to the branches and the bark, with a few straggling over the leaves or suspended from them by lines. These pests are so annoying to children as well as destructive to the foliage, that it is often necessary to singe them off the trees by a flambeau raised on the extremity of a pole; and as they fall to the ground they are eagerly devoured by the crows and domestic fowls.[2]

With the exception of the old church built by the Netherlands East India Company, the town of Galle

---

[1] The species of moth with which it is identified has not yet been determined, but it most probably belongs to a section of Boisduval's genus Bombyx near Cnethocampa *Stephens*.

[2] Another caterpillar which feeds on the jasmine-flowering Carissa, stings with such fury that I have known a gentleman to shed tears while the pain was at its height. It is short and broad, of a pale green, with fleshy spines on the upper surface, each of which seems to be charged with the venom that occasions this acute suffering. The moth which this caterpillar produces, *Neæra lepida*, Cramer; *Limacodes graciosa*, Westw., has dark brown wings, the primary traversed by a broad green band. It is common in the Western side of Ceylon. The larvæ of the genus *Adolia* are also hairy, and sting with virulence.

contains no remarkable buildings, and the streets at the present day differ little in their aspect from that which they presented during the presence of the Dutch. The houses are spacious, but seldom higher than a single story, and each has, along the entire line of the front, a deep verandah supported on pillars to create shade for the rooms within.

At the close of the day we drove with the principal government officer, Mr. Cripps, through the native town, which extends beyond the walls of the fort, and thence through some native villages along the margin of the bay, in the direction of Matura, the road being one continuous avenue of coco-nut trees. The enjoyment of the scene was indescribable; the cool shade of the palm groves, the fresh verdure of the grass, the bright tint of the flowers that twined over every tree, the rich copper hue of the soil, and the occasional glimpse of the sea through the openings in the dense wood; all combined to form a landscape unsurpassed in novelty and beauty.

The suburbs consist chiefly of native huts, interspersed here and there with the decaying villas of the old Dutch burghers, distinguished by quaint doorways and fantastic entrances to the compounds and gardens. The latter contained abundance of fruit-trees, oranges, limes, pappaws, bread-fruits, and plantains, and a plentiful undergrowth of pine-apples, yams, and sweet potatoes. Of these by far the most remarkable tree is the jak, with broad glossy leaves and enormous yellow fruit, not growing on the branches, but supported by powerful stalks from the trunk of the tree.[1]

I was struck with the extraordinary numbers of the

[1] The jak, *Artocarpus integrifolia*, would seem to be the tree which Pliny says the Indians called *Pala* and *ariena*, putting forth fruit from its bark, one of which was sufficient to furnish a meal for four persons, "fructum cortice mittit ut uno quaternos satiet."—xii. 12. Sprengel and Bauhin supposed Pliny to mean the plantain; but the description quoted applies to the jak.

beautiful striped shells of the *Helix hæmastoma*, on the stems of the coco-nut palms on the road as we drove towards Matura, and stopping frequently to collect them, I was led to observe that each separate garden seemed to possess a variety almost peculiar to itself; in one the mouth of every individual shell was red, in another separated from the first only by a wall, black, and in others (but less frequently) pure white; whilst the varieties of external colouring were equally local; in one enclosure they were nearly all red, and in an adjoining one all brown.[1]

The southern coast, from Galle to Hambangtotte (which I visited at a later period), is one of the most interesting and remarkable portions of Ceylon. Its inhabitants are the most purely Singhalese section of the population. It formed an important part of the ancient division of Rohuna, which was colonised at an early period by the followers of Wijayo[2], and their descendants were so far removed from Anarajapoora and the north, that they had neither intercourse nor commixture with the Malabars. Their temples were asylums for the studious and learned, and to the present day, some of the priests of Matura and Mulgirigalle are accomplished scholars in Sanskrit and Pali, and possess rich collections of Buddhist manuscripts and books.

The scenery of the coast as far as Dondera, is singularly lovely, the currents having scooped the line of the shore into coves and bays of exquisite beauty, separated by precipitous headlands covered with forests and crowned by groves of coco-nut palms.

Close by Belligam the road passes a rock, a niche

---

[1] DARWIN, in his *Naturalist's Voyage*, mentions a parallel instance of the localised propagation of colours amongst the cattle which range the pasturage of East Falkland Island; "round Mount Osborne about half of some of the herds were mouse-coloured, a tint not common anywhere else, — near Mount Pleasant dark-brown prevailed; whereas south of Choiseul Sound white beasts with black heads and feet were common." —ch. ix. p. 192.

[2] See *ante*, Vol. I. P. I. ch. iii. p. 337.

in which contains the statue of the "*Kustia Raja*," an Indian prince, in whose honour it was erected, because, according to the legend, he was the first to teach the Singhalese the culture of the coco-nut.[1]

Every building throughout this favourite district is a memorial of the Dutch. The rest-houses on the road-side, the villas in the suburbs, and the fortifications of the towns were erected by them; and Matura, with its little star-fort of coral, remains as perfect at the present day, as when it was a seat of the spice trade, and a sanitary retreat for the garrison of Galle.[2]

Dondera Head, the Sunium of Ceylon, and the southern extremity of the island, is covered with the ruins of a temple, which was once one of the most celebrated in Ceylon. The headland itself has been the resort of devotees and pilgrims, from the most remote ages;—Ptolemy describes it as *Dagana*, "sacred to the Moon," and the Buddhists constructed there one of their earliest dagobas, the restoration of which was the care of successive sovereigns.[3] But the most important temple was a shrine which in very early times had been erected by the Hindus in honour of Vishnu. It was in the height of its splendour, when, in 1587, the place was devastated in the course of the marauding expedition by which De Souza d'Arronches sought to create a diversion, during the siege of Colombo by Raja Singha II.[4] The historians of the period state that at that time Dondera was the most renowned place of pilgrimage in Ceylon; Adam's Peak scarcely excepted.

---

[1] See *ante*, Vol. I. Pt. IV. ch. xi. p. 437. The legend will be found in POWER's *Ceylon Miscellany*, vol. i. p. 250, Cotta, 1842. An engraving of the statue is given in the *Asiatic Researches*, vol. vi. p. 432.

[2] Matura was fortified in A.D. 1550, by King Dharma-pala, with the aid of the Portuguese (VALENTYN, *Oud en Nieuw Oost-Indien*, ch. vi. p. 8); but the fort still existing was erected by the Dutch in A.D. 1645.—*Ibid.*, ch. xi. p. 130.

[3] *Query* — Does Ptolemy's name *Dagana* refer to the *dagoba?* The latter was repaired, A.D. 686, by King Dapoolu, who held his court at Mahagam, to the east of Dondera (*Rajavali*, p. 248); and again, A.D. 1180, by Prakrama Bahu I.—FORBES' *Eleven Years in Ceylon*, vol. ii. p. 178.

[4] See *ante*, Vol. II. Pt. VI. ch. i.

The temple, they say, was so vast, that from the sea it had the appearance of a city. The pagoda was raised on vaulted arches, richly decorated, and roofed with plates of gilded copper. It was encompassed by a quadrangular cloister, opening under verandahs, upon a terrace and gardens with odoriferous shrubs and trees, whose flowers were gathered by the priests for processions. De Souza entered the gates without resistance; and his soldiers tore down the statues, which were more than a thousand in number. The temple and its buildings were overthrown, its arches and its colonnades were demolished, and its gates and towers levelled with the ground. The plunder was immense, in ivory, gems, jewels, sandalwood, and ornaments of gold. As the last indignity that could be offered to the sacred place, cows were slaughtered in the courts, and the cars of the idol, with other combustible materials, being fired, the shrine was reduced to ashes.[1] A stone doorway exquisitely carved, and a small building, whose extraordinary strength resisted the violence of the destroyers, are all that now remain standing; but the ground for a considerable distance is strewn with ruins, conspicuous among which are numbers of finely cut columns of granite. The dagoba which stood on the crown of the hill, is a mound of shapeless débris.

Still farther to the east are the towns of Tangalle and Hambangtotte, in the vicinity of which lie the vast marshes or *leways*, whence the island derives its principal supplies of salt.

The fire-flies and glow-worms were kindling their emerald lamps as we returned after sunset, from our evening drive, to the Fort of Galle. We had our first Singhalese dinner at the Queen's House, with seir-fish and poultry (for which latter the adjoining district of Matura is famous), followed by a dessert

---

[1] FARIA Y SOUZA, *Portuguese Asia, &c.*, vol. iii. pt. i. ch. vi. p. 53; DE COUTO, *Asia, &c.*, dec. x. ch. xv. vol. vi. pt. ii. p. 648.

in which rambutans[1], custard apples[2], and country almonds[3], were the most agreeable novelties. The only drawbacks to enjoyment were the heat and the mosquitoes; and from either it was hopeless to escape. Next to the torture and apprehension it inflicts, the most annoying peculiarities of the mosquito are the booming hum of its approach, its cunning, its audacity, and the perseverance with which it renews its attacks however frequently repulsed; and these characteristics are so remarkable as fully to justify the conjecture that the mosquito, and not the ordinary fly, constituted the plague inflicted upon Pharaoh and the Egyptians.[4]

---

[1] This delicious fruit, which is a species of Nephelium, takes it name from the Malay word *rambut*, "the hair of the head," which describes the villose covering that envelopes it.

[2] *Anona reticulata.*

[3] From the Terminalia Catappa; called *Kath-badam* in Bengal. The tree is exotic; and was probably introduced into Ceylon from Java.—See BUCHANAN'S *Survey of Behar*, vol. i. p. 233.

[4] The precise species of insect by means of which the Almighty signalised the plague of flies, remains uncertain, as the Hebrew term *arob* or *orov*, which has been rendered in one place, "divers sorts of flies," Ps. cv. 31; and in another, "swarms of flies," Exod. viii. 21, &c., means merely an "assemblage," a "mixture," or a "swarm," and the expletive "*of flies*" is an interpolation of the translators. This, however, serves to show that the fly implied was one easily recognisable by its habit of *swarming*: and the further fact that it *bites*, or rather stings, is elicited from the expression of the Psalmist, Ps. lxxviii. 45, that the insects by which the Egyptians were tormented "devoured them," so that here are two peculiarities inapplicable to the domestic fly, but strongly characteristic of gnats and mosquitoes.

Bruce thought that the fly of the fourth plague was the "zimb" of Abyssinia which he so graphically describes; and WESTWOOD, in an ingenious passage in his *Entomologist's Text-book*, p. 17, combats the strange idea of one of the bishops, that it was a cockroach! and argues in favour of the mosquito. This view he sustains by a reference to the habits of the creature, the swarms in which it invades a locality, and the audacity with which it enters the houses; and he accounts for the exemption of "the land of Goshen in which the Israelites dwelt," by the fact of its being sandy pasture above the level of the river; whilst the mosquitoes were produced freely in the rest of Egypt, the soil of which was submerged by the rising of the Nile.

In all the passages in the Old Testament in which flies are alluded to, otherwise than in connection with the Egyptian infliction, the word used in the Hebrew is *zevov*, which the Septuagint renders by the ordinary generic term for flies in general, μυια "*musca*" (Eccles. x. 1, Isaiah vii. 10); but in every instance in which mention is made of the miracle of Moses, the Septuagint says that the fly produced was the κυνομυια, the "dog-fly." What insect was meant

The great problem which must occupy the attention of those interested in the future destiny of Point de Galle, involves the means of rendering the harbour sufficiently commodious and secure for the reception of the great and increasing number of steam-vessels, which now make it their resort. The magnitude of the interests concerned expands the question to imperial dimensions; and if Galle is to become the great civil arsenal of the East; the rendezvous for the packets and passenger ships from India, Australia, and China; as well as for the merchantmen, which touch there for telegraphic orders by which their further course is to be guided; the enlargement of the area of the harbour, as well as its protection from the swell of the monsoon, must be speedily secured by the construction of the necessary works. And, in the consideration of this, the further question arises of the comparative advantages of Trincomalie, and the practicability of adapting the unrivalled bay of the latter to all the requirements of commerce by a system of railways connecting the eastern and western coasts of Ceylon.

Elsewhere I have alluded very briefly to the phenomena of the tides around the island[1], and I have given the particulars of the "establishment" at a few of the ports most frequented by seamen. In noticing this subject in connection with Galle, there are two peculiarities which cannot fail to excite attention; the very slight variation in altitude between high and low water at all

by this name it is not now easy to determine, but Ælian intimates that the dog-fly both inflicts a wound and emits a booming sound, in both of which particulars it accords with the mosquito (lib. iv. 51); and PHILO-JUDÆUS, in his *Vita Mosis*, lib. i. ch. xxiii., descanting on the plague of flies, and using the term of the Septuagint, *κυνομυῖα*, describes it as combining the characteristic of "the most impudent of all animals, the fly and the dog, exhibiting the courage and the cunning of both, and fastening on its victim with the noise and rapidity of an arrow"—*μετὰ ῥοίζου καθάπερ βέλος*. This seems to identify the dog-fly of the Septuagint with the description of the Psalmist, Ps. lxxviii. 45, and to vindicate the conjecture that the tormenting mosquito, and not the harmless house-fly, was commissioned by the Lord to humble the obstinacy of the Egyptian tyrant.

[1] Vol. I. Pt. I. ch. i. p. 52.

points round the coast, and the discrepant hours at which the former occurs on the east and west coasts respectively. The difficulties which arose in my own mind on the subject, and the doubts I entertained as to the accuracy of the ordinary authorities, have been so satisfactorily removed by a communication from Admiral Fitzroy, that I regret my inability to incorporate at length the valuable information with which he has supplied me.

His opinion is, that Ceylon, as a prolongation of the great Indian peninsula, projects so far into the Indian Ocean as to oppose an effectual barrier to the free and simultaneous action of its waters, under the attraction of the moon. Hence they may be considered as broken into two independent sections or zones, each with a time peculiar to itself, and a tide-wave moving from east to west;—and each more or less influenced by superadded phenomena, differing essentially according to the local features of the respective shores. Thus the most easterly tide impinges on the coast of Ceylon, reaching Batticaloa about four o'clock in the afternoon, Trincomalie about two hours later, and thence passing towards Coromandel and Madras. Whilst this wave is pursuing its course, the moon has been already acting on the opposite side of India, and forming another tide-wave already in motion towards the coast of Arabia and Africa; consequently withdrawing the waters, and depressing their level in the Gulf of Manaar. But before they can be much reduced on the west they are overtaken by the wave from the east, which arrests their further fall, and limits the change of level to something less than thirty inches.

Again on the moon ceasing to influence the western section of the sea, the tendency of the tide-wave when released from her attraction is to return towards, and (because of acquired momentum) even *beyond*, its former position of equilibrium, while receding towards the coast of Malabar and Ceylon. Hence a continuance of oscillation, of advance and retrogression, must be presumed until the earth's attraction and the effects of friction shall have quite checked the movement.[1] Thus the periods within which the principal tide-waves succeed one another, and the oscillations to which they give rise, originate derivative tide-waves of form and character so peculiar as to call for a more attentive investigation than has hitherto been devoted to them.[2]

It must not, however, be forgotten, that the tidal phenomena which affect the limited zones of waters, on either side of the Indian peninsula (waters which, if left to themselves, would have a tendency, when unaffected by the attraction of the moon, to be restored to a condition of normal equilibrium), receive still further complication from the marginal efflux of the tide-wave of the great Indian Ocean. This tide-wave itself is not free, but modified in its turn by impingement against the African continent, and by the deportment of that continuous swell, "immensely broad and excessively flat,"[3] which sweeps comparatively unchecked round the world between the parallels of 40° and 60° south. In our present limited knowledge of facts, we are not in a position to determine what changes of level or of "stream" (not necessarily co-existent phenomena) may result from these various sources of disturbance.

In the harbour of Galle, the daily period of high-water is so materially modified by the phase of the monsoon, and the strength and direction of the currents, as well as of the off and on shore winds, that the very moderate ascent and depression of level (somewhat less than two feet) produced by luni-solar influences, have hitherto attracted but little attention from any except the more scientific seamen, who may have made sustained observations in order to eliminate these accidental variations

---

[1] Vide Appendix to the *Voyage of the Beagle*, vol. iv. p. 277.

[2] BABBAGE, *Ninth Bridgewater Treatise*, Appendix, p. 218.

[3] HERSCHEL, *Outlines, &c.*, p. 497.

from the general results, and establish a correct theory of the movement of the waters in the Indian Ocean. It is now nearly a quarter of a century, since Dr. Whewell laid the foundation of the inquiry and endeavoured to elicit the co-operation of practical men in its solution; and though much has been done to accumulate facts, still observations have not yet been made in sufficient number to lead to an inference as to the probable truth of any hypothesis based upon those already recorded.[1]

[1] That the question is not unworthy of the attention of intelligent officers in Ceylon, hampered as the coast-carrying trade of the island is by those singular sand-barriers, to which I have referred in a former passage (see Vol. I. Pt. I. ch. i. p. 45), is shown by a recent report, an extract from which has fallen into my hands while this volume is passing through the press. Lieut. TAYLOR, of the Indian Navy, in remarking on similar accumulations of sand which obstruct the navigation at Cochin, observes, "that a minute knowledge both of the set of the tides and of the prevailing ocean currents, as also of the heaviest swell of the south-west monsoon, is indispensable to a right judgment" in regard to any projected improvements at the former port. He enters into a minute examination of the question, supporting his view by reference to facts respecting the tides on the west side of India. That the materials derived from other authority than his own were meagre and inadequate, would be seen by a perusal of his Report; nor can much be done to assist in arriving at more mature conclusions, until the authorities recognise the importance of the inquiry, or enterprising officers, with adequate means at their disposal, go to the very moderate expense of fitting up self-registering tide-gauges at points along the coast.

CHAP. II.

GALLE TO COLOMBO. — ADAM'S PEAK.

AT sunrise, on the 30th November, as the morning gun was firing, we passed under the fort-gate, and crossed the drawbridge of Galle, *en route* for Colombo; having secured for our party the two primitive vehicles which carry the government mails, and which then performed the journey in less than twelve hours[1]; crossing the broad estuaries of three rivers in ferry boats, the Gindura, the Bentotte, and the Kalu-ganga; besides an arm of the Pantura-lake.

When the British took possession of Ceylon, and for many years afterwards, no road deserving the name was in existence, to unite these important positions.[2] Travellers were borne along the shore in palankins, by paths under the trees; troops on the march dragged their guns with infinite toil over the sand; and stores, supplies, and ammunition were carried on men's shoulders through the jungle. Since then, not only has a highway unsurpassed in construction been completed to Colombo, but continued through the mountains to the central capital at Kandy, and thence higher still to Neuera-ellia, at an elevation of six thousand feet above the sea. Nor is this all: every town of importance in the island

[1] Since then all these rivers have been bridged.

[2] PERCIVAL, p. 145. An idea of the toil of travelling this road in the year 1800 may be collected from the number of attendants which the governor was forced to take on his journey from Colombo to Galle when starting on a tour round the island; one hundred and sixty palankin bearers, four hundred coolies to carry the baggage, two elephants, six horses, and fifty lascars to take care of the tents. —CORDINER, ch. vi. p. 168.

is now connected with the two principal cities, by roads either wholly or partially macadamised. One continuous line, seven hundred and sixty-nine miles in length, has been formed round the entire circuit of the coast, adapted for carriages where it approaches the principal places, and nearly everywhere available for horsemen and wayfarers. Of upwards of three hundred miles of roads in all directions, nearly two-thirds may be considered as open and traversable at all seasons, but the others, during the rains which accompany the monsoons, are impassable from want of drainage and bridges.

No portion of British India can bear comparison with Ceylon, either in the extent or the excellence of its means of communication; and for this enviable pre-eminence the colony is mainly indebted to the genius of one eminent man, and the energy and perseverance of another. Sir Edward Barnes, on assuming the government in 1820, had the penetration to perceive that the sums annually wasted on hill-forts and garrisons in the midst of wild forests, might, with judicious expenditure, be made to open the whole country by military roads, at once securing and enriching it. Before the close of his administration, he had the happiness of witnessing the realisation of his policy; and of leaving every radius of the diverging lines, which he had planned, either wholly or partially completed. One officer who had been associated with the enterprise from its origin, and with every stage of its progress, remained behind him to consummate his plans. That officer was Major Skinner, the present Commissioner of Roads in Ceylon. To him more than to any living man, the colony is indebted for its present prosperity; and in after years, when the interior shall have attained the full development of its productive resources, and derived all the advantages of facile communications with the coast, the name of this meritorious public servant will be gratefully honoured, in close association with that of his illustrious chief.[1]

In its peculiar style of beauty, nothing in the world can exceed in loveliness the road from Point de Galle to Colombo; it is literally an avenue of palms nearly seventy miles long, with a rich under-growth of tropical trees, many of them crimson with flowers, and over-run with orchids and climbing plants[2], whose tendrils descend in luxuriant festoons. Birds of gaudy plumage dart amidst the branches, gay butterflies hover over the shady foliage, and insects of metallic lustre glitter on the leaves. Bright-green lizards dash over the banks and ascend the trees, and the hideous but harmless iguano[3], half familiar with man, moves slowly across the high-road out of the way of the traveller's carriage, and hisses as it retreats to allow him to pass. Where a view of the landscape can be caught through an opening in the thick woods, it is equally grand and impressive on every side. On one hand is seen the range of purple hills, which form the mountain-zone of Kandy, and stretch far as the eye can reach, till they are crowned by the mysterious summit of Adam's Peak.

> "Olha em Ceilaõ, que o monte se alevanta
> Tanto que as nuvens passa, ou a vista engana:
> Os naturaes o tem por cousa santa,
> Por a pedra em que está a pégada humana."[4]

To the left glitters the blue sea, studded with rocky islets, over which, even during sunny calms, the swell from the Indian Ocean rolls volumes of snowy

---

[1] Since the above was written, her Majesty's Secretary of State for the Colonies, on the recommendation of the governor, Sir Henry G. Ward, has conferred on Major Skinner an appropriate recognition of his great services by raising him to the rank of a Member of Council, with the important appointment of Auditor-General of the colony; an office for which his previous experience invested him with paramount qualifications.

[2] One of the most wonderful of these, the *gloriosa superba*, is abundant near Galle, and such is the splendour of its red and amber flowers, that even the most listless stranger cannot resist the temptation to stop and wonder.

[3] *Monitor dracæna*, Gray. For an account of this large lizard, see Vol. I. Pt. II. ch. iii. p. 182.

[4] CAMOENS, *Lusiad*, canto x. st. 136.

foam. The beach is carpeted with verdure down the line of the yellow sand; and occasionally the level sweeps of the coast are diversified by bold headlands which advance abruptly till they overhang the waves, and form sheltering bays for the boats of the fishermen, which, all day long, are in motion within sight of the shore.

Arboured in the shades of these luxuriant groves, nestle the white cottages of the natives, each with its garden of coco-nuts and plantains, and in the suburbs of the numerous villages, some of the more ambitious dwellings, built on the model of the old Dutch villas, are situated in tiny compounds [1], enclosed by dwarf walls and lines of arecas.

In this particular, the taste of the low-country Singhalese, who like to place their houses in open and airy situations, contrasts with that of the Kandyans, who are fond of seclusion, and build their villages in glens and recesses where their existence would be unsuspected, were it not indicated by the coco-nut palms which are planted beside them.

Towards Galle, the majority of this rural population are of the Chalia caste [2], whose members, though low in conventional rank, are amongst the most useful of the Singhalese population. They appear to have arrived originally from the coast of India, as embroiderers and weavers, and to have settled at Barberyn in the thirteenth century.

---

[1] From *campinho*, a little field (Portuguese).

[2] PTOLEMY gives to the inhabitants of Taprobane the name of Salœ, Σάλαι, and to the island itself Salice, Σαλίκη (lib. vii. iv.), which WILFORD says is a derivative from the Sanskrit Sala. (*Essay on the Sacred Isles of the West*, *As. Res.*, vol. x. p. 124.) An ancient name of Adam's Peak is *Salmala*, or the "Mountain of Sala." FRA BARTOLEMEO traces the origin of all these names to the *Saleyas*, an Indian tribe, called in the Puranas "Salavas," and it is a curious coincidence, that the Chalia caste, who still inhabit the district surrounding Galle, and extending thence to Negombo, claim to call themselves Salias, and say that their ancestors came originally from Hindustan. The legend is set out at length in an historical sketch of the Chalias, written by ADRIAN RAJAPAKSA, a chief of the caste, and embodied in a memoir "*On the Religion and Habits of the People of Ceylon*," by M. JOINVILLE. *As. Res.*, vol. vii. p. 399.

The most satisfactory account of this singular race, that I have seen, is in the *Asiatic Journal* for 1833, vol. xl. p. 269.

At a much later period they betook themselves to the trade of peeling cinnamon; an art of which they soon secured the virtual monopoly. The Portuguese, alive to the importance of the duties in which this hardy class was engaged, of penetrating the hills in search of the coveted spice, induced the kings of Cotta to institute a regular organisation of the caste, and to assign certain villages for their residence, at various points along the coast from Negombo to Matura. The Dutch, though treating the Chalias with the most heartless severity, preserved the system as they inherited it from their predecessors [1]; and to the present day, they thrive on the southern coast, engaging in every branch of industry that gives activity and prosperity to the district.

There is no quarter of the world in which the coco-nut flourishes in such rich luxuriance as in this corner of Ceylon. Here it enjoys a rare combination of every advantage essential to its growth,—a loose and friable soil, a free and genial air, unobstructed solar heat, and an atmosphere damp with the spray and moisture from the sea, towards which the crown of the tree is always more or less inclined.[2]

Of late years, its cultivation has been vastly increased. Some idea may be formed of its importance, from the fact that, at the time when the English took possession of Colombo, it was estimated that the single district lying between Dondera Head and Calpentyn contained ten millions of coco-nut trees [3]; and such has been the in-

[1] VALENTYN, *Oud en Nieuw Oost-Indien, &c.*, ch. xii. p. 135; ch. xv. p. 316.

[2] A writer in the *Journal of the Indian Archipelago* for 1850 observes, that this tendency to bend above the sea, causing its fruit to drop into the water, appears to account for its extension to the numerous islands and atolls "to which the nut is floated by the winds and tide."—Vol. iv. p. 103. A curious illustration of the passion of the coco-nut for the sea is mentioned by DAMPIER, in connection with the little island of Pulo-Mega, off the coast of Sumatra, which, he says, "is not a mile round, and so low that the tide flows over it. It is of a sandy-soil, and full of coco-nut trees, notwithstanding that at every spring tide the salt water goes clear over the island."—*Voyage, &c.*, vol. i. p. 474, quoted by CRAWFURD, in his *Dictionary of the Indian Islands*.

[3] BERTOLACCI, pt. iv. p. 324. The *Ceylon Observer* of the 25th Decem-

crease since, that the total number in the island cannot be less than twenty millions.

All that has ever been told of the bread fruit or any other plant contributing to the welfare of man, is as nothing compared with the blessings conferred on Ceylon by this inestimable palm. The Singhalese, in the warmth of their affection for their favourite tree, avow their belief that it pines when beyond the reach of the human voice [1]; and recount with animation the "hundred uses" for which its products are made available.[2]

---

ber 1858, contains the following summary of the extent of coco-nut cultivation in the island: —"In the quinquennial period ending 1841, the average export of coco-nut oil did not greatly exceed 400,000 gallons, the value being under 26,000*l.* In 1857, the export rose to the enormous figure of 1,767,413 gallons, valued at 212,184*l.* At 40 nuts to a gallon of oil, the above export represents no fewer than 70,696,520 coco-nuts. We should think that at least as much oil is consumed in the colony as is sent out of it. *If so, we get* 141,393,040 *nuts,* converted into 3,534,826 gallons of oil, besides poonack or oil-cake, which is valuable as food for animals and as manure. *Say that there are* 20,000,000 *of coco-nut trees in Ceylon,* oil would seem to be made from the product of one sixth of them, say 3,500,000. We should think that not less than 5,000,000 more of the trees are devoted to 'Toddy' drawing, the liquor being drunk fermented, distilled into arrack or converted into sugar. We should then have 11,500,000 of trees yielding 460,000,000 of nuts to meet the food requirements of the people, besides the quantity exported in their natural state or as copperah."

[1] That the coco-nut grows more luxuriantly in the vicinity of human dwellings is certain; but then it finds a soil artificially enriched there: and it is equally certain that the tree is never found wild in the jungles; but this may be owing to the destruction of the young plants by elephants, which are fond of the tender leaves. The same reason serves to account for its rarity in the Kandyan country, which cannot be ascribed solely to remoteness from the sea, since the coco-nut palm grows a hundred leagues from the coast in Venezuela, and it is even said to have been seen at Timbuctoo.

[2] The list is, of course, extended to the full hundred; but to eke out this complement requires some ingenious subdivision. Thus, the *trunk* furnishes fourteen appliances for building, furniture, firewood, ships, fences, and farming implements; the *leaves,* twenty-seven for thatch, matting, fodder-baskets, and minor utensils; the *web* sustaining the footstalks serves for strainers and flambeaux; the *blossom,* for preserves and pickles; the *fruit-sap,* for spirits, sugar, and vinegar; the *nut and its juices,* for food and for drinking, for oil, curries, cakes, and cosmetics; the *shell,* for cups, lamps, spoons, bottles, and tooth-powder; and the *fibre* which surrounds it, for beds, cushions, and carpets, brushes, nets, ropes, cordage, and cables. — See *ante,* Vol. I. Pt. I. ch. iii. p. 110. One pre-eminent use of the coco-nut palm is omitted in all these popular enumerations: it acts as a *conductor in protecting their houses from lightning.* As many as 500 of these trees were struck in a single *patoo* near Putlam during a succession of thunder-storms in April 1859.—*Colombo Observer.*

There is hardly one of these multifarious uses that may not be seen in active illustration during the drive between Galle and Colombo. Houses are timbered with its wood, and roofed with its plaited fronds, which, under the name of *cajans*, are likewise employed for constructing partitions and fences. The fruit, in all its varieties of form and colour[1], is ripened around the native dwellings, and the women may be seen at their doors rasping its white flesh to powder, in order to extract from it the milky emulsion which constitutes the essential excellence of a Singhalese curry.[2] In pits by

[1] Though unfamiliar to the eye of a stranger, the Singhalese distinguish five varieties of the nut. One bright orange in the colour of the outer husk, known as the "King coconut," is generally planted near the temples: it contains a fluid so delicate that a draught of it is offered by the priests to visitors of distinction as an honour. The other four vary from light yellow to dark green, and are also distinguished by shape and size. The wonderful double coco-nut from the Seychelles, *Lodoicea Seychellarum*, has been introduced into Ceylon, but I am not aware that it has yet fruited there. In size it exceeds the ordinary coconut many fold, with the added peculiarity of presenting a double form. One specimen which I obtained in Ceylon exhibits a triple formation. In the subjoined sketch an orange is introduced to exhibit the extraordinary size of these singular coco-nuts, even after being deprived of the outward husk.

Drifted by the waves from some unknown shore, this mysterious fruit was at one time believed to grow beneath the sea, and was thence called the *Coco de Mer*. Medicinal virtues were then ascribed to it, and so much as 4000 florins were offered by the Emperor Rodolf II. for a single specimen (MALTHE BRUN, vol. iv. p. 420). It is to this singular plant that Camoens alludes in the *Lusiad*:—

> "Nas ilhas de Maldiva nasce a planta
> No profundo das aguas, soberana,
> Cujo pomo contra o veneno urgente
> He tido por antidoto excellente."
> Canto x. st. 136.

[2] In a note to Vol. I. Pt. IV. ch. ii. p. 436, I have shown the error of the belief prevalent amongst Europeans, that the use of curry was introduced by the Portuguese, and that the word itself is derived from that language. In addition to the evidence there stated, it may be mentioned that IBN BATUTA, two hundred years before the Portuguese had appeared in the Indian Seas, describes the natives of Ceylon eating curry, which he calls in Arabic *couchan*, off the leaves of the plantains, precisely as they do at the present day: "Ils apportaient aussi des feuilles de bananier sur lesquelles ils plaçaient le riz qui forme leur norriture. Ils répandaient sur ce riz de *couchân*, qui sert d'assaisonnement * * * * qui est composé de poulets, de viande, de poisson, et de légumes.

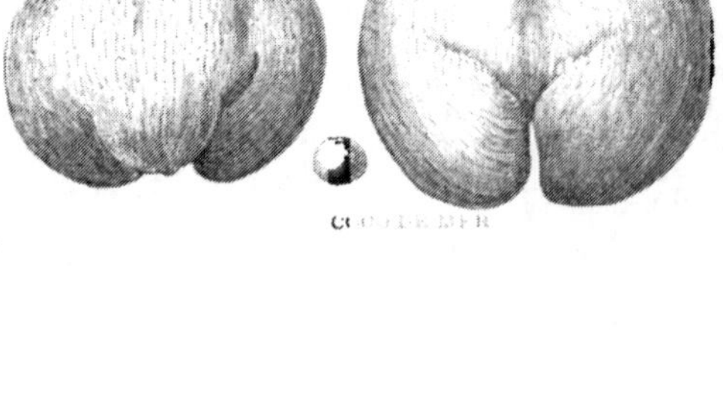

COCO DE MER

the roadside the husks of the nut are steeped to convert the fibre into coir[1], by decomposing the interstitial pith; — its flesh is dried in the sun preparatory to expressing the oil[2]; vessels are attached to collect the juice of the unexpanded flowers to be converted into sugar, and from early morn the toddy drawers are to be seen ascending the trees in quest of the sap drawn from the spathes of the unopened flowers to be distilled into arrack, the only pernicious purpose to which the gifts of the bounteous tree are perverted.

The most precious inheritance of a Singhalese is his ancestral garden of coco-nuts: the attempt to impose a tax on them in 1797, roused the populace to rebellion; and it is curiously illustrative of the minute subdivision of property in Ceylon, that in a case which was decided in the district court of Galle, within a very recent period, the subject in dispute was a claim to the 2,520th *part of ten coco-nut trees!*

At Hiccode[3], twelve miles from Galle, where our horses were changed, the Moodliar and his suite, in full costume, were waiting to offer us early coffee; and at the rest-house[4] of Amblangodde, seven miles farther on, we were gratified with a present of freshly gathered oranges and pines. As we approached the latter village, a rock-snake, *python reticulatus*, the first we had seen, a beautiful specimen at least ten feet long, was disturbed by our approach as he basked on a sunny bank, and gracefully uncoiling his folds he passed across the fence into the neighbouring enclosure.

---

[1] The term *coir* is a corruption of the Maldive term *kanbar*, by which ABOUFELDA says the natives of those islands designated the cords made from the coco-nut, with which they sewed together the planks of their shipping. The best coir is made from the *unripe* nuts. *Cāyĕr* is also the Tamil name for "rope" of any kind.

[2] The coco-nut when thus dried is called *copera*, from the Tamil term *cobri*.

[3] Spelled *Hiocadowe*.

[4] The choultries erected for the accommodation of travellers in Ceylon are styled *rest-houses*, and afford all the essential requirements for refreshment and sleep on a very moderate scale, and for a proportionately moderate cost. They are always under the control of the chief civil officer of the district, who sanctions the tariff of charges.

On lifting the sand from the sea-shore, at the back of the rest-house, I was surprised to find amongst it numerous fragments of red coral, similar to that brought by the fishermen of Naples from the straits of Messina. The *Mahawanso* alludes to the finding of such coral in the Gulf of Manaar in the *second* century[1], but it has never in modern times been sought for systematically. The ordinary white coral is found in such quantities on this part of the coast that an active trade exists in shipping it to Colombo and Galle, where, when calcined, it serves as the only species of lime used for buildings of all kinds.

During the course of the memorable siege of Colombo, by Raja Singha I., in 1587, the Portuguese, hoping to effect a diversion, directed numerous expeditions against the unprotected villages on this part of the coast, destroying the gardens, firing the dwellings, and carrying away the peasantry to be sent into slavery in India. Faria y Souza relates a touching incident which occurred on this occasion at Cosgodde, a hamlet a few miles south of Bentotte:—"Among the prisoners taken at *Cosgore*, was a bride; and as the ships were ready to weigh anchor, there ran suddenly into that in which she was, a young man, and embracing her, and she him, they said many words not understood. By the help of an interpreter, it was known that that man was the bridegroom, who being abroad when the bride was taken, he came to be a slave with her rather than live without her. And she said that since he, by that demonstration of love, had made her happier than all the Chingala women (for they were of those people), she esteemed her slavery rather a blessing than a misfortune. Souza de Arronches,

[1] *Mahawanso*, ch. xxviii. p. 168. The Portuguese were aware of the existence of red coral on the coast: "Quand la mer est grosse, elle en pousse sur les bords une quantité prodigieuse de corail, et en plusieurs endroits, ce corail noir est plus estimé que le rouge."—Ribeyro, lib. i. ch. xxii. p. 172.

hearing hereof, resolved not to part them, and taking hold of both their hands, said, 'God forbid two such lovers, for my private interest, should be made unhappy. I freely give you your liberties.' Then he ordered them to be set ashore; but they two, seeing his unexpected bounty, requited it by despising their liberties, and replied, 'they only desired to be his, and die in his service.' They lived afterwards in Colombo, where the man, on sundry occasions, faithfully served the Portuguese." [1]

The rest-house at Bentotte is one of the coolest and most agreeable in Ceylon. It is situated within a little park, deeply shaded by lofty tamarind-trees on the point of the beach where the river forms its junction with the sea. Its attractions were enhanced by a breakfast for which we were indebted to the hospitable attention of the civil officer, Mr. T. L. Gibson, whose table was covered with all the luxuries of the province; fruits in great variety, curries, fish fresh from the sea, and the delicacy for which Bentotte has a local renown, oysters taken off the rocks in the adjoining estuary [2], which, though small and somewhat bitter, were welcome from their cool associations.

After leaving Bentotte, as the coast approaches Colombo the numbers of the fishing-boats perceptibly increase, and the *karâwe* [3], or fisher caste, form the most numerous section of the village population. Like other castes, they are divided into classes [4], distinguished by the implements they employ, and the department of the

---

[1] *Asia Portug.* STEVEN's transl. vol. iii. pt. i. ch. vi. p. 53.

[2] COSMAS INDICO-PLEUSTES, describing a place on the west coast of Ceylon, which he calls Marallo, says it produced κοχλίους, which THEVENOT translates "oysters;" in which case Marallo might be conjectured to be Bentotte. But the shell in question was most probably the chank (*turbinella rapa*), and Marallo, Mantotte, off which it is found in great numbers. THEVENOT, vol. i. p. 21.

[3] The *parawas*, a section of the fisher caste, in the north and north-west of the island, are of Tamil descent, and came originally from Tuttacorin.

[4] For an account of caste as it manifests itself in Ceylon, its introduction, and influence, see Vol. I. Pt. IV. ch. i. p. 425.

craft to which they addict themselves. Thus there are the *Madell Karâwe* and the *Baroodell*, who cast nets; the *Dandu*, who carry the rod; the *Kisbai*, who catch turtle; the *Oroo*, who fish in boats; and the *Gode kawoolo*, who fish from the rocks; with others of inferior rank. The conventional distinction socially respected between these different classes is as marked and imperative as between different castes; so much so that intermarriages are not permitted except between individuals of the five first named divisions. Their means of living, however, are not restricted to fishing alone; many engage in agriculture and trade, and numbers are employed in everything connected with the building and management of boats, catamarans, and coasting vessels. To the fisher caste also belong the carpenters and cabinet-makers inhabiting the villages and towns on the southern coast, from Matura to Colombo, who produce the carved ebony furniture, so highly prized by Europeans.

So abundant was the capture of fish along the shores of Ceylon, that the Portuguese, when in possession of the island, converted it into a source of revenue by levying a tax of one-fourth on the quantity caught. This was collected by special officers who in return for the payment, undertook to protect the fishermen, to assist them in cases of emergency and in times of distress, to regulate all the affairs of the caste, and to fix the periods of fishing. The Dutch perpetuated the fish-tax in the form in which it had been levied by the Portuguese, but the British on gaining possession of the island sought to commute it by substituting a licence for the boat. The change, however, proved most distasteful to the men for whose benefit is was designed; they disliked the direct payment in money, and preferred their ancient system of payment in kind. They grew indolent and indifferent, and the market ceased to be supplied, owing to the reluctance of the fishermen to take out a licence for their boats. The prejudices of the native in favour of his ancestral custom having been found insurmountable, the experiment, attempted[1] in three instances, was in each unsuccessful; and the fish-tax, with all its inquisitorial and vexatious incidents, was restored amidst the acclamations of the fishermen.

Notwithstanding these repeated disappointments, the tax was eventually reduced from a *fourth* to a *sixth* in 1834, from a *sixth* to a *tenth* in 1837, and finally abolished in 1840. But it is a singular fact, illustrative of the unchanging habits of an Eastern people, that every diminution of the duty, instead of leading to an increase of the trade, or adding to the Colonial Exchequer, had in each successive instance the directly contrary effect; — the fishermen having no longer their accustomed stimulus to exertion, the number of fishing-boats became annually reduced, the quantity of fish taken diminished, and the price rose to more than double what it had been during the existence of the fish-tax.[2] But though abandoned by the government, the tax was not allowed to be altogether abolished; those of the fishers who were Roman Catholics[3] trans-

---

[1] In 1812, 1820, and 1827.

[2] A note in elucidation of a result so contrary to the principles of political economy, will be found, Note A, in the Appendix to this chapter.

[3] I have elsewhere alluded to the singular fact, that the fisher caste have been in every country in India the earliest converts to the Roman Catholic Church;—so much so as to render it worthy of inquiry whether it be only a coincidence or the result of some permanent and predisposing cause. The Parawas of Cape Comorin were the earliest converts of St. Francis Xavier. It was by the "fisher caste" of Manaar that he was invited to Ceylon in 1544 A.D.; and notwithstanding the martyrdom inflicted on his converts by the Raja of Jaffna, and the continued persecution of the Dutch, that district is to the present day one of the strongholds of the Roman Catholic Church in Ceylon, and the fishermen along the whole of the South-western coast as far south as Barberyn, are in the proportion of one half Roman Catholics. Is it that there is an habitual tendency to veneration of the Supreme Being amongst those "who go down to the sea in ships, and see his power in the great deep?" Is it that being a low caste themselves, the fishers of India and Ceylon acquire a higher status by espousing Christianity? or have they some sympathy with a religion whose first apostles and teachers were the fishermen of Galilee?"—Sir J. EMERSON TENNENT'S *History of Christianity in Ceylon*, ch. i. p. 20.

ferred the payment, not only unaltered in form, but in some instances increased in amount, to the Roman Catholic Church, and the privilege of its collection is to the present day farmed out by the clergy, and yearly put up to auction at the several churches along the coast.

Approaching Caltura from Barberyn, the country becomes less level, and from openings in the woods magnificent views are obtained of Adam's Peak [1], and the hills which surround it, which here make their closest approach to the sea. The veneration with which this majestic mountain has been regarded for ages, took its rise in all probability amongst the aborigines of Ceylon, whom the sublimities of nature, awaking the instinct of worship, impelled to do homage to the mountains and the sun.[2] Under the influence of such feelings the aspect of this solitary alp, towering above the loftiest ranges of the hills, and often shrouded in storms and thunder-clouds, was calculated to convert awe into adoration.

In a later age the religious interest became concentrated on a single spot to commemorate some individual identified with the national faith, and thus the hollow in the lofty rock that crowns the summit, was said by the Brahmans to be the footstep of Siva [3], by the

---

[1] This name was given by the Portuguese, who called the mountain the "*Pico de Adam.*"

[2] PTOLEMY places the Solis Portus on the east of Ceylon, and "Dagana, Lunæ sacra," on the south; and PLINY, lib. vi. ch. xxiv., says, the ambassador to Claudius described the island of the sun, "solis insula," as lying to the west of it. JACOB BRYANT, in his *New System of Mythology*, Camb. 1767, traces the veneration for Adam's Peak to the worship of Amun (the sun), in Egypt, and availing himself of the word "Hamalel," said to be one of the names of the Peak, he says, "this, without any change, is Hamal-eel, Ham the sun." But Hamal-eel is merely an European corruption of the Singhalese name *Samanhela.* BRYANT seems to have found it in VALENTYN, *Oud en Nieuw Oost-Indien*, ch. xvi. p. 378, who quotes from DE COUTO, but the latter spells it Hamanelle, which does not harmonize with BRYANT's conjecture.

[3] HARDY's *Buddhism, &c.*, p. 212, MARSDEN, in his notes to Marco Polo p. 671, quotes a passage from a Malay version of the *Ramayana,* in which the mountain of Serendib is

Buddhists, of Buddha[1], by the Chinese, of Foë[2], by the Gnostics, of Ieû[3], by the Mahometans, of Adam[4], whilst the Portuguese authorities were divided between the conflicting claims of St. Thomas[5], and the Eunuch of Candace Queen of Ethiopia.

The phases of this local superstition can be traced with curious accuracy through its successive transmitters. In the Buddhist annals, the sojourn of Buddha in Ceylon, and the impression of the "*sri-pada*," his sacred foot-mark left on departing, are recorded in that portion of the *Mahawanso* which was written by Mahanaama prior to B.C. 301[6], and the story is repeated in the other sacred books of the Singhalese. The *Raja-*

---

spoken of as containing the footstep of Adam; but this is an interpolation of the Mahometan translator, and the *Ramayana* makes no mention of Adam. The Hindus describe Adam's Peak by the term *Swangarrhanam*, "the ascent to heaven."

[1] *Mahawanso*, ch. i. p. 7. ch. xv. p. 92. ch. xxxii. p. 197. *Rajaratnacari*, p. 9. See also the *Sadharmaratnakari*.

[2] FA HIAN, *Foë-Kouë Ki*, ch. xxxviii. p. 332.

[3] *Pistis Sophia*, MS. Brit. Mus. No. 5114, fol. 148. Transl. Schwartze, p. 221.

[4] SOLEYMAN, A.D. 851. REINAUD, *Voyages Arabes, &c.*, t. i. p. 5.

[5] "Haud absimile videtur, in eo vestigio coli Eunachum Candaces Æthiopum Reginæ quem Dorotheus Tyri Episcopus in Taprobana Christi Evangelium promulgasse testatur." MAFFEI, *Histor. Indie*, lib. iii. p. 61. But DE COUTO pleads more earnestly in favour of St. Thomas, "nos parece que poderá ser do bemaventurado Apostolo S. Thomé," because it appears that in the time of the Portuguese, there was a stone in a quarry at Colombo deeply impressed with the *mark of the knees* of this saint, and closely resembling a similar indentation on a rock at Meliapore, and believed to be equally the physical result of his devotions. The rock at Meliapore is described by ANDREA CORSALI in his letter to Julian de Medicis, 5th January, 1515: what stone at Colombo DE COUTO means, it is not easy to conjecture, as no such relic is to be found there at present; but possibly he may allude to the alleged existence of a footstep at Kalany, which however is supposed to be covered by the waters of the river. DE COUTO fortifies his own theory by appeals to the many similar phenomena in Christendom, such as the hollows worn in the steps of the Santa Casa of Jerusalem on the spot covered by the church of the Ascension at the Mount of Olives, and on the rock on which the three disciples reclined in the garden of Gethsemane. DE COUTO, *Asia, &c.*, dec. v. lib. vi. ch. ii.

[6] In the work edited by WAGENFELDT in 1837, professing to be the Phœnician History of Sanchoniathon in the Greek version of Philo, allusion is made to the footstep of Bauth (Buddha) still extant in Ceylon, "ἧς καὶ ἴχνος ἐστὶν ἐν τοῖς ὄροις."—SANCHONIATHON, lib. vii. ch. 12, p. 162. Moses of Chorene disposes of the pretensions of all other claimants, by pronouncing it to be the footstep of the devil, "ibidem *Satanæ* lapsum narrant."—*Hist. Armeniæ et Epitome Geogr.*, p. 367.

Tarangini states that in the first century of the Christian era, a king of Kashmir, about the year 24, resorted to Ceylon to adore the relic on Adam's Peak.[1] The Chinese traveller, Fa Hian, who visited Ceylon A.D. 413, says that two foot-marks of Foĕ were then venerated in the island, one on the sacred mountain, and the second towards the north of the island.[2] On the continent of India both Fa Hian and Hiouen Thsang examined many other sri-padas[3]; and Wang Ta-youen[4] adheres to the story of their Buddhist origin, although later Chinese writers, probably from intercourse with Mahometans, borrow the idea that it was the footprint of Pwan-koo, "the first man," in their system of mythology.[5] In the twelfth century, the patriot King Prakrama Bahu I. "made a journey on foot to worship the shrine on Samanhela, and caused a temple to be erected on its summit,"[6] and the mountain was visited by the King Kirti Nissanga, for the same devout purpose, in A.D. 1201[7], and by Prakrama III. A.D. 1267.[8] Nor was the faith of the Singhalese in its sanctity shaken even by the temporary apostacy and persecution of the tyrant Raja Singha I., who, at the close of the sixteenth century, abjured Buddhism, adopted the worship of Brahma and installed some Aandee fakirs in the desecrated shrine upon the Peak.[9]

Strange to say the origin of the Mahometan tradition as to its being the footstep of Adam, is to be traced to

---

[1] *Raja-Tarangini*, book iii. sl. 71—79.

[2] No second original footstep of Buddha is now preserved in Ceylon, although models of the great one are shown at the Alu Wihara, at Cotta, and at other temples on the island; but a sri-pada is said in the sacred book to be concealed by the waters of the Kalany-ganga. Reinaud conjectures, from the great distance at which Fa Hian places it to the north, that the second one alluded to by him must have been situated in Madura.—*Notes to Fa Hian*, p. 342.

[3] *Foĕ-Kouĕ Ki*, ch. xxxviii. p. 332. For accounts of other sacred footsteps in Behar, see *Trans. Roy. Asiat. Soc.*, vol. i. p. 523; and in Siam, *Ibid.*, vol. iii. p. 57.

[4] *Taou-e Chè-lëŏ*, or "Account of Island Foreigners," A.D. 1350.

[5] *Po-wouh yaou-lan*, or the "Philosophical Examiner," written during the Myng Dynasty, about the year 1400, A.D.

[6] *Rajavali*, p. 254.

[7] *Mahawanso*, ch. lxxix.

[8] *Ibid.*, ch. lxxxiii.

[9] TURNOUR'S *Epitome, &c.*, p. 51.

a Christian source. In framing their theological system, the Gnostics, who, even during the lifetime of the Apostles, corrupted Christianity by an admixture of the mysticism of Plato[1]; assigned a position of singular preeminence to Adam, who, as "*Ieû, the primal man,*" next to the "*Noos*" and "*Logos,*" was made to rank as the third emanation from the Deity. Amongst the details of their worship they cultivated the veneration for monumental relics; and in the precious manuscript of the fourth century, which contains the Coptic version of the discourse on "*Faithful Wisdom,*"[2] attributed by Tertullian to the great gnostic heresiarch Valentinus, there occurs the earliest recorded mention of the sacred foot-print of Adam. The Saviour is there represented as informing the Virgin Mary that he has appointed the spirit Kalapataraoth as guardian over the footstep (skemmut) "*impressed by the foot of Ieû,* and placed him in charge of the books of Ieû, written by Enoch in paradise."[3]

The Gnostics in their subsequent dispersion under the persecution of the emperors, appear to have communicated to the Arabs this mystical veneration for Adam[4] as the great *protoplast* of the human race; and in the religious code of Mahomet, Adam, as the pure creation of the Lord's breath, takes precedence as the *Ewel' ulenbiya,* "the greatest of all patriarchs and prophets,"

---

[1] GIBBON, *Decline and Fall,* ch. xv. xxi. xlvii.

[2] Ἡ Πιστὴ Σοφία. *MSS. Brit. Mus.* No. 5114. A Latin translation by Schwartze, of this unique manuscript (probably one of the most ancient in existence) was published at Berlin, 1851, under the title of *Pistis Sophia.* The passage adverted to above is as follows: "Et posui Καλαπαταραυωθ *αρχοντα super skemmut in quo est pes Ieû,* et iste circumdat *αιωνας* omnes et *ειμαρμενας*. Illum posui custodientem libros Jeû," &c., p. 221. In previous passages Ieû is described as "primus homo."

[3] Schwartze has left the Coptic word "skemmut" untranslated, but DULAURIER, in the *Journal Asiatique* for September, 1846, p. 176, renders it the "footstep," trace.

[4] Adam was not the only scriptural character whose footsteps were venerated by the Mahometans. Ibn Batuta, early in the 14th century, saw at Damascus "*the Mosque of the Foot,* on which there is a stone, having upon it the print of the foot of Moses."—IBN BATUTA, ch. v. p. 30, LEE'S *Transl.*

and the *Kalifé y-Ekber*, "the first of God's vicegerents upon earth."[1] The Mahometans believe that on his expulsion from Paradise, Adam passed many years in expiatory exile upon a mountain in India[2] before his re-union with Eve on Mount Arafath, which overhangs Mecca. As the Koran[3], in the passages in which is recorded the fall of Adam, makes no mention of the spot at which he took up his abode on earth, it may be inferred that in the age of Mahomet, his followers had not adopted Ceylon as the locality of the sacred foot-step[4]; but when the Arab seamen, returning from India, brought home accounts of the mysterious relic on the summit of *Al-rahoun*[5], as they termed Adam's Peak, it appears to have fixed in the minds of their countrymen the precise locality of Adam's penitence. The most ancient Arabian records of travel that have come down to us mention the scene with solemnity[6]; but it was not till the tenth century that Ceylon became the established resort of Mahometan pilgrims, and Ibn Batuta, about the year 1340, relates that at Shiraz he visited the tomb of the Imam Abu-Abd-Allah, who first taught the way to Serendib.[7]

---

[1] D'OHSSON, vol. i. p. 68.

[2] FABRICIUS, *Codex Pseudepigraphus*, vol. ii. p. 20.

[3] SALE'S *Al-koran*, ch. ii. p. 5; ch. vii. p. 117.

[4] Yet Mr. DUNCAN, in a paper in the Asiatic Researches, containing "*Historical Remarks on the Coast of Malabar*," mentions a native chronicle in which it is stated, that a Pandyan who was "*contemporary with Mahomet*," was converted to Islam by a party of dervishes on their pilgrimage to *Adam's Peak*, vol. v. p. 9.

[5] Rohuna or Rohana was the ancient division of the island in which Galle is situated, and from which Adam's Peak is seen. Hence the name Al Rahoun, given by them to the mountain.

[6] SOLEYMAN and ABOU-ZEYD. See REINAUD, *Voyages Arabes et Persans dans le* ix. *Siècle*, vol. i. p. 5. TABARI "the Livy of Arabia," who lived in the ninth century, describes the descent of Adam on Serendib. See Sir W. OUSELEY'S *Travels*, vol. i. p. 35.

[7] "C'est lui qui enseigna le chemin de la montagne de Serendib dans l'île de Ceylan."—IBN BATUTA, tom. ii. p. 79. GILDEMEISTER, in the commentary prefixed to his *Scriptores Arabi*, says Abu Abdallah ben khafif, "doctor inter Cûfios clarissimus," died anno Hej. 331, 14th Sept., 942 A.D. (p. 54). IBN BATUTA tells a marvellous tale of this Imam and a party of thirty fakirs, his first companions, who being in want of provisions in the forest at the foot of Adam's Peak, killed and ate a young elephant, the Imam refusing to partake of the unclean food. In the night the herd surprised and destroyed the fakirs, but the leader, raising the Imam on his back by means of his

At the present day, the Buddhists are the guardians of the sri-pada, but around the object of common adoration the devotees of all races meet, not in furious contention, like the Latins and Greeks at the Holy Sepulchre in Jerusalem, but in pious appreciation of the one solitary object on which they can unite in peaceful worship.

The route taken to the mountain from the western side of the island, is generally from Colombo to Ratnapoora by land, and thence by jungle paths to the Peak; and on the return, visitors usually descend the Kaluganga in boats to Caltura. The distance from the sea to the summit is about sixty-five miles, for two-thirds of which the road lies across the lowlands of the coast, traversing rice lands and coco-nut groves, and passing by numerous villages with their gardens of jak-trees, arecas, and plantains.[1] After leaving Ratnapoora, the traveller proceeds by bridle-roads to climb the labyrinth of hills which cluster round the base of the sacred mountain. These form what is called the "wilderness of the Peak," and are covered with forests frequented by elephants, wild boars, and leopards. There the track winds under overarching trees, whose shade excludes the sun; across brawling rivers; through ravines so deep, that nothing but the sky is seen above, and thence the road reascends to heights from which views of surpassing grandeur are obtained over the hills and plains below. In these moist regions the tormenting land leeches swarm on the damp grass, and almost defy every precaution, however vigilant, against insidious attacks.[2]

Ambelams and rest-houses for travellers have been piously erected at various points along the weary journey, where the green sward presents a suitable locality, and

---

trunk carried him safely to a village on the banks of a river called Khaïzoran, or the river of "bamboos."—Tom. ii. p. 81.

[1] LASSEN says that the early Christian travellers believed that Adam lived on the plantain, and clothed himself with its broad leaves.—*Indische Alterthumskunde*, vol. i. p. 261.

[2] For a detailed account of the land-leech of Ceylon, see *ante*, Vol. I. Pt. II. ch. vii. p. 311.

temples in solitary spots invite the devotion of pilgrims. In one of these, at Palabaddula, a model is preserved, exhibiting in brass a fac-simile of the golden cover which once protected the sacred footstep, and which VALENTYN says was shown to some subjects of Holland who ascended the Peak in 1654 [1], but it has long since disappeared.

The country rises so rapidly, that between Gillemale and the Peak, the entire ascent, upwards of 7000 feet, is made in less than nine miles. As the path ascends it skirts round scarped acclivities, so steep that a stone allowed to drop is heard bounding from rock to rock long after it has been hidden from sight by the trees that clothe the face of the precipice below.[2]

During the greater part of this upward journey, the summit of the mountain, the object of so much solicitude and toil, is seldom visible, being hidden by the overhanging cliffs; but, at last, on reaching a little patch of table-land at Diebetne, with its ruinous rest-house, the majestic cone is discerned towering in unsurpassed sublimity, but with an intervening space of three miles of such acclivity that the Singhalese have conferred on it the appropriate name of *aukanagaou*, literally, "the sky league." Here descending into one of the many ravines, and crossing an enormous mass of rounded rock overflowed by perpetual streams, the ascent recommences by passages so steep as to be accessible only by means of steps hewn in the smooth stone. On approaching the highest altitude, vegetation suddenly ceases; and, at last, on reaching the base of the stupendous cone which forms the pinnacle of the

---

[1] *Oud en Nieuw Oost-Indien*, ch. xvi. p. 376.

[2] DE COUTO, in confirmation of the pious conjecture that the footstep on the summit was that of St. Thomas, asserts that all the trees on the Peak, and for half a league on all sides around it, *bend their crowns in the direction of the relic*; a homage which could only be offered to the footstep of an Apostle: "todas por todas as partes fazem com suas copas hum inclinacão pera a serra," &c.—*Asia, &c.*, dec. v. lib. vi. ch. ii.

peak, further progress is effected by the aid of chains securely riveted in the living rock.[1] As the pillar-like crag rounds away at either side, the eye, if turned downwards, peers into a chasm of unseen depth; and so dizzy is the elevation, that the guides discourage a pause, lest a sudden gust of wind should sweep the adventurous climber from his giddy footing, into the unfathomable gulfs below.[2] An iron ladder, let into the face of a perpendicular cliff upwards of forty feet in height, lands the pilgrim on the tiny terrace which forms the apex of the mountain; and in the centre of this, on the crown of a mass of gneiss and hornblende, the sacred footstep is discovered under a pagoda-like canopy, supported on slender columns, and open on all sides to the winds.

---

[1] The iron chains at Adam's Peak are relics of so great antiquity, that in the legends of the Mahometans they are associated with the name of Alexander the Great. IBN BATUTA, in his account of his ascent of the Peak in the fourteenth century, speaks of coming "to a place called the 'Seven Caves,' and after this to the 'Ridge of Alexander,' at which place is the entrance to the mountain. The mountain of Serendib is one of the highest in the world; we saw it from sea, at the distance of nine days. When we ascended it, we saw the clouds passing between us and its foot. On it is a great number of trees, the leaves of which never fall. There are also flowers of various colours, with the red rose (*Rhododendron?*). There are two roads on the mountain leading to the Footprint; the one is known as 'the way of Baba,' the other as 'the way of Mama,' by which they mean Adam and Eve. At the foot of the mountain there is a minaret named after Alexander, and a fountain of water. The ancients have cut something like steps, upon which one may ascend, and have fixed in iron pins, to which chains are appended, and upon these those who ascend take hold. Of these chains there are ten in number, the last of which is termed 'the chain of witness,' because when one has arrived at this and looks down, the frightful notion seizes him that he will fall."—LEE'S *Translation*, ch. xx. p. 189.

ASHREF, a Persian writer of the fifteenth century, in a poem, quoted by Sir William Ouseley, in which he celebrates the exploits of Alexander the Great, "*Zaffer Namah Sekanderi*," introduces an episode, in which the conqueror and his companion Bolinus (by whom is supposed to be meant Apollonius of Tyana) devise means whereby they may ascend the mountain of Serendib, "fixing thereto chains with rings and rivets made of iron and brass, the remains of which exist even at this day, so that travellers, by their assistance, are enabled to climb the mountain and obtain glory by finding the sepulchre of Adam, on whom be the blessing of God."—*Travels*, vol. i. p. 57.

[2] Incredible as it may seem, elephants make their way to this frightful elevation; and Major Skinner assures me that on one occasion, in 1840, the unmistakeable traces of one were found on the neck of the fearful rock which sustains the sacred Footstep.

The indentation in the rock is a natural hollow artificially enlarged, exhibiting the rude outline of a foot

about five feet long, and of proportionate breadth; but it is a test of credulity, too gross even for fanaticism to believe that the footstep is either human or divine. The worship addressed to it consists of offerings, chiefly flowers of the rhododendron, presented with genuflexions, invocations, and shouts of *Saadoo!*[1] The ceremony concludes by the striking of an ancient bell[2], and

[1] Amen!

[2] Bells are mentioned in Ceylon in the second century B.C. (see *ante*, Vol. I. Pt. IV. ch. v. p. 458), so that it is unnecessary to conjecture that the original bell on Adam's Peak may have been a gift from the devout Buddhists of China. The custom of striking it has prevailed from time immemorial, and was described by the Portuguese, "los passageros dan golpes."—RODRIGUES DE SAA, *Rebellion de Ceylon*, Lisbon, 1681, p. 17. For the subjoined plan of the summit, made in 1841, I am indebted to Mr. Ferguson, of the Surveyor-General's Department, Colombo. He makes the area of the terrace 64 feet by 45.

a. a. a. Level space.
b. The Pagoda.
c. Belfry.
d. d. d. Wall 5 feet high.
e. Shed for offerings.
f. House of the priest.
g. g. The rock.
i. The Foot-print.
o. Opening towards Ratnapoora.
n. Opening towards Kandy.
m. Opening to the well.

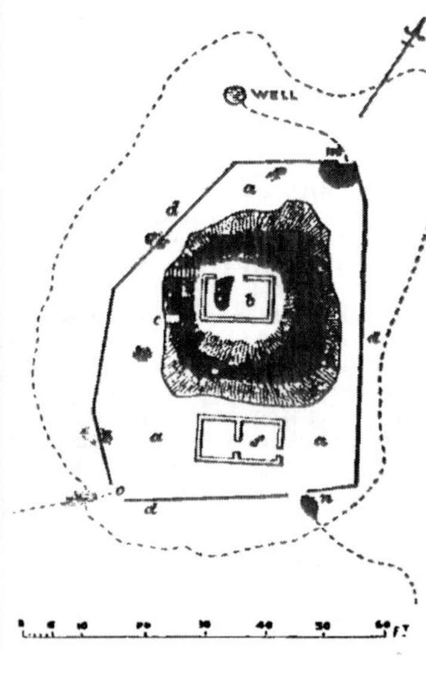

a draught from the sacred spring, which runs within a few feet of the summit.

The panorama from the summit of Adam's Peak is, perhaps, the grandest in the world, as no other mountain, although surpassing it in altitude, presents the same unobstructed view over land and sea.[1] Around it, to the north and east, the traveller looks down on the zone of lofty hills that encircle the Kandyan kingdom, whilst to the westward the eye is carried far over undulating plains, threaded by rivers like cords of silver, till in the purple distance the glitter of the sunbeams on the sea marks the line of the Indian Ocean.[2]

The descent of the Kalu-ganga from Ratnapoora to Caltura is effected with great ease in the boats which bring down rice and areca nuts to the coast, and the scenery includes everything that is characteristic of the western lowlands; temples, reached by ghauts, rising from the edge of the river; and villages surrounded by groves of tamarind and jak-trees, talipats, coco-nuts, and kitools. Along the banks, the yellow stemmed bamboo waves its feathery leaves, and on approaching the sea the screw pines and mangroves grow in dense clusters, and over-arch the margin of the stream.

Caltura has always been regarded as one of the sanitaria of Ceylon, and as it faces the sea breeze from the south-west, the freshness of its position, combined with the beauty and grandeur of the surrounding scenery, rendered it the favourite resort of the Dutch, and afterwards of the British. A fort, built on a green eminence, commanded the entrance of the river, but this is now dismantled, and forms a residence for one of the civil officers. Game is abundant; and within a very few miles the in-

---

[1] "Adam's Peak is not higher than the mountains which travellers ascend in Switzerland; but nowhere in that land *can the eye measure the height by comparison with a surrounding plain* nearly on the level of the sea."—HOFFMEISTER, *Travels, &c.*, p. 181.

[2] The first Englishman who ascended Adam's Peak was Lieut. Malcolm, of the 1st Ceylon Regiment, who reached the summit on the 27th April, 1827.—*Asiatic Journ.*, vol. i. p. 442.

land lake of Bolgodde is the resort of prodigious numbers of wild fowl, which breed in the luxuriant woods that encircle it. Caltura was one of the most promising localities in which the cultivation of the sugar-cane was attempted, but hitherto the success of the experiment has not been such as to render it commercially remunerative.

From the great extent of the coco-nut groves which surround it, Caltura is one of the principal places for the distillation of arrack. The trees, during the process of drawing the toddy, are frequented by the great bats (*pteropus*), called by the Europeans, "flying foxes."[1] They are attracted in numbers by the fermenting juice, and drink from the earthen chalices which are suspended to collect it. A friend of mine, who was at Caltura in 1852, had his attention frequently drawn to the unusual noises occasioned in some of the topes by the revels of these creatures. It assumed at the beginning the appearance of an ordinary quarrel, but grew by degrees so "fast and furious," as to become manifestly a drunken riot. The natives are well aware of this propensity of the bats, and attributed these demonstrations to their inebriety.

At Pantura, after being ferried across the arm of the lake, which here debouches on the sea, we found the carriages of the governor, which his excellency had been good enough to send to convey us to Colombo. The road lay along a broad embankment of sand, which runs for several miles between the sea and the lake of Pantura, one of those estuaries described by the Arab navigators under the name of the "*gobbs* of Serendib," into which, when the south-west monsoon was rolling a surf upon the coast, their seamen were accustomed to withdraw their frail vessels and spend "two months or more in the shade of forests and gardens, and in the enjoyment of a tem-

[1] See Vol. I. Pt. II. ch. i. p. 135.

perate coolness."[1] The Dutch took advantage of this calm sheet of water to facilitate the system of canals by which they opened a continuous line of navigation from Caltura to Negombo. The works still exist, but their utility, however it may have been appreciated two centuries ago, when the country was as yet unopened by roads, is less demonstrable at the present day, when metalled highways have been constructed in their immediate vicinity.

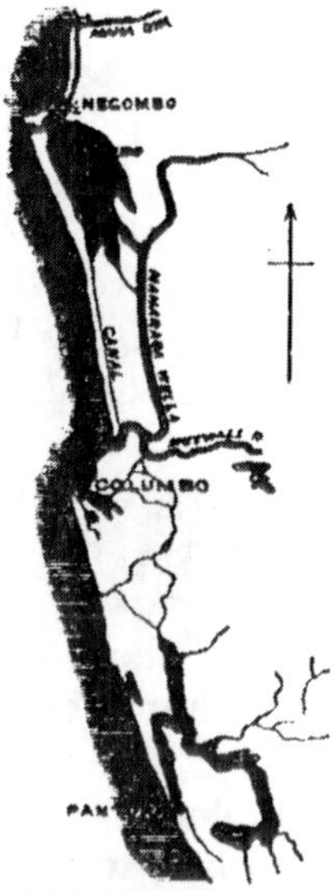

"GOBBS" ON THE WEST COAST.

At Morottu, a few miles from Pantura, the region of cultivated cinnamon begins; and thence to Colombo, for a distance of eight or ten miles, the road passes between almost continuous gardens of this renowned laurel, once guarded among the treasures of the Indies, but now comparatively neglected for the homely, but more profitable, cocoa-nut palm. The village of Morottu, which contains a population of 12,000, is chiefly inhabited by carpenters of the fisher caste, who devote themselves to the making of furniture from the jak-tree, the wood of which, though yellow when first cut, acquires in time the dark tint and markings of mahogany.

Another source of the prosperity of this thriving community is the recent adoption of barrels instead of gunny-bags for the export of coffee. The making of these, as well as of casks for the shipment of coco-nut oil, has afforded a new source of industrial employment and wealth. One eminent native of the village, Jeronis de

---

[1] IBN WAHAB, in the *Voyages Arabes et Persans*, tom. i. p. 129; ALBYROUNY, in REINAUD'S *Fragmens Arabes, &c.*, p. 119. For a full account of these "gobbs," as they exist in Ceylon, see the present work, Vol. I. Pt. I. ch. i. p. 44.

Soyza, has built, adjoining to it, a dwelling house, which may be regarded as the model of a Singhalese mansion with its gardens and oriental grounds. The entire district has benefited by the generosity of this public-spirited man, and in recognition of his patriotism in opening roads and promoting the welfare of the inhabitants, he has recently had conferred upon him the rank of Moodliar of the Governor's Gate.

On a rocky headland, which projects into the sea a few miles from Morottu, are the remains of what was once the marine palace of the governors of Ceylon; an edifice in every way worthy of the great man by whom it was erected — Sir Edward Barnes. But in one of those paroxysms of economy which are sometimes not less successful than the ambition of the Sultan in the fable, in providing haunts for those birds that philosophise amidst ruins, the edifice at Mount Lavinia had scarcely been completed at an expense which has been estimated at 30,000*l.*, when it was ordered to be dismantled, and the buildings were disposed of for less than the cost of the window frames.

At Galkisse the traveller has the opportunity of seeing a temple which may serve as an example of modern Buddhist buildings of this class in Ceylon. It is situated on a gentle eminence close by the high road, surrounded by groves of iron wood [1], murutas [2], champacs [3], and other trees, offerings of whose flowers form so remarkable a feature in the worship of the Singhalese. The modest pansela in which the priests and their attendants reside [4] is built in the hollow, and the ascent to the Wihara above it is by steps excavated in the hill. The latter is protected by a low wall decorated with mythological symbols, and the edifice itself is of the humblest dimensions, with whitened walls and a projecting tiled

[1] *Messua nagaha.*

[2] *Lagerstrœmia regina.*

[3] *Michelia champaca.*

[4] For an account of a Buddhist temple and its buildings, see *ante*, Vol. I. Pt. III. ch. iv. p. 349.

roof. In an inner apartment dimly lighted by lamps, where the air is heavy with the perfume of the yellow champac flowers, are the *pilamas* or statues of the god. One huge recumbent figure, twenty feet in length, represents Buddha, in that state of blissful repose which constitutes the elysium of his devotees; a second shows him seated under the sacred bo-tree in Uruwela; and a third erect, and with the right hand raised and the two fore fingers extended (as is the custom of the popes in conferring their benediction), exhibits him in the act of exhorting his earliest disciples. One quadrangular apartment which surrounds the enclosed adytus is lighted by windows, so as to exhibit a series of paintings on the inner wall illustrative of the narratives contained in the *jatakas*[1], or legends of the successive births of Buddha; the whole executed in the barbarous and conventional style which from time immemorial has marked this peculiar school of ecclesiastical art.[2]

As usual, within the outer enclosure there is a small Hindu *dewale* (which in this instance is dedicated to the worship of the Kattragam deviyo), and near to it grows one of the sacred bo-trees, that, like every other in Ceylon, is said to have been raised from a seed of the patriarchal tree planted by Mahindo, at Anarajapoora, more than two thousand years ago.[3] The whole establishment is on the most unpretending scale[4]; for nine months of the year the priests visit the houses of the villagers in search of alms, and during the other three, when the violence of the rains prevents their perambulations, their food is brought to them in the pansela;

---

[1] For an account of the Pansiya-panas-jataka-pota, with the 550 births of Buddha, see *ante*, Vol. I. Pt. IV. ch. X. p. 514.

[2] On the subject of the early paintings of the Singhalese temples, see *ante*, Vol. I. Pt. IV. ch. vii. p. 472.

[3] B.C. 289. For an account of its planting, see Vol. I. Pt. III. ch. iii. p. 341; and for a description of the tree, as it exists at the present day, Vol. II. Pt. X. ch. ii.

[4] In a Buddhist temple, as in the original temple of the Jews, "all the vessels thereof are of brass."—Exod. xxvii. 19.

or else they reside with some of their wealthier parishioners, who provide them once a year with a set of yellow robes.[1]

Towards sunset we had evidences of our approach to the capital by the increased number of vehicles on the road: bullock bandies covered with cajans met us; coolies, heavily laden with burdens of fish fresh from the sea, hurried towards the great town, native gentlemen, driving fast-trotting oxen in little hackery cars, hastened home from it[2]; and as we passed through the long line of villas, each in its *compound* of flowers, which forms the beautiful suburb of Colpetty, the European population of the Fort were pouring forth to enjoy their evening promenade, on horseback and in carriages, each horse attended by a Malabar groom in picturesque costume. Our way lay across the Galle-face[3], an open plain to the south of the fortifications, which at this hour is the favourite lounge of the inhabitants; the band of the regiments of the garrison adding to its afternoon attractions. When we crossed it the sward was already green after the shower of the north-west monsoon, and the tendrils of the goat's-foot convolvulus, with which the surface is closely matted, were beginning to be covered with buds. A month afterwards we were amazed to see it crimsoned by myriads of the full-blown flowers, which had expanded in the interim and covered it as closely as if it had been powdered with carmine. It realised the beauty of the scene which Darwin describes on the La Plata, where the tracts around Maldonado are so thickly overrun by *verbena melindres* as to appear a gaudy scarlet.[4]

Crossing the drawbridge and entering the Fort of Co-

---

[1] The ceremonies connected with the robes of the priesthood are described, Vol. I. Pt. IV. ch. iv. p. 452.

[2] The hackery is a light conveyance, with or without springs, in which a well-trained bullock will draw two persons at the rate of eight miles an hour.

[3] Galle-face or *Galle-faas* (Dutch), the *faas*, or front, of the fortification facing the direction of *Galle*.

[4] *Naturalist's Voyage, &c.*, ch. iii.

lombo by the old Dutch gate beneath the Middelburg bastion, we drove along the main street, shaded by rows of luxuriant hibiscus; and were received by Sir Colin Campbell under the hospitable portico of the old Government House.

PORTICO OF THE OLD QUEEN'S HOUSE, COLOMBO.

NOTE TO CHAPTER.

THE FISH-TAX IN CEYLON.

In a report which I framed in 1846, on the finances and revenue of Ceylon, I adverted to the characteristic incident alluded to at p. 131 in connection with the fish-tax, to illustrate the caution which it behoves us to exercise in relying on European theories when dealing with the habits and customs of an Oriental people, whose energies seldom respond to encouragement, and whose apathy prevents the realisation of our most familiar maxims of political economy. In the instance above alluded to, the abolition of the fish-tax had failed to supply a motive for increased activity on the part of the fishermen; it secured no advantage to the public, whose *supply of fish diminished, whilst the cost was more than doubled*; and it failed to benefit the revenue, since the receipts from the tax fell off nearly *one-third*. In proof of this I showed, that on an average of four years from 1830 to 1833, whilst the tax was *one-fourth* per cent., the average amount of duty was 7389*l*. From 1834 to 1837, when it was reduced to *one-sixth*, the average was 6694*l*., and from 1831 to 1840, whilst the duty was but *a tenth*, the receipts fell off to 4821*l*.

My report, when laid before Parliament in 1847, was accompanied by the comment of a Committee, to whom it had been referred by Earl Grey, consisting of Sir Benjamin Hawes, the Right Honourable H. Tufnell, Mr. J. Shaw Lefevre, and Mr. Bird. On this passage they remarked that my inference was "an obvious mistake," the amounts of revenue as given above, "proving not that there is anything peculiar in the Ceylon fishermen; but that their trade follows the usual course of all other trades, since with a duty of 25 per cent., the value of the fish taken was - - - - - £29,556
With a duty of 16⅔ per cent. do. - - - 40,164
do. 10 do. - - - - 48,210

The "obvious error" is, however, in the criticism, and not in my statement, which is strictly correct. Had "the usual course of all other trades" followed the several reductions of the fish-tax, the result would have been an increased demand, creating an increased supply; the price would have fallen to the consumer at least in proportion to the fall of the duty; and the revenue would have benefited by the greater quantity brought to sale. But the Committee overlooked the several passages in which I had stated that the very reverse had occurred in each particular, and that *the price of the article had doubled* after the reduction of the tax.

In 1833, under the old system, the duty of 25 per cent. yielded an income of 7389*l.* on a gross value of 29,556*l.*, which at one penny per pound showed a quantity equal to 7,093,440 pounds weight of fish as the ordinary supply under the fish-tax. But in 1837, when the duty was reduced to 16⅔ per cent., the price rose 50 per cent., so that the duty then received (6694*l.*) represented a gross value of 40,164*l.*, which at *three halfpence* per pound, *then the price in the market*, shows that the quantity caught had fallen to 6,426,240 pounds. Again, in the last stage, in which the tax was reduced to 10 per cent. in 1840, the price had risen to two pence and upwards, and the duty therefore (4821*l.*) represents, on a gross value of 48,210*l.*, only 5,785,200 pounds of fish taken. In other words, had not the price risen after the first reduction of the tax in 1833, the sum expended by the public in 1837, ought to have given 9,639,360 pounds instead of 6,426,240 pounds, and in 1840, 11,570,400 pounds instead of 5,785,200 pounds. (*See* PARLIAMENTARY PAPERS 1848, *Report on the Finance and Commerce of Ceylon*, p. 15, 51.)

In the early part of the last century, a tax on the fishermen at Lisbon produced a considerable annual sum to the Portuguese treasury; and it is a curious coincidence that the effect of its abolition was in every respect similar to that produced by the repeal of the fish-tax in Ceylon. The Regency issued a decree in November, 1830, abolishing all dues on fishing. It came into operation in 1833, and continued in force for ten years. By this measure a tax equivalent to 30 per cent. was taken off fish, but so far from increasing, the supply diminished, and the price rose in consequence. A duty of 6 per cent. was restored in 1843, together with the former regulations established for protecting and aiding the fishermen; and I ascertained at Lisbon, that since the last change the improvement in the market has been striking, the supply has become regular and abundant, and the price has fallen in consequence.

COLOMBO, FROM THE GALLE ROAD.

CHAP. III.

COLOMBO.

COLOMBO, as a town, presents little to attract a stranger. It possesses neither the romance of antiquity nor the interest of novelty. The rocky headland near which it stands, was the "Cape of Jupiter," the "*Jovis Extremum*" of Ptolemy[1], remarkable only as one of the great landmarks by which the early navigators in their coasting voyages directed their course towards the "Promontory of Birds,"[2] which marked the entrance to the harbour of Galle.

The modern fortifications are Dutch; said to have been constructed after a plan of Cohorn, and so designed as to turn to the utmost advantage the natural strength of the position, lying as it does between the lake at one side, and the rocks, which form the harbour, on the other. The works include "four bastions on the land side, with counter-scarps and ravelins, and seven batteries towards the sea, adapted to the rock line of the coast."[3] The modern buildings within the Fort are a clumsy application of European architecture to tropical requirements; outside the walls are the modest dwellings of the Dutch and Portuguese Eur-Asians, and the houses of the Singhalese, Tamils, Moors, and Malays, constructed of white-washed mud, and either covered with red tiles or thatched with the plaited fronds of the coconut palm.

The only ancient quarter is the pettah or "Black town," inhabited by the native races, and extending

---

1 *Διὸς ἄκρον.* The coincidence of Colombo with the *Jovis Extremum* of Ptolemy has been already commented on, see Vol. I. Pt. v. ch. i. p. 535.

2 Ὀρνεων ἄκρον, "*Avium Promontorium,*" PTOL.

3 From the App. to PRIDHAM'S *Ceylon*, p. 873.

to the banks of the Kalany-ganga. Hence from its contiguity to the river, the city obtained the early name of *Kalan-totta*, the "Kalany Ferry," by which it is mentioned in the *Rajavali*. To the Singhalese, always uninterested in shipping, the roadstead, and the headland which protects it, were matters of indifference; but in the twelfth and thirteenth centuries, the Moors appear to have taken possession of the beach and harbour, and converted the name to *Kalambu*, under which it is described by IBN BATUTA about the year A.D. 1340, "as the finest and largest city in Serendib."[1] They built the tomb of one of their Santons on the rocks at the Galle-baak[2], and its desecration by the Portuguese when they erected their fortified factory near the spot in 1517[3], served to exasperate the already jealous Mahometans. The designation of the city had then been further changed to *Kolamba* or *Columbu*, and the Portuguese, probably pleased to discover that the name of their new settlement so nearly approached that of Columbus[4], rendered the resemblance still more close by writing it *Colombo*, whence is derived the name borne by the fortress at the present day.[5]

The houses in the Pettah were formerly clustered close under the fortifications; but on the outbreak of hostilities with the English in 1795, the last Dutch

---

[1] "Urbs quam Ibn Batuta maximam insulæ invenit *Kalambu* nomen hucusque servavit." — GILDEMEISTER, *Script. Arab.* p. 54.

[2] Galle-baak or Galle-*baaken* (Dutch), the "beacon" on the "rocks" close by the present lighthouse.

[3] *Query*. Did the stone with the Cufic inscription of the tenth century, which in 1827 formed a door-step in the Pettah at Colombo, form any portion of the Moorish buildings at the Galle-baak? See *Trans. Roy. Asiat. Soc.*, vol. i. p. 545. GILDEMEISTER, *Script. Arab.*, p. 59.

[4] KNOX, part i. p. 3.

[5] This explanation is more simple than that of Valentyn and the Dutch writers, who imagined that Colombo was derived from Col-amba, the leaf of the mango-tree, "Gennamd *Col Amba* of't Mangaas-blad afnamen:" —*Oud en Nieuw Oost-Indien*, ch. xv. p. 275. But this fanciful derivation is unsound, as the place bears no resemblance to a leaf, and the mango-tree was then unknown in the locality. Perhaps a better derivation than either is that in the *Sidath Sangara*, where one of the meanings of the word *Kolamba* is said to be a "harbour."—DE ALWIS, p. 4.

governor caused a space to be cleared between the cemetery and the walls, and this wise precaution was afterwards maintained by the British commanders.[1]

With the exception of the military officers, whose duties require their presence within the fort, the English in general have fixed their residences either in the environs, in villas overlooking the bay; in the cinnamon gardens; or under the cool shade of the coco-nut groves by the shore in the hamlet of Colpetty. The site of this beautiful suburb is on the sandy embankment which forms the natural bund of the lake of Colombo, one of the "gobbs of Serendib," formed by an ancient arm of the Kalany-ganga, which at one period must have had its opening to the sea, at the point now occupied by the Galle-face.[2] Outside the walls, every building of importance is modern, as the Dutch, owing to the precarious nature of their relations with the people of Kandy, were careful not to erect their dwellings beyond the guns of the fortress. In the suburbs the better houses seldom rise to a second story, but the area which each of them covers is large. Their broad verandahs are supported on columns; their apartments are lofty, and cooled by Indian punkas; their floors are tiled, and the doors and windows formed of Venetian jalousies[3], opening to the ground for the sake of freshness and air. The only inconvenience arising from the latter arrangement is the rather too free entrance afforded to reptiles, snakes[4],

---

[1] TOMBE, *Voyage aux Indes*, t. ii. p. 184.

[2] The Galle-face has still such attractions for the marine crustacea that it is infested by myriads of the little crabs (*ocypode*), which employ themselves in hollowing out deep burrows seriously injurious to the safety of the horsemen who make it their promenade. From these holes the crabs emerge each with an armful of sand, scatter it in a circle by a jerk, look round on all sides, and hurry down for another burthen.

[3] On the arrival of the English, in 1796, they found the Dutch houses at Colombo suffocatingly hot, in consequence of the windows being all closed with *glass*. CORDINER, p. 32. The substitution of lattice-work was a recent improvement.

[4] The Ceylon boa (*python reticulatus*) is found of great size in the cinnamon gardens. A specimen was brought to me nineteen feet long, which some coolies had secured by fastening it to a bamboo, in which condition they carried it into the Fort. It had swallowed one of the small meminna deer.

lizards and scorpions, which occasionally resort to the rooms, and take up their abode in the ceilings;—whilst the monkeys, in their mischievous curiosity, lift the tiles to discover what they conceal.[1] Spiders of enormous size haunt the wine cellars and other darkened store-rooms, and ants in myriads beset every crevice and corner in the exercise of their useful vocation as domestic scavengers.

But the chief inconvenience of a mansion in Ceylon, both on the coast and in the mountains, is the prevalence of damp and the difficulty of protecting articles liable to injury from this source. Books, papers, and manuscripts rapidly decay; especially during the south-west monsoon, when the atmosphere is laden with moisture. Unless great precautions are taken, the binding fades and yields, the leaves grow mouldy and stained, and letter-paper, in an incredibly short time, becomes so spotted and spongy as to be unfit for use. After a very few seasons of neglect, a book falls to pieces, and its decomposition attracts hordes of minute insects, that swarm to assist in the work of destruction. The concealment of these tiny creatures during daylight renders it difficult to watch their proceedings, or to discriminate the precise species most actively engaged; but there is every reason to believe that the larvæ of the death-watch and numerous acari are amongst those most active. As nature seldom peoples a region supplied with abundance of suitable food, without, at the same time, taking measures of precaution against the disproportionate increase of individuals; so have these vegetable depredators been provided with foes who pursue and feed greedily upon them. These are of widely different genera; but instead of their services being gratefully recognised, they are popularly branded as accomplices in the work of destruction. One

[1] A malicious device of the natives, in order to annoy a neighbour, is to scatter rice over his roof, in the search for which the monkeys will so displace the tiles as to let in the rain.

of these ill-used creatures is a tiny, tail-less scorpion (*chelifer*), and another is the pretty little silvery creature (*lepisma*), called by Europeans the "fish-insect."[1]

The latter, which is a familiar genus, comprises several species, of which only two have as yet been described[2]; one, of large size, is most graceful in its movements, and singularly beautiful in appearance, owing to the whiteness of the pearly scales from which its name is derived. These, contrasted with the dark hue of the other parts, and its tri-partite tail, attract the eye as the insect darts rapidly along. Like the chelifer, it shuns the light, hiding in chinks till sunset, but is actively engaged throughout the night feasting on the acari and soft-bodied insects which assail books and papers.

The close proximity of the lake to Colombo is productive of other inconveniences; the nightly serenade of frogs (some of which are of gigantic dimensions), the tormenting profusion of mosquitoes, and the incredible swarms of more ignoble flies, cause a nuisance sometimes intolerable. So multitudinous are these insects at certain seasons, that in some of the mansions on Slave Island and its vicinity, the flies invade the apartments in such numbers as literally to extinguish the lights. On the occasion of dinner parties it is the custom to light fires on the lawn to draw away the flies from the reception rooms, which

---

[1] Of the first of these, three species have been noticed in Ceylon, all with the common characteristics of being nocturnal, very active, very minute, of a pale chesnut colour, and each armed with a crab-like claw. They are

Chelifer Librorum, Temp.
" *Oblongus*, Temp.
" *Acaroides*, Hermann.

Dr. Templeton appears to have been puzzled to account for the appearance of the latter species in Ceylon so far from its native country, but it has most certainly been introduced from Europe, in Dutch or Portuguese books.

[2] *Lepisma niveo-fasciata*, Templeton, and *L. niger*, Temp. It was called "Lepisma" by Fabricius, from its fish-like scales. It has six legs, filiform antennæ, and the abdomen terminated by three elongated setæ, two of which are placed nearly at right angles to the central one. LINNÆUS states that the European species, with which book collectors are familiar, was first brought in sugar ships from America. Hence, possibly, these are more common in seaport towns in the South of England and elsewhere, and it is almost certain that, like the chelifer, one of the species found on book-shelves in Ceylon has been brought thither from Europe.

are kept darkened and with closed windows till the arrival of the guests.

Great pains have been taken with the gardens of these bungalows: the rarest and most beautiful flowering plants of the island have been planted around them, along with fruit trees of every variety; and exotics from the Eastern Archipelago, Australia, and India have been introduced in such numbers as to justify the exclamation of Prince Soltykoff that Colombo was "un jardin botanique sur une échelle gigantesque."[1]

Of the various races which inhabit Colombo, the bulk of the Singhalese are handicraftsmen[2] and servants; the Parsees are exclusively merchants; the Moors retail dealers; the Malays soldiers and valets; the Tamils labourers and coolies; and the Caffres excavators and pioneers. The majority of the Portuguese descendants consist of impoverished artisans and domestics, and some few of them are successfully engaged in trades and professions. But the Dutch Burghers, and the offspring of the English by intermarriages with the natives, form essentially the middle class in all the towns in Ceylon. They have risen to eminence at the Bar, and occupied the highest positions on the Bench. They are largely engaged in mercantile pursuits, and as writers and clerks they fill places of trust in every administrative establishment from the department of the Colonial Secretary to the humblest police court. It is not possible to speak too highly of the services of this meritorious body of men, by whom the whole machinery of government is put into action under the orders of the civil officers. They may fairly be described in the lan-

[1] PRINCE SOLTYKOFF, *Voyage dans l'Inde*, p. 39.

[2] It is a curious trait, not unfrequent amongst the Singhalese of a rank above artisans, to encourage the growth of a nail on one of their fingers; which denotes by its extraordinary length that the individual is not addicted to labour. A similar practice is observable amongst certain classes in China and the Philippines. In Borneo the nail selected is that of the right thumb.

guage of Sir Robert Peel as the "brazen wheels of the executive which keep the golden hands in motion."

Amongst the pure Singhalese, the ascendancy of caste still exercises a baneful influence over the intellectual as well as the material prosperity of the nation. Its origin has been elsewhere alluded to[1] as directly traceable to the Brahmanical conquerors of Ceylon under Wijayo, by whom the system was introduced from the continent of India. It was unknown amongst the aborigines of the island, and although condemned by the precepts of Buddha[2], and the example of his priesthood, so attractive were the distinctions of civil rank which it conferred, that in later times, in spite of religious injunction, and in defiance of the efforts of every European government, Portuguese, Dutch, and British, to discountenance and extinguish it, no appreciable progress has yet been made towards its modification or abandonment.

A reluctant conformity is exhibited on the part of high-caste persons placed officially under the orders of low-caste headmen; but their obedience is constrained, with no effort to conceal impatience; and in the relations of private life the impassable barrier is still maintained. There is no familiar intercourse between individuals of incongruous castes, no friendly domestic meetings, and no association even in the formal festivities of wed-

---

[1] See Part IV. ch. i. p. 425.

[2] A paper by TURNOUR in the *Asiat. Soc. Journ. Beng.*, vol. ii. p. 693, contains a translation of the discourse in which Buddha exposes and denounces the folly and evils of caste. It is taken from the *Agganna Suttan* in the *Dighanikaya* section of the *Pittakas*; and enforces the eligibility of all castes, however low, to the office of the priesthood, which commands the homage of the highest. The same doctrine is repeated in the *Madhura Suttan*; and the *Wasala Suttan* contains the stanza, beginning with "Majachcha wasalo hoti," &c., which runs thus,

"A man does not become low caste by birth.
Nor by birth does one become high caste;
High caste is the result of high actions—
And by actions does a man degrade himself to caste that is low."

Still Buddhism, even when in the zenith of its power, had not the influence, or perhaps the inclination, to extinguish these distinctions; and caste continued to be tolerated under the Singhalese kings as a *social institution*. In other Buddhist countries Burmah, Siam, and Thibet, caste does not exist in any similar form.

dings, or the solemnities that do honour to the dead. The social segregation is carried to such an extreme, that members of the several classes into which each caste is subdivided, with a distinctive rank for each, refuse to associate together; and a Vellale of the first class would shrink from the communication with a Vellale of a lower order, with as much sensitiveness as he would avoid contact with a washer or a Chalia.

Doubtless in time education and civilisation will manifest their power; but in opposition to their progress no obstacle has yet been interposed so powerful as caste. It interferes with the discipline of schools, it mars the harmonising efforts of Christianity, it discountenances social improvement, and deprives the civil authority of its most efficient agents, who, however endowed with the essentials of usefulness, would be paralysed in their functions by the disqualification of conventional rank. The only great measure likely to be productive of effect in equalising the pretensions of caste is the establishment of trial by jury, on which all are entitled to serve on a footing of perfect equality. But the inference from past experiments of the government, suggests the propriety of abstaining from direct interference, and leaving the abatement of the evil to the operation of time and the gradual growth of intelligence.

Of a thing so fluctuating as European society in a colony, it almost partakes of injustice to place on record any expression of opinion, the result of limited experience. It is unhappily the tendency of small sections of society to decompose, when separated from the great vital mass, as pools stagnate and putrify when cut off from the invigorating flow of the sea. But the process is variable, both in its agents and its manifestations. What seems repulsive in colonial society to-day, may become attractive to-morrow, by a few timely departures; and on the other hand, experience has unhappily demonstrated that one ungenial arrival may be sufficient to convert peace into pandemonium.[1] Nothing can be more charming than the accounts which have reached us of the social harmony of the first British community, after the capture of the island[2]; but at that period, the purity of English feeling was still untainted, and the unity of Christian fellowship had not yet been rent in sunder by ecclesiastical jarring. It is to be hoped that some future narrator will find a moment more propitious than I did to delineate the aspect of society at Colombo.

The high cost of living has been a subject of complaint ever since our occupation of the island, and the grievance is as severely felt at the present day as when Percival lamented it in 1803. The scarcity of pasture, and the injury to which cattle are exposed from leeches, render meat scarce and dear; milk is difficult to procure[3], fresh butter is almost unknown, and poultry ex-

---

[1] "Frequent scarifications render most colonial skins so impenetrably thick, that the utmost vituperation makes hardly any impression. Recourse therefore is had to something sharper than Billingsgate. It is a general custom in colonies, when your antagonist withstands abuse, to hurt him seriously if you can, and even to do him a mortal injury; either in order to carry your point or to punish him for having carried his. In every walk of colonial life, every body strikes at his opponent's heart. If a governor or high officer refuses to comply with the wish of some leading parties, they instantly try to ruin him by getting him recalled with disgrace. If two officials disagree, one of them is very likely to be tripped up and destroyed by the other. If an official or a colonist offends the official body, the latter hunt him into jail or out of the colony. If two settlers disagree about a road or a watercourse, they will attack each other's credit at the bank, rake up ugly old stories, get two newspapers to be the instruments of their bitter animosity, and perhaps ruin each other in desperate litigation. Disagreement and rivalry are more tiger-like in a colony than disagreement and rivalry at home." —WAKEFIELD on *Colonization*. Letter xxix., p. 188.

[2] CORDINER'S *Ceylon, &c.*, p. 76.

[3] Linnæus has described the peculiar effects produced on the milk of the reindeer and the cow by the leaves of the *Pinguicula vulgaris*, a small plant common in marshes in Britain. In many parts of the coast of Ceylon there is a thorny fruited plant, with dark orange-coloured roots and primrose-like flowers, which has equally wonderful effects on milk and on water, though of a different nature. It is known to the Singhalese as the bakatoo (*Pedalium murex*), and if bits of the stem, leaves, and roots be mixed for a few seconds in milk or water, the liquid turns thick and mucilaginous, so much so, that water in this state can be raised by the hand several feet out of a bason and will fall back without noise; and this without imparting any colour, taste, or smell to the fluid, which returns to its natural state in about ten or fifteen minutes afterwards.

pensive.[1] The wages of servants are increased, owing to the necessity of importing rice from the coast of India, and the cost of keeping horses at Colombo (ascribable to the same cause) is nearly double the outlay required at Madras. Fruit alone is abundant; a pineapple of two or three pounds weight costs but a penny; and freshly-gathered oranges sell at a similarly cheap rate. Excellent stores within the Fort supply articles imported from Europe; and those who bring outfits from England, generally find they could have obtained the same articles on the spot, if not more economically, at least more judiciously chosen, as regards adaptation to the climate. Besides, the Moors in the Pettah have shops which are certainly amongst the "wonders of Serendib," from the habits of their owners and the multiform variety of their contents. Here everything is procurable that industry can collect from the looms of Asia and the manufactories of Europe; but the stocks have accumulated so long, that an antiquary estimating the date by the fashion, might fix the period of their importation in the early times of the Dutch.[2]

The domestic economy of the great body of the Singhalese, who inhabit Colombo and the other towns of the island, is of the simplest and most inexpensive character. In a climate, whose chief requirement is protection from heat, their dwellings are as little encumbered with furniture as their persons with dress; and the coolness of the earthen floor renders it preferable to a bed. Two

---

The Singhalese take advantage of this peculiarity of the *bakatoo* to thicken the milk sent round for sale to Europeans.

[1] The Malabar poultry is common at Colombo; in which the colour of the bones and skin is a disagreeable black. In other respects they are excellent.

[2] "The Moormen shopkeepers have such unpronounceable names, that by common consent their English customers designate them by the *numbers of their shops*. In this way one, a small portion of whose name consists of Meera Lebbe Hema Lebbe Tamby Ahamadoe Lebbe Marcair, is cut down to 'Number Forty-eight,' while his rival in trade is similarly symbolized as 'Number Forty-two.'"—*Household Words*, vol. viii. p. 19.

articles furnish the basis of their cookery, — rice and the flesh of the coco-nut;—*appas*[1] (cakes made of the former) supply their morning repast, with a scanty allowance of coffee; and curries, in all their endless variety, furnish their afternoon meal. The use of metal of any kind scarcely enters into their arrangements; their houses are framed without iron, their implements fashioned in wood, and their cooking utensils are clay. The broad leaves of the plantain serve as a substitute for plates; and in further illustration of their vegetable economy, the nuts of the *penela* tree[2] furnish them with a substitute for soap, and possess all its detergent qualities.[3]

But the residences of the headmen are of a very different class, and exhibit European taste engrafted on Singhalese customs. A dinner at which my family were received by the Maha Moodliar de Sarem, the Chief of highest rank in the maritime provinces, was one of the most refined entertainments at which it was our good fortune to be present in Ceylon; the furniture of his reception-rooms was of ebony richly carved, and his plate, chiefly made by native artists, was a model of superior chasing on silver. The repast, besides pastry and dessert, consisted of upwards of forty dishes; and, amongst other triumphs of the native cuisine, were some singular, but by no means inelegant, *chefs d'œuvre*,— brinjals boiled, and stuffed with savoury meats, but exhibiting *ripe and undressed fruit, growing on the same branch*, and bread-fruit, baked and seasoned *with the green leaves and flowers, fresh and uninjured by the fire.*

The present aspect of the "cinnamon gardens," which

[1] Called "hoppers" by the English.

[2] *Sapindus emarginatus*, Wahl. It is generally preferred by the horse-keepers, who say that soap renders dark horses grey.

[3] Another useful seed in Ceylon is the marking nut, the produce of the *Kiri-badulla* tree (*Semecarpus Anacardium*, Linn.), between the kernel and the pericarp of which is contained a semi-fluid varnish, as black and as durable as the nitrate of silver. It is plentiful in the bazaars of Colombo.

surround Colombo on the land-side, exhibits the effects of a quarter of a century of neglect, and produces a feeling of disappointment and melancholy. The beautiful shrubs which furnish the renowned spice have been allowed to grow wild, and in some places are scarcely visible, owing to undergrowth of jungle, and the thick envelopment of climbing plants, bignonias, ipomœas, the quadrangular vine, and the marvellous pitcher-plant, (*Nepenthes distillatoria*), whose eccentric organisation is still a scientific enigma. One most interesting flower, which encumbers the cinnamon trees, is a night-blowing convolvulus, the moon-flower of Europeans, called by the natives *alanga*[1], which never blooms in the day, but opens its exquisite petals when darkness comes on, and attracts the eye through the gloom, by its pure and snowy whiteness.

Less than a century has elapsed since these famous gardens were formed by the Dutch, and already they are relapsing into wilderness. Every recent writer on Ceylon has dwelt on their beauty and luxuriance, but henceforward it will remain to speak only of their decay. The history of the cinnamon laurel has been exhausted by Nees Von Esenbach and his brother; who, in the erudite disquisition[2] which they contributed to the *Amœnitates Botanicæ*, condensed all the learning of ancients and moderns regarding this celebrated tree.[3]

---

[1] *Colonyction speciosum*, Choisy (*Ipomœa bonanox*, L.). It is the Munda-valli of Van Rheede. *Hortus Malabar.* vol. ii. tab. 50.

[2] *De Cinnamomo Disputatio*, by C. G. and T. F. L. NEES VON ESENBACH. Bonne, 1823.

[3] Relative to the growth and cultivation of cinnamon and the method pursued by the chalias for "peeling" and preparing it for market, little could be added to the copious details of VALENTYN, during the time of the Dutch, and of PERCIVAL (chap. xvi. p. 340), and CORDINER (chap. xiii. p. 405), under the early government of the British. A very able and accurate essay on the same subject was contributed in 1817, to the *Annals of Philosophy*, vol. lviii., by HENRY MARSHALL, F.R.S.E., who served on the medical staff in Ceylon, and communicated the results of personal observation and inquiry. There is an interesting paper in the *Journal of the Royal Asiatic Society* (London), for 1846, "*On the Cinnamon Trade of Ceylon, its progress and present state*, by JOHN CAPPER, Esq."

The trade in its products was at its height[1] when Esenbach wrote; but opinion was already arraying itself against the rigidly exclusive system under which it was conducted. This was looked on as the more unjustifiable, owing to the popular belief that the monopoly was one created by nature; and that prohibitions became vexatious where competition was impossible. Accordingly, in 1832, the odious monopoly was abandoned; the Government ceased to be the sole exporters of cinnamon, and thenceforward the merchants of Colombo and Galle were permitted to take a share in the trade, on paying to the crown an export duty of *three shillings* a pound, which was afterwards reduced to *one*. But the revolution came too late to benefit those for whose advantage it was designed. The delusion of a "natural monopoly" of the spice was demonstrated by the fact, that not alone India, Java, and China, but also Guiana, Martinique, and Mauritius were found capable of producing it; and such was the stimulus to rivalry engendered by exorbitant prices, that supplies from these quarters were already supplanting the cinnamon of Ceylon in the markets of the world. Cassia, a still more formidable competitor, was arriving in Europe in large quantities; and thus the great experiment of free trade in this precious article led at first to disappointment and loss; the prices undergoing a decline as the quantity exported was suddenly increased.

The adoption of the first step inevitably necessitated a second. The merchants felt, and with justice, that the struggle was unequal so long as the Government, with its great estates and large capital, was their opposing competitor; and hence, in 1840, the final expedient was adopted by the crown of divesting itself altogether of its property in the plantations. The cinnamon gardens were offered for sale; and Ekelle

[1] The extent of the trade may be inferred from the fact, that the five principal cinnamon gardens around Negombo, Colombo, Barberyn, Galle, and Matura, were each from fifteen to twenty miles in circumference.

Kaderani and Morottu passed at once into private hands. But so depressing was the prospect, that Marandhan, from its vicinity to the capital, was felt to be more profitable as a speculation for building villas than for cultivating cinnamon. It was disposed of in lots; but not before neglect and decay had so depreciated its value that the price for which it sold was almost nominal.

One only source of income from cinnamon still remained in the hands of the Government—the *one shilling* duty on its export. But even this, as it was equivalent to 100 per cent. on the value, became in a very few years intolerable; and such was the peril which menaced the trade on my arrival in Ceylon, in 1845, that one of my earliest acts was to recommend to Her Majesty's Government an instant reduction of the tax, preparatory to its early and total abolition[1] — a measure which was afterwards consummated by Viscount Torrington.

But, like every previous reform, in relation to this ill-fated article, the relief came too late to be effectual. Had no export duty upon cinnamon been imposed when the monopoly of the growth was surrendered, in 1833, it may admit of a doubt whether Java would have been enabled to compete with the produce of Ceylon; which, in fineness and quality, was unsurpassed; but the time for the trial was past; the European consumers had become satisfied with the cheaper substitute of cassia, and Singhalese cinnamon could no longer be cultivated with advantage as of old. Under these circumstances, less care has been given of late years to the production of the finest qualities for the European market, and the coarser and less valuable shoots have been cut and peeled in larger proportion than formerly. Hence the gross quantity exported has been increasing,

---

[1] Sir J. EMERSON TENNENT'S *Report on the Finances and Commerce of Ceylon.* Presented to Parliament 1848, pp. 76, 78.

although the general character has deteriorated, and the price has proportionally declined. Excellence has ceased to be appreciated as of old; the cheaper substitute is received with sufficient favour, and the ancient staple of Ceylon is threatened with the loss of emolument, as it has already parted with its old renown.[1]

The adoption of Colombo, as the site for the Capital and the seat of Government, is altogether anomalous. The locality presents no single advantage to recommend it. Compared with other parts of the island, the country surrounding it is unproductive, the coast is low and unsheltered, and the port is less a harbour than a roadstead. None but light native craft venture close to the wharves and the fort, and ships waiting for cargo are forced to anchor in the offing where disasters have frequently occurred during the violence of the Monsoons.

It was the vicinity of the cinnamon country, and the accidental residence of the Singhalese sovereign at Cotta, that induced the Portuguese in the sixteenth century to establish themselves at this point, and the decision became irreversible when the Dutch had completed their

---

[1] The export of cinnamon from Ceylon in 1857 was nearly double that of 1841, but the gross value, instead of bearing the same ratio, exhibits a relative decrease of *nearly one third*. One explanation of this is referable to the fact of the shipment of coarse cinnamon in greatly increased proportion to fine, and the consequent reduction of the average price of the whole. Hence the phenomenon, that whilst fine cinnamon was formerly displaced by cassia, cassia is being now driven out of the market by the coarser qualities and reduced prices of cinnamon! This curious result will be discerned from the following return:

Year.	CINNAMON.		CASSIA.	
	Quantity imported from Ceylon.	Average price in London.	Quantity exported from the United Kingdom.	Average price in London.
		s. d.		s. d.
1841	452,039 lbs.	5 1 per lb.	1,262,164 lbs.	0 10[illegible] per lb.
1846	408,211 „	2 9 „	950,255 „	0 6[illegible] „
1850	733,781 „	2 10 „	753,915 „	0 10[illegible] „
1855	784,284 „	1 3½ „	454,925 „	1 1[illegible] „
1856	877,547 „	1 6 „	615,703 „	0 11[illegible] „
1857	887,959 „	1 6 „	766,691 „	0 11[illegible] „

fortifications and surrounded them on all sides with valuable plantations of the spice. Now that cinnamon has become secondary in importance; and the great central mountains adapted for the culture of coffee may be rendered equally accessible from the harbours of Galle or Trincomalie; the question will at no distant day demand solution, whether the vastly increased commerce of Ceylon, can be adequately accommodated at Colombo; and whether the interests of the island may not necessitate the transfer of the capital to some more suitable and commodious seaport.

The most picturesque spots in the environs of the town lie to the north of the fort on the angle between it and the embouchure of the river Kalany; and here, after a visit of a few weeks to the Governor, we took up our residence at Elie House, a mansion built by Mr. Anstruther, my predecessor in office. It stands on the ridge of a projecting headland, commanding a wide prospect over the Gulf of Manaar; and in the midst of a garden containing the rarest and most beautiful trees of the tropics, tamarinds, jambus, nutmegs, guavas, mangoes, and oranges, the graceful *casuarinas* of Australia, and the beautiful traveller's palm[1] of Madagascar.

ELIE HOUSE, COLOMBO.

[1] *Ravenala speciosa.*

CHAP. IV.

COLOMBO TO KANDY.

THE day after my arrival in Colombo, I took the oaths as a member of the executive council, the body which acts as the cabinet of the Governor; consisting of the Queen's Advocate, the three principal officers of the colony[1], and (when the head of the administration is a civilian) the General in command of the forces.

In a Crown colony such as Ceylon (the official term for possessions obtained by conquest or cession), the powers of the Governor constitute a "paternal despotism," modified only by the distant authority of the Queen. The functions of his councils are consultative, but the adoption or rejection of their recommendations rests exclusively with himself. The Executive Council is the body, by whose advice his measures are originally framed preparatory to their submission to the Legislative Council, by whom they are finally discussed with all the forms of parliamentary debate. But, although the latter assembly, in addition to official members, contains representative men, selected by the Crown with becoming regard to the various races and interests in the island[2], still the paramount authority of the

[1] The Colonial Secretary, the Treasurer, and Auditor-General.

[2] The Legislative Council of Ceylon, in addition to the members of the executive, includes the two principal civil officers of the Western and Central Provinces, the Surveyor-General, and the Collector of Customs. Three unofficial members are nominated from the planting and commercial interests, and three may be held to represent the principal native races — Mr. Lorenz, the Eur-Asians; Mr. Diaz, the Singhalese; and Mr. S. Ederemenesingam, the Tamils.

Governor can over-rule their deliberations, and their labours may be nullified by the interposition of his veto.

The most important duties of the Legislative Council are necessarily those which involve the expenditure of an annual revenue, which of late years has exceeded *half a million* sterling. So far as that income is drawn from land and its produce, although much that was unjust and vexatious in the mode of its collection, has been modified or removed since the establishment of the British authority, the system in its main features is still identifiable with that which was organised by the Portuguese and perpetuated by the Dutch.[1]

By the policy of both these nations, one legitimate source of income was stifled; since by ignoring foreign trade they deprived themselves of customs' duties[2] and port charges which, owing to the judicious reforms of Viscount Torrington in 1847, yield at the present day nearly one-third of the whole receipts of the colony.

The rents and proceeds from the sales of land cleared for coffee cultivation and other purposes, form another resource altogether unknown to the Dutch, and even to

---

[1] The results of an examination into the various sources of revenue in Ceylon, and their influence upon the industry and trade of the island, will be found in the *Report of* Sir J. EMERSON TENNENT, *on the Finances and Commerce of Ceylon*, presented to Parliament in 1848.

[2] The following table exhibits the several sources of Ceylon Revenue for the year ending 31st December, 1857:—

	£	s.	d.
Customs' port and harbour dues - -	164,126	15	0
Land sales and rents - - -	30,708	2	8¼
Pearl fishery - - - -	20,550	15	6
Chanks - - - - -	188	9	0
Salt - - - - -	53,542	16	7¾
Distillation and sale of arrack and spirits -	79,811	9	5
Tax on rice, fine grain, and gardens - -	60,449	10	0¼
Tolls at bridges and ferries - - -	44,705	19	6
Stamps - - - - -	36,755	15	1
Postage - - - - -	5,700	19	8¼
Taxes on carriages and carriers - -	3,454	10	0
Royalties and miscellaneous receipts - -	16,420	9	8
Police tax - - - - -	5,075	12	1
Sale of stores, stoppages, and reimbursements	47,556	2	6¼

the British before 1812, when the rule was relaxed which forbade the tenure of land by Europeans.

Monopolies are to the present day a prominent feature of the Ceylon revenue. The fishery of pearls and chanks has been from time immemorial in the hands of the sovereign, as well as the right to collect salt; and to these in later times has been added the privilege of distilling arrack from the juice of the coco-nut palm.

Odious as the name of monopoly sounds, its reality could scarcely be less offensive than in the instances in which it prevails in Ceylon. The supposed injustice of keeping guard over the *pearl banks* has been the theme of a political romance [1], and adduced as an illustration of the wrong assumed to be inflicted on those whom it apparently excludes from legimate labour. But the employment it affords does not extend beyond a few weeks at uncertain periods, and generally with intervals of many years interposed. Besides, when a pearl fishery is proclaimed, although every individual is enabled to participate to the extent of his capital, so indifferent are the Singhalese, that few ever engage in it, and the divers and boatmen employed come chiefly from the opposite coast of India. The monopoly of *salt* as it prevails in Ceylon is common to every country of the East, and seems the only expedient by which oriental sovereigns have ever succeeded in obtaining a minimum of taxation from classes incapable of bearing in any other shape an equitable share of the public burthens;— and the restrictions on *distillation*, if properly administered, are susceptible of being used as an effectual check on the ruinous abuse of arrack.

But a tax more objectionable than these ancient monopolies, is the heavy impost laid by the Ceylon government, not only on the import of rice and grain, but on its home cultivation. The duty on foreign

---

[1] *Cinnamon and Pearls*, by Miss Martineau; *Illustrations of Political Economy*, vol. vii. p. 149.

rice[1] was originally instituted as an encouragement to native agriculture, but with strange inconsistency the tax

---

[1] In an island so peculiarly circumstanced as Ceylon, owing to its dependence on India for supplies of immigrant labour, the policy seems almost suicidal of raising revenue by a duty of *fifty per cent.* on the importation of food. But when it is borne in mind that for upwards of three centuries since Barthema and Barbosa visited Ceylon in the 16th century, there has been a sustained complaint of the deficiency of home cultivation, and the dependency of the population on foreign countries for rice; the error is glaring and indefensible of so loading native agriculture with vexatious taxes as to discourage and virtually check its extension. In a case so peculiar and anomalous, it might be questionable whether in any general scheme of a land-tax for the whole colony, it might not be judicious to encourage the growth of corn by *exempting* from its operation such lands as had been brought under cultivation for rice, or at least by subjecting them to the payment of only a modified amount; but in strong contrast to such a policy, the lands employed in the production of rice are not only the *only* ones which have been made subservient to the purpose of revenue, but a special legal provision made public in 1824, for exempting from assessment the produce of all other lands throughout the island which might be brought into cultivation for coffee, cotton, or pepper, pertinaciously re-enacts the assessment upon the cultivation of *grain!*

The mode of collecting the tax on rice is even more mischievous than the impost itself. With some slight modifications in different districts, it is this: "When the crop is sufficiently advanced to enable an estimate to be formed of its possible produce, the Government Assessors proceed to calculate its probable value, and a return is made to the Government Agent of the amount liable upon every field. The farm of the tax of each district is then sold by public auction; and as the harvest approaches the cultivator is obliged to give five days' notice to the purchaser of his intention to cut; two days' notice if he finds it necessary to postpone; if the crop be not threshed immediately the renter is entitled to a further notice of the day fixed for that purpose; and for any omission or irregularity he has a remedy, by suing for a penalty in the District Court.

"It would be difficult to devise a system more pregnant with oppression, extortion, and demoralization than the one here detailed. The cultivator is handed over helplessly to two successive sets of inquisitorial officers, the assessors and the renters; whose acts are so uncontrolled that abuses are inevitable, and the intercourse of the two parties is characterised by rigour and extortion on the one side, and cunning and subterfuges of every description on the other. Every artifice and disingenuous device is put in practice to deceive the headmen and assessors as to the extent and fertility of the land and the actual value of the crop; and they, in return, resort to the most inquisitorial and vexatious interference, either to protect the interest of the Government, or privately to further their own. Between these demoralizing influences, the character and industry of the rural population are deteriorated and destroyed. The extension of cultivation by reclaiming a portion of waste land only exposes the harassed proprietor to fresh visits from the headmen, and a new valuation by the Government Assessor, and where annoyance is not the leading object, recourse is had to corruption, in order to keep down the valuation.

"But no sooner has the cultivator got rid of the assessor than he falls into the hands of the renter, who, under the authority with which the law invests him, finds himself possessed

on the latter has been enforced with such rigour as effectually to check cultivation. The evils of this anomalous system are so obvious that it is difficult to justify the policy which has so long postponed the application of a remedy.

Another questionable means of raising a revenue is the toll on bridges and ferries; a tax which, however justifiable so far as the proceeds are applicable to the improvement of communication, is not defensible as a means of profit to the discouragement of traffic. From the love of litigation which characterises the Singhalese, the duty on *stamps* has been singularly productive, and these, with sundry receipt from a variety of minor subjects, postage, carriage duties, royalties, licences for arms and other items of less importance, are the sources of colonial income.[1] In addition to these, certain sums are enumerated in the public accounts as apparent receipts which are in realily reimbursements for previous expenditure incurred in advances for the use of the military and public departments. But exclu-

---

of unusual powers of vexation and annoyance. He may be designedly out of the way when the cultivator sends notice of his intention to cut; and if the latter, to save his harvest from perishing on the stalk, ventures to reap it in his absence, the penalties of the law are instantly enforced against him. Under the pressure of this formidable control, the agricultural proprietor, rather than lose his time or his crop in dancing attendance on the renter, or submitting to the multiform annoyances of his subordinates, is driven to purchase forbearance by additional payments; and it is generally understood that the share of the tax which eventually reaches the Treasury does not form *one-half* of the amount which is thus extorted by oppressive devices from the helpless proprietors."

The same process which is here described for the collection of the tax upon rice lands in the valleys is resorted to for realising that upon dry grain in the uplands and hills; and it is a striking confirmation of the discouragement to the extension of agriculture, which is inseparable from a system so vexatious and so oppressive, that by a return of the produce of the paddi tax and that on dry grain for the years prior to 1846, during which the cultivation of every other description of produce had been making extensive advances, it was shown that the production of corn had been for some time stationary in Ceylon; and the increase has been very inconsiderable since. See Sir J. EMERSON TENNENT'S *Report, &c.*, 1847, p. 68.

[1] There is a tax on immovable property in towns amounting to upwards of 5,000*l.* per annum, but it is applicable only to the maintenance of local police.

sive of these, the realised income of Ceylon is upwards of 500,000*l.* per annum, and is annually augmenting.

As to expenditure, one half of this sum is absorbed by the salaries and contingent expenses, and the pensions of the civil departments.[1] This amount is sufficient to cover the costs for the collection of revenue, the administration of justice, the preservation of peace and health, the maintenance of public worship, and the extension of education, unbiassed by sectarian influences. The balance of the colonial income is more than sufficient for the construction of roads, the erection of public buildings, the repair of fortifications, and the pay and allowances of the military employed in the island.

The *civil service* of the colony, properly so called, was organised on the model of the great institution by which India had so long been governed, and all the superior offices comprised within its functions are reserved exclusively for the members of the privileged body.[2] But the result was unsatisfactory, chiefly owing to the cir-

---

[1] In 1857, the proportions were as follows:—

	£	s.	d.
Civil establishments; including that of the Governor and principal officer - -	119,740	17	9½
Judicial: Chief Justice, Puisne Judges, Queen's Advocate, &c. - - - -	39,731	11	0
Ecclesiastical: Episcopal and Presbyterian Churches - - - - - -	9,921	10	0
Educational - - - - - -	8,054	10	0
Medical - - - - - -	8,034	3	0
Police - - - - - -	9,504	4	0
Fiscal's Establishment - - - -	8,453	0	9
Pensions - - - - - -	25,380	8	2
	£228,820	4	8½

[2] The advocates of Administrative Reform, when their labours shall have been successfully closed at home, will find an inviting field for exertion in reconstructing the system on which colonial business is conducted in Ceylon. So far as I am aware, no change of any importance has been effected since the following description was written in 1847: "Taken as a whole, the machinery of the executive Government is at once cumbrous and embarrassed, complicated in its processes, and slow and unsatisfactory in its performance. It is in reality a relic of the old Dutch system, patched and altered by successive governments to meet emergencies; but re-

cumscribed area within which the experiment was tried. Like the miniature oak which the Chinese can raise in a flower-pot, the dwarfed plant had every characteristic of the great tree, except its strength and solidity.

---

quiring, at the present day, fundamental changes to adapt it to the transition through which the colony is passing.

"The grand error appears to be this,—that as the business of each department increased beyond its strength the difficulty was met, not by simplifying the system, but by adding clerk after clerk to the establishment, to try to grapple with the details; forgetful that the same arrangement which may have been found effectual at some early period in controlling a small annual expenditure, can only lead to confusion and insecurity, when applied to the disbursement of half a million per annum.

"Two defects in the present system are so palpable as to be sufficient in themselves to account in a great degree both for its imperfection and expense. In the first place, all the payments in the colony, from the salary of the Governor to the wages of a pioneer, are issued *monthly*, instead of quarterly, from the Treasury, on monthly applications for the same sums from the various heads of departments sustained by monthly vouchers and accounts, and authorised by monthly warrants elaborately prepared, and signed formally by the Governor. It is impossible to conceive the multiplication of forms, documents, and securities, to which this monthly excitement gives rise; and as every instrument has to be prepared in triplicate and sometimes in quadruplicate, as these monthly applications ascend in the same monotonous succession to the Audit Office and the Treasury through the local department, the Government Agent, the Colonial Secretary, and the Governor, it is easy to imagine the multitude of writers and clerks who become indispensable in every department for the mere copying, comparing, and recording these superfluous documents. On the occasion of a visit which I made to the province of Oovah, I found all the clerks in the Badulla cutchery engaged, without pause, in making *eight thousand copies* of pay lists in quadruplicate, in order to close the road accounts of an officer who had just died.

"As to the contingent expense of the various departments, the system is even more cumbrous and annoying. For every one of these, even the most trivial in amount, the responsible officer must apply formally for the previous and special authority of the Governor, conveyed through the Colonial Secretary. The practice has now become so oppressive in the quantity of details which are brought under the Secretary's notice, that it is absurd to require that officer to devote time to such matters to the prejudice of grave and important business. Within the last twelve months I have had despatches from the remotest parts of the island, asking permission to expend 1*s.* for a gallon of oil, or 2*s.* 6*d.* for the repair of a table. I have had applications, requiring formal and recorded answers, for a flat ruler for the assistant agent at an out-station, and for two skeins of thread to sew the records of a district court; and within the last few months I had a correspondence, extending to 13 despatches, in regard to a pewter inkstand for a police-office, which could not be got at the Commissariat Store, and had to be bought by private contract at the bazaar."—SIR J. EMERSON TENNENT'S *Report, &c.*, p. 85.

Ceylon has trained but few civil servants of distinguished ability; and the failure has been aggravated by the pernicious system of promotion by mere seniority. Exertion was felt to be ineffectual when advancement was guaranteed to mediocrity, without an effort; and aspiring ability was chilled by the consciousness that no services, however zealous, were sufficient to achieve distinction when opposed to the claims of ante-dated incompetence. On more than one occasion, when offices had fallen vacant requiring talents of a higher order than those developed by routine, the Governor was unable to recommend the advancement of any one of the individuals then serving in the island; and the duty devolved on the Secretary of State of nominating persons duly qualified from home.

Impressed with the necessity for a remedy, the Earl of Derby, in 1845, directed merit instead of seniority to be the basis of promotion; and in order to extend the area of selection, he increased the number of the civil servants to upwards of seventy. The experiment is still in progress; but coupled with the higher test of preliminary qualification which has since been required from candidates for office, there is no reason to doubt its ultimate success; especially since the recent revision of salaries has to some extent removed a just cause of complaint on the part of the civil service, as to the inadequacy of their emoluments, still singularly disproportionate to those awarded to corresponding functionaries in India.

Once in each year, shortly after the setting in of the south-west monsoon, a fleet of small vessels arrives at Galle from the Maldive Islands, the commander of which is invested for the occasion with the dignity of ambassador. He is the bearer of presents and a letter from the Sultan to the Governor of Ceylon, soliciting the continued protection of England, and giving assurances in return of his Highness's anxiety to afford every succour to vessels in the event of shipwreck.

This custom has continued from time immemorial; at least from the remote period when the Chinese, in right of their supremacy over Ceylon [1], claimed the sovereignty of the Maldives.[2] The Portuguese asserted a similar right, and erected a fort in an island on one of the atolls.[3] Unfaltering in their adherence to their ancestral pursuits, the commodities which the islanders produce at the present day consist of precisely the same articles which they exported a thousand years ago, when, according to the Persian author of the *Modjmel-alte-varyke* (a History of the kings of India, written in the year of the Hejira 417), one group of the Maldives was called Diva-Kouzah, from the abundance of cowries; and another Diva-Kanbar, from the coco-nut *coir*, which the islanders spun into cordage.[4]

The boats, in addition to these, are laden with dried fish and tortoise-shell. The white cowries (*Cypræa moneta*), which they bring, are sent to Africa, where they still take the place of coin, and along with them the Maldives supply quantities of the great shell, the *Cassis rufa*, which is exported to Italy for the manufacture of cameos.

The Maldive ambassador is received by the Governor with every mark of respect; he is preceded by a guard

---

[1] See *ante*, Vol. I. Pt. v. ch. iii. p. 601.

[2] DE BARROS, *Asia*, *&c.*, dec. iii. tom. iii. pt. ii. ch. i. p. 3.

[3] *Ib.* tom. i. pt. ii. p. 423; tom. iii. pt. i. p. 300.—PYRARD DE LAVAL, *Voyage*, *&c.*, p. 170. — VALENTYN, *Oud en Nieuw Oost-Indien*, ch. xii. p. 161.

[4] The *Modjmel* is a Persian version of an Arabic translation from Sanskrit, written in the year 1026 A.D. by Abul-Hassan, of Djordjan, near the Caspian. The only portion of it which has been rendered into a European language is the chapter from which the following extract is taken, contained in the *Fragmens Arabes et Persans* of Reinaud :—"Ces îles se divisent en deux classes, suivant la nature de leur principal produit. Les unes sont nommées *Diva-Kouzah*, c'est-à-dire îles des *cauris*, à cause des cauris qu'on ramasse sur les branches des cocotiers plantés dans la mer. Les autres portent le nom de *Diva-Kanbar*, du mot *kanbar* (coir), qui désigne le fil que l'on tresse avec les fibres du cocotier et avec lequel on coud les navires."—*Fragm. Arab. et Pers.* pp. 93—124. See also DULAURIER, *Journ. Asiat.* vol. xlix. p. 171. DE BARROS describes the mode of fishing for cowries at the Maldives in the time of the Portuguese as identical with that narrated in the *Modjmel*.—*Asia, &c.*, tom. iii. pt. i. p. 312.

of honour, and introduced with his interpreters; his presents are accepted and reciprocated by suitable equivalents (one of which is a piece of scarlet cloth for the Sultan); and on the conclusion of the ceremonial he re-embarks with his little fleet, and proceeds on his voyage to the Coromandel coast.

To avoid the hot season in the low country, official residences have been provided at Kandy for the Governor and the Colonial Secretary; and early in March, 1846, we left Colombo for the hills.[1] Already the luxuriant verdure of the plains, which the south-west monsoon had so recently called forth, was converted to yellow stubble; the lake was evaporated to partial dryness, and the motionless leaves of the trees were powdered with red dust from the cleft and arid earth.

In driving through the native town to Grand Pass, on the way to the bridge of boats, which there connects the opposite banks of the Kalany-ganga, many of the houses will be seen to have an earthen vase, painted white, placed in a conspicuous position on the roof. These are evidences of the prevalence in Ceylon of that most ancient of all superstitions, the belief in the *evil eye*, which exists in every country in the universe, from China to Peru. The Greeks of the present day entertain the same horror of the κακὸ 'μάτι as their ancestors did of the βάσκανος ὀφθαλμὸς, and the *mal occhio* of moderns Italy is the traditional *fascinatio* of the Romans. The Malabars and Hindus, like the Arabians and Turks, apologise for the profusion of jewels with which they decorate their children, on the plea that

[1] It is to be hoped that the journey from Colombo to Kandy, still performed on the noble road made by Sir Edward Barnes, will shortly be facilitated by the railway now in process of formation, under the direction of Mr. DOYNE, and which, if its construction can be completed throughout the entire distance for a moderate sum, will be a signal advantage to the coffee districts. But the line that I would gladly have seen adopted is one which, skirting the Kandyan zone, with a branch to communicate with the coffee regions, would have opened a communication from sea to sea, from Colombo to Trincomalie, thus extending the advantages of so grand a work to the native races as well as the European communities.

they are intended to draw aside the evil eye; the Mahometans suspend objects from the ceilings of their apartments for the same purpose; and the object of the Singhalese in placing these whitened chatties on their gables, is to divert the mysterious influence from their dwellings.[1]

It is chiefly from the country north of the Kalany that supplies of provisions are brought to the bazaars of Colombo; and however scrupulously the disciples of Buddha may observe his injunction to abstain from taking life, a stranger in travelling this road is shocked at the callous indifference to the infliction of pain which characterises their treatment of animals intended for market. Pigs are suspended from a pole, passed between the fore and hind legs, and evince by incessant cries the torture which they endure from the cords; fowls are brought from long distances hanging by their feet; and ducks are carried by the head, their necks bent over the bearers' fingers to stifle their noise.

But the most repulsive exhibition of all, is the mode in which the flesh of the turtle is sold piece-meal whilst it is still alive, by the families of the Tamil fishermen at Jaffna. The creatures are to be seen in the market-place undergoing this frightful mutilation; the plastron and its integuments having been previously removed, and the animal thrown on its back, so as to display all the motions of the heart, viscera, and lungs. A broad knife, from twelve to eighteen inches in length, is first inserted at the left side, and the women, who are generally the operators, introduce one hand to scoop out the blood, which oozes slowly. The blade is next passed round, till the lower shell

[1] Amongst the Tamils at Jaffna the same belief prevails as amongst the Irish and Scotch, that their cattle are liable to injury from the blight of an evil eye, thus recalling the exclamation of Virgil's Shepherd, "Nescio quis teneros oculus mihi fascinat agnos!" *Query.* Is there any mysterious connection between the prohibition to *covet* contained in the tenth commandment, and the horror of the *evil eye*, so often alluded to in the Old and New Testaments, especially Proverbs xxviii. 22, and Mark vii. 22?

is detached and placed to one side, and the internal organs exposed in full action. Each customer, as he applies, is served with any part selected, which is cut off as ordered, and sold by weight. Each of the fins is thus successively removed, with portions of the fat and flesh, the turtle showing, by its contortions, that each act of severance is productive of agony. In this state it lies for hours, writhing in the sun, the heart[1] and head being usually the last pieces selected, and till the latter is cut off the snapping of the mouth, and the opening and closing of the eyes, show that life is still inherent, even when the shell has been nearly divested of its contents.

The woods on the right bank of the river, in passing the picturesque Bridge of Boats, conceal the remains of Kalany and its temple, a place so ancient that it confers its own name on the river which flows by its ruins. The *Mahawanso* refers to it as contemporary with Buddha[2], and connects its history with the partial submersion of the western shore of Ceylon, in the reign of Devenipiatissa, A.D. 164. The original dagoba was built five hundred years before the Christian era, and enlarged three centuries later. But the one which is now standing was constructed between the years 1240 and 1267, and rebuilt about A.D. 1301.[3]

Kalany is remarkable as the only Buddhist temple of importance in the vicinity of Colombo. So inveterate was the religious intolerance of the Dutch, that they abolished every idolatrous establishment within the range of their guns, and not content with this, they prohibited, in 1692, the celebration of the Buddhist worship at Kalany, and ordered the priests to withdraw from the temple.[4] At the present day, so sacred is the spot, that it is the resort of pilgrims from distant

---

[1] ARISTOTLE was aware of the fact that the turtle will live after the removal of the heart.—*De Vita et Morte*, ch. ii.

[2] *Mahawanso*, ch. ii. p. 9; ch. xv. p. 96; ch. xxii. p. 130; ch. lxxx. p. 20. UPHAM.

[3] *Rajavali*, pp. 257—259.

[4] Sir J. EMERSON TENNENT'S *Hist. of Christianity in Ceylon*, ch. ii. p. 55.

places, who annually pay their devotions before the great statue during the festival in July, when the ceremonies are solemnised by torchlight.[1]

For some miles the road crosses the marshy plains that lie between the river and the sea, on an embankment, whose sides are shaded by long lines of teak, a tree which it has been attempted to naturalise in the island. So long as it runs within a moderate distance of the sea, the groves of coco-nut trees continue to surround every hamlet; but on turning more inland, these gradually disappear, and are succeeded by the graceful arecas, mixed with the kitool or jaggery palm.[2] But what most excites the wonder of a stranger, are the flowering trees which adorn the landscape: the murutu [3], with its profusion of lilac blossoms, and the gorgeous imbul [4], whose crimson petals thickly strew the ground, when making way for the oblong pods that contain the silky cotton, for which the tree is prized.

In the numerous streams which are passed on this route, the Singhalese are to be seen at all hours of the day, indulging in their passion for the bath, in which they imitate the Hindus; and such is the discipline to which their skins are subjected, that it is not unusual to have

---

[1] About thirty miles further eastward, on a tributary of the Kalany, are situated the remains of the old city of Sita-wacca, one of the most ancient in Ceylon, if we are to accept the tradition that it owes its appellation to Sita, the Helen of the *Ramayana*. Whilst the Portuguese were at war in defence of their ally the King of Cotta, Sita-wacca was the stronghold of their daring opponents, Maaya Dunnai and Raja Singha; and it was eventually destroyed by their relentless general Azavedo, at the close of the 16th century. The vestiges of the palace and temple are still traceable; they are constructed of hewn granite, and in one place a deep moat is crossed by a bridge composed of five slabs fourteen feet long and of more than proportionate thickness. A striking account of the ruins, as they appeared in the year 1675, will be found in VALENTYN'S *Oud en Nieuw Oost-Indien*, pp. 207—229. The little fort of Ruanwelle (*Rang-Welli*, the "Golden sand"), which was once so important on the frontier of the kings of Kandy, stands on an eminence above the Kalany, a few miles east of Sita-wacca. It is now the residence of the civil officer in charge of the district. The country around it is magnificent, commanding noble views of the mountains near Adam's Peak and the cataracts which descend from them.

[2] *Caryota urens.*

[3] *Lagerstrœmia Reginæ.*

[4] *Bombax Malabaricus.*

them rubbed with a porous stone, in the same way that the mahouts scrub the hide of the elephant, previous to anointing them with oil, — not the precious spikenard of antiquity, but the more homely produce of the coco-nut palm.

The number of bullock-carts encountered between Colombo and Kandy, laden with coffee from the interior, or carrying up rice and stores for the supply of the plantations in the hill-country, is quite surprising. The oxen thus employed on this single road, are estimated at upwards of twenty thousand. The bandy to which they are yoked is a barbarous two-wheeled waggon, with a covering of plaited coco-nut leaves, in which a pair of strong bullocks will draw from five to ten hundred weight, according to the nature of the country; and with this they will perform a journey of twenty miles a day on a level.

A few of the large humped cattle of India are annually imported for draught; but the vast majority of those in use are small and dark-coloured, with a graceful head and neck, and elevated hump, a deep silky dewlap, and limbs as slender as a deer. They have neither the strength nor weight requisite for this service; and yet the entire coffee crop of Ceylon, amounting annually to upwards of half a million hundred weight, is year after year brought down from the mountains to the coast by these indefatigable little creatures, which, on returning, carry up proportionally heavy loads of rice and implements for the estates.[1] There are two varieties of the native bullock; one a somewhat coarser animal, of a deep red colour, the other, the high-bred black one I have just described. So rare was a white one of this species, under the native kings, that the Kandyans were compelled to set them apart for the royal herd.[2]

---

[1] A pair of these little bullocks carry up about twenty bushels of rice to the hills, and bring down from fifty to sixty bushels of coffee to Colombo.

[2] WOLF says that, in the year 1763,

Although bullocks may be said to be the only animals of draught and burden in Ceylon (horses being rarely used except in spring carriages), no attempt has been made to improve the breed, or even to better the condition and treatment of those in use. Their food is indifferent, pasture in all parts of the island being rare, and cattle are seldom housed under any vicissitudes of weather.

The labour to which they are best adapted, and in which, before the opening of roads, these cattle were formerly employed, is in traversing the jungle paths of the interior, carrying light loads as pack-oxen in what is called a "*tavalam*,"—a term which, substituting bullocks for camels, is equivalent to a "caravan."[1] The class of persons engaged in this traffic in Ceylon resemble in their occupations the "Banjarees" of Hindustan, who bring down to the coast corn, cotton, and oil, and take back cloths and iron and copper utensils to the interior. In the unopened parts of the island, and especially in the eastern provinces, this primitive practice still continues; and when travelling in these districts we have often encountered long files of pack-bullocks toiling along the mountain paths, their bells tinkling musically as they moved; or halting during the noonday heat beside some stream in the forests, their burdens piled in heaps near the drivers, who had lighted their cooking fires, whilst the bullocks were permitted to bathe and browse.

The persons engaged in this wandering trade are chiefly Moors, and the business carried on by them consists in bringing up salt from the government depôts

---

he saw in Ceylon two white oxen, each of which measured upwards of eight feet high. They were sent as a present from the King of Atchin.—*Life and Adventures*, p. 172.

[1] Attempts have been made to domesticate the camel in Ceylon; but, I am told, they died of ulcers in the feet, attributed to the *too great moisture* of the roads at certain seasons. This explanation seems insufficient if taken in connection with the fact of the camel living in perfect health in climates equally, if not more, exposed to rain. I apprehend that sufficient justice was not done to the experiment.

on the coast to be bartered with the Kandyans in the hills for "native coffee," which is grown in small quantities round every house, but without systematic cultivation. This they carry down to the maritime towns, and the proceeds are invested in cotton cloths and brass utensils, dried fish, and other commodities, with which the *tavalams* supply the secluded villages of the interior.

The mode of life both of the conductors of these caravans and of the Singhalese drivers of bandies, is a succession of travel and adventure resembling that of the mule-drivers of Spain. Like the "arrieros" of Andalusia, they move by night, or in the dusk, and rest during the day in the cool shade of the trees, passing their time in games of chance, to which they are passionately devoted, and resuming their journey at night-fall.

At Veangodde, twenty-five miles from Colombo, the residence of Don Solomon Dias Bandarnayeke, one of the Moodliars of the Governor's Gate, affords the most agreeable example of the dwelling of a low-country headman, with its broad verandahs, spacious rooms, and extensive offices, shaded by palm-groves and fruit trees. The chief himself, now upwards of eighty years[1] of age, is a noble specimen of the native race, and in his official costume, decorated with the gold chains and medals by which his services have been recognised by the British Government, his tall and venerable figure makes a striking picture.

DON SOLOMON DIAS BANDARNAYEKE.

[1] Don Solomon died in 1859, whilst the first edition of this work was in press.

On the occasion of our visit, we were received by him with the honours of the white cloth, the approach to his house being covered with long pieces of cotton to the porch. Tom-tom beaters and musicians[1] were stationed along the avenue, groups of boys exhibited national dances, and beat time by clashing together sticks of hard wood, and after them a band of devil dancers from an adjacent temple, with masks and grotesque dresses, went through a performance which, in contortion and enthusiasm, resembled the fury of the Corybantes.

Half way between Colombo and Kandy is the picturesque rest-house of Ambepusse, one of those treacherously beautiful spots which have acquired a bad renown from the attractions of the scenery and the pestilent fevers by which the locality is infested.

THE REST-HOUSE AT AMBEPUSSE.

After leaving the village, the road crosses the spurs of the hills which descend from the mountain zone, and the aspect of the country gradually changes from maritime plains to the ruder and less cultivated Kandyan highlands. Instead of broad inundated paddi-fields, rice is grown in the moist crannies of the hills, and dry grain is cultivated on their slopes. The majestic crowns

[1] Two of these musicians, who played on a rude pipe like a flageolet, had the faculty of keeping up a sustained and monotonous note for many minutes without intermission, by inhaling through the nostrils whilst they blew with the lips.

of the Talipat palm begin to appear near the villages, and graceful bamboos wave their feathery plumes in every hollow.

The forests become so dense that troops of monkeys venture in sight, and flocks of plumb-headed paroquets romp and scream amongst the branches.[1] Buddhist temples appear in secluded spots, and picturesque *maduas* for preaching *bana*, built with pagoda-like roofs rising tier above tier. Shaven priests in yellow robes, and carrying ivory fans, plod on their errand of poverty, to collect food in the villages. The houses, instead of groves of coco-nuts, are surrounded by a fence of coffee-bushes, with their polished green leaves and wreaths of jasmine-like flowers, and everything indicates the change from the low-country and its habits to the hills and their hardier peasantry.

As this was one of the idle seasons of the year, during which labour is suspended, whilst waiting for the rains of the monsoon, ere recommencing the sowing of rice, the Kandyans were lounging about their villages or gathered in groups by the roadside, engaged in listless and sedentary amusements. In one place a crowd was collected to watch the feats of a juggler, who, to our surprise, commenced his performances by jumping up on to a pole, and placing his feet upon a cross bar six feet from the ground. On this he coursed along the road by prodigious leaps, and returning to the audience, steadied himself on his

[1] A white monkey, taken between Ambepusse and Kornegalle, where they are said to be numerous, was brought to me to Colombo. Except in colour, it had all the characteristics of *Presbytes cephalopterus*. So striking was its whiteness that it might have been conjectured to be an albino, but for the circumstance that its eyes and face were black. I never saw another specimen; but the natives say they are not uncommon, and KNOX, who alludes to the fact, adds, that they are "milk-white both in body and face; but of this sort there is not such plenty."—Pt. i. ch. vi. p. 25. The Rev. R. SPENCE HARDY mentions, in his learned work on *Eastern Monachism*, that on the occasion of his visit to the great temple of Dambool, he encountered a troop of white monkeys on the rock in which it is situated—which were doubtless a variety of the Wanderoo. (*Eastern Monachism*, ch. xix. p. 204.) PLINY was aware of the fact that white monkeys are occasionally found in India. (*Nat. Hist.* lib. viii. ch. xxxii.)

perch, and then opened his exhibition. This consisted of endless efforts of legerdemain: catching pebbles thrown up to him by his confederate below, which, upon opening his closed hand, flew away as birds; breaking an egg-shell, and allowing a small serpent to escape from it; and keeping a series of brass balls in motion by striking them with his elbows, as well as his hands. Balancing on his nose a small stick with an inverted cup at top, from which twelve perforated balls were suspended by silken cords, he placed twelve ivory rods in his mouth, and so guided them by his lips and tongue, as to insert the end of each in a corresponding aperture in the ball, till the whole twelve were sustained by the rods, and the central support taken away. This and endless other tricks he performed, *balancing himself all the while on the single pole on which he stood.* He took a ball of granite, six or seven inches in diameter, and probably fourteen pounds' weight, and standing with his arms extended in line, he rolled it from the wrist of one hand across his shoulders to the wrist of the other backwards and forwards repeatedly, apparently less by raising his arms than by a vigorous effort of the muscles of his back; then seizing it in both hands, he flung it repeatedly twenty feet high, and watching it in its descent till within a few inches of his skull, he bent forward his head, and caught the ball each time between his shoulders; then bounding along the road, still mounted on his pole, he closed his performance amidst the smiles of the audience.[1]

---

[1] The artists on these occasions are always Tamils; and it may be regarded as a further evidence of the error already adverted to (*ante*, Vol. I. Pt. v. ch. i. p. 532) in supposing that the story of Jambulus, as told by Diodorus, relates to Ceylon — that the Singhalese have never been noted for their skill in jugglery and legerdemain, although these arts are brought to high perfection in Hindustan and other countries around them. DIODORUS, in speaking of the performers in the island, described by Jambulus, says, the flexibility of their limbs was such, that they seemed to consist of muscle rather than bone: *Τὰ δὲ ὀστεᾶ τοῦ σώματος ἔχειν ἐπὶ ποσὸν καμπτόμενα καὶ πάλιν ἀποκαθιστάμενα παραπλησίως τοῖς νευρώδεσι.* The passage is further remarkable, as it evidently describes an exhibition of *ventriloquism*, and is probably the earliest mention of that art upon record. Such appears to have been their skill, that Jambulus was im-

The last thirty miles of this wonderful road passes through scenery which combines the grandeur of Alps with the splendour of tropical vegetation. It is an Oriental Simplon, climbing hills, crossing torrents; and following the windings of ravines, till it reaches its extreme altitude at the pass of Kaduganawa, one of those romantic glens which the former kings of Kandy jealously guarded as an entrance from the low country.

Some prophet had foretold that the "Kandyan kingdom would perish when a bullock should be driven through a certain hill, and a horseman ride through a rock." Sir Edw. Barnes carried a tun-

pressed with the belief that they had each two tongues, and were enabled to conduct two distinct discourses simultaneously: Ἴδιον δέ τι καὶ περὶ τὴν γλῶτταν αὐτοὺς ἔχειν, τὸ μὲν φυσικῶς αὐτοῖς συγγεγεννημένον, τὸ δ' ἐξ ἐπινοίας φιλοτεχνούμενον· δίπτυχον μὲν γὰρ αὐτοὺς ἔχειν τὴν γλῶτταν ἐπὶ ποσόν, τὰ δ' ἐνδοτέρω προσδιαιρεῖν, ὥστε διπλῆν αὐτὴν γίνεσθαι μέχρι τῆς ῥίζης * * * * τὸ δὲ πάντων παραδοξότατον, ἅμα πρὸς δύο τῶν ἐντυγχανόντων λαλεῖν ἐντελῶς, ἀποκρινομένους τε καὶ ταῖς ὑποκειμέναις περιστάσεσιν οἰκείως ὁμι-

nel under the hill, and the Kandy mail drives through an archway in the rock.[1]

A little beyond the top of the pass, where the road begins to descend towards the Mahawelli-ganga, a colony of the degraded tribe, the Rodiyas, have established one of their hamlets or *kuppiyames*, meaning literally a "collection of huts;" for, as one of the incidents of their infamy, they were not permitted to call their places of residence, villages. The condition of the Pariahs, the Niadis, Porleahs, and other debased races in India, presents nothing more dreadful than the unresisting degradation of this abhorred community.

Their expulsion from the pale of society took place in an age so remote, that even the traditions as to its cause are confused or forgotten.[2] One legend describes them as a branch of the Veddahs, condemned to never-ending degradation for having supplied a king's table with human flesh instead of vension[3]; but a difference in their height and figure suggests the more probable idea that they may have been immigrants from the coast of India, of the Chandala blood[4], a people so degraded, that water over which their shadows had passed was held to be defiled till purified by sun light.

The language of the Rodiyas, mingled with corrupted Singhalese, contains unintelligible words indicative of a foreign descent. They are found only in the Kandyan districts; at Saffragam, Doombera, and Wallepane and a few other places in the interior; their numbers do not probably exceed a thousand, and are said to be decreasing.

λοῦντας· τῇ μὲν γὰρ ἑτέρᾳ πτυχὶ πρὸς τὸν ἕνα, τῇ δ' ἄλλῃ πάλιν ὁμοίως πρὸς τὸν ἕτερον διαλέγεσθαι.—DIOD. SIC. lib. ii.

[1] More than ten years were occupied in the construction of the Kandy road, which was begun in 1820, and not thoroughly completed till 1831. A column, erected on the face of the cliff, commemorates the services of the officer under whose immediate care the road was formed, and whose premature death was accelerated by exposure during its progress. The pedestal bears the inscription:

CAPTAIN DAWSON,
During the government of Sir Edward Barnes,
K.C.B. &c.
Commanding Royal Engineers, Ceylon,
whose science and skill planned and executed
this Road,
and other works of public utility,
Died at Colombo, 28th March, 1829.
By subscription this Monument was erected
to his memory by his friends and admirers.

[2] The *Rajavali* mentions Rodiyas 204 B.C. (p. 188); and the *Mahawanso*, A.D. 589 (ch. xlii.).

[3] KNOX, pt. iii. ch. ii. p. 70.

[4] The *Mahawanso* mentions a village of outcasts in Ceylon, A.D. 437, of Hindu origin (ch. x. p. 66).

Under the Kandyan kings their humiliation was utter and complete. The designation Rodiya, or *rodda*, means, literally, "filth." They were not permitted to cross a ferry, to draw water at a well, to enter a village, to till land, or learn a trade, as no recognised caste could deal or hold intercourse with a Rodiya. Formerly they were not allowed to build houses with two walls or a double roof, but hovels in which a hurdle leaned against a single wall and rested on the ground.[1] They were forced to subsist on alms or such gifts as they might receive for protecting the fields from wild beasts or burying the carcases of dead cattle; but they were not allowed to come within a fenced field even to beg. They converted the hides of animals into ropes, and prepared monkey-skins for covering tom-toms and drums, which they bartered for food and other necessaries. They were prohibited from wearing a cloth on their heads, and neither men nor women were allowed to cover their bodies above the waist or below the knee. If benighted they dare not lie down in a shed appropriated to other travellers, but hid themselves in caves or deserted watch-huts. They could not enter a court of justice, and if wronged had to utter their complaints from a distance. Though nominally Buddhists (but conjointly demon-worshippers), they were not allowed to go into a temple, and could only pray "standing afar off."

Although they were permitted to have a headman, who was styled their *hollo-walhia*, his nomination was stigmatised by requiring the sanction of the common jailor, who was likewise the sole medium of communication between the Rodiyas and the rest of the human race. So vile and valueless were they in the eyes of the community, that, under the Kandyan rule, when it was represented to the king that the Rodiyas had so multiplied as to be a nuisance to the villagers, an order was given to reduce their numbers by shooting a certain proportion in each

---

[1] VALENTYN, *Oud en Nieuw Oost-Indien*, Introd. p. 7.

kuppiyame.[1] The most dreaded of all punishments under the Kandyan dynasty was to hand over the lady of a high caste offender to the Rodiyas; and the mode of her adoption was by the Rodiya taking betel from his own mouth and placing it in hers, after which till death her degradation was indelible.[2]

Under the rule of the British, which recognises no distinction of caste, the status of the Rodiyas has been nominally, and even materially, improved. Their disqualification for labour no longer exists; but after centuries of mendicancy and idleness they evince no inclination for work. Their pursuits and habits are still the same, but their bearing is a shade less servile, and they pay a profounder homage to a high than a low caste Kandyan, and manifest some desire to shake off the opprobrious epithet of Rodiyas. Their houses are better built, and contain a few articles of furniture, and in some places they have acquired patches of land and possess cattle. Even the cattle share the odium of their owners, and to distinguish them from the herds of the Kandyans, their masters are obliged to suspend a coco-nut shell from their necks by a leathern cord.[3]

Socially their hereditary stigma remains unaltered; their contact is still shunned by the Kandyans as pollution, and instinctively the Rodiyas crouch to their own degradation. In carrying a burden they still load the pingo (yoke) at one end only, instead of both, like other natives. They fall on their knees with uplifted hands to address a man of the lowest recognised caste; and they shout on the approach of a traveller, to warn him to stop till they can get off the road and allow him to pass without the risk of too close a proximity to their persons.

---

[1] From a MS. *Memorandum on the Rodiyas* by Mr. MITFORD, C.C.S., DAVY relates that shortly after the British got possession of Kandy, some police Vidahns, who were ordered to arrest certain Rodiyas for murder, refused to pollute themselves by laying hands on them, but offered *to shoot them down from a distance.* (Ch. iv. p. 131.)

[2] Rev. R. SPENCE HARDY, *The Friend*, vol. ii. p. 15.

[3] CASIE CHITTY, *Ceylon Miscell.* 1853, p. 240.

Their habits are filthy, and their appetites omnivorous. Carrion is as acceptable to them as the flesh of monkeys, squirrels, the civet-cat, mongoos, and tortoises [1]; and they hover near ceremonies and feasts in hope of obtaining the fragments. The men are employed occasionally on the coffee estates, and in making roads, but they are generally stigmatised as imbecile, and shunned as reputed thieves. The character of the women is still more disreputable; they wander as jugglers, and at feasts perform dances, during which they keep two polished brass plates rotating, one on the top of each fore-finger.

RODIYAS.

The Rodiyas who have established themselves in the village of Kaduganawa, are remarkable for the beauty and fine figures of the females, which are displayed to advantage by the lightness of their conventional costume.

[1] CASIE CHITTY in *Ceylon Miscell.*, p. 238.

As if to demonstrate that within the lowest depths of degradation there may exist a lower still, there are two races of outcasts in Ceylon, who are abhorred and avoided even by the Rodiyas. These are the Ambetteyos, or barbers, and the Hanomoreyos, or betel-box makers, of Oovah, who are looked on as so vile that no human being would touch rice that had been cooked in their houses; and the Rodiyas, on the occasion of festivals, tie up their dogs to prevent them prowling in search of food to the dwellings of these wretches.

In contemplating the position and treatment of the Rodiyas of Ceylon, one is struck with its similarity to that of the Cagots and Caqueux, "the Pariahs of the West," who, from time immemorial, have been held in abhorrence in the valleys of the Pyrenees, and the plains of Bretagne, Poitou, and Guienne. The origin of either race is alike obscure, and it remains uncertain whether the Cagots were extruded from human sympathy and association as the descendants of Gothic or Moorish oppressors; or whether they were shunned from religious hatred, as the offspring of Arians, Jews, or Mahometans. For more than a thousand years, there are records of their social proscription, with every accompaniment of infamy and abhorrence. Their persons were believed to be contaminating, and their smell an abomination. Like the Rodiyas, they were compelled to stand aside on the highway to allow travellers to pass; they were punished for coming between the wind and a free citizen; they durst not draw water from a public fountain, or touch the parapet of a bridge with their uncovered hand. To protect the earth from the pollution of their feet, they were forced to wear shoes, and to enable all comers to avoid them, the law ordered them to carry a red mark (*pied d'oye*) upon their shoulders. They were forbidden to touch an article of food in the market-place before it had been sold and delivered to them. Their dwellings were huts and hovels in spots avoided by the rest of mankind; and though permitted to embrace

Christianity, they had to enter stooping through a separate porch into the churches, to touch the holy water in a separate *bénitier*, to pray in a separate recess, and after death their dishonoured remains were interred in a separate cemetery; in one of which, as if to taunt them with the perpetual remembrance that death was their only escape from an existence in which enjoyment was unknown, a column still remains with the inscription, "*absit gloriari, nisi in cruce Domini.*"

But the most curious coincidence between the case of the Rodiyas and that of the outcasts of France was, that both tribes were doomed to the revolting employment of skinning dead cattle, and steeping hemp to be made into ropes and cordage. Hence the Caqueux were known as the rope-makers ("cordiers") of Basse-Bretagne, and their villages were called "corderies," whilst the Cagots were almost universally carpenters;—the two trades being alike infamous at an early period, because those who pursued the one were expected to furnish gibbets and instruments of torture, whilst the other provided the halters for the executioner.[1]

From the Rodiya village at Kaduganawa, there is a gentle descent, for eight or nine miles, towards the banks of the Mahawelli-ganga; a bend of which flows around Kandy, surrounding the city, as the Singhalese say, "like a necklace of pearls."[2] The road still passes through rich and romantic scenery; mountains forest-clad to their summits; valleys brightened by fertilising streams, and villages and hamlets embosomed

---

[1] MICHEL, in his *History of the Outcast Races of France and Spain*, thus accounts for this popular prejudice: "Les Caqueux de la Brétagne ne pouvaient exercer d'autre état que celui de *cordier;* mais il était infame comme je suppose que celui de charpentier l'était dans le sud-ouest de la France; et cela apparemment par la même raison—car si les charpentiers dressaient les gibets et les autres instruments de supplice, les cordiers fournissaient les harts destinés à mettre un terme à la vie des criminels condamnés à être pendus."—*Histoire des Races Maudites de la France et de l'Espagne*, ch. v. tom. i. p. 316, &c.

[2] "And, moreover, by the side of the Mahawelli-ganga, which is like *a necklace of pearls round the neck of a queen of Ceylon*, the King," &c.—*Rajaratnacari*, p. 130.

amidst trees. A bridge of satin-wood crosses the river at Peradenia, and a drive of a few miles through a continuous line of cottages and bazaars, leads to the entrance of the Demesne, in which stands the Pavilion, the stately residence of the Governor at the central capital.

CHAP. V.

KANDY AND PERADENIA.

KANDY presents no architectural monument with any pretension to antiquity. Its singularly secure position, in a peninsula formed by a sweep of the great river and surrounded by a double circumvallation of mountains, may, at a very early period, have rendered it a stronghold of the princes of Maya; but the first mention of it as a city is at the beginning of the fourteenth century[1], when a temple was built there to contain the dalada and other relics. From possessing these it became an important seat of the Buddhist hierarchy, and eventually the residence of branches of the royal family. But it was not till the close of the sixteenth century that it was adopted as the capital of the island, after the destruction of Cotta and the defeat of Raja Singha II., by Wimala Dharma, A.D. 1592. The town at that time probably occupied in part the valley afterwards submerged by the construction of the Kandy Lake, which was formed by the last king, in 1807. During the wars with the Portuguese and the Dutch, Kandy was so repeatedly burned and otherwise destroyed that scarcely any part of the ancient buildings, except the temples and the royal residence, was remaining when the English obtained possession of the city in 1815.[2]

---

[1] In the reign of Pandita Prakrama Bahu III., between 1267 and 1301 A.D.—*Mahawanso*, ch. lxxxiii.; *Rajaratnacari*, p. 104.

[2] The Portuguese captured Kandy in A.D. 1592, and they burned it in A.D. 1627 (RIBEYRO, pt. ii. ch. i. p. 192); and again in A.D. 1637 (FARIA Y SOUZA, pt. iv. ch. viii. p. 375). The Dutch occupied it after its destruction by its own inhabitants in A.D. 1764;—and it was partially burnt by the king on the approach of the English in A.D. 1803.

The palace, a wing of which is still occupied by the chief civil officer of the province, is popularly believed to be much older than it really is. It was built by Wimala Dharma, about the year 1600, and Spilberg, the Dutch admiral, who visited Kandy in 1602, says that the king employed the services of his Portuguese prisoners in its erection; — a circumstance which may serve to account for the European character which pervades the architecture of some portions still remaining[1]; such as the tower adjoining the Malagawa temple, in which the sacred tooth is deposited.

TEMPLE OF THE DALADA, KANDY.

As to the streets and the dwellings of the natives, they were wretched at all times; the barbarous etiquette of the Kandyan kings reserving the luxury of windows, whitened walls, and tiles for the members of the royal family, and prohibiting their use to subjects.[2] One quarter of the town, leading from the Lake to the Mahawelli-ganga, contained houses of this privileged construction; and Boyd, on the occasion of his embassy

[1] "Don Juan a fait bâtir un magnifique palais à Candy, et plusieurs tours et pagodes à quoi il a emploie les Portugais qu'il avait fait prisonniers." — SPILBERG, *Voyage*, tom. ii. p. 443. There is no reason to believe that any vestige now remains of the original temple built for the reception of the Tooth by Pandita Prakrama Bahu III. A.D. 1767. — *Mahawanso*, ch. lxxxiv.

[2] VALENTYN, *Oud en Nieuw Oost-Indien*, ch. iii. p. 46.

in 1782, found the principal street so broad, that it afforded space for elephant-fights, which were held there to amuse the king. To avoid mischief from the enraged animals, the houses were approached by flights of steps, which gave them the appearance of two stories, although they consisted of but one.[1] The British, on their entrance into the city in 1815, were astonished at the misery of the place[2]; — but the wretched buildings have since been replaced by others more indicative of the improved civilisation and increasing prosperity of the inhabitants.

The Palace originally covered a considerable area, but its buildings were mean, its passages intricate and dark, and its chambers gloomy, confined, and filthy in the extreme. Of the rooms which still remain, the principal have been altered and adapted to European tastes, but their style of decoration, and the frequent recurrence of the sacred goose amongst the ornaments on the walls, bespeak their Buddhistical origin. Externally, the façade is rather imposing; the space which it occupies is screened by a crenellated wall, connecting it with the temple and its octagonal tower. In front is a moat, which has been recently levelled, but was formerly filled with water; — this was crossed by a bridge, that led to the grand gate; it was flanked by elephants sculptured in granite, and communicated with the palace by a broad flight of stone steps.

The only existing structure which seems worthy of its original destination, is the Audience Hall, at present used as the district court-house; a spacious apartment supported on richly carved columns of teak-wood, the bracketed capitals being admirable specimens of florid Hindu architecture. Public receptions were held by night[3], when the hall was lighted with wax, the colonnades on each side crowded with crouching courtiers;

---

[1] BOYD'S *Embassy to Kandy. Miscell. Works*, vol. ii. p. 209.

[2] *Asiat. Journ.*, vol. i. p. 44.

[3] DAVY'S *Ceylon*, p. 178.

and in a dim, and studiously darkened alcove, the king, reclining on a throne, was approached by his ministers, "on all fours, with their faces close to the floor, and almost literally licking the dust." [1]

The temples of Kandy, both Buddhist and Hindu, are dilapidated edifices, apparently perishing from unarrested decay. They are situated in enclosed court-yards, and, under the shade of the groves that surround them, crumble the neglected monuments of the later sovereigns of Kandy.[2] All the Buddhist priests in Ceylon belong ostensibly to one or other of the two great establishments at Kandy, the Asgiri and Malwatté. In doctrines and discipline they are identical, but they differ somewhat in territorial authority, the ecclesiastical jurisdiction of the Asgiri being understood to extend over the northern parts of the island, and that of the Malwatté chiefly over the temples to the south. With the extinction of the national dynasty, the status and influence of the priesthood have undergone a rapid decline;—not that their possessions have diminished, nor that the protection of the chiefs has been less generous than before; but in the eyes and estimation of the people they have endured a diminution of dignity from the loss of the royal presence, in which it was their privilege to bask. Even their ritual pomp and ceremonials no longer command the same homage from the populace, and the great annual procession of the Perahara, with its torchlights, its solemn music, and capari-

[1] BOYD'S *Embassy, &c. Miscell. Works*, vol. ii. p. 214.

[2] After burning the bodies of the deceased kings, their ashes were carried by a man in a black mask, to the Mahawelli-ganga, where he embarked in a canoe. At the deepest part of the river he clove the vase with a sword, scattered the ashes on the stream, and plunging headlong after them, dived and rose near the opposite bank, whence he fled to the forest and was presumed to be never more seen. The canoe was allowed to drift away; the horses and elephants that accompanied the procession were set at liberty in the woods; and the females who strewed rice over the coffin, were transported across the river and forbidden ever to return.—DAVY'S *Ceylon*, p. 162.

soned elephants, is spiritless and unimpressive, if contrasted with occasions within memory, when it was hallowed by the divine presence of a king.[1]

At the present day nothing can be less obtrusive than the Buddhist worship, or less ostentatious than the demeanour of its priesthood. One is only reminded of their vicinity when, at sunset or in the early morning, the silence is broken by the noise of tom-toms and the plaintive notes of the flute, mingled with the discordant blare of the chank shells, which are sounded as an accompaniment to the melancholy chaunting of their choir.

But the most remarkable object at Kandy is unquestionably the *dalada*, asserted to be the "sacred tooth" of Buddha, which for so many centuries has commanded the unreasoning homage of millions of devotees. An allusion has been elsewhere made to the traditional history of this relic[2], its rescue from the flames after the cremation of the mortal remains of Gotama Buddha at Kusinara, B.C. 543, and its preservation for eight hundred years at Dantapura in Kalinga, whence it was brought to Ceylon in the fourth century after Christ.[3] It was afterwards captured by the Malabars about the year 1315, and again carried to India, but recovered by the prowess of Prakrama Bahu III. During the troublous times which followed, the original tooth was hidden in different parts of the island, at Kandy, at Delgamoa in Saffragam, and at

[1] An account of the Pera-hara, and the historical event which it commemorates, will be found in *The Friend*, published at Colombo in 1839, vol. iii. p. 41. A description of the procession, as it was celebrated two centuries ago, is contained in the truthful narrative of KNOX, pt. iii. ch. iv. p. 78.

[2] See Vol I. Pt. III. ch. ix. p. 388.

[3] A.D. 311, *Mahawanso*, ch. xxxvii. p. 241; *Rajavali*, p. 240. MAHANAMO, who wrote his portion of the *Mahawanso*, between A.D. 459 and 477, quotes as his authority for the history of the tooth, a work which is extant to the present day, called the *Dalada-wanso*, or *Chronicle of the Dalada*, and from it and other sources TURNOUR drew the materials for a memoir, which he communicated in 1837 to the Asiatic Society of Bengal, on "*The Tooth-relic of Ceylon*," *Asiat. Soc. Journ. Beng.*, vol. vi. p. 856. Forbes published a paper on the history of the tooth, in the *Ceylon Calendar* for 1835.

Kotmalie; but at last in 1560 it was discovered by the Portuguese [1], taken to Goa by Don Constantine de Braganza, and burned by the Archbishop in the presence of the Viceroy of India and his court.

The fate of this renowned relic is so remarkable, and its destruction is related with so much particularity by the Portuguese annalists of the period, and their European contemporaries, that no historical doubt can be entertained, even were internal evidence wanting, that the tooth now exhibited at Kandy is a spurious and modern substitute for the original, destroyed in 1560.

The story as told by De Couto [2] is curiously illustrative of the genius and faith of the Bhuddist races. No sooner was it ascertained that the relic had been seized by Don Constantine, than the sovereign of Pegu, who had previously despatched annual embassies to offer homage at its shrine, sent in anxious haste to redeem it by an exchange of treasure and political services. The fidalgos of Goa were eager to replenish their exhausted treasury on the generous terms which he offered; but the piety of the Roman Catholic prelates was triumphant, the idolatrous object was consumed, and its ashes scattered on the sea.[3]

But a very few years elapsed before the delusion was

---

[1] For the particulars of the siege and capture of Jaffna in 1560, see Vol. II. Pt. VI. ch. i. p. 28.

[2] The account of the capture and subsequent fate of the Dalada is so important an incident in the religious annals of Ceylon, and at the same time has so significant a bearing on the veneration still paid to the supposed relic at Kandy, that I have thought it necessary to translate the passage as it is given by DE COUTO, in his *History of the Conquest of India by the Portuguese*. It will be found in the Appendix to this chapter.

[3] The narrative of DE COUTO is circumstantial and minute as to the mode of its destruction: "Assentado isto, mandou o Viso-Rey ao Thesoureiro que trouxesse o dente: e o entregou ao Arcebispo, que alli presentes todos o lançou em hum almofariz, e com sua propria mão o pizou, e desfez em póz, e os deitou em hum brazeiro, que pera isso mandou trazer, e as cinzas, e carvões mandou lançar no meio do rio a vista de todos, que assomáram ás varandas, e janellas que cahiam sobre o mar." — DE COUTO, Dec. vii. lib. ix. ch. xvii.; see also RODRIGUES DE SAA, *Rebelion, &c.*, p. 18—99; VALENTYN, ch. xvi. p. 383.

revived, and not only a duplicate, but a triplicate of the desecrated relic were regarded with undiminished adoration both in Pegu and Ceylon. The story of the resuscitated imposture is related by De Couto. The king of Pegu, in 1566, having been told by the astrologers that he was to wed a Singhalese princess, sent to demand her in marriage; but the reigning sovereign, Don Juan Dharma Pala, having unfortunately no child, the prophecy was on the point of discomfiture; when his chamberlain, a nobleman of the blood royal, suggested the substitution of his own daughter, and added impiety to fraud by feigning to the Peguan envoys that he still held in secret the genuine *dalada*, falsely supposed to have been destroyed by the Christians at Goa. The device was successful, the supposititious princess was received in Pegu with all the nuptial honours of royalty; and ambassadors were despatched to Ceylon, to obtain possession of the sacred tooth, which was forthwith transferred to Arracan.

The king of Kandy, Wikratna Bahu, on learning the deception which had been perpetrated by his cousin of Cotta, apprised the Peguan sovereign of the imposture which had been practised upon him; and to redress it he offered him his own daughter in marriage, and proposed as her dowry to send the veritable tooth, affirming that both the one recently obtained from Colombo, and the other formerly pulverised at Goa, were counterfeit, his alone being the genuine relic of Buddha.[1] But the prince of Pegu was too devout to confess himself a dupe; "he gave ear to the ambassadors," says Faria y Souza, "but not to their information, and thus had Don Constantine de Braganza sold the tooth, as he was

[1] The Singhalese never seem to have been scrupulous about multiplying Buddha's teeth. For Marco Polo says the Great Khan Khubla sent to demand one in the year 1281, "and obtained from the king (of Ceylon) two large back teeth, together with some of his hair and a handsome vessel of porphyry."—MARCO POLO, *Travels, &c.*, b. iii. ch. xxiii. p. 671.

advised, there had not been *two* set up to be adored by so many people."[1]

The incidents of this narrative are too minute, and their credibility is established by too many contemporary and concurrent authorities[2], to admit of any doubt that the authenticity of the tooth now preserved in the Malagawa at Kandy is no higher than its antiquity, and that the supposed relic is a clumsy substitute, manufactured by Wikrama Bahu in 1566, to replace the original *dalada* destroyed by the Portuguese in 1560.[3] The dimensions and form of the present *dalada* are fatal to any belief in its identity with the one originally worshipped, which was probably human[4], whereas the object now shown is a piece of discoloured ivory, about two inches in length, and less than one in diameter, resembling the tooth of a crocodile rather than that of a man.

THE TOOTH.

---

[1] FARIA Y SOUZA, vol. ii. pt. iii. ch. ii. p. 251; DE COUTO, Dec. viii. vol. v. pt. i. ch. xii., xiii. p. 74.

[2] The fact of the destruction of the tooth in 1561 by Don Constantine de Braganza is confirmed by the authority of RODRIGUES DE SAA Y MENEZES, who in 1678 wrote his "*Rebelion de Ceylan*" to commemorate the exploits and death of his father Constantine de Saa y Noroña, who perished in the expedition to reduce the Kandyans at Badulla, A.D. 1630.—*Rebelion, &c.*, ch. i. p. 18: ch. vii. p. 99. The story, which must have created a sensation throughout India, is related by Sir THOMAS HERBERT, whose travels were published in 1634, and by FRANCOIS PYRARD DE LAVAL, who visited Ceylon about 1608 A.D. *Voyage, &c.*, tom. ii. ch. x. p. 89. VALENTYN records the fate of the tooth, and says it had been kept near Adam's Peak till 1554. *Oud en Nieuw Oost-Indien*, ch. xvi. p. 382. In the *Narrative of the Mission sent by the Governor-General of India to the Court of Ava in* 1855, by Captain Yule, the envoy and his suite pointed out to him near the palace at Amarapoora "a square edifice, representing the depository of the tooth of Gotama, which, in ancient times, was preserved within the royal precincts," p. 136. In descending the river to Rangoon on the return of the Mission, they were shown at Nyoungoo, the Zeegoong pagoda, which "enshrines a *fac-simile* of one of Gotama's teeth."—Pp. 33, 196.

[3] The powers of the tooth as a national palladium, and the exemption of Ceylon from foreign domination, so long as it possessed the relic and the sacred tree at Anaraja-poora, are propounded in the *Rajaratnacari*, UPHAM's version, ch. i. p. 2.

[4] FARIA Y SOUZA says it was said to be the tooth of an ape, but this arises from confounding Buddha and Hanuman the Sacred Monkey, vol. ii. pt. ii. ch. xvi. p. 207.

Its popular acceptance, notwithstanding this anomalous shape, may probably be accounted for by the familiarity of the Kandyans, under their later kings, with the forms of some of the Hindu deities, amongst whom Vishnu and Kali are occasionally depicted with similarly projecting canines.[1]

The apartment in which it is deposited is in the inmost recess of the Wihara, a small chamber without windows, in which the air is stiflingly hot, and heavy with the perfume of flowers. The frames of the doors are inlaid with carved ivory, and on a massive silver table stands the bell-shaped *carandua*, the shrine, which encloses the relic, encrusted with gems, and festooned with jewelled chains. The outer case contains a number

SHRINE OF THE SACRED TOOTH.

of others, similarly wrought, but diminishing in size, till on removing the inner one a golden lotus is disclosed, in the centre of which reposes the mysterious tooth.

[1] See MOOR's *Hindu Pantheon*, pl. xxviii. L.

The antiquity of these caranduas is doubtful, but their fashion and form appear to be identical with those described in the *Rajaratnacari* as having been made for the relic by successive sovereigns between 1267 and 1464 A.D.[1]

Nothing can be more picturesque than the situation and aspect of Kandy, on the banks of a miniature lake, overhung on all sides by hills, which command charming views of the city, with its temples, and monuments below. In the lake, a tiny island is covered by a picturesque building, now a powder magazine, but in former times a harem of the king. A road, which bears the name of "*Lady Horton's Walk*," winds round one of those hills; and on the eastern side, which is steep and almost precipitous, it looks down into the valley of Doombera, through which the Mahawelliganga rolls over a channel of rocks, presenting a scene which nothing in the tropics can exceed in majestic beauty.

In a park at the foot of this acclivity is the pavilion of the governor, one of the most agreeable edifices in India, not less for the beauty of its architecture than for its judicious adaptation to the climate. The walls and columns are covered with chunam, prepared from calcined shells, which in whiteness and polish rivals the purity of marble. The high ground immediately behind is included in the demesne, and so successfully have the elegancies of landscape gardening been combined with the wildness of nature, that during my last residence at Kandy a leopard from the forest above came down nightly, to drink at the fountain in the parterre.

My own official residence, from its vicinity to the same jungle, was occasionally entered by equally unexpected visitors. Serpents are numerous on the hills, and as the house stood on a terrace formed out of one of its steepest sides, the cobra de capello and the green cara-

[1] *Rajaratnacari*, pp. 103, 113.

KANDY FROM THE WESTERN REDOUBT.

wella frequently glided through the rooms on their way towards the grounds. During the residence of one of my predecessors in office, an invalid, who lay for some days on a sofa in the verandah, imagined more than once that she felt something move under the pillow; and on rising to have it examined, a snake was discovered with a brood of young, which from their being born alive were most probably venomous. A lady residing in the old palace adjoining, going to open her piano was about to remove what she thought to be an ebony walking-stick that lay upon it, but was startled on finding that she had laid hold of a snake.

One day when the carriage had come to the door, and I was about to hand a lady in, a rat-snake uncoiled itself on the cushion, and glided leisurely down the steps. These creatures, however, are perfectly harmless, and are encouraged by the horse-keepers to take up their abode about the offices and stable-yard, which they keep free of vermin. In colour they are brown, with a tinge of iridescent blue.

Another less formidable intruder was the great black scorpion[1], as large as a little cray-fish, which sometimes when disturbed in the daylight made its way across the floor with its venomed tail arched forward, prepared to encounter any assailant. Its habits are crepuscular, lurking by day under stones and in ruined walls and cellars, and issuing at dusk in search of orthopterous larvæ and succulent insects. Exaggerated apprehensions prevail as to the effects of its wound, which is neither dangerous nor very painful, but after occasioning some inflammation, yields to the free use of hartshorn and cooling lotions.[2]

A small yellow scorpion[3] is common in all parts of the island, flat, narrow, and about two inches in length.

---

[1] *Buthus Afer*, Linn.

[2] Dr. Davy says, that in Ceylon the poison of the scorpion is very little if at all more active than that of the bee or wasp. He adds, that in two or three instances, when he tried the sting of the large black scorpion on fowls, it appeared to have no effect. (DAVY'S *Ceylon*, p. 101.)

[3] *Scorpio linearis*, Temp.

It frequents the sleeping apartments and wardrobes, and conceals itself in the folds of loose dresses. It is regarded as noxious, but I believe unjustly, as I never heard of any injury arising from its sting.

The temperature of Kandy is believed to have increased in warmth since the surfaces of the surrounding mountains have been dried by the felling of the trees, to convert the forests into plantations of coffee [1]; — and it is certainly remarkable that although grapes will not ripen there now, as the vine requires a winter repose [2], wine from grapes grown on the spot was produced in the time of the Dutch. Spilberg, who drank of it in 1602, describes its quality as excellent; and Valentyn at a later period speaks of it in similar terms.[3]

KANDYAN CHIEFS

The costumes of the groups of Kandyans who, on occasions of ceremony, present themselves to the governor

[1] For an analysis of the climate of Kandy, see *ante*, Vol. I. Pt. I. ch. ii. p. 70.

[2] See Vol. I. Pt. I. ch. iii. p. 80, and Vol. II. p. 589.

[3] "Tout ce que l'on récueille dans les autres païs, soit huile, froment, vin, y peut croître et produire encore mieux qu'ailleurs. *Nous y avons bu de très bons vins du crû du païs.*" — SPILBERG, tom ii. p. 452. VALENTYN says, the wine of Kandy was equal to any in Portugal: "en die in zich zelve zoo goed was, als eenige wyn in Portugal gewasschen." — *Oud en Nieuw Oost-Indien*, ch. viii. p. 104.

at the Pavilion, or lounge in front of the chief civil officer's cutcherry, are even more curious than those of the low-country Singhalese at Galle and Colombo. The priests of Buddha, moody and abstracted, draw their yellow robes around them, and walk with downcast eyes, their ears appearing unnaturally large, from their heads being closely shaven. The coralles and other petty headmen are distinguished only by a flattened cap of white calico, but the great chiefs, the Rate-mahatmeyas[1], and the nearly extinct rank of Dissave, wear a singularly ungraceful dress of stiffened white muslin, with gigot sleeves, a goffred Vandyck, and their waist girt by an embroidered belt. Each is accompanied by an attendant bearing an umbrella of state, or an ornamented fan of the talipat-leaf inlaid with talc, as an emblem of his dignity.

From Kandy to the Royal Botanic Garden at Peradenia, the road for nearly four miles passes through a continuous suburb, in which almost every house is surrounded by a little garden of coco-nut palms, bread-fruit, and coffee-trees. The *Rajaratnacari* records that in the year 1371 " the king, Wikrama Bahu III., ascended the throne, and kept his court at Pira-deniya, situated near the river Mahawelli-ganga,"[2] but no traces now remain of the buildings of that period.

A large tract by the banks of the river has been converted into a sugar plantation, originally stocked with canes from Mauritius; but the experiment has not been attended with the anticipated success, the produce barely sufficing for the supply of the central province. The mediocrity of the soil, and the necessity of frequently changing the plants, coupled with a superabundance of merely watery fluid in the canes, and disproportionate yield of saccharine, have hitherto contributed to discourage the extension of the enterprise. The same unsatisfactory result has unfortunately characterised all similar attempts in other parts of the island.

---

[1] Literally, "country-gentlemen." | [2] *Rajaratnacari*, p. 111.

The cultivation of sugar was introduced by the Dutch, and has been attempted by the English[1], at various places in the vicinity of Negombo, Caltura, and Galle. Of these almost the only estates on which the effort has been energetically persevered in, are a few in the southern province, one especially on the Matura river; but the series of previous disappointments deadens the hope of any very decided ultimate success.

The entrance to the Peradenia Garden is through a noble avenue of India-rubber trees (*Ficus elastica*), and the first object that arrests the admiration of a stranger on entering is a group of palms, which is, I apprehend, unsurpassed both in variety and grandeur. It includes nearly all those indigenous to the island,— the towering talipat, the palmyra, the slender areca, and the kitool, with its formidable thorny congener, the *Caryota horrida*, and numerous others less remarkable. Amongst the exotic species are the date-palm, the *Livistona chinensis*, some species of *Calamus*, and the wonderful Coco-de-mer of the Seychelles.[2] Close beside these are marvellous specimens of the symmetrical traveller's tree of Madagascar[3], upwards of fifty feet high, surrounded by *Yuccæ* and *Scitaminiæ*. Nothing in Ceylon so forcibly impresses a traveller with the glory of tropical vegetation, as this luxuriant and unrivalled display.

The garden, covering an area of nearly one hundred and fifty acres, overlooks the noble river that encircles it on three sides; and, surrounding the cultivated parterres, the tall natural woods afford a favourable opportunity for exhibiting some of the wonders of the Ceylon flora,—orchideæ, festoons of flowering creepers (*ipomœas* and *bignonias*), the *guilandina bonduc*, with

---

[1] Sir Edward Barnes, with his characteristic vigilance, formed one of the first sugar plantations at Veangodde, between Colombo and Kandy.

[2] See *ante*, Vol. II. Pt. VII. ch. ii. p. 176.

[3] *Ravenala speciosa.*

its silicious seeds, the powerful jungle-rope (*Bauhinia scandens*), and the extraordinary climber[1], whose strong stays, resembling in form and dimensions the chain-cable of a man of war, lash together the tall trees of the forest.

The nurseries, the spice ground, the orchards and experimental garden, are all in high vigour; and since the formation of this admirable institution, about thirty[2] years ago, the benefits which it has conferred on the colony have more than realised the anticipations of its founders. European and other exotic plants have been largely introduced; the valuable products of the eastern Archipelago, cloves, nutmegs, vanilla, and other spices, have been acclimatised; foreign fruits without number, mangoes, durians, lichees, loquats, granadillas, and the avocado pear, have been propagated, and their cultivation extended throughout the island; and the tea shrub, the chocolate, arrow-root, tapioca, West Indian ginger, and many others have been domesticated. The present able and accomplished director has already commenced the publication of a Singhalese Flora, the completion of which will place the savans of Europe in possession of accurate information as to the botany of the island. But in any allusion to the gardens of Peradenia, the name and services of Dr. Gardner, to whose memory a modest monument has been erected in the grounds, will always be associated with agreeable recollections of one whose genius was as remarkable in acquiring as his gentle manners were successful in popularising science in Ceylon.

At times there has been the murmur of ill-informed utilitarianism against the expenditure bestowed upon

[1] *Bauhinia racemosa?*

[2] The first botanic garden in Ceylon was established by Mr. North, in 1799, at Ortafula, on the banks of the Kalany, at Colombo, and M. Joinville was named its curator. In 1810 it was transferred to a portion of Slave Island, which thence acquired the name of "Kew," and in 1813 it was again removed to Caltura, where Moon, the author of the first English *Catalogue of Ceylon Plants*, was superintendent, and under him the present gardens were eventually laid out at Peradenia.

the botanic garden of Peradenia. But the object of such institutions, and the functions of their curators, are still imperfectly appreciated even in the localities to whose welfare they are most conducive; owing chiefly to an ignorant impatience for results which in their very nature must be prospective. The fact is overlooked, that such foundations are designed not for individual benefit, but for the collective advantage of communities by the gradual application of science to material development.

Objects at first despised and insignificant, become sources of colonial wealth under the auspices of the botanist; and, on the other hand, productions upon which the prosperity of a region may be dependent, are liable to destruction and decay in the absence of his experience and counsels.[1] It is wise policy in the government of a country, and most of all of a new and unexplored one, to encourage the cultivation of science for its own sake, confident that its labours, if not remunerative at the moment, will prove infallibly productive in the future.

The colonial botanist, in addition to the care and nomenclature of plants, useful, rare, and ornamental, and

[1] Witness the wholesale destruction of the forests of India for immediate profit; the expenditure on unremunerative cultivation; the waste of money and labour in useless draining and planting; the neglect of invaluable products, and the substitution of those that are worthless; all ascribable to the want of scientific knowledge and guidance. Dr. HOOKER remarks (preface to the *Flora of New Zealand*): "During a residence of some years in our colonies and foreign possessions, I have observed that the inhabitants are invariably anxious to acquire the names of the plants around them; they regret not having learnt the rudiments of botany in their youth, and are most desirous that their children should be instructed in them, feeling that their practical information, however accurate and extensive, is useless beyond their own sphere. On my return to England, I was no less struck with the fact (which as a juror was prominently brought before me) that, for want of a little botanical knowledge on the part of the exhibitors, large collections of vegetable produce, sent to the Great Exhibition, were rendered all but valueless." In these instances, had the scientific names been attached, it would have been easy to have given such a popular and accurate account of the articles in question, that they might have been recognised by any one acquainted with the rudiments of botany, and thus direct benefit would have accrued to the colonies producing them.

the collection of fruits and products of all kinds, for an œconomic museum of botany, should take upon himself the selection of a library and the formation of a *hortus siccus* for consultation and reference. These duties, together with his foreign correspondence and exchanges, the reception of scientific strangers, the journeys of himself and his assistants to explore the country and collect botanical specimens, and occasional publications to excite and sustain popular interest in his pursuits, ought to constitute the functions of a botanical officer, and no colony can fail to reap the benefit of such labours if judiciously discharged.

But the dissatisfaction which has occasionally manifested itself in Ceylon, arises not alone from a want of due appreciation of the legitimate duties of a superintendent, but also from an unreasonable expectation of services not legitimately within his province. A knowledge of agriculture, horticulture, forestry, pharmacy, and toxicology have each been demanded, as well as the philosophy of climates, the geologic nature of rocks and soils, the chemistry of manures, and the œconomic habits of animals, birds, and insects; and it is within my own knowledge that from the coffee planters, there have been remonstrances to the local government as to the propriety of applying public funds for the maintenance of an institution from which, in regard to their own estates, they had failed individually to obtain assistance in connection with these and similar subjects.[1] A man of generous education may, no doubt, be more or less familiar with such studies, but even if a scientific botanist felt diffident in propounding opinions or offering directions in relation to them, his peculiar attainments must be of signal advantage in modifying the views or facilitating the operations of others. So charming is the sphere of his duties, that those who cannot estimate their importance

[1] In some colonies, by a still more unreasonable requirement, the curator of the botanic garden has been expected to grow vegetables for the table of the governor, his officers, and staff.

except by the value of their ostensible results, are liable to ignore their latent utility in the contemplation of their ornamental attractions. But observation and experience cannot fail to dissipate false expectations; and looking to the present transitional aspect of Ceylon, and the future which is already dawning for the island, my conviction is strong that no establishment in the colony is so essential to its interest as the Royal Botanic Gardens of Peradenia.

NOTE TO CHAPTER V.

STORY OF THE DESTRUCTION OF THE SACRED TOOTH.

Translated from the Portuguese of Diego de Couto, *Asia, &c.* Decade vii. lib. ix. ch. 2, &c.

After describing the siege and reduction of Jaffna, in 1560, by the viceroy Don Constantine de Braganza, in the 2nd chapter of the vii. decade, book ix., the narrative proceeds as follows: —

* * * * * * *

"Amongst the spoils of the principal temple they brought to the viceroy a *tooth* mounted in gold, which was generally said to be the tooth of an ape, but which these idolaters regarded as the most sacred of all objects of adoration. The Viceroy was immediately made aware that its value was inestimable, as the natives would be sure to offer vast sums to redeem it. They believed it to be the tooth of their great saint Buddha. This Buddha, so runs their legend, after visiting Ceylon, travelled over Pegu and the adjacent countries, converting the heathen and working miracles; and, death approaching, he wrenched this tooth from its socket, and sent it to Ceylon as the greatest of relics. So highly was it venerated, by the Singhalese and by all the people of Pegu, that they esteemed it above all other treasures." * * * *

CHAP. XVII.

How the King of Pegu sent to offer a sum of gold to the Viceroy Don Constantine for the ape's tooth, which was taken at Jaffna-patam, and of the decision of the divines thereupon, and how it was resolved to destroy it by fire.

"Martin Alfonso de Mello happened to be in Pegu with his ship on business, when the Viceroy, Don Constantine, returned (to Goa) from Jaffna-patam, and the king, hearing that the 'tooth' which was so profoundly revered by all Buddhists had been carried off, summoned Martin Alfonso to his presence, and besought him, on his return to India, to entreat the Viceroy to surrender it, offering to give in exchange whatever might be demanded for it. And those who know the Peguans, and the devotion with which they regard this relic of the devil, affirmed that the king would have given *three* or even *four hundred thousand cruzadoes* to obtain possession of it. By advice of Martin Alfonso, the king despatched ambassadors to accompany him to the Viceroy on this affair, and empowered them to signify his readiness to ratify any agreement to which they might assent on his behalf.

"Martin Alfonso, on reaching Goa, in April 1561, apprised the Viceroy of the arrival of the envoys, who, after their reception, opened the business for which they were accredited, making a request for the tooth on behalf of their sovereign; offering in return any terms that might be required, with a proposal for a perpetual alliance with Portugal, and an undertaking to provision the fortress of Malacca at all times when called upon; together with many other conditions and promises. The Viceroy promised an early reply, and, in the meantime, communicated with his veteran captains and fidalgos, all of whom were in favour of accepting an offer which would recruit the exhausted treasury; and so eager were they, that the question seemed to be decided.

"But the matter having reached the ear of the Archbishop, Don Gaspar, he repaired instantly to the Viceroy, and warned him that he was not to permit this tooth to be ransomed for all the treasures of the universe; since it would be dishonouring to the Lord, and would afford an opportunity to these idolaters to pay to that bone the worship which belonged to God alone. The Archbishop wrote memorials on the subject, and preached against it from the pulpit, in the presence of the Viceroy and his court, so that Don Constantine, who as a conscientious Catholic feared God and obeyed the Church, hesitated to proceed with the affair, or to take any step that was not unanimously approved. He thereupon convened an assembly of the Archbishop, the prelates, and heads of the religious orders, together with the captains and senior fidalgos, and other officers of the Government: he laid the matter before them, the large offers of money that had been made for the tooth, and the pressing wants of the service, all of which could be provided for out of so great a ransom. After mature deliberation, a resolution was come to that it was not competent to part with the tooth, since its surrender would be an incitement to idolatry, and an insult to the Almighty; crimes which could not be contemplated, though the state, or even the world itself, might be imperilled. Of this opinion were the prelates, the inquisitors, the vicar-general of the Dominicans, Fra Manuel de Serra of the same order, the prior of Goa, the Father Custodian of the Franciscans, Padre Antonio de Quadros of the Company of Jesus, the Provincial of India, and others of the Society of the Jesuits.

"This resolution having been come to and committed to writing, to which all attached their signatures (and a copy of which is now in our possession in the Record Office), the Viceroy called on the treasurer to produce the tooth. He handed it to the Archbishop, who, in their presence, placed it in a mortar, and with his own hand reducing it to powder, cast the pieces into a brazier, which stood ready for the purpose; after which, the ashes and the charcoal together were cast into the river, in sight of all, they crowding to the verandahs and windows which looked upon the water.

"Many protested against this measure of the Viceroy, since there was nothing to prevent the Buddhists from making other idols; and out of a piece of bone they could shape another tooth in resemblance of the one they had lost, and extend to it the same worship; whilst the gold that had been rejected would have repaired the pressing necessities of the state. In Portugal itself much astonishment was expressed that these proceedings should have been assented to.

"To commemorate the event, and to illustrate the spirit which had dictated an act approved by the Fathers of the Company, and signalised by zeal for Christianity and the glory of God, a device was designed as follows:—On an escutcheon was a representation of the Viceroy and the Archbishop surrounded by the prelates, monks, and divines who had been present on the occasion, and in the midst was the burning brazier, together with Buddhists offering purses of money. Above the letter C, being the initial of Don Constantine, was repeated five times thus—

C C C C C

and below it the five words —

Constantinus cœli cupidine
crumenas cremavit,

the interpretation being that 'Constantine devoted to heaven, rejected the treasures of earth.'"

DECADE VIII.

CHAPTER XII.

How the King of Pegu sent to the King of Ceylon to demand his daughter in marriage.

* * * "At the birth of Brama, king of Pegu, the astrologers who cast his nativity, predicted that he should marry a daughter of the king of Ceylon, who was to have such and such marks and features, and certain proportions of limbs and figure. Brama, desirous to fulfil the prediction, sent ambassadors to Don Juan (the king of Cotta), whom he addressed as the sole inheritor of the royal blood and the only legitimate sovereign of the island; and sought his daughter in marriage, accompanying the demand by a ship load of rich presents, consisting of things unknown in Ceylon, besides woven cloth and precious stones. The envoys arrived about the time that the king had abandoned Cotta to take up his residence within the Fort of Colombo (A. D. 1564). He received the ambassadors with much distinction, and learning the purpose of their coming, he concealed from them the fact that the astrologers were in error, as he was childless. He had, however, brought up in his palace a daughter of his great chamberlain, a prince of the blood royal, who had embraced Christianity through the instrumentality of the governor Francisco Barreto, whose name he assumed; and such was the influence of this man, in addition to the claim of relationship, that in all things the king was directed by his counsels. This girl the king treated with every honour as his own child: on the arrival of the envoys she had a place assigned to her at the royal table, and was addressed as his daughter, and under that designation he sought to render her wife to the king of Pegu. The opposition which he appre-

hended was from the captain-general of Colombo and the Franciscans, who, although the girl was a Buddhist, might nevertheless regard her as a lamb within their fold, whom they could any day induce to become a Christian, and they were, therefore, likely to interfere to prevent her leaving the island. Discussing these considerations with the great chamberlain, who was a man of resources and tact, the latter pointed out to the king, who relied on his judgment in all things, that although forced to abandon Cotta and reduced to poverty, he might, through this alliance, open up a rich commerce with Pegu, and he accordingly assented that the girl should be despatched to the king, provided she was conveyed away secretly and without the knowledge of the Portuguese at Colombo.

"But the chamberlain did more; in concert with the king, he caused to be made out of a stag's horn, a *fac-simile* of the ape's tooth carried off by Don Constantine, and mounting it in gold, he enclosed it in a costly shrine richly decorated with gems. Conversing one day with the Paguan ambassador and the Buddhist priests (talapoens) in his suite, who were about to set out to worship and make offerings at the sacred footprint on Adam's Peak, the chamberlain, who was a Buddhist at heart, disclosed to them in confidence that Don Juan, the Singhalese king, was still in possession of the genuine tooth of Buddha[1], that which was seized by Don Constantine being a counterfeit, and that he, the great chamberlain, kept it concealed in his house, the king of Ceylon having become a Christian. The ambassador and the talapoens evinced their delight on this intelligence, and besought him to permit them to see it; he consented reluctantly, and first obliging them to disguise themselves, he conducted them by night to his residence, and there exhibited the tooth in its shrine, resting on an altar, surrounded by perfumes and lights. At the sight they prostrated themselves on the ground, and spent the greater part of the night in ceremonies and superstitious devotion; afterwards, addressing the great chamberlain, they entreated him to send the relic to the king of Pegu, at the same time with the princess; undertaking that as a part of the splendour and pomp

---

[1] DE COUTO, who originally describes it as the tooth of Buddha, calls it in this passage, "*Dente do seu idolo Quijay;*" and in another place "do *Quiar*," probably a corrupt spelling of the Burmese word for a Buddha "*Phra*," or possibly a modification of the Chinese name for Gotama, "*Kiu-tan.*"

of the marriage, Brama would send him a million of gold, and year by year despatch to Ceylon a present of a ship laden with rice and such other articles as might be required. All this was negotiated privately, the king and the great chamberlain alone being in the secret.

"When the time arrived for the young lady to take her departure, it was so cunningly arranged, that neither the captain of Colombo, Diego de Mello, nor the priesthood, suspected anything. Andrea Bayam Moodliar accompanied her as ambassador from the sovereign of Ceylon, and after a prosperous voyage, they landed at a port to the south of Cosmi[1], and announced their success and the arrival of the queen to the delight of the king and his nobles. * * * The son and heir of the king received her as she disembarked * * * the king met her at the gates of the palace which was assigned to her as a residence, gorgeously furnished in chamber, ante-chamber, and ward-room with all that became the consort of so rich and powerful a monarch, who conferred upon her immense revenues to defray the charges of her household. For days he devoted himself to her society, conducted her to the royal residence, and with great solemnity required the people to swear allegiance to her as their queen. The eunuchs who waited on her, imparted these particulars to Antonio Toscano, with whom they were intimate, and who communicated them to me.

"But as in these countries no secret is long preserved which is in any one's keeping, king Brama came at length to discover that his wife was the daughter, not of the king, but of his chamberlain; for it seems that Andrea Bayam, the Singhalese ambassador, who, as the proverb says, could not keep his tongue within his teeth, divulged it to some Chinese at Pegu, who acquainted the king. He, however, was little moved by the discovery, especially as the talapoens and ambassadors gave him an account of the ape's tooth, and of the veneration with which it was preserved, and of the arrangement which they had concerted with the person in charge of it. This excited the desire of Brama, who regarded it as the tooth of his idol[2], and reverenced it above everything in life; even as we esteem the

---

[1] Probably Casmin, on a branch of the Irawaddi.
[2] "Dente do seu idolo *Quijay*."

tooth of St. Apollonia (though I shall not say much of the tooth of that sainted lady); more highly than the nail which fastened our Saviour to the cross; the thorns which encircled his most sacred head; or the spear which pierced his blessed side, which remained so long in the hands of the Turks, without such an effort on the part of the monarchs of Christendom to rescue them as king Brama made to gain possession of this tooth of Satan, or rather of a stag. He immediately despatched the same ambassadors and talapoens in quest of it, and sent extraordinary presents by them to the king of Ceylon, with promises of others still more costly. The ambassadors reached Colombo, negotiated secretly with Don Juan, who placed the tooth with its shrine in their hands with much solemnity and secrecy, and with it they took their departure in the same vessel in which they had arrived."

CHAPTER XIII.

Of the magnificence and splendour with which this tooth was received in Pegu.

"In a few days they drew near to Cosmi, a port of Pegu, whence the news spread quickly, the priesthood (talapoens) assembled, and the people crowded devoutly to offer adoration to the tooth. For its landing they collected vast numbers of rafts elaborately and richly ornamented, and when they came to carry the accursed tooth on shore it rested on gold and silver and other costly rarities. Intelligence was instantly sent to Brama to Pegu, who despatched all his nobles to assist at its reception, and he superintended in person the preparation of a place in which the relic was to be deposited. In the arrangements for this he displayed to the utmost all the resources and wealth at his command. In this state the tooth made the ascent of the river, which was covered with rich boats encircling the structure, under which rested the shrine, so illuminated that it vied with the brightness of day.

"The king, when all was prepared, seated himself in a boat decorated with gilding and brocaded silks; he set out two days in advance to meet the procession, and on coming in sight of it he retired into the cabin of his galley, bathed, sprinkled himself with perfumes, assumed his most costly dress, and on touching the raft which bore the tooth he prostrated himself before it with all the gestures of profound adoration, and on his knees approaching the altar on which rested the shrine, he received the tooth from those who had charge of it, and raising it aloft, placed it on his head many times with adjurations of solemnity and awe; then restoring it to its place, he accompanied it on its way to the city. As it passed along, the river was perfumed with the odours which ascended from the barges, and as it reached the shore the talapoens and nobles of the king and all the chief men advancing into the water took the shrine upon their shoulders and bore it to the palace, accompanied by an impenetrable multitude of spectators. The grandees taking off their costly robes, spread them on the way in order that those who carried that abominable relic might walk upon them.

"The Portuguese who happened to be present were astonished on witnessing this barbarous pomp; and Antonio Toscano, who I have stated elsewhere was of the party, has related to me such extraordinary particulars of the majesty and grandeur with which the tooth was received, that I confess I cannot command suitable language to describe them. In fact, everything that all the emperors and kings of the universe combined could contribute to such a solemnity, each eager to display his power to the utmost, all this was realised by the acts of this barbarian king.

"The tooth was at last deposited in the centre of the courtyard of the palace, under a costly tabernacle, upon which the monarch and all his grandees presented their offerings, declaring their lineage, all which was recorded by scribes nominated for that duty. Here it remained two months, till the wihare (*varela*), which they set about erecting could be constructed, and on which such expenditure was lavished as to cause an insurrection in the kingdom.

"To end the story, I shall here tell of what occurred in the following year, between the king of Kandy and Brama, king of Pegu, respecting these proceedings of Don Juan, king of Ceylon. These matters which Don Juan had transacted so secretly touching the marriage of his pretended daughter with the king of Pegu, as well as the affair of the tooth, soon reached the ear of the king of Kandy, who learning the immense amount of treasure which Brama had given for it, was influenced with envy, (for he was a connection of Don Juan, having married his sister, or as some said his daughter,) and immediately despatched an envoy to Pegu, whom the king received with distinction. He opened the object of his mission, and disclosed, on the part of his master, that the lady whom Don Juan had passed off as his own child, was in reality the daughter of the great chamberlain, and that the tooth, which had been received with so much pomp and adoration, had been fabricated out of the horn of a deer; but he added that the king of Kandy, anxious to ally himself with the sovereign of Pegu, had commissioned him to offer in marriage a princess who was in reality his own offspring, and not supposititious; besides which he gave him to understand that the Kandyan monarch was the possessor and depositary of the genuine tooth of Buddha, neither the one which Don Constantine had seized at Jaffna-patam, nor yet that which was held by the king of Pegu, being the true one,—a fact which he was prepared to substantiate by documents and ancient olas.

"Brama listened to his statement and pondered it in his mind; but seeing that the princess had already received the oaths of fidelity as queen, and that the tooth had been welcomed with so much solemnity, and deposited in a wihare, specially built for it, he resolved to hush up the affair, to avoid confessing himself a dupe, (for kings must no more admit themselves to be in error in their dealings with us, than we in our dealings with them). Accordingly, he gave as his reply, that he was sensible of the honour designed for him by the proffered alliance with the royal family of Kandy, and likewise by the offer of the tooth; that he returned his thanks to the king, and as a mark of consideration would send back by his ambassadors a ship laden with presents. He caused two vessels to be prepared for sea, with cargoes of rice and rich cloths, one for Don Juan, and the other for the king of Kandy; and in that for Don Juan, he embarked all the Portuguese subjects whom he had held in captivity, and amongst them Antonio Toscano, who has told me these things many times. These ships having arrived at Ceylon, the one which was for the Kandyan port had her cables cut and was stranded before she could discharge her cargo, so that all was lost and the ambassador drowned; some said that this was done by order of the Singhalese king, Don Juan, and if so, it was probably a stratagem of the great chamberlain, for the king himself had no genius for plots. Thus things remained as they were, nothing farther having been attempted or done."

CHAP. VI.

GAMPOLA AND THE COFFEE REGIONS.

THE great road from Kandy to the Sanitarium of Neuera-ellia, a distance of nearly fifty miles, is carried to the height of six thousand feet above the sea, and passes, for the greater part of the ascent, through the mountain districts, which have recently been enriched by the formation of plantations of coffee. For the first twelve miles it runs within a short distance of the Mahawelli-ganga, crossing it by the bridge of Peradenia, which here spans the river with a single arch of more than two hundred feet, and its crown nearly seventy feet above the stream. Such is the volume and violence of the torrent that rushes through this narrow channel during the deluge of the monsoons, that in 1834 the waters rose sixty feet above the ordinary level, hurrying along the trunks of forest trees, and the carcases of buffaloes, elephants, and deer.

The drive from Kandy to Gampola is calculated to convey a favourable impression of the wealth and comfort of the peasantry. The road is lined with bazaars for the sale of European as well as native commodities; and it winds between farm-houses and granaries, and fields rich in cattle for the labour of the rice-lands.

But the dwellings visible from the highway are principally occupied by low-country Singhalese, who have resorted to the hills as dealers; the genius of the Kandyans being morbidly opposed to traffic of all kinds, and to intercourse with strangers. In conformity with this feeling, the villages are concealed in glens and woods, and, wherever it is practicable, the houses are built in nooks and hollows, where they would escape observation, were it not that their position is betrayed by the crowns of the few coco-nut palms with which they are ordinarily surrounded, or the delicate green hue of the terraces for the cultivation of rice.

Coupled with this love of retirement and impatience of intrusion, one of the main features in the general character of the Kandyans is their feudal subserviency to the conventional authority of their chiefs, and the unreasonable devotion with which they worship rank. Although all real power for oppression or coercion has been abolished under the mild rule of the British, this form of traditionary subjection remains unaltered, and apparently indelible in the national instincts of the peasantry.

In intelligence and acuteness they are inferior to the people of the low country, whose faculties have been sharpened as well by longer intercourse with Europeans, as by educational training; but it is doubtful, whether in moral and social qualities, the Kandyans, with all their vices, are not superior to the Singhalese.[1] Tyranny has made both races cowardly, and cowardice false, till such is the prevalence of prevarication, that shame has ceased to operate; judges estimate the truth of evidence by probability; and during my own tenure of office, a chief, with the native title of *Banda*, equivalent to the rank of a "prince," petitioned for the remission of his punishment for perjury, on the ground

---

[1] A sketch of the national character of the Singhalese will be found in Sir J. EMERSON TENNENT'S *History of Christianity in Ceylon*, ch. vi. p. 249. DE QUINCEY, in an article on Ceylon, in *Blackwood's Magazine* for November, 1843, which has since been embodied in the collected edition of his works, has described the Kandyans as "a desperate variety of the tiger-man, agile and fierce, but smooth, insinuating, and full of subtlety as a snake." As compared with the low-country Singhalese, whom he paints as soft and passive, the Kandyan is represented as "a ferocious little bloody coward, full of mischief as a monkey, grinning with desperation, and laughing like a hyena."—DE QUINCEY, *Works*, p. 14. The extreme exaggeration and inaccuracy of these passages are accounted for by the personal inexperience of the author, De Quincey having applied to the normal condition of a race, epithets merited by rare barbarities, such as the massacre of Major Davie's companions.

that such a crime was notoriously venial amongst his countrymen.

Amidst so many vices, one redeeming virtue which elevates the people of Ceylon, especially the highlanders of Kandy, above the corresponding classes in India, is the strong affection which binds together those of the same family, and the reverence and tender regard with which old age is honoured and watched over by youth. During the rebellion of 1817, instances occurred of sons and brothers who voluntarily delivered themselves up to the British in broken-hearted despair on learning the fate of their kindred; and one of the ceremonies which leads pilgrims to the summit of Adam's Peak, is the desire to renew the vows of attachment between relatives and friends, and to solemnise, by a reverential salutation at the sacred shrine, the love of the young for their parents.[1]

Gampola, the ancient *Ganga-sri-poora*, "the stately city by the river," was the last of the native capitals of Ceylon before the expiring dynasty removed to Cotta about the year 1410. It was built in the middle of the fourteenth century, and it was here that Ibn Batuta shortly afterwards visited the king by whom it was founded[2]; whose palace he says was situated near a bend of the river called "the estuary of rubies." It was at this spot that his successor, in 1405, was defeated by the Chinese general Ching Ho, and carried captive to Nankin.[3] No ruins or an-

[1] Dr. DAVY, after describing the religious ceremonial at the Sacred Footstep says, "an interesting scene followed, wives affectionately saluted their husbands, children their parents, and friends one another. A grey-headed woman first made her salaam to a venerable old man; — she was moved to tears, and almost kissed his feet. He raised her affectionately, and several middle-aged men then saluted the patriarchal pair. These were salaamed in return by the younger men, who had first paid their respects to the old people, and lastly those of nearly the same standing saluted each other and exchanged betel leaves. The intention of these salutations was of a moral kind; to confirm the ties of friendship, to strengthen family kindness, and remove animosities."— DAVY, pt. ii. ch. ii. p. 345.

[2] BHUWANEKA BAHU IV., about A.D., 1347, *Rajaratnacari*, p. iii.; IBN BATUTA, LEE'S Transl. 4to., ch. xx. p. 186.

[3] For an account of this event see Vol. I. Pt. v. ch. iii. p. 598.

tiquities remain to mark the site of ancient edifices, and the city, like the generality of those in the East, where domestic buildings were formed of such humble materials as wood and earth, has long since crumbled into dust.

But Gampola has a higher modern interest, inasmuch as it was one of the first places in Ceylon at which the systematic culture of coffee was attempted[1]; and it is at the present day one of the most important localities in the district, as the point at which the great roads converge which connect the rich districts of Pusilawa, Dimboola, Kotmalie, and Ambogammoa with Kandy and Colombo.

The rest-house of Gampola is one of the most frequented in Ceylon; and whilst halting here a servant showed me his hand swollen and inflamed with the appearance of a puncture between the thumb and forefinger, caused, as he stated, by a "tarantula," as the huge spider *Mygale fasciata* is vulgarly and erroneously called in Ceylon. It bit him, he said, in the wine cellar, when lifting a bottle in the dark; but it is more than probable that he had mistaken the bite of a centipede or the nip from the chelæ of a scorpion for that of a spider; for although it is certain that the mandibles of the latter are furnished with a poisonous venom, I have never heard of any well-authenticated instance of injury resulting from its attacks. In fact, from the position and direction of the jaws the creature would most likely have to turn over in some awkward way in order to inflict a wound, and even then its jaws could scarcely embrace an object of such size as the finger or hand of a man.

The largest specimens I have seen of the mygale were at Gampola and its vicinity, and one taken in the godown of this rest-house nearly covered with its legs an ordinary-sized breakfast plate.

This hideous creature does not weave a broad web or net like other spiders, but nevertheless it forms a

[1] The first plantation was opened at Gampola by Mr. George Birch.

comfortable mansion in the wall of a neglected building, the hollow of a tree, or the eaves of an overhanging stone. This it lines throughout with a tapestry of silk of a tubular form; and a texture so exquisitely fine and closely woven, that no moisture can penetrate it. The extremity of the tube is carried out to the entrance, where it expands into a little platform, stayed by braces to the nearest objects that afford a firm hold. In particular situations, where the entrance is exposed to the wind, the mygale, on the approach of the monsoon, extends the strong tissue above it so as to serve as an awning to prevent the access of rain.

The construction of this silken dwelling is exclusively designed for the domestic luxury of the spider; it serves no purpose in trapping or securing prey, and no external disturbance of the web tempts the creature to sally out to surprise an intruder, as the epeira and its congeners would.

As to the stories told of the mygale catching and killing birds, I am satisfied, both from inquiry and observation, that at least in Ceylon they are destitute of truth, and that (unless in the possible case of acute suffering from hunger) this creature shuns all descriptions of food except soft insects and annelides. A lady at Marandan, near Colombo, told me that she had, on one occasion, seen a little house-lizard (*gecko*) seized and devoured by one of these ugly spiders.

The soil and situation of Gampola have proved unfavourable for the growth of coffee; but there is hardly one of the magnificent hills seen from it that has not been taken possession of by European settlers within a very recent period. Although the coffee plant, the *kăwăh* of the Arabs, which is a native of Africa, was known in Yemen at an early period, it is doubtful whether there, or in any other country in the world, its use as a stimulant had been discovered before the beginning of the fifteenth century. The Arabs introduced it early into India, and before the arrival of the Portuguese or Dutch, the tree had been grown in

Ceylon; but the preparation of a beverage from its berries was totally unknown to the Singhalese[1], who only employed its tender leaves for their curries, and its delicate jasmine-like flowers for ornamenting their temples and shrines.

The Dutch carried the coffee tree to Batavia in 1690[2], and about the same time they began its cultivation in Ceylon. But as their operations were confined to the low lands around Negombo and Galle, the locality proved unsuitable, both in temperature and soil. The natives, too, were unfavourably disposed to the innovation; and although the quality of the coffee is said to have been excellent[3], it was found that it could not be raised to advantage in comparison with that of Java, where the experiment proved eminently successful. At length, in 1739, the effort was suspended[4]; but the culture, although neglected by the government, was not abandoned by the Singhalese, who, having learned the commercial value of the article, continued to grow it in small quantities, and after the British obtained possession of Ceylon, the Moors, who collected it in the villages, brought it into Colombo and Galle to be bartered for cutlery, cotton, and trinkets.[5]

On the occupation of Kandy, after its cession in 1815, the English found the coffee tree growing in the vicinity of the temples; and gardens had been formed of it by

---

[1] CHRISTIAN WOLF, *Life and Adventures*, p. 117.

[2] CRAWFURD, in his *Dictionary of the Indian Island*, says, a single plant of coffee grown in a garden at Batavia, about A.D. 1690, was sent by the Governor-General to Holland, as a present to the Governor of the Dutch East India Company. It was planted in the Botanic Gardens at Amsterdam, where it flourished, bore fruit, and the fruit produced young plants. Some of the latter were sent to the Colony of Surinam, where coffee began to be cultivated as an article of trade, A.D. 1718, and from thence the first coffee plants were taken to the English and French West India Islands. From Java the cultivation of coffee has been extended to Sumatra, Celebes, Bali, and several of the Philippine Islands.

[3] See *Memoir*, by M. BURNAND, *Asiatic Journal*, vol. xii. p. 444.

[4] *Memoir* of Governor SCHREUDER, Appendix to LEE'S *Ribeyro*, p. 193.

[5] BERTOLACCI gives the export of coffee from Ceylon, in
1806, 189½ candies, about 94,500 lbs.
1810, 435 ,, 217,500 lbs.
1813, $432\frac{2}{3}$,, 216,500 lbs.

the king on the banks of the Mahawelli-ganga, and close to his palace at Hanguran-ketti.

So soon as Sir Edward Barnes had made such progress with the great central high road as to open a communication with the hill country, it was obvious to his clear and energetic mind that so grand a work would be a reproach instead of a trophy, were its uses to be limited to mere military exigencies, without conducing to the material prosperity of the island. Hence, even before its final completion, his measures were taken to emulate in Ceylon the industrial enterprise of India. The preparation of indigo was attempted, but unsuccessfully, near Veangodde; that of sugar was encouraged on the alluvial lands of the interior; and, taught by experience the inaptitude of the lowlands for the profitable cultivation of coffee [1], Sir Edward formed the first upland plantation about 1825, on his own estate at Gangaroowa, adjoining the gardens of Peradenia.

The moment was rendered propitious by a concurrence of favourable circumstances; the use of coffee had been largely increased in the United Kingdom by the remission of one half the import duty in 1825, — a measure under the impetus of which the consumption nearly doubled itself within three years [2], and went on augmenting till it outstripped the powers of production in the West Indies, and raised the value of coffee to such a pitch that the produce of India and Ceylon came into rapid demand at highly remunerative prices.[3]

Coupled with these fiscal facilities, another important change was in progress, which vastly enlarged the

[1] The first attempts by British speculators to cultivate coffee in Ceylon, were made on the banks of the Gindura, about sixteen miles from Galle. The failure was so signal, that the plants were taken up to put down sugar cane, and these in turn made way for coco-nut palms. —LEWIS' *Coffee Planting in Ceylon.* Colombo, 1855, p. 5.

[2] Consumption of Coffee in the United Kingdom,

1824	7,993,040 lbs.
1825	10,766,112 „
1826	12,724,139 „
1827	14,974,373 „

[3] PORTER'S *Progress of the Nation,* p. 373, 549.

demand for coffee, not only in Great Britain, but over a great part of Western Europe; and especially in Belgium and France;—this was the annually diminishing consumption of wine concurrently with an increasing consumption of coffee[1] and tea. In England coffee had come to be a necessary of life for the poor, as well as a luxury to the opulent classes.

Almost before the first crops of Ceylon could be shipped, the industry of her most formidable rivals in Jamaica, Dominica, and Guiana was paralysed by the conduct of the slaves subsequent to emancipation; and the production of these islands began to decline at the moment when Geylon was entering on her new career.[2] It was under these circumstances that an experiment was inaugurated in the Kandyan highlands, which, within less than a quarter of a century, has effected an industrial revolution in the island, converting Ceylon from a sluggish military cantonment into an enterprising British colony, and transferring the supply of one of the first requisites of society from the western to the eastern hemisphere.

The example of the Governor was speedily followed; plantations were opened at Gampola and elsewhere,

---

[1] *Enquête Legislative sur l'Impôt des Boissons.* Paris, 1851, *Rapport*, p. 35. So great has been the change of manners and habits in the United Kingdom, even within the last twenty years, that had the population in 1854, taking it at 27,600,000, drunk coffee, tea, and cocoa in the same proportion as the population of 1835-6 (the latter being about 24,350,000), the increase in the consumption of these articles would have been only 8,125,000 lbs., *whereas it has actually been* 42,918,215 lbs. In 1801 the individual consumption of coffee in Great Britain was one ounce per annum for each person, in 1831 it had risen to 1 lb. 5½ oz.

[2] The Imports of Coffee into the United Kingdom.

Year.	From the West Indies.	Exports from Ceylon.
1827	29,419,598 lbs.	1,792,448 lbs.
1837	15,577,888 „	6,756,848 „
1847	5,259,449 „	19,475,904 „
1857	4,054,028 „	67,453,680 „

and the first attempt, though begun in a comparatively low altittide sufficed to demonstrate the superiority of the hill country over the low land, for cultivation, both in the quality and the abundance of the produce.

At this crisis the fate of the experiment was decided, by the adoption, in 1835, of a measure which Sir Edward Barnes had urged on the home government in 1826; the duty was equalised upon East and West India coffee, imported into the United Kingdom, at the moment when the failing supply of the latter turned attention eagerly and anxiously towards Ceylon. In the very next year nearly four thousand acres of mountain forest were felled and planted, and in an incredibly short time the sale of crown lands exceeded forty thousand acres per annum.[1]

The mountain ranges on all sides of Kandy became rapidly covered with plantations; the great valleys of Doombera, Ambogammoa[2], Kotmalie, and Pusilawa were occupied by emulous speculators; they settled in the steep passes ascending to Neuera-ellia; they penetrated to Badulla and Oovah, and coffee trees quickly bloomed on solitary hills around the very base of Adam's Peak.

The first ardent adventurers pioneered the way through

---

[1] The sales of crown lands between 1837 and 1845 were as follows:

1837 . . .	3,661 acres.
1838 . . .	10,401 ,,
1839 . . .	9,570 ,,
1840 . . .	42,841 ,,
1841 . . .	78,685 ,,
1842 . . .	48,533 ,,
1843 . . .	58,336 ,,
1844 . . .	20,415 ,,
1845 . . .	19,062 ,,

Much of this land was bought on speculation, and not with a view to immediate cultivation.

[2] Of these districts, one of the first towards which the rush of enterprise was directed was the beautiful region of Ambogammoa, the altitude of which, combined with its vicinity to the Kalany river, which is navigable for a great distance above Colombo, promised the utmost amount of success to the experiment. A new road was constructed to connect it with the capital, and thousands of acres of crown lands were eagerly bought up for future speculation. But in no quarter of the island has disappointment been so great as in these favourite valleys. The quality of the soil proved deceptive, a large proportion of the estates opened were allowed to return to their original wildness, and at the present moment, although the number of plantations is still large, the average produce of the district is the lowest in Ceylon.

pathless woods, and lived for months in log-huts, whilst felling the forest and making their preliminary nurseries preparatory to planting; but within a few years the tracks by which they came were converted into highways, and their cabins replaced by bungalows, which, though rough, were picturesque and replete with European comforts. The new life in the jungle was full of excitement and romance, the wild elephants and leopards retreated before the axe of the forester; the elk supplied their table with venison, and jungle fowl and game were within call and abundant.

The coffee mania was at its climax in 1845. The Governor and the Council, the Military, the Judges, the Clergy, and one half the Civil Servants penetrated the hills, and became purchasers of crown lands. The East India Company's officers crowded to Ceylon to invest their savings, and capitalists from England arrived by every packet. As a class, the body of emigrants was more than ordinarily aristocratic, and if not already opulent, were in haste to be rich. So dazzling was the prospect that expenditure was unlimited; and its profusion was only equalled by the ignorance and inexperience of those to whom it was entrusted. Five millions sterling are said to have been sunk within less than as many years; but this estimate is probably exaggerated. The rush for land was only paralleled by the movement towards the mines of California and Australia, but with this painful difference, that the enthusiasts in Ceylon, instead of thronging to disinter, were hurrying to bury their gold.

In the midst of these visions of riches, a crash suddenly came which awoke victims to the reality of ruin. The financial explosion of 1845 in Great Britain speedily extended its destructive influence to Ceylon; remittances ceased, prices fell, credit failed, and the first announcement on the subsidence of turmoil, was the doom of protection, and the withdrawal of the distinctive duty, which had so long screened British plantations from competition with the coffee of Java and Brazil.

The consternation thus produced in Ceylon was proportionate to the extravagance of the hopes that were blasted; estates were forced into the market, and madly sold off for a twentieth part of the outlay incurred in forming them.[1] Others that could not even be sacrificed, were deserted and allowed to return to jungle. For nearly three years the enterprise appeared paralysed; the ruined disappeared, and the timid retreated; but those who combining judgment with capital persevered, succeeded eventually, not alone in restoring energy to the enterprise, but in imparting to it the prudence and experience gleaned from former disasters.

The crisis, had it not been precipitated by the calamities of 1845, must inevitably have ensued from the indiscretions of the previous period; and the healthy condition in which coffee-planting appears at the present day in Ceylon, results from the correction of the errors then committed. It is no exaggeration to say, that there is not a single well-established principle which now guides the management of estates, and the conduct of their proprietors, that was not preceded by a directly opposite policy prior to 1845. Observation has since discerned the true tests of soil and aspect; former delusions as to high altitudes have been exploded; unprofitable districts avoided, unproductive estates abandoned; and in lieu of the belief that a coffee-bush, once rooted, would continue ever after to bear crops without manure, and to flourish in defiance of weeds and neglect, every

---

[1] A writer in the *Calcutta Review*, for March, 1857, cites numerous instances in which valuable estates were sold in the panic for nominal sums: two estates in Badulla which had cost 10,000*l*. were sold for 350*l*.; the Hindugalla plantation, which cost 10,000*l*., produced 500*l*. Mr. AUSTIN, in an able paper attached to LEES' *Translation of Ribeyro*, says "an estate that was sold in 1843 for 15,000*l*. was knocked down last month (1847) for 40*l*. only." — p. 229. Mr. RIGG, in the *Journal of the Indian Archipelago* for 1852, p. 130, describes the loss in Ceylon between 1841 and 1847 as *ninety* per cent. of the gross amount previously invested in coffee planting, but this is an excessive estimate. Mr. FERGUSON'S calculation is probably nearer the truth, that in addition to the money wasted by extravagant management, the extent of abandoned estates was equal to *one tenth* of those originally opened. — *Colombo Observer*, 1857.

estate is now tended like a garden, and the soil enriched artificially in proportion to the produce it bears. Expenditure has been reduced within the bounds of discretion; an acre of forest-land can be brought under crop in 1857 for one tenth what it cost in 1844; and although the extravagant prices, and still more extravagant expectations, of that period, have been dissipated, coffee-planting at the present day, under careful supervision, promises to be as sound an investment as moderate enterprise can hope for.

But whatever may be the ascertained advantages of Ceylon in point of soil, temperature, and moisture; and however bountiful may be the yield of the plants, the speculation must always be estimated in connection with the cost and vicissitudes with which it is unhappily associated. Anxiety must be inseparable from an undertaking exclusively dependent on immigrant labour; and liable to be affected at the most critical moment by its capricious fluctuations. No temptation of wages, and no prospect of advantage, has hitherto availed to overcome the repugnance of the Singhalese and Kandyans to engage in any work on estates, except the first process of felling the forests. Every subsequent operation must be carried on by coolies from Malabar and the Coromandel coast, whose arrival is uncertain, and whose departure being influenced by causes arising in India, may be precipitated by the most unforeseen occurrences.[1] These labourers have to be remunerated at high rates in the silver currency of India, the value of which fluctuates with the exchanges; and fed on rice imported for their exclusive consumption, burthened with all the charges of freight, duty, and carriage to the hills. The crop, when saved on the estate, has either to encounter the risks incident to transport by hand, through mountains as yet un-opened by roads; or the

[1] In 1858 the number of Tamil labourers arriving in Ceylon was 96,000. The number taking their departure from the island was 50,000.

chances of deterioration to which it is exposed in bullock-carts during long journeys to the coast.

Evils still more formidable from natural causes beset the trees during their growth: eddying winds in the mountain valleys loosen the plants, and injure the bark; wild cats, monkeys, and squirrels prey upon the ripening berries; caterpillars devour the leaves, and at intervals, a plague of insects, known to planters as the *coffee-bug*, but in reality a species of coccus [1], establish themselves on the young shoots and buds, and cover them with a noisome incrustation of scales, enclosing their larvæ, from the pernicious influence of which the fruit shrivels and drops off.[2]

At other seasons, the golunda rats [3], when the seeds of the nilloo (*strobilanthes*), on which they feed, are exhausted [4], invade the plantations in swarms, gnaw off the young branches, and divest the tree of buds and bloom. As many as a thousand of these vermin have been killed in a day on a single estate, and the Malabar coolies esteem them a luxury, and eat them roasted or fried in coco-nut oil.

Still, in defiance of all risks and discouragement, the rapid extension of the cultivation of coffee in Ceylon is the most irrefragable test of the suitability of the island for its growth and the profit at which it may be conducted By far the most valuable statistical record on this subject, is a document prepared by Mr. A. M. FERGUSON, from data collected by the Planters' Association, exhibiting in detail the number of estates in 1857, the proportion of acres under bearing, the amount of their produce, and the

---

[1] *Lecanium Coffeæ*, Walker.

[2] The history of these insects is so remarkable, that I have appended as a note to this chapter an account of them prepared chiefly from a report drawn up by the late Dr. GARDNER, shortly after attention had been attracted to the ravages occasioned by their visitations in the coffee estates of the interior.

[3] *Golunda Elliotti*, Gray. See KELAART'S *Fauna Zeylan.*, p. 67.

[4] See *ante*, Vol. I. Pt. I. ch. iii. p. 91.

labour required on each during crop-time.[1] The general result is, that on 404 estates (irrespective of large tracts of unfelled forest, reserved for future extension), the area yielding coffee was 63,771 acres, and that planted, but not yet bearing, 17,179. The number of Malabar coolies employed, estimating them at two to each acre in crop-time, was 129,200, and the produce on an average of the two previous years, 347,100 cwt. of coffee.[2]

This is, of course, exclusive of the quantity grown by the natives around their villages and detached dwellings, of which in the same year 160,000 cwt. were exported, besides the quantity retained for home consumption. Estimating the area, therefore, by the produce, and taking the latter at the average of 5½ cwt. to each acre, it would appear that not less than 130,000 acres of land were yielding coffee in 1857, of which 50,000 at least were held by natives of Ceylon.

As to the future prospect of the colony, Mr. FERGUSON calculates that, suitable lands yet to be brought under cultivation may add *treble* to the present acreage, and the produce, by improved processes, may be increased at least twenty-five per cent. Should prices in Europe continue such as to encourage enterprise in Ceylon, and no unforeseen occurrences obstruct the influx of immigrant labour from India, Mr. FERGUSON looks forward to the day when a quarter of a million of cultivated acres, together with the native crops, may furnish *two* million cwt. of coffee as the annual production of the island.[3]

However large this estimate may seem, it must be borne in mind that the actual expansion of the trade has hitherto justified every previous conjecture as to the capabilities of the colony: within twenty years, the

[1] This table is so valuable as an historic record, that I have appended it to the present chapter, together with a map, by Mr. Arrowsmith, showing the locality of each estate.

[2] This, it will be observed, is at the rate of but 5½ cwt. per acre.

[3] Colombo Observer, 1857.

value of the coffee exported has risen from 107,000*l.* in 1837 to 1,296,736*l.* in 1857; and whatever uncertainty may be felt for the future, as to the probable consumption of a production so immensely augmented, it must be borne in mind that already markets are opening in which the demand seems susceptible of almost infinite extension. France, last year, received more than one-third of the coffee sent from Ceylon; a very considerable quantity is shipped annually to Holland (a portion of it probably in transit to Belgium and Germany); Australia is an increasing consumer; the United States take a yearly supply; Singhalese coffee has been sent to South America; Calcutta and Madras received it from Colombo, and even the Arabian and Persian races have, in recent years, been transferring their taste from the berry of Mocha, to that of Malabar and Ceylon.

Where circumstances enable the proprietor to be resident on his own estate, and to superintend its operations and control its expenditure in person, few colonial pursuits present attractions superior to these exhibited by Ceylon, either as to actual enjoyment or reasonable returns for investment. But where the capitalist is helplessly reliant on the honour and services of a representative on his distant possessions; under circumstances in which few have the resolution to resist stimulants and the usual devices for diversifying monotony and overcoming the ennui attendant on isolation and solitude; property of this kind is accompanied by inextricable risks and anxieties; and the owner will be often tempted to ascribe to bad faith or neglect, the disappointments, outlay, and losses which are in reality attributable to ordinary vicissitudes rather than to the infidelity of agents.

Amongst the many public works by which Sir Henry G. Ward has signalised his government of Ceylon one of the most important is the suspension-bridge which he has succeeded in throwing across the Mahawelli-ganga at Gampola; it completes the communication between the central capital and the coffee districts of the Southern Zone, and an object of the highest value to the planting interests. But the early settlers in these hills will long remember with interest, the ancient ferry, the passage of which was frequently attended with danger; when the river, swollen by sudden rains in the mountains, swept past in a torrent, sometimes raised thirty feet above the customary level.

THE OLD GAMPOLA FERRY.

STATISTICS OF CEYLON COFFEE

(From the "Ceylon

Number.	Names of Districts.	Number of Estates.	Bearing.	Not yet Bearing.	Total in Cultivation.	Average Crop last two Years.	Crop per Acre.	Average Cultivation on Estates.
			Acres.	Acres.	Acres.	Cwt.	Cwt.	Acres.
1	ALLAGALLA .	14	1,900	400	2,300	7,000	3·7	164
2	AMBOGAMMOA .	21	4,340	290	4,630	12,000	2·7	220
3	BADULLA . .	23	2,300	500	2,800	13,000	5·6	122
4	DIMBOOLA, LOWER	7	1,590	170	1,760	8,500	5·3	251
5	DIMBOOLA, UPPER	7	1,110	330	1,440	3,500	3·1	206
6	DOLLASSBAGE .	18	2,900	370	3,270	9,500	3·3	182
7	DOOMBERE .	9	1,520	250	1,770	16,000	10·5	197
8	HANTANNE . .	22	4,090	700	4,790	16,000	3·9	217
	Carried forward	121	19,750	3,010	22,760	85,500		

PLANTATIONS, 1857. BY A. M. FERGUSON, Esq.

Observer," 11*th July*, 1857.

Probable Crop in 1857-58.	Labourers required during Crop time.	Names of Estates to which the foregoing Statistics apply.
Cwts.	Coolies.	
8,000	4,000	Coodoogalle, Peak, Kirimittie, Allagalla, Oolankanda, Dekinde, Moragaha, Wyrley Grove, Amanapoora, Kadaganava, Gangarooa, Ingrogalla (?) (?).
13,000	6,000	Imboolpittia, Hyndford, Wattewelle, Mount Jean, Inchyra, Trafalgar, Agrawatte, Wadiacadoola, Deekoya, Gangawatte, Templestowe, Woodstock, Galbodde, Koorookoodia, Atherton, Barcaple, Gilston, Henawella, Mookalana, Hangran-Oya, Dahanaike.
15,000	5,000	Wayvelhena, Ootoombye, Gourakelle, Passera Polligolle, Kottugodde, Oodoowerra, Gongaltenne, Glen Alpin, Baddegamme or Spring Valley, Cannavarella, Nahavella, Weweise, Debedde, Dickbedde, Kahagalle, Happotella, Unugalla, Redipanne, Elizabeth, Cooroondokelle (?) (?) (?).
9,000	3,000	Kellewatte, Bogahapatne, Niagara, Union, Hudson, Stoneycliff, Hunugalle.
4,200	2,000	Wattegodde, Scalpa, Louisa, Ratmalkelle, Radella, Palaradella, Hopewell.
10,400	5,000	Kooroondawatte, Paragalle, Hillside, Barnagalla, Raxawa, Madoolhena, Malgolla, Natakanda, Allakolla, Dorset, Windsor Forest, Penylan, Kellie, Kelvin, Kattaram, Hormusjie, Miroote, Oorakande.
18,000	3,500	Rajewelle No. 1, Rajewelle No. 2, Mahaberia, Ambecotta, Cangawatte, Deegalla, Teldenia, Kondissally, Palikelle.
19,000	7,000	Doonomadalawa, Faricland, Hendrick's, Hantenne, Primrosehill, Peradenia, Govinda, Mount Pleasant, Dodangwella, Richmond, Shrub's Hill, Hindogalla, Amblamana, Gallaha, Ingrogalla, Ooragalle, Horagalle, Kitoolmoola, Oodoowella, Maha Oya, Dunally, Galoya.
96,600	35,500	

Number.	Names of Districts.	Number of Estates.	Bearing.	Not yet Bearing.	Total in Cultivation.	Average Crop last two Years.	Crop per Acre.	Average Cultivation on Estates.
			Acres.	Acres.	Acres.	Cwt.	Cwt.	Acres.
	Brought forward	121	19,750	3,010	22,760	85,500		
9	Hewáhette, Lower	17	2,550	720	3,270	16,000	6·3	192
10	Hewahette, Upper	11	1,790	944	2,734	9,000	5·6	249
11	Hunasgeria .	17	3,661	558	4,219	28,000	7·6	248
12	Kaduganava .	20	3,976	1,651	5,627	17,000	4·3	281
13	Kalibokka .	13	2,660	770	3,430	20,000	7·5	264
14	Kornegalle .	20	2,500	750	3,250	10,000	4·0	162
15	Kotmalie . .	22	3,800	260	4,060	18,000	4·7	184
16	Knuckles . .	16	2,045	792	2,837	12,000	5·9	177
17	Matelle, East	27	3,291	1,712	5,003	26,000	7·9	185
	Carried forward	284	46,023	11,167	57,190	241,500		

Probable Crop in 1857–58.	Labourers required during Crop time.	Names of Estates to which the following Statistics apply.
Cwts.	Coolies.	
96,600	35,500	
20,000	6,000	Charlemont, Medegamma No. 1, Medegamma No. 2, Bowlana, Maousakella, Belwood, Galantenne, Deltotte, Great Valley, Little Valley, Bopitia, Puttiagamma, Naranghena, Waloya, Lool-Condura, Codugalla, Kalloogalpatne.
11,000	5,000	Gonavey, Hope, Mooloya, Nathoongodde, Yakabendakelly, Rickellegascadde, Wevatenne, Hangurankette, Pookeloya, Gallela, Cavinella.
32,000	8,000	Galgawatte, Happoowidde, Nilocanda, Kittoolgalla, Hunugalla, Halgolla, Horagalla, Mahatenna, Dotallagalla, Elkadua, Algooltenne, Waygalla, Hunasgeria, Patampahi, Udogodde, Gavatenne, Ellagalla.
22,000	8,000	De Soysa's, Mahabelongalla, Solomon's, Churchhill, Franklands, Alpittykanda, Providence Mount, Prospect, Cottagalla, Kallagalla, Wackittiatenne, Gona-Adica, Gadadessa, Hunegalla, Ambelawa, Sinipitia, Ashbourne, Bokanda, Villakande, Kehelwatte.
23,500	6,000	Relugas, Hoolankanda, Deyanilla, Galheria, Nillomally, Hunnnagalla, Maousakelle, Madoolkelley, Hatella, Wattikelley, Malwattey, Ratnatenne, Lagallakanda.
13,000	5,000	Handrookanda, Bulatvellekanda, Kattuwella, Moorootikanda, Dodangtalawa, Goongannua, Paragodde, Ambacoombra, Oodahena, Morrakanda, Katookitool, Dunira, Rockhill, Greenwood, Galgedera, Boldegalla, Tallatenne, Hatbowe, Doolwella, Belloongodde.
19,000	7,000	Bowhill, Kadianlena, Baharundra, Kataboola, Kooroowakka, Oonoocotooa, Telesangalla, Yallebende, Hennwelle, Oonoogalpatne, Harangolla, Tyspane, Bellevue, Queensberry, Doombegastalawa, Habogastalawa, Doonuwille, Kolapatna, Gigiranoya, Gongolla Fettercairn, Cattoogalla.
16,000	5,000	Allakolla, Kandekettia, Leangolla, Madakelle, Katooloya, Kootooatenne, Tunisgalla, Dalookoya, Bellses, Bambraella, Battagalla, Middleton, Moraga, Goomera, Lebanon, Gouragalla.
37,000	8,000	Nagalla, Gammadua, Kensington, Mitchell's, Callagalla, Opalgalla, Ellagalla, Cattaratenne, Dankande, Midland Attgodde, Bambragalla No. 1, Cabroosa Ella, Bambragalla No. 2, Oodelamana, Nicholoya, Poengalla, Cabragalla, Petikanda, Sylva Kande, Kinrara, Damboolagalla, Kandenewera, Maousagalla, Wiriapolle, Godapolla No. 1, Godapolla No. 2.
290,100	93,500	

Number.	Names of Districts.	Number of Estates.	Bearing.	Not yet Bearing.	Total in Cultivation.	Average Crop last two Years.	Crop per Acre.	Average Cultivation on Estates.
			Acres.	Acres.	Acres.	Cwt.	Cwt.	Acres.
	Brought forward	284	46,023	11,167	57,190	241,500	"	"
18	MATEILE, WEST	16	2,100	830	2,930	15,500	7·4	183
19	MATURATTE .	10	330	890	1,220	2,600	7·9	122
20	MEDAMAHANEWERA	9	895	450	1,345	4,500	5·0	149
21	NILAMBE . .	9	2,180	390	2,570	14,000	6·4	285
22	PUSILAWA . .	28	6,330	570	6,900	40,000	6·3	246
23	RANGBODDE .	19	1,411	952	2,363	7,000	5·0	124
24	RANGALLA . .	8	1,095	820	1,915	9,000	8·0	239
25	SAFFRAGAM .	7	1,200	500	1,700	5,000	4·2	243
26	WALIAPANE .	5	777	30	807	4,500	5·8	161
27	YACDESSA . .	8	1,430	580	2,010	3,500	2·4	251
	Totals & Averages	403	63,771	17,179	80,950	347,100	5·5	200

Probable Crop in 1857–58.	Labourers required during Crop time.	Names of the Estates to which the following Statistics apply.
Cwt.	Coolies.	
290,100	93,500	
20,000	5,000	Kent, Amboka, Seligamma, Beradowella, Vicarton, Borders, Ettapolla, Berkshire, Wiltshire, Hampshire, Madua, Madewelle, Ancoombra, Ballacadua, Gorala Ella, Lagahaella.
8,500	2,000	Goodwood, Gonapatna, Mormon Hill, Allakollawewa, Smiths's Maduren, Newera, Manapitia, Seaton, Alma, Bartholomeuz.
6,500	2,000	Nugatenne, Gallakella, California, Ellen Maria, Alea Vittene, Dodangalla, Woodside, Watte Kelle, Hangrogamme.
15,000	4,000	Wattegodde, Haaloya, Wariagalla, Nilambe, Vedchettia, Colgrain, Nawagalla, Galloway, Knowe, Goorookelle.
42,000	10,000	Moneragalla, Rothschild, Gouracodde, Waygahapittiya, Niapana, Harmony, Katookelle, Yattepiangalla, Doragalla, Dowategas, Peacock, Kalloogalla, Moragalla, Melfort, Blackforest, Delta, Glenlock, Whyddon, Hallebodde, Kattookitool, Kandalawa, Stellenberg, Newmarket, Proprasse, Caragastalawa, Meegolla, Peak, and Peak Forest.
11,000	3,500	Condagalla, Labookelle, Pallagalla, Rangbodde, Bluepills, Rambodde, Weddemulla, Poojagodde, Wavendon, Eyrie, Willisfords's, Sabonadiere's, Tavalamtenne, Poondelloya, Harrow, Eton, Robertson's, Neitner's, Meeriscotoakelle.
15,500	3,600	Cotaganga, Girinde Elle, Lovegrove, Gallebodde, Ranwella, Battagalla, Rangalle No. 1, Rangalle No. 2.
7,000	2,000	Massena, Patigalla, Hatarebage, Springwood, Evarton, Barra, Palamcottah.
4,800	1,200	Alnwick, St. Margaret's, Tulloes, Kirklees (?)
4,500	2,500	Horagalla, Yacdesse, Dotola, Nagastenne, Burn, Galamudina, Bennetsfield, Stenshells.
424,700	129,200	

NOTE.

THE COFFEE BUG.

(*Lecanium Coffeæ*, Walker.)

THE following notice of the *Coccus*, known in Ceylon as the "coffee-bug," and of the singularly destructive effects produced by it on the plants, has been prepared chiefly from a memoir presented to the Ceylon Government by the late Dr. Gardner, in which he traces the history of the insect from its first appearance in the coffee districts, until it had established itself more or less permanently in all the estates in full cultivation throughout the island.

The first thing that attracts attention on looking at a coffee tree which has for some time been infested by this coccus, is the number of brownish wart-like bodies that stud the young shoots and occasionally the margins on the underside of the leaves. Each of these warts or scales is a transformed female, containing a large number of eggs which are hatched within it.

When the young ones come out from their nest, they run about over the plant looking very much like diminutive wood-lice, and at this period there is no apparent distinction between male and female. Shortly after being hatched the males seek the underside of the leaves, while the females prefer the young shoots as a place of abode. If the under surface of a leaf be examined, it will be found to be studded, particularly on its basal half, with minute yellowish-white specks of an oblong form. These are the larvæ of the males undergoing transformation into pupæ, beneath their own skins; some of these specks are always in a more advanced state than the others, the full-grown ones being whitish and scarcely a line long. Some of this size are translucent, the insect having escaped; the darker ones have it still within, of an oblong form, with the rudiment of a wing on each side attached to the lower part of the thorax and closely applied to the sides; the legs are six in number, the four hind ones being directed backwards, the anterior forwards (a peculiarity not occurring in other insects); the two antennæ are also inclined backwards, and from the tail protrude three short bristles, the middle one thinner and longer than the rest.

When the transformation is complete, the mature insect makes its way from beneath the pellucid case[1], all its organs having then attained their full size: the head is subglobular, with two rather prominent black eyes, and two antennæ, each with eleven joints, hairy throughout, and a tuft of rather longer hairs at the apices; the legs are also hairy, the wings are horizontal, of an obovate oblong shape, membranous, and extending a little farther than the bristles of the tail. They have only two nerves, neither of which reaches so far as the tips; one of them runs close to the costal margin, and is much thicker than the other, which branches off from its base and skirts along the inner margin; behind the wings is attached a pair of minute halteres of peculiar form. The possession of wings would appear to be the cause why the full-grown male is more rarely seen on the coffee bushes than the female.

The female, like the male, attaches herself to the surface of the plant, the place selected being usually the young shoots; but she is also to be met with on the margins of the undersides of the leaves (on the upper surface neither the male nor female ever attach themselves); but, unlike the male, which derives no nourishment from the juices of the tree (the mouth being obsolete in the perfect state), she punctures the cuticle with a proboscis (a very short three-jointed *promuscis*), springing as is were from the breast, but capable of being greatly porrected, and inserted in the cuticle of the plant, and through this she abstracts her nutriment. In the early pupa state the female is easily distinguishable from the male, by being more elliptical and much more convex. As she increases in size the skin distends and she becomes smooth and dry; the rings of the body become effaced; and losing entirely the form of an insect, she presents, for some time, a yellowish pustular shape, but ultimately assumes a roundish conical form, of a dark brown colour.[2]

---

[1] Mr. WESTWOOD, who observed the operation in one species, states that they escape backwards, the wings being extended flatly over the head.

[2] There are many other species of the Coccus tribe in Ceylon, some (Pseudococcus?) never appearing as a scale, the female wrapping herself up in a white cottony exudation; many species nearly allied to the true Coccus infest common plants about gardens, such as the Nerium Oleander, Plumeria Acuminata, and others with milky juices: another subgenus (Ceroplastes?), the female of which produces a protecting waxy material, infests the Gendurassa Vulgaris, the Furcræa Gigantea, the Jak tree, Mango, and other common trees.

Until she has nearly reached her full size, she still possesses the power of locomotion, and her six legs are easily distinguishable in the under surface of her corpulent body; but at no period of her existence has she wings. It is about the time of her obtaining full size that impregnation takes place (Réaumur has described the singular manner in which this occurs, *Mém.*, tom. iv.), after which the scale becomes somewhat more conical, assumes a darker colour, and at length is permanently fixed to the surface of the plant, by means of a cottony substance interposed between it and the vegetable cuticle to which it adheres. The scale, when full grown, exactly resembles in miniature the hat of a Cornish miner, there being a narrow rim at the base, which gives increased surface of attachment. It is about $\frac{1}{8}$-inch in diameter, by about $\frac{1}{12}$ deep, and it appears perfectly smooth to the naked eye, but it is in reality studded over with a multitude of very minute warts, giving it a dotted appearance; it is entirely destitute of hairs, except the margin, which is ciliated. The number of eggs contained in one of the scales is enormous, amounting in a single one to 691. The eggs are of an oblong shape, of a pale flesh colour, and perfectly smooth. A few small yellowish maggots are sometimes found with the eggs; these are the larvæ[1] of insects, the eggs of which have been deposited in the female while the scale was soft. They escape when mature by cutting a small round hole in the dorsum of the scale.

It is not till after this pest has been on an estate for two or three years that it shows itself to an alarming extent. During the first year, a few only of the ripe scales are seen scattered over the bushes, generally on the younger shoots; but that year's crop does not suffer much, and the appearance of the tree is little altered. The second year, however, brings a change for the worse; if the young shoots and the underside of the leaves be now examined, the scales will be found to have become much more numerous, and with them appear a multitude of white specks, which are the young scales in a more or less forward state. The clusters of berries now assume a black sooty look, and a great number of them fall off before coming

[1] Of the parasitic Chalcididiæ, many genera of which are well known to deposit their eggs in the soft Coccus, viz.: Encystus, Coccophagus, Pteromalus, Mesosela, Agonioneurus; besides Aphidius, a minutely sized genus of Ichneumonidæ. Most, if not all, these genera are Singhalese.

to maturity; the general health of the tree also begins to fail, and it acquires a blighted appearance. A loss of crop is this year sustained, but to no great extent.

The third year brings about a more serious change, the whole plant acquires a black hue, appearing as if soot had been thrown over it in great quantities; this is caused by the growth of a parasitic fungus[1] over the shoots and the upper surface of the leaves, forming a fibrous coating, somewhat resembling velvet or felt. This never makes its appearance till the insect has been a long time on the bush, and it probably owes its existence there to an unhealthy condition of the juices of the leaf, consequent on the irritation produced by the coccus, since it never visits the upper surface of the leaf until it has fully established itself on the lower. At this period the young shoots have an exceedingly disgusting look from the dense mass of yellow pustular bodies forming on them, the leaves get shrivelled, and the trees become conspicuous in the row. The black ants are assiduous in their visits to them. Two-thirds of the crop is lost, and on many trees not a single berry forms.

As far as it is possible to ascertain, the coffee bushes were not affected before 1843, when Captain Robertson first observed the pest on his estate at Lapalla Galla, whence it spread eastward through other estates, and finally reached all the other estates in the island. It or a very closely allied species has been observed in the Botanic Garden at Peradenia, on the *Citrus acida, Psidium pomiferum, Myrtus Zeylanica, Rosa Indica, Careya arborea, Vitex Negundo,* and other plants. The coffee coccus has generally been first observed in moist hollow places sheltered from the wind; and thence it has spread itself even over the driest and most exposed parts of the island, and in some estates, after attaining a maximum, it has gradually declined, but has shown a liability to reappear, especially in low sheltered situations, and it is believed to prevail most extensively in wet seasons. It is easily transmitted from one estate to another, while in its earlier stages, on the clothes of human beings, and in various other ways, which will readily suggest themselves. Dr. Gardner, after careful consideration and minute examination of estates, arrived at the conclusion, that all

[1] *Racodium?* Species of this genus are not confined to the coffee plant alone in Ceylon, but follow the "bugs" in their attacks on other bushes. It appears like a dense interlaced mesh of fibres, each made up of a single series of minute oblong vesicles applied end to end.

remedies suggested up to that time had utterly failed, and that none at once cheap and effectual was likely to be discovered. He seems also to have been of opinion that the insect was not under human control; and that even if it should disappear, it would only be when it should have worn itself out as other blights have been known to do in some mysterious way. Whether this may prove to be the case or not, is still very uncertain, but everything observed by Dr. Gardner tended to indicate the permanency of the pest.

CHAP. VII.

PUSILAWA AND NEUERA-ELLIA.

From the right bank of the Mahawelli-ganga at Gampola, the road which up to that point keeps the level of the river, begins at once to ascend; and thence to Pusilawa, it winds among the mountains in the most picturesque contortions; sometimes hidden in recesses, into which it retires in search of a passage across a rocky stream, and again emerging to clamber over the opposing hills. For the greater part of the way it is carried along the face of steep acclivities with the scarped cliff on one hand, and on the other a precipitous bank; and in the depths below the Gallatta river is seen, gliding beneath over-arched woods, or foaming amongst reefs and fallen rocks.

The vegetation is as varied as the scenery; — strange trees attract the eye in the forests: the *goraka*[1], with stem and branches yellow from the exudation of gamboge, the *imbul* blazing with crimson blossoms, and the *datura* covered with its snowy flower bells. The banks of the streams glow with the rosy oleander, and the damp ground adjoining them is feathered with tree-ferns[2], which here attain a height of fifteen to twenty feet.

The sides of the mountains here exhibit that strange peculiarity to which I have before alluded[3] of smooth verdant slopes known as *patenas*, occurring capriciously in the midst of forest land; covered with rank lemon-grass, and avoided by all trees except the stunted

[1] *Garcinia cambogia.*

[2] *Alsophila gigantea.*

[3] See *ante*, Vol. I. ch. i. p. 24.

cahatta and the *amusada-nelli*[1], whose thick and pungent bark supplies tannin to the Kandyans.

In these high altitudes the air is so undisturbed, and the silence so profound, that individual sounds, the hum of insects, the voice of birds, or the shrill call of the squirrels, are caught with surprising clearness. Standing at sunset on one of the mountains at Ambogammoa, one can hear distinctly the evening guns fired at Colombo and Kandy, the one thirty and the other twenty miles distant in opposite directions.

At the time of my first visit in 1846, these mountains exhibited a scene of wonderful activity and interest; the woodman's axe resounded in all directions, and the white smoke ascended in clouds from the slopes where the felled trees[2], after being withered and dried by the scorching sun, were fired to get rid of the fallen timber and clear the ground for the reception of the young coffee plants.

At Pusilawa our home on many occasions was the hospitable bungalow of Mr. Worms and his brother, the proprietors of one of the finest plantations in the island. Their estate, which now consists, besides unfelled forest, of upwards of one thousand acres of coffee trees in full bearing, was commenced by themselves in 1841, when the new enterprise was still in its infancy. Their practical knowledge of planting was therefore acquired during its experimental stages; and no capitalists in the colony have contributed more to its advancement by judgment and moderation in times of excitement, and firmness and perseverance in periods of difficulty. Hereafter, when the great project to which they have devoted their lives, shall have attained its full development, Ceylon, in the plenitude of commercial success, will remember with gratitude the names of

[1] *Careya arborea* and *Emblica officinalis.*

[2] For a description of the curious process adopted by the Kandyans for prostrating a whole forest simultaneously, see *ante,* Vol. I. Pt. I. ch. iii. p. 105.

men like these, who were the earliest pioneers of its prosperity.

It is difficult to imagine a scene of greater natural grandeur than that in the midst of which their estates have been formed. The valley of Pusilawa[1] is overhung on its south-eastern side by a chain of wooded hills, the last of which, known as Moonera-galla, or the "Peacock rock," rises upwards of 4000 feet above the level of the sea, and commands a prospect of indescribable beauty and magnificence; embracing far and wide mountains, forests, rivers, cataracts, and plains. The plantations of the Messrs. Worms extend to the very crown of Moonera-galla, and the undulating sides of the hills, which fifteen years ago were concealed by the trees of the Black Forest, are now fenced with roses and covered in all directions with luxuriant coffee bushes.

A plantation of coffee is at every season an object of beauty and interest. The leaves are bright and polished like those of a laurel, but of a much darker green; the flowers, of the purest white, grow in tufts along the top of the branches, and bloom so suddenly, that at morning the trees look as if snow had fallen on them in wreaths during the night. Their jasmine-like perfume is powerful enough to be oppressive, but they last only for a day, and the bunches of crimson berries which succeed resèmble cherries in their brilliancy and size. Within the pulp, concealed in a parchment-like sheath, lies the double seed, which by a variety of processes is freed from its integuments, and converted into coffee.

On this fine estate an attempt has been made to grow tea: the plants thrive surprisingly, and when I saw them they were covered with bloom. But the experiment was defeated by the impossibility of

[1] *Pusilawa* is said to mean the "valley of flowers." Another conjecture is, that the name is derived from the great climbing plant, the *pus-wael* (Entada Pursetha), whose gigantic pods five feet long excite astonishment in passing through the forest. See *ante*, Vol. I. Pt. I. ch. iii. p. 106.

finding skilled labour to dry and manipulate the leaves. Should it ever be thought expedient to cultivate tea in addition to coffee in Ceylon, the adaptation of the soil and climate has thus been established, and it only remains to introduce artisans from China to conduct the subsequent processes.

It will readily be inferred that if the life of a successful planter in these mountains be fraught with anxieties, these are compensated by enjoyment. One can imagine the satisfaction with which he must contemplate the rich prospects that his own energies have created, peopling the solitudes with industry, and teaching the desert to blossom like the rose.

Pusilawa and the surrounding valleys and forests have furnished large collections of objects, illustrative of the zoology of the island; but this is a source of enjoyment of which the successors of the present generation will be deprived, by the felling of the forests and the destruction of the jungle, which now affords protection to multitudes of animals, birds, reptiles, and insects. Their numbers are already declining in this particular spot; but still, such is their profusion in the forests and throughout the region surrounding the coffee estates, that opportunities exist for observing their instincts, under most inviting circumstances, and even the apathetic become interested in watching their habits. These are so striking that they impress themselves on every sense, and stand out clear and illustrative in our recollections of the day and its progress. It is not alone that their crowded associations almost overpower the memory, it is not that they form at all times the incidents and life of the landscape — imparting vivacity to the foliage, and rendering the air harmonious with their motion and their music; but there is a degree of order in their arrangements, and almost of system in their hours of appearing and retiring, that serves, when experience has rendered them familiar, to identify each period of the day with its accustomed visitants, and assigns to morning, noon, and twilight their peculiar symbols.

With the first glimmering of dawn the bats and nocturnal birds retire to their accustomed haunts, in which to hide them from "day's garish eye;" the jackal and the leopard steal back from their nightly chase; the elephants return timidly into the shade of the forest, from the water pools in which they had been luxuriating during the darkness; and the deep-toned bark of the elk resounds through the glens as he retires into the security of the forest. Day breaks, and its earliest blush shows the mists tumbling in turbulent heaps through the deep valleys. The sun bursts upwards with a speed beyond that which marks his progress in the cloudy atmosphere of Europe, and the whole horizon glows with ruddy lustre:

> "Not, as in northern climes, obscurely bright,
> But one unclouded blaze of living light."

At no other moment does the verdure of the mountain woods appear so vivid; each spray dripping with copious dew, and a pendant brilliant twinkling at every leaf; the grassy glade is hoar with the condensed damps of night, and the threads of the gossamer sparkle like strings of opal in the sunbeams.

The earliest members of the animated world that catch the eye as they move abroad, are the *Hesperidæ;* the first butterflies, that, with abrupt gesture, pay their morning visit to the flowers. To them succeed the *Theclæ*, distinguished by the blue metallic lustre of their wings; and the *Polyommati*, the minutest and most delicate of the diurnal lepidoptera. The other species make their appearances with unerring certainty at successive stages of the morning; the *Theclæ* are followed by the *Vanessæ*, and these by the gaudy *Papilios*, till, as day advances, the broad-leaved plants and flowering shrubs are covered by a dancing cloud of butterflies of every shape and hue. The bees hurry abroad in all directions, and the golden beetles clamber lazily over the still damp leaves.

The earliest bird upon the wing is the crow[1], which leaves his perch almost with the first peep of dawn, cawing and flopping his wings in the sky. The parroquets follow in vast companies, chattering and screaming in exuberant excitement. Next the cranes and waders, which fly inland to their breeding places at sunset, rise from the branches on which they had passed the night, waving their wings to disencumber them of the dew; and, stretching their awkward legs behind, they soar away in the direction of the rivers and the far sea-shore.

The songster that first pours forth his salutation to the morning is the dial-bird (*Copsychus saularis*), and the yellow oriole, whose mellow flute-like voice is heard far through the stillness of the dawn. The jungle cock, unseen in the dense cover, shouts his reveille; not with the shrill clarion of his European type, but in a rich melodious call, that ascends from the depths of the valley. As light increases, the grass warbler[2] and maynah[3] add their notes; and the bronze-winged pigeons make the woods murmur with their plaintive cry, which resembles the distant lowing of cattle. The swifts and swallows sally forth as soon as there is sufficient warmth to tempt the minor insects abroad: the bulbul lights on the forest trees, and the little gem-like sun birds[4] (the humming-birds of the East) quiver on their fulgent wings above the opening flowers.

At length the fervid moon approaches, the sun mounts high, and all animated nature begins to yield to the oppression of his beams. The green enamelled dragonflies still flash above every pool in pursuit of their tiny prey; but almost every other winged insect instinctively seeks the shade of the foliage. The hawks and

---

1 *Corvus culminatus.*
2 *Cisticola cursitans.*
3 *Hetærornis cristatella.*
4 *Nectarinia Zeylanica.*

falcons now sweep through the sky to mark the smaller birds which may be abroad in search of seeds and larvæ. The squirrels dart from bough to bough uttering their shrill, quick cry; and the cicada on the stem of the palm-tree raises the deafening sound whose tone and volubility have won for him the expressive title of the "Knife-grinder."

It is during the first five hours of daylight that nature seems literally to teem with life and motion, the air melodious with the voice of birds, the woods resounding with the simmering hum of insects, and the earth replete with every form of living nature. But as the sun ascends to the meridian the scene is singularly changed, and nothing is more striking than the almost painful stillness that succeeds the vivacity of the early morning. Every animal disappears, escaping under the thick cover of the woods; the birds retire into the shade; the butterflies, if they flutter for a moment in the blazing sun, hurry back into the damp shelter of the trees as though their filmy bodies had been parched by the brief exposure; and, at last, silence reigns so profound that the ticking of a watch is sensibly heard, and even the pulsations of the heart become audible. The buffalo now steals to the tanks and watercourses, concealing all but his gloomy head and shining horns in the mud and sedges; the elephant fans himself languidly with leaves to drive away the flies that perplex him; and the deer cower in groups under the over-arching jungle. Rustling from under the dry leaves the bright green lizard springs up the rough stems of the trees, and pauses between each dart to look inquiringly around. The woodpecker makes the forest re-echo with the restless blows of his beak on the decaying bark, and the tortoise drops awkwardly into the still water which reflects the bright plumage of the kingfisher, as he keeps his lonely watch above it.

So long as the sun is about the meridian, every living creature seems to fly his beams and linger in the closest shade. Man himself, as if baffled in all devices to escape the exhausting glare, suspends his toil; and the traveller abroad since dawn reposes till the mid-day heat has passed. The cattle pant in their stifling sheds, and the dogs lie prone upon the ground, their legs extended far in front and behind, as if to bring the utmost portion of their body into contact with the cool earth.

As day declines nature recovers from her languor and exhaustion, the insects again flutter across the open glades, the birds venture once more upon the wing, and the larger animals saunter from under cover, and move away in the direction of the ponds and pasture. The traveller recommences his suspended journey, and the husbandman, impatient to employ the last hours of fading night, hastens to resume the interrupted labours of the morning. The birds which had made distant excursions to their feeding-grounds are now seen returning to their homes; the crows assemble round some pond to dabble in the water, and readjust their plumes before retiring for the night; the parroquets settle with deafening uproar on the crowns of the palm-trees near their nests; and the pelicans and sea-birds, with weary wing, retrace their way to their breeding-place near some solitary watercourse or ruined tank. The sun at last

"Sinks, as a flamingo
Drops into her nest at nightfall;"

twilight succeeds, and the crepuscular birds and animals awaken from their mid-day torpor and prepare to enjoy their nightly revels. The hawk-moths now take the place of the gayer butterflies, which withdraw with the departure of light; innumerable beetles make short and uncertain flights in the deepening shade, and in pursuit of them and the other insects that frequent the dusk, the night-jar[1], with expanded

[1] *Caprimulgus Asiaticus.*

jaws, takes low and rapid circles above the plains and pools.

Darkness at last descends, and every object fades in night and gloom; but still the murmur of innumerable insects arises from the glowing earth. The fruit-eating bats launch themselves from the high branches on which they have hung suspended during the day, and cluster round the mango-trees and tamarinds; and across the grey sky the owl flits in pursuit of the night moths on a wing so soft and downy that the air scarcely betrays its pulsations.

The palm-cat now descends from the crest of the coco-nut where she had lurked during the day, and the glossy genette emerging from some hollow tree, steals along the branches to surprise the slumbering birds. Meanwhile, among the grass already damp with dew, the glow-worm lights her emerald lamp[1], and from the shrubs and bushes issue showers of fire-flies, whose pale green flashes sparkle in the midnight darkness till day returns and morning "pales their ineffectual fires."

Still ascending towards Neuera-ellia, the road from Pusilawa winds through the valley skirting the bases of the hills till it reaches an apparently insurmountable barrier of mountains in the glen of Rangbodde. Here the acclivities that bound the ravine are overcome by a series of terraced windings cut out of the almost precipitous hill, and so narrow is the gorge, that the road enters between two cataracts that descend on either side of the pass. Some of the finest coffee in the island is produced at Rangbodde, and the estate of General Fraser presents a suitable illustration of the splendid scenery amidst which these plantations have been formed.

---

[1] The glow-worm of Ceylon, the female of the *Lampyris*, attains a size far exceeding anything I have heard of elsewhere. I have seen it near Pusilawa *three* inches in length, but without a proportionate increase of splendour. It feeds principally on snails, making its way into the shells and devouring the soft parts.

GENERAL FRASER'S ESTATE AT RANGBODDE.

In the damp shade near these water-falls the delicate spectre butterfly[1] is seen in unusual numbers, its broad and limber wings undulating as if unequal to sustain its weight, and over the streams the brilliant green dragon-fly[2] dashes from place to place, on wings that flash like sliced emeralds set in gold.

Pusilawa is a favourite haunt of a curious species of long-legged spider[3], that congregates in groups of from fifty to a hundred, in hollow trees and in holes in the banks by the roadside, and to a casual observer would seem bunches of horse-hair. This appearance is produced by the long and slender legs of these creatures, which are a shining black, whilst their bodies, so small as to be mere specks, are concealed beneath them. The same spider is found in the low country near Galle, but there it shows no tendency to become gregarious. Can

[1] *Hestia Jasonia.*
[2] *Euplœa splendens.*
[3] *Phalangium bisignatum.*

it be that they thus assemble in groups in the hills for the sake of accumulated warmth at the cool altitude of 4000 feet?

The lowland Singhalese have a horror of the cold in these elevated situations, and still more of the rain, to avoid the pattering of which on their skins they would at any time crouch under water in a stream or a tank. It is difficult to tempt them to the hills, and even the Malabar coolies shrink with apprehension from the chills of Neuera-ellia. To provide labour for these mountain roads the Government retain in their pay a body of Caffres as pioneers, the remnant of a force which was originally incorporated by the Portuguese, who introduced them from their African settlements at Mozambique. The Dutch succeeded in keeping up its strength by an immigration from the Cape, and the British maintained it by purchasing slaves from the Portuguese at Goa. At present the Caffres show no inclination to resort to the island, and this valuable force is threatened with extinction in consequence.

On the occasion of my first ascent, the Rangbodde pass was rendered dangerous by the presence of a "rogue" elephant which infested it. He concealed himself by day in the dense forests on either side of the road, making his way during the darkness to the river below; and we saw, as we passed, marks on the trunks of the trees where he had rubbed off the mud, after returning from his midnight bath. On the morning when I crossed the mountain, a poor Caffre, one of the pioneer corps, proceeding to his labour, came suddenly upon this savage at a turning in the road, when the elephant, alarmed by the intrusion, lifted him with its trunk and beat out his brains against the bank.

After a slow and toilsome journey to an elevation of more than 6000 feet[1], a sight is obtained of the plain of

[1] The rest-house on the plain at Neuera-ellia is 6222 feet above the sea.

Neuera-ellia. The first visit of Europeans to this lofty plateau was made by some English officers, who, in 1826, penetrated so far in pursuit of elephants.[1] Struck with its freshness and beauty, they reported their discovery to the Governor, and Sir Edward Barnes, alive to its importance as a sanitary retreat for the troops, took possession of it instantly, and commenced the building of barracks, and of a bungalow for his own accommodation. He directed the formation of a road; and within two years Neuera-ellia was opened (in 1829) as a convalescent station. In the estimation of the European and the invalid it is the Elysium of Ceylon. At this elevation, and encircled by mountains (which on the northern side rise 2000 feet higher still), in the midst of a grassy plain, watered by crystal streams, and surrounded by hills covered with luxuriant vegetation, stands the little hamlet; the smoke curling above the thatch of its white cottages in the midst of gardens of roses and mignonette; and even of some European fruit-trees, that charm with their foliage, though they rarely bring their fruit to maturity. It is difficult to imagine a higher enjoyment than to mount almost between sunrise and sunset from the sultry calm of Colombo to the cool and delicious breezes of this mountain plateau; to leave the flaming noon and the suffocating nights of the coast, and after a journey of less than a hundred miles along admirable roads, and through scenery unsurpassed in its loveliness and grandeur, to rest in an English cottage, with a blazing wood fire, to sleep under blankets, and awake in the morning to find thin ice on the water and hoar-frost encrusting the herbage.

The temperature of Neuera-ellia, according to Davy, ranges from 36° to 81°, with a mean daily variance of

[1] Neuera-ellia was of course previously known by the natives. It had been the retreat of one of the Kandyan kings, who fled thither from the Portuguese about the year 1610, and from the circumstance of its having thus become an imperial residence, "nuwara," it obtained its present appellation *Nuwara-e'lia,* the "royal city of light."

11°), but the latter is higher than is shown by recent experiment, the average at noon being now ascertained to be about 62°, and the highest observation of the unexposed thermometer 70°.

At this elevation there is a perpetual breeze, but of the two winds, the residents, in spite of the greater moisture and more frequent showers, prefer the south-west, to the dry and parching breeze from the north and east. The quantity of rain, of course, varies in a series of years; but it is by no means so great as in the lower range of the hills, and does not much exceed the ordinary average on the western coast.[1] During the transitional periods of the monsoons the fall is less equable, and the intervals of suspension longer; on the other hand, rain has been known about this period to descend without intermission for fourteen days. Except during these violent outbursts there is scarcely a day when outdoor exercise is not practicable. Even at noon the clouds which collect round the summit of these lofty hills serve to ward off the sun, and out-door life is as enjoyable as summer at home. Here the troops never change woollen for other clothing[2], and European visitors are glad to recall associations of England by producing their winter muffling and surtouts.

In the early part of the year, from December to March, the mornings are bracing and frosty, and one is tempted to take the chill off the water on stepping into the accustomed bath before breakfast. The noon-day warmth adds a zest to the evening fire, and the nights are so brilliant that a book may be read by moonlight.

---

[1] The quantity of rain falling at Neuera-ellia has perceptibly decreased of late years, probably owing to the extensive clearing of the surrounding forests, to prepare them for coffee planting.

[2] It may seem to modify the popular opinion as to great changes of temperature being in themselves prejudicial to health, that the medical officers in charge of troops at Neuera-ellia have remarked that, notwithstanding the sudden variation, from the heat of the sun which is sometimes oppressive in the afternoon, to chill breezes and hoar frost at night, the men never suffer from this cause alone; without some incautious act on the part of those exposed.

May or June ushers in the boisterous monsoon, with its thunder and torrents, the solemnity of which is increased by storms of wind such as are unknown in the low country. From July to November, when the monsoon again changes, the plain presents the same characteristics of climate and verdure; flowers spring up after the rains, and day after day invalids enjoy their healthful drive round the base of the hills that encircle the valley, and excursionists make their pilgrimages to the top of Pedurutalla-galla[1], an elevation of 8280 feet, from which there is a view of surpassing magnificence over the lower range of mountains and the plains beneath, threaded by the silvery line of the rivers, and stretching away till it meets the sea on the far horizon.

In these invigorating heights the newly arrived visitor, escaping in a single night from the sultry languor of the low country is surprised by the unexpected importunities of his recovered appetite, and seizes with a relish dishes he would have declined with averted face the day before. In a temperature resembling that of an English autumn, the skin moist, but no longer sodden, the chest expanding in a lighter atmosphere, and the enlivened circulation imparting an unaccustomed glow and colour to the surface; he addresses himself with vigour to pedestrian excursions among the surrounding hills. Here a slight difficulty of breathing surprises a stranger — arising from the high rarefaction of the air—but it soon passes off.

To those delicate constitutions which, without the presence of actual disease, are nevertheless debilitated from long exposure to tropical heat, the change produced by the lofty climate of Neuera-ellia is still more remarkable; muscular tenuity disappears, the limbs recover their elasticity and roundness, the spirits rise

[1] Generally called "Pedro-talla-galla." It takes this name from producing some plants suitable for the weaving of *peduru*, "mats,"—these serve as a substitute for the "*talla*" or strips of leaves; and they grow amongst the rocks "*galla*," near its summit.

with the renewal of strength, the pallor of the features disappears, and after a few weeks of out-door excitement the visitor returns to the coast with a complexion as clear as if freshly imported from Europe.

But whilst thus adapted to the preservation of health, and to the stage of weakness consequent on the subsidence of disease, Neuera-ellia, as a sanatarium, is little to be relied on for the relief of active ailments, especially such as are incident to the island. Derangements of the liver and internal organs are likely to be aggravated there by congestion, and the diminution of that quietude which is essential to the work of reparation; and in affections of the lungs there is an increase of uneasiness in the chest from breathing such highly rarefied air.

Only one class of sufferers seem to derive a relief at once rapid and effectual, — those with cutaneous abrasions or ulcerations by leech-bites. These wounds in the low country are sluggish and slow to heal, but in the tonic air of the mountain they quickly close, to the surprise of the patient, and almost without the intervention of surgical skill.

But however limited its sanative effects, the blessing with which Providence has endowed the island, in placing such a climate within reach of the sultry coast, has never been duly estimated by Europeans, nor availed of as a preventive *against the approaches of disease.* By the military, especially, its value has been inadequately appreciated as a prophylactic. Soldiers are only allowed to visit it after becoming pronounced invalids: when health might have been preserved comparatively unimpaired, had they been sent there as a precaution, on the earliest symptom of that exhaustion and debility which ordinarily prelude actual seizure. After the attack has subsided the influence of the plain on convalescents is something magical; and in cases of fever no effort should be spared to enable the patient to reach it. Instances have occurred in which it might be apprehended that the sufferer would die upon the road, when he has rallied and recovered after reaching Neuera-ellia, as if the breezes of the mountain were the elixir of St. Leon.

As preventive of illness, therefore, the advantages of Neuera-ellia cannot be too highly lauded. To the hypochondriac and the valetudinarian,

> "When nature, being oppress'd, commands the mind
> To suffer with the body,"

the valley is a paradise; to the languid and exhausted dweller on the coast a visit to this elevated region acts like the touch of his mother earth, strengthening him to wrestle with the heats below; and children after rejoicing in the bracing breezes descend as rosy and bright as on their first arrival from England.

European vegetables have been grown after infinite pains and attention at Neuera-ellia, and attempts have been made to cultivate English grain [1]; but the result has been unsatisfactory, — the seed was destroyed by the multitude of larvæ and other depredators in a soil that had never before been disturbed; and although the experiment may eventually prove successful, the labour and cost in the intermediate stages must for some time to come discourage the enterprise as a remunerative speculation.

As the plain is entirely formed of débris from the hills, it has been largely productive of precious stones embedded in the alluvial deposit, and is still covered with pits sunk by the gem-finders. One of the amusements of visitors is jewel-hunting, and they are frequently requited by the discovery of small rubies, sapphires, and topazes.

From Neuera-ellia to Badulla the road makes a descent of more than 3000 feet within forty miles, and com-

---

[1] An account of these experiments and their results will be found in Mr. BAKER'S *Eight Years' Wanderings in Ceylon*, 8vo. Longmans, 1855, ch. ii. p. 14, &c.

mands at every point splendid views over the hills and undulating plains of Oovah. This fertile region was formed into a principality by King Senerat, who, at his decease in 1635, bequeathed it to his step-son; and it was here that the Portuguese commander, Don Constantine de Sa y Noroña, being tempted to invade the high country, in 1630, was led into an ambuscade, and mercilessly slaughtered by the Kandyans. This gloomy episode in the history of the Europeans in Ceylon forms the subject of a touching narrative written by his son Rodrigues de Sa y Menezes to vindicate the memory of his father [1], who alone of all the Portuguese governors of the island appears to have been kindly remembered for some endearing qualities in his disposition.

The general aspect of the province presents grassy plains, which afford better pasturage for cattle than any others in the island; and fertile rice-lands, in the management of which the people of Oovah are pre-eminent, from their skill in leading streams from great distances for purposes of irrigation.[2] Cattle are abundant, and especially buffaloes, which are universally employed for tillage; and amongst the objects of cultivation to which the climate is adapted are Indian corn, millet, yams, potatoes, and cassava. Large quantities of materials are grown for the preparation of curry; turmeric, capsicums, onions and garlic, as well as cardamoms and pepper. Vegetable oils are expressed from numerous plants; indigo, madder, sapan-wood and arnotto furnish dyes; and the hills, long before European planters had established themselves around Kandy, were celebrated for yielding the finest native coffee in Ceylon. At the

---

[1] *Rebelion de Ceylan, &c.* Lisbon, A.D. 1681. For an account of this ill-fated expedition, see *ante*, Vol. II. Pt. IV. ch. ii. p. 40.

[2] The sources of these streams are chiefly in the hills surrounding Neuera-ellia; "therefore," says Mr. BAKER, in his *Eight Years' Wanderings in Ceylon*, "the king in possession of Neuera-ellia had the most complete command over his subjects in Oovah, as he could either give or withhold the supply at pleasure by allowing its free exit or altering its course." Ch. iii. p. 49.

present moment there are upwards of three thousand acres in bearing, and the ascertained portion of forest land suitable for plantations is not less than thirty thousand more.

The climate is one of the most salubrious in Ceylon; and owing to this singular combination of capabilities there can be little doubt that, with the extension of roads and enlarged means of communication with the capitals and the coast, Oovah, as it is already one of the richest districts in the island, is destined at no distant date to be one of the most prosperous and frequented.

Badulla, the capital of the principality, lies in a valley, on one side of which rises the mountain of Namoone-koole, whose summit is nearly 7000 feet high. No scene in nature can be more peaceful and lovely,

BADULLA.

but the valley has been so often desolated by war, that nothing remains of the ancient city except its gloomy temples and the vestiges of a ruined dagoba. The British have converted an ancient residence of the prince of Oovah into a fort, defended by earth-works; and the modern town, in the activity of its bazaars and the comfort and order of its dwellings, generally surrounded by gardens of coco-nuts, coffee, and tobacco, attests the growing prosperity and contentment of the district.

About four hundred yards from the Fort is the tepid spring, called by the natives "the smoke-mouthed well," which is held in equal veneration by Buddhists, Hindus, and Mahometans. The Hindus believe that two chank shells, still preserved in an adjacent dewale which is dependent on the great temple of Kattragam, were obtained from two cobra de capellos, which rose with them from the depths of this well; and the Mahometans have a tradition that a devout Santon, on his prilgrimage to Adam's Peak, died, and was buried near the spring. It is remarkable, too, that in the mountains of Ooda-Kinda, in western Oovah, there is a small community known as the "*Padu-guruwas*," who profess Islam, but conform to Kandyan customs; and it seems to be doubtful whether they are Mahometan converts, or the descendants of a tribe from the continent of India.

I have mentioned elsewhere [1], the existence in Oovah of a race of out-castes, the *Ambatteyos*, so degraded, that even the Rodiyas prevent their dogs from eating the fragments of food cooked by them. It is further illustrative of the development of caste in Ceylon, that, in the neighbourhood of Badulla, there is a class known as *Pareyos*, or "strangers," and sometimes as *Weediye-ettos*, or "people of the high road," who are believed to be the offspring of some Portuguese captives, made slaves after the massacre of Constantine de Sa y Noroña. They were permitted to intermarry with women of rank who had been expelled from Kandy for crimes; but these, as a less punishment than consigning them to the Rodiyas, were degraded to the condition of royal

---

[1] See *ante*, Vol. II. Pt. VII. ch. iv. p. 191.

serfs, and condemned to menial services in the rice-lands and granaries.

Perhaps there is not a scene in the world which combines sublimity and beauty in a more extraordinary degree than that which is presented at the Pass of Ella, where, through an opening in the chain of mountains, the road from Badulla descends rapidly to the lowlands, over which it is carried for upwards of seventy miles, to Hambangtotte, on the south coast of the island. The ride to Ella passes for ten or twelve miles along the base of hills thickly wooded, except in those spots where the forest has been cleared for planting coffee. The view is therefore obstructed, and at one point appears to terminate in an impassable glen; but on reaching this the traveller is amazed at discovering a ravine through which a torrent has forced its way, disclosing a passage to the plains below, over which, for more than sixty miles, the prospect extends, unbroken by a single eminence, till, far in the distance, the eye discerns a line of light, which marks where the sunbeams are flashing on the waters of the Indian ocean.

PART VIII.

THE ELEPHANT.

CHAPTER I.

STRUCTURE AND FUNCTIONS.

During my residence at Kandy, I had twice the opportunity of witnessing the operation on a grand scale of capturing wild elephants, intended to be trained for the public service in the establishment of the Civil Engineer;—and in the course of my frequent journeys through the interior of the island, I succeeded in collecting so many particulars relative to the habits of these interesting animals in a state of nature, as has enabled me not only to add to the information previously possessed, but to correct many fallacies popularly received regarding their instincts and disposition. These I am anxious to place on record before proceeding to describe the scenes of which I was a spectator, during the progress of the elephant hunts in the district of the Seven Corles, at which I was present in 1846, and again in 1847.

With the exception of the narrow but densely inhabited belt of cultivated land, which extends along the sea-borde of the island from Chilaw on the western coast to Tangalle on the east, there is no part of Ceylon in which elephants may not be said to abound; even close to the environs of the most populous localities of the interior. They frequent both the open plains and the deep forests; and their footsteps are to be seen wherever food and shade, vegetation and water[1], allure

[1] M. Ad. Pictet has availed himself of the love of the elephant for water, to found on it a solution of the long-contested question as to the etymology of the word "elephant,"—a term which, whilst it has passed into almost every dialect of the West, is scarcely to be traced in

them, alike on the summits of the loftiest mountains, and on the borders of the tanks and lowland streams.

From time immemorial the natives have been taught to capture and tame them, and the export of elephants from Ceylon to India has been going on without interruption from the period of the first Punic War.[1] In later times all elephants were the property of the Kandyan crown; and their capture or slaughter without the royal permission was classed amongst the gravest offences in the Kandyan code.

In recent years there is reason to believe that their numbers have become considerably reduced. They have entirely disappeared from districts in which they were

---

any language of Asia. The Greek ἐλέφας, to which we are immediately indebted for it, did not originally mean the animal, but, as early as the time of Homer, applied only to its tusks, and signified *ivory*. BOCHART has sought for a Semitic origin, and seizing on the Arabic *fil*, and prefixing the article *al*, obtains *alfil*, akin to ελεφ; but to this the objection lies that it excludes the other two syllables αντος. Rejecting this, BOCHART himself resorts to the Hebrew *eleph*, an "ox"—and this conjecture derives a certain degree of countenance from the fact that the Romans, when they obtained their first sight of the elephant in the army of Pyrrhus, in Lucania, called it the *Luca bos*. But the αντος is still unaccounted for; and POTT has sought to remove the difficulty by introducing the Arabic *hindi*, Indian, thus making *eleph-hindi*, "*bos Indicus*." The conversion of *hindi* into αντο is an obstacle, but here the example of "tamarind" comes to aid; *tamar hindi*, the "Indian date," which in mediæval Greek forms ταμαρεντι. A theory of BENARY, that ἐλέφας might be compounded of the Arabic *al*, and *ibha*, a Sanskrit name for the elephant, is exposed to still greater etymological exception. PICTET's solution is, that in the Sanskrit epics the King of Elephants, who has the distinction of carrying the god Indra, is called *airavata* or *airavana*, a modification of *airavanta*, "son of the ocean," which again comes from *iravat*, "abounding in water." "Nous aurions donc ainsi, comme corrélatif du grec ἐλέφαντο, une ancienne forme, *âirâvanta* ou *âilâvanta*, affaiblie plus tard en *âirâvata* ou *âirâvana* . . . . On connaît la prédilection de l'éléphant pour le voisinage des fleuves, et son amour pour l'eau, dont l'abondance est nécessaire à son bien-être." This Sanskrit name, PICTET supposes, may have been carried to the West by the Phœnicians, who were the purveyors of ivory from India; and, from the Greek, the Latins derived *elephas*, which passed into the modern languages of Italy, Germany, and France. But it is curious that the Spaniards acquired from the Moors their Arabic term for ivory, *marfil*, and the Portuguese *marfim*; and that the Scandinavians, probably from their early expeditions to the Mediterranean, adopted *fill* as their name for the elephant itself, and *fil-bein* for ivory; in Danish, *fils-ben*. (See *Journ. As'at.* 1843, t. xliii. p. 133.) The Spaniards of South America call the palm which produces the vegetable ivory (*Phytelephas macrocarpa*) *Palma de marfil*, and the nut itself, *marfil vegetal*.

[1] ÆLIAN, *de Nat. Anim.* lib. xvi. c. 18; *Cosmas Indicopl.* p. 128.

formerly numerous[1]; smaller herds have been taken in the periodical captures for the public service, and hunters returning from the chase report them to be more scarce. In consequence of this diminution the peasantry in some parts of the island have even suspended the ancient practice of keeping watchers and fires by night to drive away the elephants from their growing crops.[2] The opening of roads and the clearing of the mountain forests of Kandy for the cultivation of coffee, have forced the animals to retire to the low country; where again they have been followed by large parties of European sportsmen; and the Singhalese themselves, being more freely provided with arms than in former times, have assisted in swelling the annual slaughter.

Had the motive which incites to the destruction of the elephant in Africa and India prevailed in Ceylon, and had the elephants there been provided with tusks, they would long since have been annihilated for the sake of their ivory.[3] But it is a curious fact that,

---

[1] LE BRUN, who visited Ceylon A.D. 1705, says that in the district round Colombo, where elephants are now never seen, they were then so abundant, that 160 had been taken in a single corral. (*Voyage, &c.*, tom. ii. ch. lxiii. p. 331.)

[2] In some parts of Bengal, where elephants were formerly troublesome (especially near the wilds of Ramgar), the natives got rid of them by mixing a preparation of the poisonous nepal root called *dakra* in balls of grain, and other materials, of which the animal is fond. In Cuttack, above fifty years ago, mineral poison was laid for them in the same way, and the carcases of eighty were found which had been killed by it. (*Asiat. Res.*, xv. 183.)

[3] The annual importation of ivory into Great Britain alone, for the last few years, has been about *one million* pounds; which, taking the average weight of a tusk at sixty pounds, would require the slaughter of 8,333 male elephants.

But of this quantity the importation from Ceylon has generally averaged only five or six hundred weight; which, making allowance for the lightness of the tusks, would not involve the destruction of more than seven or eight in each year. At the same time, this does not fairly represent the annual number of tuskers shot in Ceylon, not only because a portion of the ivory finds its way to China and to other places, but because the chiefs and Buddhist priests have a passion for collecting tusks, and the finest and largest are to be found ornamenting their temples and private dwellings. The Chinese profess that for their exquisite carvings the ivory of Ceylon excels all other, both in density of texture and in delicacy of tint; but in the European market, the ivory of Africa, from its more distinct graining and other causes, obtains a higher price.

whilst in Africa both sexes have tusks, with some slight disproportion in the size of those of the females; and whilst in India the females are provided with them, though of much less dimensions than the males; not one elephant in a hundred is found with tusks in Ceylon, and the few that possess them are exclusively males. Nearly all, however, have those stunted processes which are called *tushes*, about ten or twelve inches in length and one or two in diameter,—these I have observed them to use in snapping off small branches and climbing plants; and hence tushes are seldom seen without a groove worn into them near their extremities.[1]

Amongst other surmises more ingenious than sound, the general absence of tusks in the elephant of Ceylon has been associated with the profusion of rivers and streams in the island; whilst it has been thrown out as a possibility that in Africa, where water is comparatively scarce, the animal is equipped with these implements in order to assist it in digging wells in the sand and in raising the juicy roots of the mimosas and succulent plants for the sake of their moisture. In support of this hypothesis, it has been observed, that whilst the tusks of the Ceylon species, which are never required for such uses, are slender, graceful and curved, seldom exceeding fifty or sixty pounds' weight, those of the African species are straight and thick, weighing occasionally one hundred and fifty, and even three hundred pounds.[2]

---

[1] The old fallacy is still renewed, that the elephant sheds his tusks. ÆLIAN says he drops them once in ten years (lib. xiv. c. 5); and PLINY repeats the story, adding that, when dropped, the elephants hide them under ground (lib. viii.); whence, SHAW says, in his *Zoology*, "they are frequently found in the woods," and exported from Africa (vol. i. p. 213); and Sir W. JARDINE, in the *Naturalist's Library* (vol. ix. p. 110), says, "the tusks are shed about the twelfth or thirteenth year." This is erroneous: after losing the first pair, or, as they are called, the "milk tusks," which drop in consequence of the absorption of their roots, when the animal is extremely young, the second pair acquire their full size, and become the "permanent tusks," which are never shed.

[2] Notwithstanding the inferiority in weight of the Ceylon tusks, as compared with those of the elephant of India, it would, I think, be precipi-

But it is manifestly inconsistent with the idea that tusks were given to the elephant to assist him in digging for his food, to find that the females are less bountifully supplied with them than the males, whilst the necessity for their use extends equally to both sexes. The same argument would serve to demonstrate the fallacy of the conjecture, that the tusks of the elephant were given to him as weapons of offence, for if such were the case the vast majority in Ceylon, males as well as females, would be left helpless in presence of an assailant. But although in their conflicts with one another, those which are provided with tusks may occasionally push with them clumsily at their opponents; it is a misapprehension to imagine that tusks are designed specially to serve "in warding off the attacks of the wily tiger and the furious rhinoceros, often securing the victory by one blow which transfixes the assailant to the earth." [1]

So harmless and peaceful is the life of the elephant, that

---

tate to draw the inference that the size of the former was uniformly and naturally less than those of the latter. The truth, I believe to be, that if permitted to grow to maturity, the tusks of the one would, in all probability, equal those of the other; but, so eager is the search for ivory in Ceylon, that a tusker, when once observed in a herd, is followed up with such persevering impatience, that he is almost invariably shot before attaining his full growth. General DI LIMA, when returning from the governorship of the Portuguese settlements at Mozambique, told me, in 1848, that he had been requested to procure two tusks of the largest size and straightest possible shape, which were to be formed into a cross to surmount the high altar of the cathedral at Goa: he succeeded in his commission, and sent two, one of which was 180 pounds, and the other 170 pounds' weight, with the slightest possible curve. In a periodical, entitled *The Friend*, published in Ceylon, it is stated in the volume for 1837 that the officers belonging to the ships Quorrah and Alburhak, engaged in the Niger Expedition, were shown by a native king two tusks, each two feet and a half in circumference at the base, eight feet long, and weighing upwards of 200 pounds. (Vol. i. p. 225.) BRODERIP, in his *Zoological Recreations*, p. 256, says a tusk of 350 pounds' weight was sold at Amsterdam, but he does not quote his authority.

[1] *Menageries, &c.*, published by the Society for the Diffusion of Useful Knowledge, vol. i. p. 68: "The Elephant," ch. iii. It will be seen that I have quoted repeatedly from this volume, because it is the most compendious and careful compilation with which I am acquainted of the information previously existing regarding the elephant. The author incorporates no speculations of his own, but has most diligently and agreeably arranged all the facts collected by his predecessors. The story of antipathy between the elephant and rhinoceros is probably borrowed from ÆLIAN, *de Nat.*, lib. xvii. c. 44.

nature appears to have left him unprovided with any weapon of offence: his trunk is too delicate an organ to be rudely employed in a conflict with other animals, and although on an emergency he may push or gore with his tusks (to which the French have hastily given the term "*défenses*,") their almost vertical position, added to the difficulty of raising his head above the level of his shoulder, is inconsistent with the idea of their being designed for attack, since it is impossible for the elephant to strike an effectual blow, or to wield his tusks as the deer and the buffalo can direct their horns. Nor is it easy to conceive under what circumstances an elephant could have a hostile encounter with either a rhinoceros or a tiger, with whose pursuits in a state of nature his own can in no way conflict.

Towards man elephants evince shyness, arising from their love of solitude and dislike of intrusion; any alarm they exhibit at his appearance, may be reasonably traced to the slaughter which has reduced their numbers; and as some evidence of this, it has always been observed that an elephant exhibits greater impatience of the presence of a white man than of a native. Were his instincts to carry him further, or were he influenced by any feeling of animosity or hostility, it must be apparent that, as against the prodigious numbers which inhabit the forests of Ceylon, man would wage an unequal contest, and that of the two one or other must long since have been reduced to a helpless minority.

Official testimony is not wanting in confirmation of this view;—in the returns of 108 coroners' inquests held in Ceylon, during five years, from 1849 to 1855 inclusive, in cases of death occasioned by wild animals; 16 are recorded as having been caused by elephants, 15 by buffaloes, 6 by crocodiles, 2 by boars, 1 by a bear, and 68 by serpents; (the great majority of the last class of sufferers being women and children, who had been bitten during the night). Little more than *three* fatal accidents annually on the average of five years, is certainly a small proportion amongst a population estimated at a million and a half, in an island abounding with elephants, with which encounters are daily stimulated by the love of sport or the hope of gain. Were the elephants instinctively vicious or even highly irritable in their temperament, the destruction of human life under the circumstances must have been infinitely greater. It must also be taken into account, that some of the accidents recorded may have occurred in the rutting season, when elephants are subject to fits of temporary fury, known in India by the term *must*, in Ceylon *mudda*, —a paroxysm which speedily passes away, but during the fury of which it is dangerous even for the mahout to approach those ordinarily the tamest and most gentle.

But, then, the elephant is said to "entertain an extraordinary dislike to all quadrupeds; that dogs running near him produce annoyance; that he is alarmed if a hare start from her form;" and from Pliny to Buffon every naturalist has recorded his supposed aversion to swine.[1] These alleged antipathies are in a great degree, if not entirely, imaginary. The habits of the elephant are essentially harmless, his wants lead to no rivalry with other animals, and the food to which he is most attached is found in such abundance that he obtains it without an effort. In the quiet solitudes of Ceylon, elephants may constantly be seen browsing peacefully in the immediate vicinity of and in close contact with other animals. I have seen groups of deer and wild buffaloes reclining in the sandy bed of a river in the dry season, and elephants plucking the branches close beside them. They show no impatience in the company of the elk, the bear, and the wild hog; and on the other hand, I have never discovered an instance in which these animals have evinced any apprehension of

[1] *Menageries, &c.*, "The Elephant," ch. iii.

them. The elephant's natural timidity, however, is such that he becomes alarmed on the appearance in the jungle of any animal with which he is not familiar; he is said to be afraid of the horse, but from my own experience I should say it is the horse that is alarmed at the aspect of the elephant; in the same way, from some unaccountable impulse, the horse has an antipathy to the camel, and evinces extreme impatience, both of the sight and the smell of that animal.[1] When enraged, an elephant will not hesitate to charge a rider on horseback; but it is against the man, not against the horse, that his fury is directed; and no instance has been ever known of his wantonly assailing a horse.

A horse, which belonged to the late Major Rogers[2], had run away from his groom, and was found some considerable time afterwards grazing quietly with a herd of elephants. Pigs are constantly to be seen feeding about the stables of the tame elephants, which manifest no repugnance to them. As to the smaller animals, the elephant undoubtedly evinces uneasiness at the presence of a dog, but this is referable to the same cause as his impatience of a horse, namely, that neither is habitually seen by him in the forest; but it would be idle to suppose that this feeling could amount to hostility against a creature incapable of inflicting on him the slightest injury.[3] The truth I apprehend to be that, when they meet, the impudence and impertinences

---

[1] This peculiarity was noticed by the ancients, and is recorded by Herodotus: "κάμηλον ἵππος φοβέεται, καὶ οὐκ ἀνέχεται οὔτε τὴν ἰδέην αὐτῆς ορέων οὔτε τὴν ὀδμὴν οσφραινόμενος" (Herod. ch. 80). Camels have long been bred by the Grand Duke of Tuscany, at his establishment near Pisa, and even there the same instinctive dislike to them is manifested by the horse, which it is necessary to train and accustom to their presence in order to avoid accidents. Mr. BRODERIP mentions, that, "when the precaution of such training has not been adopted, the sudden and dangerous terror with which a horse is seized in coming unexpectedly upon one of them is excessive."—*Note-book of a Naturalist*, ch. iv. p. 113.

[2] Major ROGERS was many years the chief civil officer of Government in the district of Oovah, where he was killed by lightning, 1845.

[3] To account for the impatience manifested by the elephant at the

of the dog are offensive to the gravity of the elephant, and incompatible with his love of solitude and ease. Or may it be assumed as an evidence of the sagacity of the elephant, that the only two animals to which he manifests an antipathy, are the two which he has seen in the company of his enemy, man?

Major Skinner, whose official duties in tracing roads involved the necessity of his being in the jungle for months together, always found that, by night or by day, the barking of a dog which accompanied him, was sufficient to put a whole herd to flight. On the whole, therefore, I am of opinion that the elephant lives on terms of amity with every quadruped in the forest, that he neither regards them as his foes, nor provokes their hostility by his acts; and that, with the exception of man, *his greatest enemy is a fly!*

These statements of the supposed animosity of the elephant to minor animals, originated with Ælian and Pliny, who had probably an opportunity of seeing, what may at any time be observed, that when a captive elephant is picketed beside a post, the domestic animals, goats, sheep and cattle, will annoy and irritate him by their audacity in making free with his provender; but this is an evidence in itself of the little instinctive dread which such comparatively puny creatures entertain of one so powerful and yet so gentle.

Amongst elephants themselves, jealousy and other causes of irritation frequently occasion contentions between individuals of the same herd; but on such occasions it is their habit to strike with their trunks and to bear down their opponents with their heads. It is doubtless correct, that an elephant, when prostrated by the force and fury of an antagonist of his own species, is often

---

presence of a dog, it has been suggested that he is alarmed lest the latter should attack *his feet*, a portion of his body of which the elephant is peculiarly careful. A tame elephant has been observed to regard with indifference a spear directed towards his head, but to shrink timidly from the same weapon when pointed at his foot.

wounded by the downward pressure of the tusks, which, in any other position, it would be almost impossible to use offensively.

Mr. Mercer, who in 1846 was the principal civil officer of Government at Badulla, sent me a jagged fragment of an elephant's tusk, about five inches in diameter, and weighing between twenty and thirty pounds, which had been brought to him by some natives, who, being attracted by a noise in the jungle, witnessed a combat between a tusker and one without tusks, and saw the latter with his trunk seize one of the tusks of his antagonist and wrench from it the portion in question, which measured two feet in length.

Here the trunk was shown to be the more powerful offensive weapon of the two; but I apprehend that the chief reliance of the elephant for defence is on his ponderous weight, the pressure of his foot being sufficient to crush any minor assailant after being prostrated by means of his trunk. Besides, in using his feet for this purpose, he derives a wonderful facility from the peculiar formation of the knee-joint in his hind leg, which, enabling him to swing his hind feet forward close to the ground, assists him to toss the body alternately from foot to foot, till he deprives it of life.[1]

A sportsman who had undergone this operation, having been seized by a wounded elephant but rescued from his fury, described to me his sufferings as he was thus flung back and forward between the hind and fore feet of the animal, which ineffectually attempted

[1] In the Third Book of Maccabees, which is not printed in our Apocrypha, but appears in the Series in the Greek Septuagint, the author, in describing the persecution of the Jews by Ptolemy Philopator, B.C. 210, states that the king swore vehemently that he would send them into the other world, "foully trampled to death by the knees and feet of elephants" (*πέμψειν εἰς ᾅδην ἐν γόνασι καὶ ποσὶ θηρίων ᾐκισμένους*. 3 Mac. v. 42). ÆLIAN makes the remark, that elephants on such occasions use their *knees* as well as their feet to crush their victims.—*Hist. Anim.* viii. 10.

to trample him at each concussion, but abandoned him without inflicting serious injury.

KNOX, in describing the execution of criminals by the state elephants of the former kings of Kandy, says, "they will run their teeth (*tusks*) through the body, and then tear it in pieces and throw it limb from limb;" but a Kandyan chief, who was witness to such scenes, has assured me that the elephant never once applied his tusks, but, placing his foot on the prostrate victim, plucked off his limbs in succession by a sudden movement of his trunk. If the tusks were designed to be employed offensively, some alertness would naturally be exhibited in using them; but in numerous instances where sportsmen have fallen into the power of a wounded elephant, they have escaped through the failure of the enraged animal to strike them with its tusks, even when stretched upon the ground.[1]

Placed as the elephant is in Ceylon, in the midst of the most luxuriant profusion of his favourite food, in close proximity at all times to abundant supplies of water, and with no enemies against whom to protect himself, it is difficult to conjecture any probable utility which he could derive from such appendages. The absence of tusks is unaccompanied by any inconvenience to those in whom they are wanting; and as regards the few who possess them, the only instance in which I am aware of their being employed in relation to the œconomy of the animal, is to assist in ripping open the stem of the jaggery palms and young palmyras to extract the farinaceous core; and in splitting the juicy shaft of the plantain. Whilst the tuskless elephant crushes the latter under foot, thereby soiling it and wasting its moisture; the other, by opening it with the point of his tusk, performs the operation with

[1] The *Hastisilpe*, a Singhalese work which treats of the "Science of Elephants," enumerates amongst those which it is not desirable to possess, "the elephant which will fight with a stone or a stick in his trunk."

delicacy and apparent ease. These, however, are trivial and almost accidental advantages: on the other hand, owing to irregularities in their growth, the tusks are sometimes an impediment in feeding[1]; and in more than one instance in the Government Studs, tusks which had so grown as to approach and cross one another at the extremities, have had to be removed by the saw, the contraction of space between them so impeding the free action of the trunk as to prevent the animal from conveying branches to his mouth.[2]

It is true that in captivity, and after a due course of training, the elephant discovers a new use for his tusks when employed in moving stones and piling timber; so much so that a powerful one will raise and carry on them a log of half a ton weight or more. One evening whilst riding in the vicinity of Kandy, towards the scene of the massacre of Major Davie's party in 1803, my horse evinced some excitement at a noise which approached us in the thick jungle, and which consisted of a repetition of the ejaculation *urmph! urmph!* in a hoarse and dissatisfied tone. A turn in the forest explained the mystery, by bringing me face to face with a tame elephant, unaccompanied by any

---

[1] Among other eccentric forms, an elephant was seen in 1844, in the district of Bintenne, near Friar's-Hood Mountain, one of whose tusks was so bent that it took what sailors term a "round turn," and then resumed its curved direction as before. In the Museum of the College of Surgeons, London, there is a specimen, No. 2757, of a *spiral* tusk.

[2] Since the foregoing remarks were written relative to the undefined use of tusks to the elephant, I have seen a speculation on the same subject in Dr. HOLLAND's "*Constitution of the Animal Creation, as expressed in structural Appendages;*" but the conjecture of the author leaves the problem scarcely less obscure than before. Struck with the mere *supplemental* presence of the tusks, the absence of all apparent use serving to distinguish them from the *essential* organs of the creature, Dr. HOLLAND concludes that their production is a process incident, but not ancillary, to other important ends, especially connected with the vital functions of the trunk and the marvellous motive powers inherent to it; his conjecture is, that they are "a species of safety valve of the animal œconomy," —and that "they owe their development to the predominance of the senses of touch and smell, conjointly with the muscular motions of which the exercise of these is accompanied." "Had there been no proboscis," he thinks, "there would have been no supplementary appendages, — the former creates the latter."— P. 246, 271.

attendant. He was labouring painfully to carry a heavy beam of timber, which he balanced across his tusks, but the pathway being narrow, he was forced to bend his head to one side to permit it to pass endways; and the exertion and inconvenience combined led him to utter the dissatisfied sounds which disturbed the composure of my horse. On seeing us halt, the elephant raised his head, reconnoitred us for a moment, then flung down the timber and forced himself backwards among the brushwood so as to leave a passage, of which he expected us to avail ourselves. My horse still hesitated: the elephant observed it, and impatiently thrust himself still deeper into the jungle, repeating his cry of *urmph!* but in a voice evidently meant to encourage us to come on. Still the horse trembled; and anxious to observe the instinct of the two sagacious creatures, I forbore any interference: again the elephant wedged himself further in amongst the trees, and waited impatiently for us to pass him; and after the horse had done so tremblingly and timidly, I saw the wise creature stoop and take up his heavy burthen, trim and balance it on his tusks and resume his route, hoarsely snorting, as before, his discontented remonstrance.

Between the African elephant and that of Ceylon, with the exception of the striking peculiarity of the absence of tusks in the latter, the distinctions are less apparent to a casual observer than to a scientific naturalist. In the Ceylon species the forehead is higher and more hollow, the ears are smaller, and, in a section of the teeth the grinding ridges, instead of being lozenge-shaped, are transverse bars of uniform breadth.[1]

---

[1] The Dutch naturalists have recently announced the discovery of some peculiarities in the elephant of Sumatra, which serve to distinguish it from that of India and Africa; and, as they allege, to entitle it to the rank of a separate species to which they have given the name of *E. Sumatrensis*. The supposed differences are said to consist in the respective number of vertebræ and ribs, and some variation in the ridges of the grinders. —CRAWFURD, *Dict. of Indian Islands*, p. 136.

The Indian elephant is stated by Cuvier to have four nails on the hind foot, whilst the African variety has but three; but amongst the perfections of a high-bred elephant of Ceylon, is always enumerated the possession of *twenty* nails, whilst those of a secondary class have but eighteen in all.

So conversant are the natives with the structure and "points" of the elephant, that they divide them readily into castes, and describe with particularity their distinctive excellences and defects. In the *Hastisilpe*, a Singhalese work which treats of their management, the marks of inferior breeding are said to be "eyes restless like those of a crow, the hair of the head of mixed shades; the face wrinkled and small; the tongue curved and black; the nails short and green; the ears small; the neck thin, the skin freckled; the tail without a tuft, and the forequarter lean and low;" whilst the perfection of form and beauty is supposed to consist in the "softness of the skin, the red colour of the mouth and tongue, the forehead expanded and hollow, the ears large and rectangular, the trunk broad at the root and blotched with pink in front; the eyes bright and kindly, the cheeks large, the neck full, the back level, the chest square, the fore legs short and convex in front, the hind quarter plump, and five nails on each foot, all smooth, polished, and round.[1] An elephant with these perfections," says the author of the *Hastisilpe*, "will impart glory and magnificence to the king; but he cannot be discovered amongst thousands, yea, there shall never be found an elephant clothed at once with *all* the excellences herein described." The "points" of an elephant are to be studied with the greatest advantage in those attached to the temples, which are always of the highest caste, and exhibit the most perfect breeding.

---

[1] A native of rank informed me, that "the tail of a high-caste elephant will sometimes touch the ground, but such are very rare."

The colour of the animal's skin in a state of nature is generally of a lighter brown than that of those in captivity; a distinction which arises, in all probability, not so much from the wild elephant's propensity to cover himself with mud and dust, as from the superior care which is taken in repeatedly bathing the tame ones, and in rubbing their skins with a soft stone, a lump of burnt clay, or the coarse husk of a coco-nut. This kind of attention, together with the occasional application of oil to the skin, gives rise to the deeper black which their hides present.

Amongst the native Singhalese, however, a singular preference is evinced for elephants which exhibit those flesh-coloured blotches which occasionally mottle the skin of an elephant, chiefly about the head and extremities. The front of the trunk, the tips of the ears, the forehead, and occasionally the legs, are thus diversified with stains of a yellowish tint, inclining to pink. These are not natural; nor are they hereditary, for they are seldom exhibited by the younger individuals in a herd, but appear to be the result of some eruptive affection, the irritation of which has induced the animal in his uneasiness to rub himself against the rough bark of trees, and thus to destroy the outer cuticle.[1]

To a European these spots appear blemishes, and the taste which leads the natives to admire them is probably akin to the feeling which has at all times rendered *a white elephant* an object of wonder to Asiatics. The rarity of the latter is accounted for by regarding this peculiar appearance as the result of albinism; and notwithstanding the exaggeration of Oriental historians, who compare the fairness of such creatures to the whiteness of snow, even in its utmost perfection, I apprehend that the tint of a white elephant is little else than a flesh-colour, rendered somewhat more conspicuous by the blanching of

[1] This is confirmed by the fact that the scar of the ancle wound, occasioned by the rope on the legs of those which have been captured by noosing, presents precisely the same tint in the healed parts.

the skin, and the lightness of the colourless hairs by which it is sparsely covered. A white elephant is mentioned in the *Mahawanso* as forming part of the retinue attached to the Temple of the Tooth at Anarajapoora, in the fifth century after Christ[1]; but it commanded no religious veneration, and like those of the kings of Siam, it was tended merely as an emblem of royalty;[2] the sovereign of Ceylon being addressed as the "Lord of Elephants."[3] In 1633 a white elephant was exhibited in Holland[4]; but as this was some years before the Dutch had established themselves firmly in Ceylon, it was probably brought from some other of their eastern possessions.

---

[1] *Mahawanso*, ch. xxxviii. p. 254, A. D. 433.

[2] PALLEGOIX, *Siam, &c.*, vol. i. p. 152.

[3] *Mahawanso*, ch. xviii. p. 111. The Hindu sovereigns of Orissa, in the middle ages, bore the style of *Gaja-pati*, "powerful in elephants." —*Asiat. Res.* xv. 253.

[4] ARMANDI, *Hist. Milit. des Elephants*, lib. ii. c. x. p. 380. HORACE mentions a white elephant as having been exhibited at Rome: "Sive elephas albus vulgi converteret ora." —HOR. *Ep.* II. 196.

CHAP. II.

HABITS WHEN WILD.

ALTHOUGH found generally in warm and sunny climates, it is a mistake to suppose that the elephant is partial either to heat or to light. In Ceylon, the mountain tops, and not the sultry valleys, are his favourite resort. In Oovah, where the elevated plains are often crisp with the morning frost, and on Pedro-talla-galla, at the height of upwards of eight thousand feet, they are found in herds, whilst the hunter may search for them without success in the jungles of the low country. No altitude, in fact, seems too lofty or too chill for the elephant, provided it affords the luxury of water in abundance; and, contrary to the general opinion that the elephant delights in sunshine, he seems at all times impatient of its glare, and spends the day in the thickest depth of the forests, devoting the night to excursions, and to the luxury of the bath, in which he also indulges occasionally by day. This partiality for shade is doubtless ascribable to his love of coolness and solitude; but it is not altogether unconnected with the position of his eye, and the circumscribed use which his peculiar mode of life permits him to make of his faculty of sight.

All the elephant hunters and natives to whom I have spoken on the subject concur in opinion that his range of vision is circumscribed, and that he relies more on his ear and his sense of smell, than on his sight, which is liable to be obstructed by the dense foliage; besides which, from the formation of his neck, he is incapable of directing the range of his eye much above the level of his head.[1]

The elephant's small range of vision is sufficient to account for his excessive caution, his alarm at unusual noises, and the timidity and panic exhibited by him at trivial objects and incidents which, imperfectly discerned, excite his suspicions for his safety.[2] In 1841 an officer[3] was chased by an elephant which he had slightly wounded; and which seizing him in the dry bed of a river, had its fore-foot already raised to crush him; but the animal's forehead being caught at the instant by the tendrils of a climbing plant which had suspended itself from the branches above, it suddenly turned and fled; leaving him badly hurt, but with no limb broken. I have heard many similar instances, equally well attested, of this peculiarity in the elephant.

---

[1] After writing the above, I was permitted by the late Dr. HARRISON, of Dublin, to see some accurate drawings of the brain of an elephant, which he had the opportunity of dissecting in 1847, and on looking to that of base, I have found a remarkable verification of the information which I collected in Ceylon.

The small figure A is the ganglion of the fifth nerve, showing the small motor and large sensitive portion.

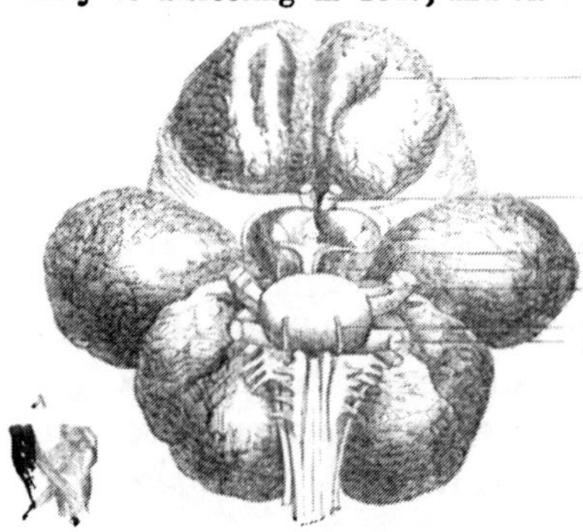

The *olfactory lobes*, from which the olfactory nerves proceed, are large, whilst the *optic and muscular nerves of the orbit are singularly small* for so vast an animal; and one is immediately struck by the prodigious size of the fifth nerve, which supplies the proboscis with its exquisite sensibility, as well as by the great size of the motor portion of the seventh, which supplies the same organ with its power of movement and action.

[2] *Menageries, &c.*, "The Elephant," p. 27.

[3] Major ROGERS. An account of this singular adventure will be found in the *Ceylon Miscellany* for 1842, vol. i. p. 221.

On the other hand, their power of smell is so remarkable as almost to compensate for the deficiency of sight. The herd are not only apprised of the approach of danger by this means, but when scattered in the forest, and dispersed out of range of sight, they are enabled by it to reassemble with rapidity and adopt precautions for their common safety. The same necessity involves a delicate sense of hearing, and the use of a variety of noises or calls, by means of which elephants succeed in communicating with each other upon all emergencies. "The sounds which they utter have been described by the African hunters as of three kinds: the first, which is very shrill, produced by blowing through the trunk, is indicative of pleasure; the second, produced by the mouth, is expressive of want; and the third, proceeding from the throat, is a terrific roar of anger or revenge."[1] These words convey but an imperfect idea of the variety of noises made by the elephant in Ceylon; and the shrill cry produced by blowing through his trunk, so far from being regarded as an indication of "pleasure," is the well-known cry of rage with which he rushes to encounter an assailant. ARISTOTLE describes it as resembling the hoarse sound of a "trumpet."[2] The French still designate the proboscis of an elephant by the same expression "trompe," which we have unmeaningly corrupted into *trunk*, and hence the scream of the elephant is known as "trumpeting" by the hunters in Ceylon. Their cry when in pain, or when subjected to compulsion, is a grunt or a deep groan from the throat, with the proboscis curled upwards and the lips wide apart.

Should the attention of an individual in the herd

---

[1] *Menageries, &c.,* "The Elephant," ch. iii. p. 68.

[2] ARISTOTLE, *De Anim.*, lib. iv. c. 9. "ὅμοιον σάλπιγγι." See also PLINY, lib. x. ch. cxiii. A manuscript in the British Museum, containing the romance of "*Alexander,*" which is probably of the fifteenth century, is interspersed with drawings illustrative of the strange animals of the East. Amongst them are two elephants, whose trunks are literally in the form of *trumpets with expanded mouths.* See WRIGHT'S *Archæological Album,* p. 176.

be attracted by any unusual appearance in the forest, the intelligence is rapidly communicated by a low suppressed sound made by the lips, somewhat resembling the twittering of a bird, and described by the hunters by the word "*prut*."

But a very remarkable noise has been described to me by more than one individual, who has come unexpectedly upon a herd of elephants during the night, when their alarm was apparently too great to be satisfied with the stealthy note of warning just described. On these occasions the sound produced resembled the hollow booming of an empty tun when struck with a wooden mallet or a muffled sledge. Major MACREADY, Military Secretary in Ceylon in 1836, who heard it by night amongst the wild elephants in the great forest of Bintenne, describes it as "a sort of banging noise like a cooper hammering a cask;" and Major SKINNER is of opinion that it must be produced by the elephant striking his sides rapidly and forcibly with his trunk. Mr. CRIPPS informs me that he has more than once seen an elephant, when surprised or alarmed, produce this sound by striking the ground forcibly with the point of the trunk, and this movement was instantly succeeded by raising the trunk, and pointing it in the direction whence the alarm proceeded, as if to ascertain by the sense of smell, the nature of the threatened danger. As this strange sound is generally mingled with the bellowing and ordinary trumpeting of the herd, it is in all probability a device resorted to, not alone for warning their companions of some approaching peril, but also for the additional purpose of terrifying unseen intruders.[1]

Extravagant estimates are recorded of the height of the elephant. In an age when popular fallacies in relation to him were as yet uncorrected in Europe by

---

[1] PALLEGOIX, in his *Description du Royaume Thai ou Siam*, adverts to a sound produced by the elephant when weary: "quand il est fatigué, *il frappe la terre avec sa* trompe et en tire un son semblable à celui du cor." —Tom. i. p. 151.

the actual inspection of the living animal, he was supposed to grow to the height of twelve or fifteen feet. Even within the last century in popular works on natural history, the elephant, when full grown, was said to measure from seventeen to twenty feet from the ground to the shoulder.[1] At a still later period, so imperfectly had the facts been collated, that the elephant of Ceylon was believed to "excel that of Africa in size and strength."[2] But so far from equalling the size of the African species, that of Ceylon seldom exceeds the height of nine feet, even in the Hambangtotte country, where the hunters agree that the largest specimens are to be found, and the ordinary herds do not average more than eight feet. WOLF, in his account of the Ceylon elephant[3], says, he saw one taken near Jaffna which measured twelve feet and one inch high. But the truth is, that the general bulk of the elephant so far exceeds that of the animals which we are accustomed to see daily, that the imagination magnifies his unusual dimensions; and I have seldom or ever met with an inexperienced spectator who did not unconsciously over-estimate the size of an elephant, shown to him whether in captivity or in a state of nature. Major DENHAM would have guessed some which he saw in Africa to be sixteen feet in height, but the largest when killed was found to measure nine feet six.[4]

For a creature of his extraordinary weight, it is astonishing how noiselessly and stealthily the elephant can make his escape from a pursuer. When suddenly disturbed in the jungle, he will burst away with a rush that seems to bear down all before him; but the noise sinks into absolute stillness so suddenly, that a novice might well be led to suppose that the fugitive had only

---

[1] *Natural History of Animals.* By Sir JOHN HILL, M.D. London, 1748-52, p. 565.

[2] SHAW'S *Zoology.* Lond. 1800, vol. i. p. 216; ARMANDI, *Hist. Milit. des Elephans,* liv. i. ch. i. p. 2.

[3] WOLF'S *Life and Adventures, &c.,* p. 164.

[4] The fossil remains of the Indian elephant have been discovered at Jabalpur, showing a height of fifteen feet.—*Journ. Asiat. Soc. Beng.* vi.

halted within a few yards of him, when further search would disclose that he has stolen silently away, making scarcely a sound in his escape; and, stranger still, leaving the foliage almost undisturbed by his passage.

The most venerable delusion respecting the elephant, and that which held its ground with unequalled tenacity, is the ancient fallacy which is explained by Sir THOMAS BROWNE in his *Pseudodoxia Epidemica*, that "it hath no joynts, and this absurdity is seconded by another, that being unable to lye downe it sleepeth against a tree, which the hunters observing doe saw almost asunder, whereon the beast relying, by the fall of the tree falls also down it-selfe and is able to rise no more."[1] Sir THOMAS is disposed to think that "the hint and ground of this opinion might be the grosse and somewhat cylindricall composure of the legs of the elephant, and the equality and lesse perceptible disposure of the joynts, especially in the forelegs of this animal, they appearing when he standeth, like pillars of flesh;" but he overlooks the fact that PLINY has ascribed the same peculiarity to the Scandinavian beast somewhat resembling a horse, which he calls a "machlis,"[2] and that CÆSAR in describing the wild animals in the Hercynian forests, enumerates the *alce*, "in colour and configuration approaching the goat, but surpassing it in size, its head destitute of horns *and its limbs of joints*, whence it can neither lie down to rest, nor rise if by any accident it should fall, but using the trees for a resting-place, the hunters by loosening their roots bring the *alce* to the ground, so soon as it is tempted to lean on

---

[1] *Vulgar Errors*, book iii. chap. 1.

[2] Machlis (said to be derived from α, priv., and κλίνω, *cubo*, quod non cubat). "Moreover in the island of Scandinavia there is a beast called *Machlis*, that hath neither ioynt in the hough, nor pasternes in his hind legs, and therefore he never lieth down, but sleepeth leaning to a tree, wherefore the hunters that lie in wait for these beasts cut downe the trees while they are asleepe, and so take them; otherwise they should never be taken, they are so swift of foot that it is wonderful."—PLINY, *Natur. Hist.* Transl. Philemon Holland, book viii. ch. xv. p. 200.

them."[1] This fallacy, as Sir THOMAS BROWNE says, is "not the daughter of latter times, but an old and grey-headed errour, even in the days of ARISTOTLE," who deals with the story as he received it from CTESIAS, by whom it appears to have been embodied in his lost work on India. But although ARISTOTLE generally receives the credit of having exposed and demolished the fallacy of CTESIAS, it will be seen by a reference to his treatise *On the Progressive Motions of Animals*, that in reality he approached the question with some hesitation, and has not only left it doubtful in one passage whether the elephant has joints *in his knee*, although he demonstrates that it has joints in the shoulders[2]; but in another he has distinctly affirmed that on account of his weight the elephant cannot bend his fore legs together, but only one at a time, and reclines to sleep on that particular side.[3]

---

[1] "Sunt item quæ appellantur *Alces*. Harum est consimilis capreis figura, et varietas pellium; sed magnitudine paulo antecedunt, mutilæque sunt cornibus, *et crura sine nodis articulisque habent;* neque quietis causa procumbunt; neque, si quo afflictæ casu conciderunt, erigere sese aut sublevare possunt. His sunt arbores pro cubilibus; ad eas sese applicant, atque ita, paulum modo reclinatæ, quietem capiunt, quarum ex vestigiis cum est animadversum a venatoribus, quo se recipere consueverint, omnes eo loco, aut a radicibus subruunt aut accidunt arbores tantum, ut summa species earum stantium relinquatur. Huc cum se consuetudine reclinaverint, infirmas arbores pondere affligunt, atque una ipsæ concidunt."—CÆSAR, *De Bello Gall.* lib. vi. ch. xxvii.

The same fiction was extended by the early Arabian travellers to the rhinoceros, and in the MS. of the voyages of the "Two Mahomedans," it is stated that the rhinoceros of Sumatra "n'a point d'articulation au genou ni à la main."—*Relations des Voyages, &c.* Paris, 1845, vol. i. p. 29.

[2] "When an animal moves progressively an hypothenuse is produced, which is equal in power to the magnitude that is quiescent, and to that which is intermediate. But since the members are equal, it is necessary that the member which is quiescent should be inflected either in the knee or in the incurvation, *if the animal that walks is without knees.* It is possible, however, for the leg to be moved, when not inflected, in the same manner as infants creep; and there is an ancient report of this kind about elephants, which is not true, for such animals as these, *are moved in consequence of an inflection taking place either in their shoulders or hips.*" —ARISTOTLE, *De Ingressu Anim.*, ch. ix. Taylor's Transl.

[3] ARISTOTLE, *De Animal.*, lib. ii. ch. i. It is curious that Taylor, in his translation of this passage, was so strongly imbued with the "grey-headed error," that in order to elucidate the somewhat obscure meaning of Aristotle, he has actually interpolated the text with the exploded fallacy of Ctesias, and after the word reclining to sleep, has inserted the

So great was the authority of ARISTOTLE, that ÆLIAN, who wrote two centuries later and borrowed many of his facts from the works of his predecessor, perpetuates this error; and, after describing the exploits of the trained elephants exhibited at Rome, adds the expression of his surprise, that an animal without joints (ἄναρθρον) should yet be able to dance.[1] The fiction was too agreeable to be readily abandoned by the poets of the Lower Empire and the romancers of the middle ages; and PHILE, a contemporary of PETRARCH and DANTE, who, in the early part of the fourteenth century, addressed his didactic poem on the elephant to the Emperor Andronicus II., untaught by the exposition of ARISTOTLE, still clung to the old delusion,

> "Πόδες δὲ τούτῳ θαῦμα καὶ σαφὲς τέρας,
> Οὓς, οὐ καθάπερ τἄλλα τῶν ζώων γένη,
> Εἴωθε κινεῖν ἐξ ἀνάρθρων κλασμάτων·
> Καὶ γὰρ στιβαροῖς συντεθέντες ὀστέοις,
> Καὶ τῇ πλαδαρᾷ τῶν σφυρῶν καταστάσει,
> Καὶ τῇ πρὸς ἄρθρα τῶν σκελῶν ὑποκρίσει,
> Νῦν εἰς τόνους ἄγουσι, νῦν εἰς ὑφέσεις,
> Τὰς παντοδαπὰς ἐκδρομὰς τοῦ θηρίου.
> * * * * * *
>
> Βραχυτέρους ὄντας δὲ τῶν ὀπισθίων
> Ἀναμφιλέκτως οἶδα τοὺς ἐμπροσθίους·
> Τούτοις ἐλέφας ἐνταθεὶς ὥσπερ στύλοις
> Ὀρθοστάδην ἄκαμπτος ὑπνώττων μένει."
>
> v. 106, &c.

SOLINUS introduced the same fable into his *Polyhistor*; and DICUIL, the Irish commentator of the ninth century, who had an opportunity of seeing the elephant which Haroun Alraschid sent as a present to Charlemagne[2] in the year 802, corrects the error, and attributes its perpetuation to the circumstance that the joints in the

---

words "*leaning against some wall or tree*," which are not to be found in the original.

[1] "Ζῶον δὲ ἄναρθρον συνιέναι καὶ ῥυθμοῦ καὶ μέλους, καὶ φυλάττειν σχῆμα φύσεως δῶρα ταῦτα ἅμα καὶ ἰδιότης καθ' ἕκαστον ἐκπληκτική."—ÆLIAN, *De Nat. Anim.*, lib. ii. cap. xi.

[2] EGINHARD, *Vita Karoli*, c. xvi. and *Annales Francorum*, A.D. 810.

elephant's leg are not very apparent, except when he lies down.[1]

It is a strong illustration of the vitality of error, that the delusion thus exposed by Dicuil in the ninth century, was renewed by MATTHEW PARIS in the thirteenth; and stranger still, that Matthew not only saw but made a drawing of the elephant presented to King Henry III. by the king of France in 1255, in which he nevertheless represents the legs as without joints.[2]

In the numerous mediæval treatises on natural history, known under this title of *Bestiaries*, this delusion regarding the elephant is often repeated; and it is given at length in a metrical version of the *Physiologus* of THEOBALDUS, amongst the Arundel Manuscripts in the British Museum.[3]

With the Provençal song writers, the helplessness of

---

[1] "Sed idem Julius, unum de elephantibus mentiens, falso loquitur; dicens elephantem nunquam jacere; dum ille sicut bos certissime jacet, ut populi communiter regni Francorum elephantem, in tempore Imperatoris Karoli viderunt. Sed, forsitan, ideo hoc de elephante ficte æstimando scriptum est, eo quod genua et suffragines sui nisi quando jacet, non palam apparent."—DICUILUS, *De Mensura Orbis Terræ*, c. vii.

[2] *Cotton MSS.* NERO. D. 1. fol. 168, b.

[3] *Arundel MSS.* No. 292, fol. 4, &c. It has been printed in the *Reliquiæ Antiquæ*, vol. i. p. 208, by Mr. WRIGHT, to whom I am indebted for the following rendering of the passage referred to,

in water ge sal stonden
in water to mid side
ðat wanne hire harde tide
ðat ge ne falle niðer nogt
ðat it most in hire ðogt
for he ne haven no lið
ðat he mugen risen wið etc.

"They will stand in the water,
in water up to the middle of the side,
that when it comes to them hard,
they may not fall down:
that is most in their thought,
for they have no joint
to enable them to rise again.
How he resteth him this animal,
when he walketh abroad,
hearken how it is here told.
For he is all unwieldy,
forsooth he seeks out a tree,
that is strong and steadfast,
and leans confidently against it,
when he is weary of walking.
The hunter has observed this,
who seeks to ensnare him,
where his usual dwelling is,
to do his will;
saws this tree and props it
in the manner that he best may,
covers it well that he (the elephant) may not be on his guard.
Then he makes thereby a seat,
himself sits alone and watches
whether his trap takes effect.
Then cometh this unwieldy elephant,
and leans him on his side,
rests against the tree in the shadow,
and so both fall together.
If nobody be by when he falls,
he roars ruefully and calls for help,
roars ruefully in his manner,
hopes he shall through help rise.
Then cometh there one (elephant) in haste,
hopes he shall cause him to stand up;
labours and tries all his might,
but he cannot succeed a bit.
He knows then no other remedy,
but roars with his brother,
many and large (elephants) come there in search,
thinking to make him get up,
but for the help of them all
he may not get up.
Then they all roar one roar,
like the blast of a horn or the sound of bell;
for their great roaring
a young one cometh running,
stoops immediately to him,
puts his snout under him,
and asks the help of them all;
this elephant they raise on his legs:
and thus fails this hunter's trick,
in the manner that I have told you."

the fallen elephant was a favourite simile, and amongst others Richard de Barbezieux, in the latter half of the twelfth century, sung [1],

> "Atressi cum l' olifans
> Que quan chai no s' pot levar."

As elephants were but rarely seen in Europe prior to the seventeenth century, there were but few opportunities of correcting the popular fallacy by ocular demonstration. Hence SHAKSPEARE still believed that,

> "The elephant hath joints; but none for courtesy:
> His legs are for necessity, not flexure:" [2]

and DONNE sang of

> "Nature's great masterpiece, an Elephant;
> The only harmless great thing:
> Yet Nature hath given him no knee to bend:
> Himself he up props, on himself relies;
> Still sleeping stands." [3]

Sir THOMAS BROWNE, whilst he argues against the delusion, does not fail to record his suspicion, that "although the opinion at present be reasonably well suppressed, yet from the strings of tradition and fruitful recurrence of errour, it was not improbable it might revive in the next generation;" [4] — an anticipation which has proved singularly correct; for the heralds still continued to explain that the elephant is the emblem of watchfulness, "*nec jacet in somno*," [5] and poets almost of our own times paint the scene when

---

[1] One of the most venerable authorities by whom the fallacy was transmitted to modern times was PHILIP de THAUN, who wrote, about the year 1121 A.D., his *Livre des Créatures*, dedicated to Adelaide of Louvaine, Queen of Henry I. of England. In the copy of it printed by the Historical Society of Science in 1841, and edited by Mr. WRIGHT, the following passage occurs: —

> "Et Ysidres nus dit ki le elefant descrit,
> * * * * * *
> Es jambes par nature nen ad que une jointure,
> Il ne pot pas gesir quant il se voit dormir,
> Ke si cuchet estait par sei nen leverait;
> Pur çeo li stot apuier, el lui del cucher,
> U à arbre u à mur, idunc dort aseur.
> E le gent de la terre, ki li volent conquere,
> Li mur enfunderunt, u le arbre enciserunt;
> Quant li elefant vendrat, ki s'i apuierat,
> La arbre u le mur carrat, e il tribucherat;
> Issi faiterement le parnent cele gent."—P. 100.

[2] *Troilus and Cressida*, act ii. sc. 3. A.D. 1609.

[3] *Progress of the Soul*, A.D. 1633.

[4] Sir T. BROWNE, *Vulgar Errors*, A.D. 1646.

[5] RANDAL HOME'S *Academy of Armory*, A.D. 1678. HOME only

> "Peaceful, beneath primeval trees, that cast
> Their ample shade on Niger's yellow stream,
> Or where the Ganges rolls his sacred waves,
> *Leans* the huge Elephant."[1]

It is not difficult to see whence this antiquated delusion took its origin; nor is it, as Sir THOMAS BROWNE imagined, to be traced exclusively "to the grosse and cylindricall structure" of the animal's legs. The fact is, that the elephant returning in the early morning from his nocturnal revels in the reservoirs and water-courses, is accustomed to rub his muddy sides against a tree, and sometimes against a rock if more convenient. In my rides through the northern forests, the natives of Ceylon have often pointed out, that elephants of considerable size must have preceded me; from the height at which their marks had been left on the trees, against which they had been rubbing. Not unfrequently the animals themselves, overcome with drowsiness from the night's gambolling, are found dosing and resting against the trees they had so visited, and in the same manner they have been discovered by sportsmen asleep, and leaning against a rock.

It is scarcely necessary to explain that the position is accidental, and that it is taken by the elephant not from any difficulty in lying at length on the ground, but rather from the coincidence that the structure of his legs affords such support in a standing position, that reclining scarcely adds to his enjoyment of repose; and elephants in a state of captivity have been known for months together to sleep without lying down.[2] So

---

perpetuated the error of GUILLIM, who wrote his *Display of Heraldry* in A.D. 1610; wherein he explains that the elephant is "so proud of his strength that he never bows himself to any (*neither indeed can he*), and when he is once down he cannot rise up again."—Sec. III. ch. xiii. p. 147.

[1] THOMSON'S *Seasons*, A.D. 1728.

[2] So little is the elephant inclined to lie down in captivity, and even after hard labour, that the keepers are generally disposed to suspect illness when he betakes himself to this posture. PHILE, in his poem *De Animalium Proprietate*, attributes the propensity of the elephant to sleep on his legs, to the difficulty he experiences in rising to his feet:

> Ὀρθοστάδην δὲ καὶ καθεύδει παννύχως,
> Ὅτ' οὐκ ἀναστῆσαι μὲν εὐχερῶς πέλει.

But this is a misapprehension.

distinctive is this formation, and so self-sustaining the configuration of the limbs, that an elephant shot in the brain, by Major Rogers in 1836, was killed so instantaneously that it died literally *on its knees*, and remained resting on them. About the year 1826, Captain Dawson, the engineer of the great road to Kandy, over the Kadaganava pass, shot an elephant at Hangwélle on the banks of the Kalany Ganga; *it remained on its feet*, but so motionless, that after discharging a few more balls, he was induced to go close to it, and found it dead.

The real peculiarity in the elephant in lying down is, that he extends his hind legs backwards as a man does when he kneels, instead of bringing them under him like the horse or any other quadruped. The wise purpose of this arrangement must be obvious to any one who observes the struggle with which the horse *gets up* from the ground, and the violent efforts which he makes to raise himself erect. Such an exertion in the case of the elephant, and the force requisite to apply a similar movement to raise his weight (equal to four or five tons) would be attended with a dangerous strain upon the muscles, and hence the simple arrangement, which by enabling him to draw the hind feet gradually under him, assists him to rise almost without a perceptible effort.

The same construction renders his gait not a "gallop," as it has been somewhat loosely described [1], which would be too violent a motion for so vast a body; but a shuffle, that he can increase at pleasure to a pace as rapid as

---

[1] *Menageries, &c.* "The Elephant," ch. i.

Sir Charles Bell, in his essay on *The Hand and its Mechanism*, which forms one of the "Bridgewater Treatises," has exhibited the reasons deducible from organisation, which show the incapacity of the elephant to *spring* or *leap* like the horse and other animals whose structure is designed to facilitate agility and speed. In them the various bones of the shoulder and fore limbs, especially the clavicle and humerus, are set at such an angle, that the shock in descending is modified, and the joints and sockets protected from the injury occasioned by concussion. But in the elephant,

that of a man at full speed, but which he cannot maintain for any considerable distance.

It is to the structure of the knee-joint that the elephant is indebted for his singular facility in ascending and descending steep acclivities, climbing rocks and traversing precipitous ledges, where even a mule dare not venture; and this again leads to the correction of another generally received error, that his legs are "formed more for strength than flexibility, and fitted to bear an enormous weight upon a level surface, without the necessity of ascending or descending great acclivities."[1] The same authority assumes that, although the elephant is found in the neighbourhood of mountainous ranges, and will even ascend rocky passes, such a service is a violation of his natural habits.

Of the elephant of Africa I am not qualified to speak, nor of the nature of the ground which he most frequents; but certainly the facts in connection with the elephant of India are all irreconcilable with the theory mentioned above. In Bengal, in the Nilgherries, in Nepaul,

---

where the weight of the body is immense, the bones of the leg, in order to present solidity and strength to sustain it, are built in one firm and perpendicular column; instead of being placed somewhat obliquely at their points of contact. Thus whilst the force of the weight in descending is broken and distributed by this arrangement in the case of the horse; it would be so concentrated in the elephant as to endanger every joint from the toe to the shoulder.

[1] *Menageries, &c.*, "The Elephant," ch. ii.

in Burmah, in Siam, and Ceylon, the districts in which the elephants most abound, are all hilly and mountainous. In the latter, especially, there is not a range so elevated as to be inaccessible to them. On the very summit of Adam's Peak, at an altitude of 7,420 feet, and on a pinnacle which the pilgrims climb with difficulty, by means of steps hewn in the rock, Major Skinner, in 1840, found the spoor of an elephant.

Prior to 1840, and before coffee-plantations had been extensively opened in the Kandyan ranges, there was not a mountain or a lofty feature of land in Ceylon which they had not traversed, in their periodical migrations in search of water; and the sagacity which they display in "laying out roads" is almost incredible. They generally keep along the *backbone* of a chain of hills, avoiding steep gradients; and one curious observation was not lost upon the government surveyors, that in crossing the valleys from ridge to ridge, through forests so dense as altogether to obstruct a distant view, the elephants invariably select the line of march which communicates most judiciously with the opposite point, by means of *the safest ford*.[1] So sure-footed are they, that there are few places where man can go that an elephant cannot follow, provided there be space to admit his bulk, and solidity to sustain his weight.

This faculty is almost entirely derived from the unusual position, as compared with other quadrupeds, of the knee joint of the hind leg; arising from the superior length of the thigh-bone, and the shortness of the metatarsus: the heel being almost where it projects in man, instead of being lifted up as a "hock." It is this which enables him, in descending declivities, to depress and adjust the weight of his hinder portions, which

---

[1] Dr. HOOKER, in describing the ascent of the Himalayas, says, the natives in making their paths despise all zigzags, and run in straight lines up the steepest hill faces; whilst "the elephant's path is an excellent specimen of engineering—the opposite of the native track,—for it winds judiciously."—*Himalayan Journal*, vol. i. ch. iv.

would otherwise overbalance and force him headlong.[1] It is by the same arrangement that he is enabled, on uneven ground, to lift his feet, which are tender and sensitive, with delicacy, and plant them with such precision as to ensure his own safety as well as that of objects which it is expedient to avoid touching.

A *herd* of elephants is a family. It is not a group

[1] Since the above passage was written, I have seen in the *Journal of the Asiatic Society of Bengal*, vol. xiii. pt. ii. p. 916, a paper upon this subject, illustrated by the subjoined diagram.

ELEPHANT DESCENDING A DECLIVITY.

The writer says, "an elephant descending a bank of too acute an angle to admit of his walking down it direct, (which, were he to attempt, his huge body, soon disarranging the centre of gravity, would certainly topple over) proceeds thus. His first manœuvre is to kneel down close to the edge of the declivity, placing his chest to the ground: one fore-leg is then cautiously passed a short way down the slope; and if there is no natural protection to afford a firm footing, he speedily forms one by stamping into the soil if moist, or kicking out a footing if dry. This point gained, the other fore-leg is brought down in the same way; and performs the same work, a little in advance of the first; which is thus at liberty to move lower still. Then, first one and then the second of the hind legs is carefully drawn over the side, and the hind-feet in turn occupy the resting places previously used and left by the fore ones. The course, however, in such precipitous ground is not straight from top to bottom, but slopes along the face of the bank, descending till the animal gains the level below. This an elephant has done, at an angle of 45 degrees, carrying a *howdah*, its occupant, his attendant, and sporting apparatus; and in a much less time than it takes to describe the operation."

whom accident or attachment may have induced to associate together; and similarity of features and caste attest that among the various individuals which compose it, there is a common lineage and relationship. In a herd of twenty-one elephants, captured in 1844, the trunks of each individual presented the same peculiar formation, — long, and almost of one uniform breadth throughout, instead of tapering gradually from the root to the nostril. In another instance, the eyes of thirty-five taken in one kraal were of the same colour in each. The same slope of the back, the same form of the forehead, is to be detected in the majority of the same group.

In the forest several herds will browse in close contiguity, and in their expeditions in search of water they may form a body of possibly one or two hundred; but on the slightest disturbance each distinct herd hastens to re-form within its own particular circle, and to take measures on its own behalf for retreat or defence.

The natives of any place which may chance to be frequented by elephants, observe that the numbers of the same herd fluctuate very slightly; and hunters in pursuit of them, who may chance to have shot one or more, always reckon with certainty the precise number of those remaining, although a considerable interval may intervene before they again encounter them. The proportion of males is generally small, and some herds have been seen composed exclusively of females; possibly in consequence of the males having been shot. A herd usually consists of from ten to twenty individuals, though occasionally they exceed the latter number; and in their frequent migrations and nightly resort to tanks and water-courses, alliances are formed between members of associated herds, which serve to introduce new blood into the family.

In illustration of the attachment of the elephant to its young, the authority of KNOX has been quoted, that "the shes are alike tender of any one's young ones as of their own."[1] Their affection in this particular is undoubted, but I question whether it exceeds that of other animals; and even the trait thus adduced of their indiscriminate kindness to all the young of the herd,—a fact to which I have myself been an eye-witness,—so far from being an evidence of the strength of parental attachment individually, is, perhaps, somewhat inconsistent with the existence of such a passion to any extraordinary degree.[2] In fact, some individuals, who have had extensive facilities for observation, doubt whether the fondness of the female elephants for their offspring is so great as that of many other animals; as instances are not wanting in Ceylon, in which, when pursued by the hunters, the herd has abandoned the young ones in their flight, notwithstanding the cries of the latter for help.

In an interesting paper on the habits of the Indian

---

[1] A correspondent of Buffon, M. Marcellus Bles, Seigneur de Moergestal, who resided eleven years in Ceylon in the time of the Dutch, says in one of his communications, that in herds of forty or fifty, enclosed in a single corral, there were frequently very young calves; and that "on ne pouvoit pas reconnaitre qu'elles étoient les mères de chacun de ces petites éléphans, car tous ces jeunes animaux paroissent faire manse commune; ils têtent indistinctement celles des femelles de toute la troupe que ont du lait, soit qu'elles aient elles-mêmes un petit en propre, soit qu'elles n'en aient point."—Buffon, *Suppl. à l'Hist. des Anim.*, vol. vi. p. 25.

[2] White, in his *Natural History of Selborne*, philosophising on the fact which had fallen under his own notice of this indiscriminate suckling of the young of one animal by the parent of another, is disposed to ascribe it to a selfish feeling; the pleasure and relief of having its distended teats drawn by this intervention. He notices the circumstance of a leveret having been thus nursed by a cat, whose kittens had been recently drowned; and observes, that "this strange affection probably was occasioned by that desiderium, those tender maternal feelings, which the loss of her kittens had awakened in her breast; and by the complacency and ease she derived to herself from procuring her teats to be drawn, which were too much distended with milk; till from habit she became as much delighted with this foundling as if it had been her real offspring. This incident is no bad solution of that strange circumstance which grave historians, as well as the poets, assert of exposed children being sometimes nurtured by female wild beasts that probably had lost their young. For it is not one whit more marvellous that Romulus and Remus in their infant state should be nursed by a she wolf than that a poor little suckling leveret should be fostered and cherished by a bloody Grimalkin."—White's *Selborne*, lett. xx.

elephant, published by Mr. CORSE, in the *Philosophical Transactions for* 1793, he says: "if a wild elephant happens to be separated from its young for only two days, though giving suck, she never after recognises or acknowledges it," although the young one evidently knew its dam, and by its plaintive cries and submissive approaches solicited her assistance.

An elephant, if by any accident he becomes hopelessly separated from his own herd, is not permitted to attach himself to any other. He may browse in the vicinity, or frequent the same place to drink and to bathe; but the intercourse is only on a distant and conventional footing, and no familiarity or intimate association is under any circumstances permitted. To such a height is this exclusiveness carried, that even amidst the terror and stupefaction of an elephant corral, when an individual, detached from his own party in the *mêlée* and confusion, has been driven into the inclosure with an unbroken herd, I have seen him repulsed in every attempt to take refuge among them, and driven off by heavy blows with their trunks as often as he attempted to insinuate himself within the circle which they had formed for common security. There can be no reasonable doubt that this jealous and exclusive policy not only contributes to produce, but mainly serves to perpetuate, the class of solitary elephants which are known by the term *goondahs*, in India, and from their vicious propensities and predatory habits are called *Hora*, or *Rogues*, in Ceylon.[1]

---

[1] The term "rogue" is scarcely sufficiently accounted for by supposing it to be the English equivalent for the Singhalese word *Hora*. In a very curious book, the *Life and Adventures of* JOHN CHRISTOPHER WOLF, *late principal Secretary of State at Jaffnapatam in Ceylon,* the author says, when a male elephant in a quarrel about the females "is beat out of the field and obliged to go without a consort, he becomes furious and mad, killing every living creature be it man or beast: and in this state is called *ronkedor*, an object of greater terror to a traveller than a hundred wild ones."—P. 142. In another passage, p. 164, he is called *runkedor*, and I have seen it spelt elsewhere *ronquedue*. WOLF was a native of Mecklenburg; who arrived in Ceylon about 1750, A. D., as Chaplain in one of the Dutch East Indiamen, and being taken into the government

These are believed by the Singhalese to be either individuals, who by accident have lost their former associates and become morose and savage from rage and solitude; or else that being naturally vicious they have become daring from the yielding habits of their milder companions, and eventually separated themselves from the rest of the herd which had refused to associate with them. Another conjecture is, that being almost universally males, the death or capture of particular females may have detached them from their former companions in search of fresh alliances.[1] It is also believed that a tame elephant escaping from captivity, unable to rejoin its former herd, and excluded from any other, becomes a "*rogue*" from necessity. In Ceylon it is generally believed that the *rogues* are all males (but of this I am not certain), and so sullen is their disposition that although two may be in the same vicinity, there is no known instance of their associating, or of a *rogue* being seen in company with another elephant.

They spend their nights in marauding chiefly about the dwellings of men, destroying their plantations, trampling down their gardens, and committing serious ravages in rice grounds and young coco-nut planta-

---

employment he served for twenty years at Jaffna, first as Secretary to the Governor, and afterwards in an office the duties of which he describes to be the examination and signature of the "writings which served to commence a suit in any of the Courts of justice." His book embodies a truthful and generally accurate account of the northern portion of the island, with which alone he was conversant, and his narrative gives a curious insight into the policy of the Dutch Government, and the condition of the natives under their dominion. WOLF does not give "*ronkedor*" as a term peculiar to that section of the island; but both there and elsewhere, it is obsolete at the present day, unless it be open to conjecture that the modern term "rogue" is a modification of *ronquedue*.

[1] BUCHANAN, in his *Survey of Bhagulpore*, p. 503, says, that solitary males of the wild buffalo, "when driven from the herd by stronger competitors for female society, are reckoned very dangerous to meet with; for they are apt to wreak their vengeance on whatever they meet, and are said to kill annually three or four people." LIVINGSTONE relates the same of the solitary hippopotamus, which becomes soured in temper, and wantonly attacks the passing canoes.—*Travels in South Africa*, p. 231.

tions. Hence from their closer contact with man and his dwellings, these outcasts become disabused of many of the terrors which render the ordinary elephant timid and needlessly cautious: they break through fences without fear; and even in the daylight a *rogue* has been known near Ambogammoa to watch a field of labourers at work in reaping rice, and boldly to walk in amongst them, seize a sheaf from the heap, and retire leisurely to the jungle. By day they seek concealment, but are to be met with prowling about the by-roads and jungle paths, where travellers are exposed to the utmost risk from their savage assaults. It is probable that this hostility to man is the result of the enmity engendered by those measures which the natives, who have a constant dread of their visits, adopt for the protection of their growing crops. In some districts, especially in the low country of Badulla, the villagers occasionally enclose their cottages with rude walls of earth and branches to protect them from nightly assaults. In places infested by them, the visits of European sportsmen to the vicinity of their haunts are eagerly encouraged by the natives, who think themselves happy in lending their services to track the ordinary herds in consideration of the benefit conferred on the village communities, by the destruction of a *rogue*. In 1847 one of these formidable creatures frequented for some months the Rangbodde Pass on the great mountain road leading to the *sanatarium*, at Neuera-ellia; and one morning, at daybreak, I rode up to the spot where he had killed one of the corps of Caffre pioneers but a few moments before, by seizing him with his trunk and beating him to death against the bank.

To return to the herd: one member of it, generally the largest and most powerful, is by common consent implicitly followed as leader. A tusker, if there be one in the party, is generally observed to be the commander; but a female, if of superior energy, is as readily obeyed as a male. In fact, in the promotion of a leader there is no reason to doubt that supremacy is almost unconsciously assumed by those endowed with vigour and courage rather than from the accidental possession of greater bodily strength; and the devotion and loyalty which the herd evince to their leader is something very remarkable. This is more readily seen in the case of a tusker than any other, because in a herd he is generally the object of the keenest pursuit by the hunters. On such occasions the elephants do their utmost to protect him from danger: when driven to extremity they place the leader in the centre and crowd so eagerly in front of him that the sportsmen have to shoot a number which they might otherwise have spared. In one instance a tusker, which was badly wounded by Major Rogers, was promptly surrounded by his companions, who supported him between their shoulders, and actually succeeded in covering his retreat to the forest.

Those who have lived much in the jungle in Ceylon, and who have had constant opportunities of watching the habits of wild elephants, have witnessed instances of the submission of herds to their leaders, which create a singular interest as to the means adopted by the latter to communicate with distinctness, orders which are observed with the most implicit obedience by their followers. The narrative of an adventure in the great central forest toward the north of the island, which has been communicated to me by Major SKINNER, who was engaged for some time in surveying and opening roads through the thickly-wooded districts there, will serve better than any abstract description to convey an idea of the conduct of a herd on such occasions: —

"The case you refer to struck me as exhibiting something more than ordinary brute instinct, and approached nearer to reasoning powers than any other instance I can now remember. I cannot do justice to the scene, although it appeared to me at the time to be so remarkable that it left a deep impression in my mind.

"In the height of the dry season in Neuera-Ka-lawa, you know the streams are all dried up, and the tanks nearly so. All animals are then sorely pressed for water, and they congregate in the vicinity of those tanks in which there may remain ever so little of the precious element.

"During one of those seasons I was encamped on the bund or embankment of a very small tank, the water in which was so dried up that its surface could not have exceeded an area of 500 square yards. It was the only pond within many miles, and I knew that of necessity a very large herd of elephants, which had been in the neighbourhood all day, must resort to it at night.

"On the lower side of the tank, and in a line with the embankment, was a thick forest, in which the elephants sheltered themselves during the day. On the upper side and all around the tank there was a considerable margin of open ground. It was one of those beautiful, bright, clear, moonlight nights, when objects could be seen almost as distinctly as by day, and I determined to avail myself of the opportunity to observe the movements of the herd, which had already manifested some uneasiness at our presence. The locality was very favourable for my purpose, and an enormous tree projecting over the tank afforded me a secure lodgment in its branches. Having ordered the fires of my camp to be extinguished at an early hour, and all my followers to retire to rest, I took up my post of observation on the overhanging bough; but I had to remain for upwards of two hours before anything was to be seen or heard of the elephants, although I knew they were within 500 yards of me. At length, about the distance of 300 yards from the water, an unusually large elephant issued from the dense cover, and advanced cautiously across the open ground to within 100 yards of the tank, where he stood perfectly motionless. So quiet had the elephants become (although they had been roaring and breaking the jungle throughout the day and evening), that not a movement was now to be heard. The huge vidette remained in his position, still as a rock, for a few minutes, and then made three successive stealthy advances of several yards (halting for some minutes between each, with ears bent forward to catch the slightest sound), and in this way he moved slowly up to the water's edge. Still he did not venture to quench his thirst, for though his fore feet were partially in the tank and his vast body was reflected clear in the water, he remained for some minutes listening in perfect stillness. Not a motion could be perceived in himself or his shadow. He returned cautiously and slowly to the position he had at first taken up on emerging from the forest. Here in a little while he was joined by five others, with which he again proceeded as cautiously, but less slowly than before, to within a few yards of the tank, and then posted his patrols. He then re-entered the forest and collected around him the whole herd, which must have amounted to between 80 and 100 individuals, — led them across the open ground with the most extraordinary composure and quietness, till he joined the advanced guard, when he left them for a moment and repeated his former reconnoissance at the edge of the tank. After which, and having apparently satisfied himself that all was safe, he returned and obviously gave the order to advance, for in a moment the whole herd rushed into the water with a degree of unreserved confidence, so opposite to the caution and timidity which had marked their previous movements, that nothing will ever persuade me that there was not rational and preconcerted co-operation throughout the whole party, and a degree of responsible authority exercised by the patriarch leader.

"When the poor animals had gained possession of the tank (the leader being the last to enter), they seemed to abandon themselves to enjoyment without restraint or apprehension of danger. Such a mass of animal life I had never before seen huddled together in so narrow a space. It seemed to me as though they would have nearly drunk the tank dry. I watched them with great interest until they had satisfied themselves as well in bathing as in drinking, when I tried how small a noise would apprise them of the proximity of unwelcome neighbours. I had but to break a little twig, and the solid mass instantly took to flight like a herd of frightened deer, each of the smaller calves being apparently shouldered and carried along between two of the older ones." [1]

In drinking, the elephant, like the camel, although preferring water pure, shows no decided aversion to it when discoloured with mud [2]; and the eagerness with which he precipitates himself into the tanks and streams attests his exquisite enjoyment of the fresh coolness, which to him is the chief attraction. In crossing deep rivers, although his rotundity and buoyancy enable him to swim with a less immersion than other quadrupeds, he generally prefers to sink till no part of his huge body is visible except the tip of his trunk, through which he breathes, moving beneath the surface, and only now and then raising his head to look that he is keeping the proper direction.[3] In the dry season the scanty streams which, during the rains, are sufficient to convert the rivers of the low country into torrents, frequently entirely disappear, leaving merely broad expanses of dry sand, which they have swept down with them from the hills. In this the elephants contrive

---

[1] Letter from Major SKINNER.

[2] This peculiarity was known in the middle ages, and PHILE, writing in the fourteenth century, says, that such is his *preference* for muddy water that the elephant *stirs it* before he drinks.

"Ὕδωρ δε πίνει συγχυθὲν πριν ἂν πίνοι
Τὸ γὰρ διειδὲς ἀκρίβῶς διαπτύει."—
PHILE *de Eleph.*, l. 144.

[3] A tame elephant, when taken by his keepers to be bathed, and to have his skin washed and rubbed, lies down on his side, pressing his head to the bottom under water, with only the top of his trunk protruded, to breathe.

to sink wells for their own use by scooping out the sand to the depth of four or five feet, and leaving a hollow for the percolation of the spring. But as the weight of the elephant would force in the side if left perpendicular, one approach is always formed with such a gradient that the water can be reached with his trunk without his disturbing the surrounding sand.

I have reason to believe, although the fact has not been authoritatively stated by naturalists, that the stomach of the elephant will be found to include a section analogous to that possessed by some of the ruminants, calculated to contain a supply of water as a provision against emergencies. The fact of his being enabled to retain a quantity of water and discharge it at pleasure has been known to every one observant of the habits of the animal; but the proboscis has always been supposed to be "his water-reservoir,"[1] and the theory of an internal receptacle has not been discussed. The truth is that the anatomy of the elephant is even yet but imperfectly understood[2], and, although some peculiarities of his

[1] BRODERIP's *Zoological Recreations*, p. 259.

[2] For observing the osteology of the elephant, materials are of course abundant in the indestructible remains of the animal: but the study of the intestines, and the dissection of the softer parts by comparative anatomists in Europe, have been up to the present time beset by difficulties, not alone from the rarity of subjects, but even in cases where elephants have died in these countries, decomposition interposes, and before the thorough examination of so vast a body can be satisfactorily completed, the great mass falls into putrefaction.

The principal English authorities are *An Anatomical Account of the Elephant accidentally burnt in Dublin*, by A. MOLYNEUX, A. D. 1696; which is probably a reprint of a letter on the same subject in the library of Trinity College, Dublin, addressed by A. Moulin, to Sir William Petty, Lond. 1682. There are also some papers communicated to Sir Hans Sloane, and afterwards published in the *Philosophical Transactions* of the year 1710, by Dr. P. BLAIR, who had an opportunity of dissecting an elephant which died at Dundee in 1708. The latter writer observes that, "notwithstanding the vast interest attaching to the elephant in all ages, yet has its body been hitherto very little subjected to

stomach were observed at an early period, and even their configuration described, the function of the abnormal portion remained undetermined, and has been only recently conjectured. An elephant which belonged to Louis XIV. died at Versailles in 1681 at the age of seventeen, and an account of its dissection was published in the *Mémoires pour servir à l'Histoire Naturelle*, under the authority of the Academy of Sciences, in which the unusual appendages of the stomach are pointed out with sufficient particularity, but no suggestion is made as to their probable uses."[1]

A writer in the *Quarterly Review* for December 1850, says that, "CAMPER and other comparative anatomists have shown that the left, or cardiac end of the stomach in the elephant is adapted, by several wide folds of

---

anatomical inquiries;" and he laments that the rapid decomposition of the carcase, and other causes, had interposed obstacles to the scrutiny of the subject he was so fortunate as to find access to.

In 1723 Dr. WM. STUCKLEY published *Some Anatomical Observations made upon the Dissection of an Elephant;* but each of the above essays is necessarily unsatisfactory, and little has since been done to supply their defects. One of the latest and most valuable contributions to the subject, is a paper read before the Royal Irish Academy, on the 18th of Feb., 1847, by Professor HARRISON, who had the opportunity of dissecting an Indian elephant which died of acute fever; but the examination, so far as he has made it public, extends only to the cranium, the brain, and the proboscis, the larynx, trachea, and œsophagus. An essential service would be rendered to science if some sportsman in Ceylon, or some of the officers connected with the elephant establishment there, would take the trouble to forward the carcase of a young one to England in a state fit for dissection.

Postscriptum.—I am happy to say that whilst the first edition of this work was passing through the press, a young elephant carefully preserved in spirits has been obtained in Ceylon, and forwarded to Prof. OWEN of the British Museum, by the joint exertions of M. DIARD, and Major SKINNER. An opportunity has thus been afforded from which science will reap advantage, of devoting a patient attention to the internal structure of this interesting animal.

[1] The passage as quoted by BUFFON from the *Mémoires* is as follows:—"L'estomac avoit peu de diamètre; il en avoit moins que le colon, car son diamètre n'étoit que de quatorze pouces dans la partie la plus large; il avoit trois pieds et demi de longueur: l'orifice supérieur étoit à-peu-près aussi éloigné du pylore que du fond du grand cul-de-sac qui se terminoit en une pointe composée de tuniques beaucoup plus épaisses que celles du reste de l'estomac; il y avoit au fond du grand cul-de-sac plusieurs feuillets épais d'une ligne, larges d'un pouce et demi, et disposés irrégulièrement; le reste de parois intérieures étoit percé de plusieurs petits trous et par de plus grands qui correspondoient à des grains glanduleux."—BUFFON, *Hist. Nat.*, vol. xi. p. 109.

lining membrane, to serve as a receiver for water;" but this is scarcely correct, for although CAMPER has figured accurately the external form of the stomach, he disposes of the question of the interior functions with the simple remark that its folds "semblent en faire une espèce de division particulière."[1] In like manner Sir EVERARD HOME, in his *Lectures on Comparative Anatomy*, has not only described carefully the form of the elephant's stomach, and furnished a drawing of it even more accurate than CAMPER; but he has equally omitted to assign any purpose to so strange a formation, contenting himself with observing that the structure is a peculiarity, and that one of the remarkable folds nearest the orifice of the diaphragm appears to act as a valve, so that the portion beyond may be considered as an appendage similar to that of the hog and the *peccary*.[2]

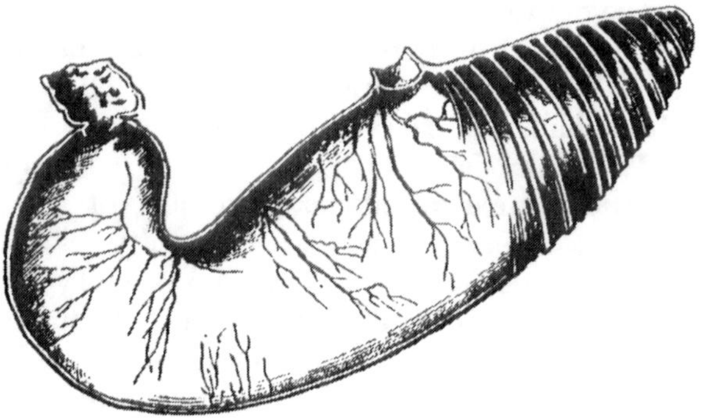

ELEPHANT'S STOMACH.

[1] "L'extrémité voisine du cardia se termine par une poche très considérable et doublée à l'intérieure du quatorze valvules orbiculaires que semblent en faire une espèce de division particulière." — CAMPER, *Description Anatomique d'un Elephant Male*, p. 37. tabl. IX.

[2] "The elephant has another peculiarity in the internal structure of the stomach. It is longer and narrower than that of most animals. The cuticular membrane of the œsophagus terminates at the orifice of the stomach. At the cardiac end, which is very narrow and pointed at the extremity, the lining is thick and glandular, and is thrown into transverse folds, of which five are broad and nine narrow. That nearest the orifice of the œsophagus is the broadest and appears to act occasionally as a valve, so that the part beyond may be considered as an appendage similar to that of the peccary and the hog. The membrane of the cardiac portion

The appendage thus alluded to by Sir EVERARD HOME is the "grand cul-de-sac," noticed by the Académie des Sciences, and the "division particulière," figured by CAMPER. It is of sufficient dimensions to contain ten gallons of water, and by means of the valve above alluded to it can be shut off from the chamber devoted to the process of digestion. Professor OWEN is probably the first who, not from an autopsy, but from the mere inspection of the drawings of CAMPER and HOME, ventured to assert, in lectures hitherto unpublished, that the uses of this section of the elephant's stomach may be analogous to those ascertained to belong to a somewhat similar arrangement in the stomach of the camel, one cavity of which is exclusively employed as a reservoir for water, and performs no function in the preparation of food.[1]

Whilst Professor OWEN was advancing this conjecture, another comparative anatomist, from the examination of another portion of the structure of the elephant, was led to a somewhat similar conclusion. Dr. HARRISON of Dublin had, in 1847, an opportunity of dissecting the body of an elephant which had suddenly died; and in the course of his examination of the thoracic viscera, he observed that an unusually close connection existed between the trachea and œsophagus, which he found to depend on a muscle unnoticed by any previous anatomist, connecting the back of the former with the forepart of the latter, along which the fibres descend and can be distinctly traced to the cardiac orifice of the stomach. Imperfectly acquainted with the habits and functions of the elephant in a state of

---

is uniformly smooth; that of the pyloric is thicker and more vascular."
—*Lectures on Comparative Anatomy*, by Sir EVERARD HOME, Bart. 4to. Lond. vol. i. p. 155. The figure of the elephant's stomach is given vol. ii. plate xviii.

[1] A similar arrangement, with some modifications, has more recently been found in the llama of the Andes, which, like the camel, is used as a beast of burden in the Cordilleras of Chili and Peru; but both these and the camel are *ruminants*, whilst the elephant belongs to the Pachydermata.

nature, Dr HARRISON found it difficult to pronounce as to the use of this very peculiar structure; but looking to the intimate connection between the mechanism concerned in the functions of respiration and deglutition,

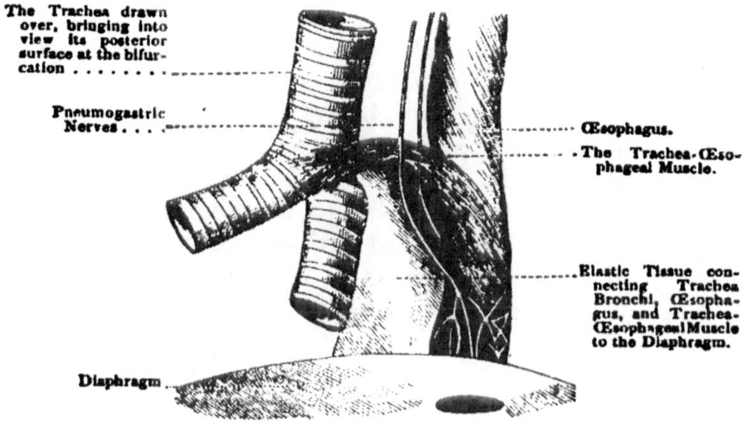

and seeing that the proboscis served in a double capacity as an instrument of voice and an organ for the prehension of food, he ventured (apparently without adverting to the abnormal form of the stomach) to express the opinion that this muscle, viewing its attachment to the trachea, might either have some influence in raising the diaphragm, and thereby assisting in expiration, "*or that it might raise the cardiac orifice of the stomach, and so aid this organ to regurgitate a portion of its contents into the œsophagus.*" [1]

Dr. HARRISON, on the reflection that "we have no satisfactory evidence that the animal ever ruminates," thought it useless to speculate on the latter supposition as to the action of the newly discovered muscle, and rather inclined to the surmise that it was designed to assist the elephant in producing the remarkable sound

---

[1] *Proceed. Roy. Irish Acad.*, vol. iv. p. 133.

through his proboscis known as "trumpeting;" but there is little room to doubt that of the two the rejected hypothesis was the correct one. I have elsewhere described the occurrence to which I was myself a witness, of elephants' inserting their proboscis in their mouths, and by the aid of the "trachea-œsophageal" muscle, described by Professor HARRISON, withdrawing gallons of water, which could only have been contained in the receptacle figured by CAMPER and HOME, and of which the true uses were discerned by the clear intellect of Professor OWEN. I was not, till very recently, aware that a similar observation as to the remarkable habit of the elephant, has been made by the author of the *Ayeen Akbery*, in his account of the *Feel Kaneh*, or elephant stables of the Emperor Akbar, in which he says, "an elephant frequently with his trunk, takes water out of his stomach and sprinkles himself with it, and it is not in the least offensive."[1] FORBES, in his Oriental Memoirs, quotes this passage of the *Ayeen Akbery*, but without a remark; nor does any European writer with whose works I am acquainted appear to have been cognisant of the peculiarity in question.

It is to be hoped that Professor OWEN'S dissection of the young elephant, recently arrived, may serve to decide this highly interesting point.[2] Should scientific investigation hereafter more clearly establish the fact that, in this particular, the structure of the elephant is assimilated to those of the llama and the camel, it will be regarded as more than a common coincidence, that an apparatus, so unique in its purpose and action, should thus have been conferred by the

---

[1] *Ayeen Akbery*, transl. of GLADWIN, vol. i. pt. i. p. 147.

[2] One of the Indian names for the elephant is *duipa*, which signifies "to drink twice" (AMANDI, p. 513). Can this have reference to the peculiarity of the stomach for retaining a supply of water? Or has it merely reference to the habit of the animal to fill his trunk before transferring the water to his mouth?

Creator on the three animals which in sultry climates are, by this arrangement, enabled to traverse arid regions in the service of man.[1]

The *food* of the elephant is so abundant, that in eating he never appears to be impatient or voracious, but rather to play with the leaves and branches on which he leisurely feeds. In riding by places where a herd has recently halted, I have sometimes seen the bark peeled curiously off the twigs, as though it had been done for amusement. In the same way in eating grass, the elephant selects a tussac which he draws from the ground by a dexterous twist of his trunk, and nothing can be more graceful than the ease with which, before conveying it to his mouth, he beats the earth from its roots by striking it gently upon his fore leg. A cocoanut he first rolls under foot, to detach the strong outer bark, then stripping off the thick layer of fibre within, he places the shell in his mouth, and swallows with evident relish the fresh liquid which flows as he crushes it between his grinders.

The natives of the peninsula of Jaffna always look for the periodical appearance of the elephants, at the precise moment when the fruit of the palmyra palm begins to fall to the ground from their ripeness. In like manner in the eastern provinces, where the custom prevails of cultivating *chena* land, by clearing a patch of forest for the purpose of raising a single crop, after which the ground is abandoned, and reverts to jungle again, although a single elephant may not be seen in the neighbourhood during the early stages of the process, the Moormen, who are the principal cultivators of this class, will predict their appearance with almost

---

[1] The buffalo and the humped cattle of India, which are used for draught and burden, have, I believe, a development of the organisation of the reticulum which enables the ruminants generally to endure thirst, and abstain from water, somewhat more marked than is found in the rest of their congeners; but nothing that approaches in singularity of character to the distinct cavities of the stomach exhibited by the three animals above alluded to.

unerring confidence so soon as the grains shall have begun to ripen; and although the crop comes to maturity at a different period in different districts, the herd are certain to be seen at each in succession, as soon as it is ready to be cut. In these well-timed excursions, they resemble the bison of North America, which, by a similarly mysterious instinct, finds its way to those portions of the distant prairies, where accidental fires have been followed by a growth of tender grass. Although the fences around these *chenas* are little more than lines of reeds loosely fastened together, they are sufficient, with the presence of a single watcher, to prevent the entrance of the elephants, who wait patiently till the rice and *coracan* have been removed, and the watcher withdrawn; and, then finding gaps in the fence, they may be seen gleaning among the leavings and the stubble; and they take their departure when these are exhausted, apparently in the direction of some other *chena*, which they have ascertained to be about to be cut.

There is something still unexplained in the dread which an elephant always exhibits on approaching a fence, and the reluctance which he displays to face the slightest artificial obstruction to his passage. In the fine old tank of Tissa-weva, close by Anarajapoora, the natives cultivate grain, during the dry season, around the margin where the ground has been left bare by the subsidence of the water. These little patches of rice they enclose with small sticks an inch in diameter and five or six feet in height, such as would scarcely serve to keep out a wild hog if he attempted to force his way through. Passages of from ten to twenty feet wide are left between each field, to permit the wild elephants which abound in the vicinity, to make their nocturnal visits to the water remaining in the tank. Night after night these open pathways are frequented by immense herds, but the tempting corn is never touched, nor is a single fence disturbed, although the merest movement of a trunk would be sufficient to demolish the fragile structure. Yet the same spots, as soon as the grain has been cut and carried home, are eagerly entered by the elephants, who resort to glean amongst the stubble.

Sportsmen observe that the elephant, even when enraged by a wound, will hesitate to charge its assailant across an intervening hedge, but will hurry along it to seek for an opening. It is possible that, in the mind of the elephant, there may be some instinctive consciousness, that owing to his superior bulk, he is exposed to danger from sources that might be perfectly harmless in the case of lighter animals, and hence his suspicion that every fence may conceal a snare or pitfall. Some similar apprehension is apparent in the deer, which shrinks from attempting a fence of wire, although it will clear without hesitation a solid wall of greater height. At the same time, the caution with which the elephant is supposed to approach insecure ground and places of doubtful[1] solidity, appears to me, so far as my own observation and experience extend, to be exaggerated, and the number of temporary bridges which are annually broken down by elephants in all parts of Ceylon, is sufficient to show that, although in captivity, and when familiar with such structures, the tame ones may, and doubtless do, exhibit all the wariness attributed to them; yet, in a state of liberty, and whilst unaccustomed to such artificial appliances, their instincts are not sufficient to ensure their safety. Besides, the fact is adverted to elsewhere[2], that the chiefs of the Wanny, during the sovereignty of the Dutch, were accustomed to take in pitfalls the elephants which they rendered as tribute to government.

---

[1] "One of the strongest instincts which the elephant possesses, is this which impels him to experiment upon the solidity of every surface which he is required to cross." —*Menageries, &c.* "The Elephant," vol. i. pp. 17, 19, 60.

[2] WOLF'S *Life and Adventures*, p. 151.

A fact illustrative at once of the caution and the spirit of curiosity with which an elephant regards an unaccustomed object, has been frequently told to me by the officers engaged in opening roads through the forest. On such occasions the wooden "tracing pegs" which they are obliged to drive into the ground to mark the levels taken during the day, will often be withdrawn by the elephants during the night, to such an extent as frequently to render it necessary to go over the work a second time, in order to replace them.[1]

As regards the general sagacity of the elephant, although it has not been over-rated in the instance of those whose powers have been largely developed in captivity, an undue estimate has been formed in relation to them whilst still untamed. The difference of instincts and habits renders it difficult to institute a just comparison between them and other animals. CUVIER[2] is disposed to ascribe the exalted idea that prevails of their intellect to the feats which an elephant performs with that unique instrument, its trunk, combined with an imposing expression of countenance; but he records his own conviction that in sagacity it in no way excels the dog, and some other species of Carnivora. If there be a superiority, I am disposed to award it to the dog, not from any excess of natural capacity, but from the higher degree of development consequent on his more intimate domestication and association with man.

One remarkable fact was called to my attention by a

---

[1] The *Colombo Observer* for March 1858, contains an offer of a reward of twenty-five guineas for the destruction of an elephant which infested the Rajawelli coffee plantation, in the vicinity of Kandy. His object seemed to be less the search for food, than the satisfying of his curiosity and the gratification of his passion for mischief. Mr. TYTLER, the proprietor, states that he frequented the jungle near the estate, whence it was his custom to sally forth at night for the pleasure of pulling down buildings and trees, "and he seemed to have taken a spite at the pipes of the water-works, the pillars of which he several times broke down—his latest fancy was to wrench off the cocks." The elephant has since been shot.

[2] CUVIER, *Règne Animal.* "Les Mammifères," p. 280.

gentleman who resided on a coffee plantation at Raxava, one of the loftiest mountains of the Ambogammoa range. More than once during the terrific thunder-bursts that precede the rains at the change of each monsoon, he observed that the elephants in the adjoining forests hastened from under cover of the trees and took up their station in the open ground, where I saw them on one occasion collected into a group; and here, he said, it was their custom to remain till the lightning had ceased, when they retired again into the jungle.[1]

When free in his native woods the elephant evinces rather simplicity than sagacity, and his intelligence seldom exhibits itself in cunning. The rich profusion in which nature has supplied his food, and anticipated his every want, has made him independent of those devices by which carnivorous animals provide for their subsistence; and, from the absence of all rivalry between himself and the other denizens of the plains, he is never required to resort to artifice for self-protection. For these reasons, in his tranquil and harmless life, he may appear to casual observers to exhibit even less than ordinary ability; but when danger and apprehension call for the exertion of his powers, those who have witnessed their display are seldom inclined to undervalue his sagacity.

Mr. Cripps has related to me an instance in which a recently captured elephant was either rendered senseless from fear, or, as the native attendants asserted, *feigned death* in order to regain its freedom. It was led from the corral as usual between two tame ones, and had already proceeded far on its way towards its destination; when night closing in, and the torches being lighted, it hesitated to go on, and finally sank to the ground apparently lifeless. Mr. Cripps ordered the fastenings to be removed from its legs, and when all attempts to raise it had failed,

[1] The elephant is believed by the Singhalese to express his uneasiness by his voice, on the approach of *rain*; and the Tamils have a proverb, —"*Listen to the elephant, rain is coming.*"

so convinced was he that it was dead, that he ordered the ropes to be collected and the carcase to be abandoned. While this was being done he and a gentleman by whom he was accompanied leaned against the body to rest. They had scarcely taken their departure and proceeded a few yards, when, to their astonishment, the elephant rose with the utmost alacrity, and fled towards the jungle, screaming at the top of its voice, its cries being audible long after it had disappeared in the shades of the forest.

CHAP. III.

ELEPHANT SHOOTING.

As the shooting of an elephant, whatever endurance and adroitness the sport may display in other respects, requires the smallest possible skill as a marksman, the numbers which are annually slain in this way may be regarded as evidence of the multitudes abounding in those parts of Ceylon to which they resort. One officer, Major Rogers, killed upwards of 1200; another, Captain Gallwey, has the credit of slaying more than half that number; Major Skinner, now the Commissioner of Roads, almost as many; and less persevering aspirants follow at humbler distances.[1]

But notwithstanding this prodigious destruction, a reward of a few shillings per head offered by the Government for taking elephants was claimed for 3500 destroyed in part of the northern province alone, in less than three years prior to 1848: and between 1851

[1] To persons like myself, who are not addicted to what is called "sport," the statement of these wholesale slaughters is calculated to excite surprise and curiosity as to the nature of a passion that impels men to self-exposure and privation, in a pursuit which presents nothing but the monotonous recurrence of scenes of blood and suffering. Mr. Baker, who has recently published, under the title of *The Rifle and the Hound in Ceylon*, an account of his exploits in the forest, gives us the assurance that "*all real sportsmen are tender-hearted men, who shun cruelty to an animal, and are easily moved by a tale of distress;*" and that although man is naturally bloodthirsty, and a beast of prey by instinct, yet that the true sportsman is distinguished from the rest of the human race by his "*love of nature and of noble scenery.*" In support of this pretension to a gentler nature than the rest of mankind, the author proceeds to attest his own abhorrence of cruelty by narrating the sufferings of an old hound, which, although "toothless," he cheered on to assail a boar at bay, but it recoiled "covered with blood, cut nearly in half, with a wound, fourteen inches in length, from the lower part of the

and 1856, a similar reward was paid for 2000 in the southern province, between Galle and Hambangtotte.

Although there is little opportunity for the display of marksmanship in an elephant battue, there is one feature in the sport, as conducted in Ceylon, which contrasts favourably with the slaughterhouse details chronicled with revolting minuteness in some recent accounts of elephant shooting in South Africa. The practice in Ceylon is to aim invariably at the head, and the sportsman finds his safety to consist in boldly facing the animal, advancing to within fifteen paces; and lodging a bullet, either in the temple or in the hollow over the eye, or in a well-known spot immediately above the trunk, where the weaker structure of the skull affords an easy access to the brain.[1] The region

---

belly, passing up the flank, completely severing the muscles of the hind leg, and extending up the spine; his hind leg having the appearance of being nearly off." In this state, forgetful of the character he had so lately given of the true sportsman, as a lover of nature and a hater of cruelty, he encouraged "the poor old dog," as he calls him, to resume the fight with the boar, which lasted for an hour, when he managed to call the dogs off, and perfectly exhausted, the mangled hound crawled out of the jungle with several additional wounds, including a severe gash in his throat. "He fell from exhaustion, and we made a litter with two poles and a horsecloth to carry him home." —P. 314. If such were the habitual enjoyments of this class of sportsmen, their motiveless massacres would admit of no manly justification. In comparison with them one is disposed to regard almost with favour the exploits of a hunter like Major Rogers, who, with the value of the ivory obtained from his encounters, bought his successive steps in the army, from a subaltern to a major, and had, therefore, an object, however disproportionate, in his slaughter of 1200 elephants.

One gentleman in Ceylon, not less distinguished for his genuine kindness of heart, than for his marvellous success in shooting elephants, avowed to me that the eagerness with which he found himself impelled to pursue them had often excited surprise in his own mind; and although he had never read the theory of Lord Kames, or the speculations of Vicesimus Knox, he came to the conclusion that the passion thus excited within him was a remnant of the hunter's instinct, with which man was originally endowed to enable him, by the chase, to support existence in a state of nature, and which, though rendered dormant by civilisation, had not been utterly eradicated.

This theory is at least more consistent and intelligible than the "love of nature and scenery," sentimentally propounded by the author quoted above.

[1] The vulnerability of the elephant in this region of the head was known to the ancients, and PLINY, describing a combat of elephants in the amphitheatre at Rome, says, that one was slain by a single blow, "pilum sub oculo adactum, in vitalia capitis venerat." (Lib. viii. c. 7.) Not-

of the ear is also a fatal spot, and often resorted to, the places I have mentioned in the front of the head being only accessible when the animal is "charging." Professor HARRISON, in his communication to the Royal Irish Academy in 1847, on the Anatomy of the Elephant, has rendered an intelligible explanation of this in the following passage descriptive of the cranium:—"it exhibits two remarkable facts; *first*, the small space occupied by the brain; and, *secondly*, the beautiful and curious structure of the bones of the head. The two tables of all these bones, except the occipital, are separated by rows of large cells, some from four to five inches in length, others only small, irregular, and honey-comb-like:—these all communicate with each other, and, through the frontal sinuses, with the cavity of the nose, and also with the tympanum or drum of each ear; consequently, as in some birds, these cells are filled with air, and thus while the skull attains a great size in order to afford an extensive surface for the attachment of muscles, and a mechanical support for the tusks, it is at the same time very light and buoyant in proportion to its bulk; a property the more valuable as the animal is fond of water and bathes in deep rivers."

Generally speaking, a single ball, planted in the forehead, ends the existence of the noble creature instantaneously: and expert sportsmen have been known to kill right and left, one with each barrel; but occasionally an elephant will not fall before several shots have been lodged in his head.[1]

withstanding the comparative facility of access to the brain, afforded at this spot, an ordinary leaden bullet is not certain to penetrate, and frequently becomes flattened. The hunters, to counteract this, are accustomed to harden the ball, by the introduction of a small portion of type-metal along with the lead.

[1] "There is a wide difference of opinion as to the most deadly shot. I think the temple the most certain, but authority in Ceylon says the 'fronter,' that is, above the trunk. Behind the ear is said to be deadly, but that is a shot which I never fired or saw fired that I remember. If the ball go true to its mark, all shots (in the head) are certain; but the bones on either side of the honey-combed passage to the brain are so thick that there is in all a 'glorious un-

Contrasted with this, one reads with a shudder the sickening details of the African huntsmen approaching *behind* the retiring animal, and of the torture inflicted by the shower of bullets which tear up its flesh and lacerate its flank and shoulders.[1]

The shooting of elephants in Ceylon has been described with tiresome iteration in the successive journals of sporting gentlemen, but one who turns to their pages for traits of the animal and his instincts is disappointed to find little beyond graphic sketches of the daring and

---

certainty' which keeps a man on the *qui vive* till he sees the elephant down."—From a paper on *Elephant Shooting in Ceylon*, by Major MACREADY, late Military Secretary at Colombo.

[1] In Mr. GORDON CUMMING's account of an *Hunter's Life in South Africa*, there is a narrative of his pursuit of a wounded elephant which he had lamed by lodging a ball in its shoulder-blade. It limped slowly towards a tree, against which it leaned itself in helpless agony, whilst its pursuer seated himself in front of it, in safety, to *boil his coffee*, and observe its sufferings. The story is continued as follows:—"Having admired him for a considerable time, *I resolved to make experiments on vulnerable points;* and approaching very near, I fired several bullets at different parts of his enormous skull. He only acknowledged the shots by a salaam-like movement of his trunk, with the point of which he gently touched the wounds with a striking and peculiar action. Surprised and shocked at finding that I was only prolonging the sufferings of the noble beast, which bore its trials with such dignified composure, I resolved to finish the proceeding with all possible despatch, and accordingly opened fire upon him from the left side, aiming at the shoulder. I first fired *six* shots with the two-grooved rifle, which must have eventually proved mortal. After which I fired *six* shots at the same part with the Dutch six-pounder. *Large tears now trickled from his eyes, which he slowly shut and opened, his colossal frame shivered convulsively, and falling on his side he expired.*" (Vol. ii. p. 10.)

In another place after detailing the manner in which he assailed a poor animal—he says, "I was loading and firing as fast as could be, sometimes at the head, sometimes behind the shoulder, until my elephant's forequarter was a mass of gore; notwithstanding which he continued to hold on, leaving the grass and branches of the forest scarlet in his wake. * * Having fired *thirty-five rounds* with my two-grooved rifle, I opened upon him with the Dutch six-pounder, and when forty bullets had perforated his hide, he began, for the first time, to evince signs of a dilapidated constitution." The disgusting description is closed thus, "throughout the charge he repeatedly cooled his person with large quantities of water, which he ejected from his trunk over his sides and back, and just as the pangs of death came over him, he stood trembling violently beside a thorn tree, and kept pouring water into his bloody mouth until he died, when he pitched heavily forward with the whole weight of his fore-quarters resting on the points of his tusks. The strain was fair, and the tusks did not yield; but the portion of his head in which the tusks were imbedded, extending a long way above the eye, yielded and burst with a muffled crash." (*Ib.* vol. ii. p. 4, 5.)

exploits of his pursuers, most of whom, having had no further opportunity of observation than is derived from a casual encounter with the outraged animal, have apparently tried to exalt their own prowess by misrepresenting the ordinary character of the elephant, describing him as "savage, wary, and revengeful." [1]

These epithets may undoubtedly apply to the outcasts from the herd, the "Rogues" or *hora allia*, but so small is the proportion of these that there is not probably one *Rogue* to be found for every five hundred of those in herds; and it is a manifest error, arising from imperfect information, to extend this censure to them generally, or to suppose the elephant to be an animal "thirsting for blood, lying in wait in the jungle to rush on the unwary passer-by, and knowing no greater pleasure than the act of crushing his victim to a shapeless mass beneath his feet." [2] The cruelties practised by the hunters have no doubt taught these sagacious creatures to be cautious and alert, but their precautions are simply defensive; and beyond the alarm and apprehension which they evince on the approach of man, they exhibit no indication of hostility or a thirst for blood.

An ordinary traveller seldom comes upon elephants unless after sunset or towards daybreak, as they go or return from their nightly visits to the tanks: but when by accident a herd is disturbed by day, they evince, if unattacked, no disposition to become assailants; and if the attitude of defence which they instinctively assume prove sufficient to check the approach of the intruder, no further demonstration is to be apprehended.

---

[1] *The Rifle and the Hound in Ceylon*; by S. W. BAKER, Esq., p. 8, 9. "Next to a rogue," says Mr. Baker, "in ferocity, and even more persevering in the pursuit of her victim, is a female elephant." But he appends the significant qualification, "*when her young one has been killed.*" — *Ibid.*, p. 13.

[2] *The Rifle and Hound in Ceylon*; by S. W. BAKER, Esq.

Even the hunters who go in search of them find them in positions and occupations altogether inconsistent with the idea of their being savage, wary, or revengeful. Their demeanour when undisturbed is indicative of gentleness and timidity and their actions bespeak lassitude and indolence induced not alone by heat, but probably ascribable in some degree to the fact that the night had been spent in watchfulness and amusement. A few are generally browsing listlessly on the trees and plants within reach, others fanning themselves with leafy branches and a few are asleep; whilst the young run playfully among the herd, the emblems of innocence, as the older ones are of peacefulness and gravity.

Almost every elephant may be observed to exhibit some peculiar action of the limbs when standing at rest ; some move the head monotonously in a circle, or from right to left; some swing their feet back and forward ; others flap their ears or sway themselves from side to side, or rise and sink by alternately bending and straightening the fore knees. As the opportunities of observing this custom have been almost confined to elephants in captivity, it has been conjectured to arise from some morbid habit contracted during the length of a voyage by sea [1], or from an instinctive impulse to substitute a motion of this kind in lieu of their wonted exercise ; but this supposition is erroneous ; the propensity being equally displayed by those at liberty and those in captivity. When surprised by sportsmen in the depths of the jungle, individuals of a herd are always occupied in swinging their limbs in this manner ; and in the several corrals which I have seen, where whole herds have been captured, the elephants, in the midst of the utmost excitement, and even after the most vigorous charges, if they stood still for a moment in stupor and exhaustion,

---

[1] *Menageries, &c.* "The Elephant," ch. i. p. 21.

manifested their wonted habit, and swung their limbs or swayed their bodies to and fro incessantly. So far from its being a substitute for exercise, those in the government employment in Ceylon are observed to practise their acquired motion, whatever it may be, with increased vigour when thoroughly fatigued after excessive work. Even the favourite practice of fanning themselves with a leafy branch seems less an enjoyment in itself than a resource when listless and at rest. The term "fidgetty" seems to describe appropriately the temperament of the elephant.

They evince the strongest love of retirement and a corresponding dislike to intrusion. The approach of a stranger is perceived less by the eye, the quickness of which is not remarkable (besides which its range is obscured by the foliage,) than by sensitive smell and singular acuteness of hearing; and the whole herd is put in instant but noiseless motion towards some deeper and more secure retreat. The effectual manner in which an animal of the prodigious size of the elephant can conceal himself, and the motionless silence which he preserves, is quite surprising: whilst beaters pass and repass within a few yards of his hiding place, he will maintain his ground till the hunter, creeping almost close to his legs, sees his little eye peering out through the leaves, when, finding himself discovered, he breaks away with a crash, levelling the brushwood in his headlong career.

If surprised in open ground, where stealthy retreat is impracticable, a herd will hesitate in indecision, and, after a few meaningless movements, stand huddled together in a group, whilst one or two, more adventurous than the rest, advance a few steps to reconnoitre. Elephants are generally observed to be bolder in open ground than in cover, but, if bold at all, far more dangerous in cover than in open ground.

In searching for them, sportsmen often avail themselves of the expertness of the native trackers; and notwithstanding the demonstration of Combe that the brain of the timid Singhalese is deficient in the organ of destructiveness [1], he shows an instinct for hunting, and exhibits in the pursuit of the elephant a courage and adroitness far surpassing in interest the mere handling of the rifle, which is the principal share of the proceeding that falls to his European companions.

The beater on these occasions has the double task of finding the game and carrying the guns; and, in an animated communication to me, an experienced sportsman describes "this light and active creature, with his long glossy hair hanging down his shoulders, every muscle quivering with excitement; and his countenance lit up with intense animation, leaping from rock to rock, as nimble as a deer, tracking the gigantic game like a bloodhound, falling behind as he comes up with it, and as the elephants, baffled and irritated, make the first stand, passing one rifle into your eager hand and holding the other ready whilst right and left each barrel performs its mission, and if fortune does not flag, and the second gun is as successful as the first, three or four huge carcases are piled one on another within a space equal to the area of a dining-room." [2]

It is curious that in these encounters the herd never rush forward in a body, as buffaloes or bisons do, but only one elephant at a time moves in advance of the rest to confront, or, as it is called, to "charge," the assailants. I have heard of but one instance in which *two* so advanced as champions of their companions. Sometimes, indeed, the whole herd will follow a leader. and manœuvre in his rear like a body of cavalry; but so large a party are necessarily liable to panic; and, one of them being turned in alarm, the entire body retreat with terrified precipitation.

As regards boldness and courage, a strange variety

---

[1] *System of Phrenology*, by GEORGE COMBE, vol. i. p. 256.

[2] Private letter from Capt. Philip Payne Gallwey.

of temperament is observable amongst elephants, but it may be affirmed that they are much more generally timid than courageous. One herd may be as difficult to approach as deer, gliding away through the jungle so gently and quickly that scarcely a trace marks their passage; another, in apparent stupor, will huddle themselves together like swine, and allow their assailant to come within a few yards before they break away in terror; and a third will await his approach without motion, and then advance with fury to the "charge."

In individuals the same differences are discernible: one flies on the first appearance of danger, whilst another, alone and unsupported, will face a whole host of enemies. When wounded and infuriated with pain, many of them become literally savage[1]; but, so unaccustomed are they to act as assailants, and so awkward and inexpert in using their strength, that they rarely or ever succeed in killing a pursuer who falls into their power. Although the pressure of a foot, a blow with the trunk, or a thrust with the tusk could scarcely fail to prove fatal, three-fourths of those who have fallen into their power have escaped without serious injury. So great is this chance of impunity, that the sportsman prefers to approach within about fifteen paces of the advancing elephant, a space which gives time for a second fire should the first shot prove ineffectual, and should both fail there is still opportunity for flight.

Amongst full grown timber, a skilful runner can escape an elephant by dodging round the trees, but in cleared land, and low brushwood, the difficulty is much increased, as the small growth of underwood which obstructs the movements of man presents no obstacle to those of an elephant. On the other hand, on level

---

[1] Some years ago an elephant which had been wounded by a native, near Hambangtotte, pursued the man into the town, followed him along the street, trampled him to death in the bazaar before a crowd of terrified spectators, and succeeded in making good its retreat to the jungle.

and open ground the chances are rather in favour of the elephant, as his pace in full flight exceeds that of man, although it is far from equal to that of a horse, as has been erroneously asserted.[1]

The incessant slaughter of elephants by sportsmen in Ceylon, appears to be merely in subordination to the influence of the organ of destructiveness, since the carcase is never applied to any useful purpose, but left to decompose and to defile the air of the forest. The flesh is occasionally tasted as a matter of curiosity: as a steak it is coarse and tough; but the tongue is as delicate as that of an ox; and the foot is said to make palatable soup. The Caffres attached to the pioneer corps in the Kandyan province were in the habit of securing the heart of any elephant shot in their vicinity, and said it was their custom to eat it in Africa. The hide it has been found impracticable to tan in Ceylon, or to convert to any useful purpose, but the bones of those shot have of late years been collected and used for manuring coffee. The hair of the tail, which is extremely strong and horny, is mounted by the native goldsmith, and made into bracelets; and the teeth are sawn by the Moormen at Galle (as they used to be by the Romans during a scarcity of ivory) into plates, out of which they fashion numerous articles of ornament, knife-handles, card racks, and presse-papiers.

---

[1] SHAW, in his *Zoology*, asserts that an elephant can run as swiftly as a horse can gallop. London, 1800–6, vol. i. p. 216.

NOTE.

AMONGST extraordinary recoveries from desperate wounds I venture to record here an instance which occurred in Ceylon to a gentleman while engaged in the chase of elephants, and which, I apprehend, has few parallels in pathological experience. Lieutenant Gerard Fretz, of the Ceylon Rifle Regiment, whilst shooting at an elephant in the vicinity of Fort MacDonald, in Oovah, was wounded in the face by the bursting of his fowling-piece, on the 22d January, 1828. He was then about thirty-two years of age. On raising him, it was found that part of the breech of the gun and about two inches of the barrel had been driven through the frontal sinus, at the junction of the nose and forehead. It had sunk almost perpendicularly till the iron plate called "the tail-pin," by which the barrel is made fast to the stock by a screw, had descended through the palate, carrying with it the screw, one extremity of which had forced itself into the right nostril, where it was discernible externally, whilst the headed end lay in contact with his tongue. To extract the jagged mass of iron thus sunk in the ethmoidal and sphenoidal cells was found hopelessly impracticable; but, strange to tell, after the inflammation subsided, Mr. Fretz recovered rapidly, his general health was unimpaired, and he returned to his regiment with this singular appendage firmly embedded behind the bones of his face. He took his turn of duty as usual, attained the command of his company, participated in all the enjoyments of the mess-room, and died *eight years afterwards*, on the 1st of April, 1836, not from any consequences of this fearful wound, but from fever and inflammation brought on by other causes.

So little was he apparently inconvenienced by the presence of the strange body in his palate that he was accustomed with his finger partially to undo the screw, which but for its extreme length he might altogether have withdrawn. To enable this to be done, and possibly to assist by this means the extraction of the breech itself through the original orifice (which never entirely closed), an attempt was made in 1835 to take off a portion of the screw with a file, but, after having cut it three parts through, the operation was interrupted, chiefly owing to the carelessness and indifference of Capt. Fretz, whose death occurred before the attempt could be resumed. The piece of iron, on being removed after his decease, was found to measure 2¾ inches in length, and weighed two scruples more than two ounces and three quarters. A cast of the breech and screw now forms No. 2790 amongst the deposits in the Medical Museum of Chatham.

CHAP. IV.

AN ELEPHANT CORRAL.

So long as the elephants of Ceylon were merely required in small numbers for the pageantry of the native princes, or the sacred processions of the Buddhist temples, their capture was effected either by the instrumentality of female decoys, or by the artifices and agility of the individuals and castes who devoted themselves to their pursuit and training. But after the arrival of the European conquerors of the island, and when it had become expedient to take advantage of the strength and intelligence of these creatures in clearing forests and making roads and other works, establishments were organised on a great scale by the Portuguese and Dutch, and the supply of elephants kept up by periodical battues conducted at the cost of the government, on a plan similar to that adopted on the continent of India, when herds varying in number from twenty to one hundred and upwards are driven into concealed enclosures and secured.

In both these processes, success is entirely dependent on the skill with which the captors turn to advantage the terror and inexperience of the wild elephant, since all attempts would be futile to subdue or confine by ordinary force an animal of such strength and sagacity.[1]

[1] The device of taking them by means of pitfalls, in addition to the difficulty of providing against that caution with which the elephant always reconnoitres suspicious or insecure ground, has the further disadvantage of exposing him to injury from bruises and dislocations in his fall. Still it was the mode of capture employed by the Singhalese, and so late as 1750 WOLF relates that the native chiefs of the Wanny, when capturing elephants for the Dutch, made "pits some fathoms deep in those places whither the elephant is wont to go in search of food, across

KNOX describes with circumstantiality the mode adopted at that time by the servants of the king to catch elephants for the royal stud. He says, "After discovering the retreat of such as have tusks, unto these they drive some *she elephants*, which they bring with them, for the purpose, which, when once the males have got a sight of, they will never leave, but follow them wheresoever they go, and the females are so used to it that they will do whatsoever, either by word or a beck, their keepers bid them. And so they delude them along through towns and countries, and through the streets of the city, even to the very gates of the king's palace, where sometimes they seize upon them by snares, and sometimes by driving them, into a kind of pound they catch them."[1]

In Nepaul and Burmah, and throughout the Chin-Indian Peninsula, when in pursuit of single elephants, either "*rogues*" detached from the herd, or individuals who have been marked for the beauty of their ivory, the natives avail themselves of the aid of females in order to effect their approaches and secure an opportunity of casting a noose over the foot of the destined captive. All accounts concur in expressing high admiration of their courage and address; but from what has fallen under my own observation, added to the descriptions I have heard from other eye-witnesses, I am inclined to believe that in such exploits the Moormen of Ceylon evince a daring and adroitness that far surpass all others.

These professional elephant catchers, or as they are called, Panickeas, inhabit the Moorish villages in

---

which were laid poles covered with branches and baited with the food of which he is fondest, making towards which he finds himself taken unawares. Thereafter being subdued by fright and exhaustion, he was assisted to raise himself to the surface by means of hurdles and earth, which he placed under foot as they were thrown down to him, till he was enabled to step out on solid ground, when the noosers and decoys were in readiness to tie him up to the nearest tree." See WOLF's *Life and Adventures*, p. 152.

[1] KNOX's *Historical Relation of Ceylon*, A.D. 1681, part i. c. vi. p. 21.

the north and north-east of the island, and from time immemorial have been engaged in taking elephants, which are afterwards trained by Arabs, chiefly for the use of the rajahs and native princes in the south of India, whose vakeels are periodically despatched to make purchases in Ceylon.

The ability evinced by these men in tracing elephants through the woods has almost the certainty of instinct; and hence their services are eagerly sought by the European sportsmen who go down into their country in search of game. So keen is their glance, that almost at the top of their speed, like hounds running "breast high" they will follow the course of an elephant, over glades covered with stunted grass, where the eye of a stranger would fail to discover a trace of its passage, and on through forests strewn with dry leaves, where it seems impossible to perceive a footstep. Here they are guided by a bent or broken twig, or by a leaf dropped from the animal's mouth, on which they can detect the pressure of a tooth. If at fault, they fetch a circuit like a setter, till lighting on some fresh marks, then go a head again with renewed vigour. So delicate is the sense of smell in the elephant, and so indispensable is it to go against the wind in approaching him, that the Panickeas, on those occasions, when the wind is so still that its direction cannot be otherwise discerned, will suspend the film of a gossamer to determine it and shape their course accordingly.

They are enabled by the inspection of the footmarks, when impressed in soft clay, to describe the size as well as the number of a herd before it is seen; the height of an elephant at the shoulder being as nearly as possible twice the circumference of his fore foot.[1]

---

[1] Previous to the death of the female elephant in the Zoological Gardens, in the Regent's Park, in 1851, Mr. MITCHELL, the Secretary, caused the measurements to be accurately made, and found the statement

On overtaking the game their courage is as conspicuous as their sagacity. If they have confidence in the sportsman for whom they are finding, they will advance to the very heel of the elephant, slap him on the quarter, and then convert his timidity into anger, till he turns upon his tormentor and exposes his front to receive the bullet which is awaiting him.[1]

So fearless and confident are they that two men, without aid or attendants, will boldly attempt to capture the largest sized elephant. Their only weapon is a flexible rope made of elk's or buffalo's hide, with which it is their object to secure one of the hind legs. This they effect either by following in his footsteps when in motion or by stealing close up to him when at rest, and availing themselves of the propensity of the elephant at such moments to swing his feet backwards and forwards, they contrive to slip a noose over his hind leg.

At other times this is achieved by spreading the noose on the ground partially concealed by roots and

---

of the Singhalese hunters to be strictly correct, the height at the shoulders being precisely twice the circumference of the fore foot.

[1] Major SKINNER, late the Chief Officer at the head of the Commission of Roads, in Ceylon, in writing to me, mentions an anecdote illustrative of the daring of the Panickeas. "I once saw," he says, "a very beautiful example of the confidence with which these fellows, from their knowledge of the elephants, meet their worst defiance. It was in Neuera-Kalawa; I was bivouacking on the bank of a river, and had been kept out so late that I did not get to my tent until between 9 and 10 at night. On our return towards it we passed several single elephants making their way to the nearest water, but at length we came upon a large herd which had taken possession of the only road by which we could pass, and which no intimidation would induce to move off. I had some Panickeas with me; they knew the herd, and counselled extreme caution. After trying every device we could think of for a length of time, a little old Moorman of the party came to me and requested we should all retire to a distance. He then took a couple of chules (flambeaux of dried wood, or coco-nut leaves), one in each hand, and waving them above his head till they flamed out fiercely, he advanced at a deliberate pace to within a few yards of the elephant who was acting as leader of the party, and who was growling and trumpeting in his rage; and flourished the flaming torches in his face. The effect was instantaneous; the whole herd dashed away in a panic, bellowing, screaming, and crashing through the underwood, whilst we availed ourselves of the open path to make our way to our tents.

leaves, beneath a tree on which one of the party is stationed, whose business it is to lift it suddenly by means of a cord, raising it on the elephant's leg at the moment when his companion has succeeded in provoking him to place his foot within its circle, the other end having been previously made fast to the stem of the tree. Should the noosing be effected in open ground, and no tree of sufficient strength at hand round which to wind the rope, one of the Moors, allowing himself to be pursued by the enraged elephant, entices him towards the nearest grove; where his companion, dexterously laying hold of the rope as it trails along the ground, suddenly coils it round a suitable stem, and brings the fugitive to a stand still. On finding himself thus arrested, the natural impulse of the captive is to turn on the man who is engaged in making fast the rope, a movement which it is the duty of his colleague to prevent by running up close to the elephant's head and provoking him to confront him by irritating gesticulations and incessant shouts of *dah! dah!* a monosyllable, the sound of which the elephant peculiarly dislikes. Meanwhile the first assailant, having secured one noose, comes up from behind with another, with which, amidst the vain rage and struggles of the victim, he entraps a fore leg, the rope being, as before, secured to another tree in front, and the whole four feet having been thus entangled, the capture is completed.

A shelter is then run up with branches, to protect him from the sun, and the hunters proceed to build a wigwam for themselves in front of their prisoner, kindling their fires for cooking, and making all the necessary arrangements for remaining day and night on the spot to await the process of subduing and taming his rage. In my journeys through the forest I have come unexpectedly on the halting place of adventurous hunters when thus engaged; and on one occasion, about sunrise, in ascending the steep ridge from the bed of the Malwatte river, the foremost rider of our party was suddenly driven back by a furious elephant, which we found picketed by two Panickeas on the crest of the bank. In such a position, the elephant soon ceases to struggle; and what with the exhaustion of rage and resistance, the terror of fire which he dreads, and the constant annoyance of smoke which he detests, in a very short time, a few weeks at the most, his spirit becomes subdued; and being plentifully supplied with plantains and fresh food, and indulged with water, in which he luxuriates, he grows so far reconciled to his keepers that they at length venture to remove him to their own village, or to the sea-side for shipment to India.

No part of the hunter's performances exhibits greater skill and audacity than this first forced march of the recently captured elephant from the great central forests to the sea-coast. As he is still too morose to submit to be ridden, and it would be equally impossible to lead or to drive him by force, the ingenuity of the captors is displayed in alternately irritating and eluding his attacks, but always so attracting his attention as to allure him along in the direction in which they want him to go. Some assistance is derived from the rope by which the original capture was effected, and which, as it serves to make him safe at night, is never removed from the leg till his taming is sufficiently advanced to permit of his being entrusted with partial liberty.

In Ceylon the principal place for exporting these animals to India is Manaar, on the western coast, to which the Arabs from the continent resort, bringing horses to be bartered for elephants. In order to reach the sea open plains must be traversed, across which it requires the utmost courage, agility, and patience of the Moor to coax their reluctant charge. At Manaar the elephants are usually detained till any wound on the leg caused by the rope has been healed, when the shipment is effected in the most primitive manner, it being next to impossible to induce the still untamed creature to walk on board, and no mechanical contrivances being provided to ship him. A dhoney, or native boat, of about forty tons burthen, is brought alongside the quay in front of the Old Dutch Fort, and being about three parts filled with the strong ribbed leaves of the Palmyra palm, it is lashed so that the gunwale may be as nearly as possible on a line with the level of the wharf. The elephant being placed with his back to the water is forced by goads to retreat till his hind legs go over the side of the quay, but the main contest commences when it is attempted to disengage his fore feet from the shore, and force him to entrust himself on board. The scene becomes exciting from the screams and trumpeting of the elephants, the shouts of the Arabs, the calls of the Moors, and the rushing of the crowd. Meanwhile the huge creature strains every nerve to regain the land; and the day is often consumed before his efforts are overcome, and he finds himself fairly afloat. The same dhoney will take from four to five elephants, who place themselves athwart it, and exhibit amusing adroitness in accommodating their own movements to the rolling of the little vessel; and in this way they are ferried across the narrow strait which separates the continent of India from Ceylon.[1]

But the feat of ensnaring and subduing a single elephant, courageous as it is, and demonstrative of the supremacy with which man wields his "dominion over

[1] In the *Philosophical Transactions* for 1701, there is "An Account of the taking of Elephants in Ceylon, by Mr. STRACHAN, a Physician who lived seventeen years there," in which the author describes the manner in which they were shipped by the Dutch, at Matura, Galle, and Negombo. A piece of strong sail-cloth having been wrapped round the elephant's chest and stomach, he was forced into the sea between two tame ones, and there made fast to a boat, on which the tame ones returned to land; he swam after the boat to the ship, where tackle was reeved to the sail-cloth and he was hoisted on board.

"But a better way has been invented lately," he says; "a large flat-bottomed vessel is prepared, covered with planks like a floor; so that this floor is almost of a height with the key. Then the sides of the key and the vessel are adorned with green branches, so that the elephant sees no water, till he is in the ship." —*Phil. Trans.* vol. xxiii. No. 227, p. 1051.

every beast of the earth," falls far short of the daring exploit of capturing a whole herd; when from thirty to one hundred wild elephants are entrapped in one vast decoy. The mode of effecting this, as it is practised in Ceylon, is no doubt imitated, but with considerable modifications, from the methods prevalent in various parts of India. It was introduced by the Portuguese, and continued by the Dutch, the latter of whom had two elephant hunts in each year, and conducted their operations on so large a scale, that the annual export, after supplying the government establishments, was from one hundred to one hundred and fifty elephants, taken principally in the vicinity of Matura, in the southern province, and marched for shipment to Manaar.[1]

The custom in Bengal is to construct a strong enclosure (called a *keddah*), in the heart of the forest, formed of the trunks of trees firmly secured by transverse beams and buttresses, and leaving a gate for the entrance of the elephants. A second enclosure, opening from the first, contains water (if possible a rivulet); and this, again, communicates with a third, which terminates in a funnel-shaped passage, too narrow to admit of an elephant turning, and within this the captives being driven in line, are secured with ropes from the outside, and led away in custody of tame ones trained for the purpose.

The *keddah* being thus prepared, the first operation is to drive the elephants towards it, for which purpose vast bodies of men fetch a compass in the forest around the haunts of the herds, contracting it by degrees, till they complete the enclosure of a certain area, round which they kindle fires, and cut footpaths through the jungle, to enable the watchers to communicate and combine. All this is performed in cautious silence and by slow approaches, to avoid alarming the herd.

---

[1] VALENTYN, *Oud en Nieuw Oost-Indien*, ch. xv. p. 272.

A fresh circle nearer to the *keddah* is then formed in the same way, and into this the elephants are admitted from the first one, the hunters following from behind, and lighting new fires around the newly inclosed space. Day after day the process is repeated; till the drove has been brought sufficiently close to make the final rush; when the whole party close in from all sides, and with drums, guns, shouts, and flambeaux, force the terrified animals to enter the fatal enclosure, when the passage is barred behind them, and retreat rendered impossible.

Their efforts to escape are repressed by the crowd, who drive them back from the stockade with spears and flaming torches; and at last compel them to pass on into the second enclosure. Here they are detained for a short time, their feverish exhaustion being relieved by free access to water; and at last being tempted by food or otherwise induced to trust themselves in the narrow outlet; they are one after another made fast by ropes, passed in through the palisade, and picketed in the adjoining woods to enter on their course of systematic training.

These arrangements vary in different districts of Bengal; and the method adopted in Ceylon differs in many essential particulars from them all; the Keddah, or, as it is there called, the corral or *korahl*[1] (from the Portuguese *curral*, a "cattle-pen") consists of but one enclosure instead of three. A stream or watering-place is not uniformly enclosed within it, because, although water is indispensable after the long thirst and exhaustion of the captives, it has been found that a pond or rivulet within the corral itself adds to the difficulty of mastering them, and increases their reluctance to

---

[1] It is thus spelled by WOLF, in his *Life and Adventures*, p. 144. *Corral* is at the present day a household word in South America, and especially in La Plata, to designate an *enclosure for cattle*.

leave it; besides which, the smaller ones are often smothered by the others in their eagerness to crowd into the water. The funnel-shaped outlet is usually dispensed with, as the animals are liable to bruise and injure themselves against the narrow stockade, and should one of them die in it, as is too often the case in the midst of the struggle, the difficulty of removing so great a carcase is extreme. The noosing and securing them, therefore, takes place in Ceylon within the area of the first enclosure into which they enter, and the dexterity and daring displayed in this portion of the work far surpasses that of merely attaching the rope through the openings of the paling, as in an Indian keddah.

One result of this change in the system is manifested in the increased proportion of healthy elephants which are eventually secured and trained out of the number originally enclosed. The reason of this is obvious: under the old arrangements, months were consumed in the preparatory steps of surrounding and driving in the herds, which at last arrived so wasted by excitement and exhausted by privation that numbers died within the corral itself, and still more died during the process of training. But in later years the labour of months being reduced to weeks, the elephants are driven in fresh and full of vigour, so that comparatively few are lost either in the enclosure or the stables. A conception of the whole operation from commencement to end will be best conveyed by describing the progress of an elephant corral as I witnessed it in 1847 in the great forest on the banks of the Alligator River, the Kimbul-oya, in the district of Kornegalle, about thirty miles north-west of Kandy.

Kornegalle, or Kurunai-galle, was one of the ancient capitals of the island, and the residence of its kings from A.D. 1319 to 1347.[1] The dwelling-house of the

[1] See *ante*, Vol. I. Pt. III. ch. xii. p. 415.

principal civil officer in charge of the district now occupies the site of the former palace, and the ground is strewn with fragments of columns and carved stones, the remnants of the royal buildings. The modern town consists of the bungalows of the European officials, each surrounded with its own garden; two or three streets inhabited by Dutch descendants and Moors; and a native bazaar, with the ordinary array of rice and curry stuffs and cooking chattees of brass or burnt clay.

But the charm of the village is the unusual beauty of its position. It rests within the shade of an enormous rock of gneiss upwards of 600 feet in height, nearly denuded of verdure, and so rounded and worn by time that it has acquired the form of a couchant elephant, from which it derives its name of Aetagalla, the Rock of the Tusker.[1] But Aetagalla is only the last eminence in a range of similarly-formed rocky mountains, which here terminate abruptly; and, from the fantastic shapes into which their gigantic outlines have been wrought by the action of the atmosphere, are called by the names of the Tortoise Rock, the Eel Rock, and the Rock of the Tusked Elephant. So impressed are the Singhalese by the aspect of these stupendous masses that in the ancient grants their lands are conveyed in perpetuity, or "*so long as the sun and the moon*, so long as Aetagalla and Andagalla shall endure."[2]

Kornegalle is the resort of Buddhists from the remotest parts of the island, who come to visit an ancient temple on the summit of the great rock, to which access is had from the valley below by means of steep paths and steps hewn out of the solid stone. Here the chief object of veneration is a copy of the sacred footstep

---

[1] Another enormous mass of gneiss is called the Kuruminia-galle, or the Beetle-rock, from its resemblance in shape to the back of that insect, and hence is said to have been derived the name of the town, *Kuruna-galle* or Korne-galle.

[2] FORBES quotes a Tamil conveyance of land the purchaser of which is to "possess and enjoy it as long as the sun and the moon, the earth and its vegetables, the mountains and the River Cauvery exist."—*Oriental Memoirs*, vol. ii. chap. ii.

hollowed in the granite, similar to that which confers sanctity on Adam's Peak, the towering apex of which, about forty miles distant, the pilgrims can discern from Aetagalla.

At times the heat at Kornegalle is extreme, in consequence of the perpetual glow diffused from these granite cliffs. The warmth they acquire during the blaze of noon becomes almost intolerable towards evening, and the sultry night is too short to permit them to cool between the setting and the rising of the sun. The district is also liable to occasional droughts when the watercourses fail, and the tanks are dried up; one of these occurred about the period of my visit, and such was the suffering of the wild animals that numbers of alligators and bears made their way into the town to drink at the wells. But the soil is prolific in the extreme; rice, cotton, and dry grain are cultivated largely in the valley. Every cottage is surrounded by gardens of coco-nuts, arecas, jak-fruit and coffee; the slopes, which they till, are covered with luxuriant vegetation, and, as far as the eye can reach on every side, there are dense forests intersected by streams, in the shade of which the deer and the elephant abound.

In 1847 arrangements were made for one of the great elephant hunts for the supply of the Civil Engineer Department, and the spot fixed on by Mr. Morris, the Government officer who conducted the corral, was on the banks of the Kimbul river, about fifteen miles from Kornegalle. The country over which we rode to the scene of the capture showed traces of the recent drought, the fields lay to a great extent untilled owing to the want of water, and the tanks, almost reduced to dryness, were covered with the leaves of the rose-coloured lotus.

Our cavalcade was as oriental as the scenery through which it moved; the Governor and the officers of his staff and household formed a long cortége, escorted by the native attendants, horse-keepers, and foot-runners. The ladies were borne in palankins, and the younger individuals of the party carried in chairs raised on poles, and covered with cool green awnings made of the fresh leaves of the talipat palm.

After traversing the cultivated lands, the path led across open glades of park-like verdure and beauty, and at last entered the great forest under the shade of ancient trees wreathed to their crowns with climbing plants and festooned by natural garlands of convolvulus and orchids. Here silence reigned, disturbed only by the murmuring hum of glittering insects, or the shrill clamour of the plumb-headed parroquet and the flute-like calls of the golden oriole.

We crossed the broad sandy beds of two rivers over-arched by tall trees, the most conspicuous of which is the Kombook[1], from the calcined bark of which the natives extract a species of lime to be used with their betel. And from the branches hung suspended over the water the gigantic pods of the huge puswel bean[2], the sheath of which measures six feet long by five or six inches broad.

On ascending the steep bank of the second stream, we found ourselves in front of the residences which had been extemporised for our party in the immediate vicinity of the corral. These cool and enjoyable structures were formed of branches and thatched with palm leaves and fragrant lemon grass; and in addition to a dining-room and suites of bedrooms fitted with tent furniture, they included kitchens, stables, and store-rooms, all run up by the natives in the course of a few days.

In former times, the work connected with the elephant hunts was performed by the "forced labour" of the natives, as part of that feudal service which under the name of Raja-kariya was extorted from the Singhalese

[1] *Pentaptera paniculata.* | [2] *Entada pursætha.*

during the rule of their native sovereigns. The system was continued by the Portuguese and Dutch, and prevailed under the British Government till its abolition by the Earl of Ripon in 1832. Under it from fifteen hundred to two thousand men used to be occupied, superintended by their headmen, in constructing the corral, collecting the elephants, maintaining the cordon of watch-fires and watchers, and conducting all the laborious operations of the capture. Since the abolition of Raja-kariya, however, no difficulty has been found in obtaining the voluntary co-operation of the natives on these exciting occasions. The government defrays the expense of that portion of the preparations which involves actual cost,—for the skilled labour expended in the erection of the corral and its appurtenances, and the providing of spears, ropes, arms, flutes, drums, gunpowder, and other necessaries for the occasion.

The period of the year selected is that which least interferes with the cultivation of the rice lands (in the interval between seed time and harvest), and the people themselves, in addition to the excitement and enjoyment of the sport, have a personal interest in reducing the number of elephants, which inflict serious injury on their gardens and growing crops. For a similar reason the priests encourage the practice, because the elephants destroy the sacred Bo-tree, of the leaves of which they are passionately fond ; besides which it promotes the facility of obtaining elephants for the processions of the the temples : and the Rate-mahat-mayas and headmen have a pride in exhibiting the number of retainers who follow them to the field, and the performances of the tame elephants which they lend for the business of the corral. Vast numbers of the peasantry are thus voluntarily occupied for many weeks in putting up the stockades, cutting paths through the jungle, and relieving the beaters who are engaged in surrounding and driving in the elephants.

In selecting the scene for the hunt, a position is chosen

which lies on some old and frequented route of the animals, in their periodical migrations in search of forage and water; and the vicinity of a stream is indispensable, not only for the supply of the elephants during the time spent in inducing them to approach the enclosure, but to enable them to bathe and cool themselves throughout the process of training after the capture.

In constructing the corral itself, care is taken to avoid disturbing the trees or the brushwood within the included space, and especially on the side by which the elephants are to approach, where it is essential to conceal the stockade as much as possible by the density of the foliage. The trees used in the structure are from ten to twelve inches in diameter; and are sunk about three feet in the earth, so as to leave a length of from twelve to fifteen feet above ground; with spaces between each stanchion sufficiently wide to permit a man to glide through. The uprights are made fast by transverse beams, to which they are lashed securely with ratans and flexible climbing plants, or as they are called "jungle ropes," and the whole is steadied by means of forked supports, which grasp the tie beams, and prevent the work from being driven outward by the rush of the wild elephants.

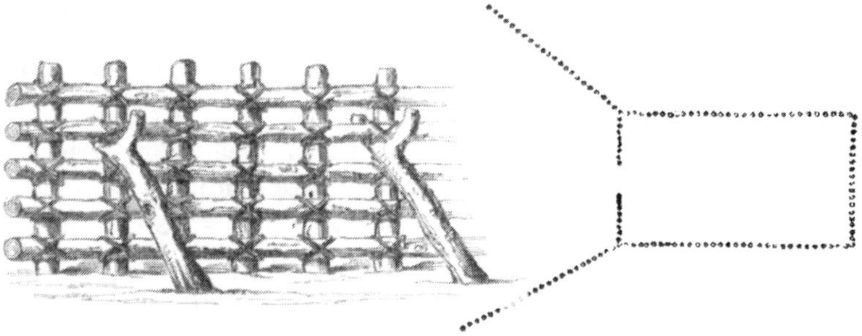

GROUND PLAN OF A CORRAL AND METHOD OF FENCING IT.

The space thus enclosed on the occasion I am now attempting to describe, was about 500 feet in length by half that width. At one end an entrance was left open, fitted with sliding bars, so prepared as to be capable of being instantly shut;—and from each angle of the end by which the elephants were to approach, two lines of the same strong fencing were continued on either side, and cautiously concealed by the trees; so that if, instead of entering by the open passage, the herd were to swerve to right or left, they would find themselves suddenly stopped and forced to retrace their course to the gate.

The preparations were completed by placing a stage for the governor's party on a group of the nearest trees looking down into the enclosure, so that a view could be had of the entire proceeding, from the entrance of the herd, to the leading out of the captive elephants.

It is unnecessary to observe that the structure here described, ponderous as it is, would be entirely ineffectual to resist the shock, if assaulted by the full force of an enraged elephant; and accidents have sometimes happened by the breaking through of the herd; but reliance is placed not so much on the resistance of the stockade as on the timidity of the captives; and their unconsciousness of their own strength, coupled with the daring of their captors and their devices for ensuring submission.

The corral being thus prepared, the beaters address themselves to drive in the elephants. For this purpose it is often necessary to fetch a circuit of many miles in order to surround a sufficient number, and the caution to be observed involves patience and delay; as it is essential to avoid alarming the elephants, which might otherwise rush in the wrong direction. Their disposition being essentially peaceful, and their only impulse to browse in solitude and security; they withdraw instinctively before the slightest intrusion, and advantage is taken of this timidity and love of retirement to cause only just such an amount of disturbance as will induce them to move slowly onwards in the direction which it is desired they should take. Several herds are by this means concentrated within such an area as will admit of their being completely encircled by the watchers; and day after day, by slow degrees, they are moved gradually onwards to the immediate confines of the corral. When their suspicions become awakened and they exhibit restlessness and alarm, bolder measures are resorted to for preventing their escape. Fires are kept burning at ten paces apart, night and day, along the circumference of the area within which they are detained; a corps of from two to three thousand beaters is completed, and pathways are carefully cleared through the jungle so as to open a communication along the entire line. The headmen keep up a constant patrol, to see that their followers are alert at their posts, since neglect at any one spot might permit the escape of the herd, and undo in a moment the vigilance of weeks. By this means any attempt of the elephants to break away is immediately checked, and on any point threatened a sufficient force can be instantly assembled to drive them back.

At last the elephants are forced onwards so close to the enclosure, that the investing cordon is united at either end with the wings of the corral, the whole forming a circle of about two miles, within the area of which the herd is detained to await the signal for the final drive.

Two months had been spent in these preparations, and they had been thus far completed, on the day when we arrived and took our places on the stage erected for us, overlooking the entrance to the corral. Close beneath us a group of tame elephants, sent by the temples and the chiefs to assist in securing the wild ones, were picketed in the shade, and lazily fanning themselves with leaves. Three distinct herds, whose united numbers were variously represented at from forty to fifty elephants, were enclosed, and were at that moment concealed in the jungle within a short distance of the stockade. Not a sound was permitted to be made, each person spoke to his neighbour in whispers, and such was the silence observed by the multitude of the watchers at their posts, that occasionally we could hear the rustling of the branches as some of the elephants stripped off their leaves.

Suddenly the signal was made, and the stillness of the forest was broken by the shouts of the guard, the rolling of the drums and tom-toms, and the discharge of muskets; and beginning at the most distant side of the area, the elephants were urged forward towards the entrance into the corral.

The watchers along the line kept silence only till the herd had passed them, and then joining the cry in their rear they drove them onward with redoubled shouts and noises. The tumult increased as the terrified rout drew near, swelling now on one side now on the other, as the herd in their panic dashed from point to point in their endeavours to force the line, but were instantly driven back by screams, guns, and drums.

At length the breaking of the branches and the crackling of the brushwood announced their close approach, and the leader bursting from the jungle rushed wildly forward to within twenty yards of the entrance followed by the rest of the herd. Another moment and they would have plunged into the open gate, when suddenly they wheeled round, re-entered the jungle, and in spite of the hunters resumed their original position. The chief headman came forward and accounted for the freak by saying that a wild pig[1], an animal which the elephants are said to dislike, had started out of the cover and run across the leader, who would otherwise have held on direct for the corral; and he intimated that as the herd was now in the highest

---

[1] Fire, the sound of a horn, and the grunting of a boar are the three things which the Greeks, in the middle ages, believed the elephant specially to dislike.

Πῦρ δὲ πτοεῖται καὶ κριὸν κερασφόρον
Καὶ τῶν μονιῶν τὴν βοὴν τὴν ἀθρόαν.
PHILE, *Expositio de Elephante*, l. 177.

state of excitement; and it was at all times much more difficult to effect a successful capture by daylight than by night when the fires and flambeaux act with double effect, it was the wish of the hunters to defer their final effort till the evening, when the darkness would lend a powerful aid to their exertions.

After sunset the scene exhibited was of extraordinary interest; the low fires, which had apparently only smouldered in the sunlight, assumed their ruddy glow amidst the darkness, and threw their tinge over the groups collected round them; while the smoke rose in eddies through the rich foliage of the trees. The crowds of spectators maintained profound silence, and not a sound was perceptible beyond the hum of an insect. On a sudden the stillness was broken by the roll of a drum, followed by a discharge of musketry. This was the signal for the renewed assault, and the hunters entered the circle with shouts and clamour; dry leaves and sticks were flung upon the watch-fires till they blazed aloft, and formed a line of flame on every side, except in the direction of the corral, which was studiously kept dark; and thither the terrified elephants betook themselves followed by the yells and racket of their pursuers.

They approached at a rapid pace, trampling down the brushwood and crushing the dry branches, the leader emerged in front of the corral, paused for an instant, stared wildly round, and then rushed headlong through the open gate followed by the rest of the herd.

As if by magic the entire circuit of the corral, which to this moment had been kept in profound darkness, now blazed with a thousand lights, every hunter on the instant that the elephants entered, rushing forward to the stockade with a torch kindled at the nearest watch-fire.

The elephants first dashed to the very extremity of the enclosure, and being brought up by the powerful fence, started back to regain the gate, but found it closed. Their terror was sublime: they hurried round the corral at a rapid pace, but saw it now girt by fire on every side;

they attempted to force the stockade, but were driven back by the guards with spears and flambeaux; and on whichever side they approached they were repulsed with shouts and discharges of musketry. Collecting into one group, they would pause for a moment in apparent bewilderment, then burst off in another direction as if it had suddenly occurred to them to try some point which they had before overlooked; but again repulsed, they slowly returned to their forlorn resting-place in the centre of the corral.

The interest of this strange scene was not confined to the spectators; it extended to the tame elephants which were stationed outside. At the first approach of the flying herd they evinced the utmost interest in the scene. Two in particular which were picketed near the front were intensely excited, and continued tossing their heads, pawing the ground, and starting as the noise drew near. At length when the grand rush into the corral took place, one of them fairly burst from her fastenings and started off towards the herd, levelling a tree of considerable size which obstructed her passage.[1]

---

[1] The other elephant, a fine tusker, which belonged to Dehigam Rate-Mahatmeya, continued in extreme excitement throughout all the subsequent operations of the capture, and at last, after attempting to break his way into the corral, shaking the bars with his forehead and tusks, he went off in a state of frenzy into the jungle. The Aratchy went in search of him a few days after with a female decoy, and waiting his approach, he sprang fairly on the infuriated beast, with a pair of sharp hooks in his hands, which he pressed into tender parts in front of the shoulder, and held him firmly till chains were passed over his legs, and he permitted himself to be led quietly away.

CHAP. V.

THE CAPTIVES.

For upwards of an hour the elephants continued to traverse the corral and assail the palisade with unabated energy, trumpeting and screaming with rage after each disappointment. Again and again they attempted to force the gate, as if aware, by experience, that it ought to afford an exit as it had already served as an entrance, but they shrunk back stunned and bewildered. By degrees their efforts became less and less frequent. Single ones rushed about here and there returning sullenly to their companions, and at last the whole herd, stupified and exhausted, formed themselves into a single group, drawn up in a circle with the young in the centre, and stood motionless under the dark shade of the trees in the middle of the corral.

Preparations were now made to keep watch during the night, the guard was reinforced around the enclosure, and wood heaped on the fires to keep up a high flame till sunrise.

Three herds had been originally entrapped by the beaters outside; but with characteristic instinct they had kept clear of each other, taking up different stations in the space invested by the watchers. When the final drive took place one herd only had entered, the other two keeping behind; and as the gate had to be instantly closed on the first division, the last were unavoidably shut out and remained still concealed in the jungle. To prevent their escape, the watches were ordered to their former stations, their fires were replenished; and all precautions being thus taken, we returned to pass the night in our bungalows by the river.

As our sleeping-place was not above two hundred yards from the corral, we were frequently awakened during the early part of the night by the din of the multitude who were bivouacking in the forest, by the merriment round the watch-fires, and now and then by the shouts with which the guards repulsed some sudden charge of the elephants in attempts to force the stockade. But at day-break, on going down to the corral, we found all still and vigilant. The fires were allowed to die out as the sun rose, and the watchers who had been relieved were sleeping near the great fence, but the enclosure on all sides was surrounded by crowds of men and boys with spears or white peeled wands about ten feet long, whilst the elephants within were huddled together in a compact group, no longer turbulent and restless, but exhausted and calm, and utterly subdued by apprehension and amazement, at all that had been passing around them.

Nine only had been as yet entrapped [1], of which three were very large, and two little creatures but a few months old. One of the large ones was a "rogue," and being unassociated with the rest of the herd, although permitted to stand near them, he was not admitted to their circle.

Outside, preparations were making to conduct the tame elephants into the corral, in order to secure the captives. The nooses were in readiness; and far apart from all stood a party of the out-caste Rodiyas, the only tribe who will touch a dead carcase, to whom,

---

[1] In some of the elephant hunts conducted in the southern provinces of Ceylon by the earlier British Governors, as many as 170 and 200 elephants have been secured in a single corral, of which a portion only were taken out for the public service, and the rest shot, the aim being to rid the neighbourhood of them, and thus protect the crops from destruction. In the present instance, the object being to secure only as many as were required for the Government stud, it was not sought to entrap more than could conveniently be attended to and trained after capture.

therefore, the duty is assigned of preparing the fine flexible rope for noosing, which is made from the fresh hides of the deer and the buffalo.

At length, the bars which secured the entrance to the corral were cautiously withdrawn, and two trained elephants passed stealthily in, each ridden by his mahout, (or *ponnekella*, as he is termed in Ceylon,) and one attendant; and, carrying a strong collar, formed by coils of rope made from coco-nut fibre, from which hung on either side cords of elk's hide, prepared with a ready noose. Along with them, and concealed behind them, the headman of the "*cooroowe*," or noosers, crept in, eager to secure the honour of taking the first elephant, a distinction which this class jealously contests with the mahouts of the chiefs and the temples. He was a wiry little man, nearly seventy years old, who had served in the same capacity under the Kandyan king, and wore two silver bangles, which had been conferred on him in testimony of his prowess. He was accompanied by his son, named Ranghanie, equally renowned for his courage and dexterity.

On this occasion ten tame elephants were in attendance; two were the property of an adjoining temple (one of which had been caught only the year before, yet it was now ready to assist in capturing others), four belonged to the neighbouring chiefs, and the rest, including the two which now entered the corral, were part of the Government stud. Of the latter, one was of prodigious age, having been in the service of the Dutch and English Governments in succession for upwards of a century.[1] The other, called by her keeper "Siri-beddi," was about fifty years old, and distinguished for her gentleness and docility. The latter was a most accomplished decoy, and evinced the utmost relish for

[1] This elephant is since dead; she grew infirm and diseased, and died at Colombo in 1848. Her skeleton is now in the Museum of the Natural History Society at Belfast.

the sport. Having entered the corral noiselessly, she moved slowly along with a sly composure and an assumed air of easy indifference; sauntering leisurely in the direction of the captives, and halting now and then to pluck a bunch of grass or a few leaves as she passed. As she approached the herd, they put themselves in motion to meet her, and the leader, having advanced in front and passed his trunk gently over her head, turned and paced slowly back to his dejected companions. Siribeddi followed with the same listless step, and drew herself up close behind him, thus affording the nooser an opportunity to stoop under her and slip the noose over the hind foot of the wild one. The latter instantly perceived his danger, shook off the rope, and turned to attack the man. He would have suffered for his temerity, had not Siribeddi protected him by raising her trunk and driving the assailant into the midst of the herd, when the old man, being slightly wounded, was helped out of the corral, and his son, Ranghanie, took his place.

The herd again collected in a circle, with their heads towards the centre. The largest male was singled out, and two tame ones pushed boldly in, one on either side of him, till the three stood nearly abreast. He made no resistance, but betrayed his uneasiness by shifting restlessly from foot to foot. Ranghanie now crept up, and, holding the rope open with both hands (its other extremity being made fast to Siribeddi's collar, and watching the instant when the wild elephant lifted its hind-foot, he succeeded in passing the noose over its leg, drew it close, and fled to the rear. The two tame elephants instantly fell back, Siribeddi stretched the rope to its full length, and, whilst she dragged out the captive, her companion placed himself between her and the herd to prevent any interference.

In order to secure him to a tree he had to be drawn backwards some twenty or thirty yards, making furious resistance, bellowing in terror, plunging on all sides, and crushing the smaller timber, which bent like reeds beneath his clumsy struggles. Siribeddi drew him steadily after her, and wound the rope round the proper tree, holding it all the time at its full tension, and stepping cautiously across it when, in order to give it a second turn, it was necessary to pass between the tree and the elephant. With a coil round the stem, however, it was beyond her strength to haul the prisoner close up, which was, nevertheless, necessary in order to make him perfectly fast;

but the second tame one, perceiving the difficulty, returned from the herd, confronted the struggling prisoner, pushed him shoulder to shoulder, and head to head, and forced him backwards, whilst at every step Siribeddi hauled in the slackened rope till she brought him fairly up to the foot of the tree, where he was made fast by the cooroowe people. A second noose was then passed over the other hind-leg, and secured like the first, both legs being afterwards hobbled together by ropes made from the fibre of the kittool or jaggery palm, which, being more flexible than that of the coco-nut, occasions less formidable ulcerations.

The two decoys then ranged themselves, as before, abreast of the prisoner on either side, thus enabling Ranghanie to stoop under them and noose the two fore-feet as he had already done the hind; and these ropes being made fast to a tree in front, the capture was complete, and the tame elephants and keepers withdrew to repeat the operation on another of the herd. As long as the tame ones stood beside him the poor animal remained comparatively calm and almost passive under his sufferings, but the moment they moved off, and he was left utterly alone, he made the most surprising efforts to set himself free and re-

join his companions. He felt the ropes with his trunk and tried to untie the numerous knots; he drew backwards to liberate his fore-legs, then leaned forward to extricate the hind ones, till every branch of the tall tree vibrated with his struggles. He screamed in his anguish with his proboscis raised high in the air, then falling on his side he laid his head to the ground, first his cheek and then his brow, and pressed down his doubled-in trunk as though he would force it into the earth; then suddenly rising he balanced himself on his forehead and his fore-legs, holding his hind-feet fairly off the ground. This scene of distress continued some hours, with occasional pauses of apparent stupor, after which the struggle was from time to time renewed abruptly, and as if by some sudden impulse, but at last the vain strife subsided, and the poor animal stood perfectly motionless, the image of exhaustion and despair.

Meanwhile Ranghanie presented himself in front of the governor's stage to claim the accustomed largesse for tying the first elephant. He was rewarded by a shower of rupees, and retired to resume his perilous duties in the corral.

The rest of the herd were now in a state of pitiable dejection, and pressed closely together as if under a sense of common misfortune. For the most part they stood at rest in a compact body, fretful and uneasy. At intervals one more impatient than the rest would move out a few steps to reconnoitre; the others would follow at first slowly, then at a quicker pace, and at last the whole herd would rush off furiously to renew the often-baffled attempt to storm the stockade.

There was a strange combination of the sublime and the ridiculous in these abortive onsets; the appearance of prodigious power in their ponderous limbs, coupled with the almost ludicrous shuffle of their clumsy gait, and the fury of their apparently resistless charge, converted in an instant into timid retreat. They rushed madly down the enclosure, their backs arched, their tails extended, their ears spread, and their trunks raised high above their heads, trumpeting and uttering shrill screams, and when one step further would have dashed the opposing fence into fragments, they stopped short on a few white rods being pointed at them through the paling; and, on catching the derisive shouts of the crowd, they turned in utter discomfiture, and after an objectless circle or two through the corral, they paced slowly back to their melancholy halting place in the shade.

The crowd, chiefly comprised of young men and boys, exhibited astonishing nerve and composure at such moments, rushing up to the point towards which the elephants charged, pointing their wands[1] at their trunks, and keeping up the continual cry of *whoop! whoop!* which invariably turned them to flight.

The second victim singled out from the herd was secured in the same manner as the first. It was a female. The tame ones forced themselves in on either side as before, cutting her off from her companions, whilst Ranghanie stooped under them and attached the fatal noose, and Siribeddi dragged her out amidst unavailing struggles, when she was made fast by each leg to the nearest group of strong trees. When the noose was placed upon her fore-foot, she seized it with her trunk, and succeeded in carrying it to her mouth, where she would speedily have severed it had not a tame elephant interfered, and placing his foot on the rope pressed it downwards out of her jaws. The individuals who acted as leaders in the successive charges on the palisades were always those selected by the noosers, and the operation of tying each, from the first approaches of the decoys, till the captive was left alone by the tree, occupied on an average somewhat less than three quarters of an hour.

It is strange that in these encounters the wild elephants made no attempt to attack or dislodge the mahouts or the cooroowes, who rode on the tame ones. They moved in the very midst of the herd; any one of whom could in a moment have pulled the riders from their seats, but no effort was made to molest them.[2]

---

[1] The fact of the elephant exhibiting timidity, on having a long rod pointed towards him, was known to the Romans; and PLINY, quoting from the annals of Piso, relates, that in order to inculcate contempt for want of courage in the elephant, they were introduced into the circus during the triumph of Metellus, after the conquest of the Carthaginians in Sicily, and *driven round the area by workmen holding blunted spears*,—"Ab operariis hastas præpilatas habentibus, per circum totam actos."—Lib. viii. c. 6.

[2] "In a corral, to be on a tame elephant, seems to insure perfect immunity from the attacks of the wild

As one after another their leaders were entrapped and forced away from them, the remainder of the group evinced increased emotion and excitement; but whatever may have been their sympathy for their lost companions, their alarm seemed to prevent them at first from following them to the trees to which they had been tied. In passing them afterwards they sometimes stopped, mutually entwined their trunks, lapped them round their limbs and neck, and exhibited the most touching distress at their detention, but made no attempt to disturb the cords that bound them.

The variety of disposition in the herd as evidenced by the difference of demeanour was very remarkable;

---

ones. I once saw the old chief Mollegodde ride in amongst a herd of wild elephants, on a small elephant; so small that the Adigar's head was on a level with the back of the wild animals: I felt very nervous, but he rode right in among them, and received not the slightest molestation." — *Letter from* MAJOR SKINNER.

some submitted with comparatively little resistance; whilst others in their fury dashed themselves on the ground with a force sufficient to destroy any weaker animal. They vented their rage upon every tree and plant within reach; if small enough to be torn down, they levelled them with their trunks, and stripped them of their leaves and branches, which they tossed wildly over their heads on all sides. Some in their struggles made no sound, whilst others bellowed and trumpeted furiously, then uttered short convulsive screams, and at last, exhausted and hopeless, gave vent to their anguish in low and piteous moanings. Some, after a few violent efforts of this kind, lay motionless on the ground, with no other indication of suffering than the tears which suffused their eyes and flowed incessantly. Others in all the vigour of their rage exhibited the most surprising contortions; and to us who had been accustomed to associate with the unwieldy bulk of the elephant the idea that he must of necessity be stiff and inflexible, the attitudes into which they forced themselves were almost incredible. I saw one lie with the cheek pressed to the earth and the fore-legs stretched in front, whilst the body was twisted round till the hind-legs extended at the opposite side.

It was astonishing that their trunks was not wounded by the violence with which they flung them on all sides. One twisted his proboscis into such fantastic shapes, that it resembled the writhings of a gigantic worm; he coiled it and uncoiled it with restless rapidity, curling it up like a watch-spring, and suddenly unfolding it again to its full length. Another, which lay otherwise motionless in all the stupor of hopeless anguish, slowly beat the ground with the extremity of his trunk, as a man in despair beats his knee with his open palm.

They displayed an amount of sensitiveness and delicacy of touch in the foot, which was very remarkable in a limb of such clumsy dimensions and protected by so thick a covering. The noosers could always force them to lift it from the ground by the gentlest touch of a leaf or twig, apparently applied so as to tickle; but the imposition of the rope was instantaneously perceived, and if it could not be reached by the trunk the other foot was applied to feel its position, and if possible remove it before the noose could be drawn tight.

One practice was incessant with almost the entire herd: in the interval of every struggle, they beat up the ground with their fore-feet, and taking up the dry earth in a coil of their trunks, they flung it dexterously over every part of their body. Even when lying down, the sand within reach was thus collected and scattered over their limbs: then inserting the extremity of their trunks in their mouths, they withdrew a quantity of water, which they discharged over their backs, repeating the operation again and again, till the dust was thoroughly saturated. I was astonished at the quantity of water thus applied, which was sufficient when the elephant, as was generally the case, had worked the spot where he lay into a hollow, to convert its surface into a thin coating of mud. Seeing that the herd had been now twenty-four hours without access to water of any kind, surrounded by watch-fires, and exhausted by struggling and terror, the supply of moisture he was capable of containing in the receptacle attached to his stomach must have been very considerable.

The conduct of the tame elephants during all these proceedings was truly wonderful. They displayed the most perfect conception of every movement, both the object to be attained, and the means of accomplishing it. They evinced the utmost enjoyment in what was going on. There was no ill-humour, no malignity in the spirit displayed, in what was otherwise a heartless proceeding, but they set about it in a way that showed a thorough relish for it, as an agreeable pastime. Their caution was as remarkable as their sagacity; there was no hurrying, no confusion, they never ran foul of the ropes, were never in the way of those noosed; and amidst the most violent struggles, when the tame ones had frequently to step across the captives, they in no instance trampled on them, or occasioned the slightest accident or annoyance. So far from this, they saw intuitively a difficulty or a danger, and addressed themselves voluntarily to remove it. In tying up one of the larger elephants he contrived, before he could be hauled close up to the tree, to walk once or twice round it, carrying the rope with him; the decoy, perceiving the advantage he had thus gained over the nooser, walked up of her own accord, and pushed him backwards with her head, till she made him unwind himself again; when the rope was hauled tight and made fast. More than once, when a wild one was extending his trunk, and would have intercepted the rope about to be placed over his leg, Siribeddi, by a sudden motion of her own trunk, pushed his aside, and prevented him; and on one occasion, when successive efforts had failed to put the noose over the leg of an elephant which was already secured by one foot, but which wisely put the other to the ground as often as it was attempted to pass the noose under it, I saw the decoy watch her opportunity, and when his foot was again raised, suddenly push in her own leg beneath it, and hold it up till the noose was attached and drawn tight.

One could almost fancy there was a display of dry humour in the manner in which the decoys thus played with the fears of the wild herd, and made light of their efforts at resistance. When reluctant they shoved them forward, when violent they drove them back; when the wild ones threw themselves down, the tame ones butted them with head and shoulders, and forced them up again. And when it was necessary to keep them down, they knelt upon them, and prevented them from rising, till the ropes were secured.

At every moment of leisure they fanned themselves with a bunch of leaves, and the graceful ease with which an elephant uses his trunk on such occasions is very striking. It is doubtless owing to the combination of a circular with a horizontal movement in that flexible limb; but it is impossible to see an elephant fanning himself without being struck by the singular elegance of motion which it displays. They too indulged themselves in the luxury of dusting themselves with sand, by flinging it from their trunks; but it was a curious instance of their delicate sagacity, that so long as the mahout was on their necks, they confined themselves to flinging it along their sides and stomach, as if aware, that to throw it over their heads and back would cause annoyance to their riders.

One of the decoys which rendered good service, and was obviously held in special awe by the wild herd, was a tusker belonging to Dehigame Rate-mahatmeya. It was not that he used his tusks for purposes of offence, but he was enabled to insinuate himself between two elephants by wedging them in where he could not force his head; besides which, they assisted him to raise up the fallen and refractory with greater ease. In some instances where the intervention of the other decoys failed to reduce a wild one to order, the mere presence and approach of the tusker seemed to inspire fear, and insure submission, without more active intervention.

I do not know whether it was the surprising qualities exhibited by the tame elephants that cast the courage and dexterity of the men into the shade, but even when supported by the presence, the sagacity, and co-operation of these wonderful creatures, the part sustained by the noosers can bear no comparison with the address and daring displayed by the *picador* and *matador* in a Spanish bull-fight. They certainly possessed great quickness of eye in watching the slightest movement of an elephant, and great expertness in flinging the noose over its foot and attaching it firmly before the animal could tear it off with its trunk; but in all this they had the cover of the decoys to conceal them; and their protection behind which to retreat. Apart from the services which from their prodigious strength the tame elephants are alone capable of rendering in dragging out and securing the captives, it is perfectly obvious that without their co-operation the utmost prowess and dexterity of the hunters would not avail them, to enter the corral unsupported, or to ensnare and lead out a single captive.

Of the two tiny elephants which were entrapped, one was about ten months old, the other somewhat more. The smallest had a little bolt head covered with woolly brown hair, and was the most amusing and interesting miniature imaginable. Both kept constantly with the herd, trotting after them in every charge; when the others stood at rest they ran in and out between the legs of the older ones; not their own mothers alone, but every female in the group, caressing them in turn.

The dam of the youngest was the second elephant singled out by the noosers, and as she was dragged along by the decoys, the little creature kept by her side till she was drawn close to the fatal tree. The men at first were rather amused than otherwise by its anger; but they found that it would not permit them to place the second noose upon its mother, it ran between her and them, it tried to seize the rope, it pushed them and struck them with its little trunk, till they were forced to drive it back to the herd. It retreated slowly, shouting all the way, and pausing at every step to look back. It then attached itself to the largest female remaining in the herd, and placed itself across her forelegs, whilst she hung down her trunk over its side and soothed and caressed it. Here it continued moaning and lamenting, till the noosers had left off securing the mother, when it instantly returned to her side; but as it became troublesome again, attacking every one who passed, it was at last secured by a rope to an adjoining tree, to which the other young one was also tied up. The second little one, equally with its playmate, exhibited great affection for its mother; it went willingly with its captor as far as the tree to which she was fastened, when it held out its trunk and tried to rejoin her; but finding itself forced along, it caught at every twig and branch it passed, and screamed with grief and disappointment.

These two little creatures were the most vociferous of the whole herd, their shouts were incessant, they struggled to attack every one within reach; and as their bodies were more lithe and pliant than those of greater growth, their contortions were quite wonderful. The most amusing thing was, that in the midst of all their agony and affliction, the little fellows seized on every article of food that was thrown to them, and ate and roared simultaneously.

Amongst the last of the elephants noosed was the *rogue.* Though far more savage than the others, he joined in none of their charges and assaults on the fences, as they uniformly drove him off and would not permit him to enter their circle. When dragged past another of his companions in misfortune, who was lying exhausted on the ground, he flew upon him and attempted to fasten his teeth in his head; this was the only instance of viciousness which occurred during the progress of the corral. When tied up and overpowered, he was at first noisy and violent, but soon lay down peacefully, a sign, according to the hunters, that his death was at hand. In this instance their prognostication was correct. He continued for about twelve hours to cover himself with dust like the others and to moisten it with water from his trunk, but at length he lay exhausted, and died so calmly, that having been moving but a few moments before, his death was only perceived by the myriads of black flies by which his body was almost instantly covered, although not one was visible a moment before.[1] The Rodiyas were called in to loose

[1] The surprising faculty of vultures in discovering carrion, has been a subject of much speculation, as to whether it be dependent on their

the ropes from the tree, and two tame elephants being harnessed to the dead body, it was dragged to a distance without the corral.

When every wild elephant had been noosed and tied up, the scene presented was one truly oriental. From one to two thousand natives, many of them in gaudy dresses and armed with spears, crowded about the enclosures. Their families had collected to see the spectacle; women, whose children clung like little bronzed Cupids by their side; and girls, many of them in the graceful costume of that part of the country, a scarf, which, after having been brought round the waist, is thrown over the left shoulder, leaving the right arm and side free and uncovered.

At the foot of each tree was its captive elephant;

---

power of sight or of scent. It is not, however, more mysterious than the unerring certainty and rapidity with which some of the minor animals, and more especially insects, in warm climates congregate around the offal on which they feed. Circumstanced as they are, they must be guided towards their object mainly if not exclusively, by the sense of smell; but that which excites astonishment is the small degree of odour which seems to suffice for the purpose; the subtlety and rapidity with which it traverses and impregnates the air; and the keen and quick perception with which it is taken up by the organs of those creatures. The instance of the scavenger beetles has been already alluded to; the promptitude with which they discern the existence of matter suited to their purposes, and the speed with which they hurry to it from all directions; often from distances as extraordinary, proportionably, as those traversed by the eye of the vulture. In the instance of the dying elephant referred to above, life was barely extinct when the flies, of which not one was visible but a moment before, arrived in clouds and blackened the body by their multitude; scarcely an instant was allowed to elapse for the commencement of decomposition; no odour of putrefaction could be discerned by us who stood close by; yet some peculiar smell of mortality, simultaneously with parting breath, must have summoned them to the feast. Ants exhibit an instinct equally surprising. I have sometimes covered up a particle of refined sugar with paper on the centre of a polished table; and counted the number of minutes which would elapse before it was fastened on by the small black ants of Ceylon, and a line formed to lower it safely to the floor. Here was a substance which, to our apprehension at least, is altogether inodorous, and yet the quick sense of smell must have been the only conductor of the ants. It has been observed of those fishes which travel overland on the evaporation of the ponds in which they live, that they invariably march in the direction of the nearest water, and even when captured, and placed on the floor of a room, their efforts to escape are always made towards the same point. Is the sense of smell sufficient to account for this display of instinct in them? or is it aided by special organs in the case of the others?

some still struggling and writhing in feverish excitement, whilst others, in exhaustion and despair, lay motionless, except that from time to time they heaped fresh dust upon their heads. The mellow notes of a Kandyan flute, which was played at a little distance, had a striking effect upon one or more of them; they turned their heads in the direction from which the music came, expanded their broad ears, and were evidently soothed with the plaintive sound. The two young ones alone still roared for freedom; they stamped their feet, and blew clouds of dust over their shoulders, brandishing their little trunks aloft, and attacking every one who came within their reach.

At first the older ones, when secured, spurned every offer of food, trampled it under foot, and turned haughtily away. A few, however, as they became more composed, could not resist the temptation of the juicy stems of the plantain, but rolling them under foot, till they detached the layers, they raised them in their trunks, and commenced chewing them listlessly.

On the whole, whilst the sagacity, the composure, and docility of the decoys were such as to excite lively astonishment, it was not possible to withhold the highest admiration from the calm and dignified demeanour of the captives. Their entire bearing was at variance with the representations made by some of the "sportsmen" who harass them, that they are treacherous, savage, and revengeful; when tormented by the guns of their persecutors, they, no doubt, display their powers and sagacity in efforts to retaliate or escape; but here their every movement was indicative of innocence and timidity. After a struggle, in which they evinced no disposition to violence or revenge, they submitted with the calmness of despair. Their attitudes were pitiable, their grief was most touching, and their low moaning went to the heart. It would not have been tolerable had they either been captured with unnecessary pain or reserved for ill treatment afterwards.

It was now about two hours after noon, and the first elephants that had entered the corral having been disposed of, preparations were made to reopen the gate, and drive in the other two herds, over which the watchers were still keeping guard. The area of the enclosure was cleared; silence was again imposed on the crowds who surrounded the corral. The bars which secured the entrance were withdrawn, and every precaution repeated as before; but as the space inside was now somewhat trodden down, especially near the entrance, by the frequent charges of the last herd, and it was to be apprehended that the others might be earlier alarmed and retrace their steps, before the barricades could be replaced, two tame ones were stationed inside to protect the men to whom that duty was assigned.

All preliminaries being at length completed, the signal was given; the beaters on the side most distant from the corral closed in with tom-toms and discordant noises; a hedge-fire of musketry was kept up in the rear of the terrified elephants; thousands of voices urged them forward; we heard the jungle crashing as they came on, and at last they advanced through an opening amongst the trees, bearing down all before them like a charge of locomotives. They were led by a huge female, nearly nine feet high, after whom dashed one half precipitately through the narrow entrance, but the rest turning suddenly towards the left, succeeded in forcing the cordon of guards and made good their escape to the forest.

No sooner had the others passed the gate, than the two tame elephants stepped forward from either side, and before the herd could return from the further end of the enclosure, the bars were drawn, the entrance closed, and the men in charge glided outside the stockade.

The elephants which had previously been made prisoners within exhibited intense excitement as the fresh din arose around them; they started to their feet, and stretched their trunks in the direction whence they winded the scent of the flying herd; and as the latter rushed headlong past, they renewed their struggles to get free and follow.

It is not possible to imagine anything more exciting than the spectacle which the wild ones presented careering round the corral, uttering piercing screams, their heads erect and trunks aloft, the very emblems of rage and perplexity, of power and helplessness.

Along with those which entered at the second drive was one that evidently belonged to another herd, and had been separated from them in the *mêlée* when the latter effected their escape, and, as usual, his new companions in misfortune drove him off indignantly as often as he attempted to approach them.

The demeanour of those taken in the second drive differed materially from that of the preceding captives, who, having entered the corral in darkness, and finding themselves girt with fire and smoke, and beset by hideous sounds and sights on every side, were more speedily reduced by fear to stupor and submission — whereas the second herd not only passed into the enclosure by daylight, bnt its area being trodden down in many places, they could discover the fences more clearly, and were consequently more alarmed and enraged at their detention. They were thus as restless as the others had been comparatively calm, and so much more vigorous in their assaults that, on one occasion in particular, their courageous leader, undaunted by the multitude of white wands thrust towards her, was only driven back from the stockade by a hunter hurling a blazing flambeau at her head. Her attitude as she stood repulsed, but still irresolute, was a study for a painter. Her eye dilated, her ears expanded, her back arched like a tiger, and her fore-foot in air, whilst she uttered those hideous screams which are imperfectly described by the term "*trumpeting*."

Although repeatedly passing by the unfortunates from

the former drove, the new herd seemed to take no friendly notice of them; they halted inquiringly for a minute, and then resumed their career round the corral, and once or twice in their headlong flight they rushed madly over the bodies of the prostrate captives as they lay in their misery on the ground.

It was evening before the new captives grew wearied with furious and repeated charges, and stood still in the centre of the corral collected into one terrified and motionless group. The fires were then relighted, the guard redoubled by the addition of the watchers, who were now relieved from duty in the forest, and the spectators retired for the night.

The business of the *third day* began by noosing and tying up the new captives, and the first sought out was their magnificent leader. Siribeddi, and the tame tusker having forced themselves on either side of her, a boy in the service of the Rate-Mahat-meya succeeded in attaching the rope to her hind foot. Siribeddi moved off, but feeling her strength insufficient to drag the reluctant prize, she went down on her fore-knees, so as to add the full weight of her body to the pull. The tusker, seeing her difficulty, placed himself in front of the prisoner, and forced her backwards, step by step, till his companion brought her fairly up to the tree, and wound the rope round the stem. Though overpowered by fear, she showed the fullest sense of the nature of the danger she had to apprehend. She kept her head turned towards the noosers, and tried to step in advance of the decoys, and in spite of all their efforts, she tore off the first noose from her fore-leg, and placing it under her foot, snapped it into fathom lengths. When finally secured, her writhings were extraordinary. She doubled in her head under her chest, till she lay as round as a hedge-hog, and rising again, stood on her fore-feet, and lifting her hind-feet off the ground, she wrung them from side to side, till the great tree above her quivered in every branch.

Before proceeding to catch the others, we requested that the smaller trees and jungle, which partially obstructed our view, might be broken away, being no longer essential to screen the entrance to the corral: five of the tame elephants were brought up for the purpose. They felt the strength of each tree with their trunks, then swaying it backwards and forwards, by pushing it with their foreheads, they watched the opportunity when it was in full motion to raise their fore-feet against the stem, and bear it down to the ground. Then tearing off the festoons of climbing plants, and trampling down the smaller branches and brushwood, they pitched them with their tusks, and piled them into heaps along the side of the fence.

Amongst the last that was secured was the solitary individual belonging to the fugitive herd. When they attempted to drag him backwards from the tree near which he was noosed, he laid hold of it with his trunk and lay down on his side immoveable. The temple

tusker and another were ordered up to assist, and it required the combined efforts of the three elephants to force him along. When dragged to the place at which he was to be tied up, he continued the contest with desperation, and to prevent the second noose being placed on his foot, he sat down on his haunches, almost in the attitude of the "Florentine Boar," keeping his hind-feet beneath him, and defending his fore-feet with his trunk, with which he flung back the rope as often as it was attempted to attach it. When overpowered and made fast, his grief was most affecting; his violence sunk to utter prostration, and he lay on the ground, uttering choking cries, with tears trickling down his cheeks.

The final operation was that of slackening the ropes and marching each captive down to the river between two tame ones. This was effected very simply. A decoy, with a strong collar round his neck, stood on either side of the wild one, on which a similar collar was formed, by successive coils of coco-nut rope; and then, by connecting the three collars together, the prisoner was effectually made safe between his two guards. During this operation, it was curious to see how the tame elephant, from time to time, used its trunk to shield the arm of its rider, and ward off the trunk of the prisoner, who resisted the placing the rope round his own neck. This being done, the nooses were removed from his feet, and he was marched off to the river, in which he was allowed to bathe; a privilege of which all eagerly availed themselves. Each was then made fast to a tree in the forest, and keepers being assigned to him, with a retinue of leaf-cutters, he was plentifully supplied with his favourite food, and left to the care and tuition of his new masters.

Returning from a spectacle such as I have attempted to describe, one cannot help feeling how immeasurably it exceeds in interest those royal battues where timid deer are driven in crowds to unresisting slaughter; or those vaunted "wild sports" the amusement of which appears to be in proportion to the effusion of blood. Here the only display of cruelty was the imposition of restraint; and though considerable mortality often occurs amongst the animals caught, the infliction of pain, so far from being an incident of the operation, was most cautiously avoided from its tendency to enrage, the policy of the captor being to conciliate and soothe. The whole scene exhibits the most marvellous example of the voluntary alliance of sagacity and instinct in active co-operation with human intelligence and courage; and nothing in nature, not even the chase of the whale, can afford so vivid an illustration of the sovereignty of man over brute creation even when confronted with force in its most stupendous embodiment.

Of the two young elephants which were taken in the corral, the least was sent down to my house at Colombo, where he became a general favourite with the servants. He attached himself especially to the coachman, who had a little shed erected for him near his own quarters at the stables. But his favourite resort was the kitchen, where he received his daily allowance of milk and plantains and picked up several other delicacies besides. He was innocent and playful in the extreme, and when walking in the grounds would trot up to me and twine his little trunk round my arm and coax me to take him to the fruit trees. In the evening, the grass-cutters now and then indulged him by permitting him to carry home a load of fodder for the horses, on which occasions he assumed an air of gravity that was highly amusing, showing that he was deeply impressed with the importance of the service intrusted to him. Being sometimes permitted to enter the dining-room, and helped to fruit at dessert, he at last learned his way to the side-board; and on more than one occasion having stolen in in the absence of the servants, he made a clear sweep of the wine-glasses and china in his endeavours to reach a basket of oranges. For these and similar pranks we were at last forced to put him away. He was sent to the Government stud, where he was affectionately received and adopted by Siribeddi, and he now takes his turn of public duty in the department of the Commissioner of Roads.

CHAP. VI.

CONDUCT IN CAPTIVITY.

The idea prevailed in ancient times, and obtains even at the present day, that the Indian elephant surpasses that of Africa in sagacity and tractability, and consequently in capacity for training, so as to render its services available to man. There does not appear to me to be sufficient ground for this conclusion.

It originated, in all probability, in the first impression created by the accounts of the elephant brought back by the Greeks after the Indian expedition of Alexander, and above all, by the descriptions of Aristotle, whose knowledge of the animal was derived exclusively from the East. A long interval elapsed before the elephant of Africa, and its capabilities, became known in Europe. The first elephants brought to Greece by Antipater, were from India, as were also those introduced by Pyrrhus into Italy. Taught by this example, the Carthaginians undertook to employ African elephants in war. Jugurtha led them against Metellus, and Juba against Cæsar; but from inexperienced and deficient training, they proved less effective than the elephants of India[1], and the his-

[1] Armandi, *Hist. Milit. des Eléphants*, liv. i. ch. i. p. 2. It is an extraordinary fact, noticed by Armandi, that the elephants figured on the coins of Alexander, and the Seleucidæ invariably exhibit the characteristics of the Indian type, whilst those on Roman medals can at once be pronounced African, from the peculiarities of the convex fore-head and expansive ears.—*Ibid.* liv. i. c. i. p. 3.

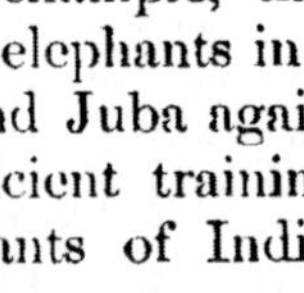

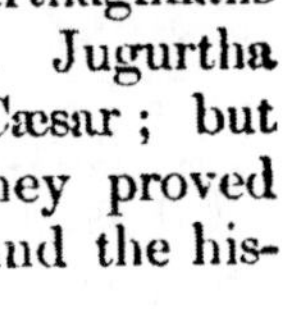

torians of these times ascribed to inferiority of race, that which was but the result of insufficient education.

It must, however, be remembered that the elephants which, at a later period, astonished the Romans by their sagacity, and whose performances in the amphitheatre have been described by Ælian and Pliny, were brought from Africa, and acquired their accomplishments from European instructors[1]; a sufficient proof that under equally favourable auspices they are capable of developing similar docility and powers with those of India.

But it is one of the facts from which the inferiority of the Negro race has been inferred, that they alone, of all the nations amongst whom the elephant is found, have never manifested ability to domesticate it, and even as regards the more highly developed races who inhabited the valley of the Nile, it is observable that the elephant is nowhere to be found amongst the animals figured on the monuments of ancient Egypt, whilst they represent the cameleopard, the lion, and even the hippopotamus. And although in later times the knowledge of the art of training appears to have existed under the Ptolemies, and on the southern shore of the Mediterranean; it admits of no doubt that it was communicated by the more accomplished natives of India who had settled there.[2]

Another favourite doctrine of the earlier visitors to the East seems to me to be equally fallacious; PYRARD, BERNIER, PHILLIPE, THEVENOT, and other travellers in the sixteenth and seventeenth centuries, proclaimed the

---

[1] ÆLIAN, lib. ii. ch. ii.

[2] See SCHLEGEL'S Essay on the Elephant and the Sphynx, *Classical Journal*, No. lx. Although the trained elephant nowhere appears upon the monuments of the Egyptians, the animal was not unknown to them, and ivory and elephants are figured on the walls of Thebes and Karnac amongst the spoils of Thothmes III., and the tribute paid to Rameses I. The Island of Elephantine, in the Nile, near Assouan (Syene) is styled in hieroglyphical writing "The Land of the Elephant"; but as it is a mere rock, it probably owes its designation to its form. See Sir GARDNER WILKINSON'S *Ancient Egyptians*, vol. i. pl. iv.; vol. v. p. 176. The elephant as figured in the sculptures of Nineveh is universally as wild, not domesticated.

superiority of the elephant of Ceylon, in size, strength, and sagacity, above those of all other parts of India[1]; and TAVERNIER in particular is supposed to have stated that if a Ceylon elephant be introduced amongst those bred in any other place, by an instinct of nature they do him homage by laying their trunks to the ground, and raising them reverentially. This passage has been so repeatedly quoted in works on Ceylon that it has passed into an aphorism, and is always adduced as a testimony to the surpassing intelligence of the elephants of that island; although a reference to the original shows that Tavernier's observations are not only fanciful in themselves, but are restricted to the supposed excellence of the Ceylon animal *in war*[2]; but the belief is pretty general that in other departments he is equally pre-eminent. I have had no opportunity of testing by personal observation the justice of this assumption; but from all that I have heard of the elephants of continental India, and seen of those of Ceylon, I have reason to conclude that the difference, if not

---

[1] This is merely a reiteration of the statement of ÆLIAN, who ascribes to the elephants of Taprobane a vast superiority in size, strength, and intelligence, above those of continental India,—"*Καὶ οἱδέ γε νησιῶται ἐλέφαντες τῶν ἠπειρωτῶν ἀλκιμώτεροί τε τὴν ῥώμην καὶ μείζους ἰδεῖν εἰσὶ καὶ θυμοσοφώτεροι δὲ πάντα πάντῃ κρίνοιντο ἄν.*"—ÆLIAN, *De Nat. Anim.*, lib. xvi. cap. xviii.

ÆLIAN also, in the same chapter, states the fact of the shipment of these elephants in large boats from Ceylon to the opposite continent of India, for sale to the king of Calinga; so that the export from Manaar, described in a former passage, has been going on apparently without interruption since the time of the Romans.

[2] The expression of TAVERNIER is to the effect that as compared with all others, the elephants of Ceylon are "plus courageux *à la guerre*." The passage is a curiosity:—

"Il faut remarquer ici une chose qu'on aura peut-être de la peine à croire, mais qui est toutefois très véritable: c'est que lorsque quelque roi ou quelque seigneur a quelqu'un de ces éléphants de Ceylan, et qu'on en amène quelqu'autre des lieux où les marchands vont les prendre, comme d'Achen, de Siam, d'Arakan, de Pegu, du royaume de Boutan, d'Assam, des terres de Cochin et de la coste du Mélinde, dès que les éléphants en voient un de Ceylan, par un instinct de nature, ils lui font la révérence, portant le bout de leur trompe à la terre et la rélevant. Il est vrai que les éléphants que les grands seigneurs entretiennent, quand on les amène devant eux, pour voir s'ils sont en bon point, font trois fois une espèce de révérence avec leur trompe, *ce que j'ai vu souvent;* mais ils sont stylés à cela, et leurs maitres le leur enseignent de bonne heure."—*Les Six Voyages de* J. B. TAVERNIER, lib. iii. ch. 20.

imaginary, is exceptional, and must have arisen in particular and individual instances, from more judicious or elaborate instruction.

The earliest knowledge of the elephant in Europe and the West, was derived from the conspicuous position assigned to it in the wars of the East: in India, from the remotest antiquity, it formed one of the most picturesque, if not the most effective, features in the armies of the native princes.[1] It is more than probable that the earliest attempts to take and train the elephant, were with a view to military uses, and that the

[1] ARMANDI has, with infinite industry, collected from original sources a mass of curious informations relative to the employment of elephants in ancient warfare, which he has published under the title of *Histoire Militaire des Eléphants depuis les temps les plus reculés jusqu'à l'introduction des armes à feu.* Paris. 1843.

The only mention of the elephant in Sacred History is in the account given in Maccabees of the invasion of Egypt by Antiochus, who entered it 170 B.C., "with chariots and elephants, and horsemen, and a great navy."—1 Maccab. i. 17. Frequent allusions to the use of elephants in war occur in both books, and in chap. vi. 34, it is stated that "to provoke the elephants to fight they showed them the blood of grapes and of mulberries." The term showed, "ἔδειξαν," might be thought to imply that the animals were enraged by the sight of the wine and its colour, but in the third Book of Maccabees, in the Greek Septuagint, various other passages show that wine, on such occasions, was administered to the elephants to render them furious. Maccab. v. 2, 10, 45. PHILE mentions the same fact, *De Elephante*, 1. 145.

There is a very curious account of the mode in which the Arab conquerors of Scinde, in the 9th and 10th centuries, equipped the elephant for war; which being written with all the particularity of an eye-witness, bears the impress of truth and accuracy. MASSOUDI, who was born in Bagdad at the close of the 9th century, travelled in India in the year A.D. 913, and visited the Gulf of Cambay, the coast of Malabar, and the Island of Ceylon, and from a larger account of his journeys he compiled a summary under the title of "*Moroudj-al-dzeheb*," or the "*Golden Meadows*," the MS. of which is now in the Bibliothèque Nationale. M. REINAUD, in describing this manuscript says, on its authority, "The Prince of Mansura, whose dominions lay south of the Indus, maintained eighty elephants trained for war, each of which bore in his trunk a bent cymetar (carthel), with which he was taught to cut and thrust at all confronting him. The trunk itself was effectually protected by a coat of mail, and the rest of the body enveloped in a covering composed jointly of iron and horn. Other elephants were employed in drawing chariots, carrying baggage, and grinding forage, and the performance of all bespoke the utmost intelligence and docility." — REINAUD, *Mémoire sur l'Inde, antérieurement au milieu du XIe siècle, d'après les écrivains arabes, persans et chinois.* Paris, M.D.CCC.XLIX. p. 215. See SPRENGER's English Translation of Massoudi, vol. i. p. 383.

art was perpetuated in later times to gratify the pride of the eastern kings, and sustain the pomp of their processions. An impression prevails even to the present day, that the process of training is tedious and difficult, and the reduction of a full-grown elephant to obedience, slow and reluctant in the extreme.[1] In both particulars, however, the contrary is the truth. The training as it prevails in Ceylon is simple, and the conformity and obedience of the animal are developed with singular rapidity. For the first three days, or till they will eat freely, which they seldom do in less time than this, the newly-captured elephants are allowed to stand quiet, or, if practicable, a tame elephant is tied near to give the wild ones confidence. Where many elephants are being trained at once, it is customary to put every new captive between the stalls of half-tamed ones, when the former soon takes to its food. This stage being attained, training commences by placing tame elephants on either side. The cooroowe vidahn, or other head of the stables, stands in front of the wild elephants holding a long stick with a sharp iron point. Two men are then stationed on either side, assisted by the tame elephants, and each holding a *hendoo* or crook[2] towards the wild one's trunk, whilst one or two others rub their hands over his back, keeping up all the while a soothing and

---

[1] BRODERIP, *Zoological Recreations*, p. 206.

[2] The iron goad with which the keeper directs the movements of the elephants, called a *hendoo* in Ceylon and *hawkus* in Bengal, appears to have retained the present shape from the remotest antiquity, and is figured in the medals of Caracalla in the identical form in which it is in use at the present day in India.

The Greeks called it ἅρπη, and the Romans *cuspis*.

Medal of Numidia.

Modern Hendoo.

plaintive chaunt, interlarded with endearing epithets, such as "ho! my son," or "oh! my father," or "my mother," as may be applicable to the age and sex of the captive. The elephant is at first furious, and strikes in all directions with his trunk; but the men in front receive all these blows on the points of their weapons, until the extremity of the trunk is so sore that the animal curls it up close, and seldom after attempts to use it. The first dread of man's power being thus established, the process of taking him to bathe between two tame elephants is greatly facilitated, and by lengthening the neck tie, and drawing the feet together as close as possible, the process of laying him down in the water is finally accomplished by the keepers pressing the sharp point of their hendoos upon the backbone.

For many days the roaring and resistance which attend the operation are considerable, and it often requires the sagacious interference of the tame elephants to control the refractory wild ones. It soon, however, becomes practicable to leave the latter alone, only taking them to and from the stall by the aid of a decoy. This step lasts, under ordinary treatment, for about three weeks, when an elephant may be taken alone with his legs hobbled, and a man walking backwards in front with the point of the hendoo always presented to the elephant's head, and a keeper with an iron crook at each ear. On getting into the water the fear of being pricked on his tender back induces him to lie down directly on the crook being only held over him *in terrorem*. Once this point has been achieved, the further process of taming is dependent upon the disposition of the creature.

The greatest care is requisite, and daily medicines are applied to heal the fearful wounds on the legs which even the softest ropes occasion. This is the great difficulty of training; for the wounds fester grievously, and many months and sometimes years will elapse before an elephant will allow his feet to be touched without indications of alarm and anger.

The observation has been frequently made that the most vicious and troublesome elephants to tame, and the most worthless when tamed, are those distinguished by a thin trunk and flabby pendulous ears. The period of tuition does not appear to be influenced by the size or strength of the animals: some of the smallest give the greatest amount of trouble; whereas, in the instance of the two largest that have been taken in Ceylon within the last thirty years, both were docile in a remarkable degree. One in particular, which was caught and trained by Mr. Cripps, when Government agent, in the Seven Corles, fed from the hand the first night it was secured, and in a very few days evinced pleasure on being patted on the head.[1] There is none so obstinate, not even a *rogue*, that may not, when kindly and patiently treated, be conciliated and trained.

The males are generally more unmanageable than the females, and in both an inclination to lie down to rest is regarded as a favourable symptom of approaching tractability, some of the most resolute having been known to stand for months together, even during sleep. Those which are the most obstinate and violent at first are the soonest and most effectually subdued, and generally prove permanently docile and submissive. But those which are sullen or morose, although

[1] This was the largest elephant that has been tamed in Ceylon; he measured upwards of nine feet at the shoulders and belonged to the caste so highly prized by the temples. Though gentle after his first capture, his removal from the corral to the stables, though only a distance of six miles, was a matter of the extremest difficulty; his extraordinary strength rendering him more than a match for the attendant decoys. He, on one occasion, escaped, and was recaptured in the forest; and he afterwards became so docile as to perform a variety of tricks. He was at length ordered to be removed to Colombo; but such was his terror on approaching the fort, that on coaxing him to enter the gate, he became paralyzed in the extraordinary way elsewhere alluded to, and *died on the spot*.

they may provoke no chastisement by their viciousness, are always slower in being tamed, and are rarely to be trusted in after life.[1]

But whatever may be its natural gentleness and docility, the temper of an elephant is seldom to be implicity relied on in a state of captivity and coercion. The most amenable are subject to occasional fits of stubbornness; and even after years of submission, irritability and resentment will unaccountably manifest themselves. It may be that the restraints and severer discipline of training have not been entirely forgotten; or that incidents which in ordinary health would be productive of no demonstration whatever, may lead, in moments of temporary illness, to fretfulness and anger. The knowledge of this infirmity led to the popular belief recorded by PHILE, that the elephant had *two hearts*, under the respective influences of which he evinced ferocity or gentleness; subdued by the one to habitual tractability and obedience, but occasionally

[1] The natives profess that the high caste elephants, such as are allotted to the temples, are of all others the most difficult to tame, and M. BLES, the Dutch correspondent of BUFFON, mentions a caste of elephants which he had heard of, as being peculiar to the Kandyan kingdom, that were not higher than a heifer (génisse), covered with hair, and insusceptible of being tamed. (BUFFON, *Supp.*, vol. vi. p. 29.) Bishop HEBER, in the account of his journey from Bareilly towards the Himalayas, describes the Raja Gourman Sing, "mounted on a little female elephant, hardly bigger than a Durham ox, and almost as shaggy as a poodle."—*Journ.* ch. xvii. It will be remembered that the elephant discovered in 1803 embedded in icy soil in Siberia, was covered with a coat of long hair, with a sort of wool at the roots; and there arose the question whether that northern region had been formerly inhabited by a race of elephants, so fortified by nature against cold; or whether the individual discovered had been borne thither by currents from some more temperate latitudes. To the latter theory the presence of hair seemed a fatal objection; but so far as my own observation goes, I believe the elephants are more or less provided with hair. In some it is more developed than in others, and it is particularly observable in the young, which when captured are frequently covered with a woolly fleece, especially about the head and shoulders. In the older individuals in Ceylon, this is less apparent; and in captivity the hair appears to be altogether removed by the custom of the mahouts to rub their skin daily with oil and a rough lump of burned clay. See a paper on the subject, *Asiat. Journ.* N. S. vol. xiv. p. 182, by Mr. G. FAIRHOLME.

roused by the other to resume his former rage and resistance.[1]

As a general rule, the presence of the tame ones may be dispensed with after two months, and the captive may then be ridden by the driver alone; and after three or four months he may be entrusted with labour, so far as regards docility, but it is undesirable and even involves the risk of life, to work the elephant too soon; as it has frequently happened that a valuable animal has lain down and died the first time it was tried in harness, from what the natives believe to be "broken heart,"—certainly without any cause inferable from injury or previous disease.[2] It is observable, that till a captured elephant begins to relish his food, and grow fat upon it, he becomes so fretted by work, that in an incredibly short space of time it kills him.

The first employment to which an elephant is put is treading clay in a brick-field, or drawing a waggon in double harness with a tame companion. But the work in which the display of sagacity renders his labours of the highest value, is that which involves the use of heavy materials; and hence in dragging and piling timber, or moving stones[3] for the construction of retaining walls and

---

[1] "Διπλῆς δὲ φάσιν εὐπορῆσαι καρδίας·
Καὶ τῇ μὲν εἶναι θυμικὸν τὸ θηρίον
Εἰς ἀκρατῆ κίνησιν ἠρεθισμένον,
Τῇ δὲ προσηνὲς καὶ θρασύτητος ξένον.
Καὶ τῇ μὲν αὐτῶν ἀκροᾶσθαι τῶν λόγων
Οὓς ἄν τις Ἰνδὸς εὖ τιθασεύων λέγοι,
Τῇ δὲ πρὸς αὐτοὺς τοὺς νομεῖς ἐπιτρέχειν
Εἰς τὰς παλαιὰς ἐκτραπὲν κακουργίας."

PHILE, *Expositio de Elephante*, l. 126, &c.

[2] Captain YULE, in his *Narrative of his Embassy to Ava in* 1855, records an illustration of this tendency of the elephant to sudden death; one newly captured, the process of taming which was exhibited to the British Envoy, "made vigorous resistance to the placing of a collar on its neck, and the people were proceeding to tighten it, when the elephant, which had lain down as if quite exhausted, reared suddenly on the hind quarters, and fell on its side—*dead!*"—P. 104.

Mr. STRACHAN noticed the same liability of the elephants to sudden death from very slight causes; "of the fall," he says, "at any time, though on plain ground, they either die immediately, or languish till they die; their great weight occasioning them so much hurt by the fall."—*Phil. Trans.* A.D. 1701, vol. xxiii. p. 1052.

[3] A correspondent informs me that on the Malabar coast of India, the elephant, when employed in dragging stones, moves them by means of a rope, which he either draws with his forehead, or manages by seizing it with his teeth.

the approaches to bridges, his services in an unopened country are of the utmost importance. When roads are to be constructed along the face of steep declivities, and the space is so contracted that risk is incurred either of the elephant falling over the precipice or of rocks slipping down from above, not only are the measures which he resorts to the most judicious and reasonable that could be devised, but if urged by his keeper to adopt any other, he manifests a reluctance which shows that he has balanced in his own mind the comparative advantages of each. He appears on all occasions to comprehend the purpose and object which he is expected to promote, and hence he voluntarily executes a variety of details without any guidance whatsoever from his keeper. This is one characteristic in which the elephant manifests a superiority over the horse; although in strength in proportion to his weight he does not equal the latter.

His minute motions when engrossed by such operations, the activity of his eye, and the earnestness of his attitudes can only be comprehended by being seen. In moving timber and masses of rock the trunk is the instrument with which he mainly goes to work, but those which have tusks turn them to account; to get a weighty stone out of a hollow he kneels down so as to apply the pressure of his head to move it upwards, then steadying it with one foot till he can raise himself, he applies a fold of his trunk to shift it to its place, and adjust it accurately in position: this done, he steps round to view it on either side, and readjust it with due precision. He appears to gauge his task by his eye, to form a judgment whether the weight be proportionate to his strength. If doubtful of his own power, he hesitates and halts, and if urged against his will, he roars and shows temper.

In clearing an opening through forest land, the power of the African elephant, and the strength ascribed to him by a recent traveller, as displayed in uprooting trees, has never been equalled or approached by anything I have seen of the elephant in Ceylon[1] or heard of them in India. Of course much must depend on the nature of the timber and the moisture of the soil; a strong tree on the verge of a swamp may be overthrown with greater ease than a small and low one in parched and solid ground. I have seen no "tree" deserving the name, nothing but jungle and brushwood, thrown down by the mere movement of an elephant without some special exertion of force. But he is by no means fond of gratuitously tasking his strength; and his food being so abundant that he obtains it without an effort, it is not altogether apparent, even were he able to do so, why he should assail "the largest trees in the forest," and encumber his own haunts with their broken stems; especially as there is scarcely anything which an elephant more dislikes than to venture amongst fallen timber.

A tree of twelve inches in diameter resisted successfully the most strenuous struggles of the largest elephant I saw led to it in a corral; and when directed by

---

[1] "Here the trees were large and handsome, but not strong enough to resist the inconceivable strength of the mighty monarch of these forests; almost every tree had half its branches broken short by them, and at every hundred yards I came upon entire trees, and these, *the largest in the forest*, uprooted clean out of the ground, and *broken short across their stems*."—*A Hunter's Life in South Africa*. By R. GORDON CUMMING, vol. ii. p. 305.—"Spreading out from one another, they smash and destroy all the finest trees in the forest which happen to be in their course. . . . I have rode through forests where the trees thus broken lay so thick across one another, that it was almost impossible to ride through the district."—*Ibid.* p. 310.

Mr. Gordon Cumming does not name the trees which he saw thus "uprooted" and "broken across," nor has he given any idea of their size and weight, but Major DENHAM, who observed like traces of the elephant in Africa, saw only small trees overthrown by them; and Mr. PRINGLE, who had an opportunity of observing similar practices of the animals in the neutral territory of the Eastern frontier of the Cape of Good Hope, describes their ravages as being confined to the mimosas, "immense numbers of which had been torn out of the ground and placed in an inverted position, in order to enable the animals to browse at their ease on the soft and juicy roots, which form a favourite part of their food. Many of the *larger mimosas had resisted all their efforts; and indeed it is only after heavy rain, when the soil is soft and loose, that they ever successfully attempt this operation*."—PRINGLE's *Sketches of South Africa*.

their keepers to clear away growing timber, the removal of even a small tree, or a healthy young coco-nut palm, is a matter both of time and exertion to the tame ones. For this reason the services of an elephant are of much less value in clearing a forest than in dragging and piling felled timber. But in the latter occupation in particular, he manifests an intelligence and dexterity which is surprising to a stranger, because the sameness of the operation enables the animal to go on for hours disposing of log after log, almost without a hint or a direction from his attendant. In this manner, two elephants employed in piling ebony and satinwood in the yards attached to the commissariat stores at Colombo, were so accustomed to the work, that they were enabled to accomplish it with equal precision and with greater rapidity than if it had been done by dock-labourers. When the pile attained a certain height, and they were no longer able by their conjoint efforts to raise one of the heavy logs of ebony to the summit, they had been taught to lean two pieces against the heap, up the inclined plane of which they gently rolled the remaining logs, and placed them trimly on the top.

It has been asserted that in these occupations "elephants are to a surprising extent the creatures of habit,"[1] that their movements are altogether mechanical, and that "they are annoyed by any deviation from their accustomed practice, and resent any constrained departure from the regularity of their course." So far as my own observation goes, this is incorrect; and I am assured by the officers in charge of them, that in regard to changing their treatment, their hours, or their occupation, an elephant evinces no more consideration than a horse, but exhibits the same pliancy and facility.

At one point, however, the utility of the elephant stops short. Such is the intelligence and earnestness he displays

---

[1] *Menageries, &c.* "The Elephant," vol. ii. p. 23.

in work, which he seems to conduct almost without supervision, that it has been assumed[1], that he would continue his labour, and accomplish his given task, as well in the absence of his keeper as during his presence. But here his innate love of ease displays itself, and if the eye of his attendant be withdrawn, the moment he has finished the thing immediately in hand, he will stroll away lazily, to browse or enjoy the luxury of fanning himself and blowing dust over his back.

His obedience to his keeper is the result of affection, as well as of fear; and although his attachment is so strong that an elephant in Ceylon has been known to remain out all night, without food, rather than return, and leave behind him his mahout, who was lying intoxicated in the jungle; he manifests little difficulty in yielding the same submission to a new driver in the event of a change of attendants. This is opposed to the popular belief that "the elephant cherishes such an enduring remembrance of his old mahout, that he cannot easily be brought to obey a stranger."[2] In the extensive establishments of the Ceylon Government, the keepers are changed without hesitation, and the animals, when equally kindly treated, are in a very short time as tractable and obedient to their new driver as to the old, so soon as they have become familiarized with his voice.[3]

This is not, however, invariably the case; and Mr. CRIPPS, who had remarkable opportunities for observing the habits of the elephant in Ceylon, mentioned to me an instance in which one of a singularly stubborn disposition occasioned some inconvenience after the death of his keeper, by refusing to obey any other, till his attendants bethought them of a child about twelve years old, in a distant village, where the animal had been formerly picketed, and to whom he had

---

[1] *Menageries, &c.* "The Elephant," c. vi. p. 138.
[2] *Ibid.*, vol. i. p. 19.
[3] *Encyclop. Brit.*, *Mammalia*, art. Elephant.

manifested much attachment. The child was sent for; and on its arrival the elephant, as anticipated, evinced extreme satisfaction, and was managed with ease, till by degrees he became reconciled to the presence of a new superintendent.

It has been said that the mahouts die young, owing to some supposed injury to the spinal column from the peculiar motion of the elephant; but such a remark does not apply to those in Ceylon, who are healthy, and as long lived as others. If the motion of the elephant be thus injurious, that of the camel must be still more so; yet we never hear of early death ascribed to this cause by the Arabs.

The voice of the keeper, with a very limited vocabulary of articulate sounds, serves almost alone to guide the elephant in his domestic occupations.[1] Sir EVERARD HOME, from an examination of the muscular fibres in the drum of an elephant's ear, came to the conclusion, that notwithstanding the distinctness and power of his perception of sounds at a greater distance than other animals, he was insensible to their harmonious modulation and destitute of a musical ear.[2] But Professor HARRISON, in a

---

[1] The principal sound by which the mahouts in Ceylon direct the motions of the elephants is a repetition, with various modulations, of the words *ur-re! ur-re!* This is one of those interjections in which the sound is so expressive of the sense that persons in charge of animals of almost every description throughout the world appear to have adopted it with a concurrence that is very curious. The camel drivers in Turkey, Palestine, and Egypt encourage them to speed by shouting *ar-ré! ar-ré!* The Arabs in Algeria cry *eirich!* to their mules. The Moors seem to have carried the custom with them into Spain, where mules are still driven with cries of *arré* (whence the muleteers derive their Spanish appellation of "arrieros"). In France the sportsman excites the hound by shouts of *hare! hare!* and the waggoner there turns his horses by his voice, and the use of the word *hurhaut!* In the North, "*Hurs* was a word used by the old Germans in urging their horses to speed;" and to the present day, the herdsmen in Ireland, and parts of Scotland, drive their pigs with shouts of *hurrish! hurrish!* closely resembling that used by the mahouts in Ceylon.

[2] *On the Difference between the Human Membrana Tympani and that of the Elephant.* By Sir EVERARD HOME, Bart., Philos. Trans. 1823. Paper by Prof. HARRISON, Proc. Royal Irish Academy, vol. iii. p. 386.

paper read before the Royal Irish Academy in 1847, has stated that on a careful examination of the head of an elephant which he had dissected, he could "see no evidence of the muscular structure of the membrana tympani so accurately described by Sir EVERARD HOME," whose deduction is clearly inconsistent with the fact that the power of two elephants may be steadily combined by singing to them a measured chant, somewhat resembling a sailor's capstan song; and in labour of a particular kind, such as hauling a stone with ropes, they will thus move conjointly a weight to which their divided strength would be unequal.[1]

Nothing can more strongly exhibit the impulse of obedience in the elephant, than the patience with which, at the order of the keeper, he swallows the nauseous medicines of the native elephant-doctors; and it is impossible to witness the fortitude with which (without shrinking) he submits to excruciating surgical operations for the removal of tumours and ulcers to which he is subject, without conceiving a vivid impression of his gentleness and intelligence. On such occasions one might almost imagine that compliance was induced by some perception of the object to be attained by temporary endurance; but this is inconsistent with the touching incident which took place during the slaughter of the elephant at Exeter Change in 1826, when after receiving ineffectually upwards of 120 balls in various

[1] I have already noticed the striking effect produced in the captive elephants in the corral, by the harmonious notes of an ivory flute; and on looking to the graphic description which is given by ÆLIAN of the exploits which he witnessed as performed by the elephants exhibited at Rome, it is remarkable how very large a share of their training appears to have been ascribed to the employment of music.

PHILE, in the account which he has given of the elephant's fondness for music, would almost seem to have versified the prose narrative of ÆLIAN, as he describes its excitement at the more animated portions, its step regulated to the time and movements of the harmony; the whole "*surprising in a creature whose limbs are without joints!*"

"Καινόν τι ποιῶν ἐξ ἀνάρθρων ὀργάνων."
—PHILE, *Expos. de Eleph.*, l. 216.

For an account of the training and performances of the elephants at Rome, as narrated by ÆLIAN, see the appendix to this chapter.

parts of his body, he turned his face to his assailants on hearing the voice of his keeper, and knelt down at the accustomed word of command, so as to bring his forehead within range of the rifles.[1]

The working elephant is always a delicate animal, and requires watchfulness and care; as a beast of burden he is unsatisfactory; for although in point of mere strength there is scarcely any weight which could be conveniently placed on him that he could not carry, it is difficult to pack it without causing abrasions that afterwards ulcerate. His skin is easily chafed by harness, especially in wet weather. Either during long droughts or too much moisture, his feet are liable to sores, which render him non-effective for months. Many attempts have been made to provide him with some protection for the sole of the foot, but from his extreme weight and peculiar mode of planting the foot, they have all been unsuccessful. His eyes are also liable to frequent inflammation, and the skill of the native elephant-doctors, which has been renowned since the time of Ælian, is nowhere more strikingly displayed than in the successful treatment of such attacks.[2] In Ceylon, the murrain among cattle is of frequent occurrence and carries off great numbers of animals, wild as well as tame. In such visitations the elephants suffer severely, not only those at liberty in the forest, but those carefully tended in the government stables. Out of a stud of about 40 attached to the department of the Commission of Roads, the deaths between 1841 and 1849 were on an average *four* in each year, and this was nearly doubled in those years when murrain prevailed.

Of 240 elephants employed in the public departments of the Ceylon Government which died in twenty-five years from 1831 to 1856, the length of time that each

---

[1] A shocking account of the death of this poor animal is given in HONE'S *Every-Day Book*, March, 1830, p. 337.

[2] ÆLIAN, lib. xiii. c. 7.

lived in captivity has only been recorded in the instances of 138. Of these there died:—

Duration of Captivity.	No.	Male.	Female.
Under 1 year	72	29	43
From 1 to 2 years	14	5	9
" 2 " 3 "	8	5	3
" 3 " 4 "	8	3	5
" 4 " 5 "	3	2	1
" 5 " 6 "	2	2	.
" 6 " 7 "	3	1	2
" 7 " 8 "	5	2	3
" 8 " 9 "	5	5	.
" 9 " 10 "	2	2	.
" 10 " 11 "	2	2	.
" 11 " 12 "	3	1	2
" 12 " 13 "	3	.	3
" 13 " 14 "	.	.	.
" 14 " 15 "	3	1	2
" 15 " 16 "	1	1	.
" 16 " 17 "	1	.	1
" 17 " 18 "	.	.	.
" 18 " 19 "	2	1	1
" 19 " 20 "	1	.	1
Total	138	62	76

Of the 72 who died in one year's servitude, 35 expired within the first six months of their captivity. During training, many of them die in the unaccountable manner already referred to, lying down suddenly and expiring, of what the natives designate *a broken heart.*

On being first subjected to work, the elephant is liable to severe and often fatal swellings of the jaws and abdomen.[1]

From these causes there died, between 1841 and 1849 . .	9
Of Cattle murrain	10
Sore feet	1
Colds and inflammation	6
Diarrhœa	1
Worms	1

[1] The elephant which was dissected by Dr. HARRISON, of Dublin, in 1847, died, after four or five days' illness, of a febrile attack, which Dr. H. says was "very like scarlatina (at that time a prevailing disease)—his skin in some cases became almost scarlet."—*Private Letter.*

Of Diseased liver	1
Injuries from a fall	1
General debility	1
Unknown	8

Of the whole, twenty-three were females, and eleven males.

The ages of those that died could not be accurately stated, owing to the circumstance of their having been captured in corral. Only two were tuskers. Towards keeping the stud in health, nothing has been found so conducive as regularly bathing the elephants, and giving them the opportunity to stand with their feet in water or in moistened earth.

On the whole, there may be a question as to the prudence or economy of maintaining a stud of elephants for the purposes to which they are now assigned in Ceylon. In the rude and unopened parts of the country, where rivers are to be forded, and forests are only traversed by jungle paths, their labour is of value, in certain contingencies, in the conveyance of stores, and in the earlier operations for the construction of fords and rough bridges of timber. But in more highly civilised districts, and wherever macadamised roads admit of the employment of horses and oxen for draught, I apprehend that the services of elephants might, with advantage, be gradually reduced, if not altogether dispensed with.

The love of the elephant for coolness and shade renders him at all times more or less impatient of work in the sun, and every moment of leisure he can snatch is employed in covering his back with dust, or fanning himself to diminish the annoyance of the insects and heat. From the tenderness of his skin and its liability to sores, the labour in which he can most advantageously be employed is that of draught; but the reluctance of horses to meet or pass elephants renders it difficult to work the latter with safety on frequented roads. Besides, were the full load which an elephant is capable of drawing in proportion to his muscular strength, to be placed upon waggons of corresponding dimension, the injury to the roads would be such that the wear and tear of the highways and bridges would prove too costly to be borne. On the other hand, by restricting it to a somewhat more manageable quantity, and by limiting the weight, as at present, to about *one ton and a half*, it is doubtful whether an elephant performs so much more work than could be done by a horse or by bullocks, as to compensate for the greater cost of his feeding and attendance.

Add to this, that from accidents and other causes, from ulcerated abrasions of the skin, and illness of many kinds, the elephant is so often invalided, that the actual cost of his labour, when at work, is very considerably enhanced. Exclusive of the salaries of higher officers attached to the government establishments, and other permanent charges, the expenses of an elephant, looking only to the wages of his attendants and the cost of his food and medicines, varies from *three shillings to four shillings and sixpence* per diem, according to his size and class.[1] Taking the average at three shillings and

[1] An ordinary-sized elephant engrosses the undivided attention of *three* men. One, as his mahout or superintendent, and two as leaf-cutters, who bring him branches and grass for his daily supplies. One of larger growth would probably require a third leaf-cutter. The daily consumption is two cwt. of green food, with about half a bushel of grain. When in the vicinity of towns and villages, the attendants have no difficulty in procuring an abundant supply of the branches of the trees to which they are partial; and in journeys through the forest and unopened country, the leaf-cutters are sufficiently expert in the knowledge of those particular plants with which the elephant is satisfied. Those that would be likely to disagree with him he unerringly rejects. His favourites are the palms, especially the cluster of rich, unopened leaves, known as the "cabbage," of the coconut, and areca; the young trunks of the palmyra and jaggery (*Caryota urens*) are torn open in search of the farinaceous matter contained in the spongy pith. Next to these come the varieties of fig-trees, particularly the sacred *Bo* (F. religiosa) which is found near every temple, and the *na gaha* (*Messua ferrea*), with thick dark leaves and a scarlet flower. The leaves of the Jak tree and bread fruit (*Artocarpus integrifolia* and *A. incisa*), the wood apple (*Ægle Marmelos*), Palu (*Mimusops indica*), and a number of others well known to their attendants, are all consumed in turn. The stems of the plantain, the stalks of the sugar-cane, and the feathery tops of the bamboos, are irresistible

nine-pence, and calculating that hardly any individual works more than four days out of seven, the charge for each day so employed would be equal to *six shillings and sixpence.* The keep of a powerful dray-horse, working five days in the week, would not exceed half-a-crown, and two such would unquestionably do more work than any elephant under the present system. I do not know whether it be from a comparative calculation of this kind that the strength of the elephant establishments in Ceylon has been gradually diminished of late years, but in the department of the Commissioner of Roads, the stud, which formerly numbered upwards of sixty elephants, has been reduced of late years to thirty-six, and is at present less than half that number.

The fallacy of the supposed reluctance of the elephant to breed in captivity has been demonstrated by many recent authorities; but with the exception of the birth of young elephants at Rome, as mentioned by ÆLIAN, the only instances that I am aware of their actually producing young under such circumstances, took place in Ceylon. Both parents had been for several years attached to the stud of the Commissioner of Roads, and in 1844 the female, whilst engaged in dragging a waggon, gave birth to a still-born calf. Some years before, an elephant, which had been captured by Mr. Cripps, dropped a female calf, which he succeeded in rearing. As usual, the little one became the pet of the keepers; but as it increased in growth, it exhibited the utmost violence when

luxuries. Pine-apples, water melons, and fruits of every description, are voraciously devoured, and a coco-nut when found is first rolled under foot to detach it from the husk and fibre, and then raised in his trunk, and crushed, almost without an effort of his ponderous jaws.

The grasses are not found in sufficient quantity to be an item of his daily fodder; the Mauritius or the Guinea grass is seized with avidity; lemon grass is rejected from its overpowering perfume, but rice in the straw, and every description of grain, whether growing or dry; grain (*Cicer arietinum*), Indian corn, and millet are his natural food. Of such of these as can be found, it is the duty of the leaf-cutters, when in the jungle and on march, to provide a daily supply.

thwarted; striking out with its hind feet, throwing itself headlong on the ground, and pressing its trunk against any opposing object.

The ancient fable of the elephant attaining the age of two or three hundred years is still prevalent amongst the Singhalese. But the Europeans and those in immediate charge of them entertain the opinion that the duration of life for about *seventy* years is common both to man and the elephant; and that before the arrival of that period, the symptoms of debility and decay ordinarily begin to manifest themselves. Still instances are not wanting in Ceylon of trained decoys that have lived for more than double the reputed period in actual servitude. One employed by Mr. Cripps in the Seven Corles was represented by the Cooroowe people to have served the king of Kandy in the same capacity sixty years before; and amongst the papers left by Colonel Robertson (son to the historian of "Charles V."), who held a command in Ceylon in 1799, shortly after the capture of the island by the British, I have found a memorandum showing that a decoy was then attached to the elephant establishment at Matura, which the records proved to have served under the Dutch during the entire period of their occupation, (extending to upwards of one hundred and forty years;) and was said to have been found in the stables by the English on the expulsion of the Portuguese in A.D. 1656.

It is perhaps from this popular belief of their almost illimitable age, that the natives generally assert that the body of a dead elephant is seldom or never to be discovered in the woods. And certain it is that frequenters of the forest with whom I have conversed, whether European or Singhalese, are consistent in their assurances that they have never found the remains of an elephant that had died a natural death. One chief, the Wannyah of the Trincomalie district, told a friend of mine, that once after a severe murrain, which had swept the province, he found the carcases of elephants that had died of the disease. On the other hand, a European gentleman, who for thirty-six years without intermission has been living in the jungle, ascending to the summit of mountains in the prosecution of the trigonometrical survey, and penetrating valleys in tracing roads and opening means of communication; one, too, who has made the habits of the wild elephant a subject of constant observation and study,—has often expressed to me his astonishment that after seeing many thousands of living elephants in all possible situations, he had never yet found a single skeleton of a dead one, except of those which had fallen by the rifle.[1]

It has been suggested that the bones of the elephant may be so porous and spongy as to disappear in consequence of early decomposition; but this remark would not apply to the grinders or to the tusks; besides which, the inference is at variance with the fact, that not only the horns and teeth, but entire skeletons of deer, are frequently found in the districts inhabited by the elephant.

The natives, to account for this popular belief, declare that the herd bury those of their companions who happen to perish.[2] It is curious that this belief was current also amongst the Greeks of the Lower Empire; and PHILE, who wrote at Constantinople early in the fourteenth century, not only describes the younger

---

[1] This remark regarding the elephant of Ceylon does not appear to extend to that of Africa, as I observe that BEAVER, in his *African Memoranda*, says that "the skeletons of old ones that have died in the woods are frequently found."—*African Memoranda relative to an attempt to establish British Settlements at the Island of Bulama.* Lon. 1815, p. 358.

[2] A corral was organised near Putlam in 1840, by Mr. Morris, the chief officer of the district. It was constructed across one of the paths which the elephants frequent in their frequent marches, and during the course of the proceedings two of the captured elephants died. Their carcases were left of course within the enclosure, which was abandoned as soon as the capture was complete. The wild elephants resumed their path through it, and a few days afterwards the headman reported to Mr. Morris that the bodies had been removed and carried outside the corral to a spot to which nothing but the elephants could have borne them.

elephants as tending the wounded, but as burying the dead:

> "Ὅταν δ' ἐπιστῇ τῆς τελευτῆς ὁ χρόνος
> Κοινοῦ τέλους ἄμυναν ὁ ξένος φέρει."[1]

The Singhalese have a further superstition in relation to the closing life of the elephant: they believe that, on feeling the approach of dissolution, he repairs to a solitary valley, and there resigns himself to death.

A native who accompanied Mr. Cripps, when hunting in the forests of Anarajapoora, intimated that he was then in the immediate vicinity of the spot "*to which the elephants came to die*," but that it was so mysteriously concealed, that although every one believed in its existence, no one had ever succeeded in penetrating to it. At the corral which I have described at Kornegalle, in 1847, Dehigame, one of the Kandyan chiefs, assured me it was the universal belief of his countrymen, that the elephants, when about to die, resorted to a valley in Saffragam, among the mountains to the east of Adam's Peak, which was reached by a narrow pass with walls of rock on either side, and that there, by the side of a lake of clear water, they took their last repose.[2] It was not without interest that I afterwards recognized this tradition in the story of *Sindbad of the Sea*, who in his Seventh voyage, after conveying the presents of Haroun al Raschid to the King of Serendib, is wrecked on his return from Ceylon and sold as a slave to a master who employs him in

[1] PHILE, *Expositio de Eleph.*, l. 243.

[2] The selection by animals of a *place to die*, is not confined to the elephant. DARWIN says, that in South America "the guanacos (llamas) appear to have favourite spots for lying down to die; on the banks of the Santa Cruz river, in certain circumscribed spaces which were generally bushy and all near the water, the ground was actually white with their bones; on one such spot I counted between ten and twenty heads."—*Nat. Voy.* ch. viii. The same has been remarked in the Rio Gallegos; and at St. Jago in the Cape de Verde Islands, DARWIN saw a retired corner similarly covered with the bones of the goat, as if it were "the burial ground of all the goats in the island."

shooting elephants for the sake of their ivory; till one day the tree on which he was stationed having been uprooted by one of the herd, he fell senseless to the ground, and the great elephant approaching wound his trunk around him and carried him away, ceasing not to proceed, until he had taken him to a place where, his terror having subsided, *he found himself amongst the bones of elephants, and knew that this was their burial place*."[1] It is curious to find this legend of Ceylon in what has, not inaptly, been described as the "Arabian Odyssey" of Sinbad; the original of which evidently embodies the romantic recitals of the sailors returning from the navigation of the Indian Seas, in the middle ages[2], which were current amongst the Mussulmans, and are reproduced in various forms throughout the tales of the *Arabian Nights*.

---

[1] *Arabian Nights' Entertainment*, LANE'S edition, vol. iii. p. 77.

[2] See a disquisition on the origin of the story of Sinbad, by M. REINAUD, in the introduction prefixed to his translation of the *Arabian Geography of Aboulfeda*, vol. i. p. lxxvi.

APPENDIX TO CHAPTER VI.

As Ælian's work on *the Nature of Animals* has never, I believe, been republished in any English version, and the passage in relation to the training and performance of elephants is so pertinent to the present inquiry, I venture to subjoin a translation of the 11th Chapter of his 2nd Book.

"Of the cleverness of the elephant I have spoken elsewhere, and likewise of the manner of hunting: I have mentioned these things, a few out of the many which others have stated; but for the present I purpose to speak of their musical feeling, their tractability and facility in learning what it is difficult for even a human being to acquire, much less a beast, hitherto so wild:—such as to dance, as is done on the stage; to walk with a measured gait; to listen to the melody of the flute, and to perceive the difference of sounds, that, being pitched low lead to a slow movement, or high to a quick one: all this the elephant learns and understands, and is accurate withal, and makes no mistake. Thus has Nature formed him, not only the greatest in size, but the most gentle and most easily taught. Now if I were going to write about the tractability and aptitude to learn amongst those of India, Æthiopia, and Libya, I should probably appear to be concocting a tale and acting the braggart, or to be telling a falsehood respecting the nature of the animal founded on a mere report, all which it behoves a philosopher, and most of all one who is an ardent lover of truth, not to do. But what I have seen myself, and what others have described as having occurred at Rome, this I have chosen to narrate, selecting a few facts out of many, to show the particular nature of those creatures. The elephant when tamed is an animal most gentle and most easily led to do whatever he is directed. And by way of showing honour to time, I will first narrate events of the oldest date. Cæsar Germanicus, the nephew of Tiberius, exhibited once a public show, wherein there were many full-grown elephants, male and female, and some of their breed born in this country. When their limbs were beginning to become firm, a person familiar with such animals instructed them by a strange and surprising method of teaching; using only gentleness and kindness, and adding to his mild lessons the bait of pleasant and varied food. By this means he led them by degrees to throw off all wildness, and, as it were, to desert to a state of civilisation, conducting themselves in a manner almost human. He taught them neither to be excited on hearing the pipe, nor to be disturbed by the beat of drum, but to be soothed by the sounds of the reed, and to endure unmusical noises and the clatter of feet from persons while marching; and they were trained to feel no fear of a mass of men, nor to be enraged at the infliction of blows, not even when compelled to twist their limbs and to bend them like a stage-dancer, and this too, although endowed with strength and might. And there is in this a very noble addition to nature, not to conduct themselves in a disorderly manner and disobediently towards the instructions given by man; for after the dancing-master had made them expert, and they had learnt their lessons accurately, they did not belie the labour of his instruction whenever a necessity and opportunity called upon them to exhibit what they had been taught. For the whole troop came forward from this and that side of the theatre, and divided themselves into parties; they advanced walking with a mincing gait and exhibiting in their whole body and persons the manners of a beau, clothed in the flowery dresses of dancers; and on the ballet-master giving a signal with his voice, they fell into line and went round in a circle, and if it were requisite to deploy, they did so. They ornamented the floor of the stage by throwing flowers upon it, and this they did in moderation and sparingly, and straightway they beat a measure with their feet and kept time together.

"Now that Damon and Spintharus and Aristoxenus and Xenophilus and Philoxenus and others should know music excellently well, and for their cleverness be ranked amongst the few, is indeed a thing of wonder, but not incredible, nor contrary at all to reason. For this reason that a *man* is a rational animal, and the recipient of mind and intelligence. But that a jointless animal (ἄναρθρον) should understand rhythm and melody, and preserve a gesture, and not deviate from a measured movement, and fulfil the requirements of those who laid down instructions, these are gifts of nature, I think, and a peculiarity in every way astounding. Added to these there were things enough to drive the spectator out of his senses; when the strewn rushes and other materials for beds on the ground were placed on the sand of the theatre, and they received stuffed mattresses such as belonged to rich houses and variegated bed coverings, and goblets were placed there very expensive, and bowls of gold and silver, and in them a great quantity of water; and tables were placed there of sweet-smelling wood and ivory very superb; and upon them flesh meats and loaves enough to fill the stomachs of animals the most voracious. When the preparations were completed and abundant, the banqueters came forward, six male and an equal number of female elephants; the former had on a male dress, and the latter a female; and on a signal being given they stretched forward their trunks in a subdued manner, and took their food in great moderation, and not one of them appeared to be gluttonous, greedy, or to snatch at a greater portion, as did the Persian mentioned by Xenophon. And when it was requisite to drink, a bowl was placed by the side of each; and inhaling with their trunks they took a draught very orderly; and then they scattered the drink about in fun; but not as in insult. Many other acts of a similar kind, both clever and astonishing, have persons described, relating to the peculiarities of these animals, and I saw them writing letters on Roman tablets with their trunks, neither looking awry nor turning aside. The hand, however, of the teacher was placed so as to be a guide in the formation of the letters; and while it was writing the animal kept its eye fixed down in an accomplished and scholarlike manner."

PART IX.

THE NORTHERN FORESTS.

CHAPTER I.

FOREST TRAVELLING IN CEYLON.

On the adjournment of the Council in the spring of 1848, I availed myself of the recess in order to acquire a personal knowledge of a part of the island which the urgency of public affairs had previously prevented me from visiting. The journey that I contemplated, extended round the unfrequented country lying to the north of the Mahawelli-ganga and the Kandyan zone, comprising that section of the island which formed, at a remote period, the division of the Singhalese Kingdom, known as Pihiti, or the Raja-ratta. It includes the ruins of two of the ancient capitals; Anarajapoora and Pollanarrua; and from the extent of its works for irrigation, and the number of its agricultural communities, it must have been, at an early period, the most productive as well as the most densely populated portion of Ceylon. This character it retained until the misery and devastation consequent on the incursions and domination of the Malabars reduced its cities to ruins, its villages to desolation, and its cultivated lands to wilderness and jungle. With the exception of those tracts which approach the coast, it is now one continuous forest, extending from sea to sea, concealing the ruins of stupendous monuments, and encircling the sites of prodigious reservoirs; some of them of dimensions so vast, that even in their decay they form artificial lakes of miles in circumference.

This singular region is so little known to Europeans that in one of the most recent Maps of Ceylon[1], it is left

[1] *Atlas of the Society for the Diffusion of Useful Knowledge.*

blank as an "*Unexplored district;*"—yet it is by no means destitute of population. Scattered throughout its recesses, there exists a semi-civilised race, whose members have little or no intercourse with the inhabitants of the rest of the island, but dwell apart in these deep solitudes, subsisting by the cultivation of rice, generally in the basins of deserted tanks, or on the margins of the neglected watercourses.

One vast expanse to the north-east of the Kandyan mountains is known by the name of the Vedda-ratta, or country of the Veddahs, a harmless and uncivilised tribe, who live in caves, or inhabit rude dwellings constructed of bark and grass. For food they are dependent upon their arrows, and they never leave the vicinity of their solitary homes, except at certain periods of the year, when they visit the confines of the civilised country in order to barter honey and dried deer-flesh for arrow-heads and other articles, essential in their rude mode of life.

The influence of the successive settlements planted in turn by Europeans, on the confines of this secluded district, has never penetrated far within its borders. Whilst the forts and the factories established by the Portuguese and the Dutch, at Batticaloa, Cottiar, and Trincomalie on the eastern coast, and at Jaffna and Manaar on the west, enabled them to maintain a sufficiently secure position for the protection of their commerce, no evidence remains of their having established, or sought to establish, their authority permanently in the interior of Neuera-kalawa or the Wanny. Even the English, till recently, devoted no attention to these outlying provinces; but a highway has lately been cut due north and south through the central forests, from Jaffna to Kandy; one branch extending eastward to Trincomalie, and a second westward through Anarajapoora to Putlam. Other roads are in progress, leading to the interior from those points on the coast where the Malabar Coolies disembark, on arriving from the continent of India, in quest of employment in the coffee plantations of the Central Province. In consequence of the opening of these, it is to be hoped that the annual current of immigration, instead of setting, as it has hitherto done, along the hot sands and inhospitable deserts of the western shore, may be tempted to pass by the central line of communication, where the facilities for obtaining shade and water will increase the comforts of their march; and the sight of vast tracts of arable but now unoccupied land may eventually lead to the permanent settlement in the island of some portion of these migratory labourers.

Another circumstance which will contribute to the improvement of the northern section of the island, is the attention recently directed to the seaborde as a suitable locality for the cultivation of the coco-nut. Within the last twenty years, large plantations of these palms have been formed at Batticaloa on the east, at Jaffna on the north, and at Chilaw and Calpentyn on the west of the great central forests; and it is reasonable to expect that the success of these will stimulate agriculture inland, settlers being encouraged by the known fertility of the soil, and by the facilities for travel, provided by the roads already in existence and to be extended hereafter by means of those now in progress.

I set out on my journey with the intention of crossing the island from west to east, from Colombo to Batticaloa. To reach the latter place, I did not avail myself of the convenient but circuitous high road by Neuera-ellia and Badulla; but made arrangements for riding across the island in a direct line from Kandy, by way of Bintenne through the country of the Veddahs, in order to become acquainted with the actual state of these wild creatures, and to enable myself to judge of the amount of success which had attended the recent attempts to introduce civilisation, and induce them to settle in villages and engage in agriculture. From Batticaloa, I proposed to turn northward to Trincomalie, and there, leaving the coast, to strike inland for the purpose of visiting the great tank of Padivil, one of the most stupendous in Ceylon. Thence I arranged to return eastward to the sea at Moeletivoe; to proceed to the peninsula of Jaffna, and finally to reach the Gulf of Manaar in time to be received on board the Government steamship, when on her way to the annual inspection of the Pearl Banks, in the Bay of Condatchy; and thus to return by sea to Colombo.

The arrangement of provisions for such a journey, forms one of the leading difficulties in all expeditions through this region of Ceylon. From time immemorial, the natives of the central and northern provinces, and especially the inhabitants of the ancient Kandyan kingdom, have been averse to trade, and indisposed either to labour for hire, or to exchange the produce of their lands for money. In fact, till a very recent period, money was almost unknown in these parts of the island; and the policy of the chiefs was inimical alike to the active industry which is creative of property, and to the process of barter which would lead to the accumulation of wealth; — either would have subverted the system of dependence, whereby the tillers of the soil were rendered subservient to their chiefs; and both were, therefore, as far as possible discouraged amongst all who were amenable to their sway. In general, the soil is the exclusive property of the headmen, and those who cultivate it, in place of paying rent to its proprietors, receive from them payment in kind. Thus, throughout the hill country, the chiefs may be said to retain sole possession of nearly all the grain that is grown; with it they remunerate their labourers, maintain their households, and, by issuing food from their baronial granaries in times of famine, rivet more closely the dependency of their people. The ambition of a chief is not to amass property, but to acquire land: and land is prized not for produce, as represented by its value in money, but in proportion to the number of retainers and dependents it will feed. Hence, the peasantry have seldom corn to dispose of: no Kandyan betakes himself to dealing or to barter, and few villages possess even the convenience of a bazaar.

In setting out therefore on any lengthened expedition, it is indispensable that Europeans should provide themselves with means for carrying from town to town the supplies of rice and other articles necessary for their own consumption, and even the *gram*[1] and paddi required for the use of their horses. On the journey of which I am speaking, our tents were carried by elephants, beds, baggage canteens, and provisions by coolies, and our party at the first encampment, including servants, horse-keepers, and grass-cutters, mustered one hundred and fifty persons. We found that milk, eggs, and fowl were to be procured at some of the villages on the route, and occasionally a sheep or a cow: and along the sea-coast we had frequently supplies of fish, but in the main we were dependent upon the guns of the party for providing our table. Throughout, venison and game were to be had in abundance, especially pea-fowl, jungle-cocks, flamingoes, and parrots, which last make excellent pies. Water, except in the vicinity of rivers, was scarce; generally bad, near the sea, owing to the prevalence of salt marshes;—and in the low-country, where streams are rare, and wells few, the only supply was derived from artificial tanks and their tributary streams and outlets, in which the sediment is liable to be stirred up at all times by cattle, and by deer and elephants which resort to them after sunset, or bathe in them during the night. To correct the impurity of the tank-water, when intended for their own use, the natives employ a horny seed, the produce of a species of strychnus, about the size of a coffee-bean, called by the Tamils *tettan-kottia*, and by the Singhalese *ingini*.[2] This they rub round the inside of the unglazed earthen chatty in

[1] *Gram* is the pea of the *Cicer arietinum*,—*paddi*, rice in the husk.

[2] Strychnus potatorum.

which the muddy water is held, till about one half of the seed is ground off, which mingling with the water, it forms a delicate mucilage. In the course of a few minutes the impure particles being seized by this, descend and form an apparently viscid sediment at the bottom, whilst the clearer fluid remains at the top, and although not altogether bright, it is sufficiently pure for ordinary purposes.

The necessity of carrying supplies for two months for so large a company, through a country which, for the first three hundred miles after leaving Kandy, was altogether destitute of roads, rendered progress toilsome and slow. Our day's journey seldom exceeded fifteen miles, as the bearers and foot-runners could not accomplish more, and even at this pace they require an occasional halt of a day or two to recruit.

For the first five or six miles after leaving Kandy, we had the advantage of a carriage-road, and for twenty more our route lay along a bridle-path, which had been formed some thirty years before, for the purpose of keeping up a military communication with the Fort of Badulla, but this has been abandoned ever since the opening of the highway across the mountains of Neuera-ellia. On leaving this rugged road, we struck into the great Eastern Forest, through which our path lay for many days, till we began to approach the low marshy plains in the vicinity of Batticaloa. For the most part, we made our way, under cover of lofty trees, along tracks with which the natives were familiar, but which it would be hazardous for a stranger to attempt to follow without the aid of an experienced guide. In fact, immediately after descending from the hills, the face of the country is so level, that no eminence arises for miles from which it would be possible for a traveller to discern any land-marks for his direction. Once or twice in our journey, we had an opportunity of ascending detached rocks from which the level forest alone was visible, stretching away to the verge of the horizon. On such occasions, the feeling experienced was rather nervous and uneasy; emerging for an instant from beneath an ocean of foliage in whose depths we were wandering, viewing its boundless green expanse extending on every side, without inequality, and apparently without end,—then descending again into the depths of the forest, and trusting to our semi-civilised guides to pilot us in safety through the endless labyrinth of woods.

There is something solemn and impressive in the majestic repose of these leafy solitudes, where the deep silence is unbroken, except by the hum of innumerable insects, whose noises, though far too fine and delicate to be individually audible, unite to form an aggregate of gentle sounds, that murmur softly on every side, and produce an effect singularly soothing and dreamy. It is a popular, but erroneous belief, that these dense woods are the dwellings of numerous animals, which find food and shelter within their deep recesses; and nothing more powerfully excites surprise in a stranger's mind, than the comparative scarcity of life in the heart of these thick forests. Even birds are rarely seen in their depths, and other creatures begin to appear only when we come to the confines of the plains, and enter those pasture lands and park-like openings, which occur in the immediate vicinity of the low country.

The fact is that the density of the forest, though capable of affording cover to the wilder carnivora, is unfavourable to the growth of any kind of herbage fitted for the support of the graminivorous animals. Quadrupeds are therefore compelled to keep for the most part on the verge of the open country, and in the vicinity of water, where the phytophagous tribes find abundance of food, and the carnivorous congregate attracted by the resort of the others.

Generally, our horses were able to ford, or to swim over, such rivers as we were obliged to cross on our route; but the more rapid and impetuous streams we passed in canoes or on rafts formed of sticks laid across two hollowed trunks of trees. Whenever it was practicable, we halted for the night in the pansela of a temple; and on the more frequented tracks, towards the coast, we had occasionally the shelter of the government rest-houses; but in the majority of instances, we spent the night either under tents, or in booths which the natives rapidly constructed of fresh branches, dexterously covered with leaves and grass.

The servants and attendants were formed into two companies, of which one was always in advance, sent forward to make arrangements for our arrival at the next halting place, so that the set of tents in which we dined and slept passed us on our subsequent march and were ready for our reception at breakfast on the following morning. We were in the saddle before sunrise, and our arrival at the scene of our mid-day rest, which was generally beside a river or a tank, was the signal for the lighting of the cooking fires, the compounding of curries, the preparation of coffee, the roasting of game on wooden spits, and the other arrangements for a morning repast. By the time that we had fully enjoyed the luxury of a bath, breakfast was ready to be eaten with the relish which morning exercise alone can secure. When the heat of noon was past, we resumed our route, to reach our next encampment after sunset, and there to dine and spend the night. Such travelling was unaccompanied with privations or discomfort; its freedom was indescribably exhilarating and enjoyable, and I shall ever look back to these journeys as the most agreeable of the many pleasant incidents that marked my residence in Ceylon.

CHAP. II.

BINTENNE. — THE NAVIGATION OF THE MAHAWELLI-GANGA. — THE CUSTOM OF POLYANDRY. — THE RESTORATION OF THE RUINED TANKS.

All preparations for our journey having been completed, the elephants with the heavy baggage were sent forward from Kandy on the 7th of February, and on the following evening we set out by the lower Badulla road, which for some distance follows the descent of the Mahawelli-ganga, afterwards turning due east, towards Bintenne, and the country of the Veddahs. Nothing can be finer than the scenery along this portion of the river; which falls 1500 feet between Kandy and Bintenne; making its way through the gorges of those wonderful hills, wooded to their highest ascents, and so steep that, when standing by the water's edge, it strains the eye to look upward to their summits. The great current is turbulent in the extreme; it rolls down long declivities and struggles between rocks of granite, with a loud roar that came up through the thick forest to the path by which we rode, so high above the river that its channel was hardly discernible in the valley below. Presently, as we journeyed along, we caught sight of it emerging from woody defiles, and spreading its waters into placid levels over deep beds of yellow sand, from the repeated occurrence of which it has acquired the name of the "great sandy river." Its banks are fringed with the graceful foliage of the bamboos, which here attain a height of fifty to sixty feet, their feathery crowns waving majestically, like ostrich plumes, above the stream.

The almost abandoned path by which we descended

presented many objects of curious interest; it was frequently crossed by rivulets from the mountains, one so densely charged with calcareous matter that it had coated the rocks in its descent with a deposit, which lay so thick as almost to form an elevated channel for the stream; others were impregnated with iron, and so highly coloured as to indicate its presence in great abundance in the hills above.

For the first ten miles after leaving Kandy, the rivers are either bridged or fordable; but, after sunset, we came to the Maha-oya, the first which presented neither of these facilities. As we rode down to its bank, a headman, the coralle of the district, appeared with his followers on the further side, and a little raft pushed off towards us, constructed of branches laid across two hollowed trees. On this we placed ourselves and our saddles, and with our horses swimming behind us, reached the opposite bank whence a ride of two miles to the top of the pass of Gonnegamme brought us to the native house, where our servants were awaiting our arrival. It was a poor hovel, its wretchedness but ill concealed by the white cloths with which, according to the native fashion, the walls and ceilings were hung in honour of strangers. It afforded us, however, cover for the night, our servants sleeping outside in the open air, and before daybreak we were again in the saddle by torchlight *en route* for the bank of the Ooma-oya[1], which we hoped to reach in time for breakfast.

The low-country Singhalese make these torches, or "chules," as they are called, out of the dry leaves of the coco-nut palm, binding them into bundles six feet long, and three or four inches in diameter, and these burn for about half an hour if dexterously carried. In the north, however, where the coco-nut is rare, the inhabitants employ an ingenious substitute, and form a much superior torch

[1] *Ganga*, in Singhalese, means a great river; *Oya* a smaller one; and *Ella*, a rivulet or stream.

generally out of a straight dried branch of the "welang tree"[1] of which the Veddahs make their arrows. This is bruised into loose strips, some of which extend the whole length of the branch, so that the bundle does not require to be tied, and at the same time is rendered so flexible and elastic that it burns freely and steadily. On a journey, a "chule" of the latter description will last for two hours: they are used everywhere in the north by travellers and foot-runners to warn bears out of the path, and by the watchers to drive away wild boars and elephants from nocturnal visits to the rice lands. A party in motion before sunrise forms a picturesque object winding down a mountain pass by torchlight, and still more so when the flames of the chules are reflected from the waters of an inland lake, as they skirt along its margin.

Instead of arriving at the Ooma-oya for breakfast as we had expected, we found the road, which for a good part of the way runs in the bed of a torrent, so much injured by the rains and the flooded streams, that it was nearly sunset before we reached our destination. In descending from the hills we had to cross several tributaries of the Mahawelli-ganga, the passage of which, owing to the rocks, we found much more troublesome than that of rivers of the same size in the low country, where the quiet depth of water enables horses to swim with ease. But it is difficult to induce a horse to swim the rapid rivers in the hill country, and nearly impossible to ford them, broken up as they frequently are into pools and obstructed by rocks. We crossed one stream of great volume and turbulence, the Koorinda-oya, or "Cinnamon river," on a tree adroitly felled, so as to fall at right angles with the stream; our horses scrambling over the rocks and through the eddies higher up.

The Ooma-oya, which we reached at sunset, and near which we halted for the night, is the deepest and largest

[1] *Pterospermum suberifolium.*

of those which flow into this portion of the Mahawelli-ganga. Our elephants were exceedingly reluctant to enter it, but their loads having been sent over on rafts, their drivers forced them to plunge in: and they swam across, burying every portion of their bodies beneath the water, with the exception of the tips of their trunks. Occasionally they raised their heads to observe their course, and then sank again, making direct for the opposite bank.

During the night rain began to fall heavily, and appeared to threaten a long continuance. This was a serious embarrassment, as we had still two of the most dangerous rivers to cross before reaching Bintenne, and if we had delayed till these had become swelled by the flood, it appeared certain that they would be impassable, as our coolies and foot-runners would have found neither a boat nor a ford. Besides, as one party of our people in charge of the stores and provisions had not yet come up, we had reason to fear that some of the streams which we had crossed the day before were already swollen into torrents. It was clear, therefore, that if we did not get on at once to Bintenne, where provisions were abundant, we were likely ere long to find ourselves enclosed between impracticable rivers on either side, without food for ourselves, rice for our people, or corn for our cattle. No time was to be lost; despite the rain we got again in motion, swam the Badulla river and the Logole-oya, which were already rolling in torrents; and by sunset reached Pangragamme in safety.

This village consists of a few mud houses built under tamarind trees of patriarchal age and prodigious size. As it is situated in a hollow, these rude dwellings were rendered uncomfortable by the rains, the floors being turned to black mud, besides which water oozed through the grass thatch in all directions. Pangragamme is inhabited chiefly if not exclusively by Moors, who have erected there a small mosque of the humblest pretensions. It is the point at which the principal road turns off to Welasse, a district whose fertility in ancient times procured for it the name *Wel-laksya*, or "the hundred thousand rice fields," which it bears to the present day; but the miserable state of its cultivation ill sustains its title to that designation. To remain in such wretched quarters longer than was absolutely necessary was by no means desirable, and by daybreak we were again on horseback for Bintenne.

On our arrival we found the large pansela, or dwelling of the priests attached to the great temple, hung with white cloth and prepared for our reception; and our tent furniture having been arranged, we took up our residence for a day or two; if not in agreeable quarters at least under shelter from the storm; with leisure to open our portmanteaus which had been wetted in fording the rivers, and to await more favourable weather for resuming our journey. The tents also were so soaked, that the elephants were unequal to their weight, and could not proceed until they had been dried in the sun.

In the district through which we had been passing the population was thin and cultivation rare. Occasionally paddi-fields were to be seen near the Mahawelli-ganga, or terraced high up in the recesses between two hills where a stream afforded the means of irrigation; and now and then we could descry, on the tops of some of the mountains, the temporary Chena villages, as they are called, of squatters, who settle there from time to time to burn down patches of the jungle and reap a single crop of dry rice or millet, after which the soil is left to fallow for a series of years before the operation can be repeated. But in the vicinity of Bintenne, the country is infinitely more rich and productive. Rice is cultivated on an extensive scale, and we found none of the usual difficulties in purchasing food for our people or fodder for our horses.

The town of Bintenne is situated in a wide level plain,

at an angle where the river, after running due east from Kandy for fifty miles, turns suddenly north to seek the sea at Trincomalie. The tracts around this spot are watered by a stream which joins the river, but is intercepted near the village of Horrabora, about three miles from Bintenne, and there serves to fill one of those stupendous tanks, the ruins of which occur so frequently throughout the north of Ceylon. If husbanded, the contents of this reservoir would be sufficient to irrigate a prodigious extent of rice land, but at present its embankment is broken, its contents are permitted to run to waste, and only a few fields are enriched by them; but even these are capable of more than supplying the wants of the declining population of Bintenne and the surrounding district.

In point of antiquity Bintenne transcends even the historic renown of Anarajapoora. Long before the Wijayan invasion, it was one of the chief cities of the aborigines, and Gotama, on his first visit to Lanka, descended "in the agreeable Mahanaga garden, the assembling place of the Yakkos;" the site of which is still marked by the ruins of a dagoba, built three hundred years before the Christian era, by the brother of King Devenipiatissa, in commemoration of that great event.[1] The city, which was then called Mahayangana, continued for many centuries to be one of the most important places in Ceylon. It was the birthplace of Sangatissa, the king who, in the year A.D. 234, placed a glass pinnacle on the spire of the Ruanwellé dagoba, at the capital,

[1] *Mahawanso*, ch. i. p. 3. According to the *Mahawanso*, Gotama gave to the chief of the devos Sumano, "a handful of pure blue locks from the growing hair of his head," and this, together with the bone of his thorax recovered from his funeral pile, was enclosed in the original dagoba, built shortly after his decease. "The younger brother of King Devenipiatissa (B. C. 307), discovering this marvellous dagoba, constructed another, encasing it thirty cubits in height; the King Duthagaminu (B. C. 164) constructed a dagoba, enclosing that one eighty cubits in height; and thus was the Mahayangana dagoba completed."—*Ibid.*, ch. i. p. 4. The existence of this dagoba and its contents, were alluded to as antiquities by Mahindo, in his conversations with Devenipiatissa, previously to the final establishment of the Buddhist religion in Ceylon.—*Ibid.*, ch. xvii. p. 104.

"to serve as a protection against lightning;"[1] and Bintenne (not Mahagam, as is generally supposed) was the *Maagrammum* of Ptolemy, which he describes as the "*metropolis*" of Taprobane, "beside the great river" Mahawelli-ganga.

The ruined dagoba stands close by the pansela in which we were lodged. It is a huge semi-circular mound of brickwork, three hundred and sixty feet in circumference, and still one hundred feet high, but so much decayed at the top, that its original outline is no longer ascertainable. When Spilberg the Dutch admiral saw it, on his way to Kandy in 1602[2], it was comparatively perfect, as white as marble, and surmounted by a "gilded pyramid."[3] There were at that time a number of other monuments, and a Buddhist monastery, the priests of which Spilberg describes as moving along the streets under the shade of large umbrellas borne by slaves. The temples were then remarkable for the richness of their decorations, but the only one remaining at the present day, is a low and mean edifice of whitened mud, enclosing a rude statue of Buddha, the exterior walls covered with barbarous mythological drawings. The village contains about thirty miserable houses, but it presents one feature, which I have seen in no other Kandyan hamlet, that the houses are built in a connected line and under one continuous roof, instead of being, as in Kandyan villages generally, a mere cluster of detached dwellings, concealed in a tope of coco-nut and jak trees, and each constructed to secure seclusion and privacy. This improvement, if it be such, in Bintenne may probably have taken place when it was a military station after the rebellion of 1817; but still it is a singular instance, and the only one I have seen, of the adoption by Kandyans of the European practice of building a street.

[1] *Mahawanso*, ch. xxxvi. p. 229. For a notice of this occurrence in the early history of Electricity, see *ante*, Vol. I. Pt. IV. ch. ix. p. 506.

[2] See *ante*, Vol. II. Pt. VI. ch. ii. p. 35.

[3] SPILBERG, *Voiage, &c.*, tom. ii. p. 426.

Even during the dominion of the Dutch, Bintenne continued to be a place of dignity and importance; they spoke of it as the "finest city in the island, with a spacious palace belonging to the emperor."[1] It was in this palace, that Spilberg was received in 1602 by one of the queens of King Senerat, at an interview, of which the admiral has left a lively description.[2] The town now contains no memorials of its former greatness, except a few carved stones that mark the site of ancient edifices.

By following a shady path for a few hundred yards from the temple, we come upon a splendid view of the Mahawelli-ganga and of the magnificent hill-country from which it here emerges on the fertile plains, across whose level it pursues its solitary course to the sea. Immediately behind are the Kandyan Mountains, and the ancient pass of *Galle-pada-hulla*, or the "path of one thousand steps,"[3] which led towards Kandy from the now forgotten city of Meda-maha-neuera; and to the left tower the lofty hills of Oovah, presenting one of the grandest imaginable examples of bold mountain scenery. At our feet rolled the great river, now swollen and turbulent from the recent rains; its stream as broad

---

[1] VALENTYN, *Oud en Nieuw Oost-Indien*, ch. ii. p. 40.

[2] SPILBERG, *Voiage, &c.*, vol. ii. p. 424. Spilberg speaks of this lady as a daughter of the late King Wimala Dharma, "fille du feu Roi de Candy qui étoit une des femmes du regnant."—*Ibid.*, p. 425. If so, it must have been a former wife, as Senerat married his widow, the Queen Donna Catharina.—See *ante*, Vol. II. Pt. VI. ch. ii. p. 36.

[3] The following description of this singular pass as it existed in 1813, will serve to give an idea of the strength of the "natural fortifications" by which the kings of Kandy considered themselves beyond the risk of invasion from the low country. "Our first labour was an ascent up the Galle-pada-hulla Pass by a path which I cannot otherwise describe than by saying that it was the most abrupt and precipitous that it has ever been my lot to see. Our horses were not merely useless but an encumbrance, from the extreme hazard to which they were exposed; and it was only by the most laborious efforts that we could prosecute our journey. After an ascent of about four miles, bringing us to an elevation of 4000 feet above the path we had left, we supposed our difficulties were ended; but in this we were mistaken, and the road was of the same description, alternately ascending and descending all the way to Kandy." — CROWTHER'S *Missionary Notices, &c.*, 1813.

as the Thames at London, and of sufficient depth at all times to be navigable for small vessels. Valentyn states that so late as the beginning of the last century, the kings of Kandy had establishments at Bintenne for building galleys and tsampans.[1] The strongest feeling awakened at this remarkable spot is that of deep regret on seeing this prodigious agent of enrichment and civilisation rolling its idle waste of waters to the sea. It sweeps through luxuriant solitudes, past wide expanses of rich but now unproductive land, and under the very shade of forests whose timber and cabinet woods alone would form the wealth of an industrious people.

At one time the possibility of rendering this noble river navigable from the coast to the interior engaged the attention of the government, and in 1832, Mr. Brooke, the Master attendant at Trincomalie, was directed by Sir Robert Horton to explore its course, ascending it *from the sea in the direction of Kandy;* in order to ascertain its probable value if employed for commercial purposes; the size of boats for which it was really available; and how far its impediments were susceptible of removal, so as to determine the extent to which it might be employed for the conveyance of troops and stores.[2]

About forty miles before it enters the sea, the Mahawelli-ganga, separates into two distinct branches,—one, the Kooroogal-ganga, continuing a northerly course till it falls into the bay of Trincomalie, west of Cottiar; the other, the Vergel-aar, diverging almost at right angles at a point called Koorangemone, and reaching the coast by several mouths north and south of Arnetivoe, or the "Island of Elephants." The tradition of the natives

---

[1] "Hier werden de beste galeyen en tsjampans des Keysers gemaakt."—*Oud en Nieuw Oost-Indien*, ch. iii. p. 40.

[2] An abstract of Mr. BROOKE'S Report on the Navigation of the Mahawelli-ganga was published in the *Journal of the Roy. Geogr. Soc.* for 1833, vol. iii. p. 223.

is that at no very remote period, the Vergel-aar was a narrow watercourse, cut by the natives for irrigating their paddi-fields, but that, the soil being light and yielding, it hollowed out and deepened its own bed with such rapidity as almost to drain the original channel of the river below the point of junction; the Vergel becoming, what it now is, one of the most tumultuous and dangerous torrents on the eastern side of Ceylon. By the same operation the original channel of the Mahawelli-ganga was rendered so shallow as to be at all times unnavigable, and even dry in many places, except during the freshes after the rains, when it resumes its original depth and importance.

Mr. Brooke, in setting out to ascend the Mahawelli-ganga from Trincomalie towards Kandy, proceeded by land to a place on the main stream called Kooroogal-gamma, thirty-two miles from the sea, up to which, owing to the level nature of the country, the river being affected by the tides, the water is always more or less salt. To this point he caused the boats to be hauled up the stream; but the channel was so dry that in many places the boatmen failed to find even the few inches of water requisite to float canoes, and were frequently obliged to drag them over long banks of dry sand. Between the sea and the junction with the Vergel, there was not a village nor a human dwelling, except the solitary shed at a ferry near Kooroogal-gamma, across which the people from the interior carry their products to the bazaar of Trincomalie. Yet, such is the fertility of the adjacent country, that, were the river rendered navigable, large quantities of grain might be carried down its course, and find a ready market at numerous places on the coast.

At the point where the main river empties its waters into the Vergel, the bed of the latter is so deep and narrow that the current rushes in with extreme impetuosity. The natives, in floating down timber to Trincomalie, whilst the river is high after the rains, approach the separation of the two streams with apprehension; since instances are frequent in which rafts have been carried into the Vergel and swept out to sea, those in charge being compelled to abandon them precipitately and swim to land.

Mr. Brooke succeeded in ascending the river to Bintenne and Pangragamme, a distance of 120 miles from the bay of Trincomalie, and describes his voyage as rendered hazardous by the rapids, in which it was difficult to steady the boats, whilst an upset would have been dangerous, owing to the multitude of crocodiles with which the river swarmed.

After passing Koorangemoné, where the two branches of the river diverge, villages became more frequent, but the inhabitants were poor and exhausted by fever, their houses being built over marshy ground and raised on piles, to obviate inconvenience from the periodical inundation of the river after the rains. The population on the left or western bank were chiefly Moors who cultivate a little rice, whilst to the right extended the vast forests of Bintenne frequented by the uncivilised Veddah tribes.

The river, as far up as Perriatorre, in the vicinity of the remarkable mountain called the Gunner's Quoin, varies from 100 to 140 yards in width, and after this point occasionally expands to upwards of 500. Its depth is from 4 to 7 feet, but rising to 25 or 30 during the rains. The chief obstructions for the first 80 miles are huge banks of sand piled up at the angles and sharp bends of the river, and occasionally collections of dead trees swept together by the floods, hang across the river, impeding the passage and helping to accumulate fresh heaps of sand and drift-wood.

At Calinga, twenty-four miles above Perriatorre, the Mahawelli-ganga loses its sandy character, and flows over rocks of granite. Here Mr. Brooke found the navigation extremely difficult, occasionally presenting rapids and falls of twelve feet and upwards, round which his boats had to be dragged along the bank. These rocky obstructions extend for fourteen miles, after which the river recovers its former character and is easily navigable as far as Bintenne and Pangragamme ; but above this the reefs become so formidable that they effectually prevented further progress ; and here Mr. Brooke terminated the portion of his journey practicable by boats, and explored the remainder of the channel to Kandy on foot.

The result of his expedition was satisfactory, in so far as it served to establish the fact that, by preventing the abstraction of the water now diverted into the Vergel, and by removing some sand banks and minor obstructions below the present junction, the Mahawelliganga might be easily rendered navigable for eighty miles from the bay of Trincomalie to Calinga, an important locality in the centre of one of the most fertile and productive districts of Ceylon, where, however, in consequence of the absence of roads, or any other means of intercommunication, the soil can scarcely be said to be under cultivation, except in the immediate vicinity of the Moorish villages, which are scattered over the district of Tamankadua. For thirty miles above Calinga, the removal of the rocks and impediments would be difficult ; but even here a communication might be established for a moderate expenditure, and inland navigation rendered possible from the eastern coast, almost to the foot of the Kandyan hills, and the vicinity of the coffee plantations in the mountain zone. To the latter the conveyance of rice and stores from the low country would be a signal advantage ; and the transport of coffee to a shipping port, at a reasonable charge, would reduce one of the most formidable difficulties with which the planters have to struggle in their competition with other countries.

To the Kandyan people the realisation of such a project would be productive of simultaneous advantage, by opening up a market for the agricultural productions of the interior, as well as an outlet for its mineral wealth. It would also afford an easy transport to the sea for the ebony, satin-wood, and other valuable timber, which now grow in neglected luxuriance and in almost exhaustless profusion throughout the forests intersected by the Mahawelli-ganga. It is a painful but convincing illustration of the evils consequent on the destitution of facilities for communication, that, notwithstanding the abundance of timber in the eastern province, it is cheaper, at Colombo, to import teak from Burmah, and jarrah wood from Australia, than to bring halmalille, beams from the forests of Neuera-kalawa. Of the large quantities of cabinet woods exported from Trincomalie only a very small portion is carried down the river, and the trees which are sent by it have first to be cut into short lengths, as there is not sufficient water in the channel to float heavy logs. Were the obstructions judiciously removed, and the water restored to the old channel below Kooroogalgammoa, the gain to Government from the exportation of timber alone would in a few years repay the outlay, not to speak of the permanent increase to the revenue which would necessarily arise, from the extension of the quantity of land brought into cultivation for rice.

At one extremity of the town of Bintenne, is the *Wellawé*, or residence of the local headman, a chief named Gonnigoddé, who formerly held the high rank of "Dissave of Bintenne." Its buildings encircle a courtyard, round which a covered verandah supported on pillars affords a communication with the several apartments. So little idea of domestic comfort or refinement have the Kandyans, even of this high rank, that the largest of these chambers are little dingy dens from ten to twelve feet square, each lighted by a single window, or rather a hole, the area of which does not exceed a square foot.

The old chief escorted us to visit the ladies of his family, who were introduced as we sat at table in the small entrance room. His wife, a rather comely person, and his daughter, came in timidly, remained standing for a few moments, and then retired. They were dressed in loose cloths, in the Kandyan fashion. Their feet were bare, but their necks, arms, and ankles were loaded with gold chains and jewels, so dirty that it was difficult to estimate their value, or discover their beauty.

In this instance the lady was the wife of one husband, but the revolting practice of *polyandry* prevails throughout the interior of Ceylon, chiefly amongst the wealthier classes; of whom, one woman has frequently three or four husbands, and sometimes as many as seven. The same custom was at one time universal throughout the island[1], but the influence of the Portuguese and Dutch sufficed to discountenance and extinguish it in the maritime provinces. As a general rule the husbands are members of the same family, and most frequently brothers. According to the notion of the Singhalese, the practice originated in the feudal times, when, as is alleged, their rice lands would have gone to destruction, during the long absences enforced on the people by the duty of personal attendance on the king and the higher chiefs, had not some interested party been left to conduct their tillage. Hence the community of property led eventually to the community of wives. An aged chief of the Four Corles, Aranpulle Ratemahatmeya, who lived under three native kings, prior to the conquest of Kandy by the British, informed me, in 1848, in reply to an inquiry addressed to him as to the origin of polyandry, that its prevalence was attributable to the services above alluded to, "when the people gave their attendance at the royal palace, and at the residences of the great headman, besides contributing

[1] The King of Cotta, Wijayo Bahu VII., who was reigning when the Portuguese built their first fort at Colombo, had one wife in common with his brother; and Raja Singha I. was born in polyandry.—VALENTYN, *Oud en Nieuw Oost-Indien*, ch. vi. p. 95.

labour on the lands of their lords, and accompanying them in their distant journeys; during such intervals of prolonged absence their own fields would have remained uncultivated and their crops uncut, had they not resorted to the expedient of identifying their representatives with their interests, by adopting their brothers and nearest relatives as the partners of their wives and fortunes." In more recent times the custom has been extenuated on the plea, that it prevents the subdivision of estates, the children of these promiscuous marriages being the recognised heirs of all the husbands, however numerous, of their mother.

But the practice of polyandry is, I apprehend, much more ancient than the system thus indicated. In point of antiquity it can be shown to have existed at a period long antecedent to the conquest of Wijayo, or the establishment of his feudal followers in Ceylon. It appears to have been encouraged amongst almost every race on the continent of India; it receives a partial sanction in the institutes of Menu; and it is adverted to without reproach in the epic of the *Maha Barat*[1], the heroine of which, Draupadi, was the wife of five Pandu brothers. It has existed from time immemorial in the valley of Kashmir[2], in Thibet, and in the Sivalik mountains: it is found in Sylhet and Kachar[3], among the Coorgs of Mysore and the Todas on the Nilgherry hills; and to the present hour it serves to regulate the laws of inheritance amongst the Nairs in the southern extremity of the Dekkan.[4]

---

[1] The odious custom would appear to have been common in Britain at the period of Cæsar's invasion. "The Britons," he says, "uxores habent deni duodenique inter se communes, *et maxime fratres cum fratribus, et parentes cum liberis.* Sed si qui sunt ex his nati, eorum habentur liberi à quibus primum virgines quæque ductæ sunt." — *De Bello Gallico*, lib. v. ch. xiv.

[2] VIGNE's *Kashmir*, vol. i. p. 37.

[3] *Journ. Asiat. Soc. Beng.*, vol. ix. p. 834.

[4] *Asiat. Res.*, vol. v. p. 13. CASTANHEDA, one of the Portuguese historians of India, ascribes the prevalence of polyandry amongst the Nairs to the design of the sovereigns, that being devoid of care and love for their children, their attention might be the more exclusively given

Although polyandry is inferentially reprobated in the *Rajavali* and *Mahawanso*[1], the Buddhist priesthood have never interposed to discourage it in Ceylon. No infamy attaches to such unions, and the offspring are regarded as equally legitimate with those born in wedlock: British courts of justice being bound to protect the rights of descent and inheritance as regulated by the local customs of the Kandyans, have been hitherto constrained to recognise its existence, but within a very recent period a law has been introduced, under the influence of which, if it can be enforced with the co-operation of the more highly educated natives of Kandy, it is to be hoped that this opprobrium will ere long cease to disgrace a possession of the British Crown.

Having expressed a wish to visit the ruined tank of Horra-bora, the most interesting object in the district of Bintenne, the old chief mounted his horse, and rode forward to show us the path through the forest. The road led for the entire distance across a succession of paddi fields, which were then under water from the previous rains; but the sight of the ruin well repaid the inconvenience of the ride. It is a stupendous work,—a stream flowing between two hills about three or four miles apart, has been intercepted by an artificial dam drawn across the valley at the point where they approach; and the water thus confined is thrown back till it forms a lake eight or ten miles long by three or four wide, exclusive of narrow branches running behind spurs of the hills. The embankment is from fifty to seventy feet high, and about two hundred feet broad at the base. But one of the most ingenious features in the work is the advantage which has been taken in its construction

---

to martial service.—CONQUISTA *da India, &c.*, ch. xiv. p. 36.

HUMBOLDT found the custom of polyandry in the island of Lancerota, one of the Canaries.—*Narrat.* ch. i.

[1] *Rajavali*, p. 168; *Mahawanso*, ch. xxxvi. p. 227, ch. xxxvii. p. 250.

of two vast masses of rock, which have been included in the retaining bund, the intervening spaces being filled up by earth-work, and faced with stone. In order to form the sluices, it is obvious that the simplest plan would have been to have placed them in the artificial portions of the bank; but the builders, conscious of the comparatively unsubstantial nature of their own work, and apprehensive of the combined effect of the weight and rush of the water, foresaw that the immense force of its discharge would speedily wear away any artificial conduits they could have constructed for its escape; and they had the resolution to hollow out channels in the solid rock; through which they opened two passages, each sixty feet deep, four feet broad at the bottom, and widening to fifteen or twenty at the top. The walls on either side still exhibit traces of the wedges by which the stone was riven to effect the openings. These passages had formerly been furnished with sluices for regulating the quantity of water allowed to escape, and the hewn stones which retain these flood-gates lie displaced, but unbroken in the bed of the channel.

The tank is now comparatively neglected, and its retaining wall would evidently have been long since worn away by the force of the escaping water, had not this precaution of its builders effectually provided against its destruction. The basin abounds with crocodiles, some of which were lying on the rocks as we rode up, and floundered into the lake on our approach. The embankment was overgrown not merely with jungle, but with forest trees, whose roots have contributed to give it solidity. Amongst these are numbers of the curious *Terminalia alata*, whose roots run above ground as thick as a man's wrist; the extremity of each, instead of terminating in a single fibre, expands into a round knob as large as a melon. The margin of the water showed the dead shells of the Unio, which abounds in the Ceylon tanks, and might become an article of food where it not for the prejudice of the natives. One species, the *U. marginalis*, produces small pearls. *Paludinæ* and *Limnæi* swarm amongst the wet sedges, and a white Planorbis (*P. indica?*) creeps up the stems of the bulrushes, and boldly launching itself on the still water, floats across it by means of its expanded foot.

The impression left on my mind by the inspection of this magnificent work, and confirmed by subsequent examination of many specimens of the ancient tanks throughout the northern divisions of the island, induced me in 1848 to submit to the Council at Colombo, a project for initiating by legislative authority, and under the control of government officers, measures for the gradual restoration of some of these important reservoirs. The suggestion was adopted[1], but occurrences which afterwards disturbed the tranquillity of the island, prevented the carrying out of my plans, and the distinction was reserved for a subsequent governor, Sir Henry G. Ward, not only to promulgate an ordinance to facilitate the revival of the ancient customs regarding irrigation[2], but to contribute to the promotion of this great national object in the eastern and southern provinces, both by the encouragement of the Government, and by the application of funds at its disposal.

The sentiments not less than the interests of the Singhalese people are deeply involved in this question. The stupendous ruins of their reservoirs are the proudest monuments which remain of the former greatness of their country, when the opulence which they engendered enabled the kings to lavish untold wealth upon edifices of religion, to subsidise mercenary armies, and to fit out expeditions for foreign conquest. Excepting the

---

[1] In the Legislative Council, 6th November, 1848, the attention of the Home Government had been previously directed to the subject of adopting preliminary measures for restoring the cultivation of rice by repairing the ruined tanks. (See Sir J. Emerson Tennent's *Report on the Finance and Commerce of Ceylon. Parliamentary Papers*, 1848, p. 69.)

[2] Ordinance, No. 9, 1856.

exaggerated dimensions of Lake Mœris in Central Egypt, and the mysterious "basin of Al Aram," the bursting of whose embankment devastated the Arabian city of Mareb [1], no similar constructions formed by any race, whether ancient or modern, exceed in colossal magnitude the stupendous tanks of Ceylon. The reservoir of Koh-rud at Ispahan, the artificial lake of Ajmeer, or the tank of Hyder, in Mysore, can no more be compared in extent or grandeur with Kala-weva, or Padivil-colom than the conduits of Hezekiah [2], the kanâts of the Persians, or the subterranean water-courses of Peru [3] can vie with the Ellahara canal, which probably connected the lake of Mineri and the "Sea of Prakrama" with the Amban-ganga river.

Reasons have been elsewhere assigned [4], why works of this nature were rendered indispensable by the peculiarities of climate, and the deficient supply of rain or river water for purposes of agriculture in the northern districts of Ceylon, whilst in the mountainous regions of the south, the deluge of the monsoons and the perennial freshness of the streams render the peasantry independent of artificial irrigation. Hence every village to the north of the Kandyan zone was provided with one tank at least; and by the provident munificence of the native sovereigns, the face of the country became covered with a network of canals to convey streams to the rice lands. So long as these precious structures remained intact cultivation was continuous and famines unknown. But their preservation was dependent not only on the maintenance of the co-operative village system (a system whose existence was contingent on the duration of peace and tranquillity), but on the supremacy of a domestic government sufficiently strong

[1] The *Koran*, ch. xxxiv.

[2] 2 Kings, ch. xx. v. 20.

[3] DARWIN, *Nat. Voy.*, ch. xvi. p. 358.

[4] See *ante*, Vol. I. Pt. I. ch. ii. p. 73.

to control the will and direct the action of these rural municipalities. This salutary authority was superseded, and eventually annihilated by the Malabar invaders. They do not appear to have molested or wantonly destroyed the village tanks; (in fact, the only recorded instance of the deliberate destruction of a tank was by the Portuguese in the sixteenth century[1];) but the presence of an enemy paralysed the organisation under which alone they could be administered for the general advantage of the community, and the gradual decline of the peasantry involved the neglect, and eventually the ruin, of the reservoirs and canals. Between the seventh century and the twelfth, agriculture was so successful, that Ceylon produced ample supplies for the sustenance of her teeming population[2]; but in the thirteenth and fourteenth centuries, when the baneful domination of the Malabars had become intolerable, industry was stifled, and the remnant of the people became helplessly reliant on the continent of India for their annual supplies of food — a dependency which has continued unrelieved to the present time.

The difficulties attendant on any attempt to bring back cultivation by the repair of the tanks are too apparent to escape notice. The effort must be made by judicious degrees. The system to be restored was the growth of a thousand years of freedom which a brief interval of despotism sufficed to destroy; and it would require the lapse of centuries to reproduce the population, and re-create the wealth in cattle and

[1] This event took place during the siege of Colombo by Raja Singha II., A. D. 1587, when Thomé de Souza d'Arronches was despatched, to make a diversion by ravaging the southern coast of Ceylon. DE COUTO recounts, amongst other atrocities then perpetrated, that after sacking the town of Bellegam, a party was sent to a river which he calls the Meliseu, where they halted *and destroyed the tank*, "no qual desembarcáram e tomaram huma tranqueira."—*Asia*, dec. x. ch. xv.; FARIA Y SOUZA, *Portuguese Asia*, vol. iii. p. 53. An account of this infamous expedition of Souza D'Arronches will be found in another part of the present work, Vol. II. Pt. VI. ch. i., and Vol. II. Pt. VII. ch. i.

[2] "La population est agglomerée, et la terre produit des grains en abondance."—HIOUEN THSANG, *Voyages, &c.*, tom. i. p. 194.

manual labour essential to realise again the agricultural felicity which prevailed under the Singhalese dynasties. But the experiment is one worthy of the beneficent rule of the British Crown, under whose auspices the ancient organisation may be revived amongst the native Singhalese. The project has been broached of initiating the experiment by colonisation from the coast of India, or by the introduction of agriculturists from China; but the suggestion is uncongenial of attempting the revival of agriculture through the instrumentality of Tamils, the very race to whose malignant influence it owes its decay; and any project, to be satisfactory as well as successful, should contemplate the benefit of the natives, and not that of strangers in Ceylon.

The Singhalese within the last three hundred years have seen three European nations in succession take possession of their country and monopolise its productions for the enrichment of foreigners. The Portuguese and Dutch extorted its cinnamon and pearls, the British have covered its mountains with plantations of coffee, and its coasts with gardens of coco-nut palms; but each has failed in turn to inaugurate a policy that would tend successfully to elevate native industry, or emancipate the people themselves from their dependence upon foreigners for food. Apathetic and impassive as they are in other particulars, the people are keenly sensitive to their wrongs in this respect. Tradition and their historical annals have familiarised them with the names of those sovereigns whose reigns were signalised by the promotion of the one paramount interest of their subjects, and whose memory is cherished with corresponding devotion. Even the rule of usurpers was submitted to not merely with patience but with gratitude, where it was characterised by generosity in the maintenance of the great works on which prosperity was so largely dependent. In the gloom of its decline the native chronicles of the island do not fail to record that, "because the fertility of the land had decreased, kings were no longer esteemed as before."[1] Nothing is more natural than the disaffection of the Kandyans to a government under which this indifference to their interests is perpetuated, and nothing would so much endear to them the name and authority of Great Britain as an energetic and successful effort, to emulate the ancient kings in the encouragement and protection bestowed on the agricultural industry of the island.

The tank at Horra-bora presents singular facilities for commencing the attempt. From its superior state of preservation its repairs might be effected at a comparatively small cost, and the experiment derives peculiar encouragement from the fact that the reservoir is surrounded by a vast expanse of government land suitable for rice cultivation, and that it lies within a distance from Kandy and the coffee estates so inconsiderable as to offer no appreciable obstacle to the ready sale of almost any amount of produce derivable from it.

---

[1] *Rajavali*, p. 230.

CHAP. III.

THE VEDDAHS.

At Bintenne I had an opportunity of acquiring the information I was so desirous to collect regarding the progress and past success of the attempt made by Government to introduce civilisation amongst the Veddahs. The district which they inhabit, about ninety miles in length by half that breadth, is situated in the south-eastern section of the island, and extends towards the sea, from the base of the Budulla and Oovah hills. Within a comparatively recent period, they ranged over a much more extended area; and in the time of the Dutch, to whom they paid a tribute in elephants[1], they were found in the Wanny, within a very short distance of the peninsula of Jaffna.

It is incorrect to apply the term *savages* to harmless outcasts like these, who neither in disposition nor in action exhibit such vices as we are accustomed to associate with that epithet. The proofs are stated elsewhere[2] which show the Veddahs to be a remnant of the Yakkos, the aboriginal inhabitants of Ceylon, who, after the conquest of the island by Wijayo and his followers, retired before the invaders into the wilds of the east and south; whence they never emerged, but, on the contrary, withdrew still deeper into the jungle in order to avoid contact with civilisation.

Here, for upwards of two thousand years, has this

[1] Valentyn, *Oud en Nieuw Oost-Indien, &c.*, ch. ii. p. 8, 32; ch. iii. p. 49.

[2] See *ante*, Vol. I. Pt. iii. ch. vii. p. 372; *Ibid.*, Vol. I. Pt. v. ch. ii. p. 569.

remarkable fragment of an ancient race remained almost unaltered as regards customs, language, and pursuits; and it exhibits, at the present day, a living portraiture of the condition of the islanders as described in the *Mahawanso* before the Bengal conquerors had taught the natives the rudiments of agriculture, and "rendered Lanka habitable for men."[1]

In relation to the mass of the Singhalese people, the Veddahs stand in a position similar to that of the scattered tribes, vestiges of the aborigines of India, still lurking in the mountain forests of Hindustan, and which for ages have shrunk from intercourse with the Aryan races, who subjugated, and whose descendants still occupy, the Peninsula.[2]

There is no lack of historical evidence to establish the identity of the Veddahs with the Yakkos.[3] The allusions of the *Mahawanso* and other native chronicles are confirmed by classical authorities[4], as well as by the direct testimony of the Chinese Buddhists, who wrote of Ceylon between the fifth and seventh centuries[5]; and in the curious tract *De Moribus Brachmanorum*, which bears the name of Palladius, and appears to have been written about the year 400, the Veddahs are alluded to almost by name, and described in terms which apply to this extraordinary tribe even at the present day.[6]

---

[1] *Mahawanso*, ch. vii. p. 49.

[2] Such are the Koolies in Guzerat, the Bheels in Malwa, the Puttoons in Cuttack, and the Khoonds in Gundwana, the Bedas in Mysore, and the still more savage hordes amongst the mountains east of Bengal. — See *Asiat. Soc. Journ. Beng.*, vol. xxvi. p. 206.

[3] LASSEN, *Indische Alterthumskunde*, vol. i. p. 200.

[4] Allusion has been made elsewhere (Vol. I. Pt. v. ch. ii. p. 569) to the concurrent testimony of Pliny, and a long chain of subsequent writers on the subject of the Veddahs and the endurance of a custom which identifies them incontrovertibly with the aborigines of Ceylon.

[5] FA HIAN, *Foë-Kouë Ki*, ch. xxxviii.; HIOUEN THSANG, *Pèlerins Bouddh.*, tom. ii. p. 146.

[6] The traveller of Thebes, from whom the author of the tract professes to have derived his information, describes the Veddahs in the following terms: "ἔφθασα ἐγγὺς τῶν καλουμένων Βισάδων. ἔθνος δέ ἐστιν ἐκεῖνο

The modern Veddahs live more or less by hunting and the use of the bow, in drawing which they occasionally employ their feet as well as their hands.[1] The "Rock Veddahs" and the "Village Veddahs" form the two grand divisions of the tribe, whose respective names serve to indicate, faintly, the difference in the amount of civilisation which is found to subsist amongst the members of this wild race. The Village Veddahs approach the confines of the European settlements on the eastern coast, where they cultivate some rude species of grain, and submit to dwell in huts of mud and bark. The Rock Veddahs[2] remain concealed in the forests, subsisting on roots, fish, honey, and the produce of the chase; lodging in caves, or under the shelter of overhanging rocks, and sometimes sleeping on stages, which they construct in the trees.[3] In the choice of their food, both classes are almost omnivorous, no carrion or vermin being too repulsive for their appetite. They subsist upon roots, grain, and fruit, when they can procure them; and upon birds, bats, crows, owls and kites, which they bring down with the bow; but for some unexplained reason, they will not touch the bear, the elephant, or buffalo, although the

---

πάνυ σμικρότατον καὶ ἀδρανίστατον· λιθίνοις σπηλαίοις ἐνοικοῦντες οἵτινες καὶ κρημνοβατεῖν ἐπίστανται διὰ τὴν τοῦ τόπου συστροφήν. **Εἰσὶ δὲ καὶ οἱ Βισάδες** *ἀνθρωπάρια, κολαβὰ, μεγαλοκέφαλα, ἄκαρτα, καὶ ἀπλότριχα.*"—Lib. iii. ch. viii. It is a remarkable coincidence that this name of *Bisadæ*, or *Besadæ* (which in mediæval Greek is pronounced Vesadæ) is applied by Ptolemy to a similar race inhabiting Northern India. A forest tribe of Mysore, known by the name of Bedas or Vedas, formed part of the army of Tippoo Sahib.

[1] See *ante*, Vol. I. Pt. IV. ch. viii. p. 499. One meaning of the word Veddah, is "an Archer." DE ALWIS, *Sidath Sangara*, p. xvii.; and the *Mahawanso*, speaking of one of the warriors of Dutugaimunu who came from the Veddah country, says, the "exercise of the bow was the profession of their caste," ch. xxiii.

[2] The term "Rock Veddahs," *galle-vedda*, is probably a modern distinction; but may not the tribe still represent the ancient "*Gallas*" who once inhabited the south of the island, and from whom it is just possible that the harbour of Galle may have acquired its name, although other derivations are more plausible?

[3] HUMBOLDT mentions a race of South American Indians, the Guaraons in the Delta of the Orinoco, who construct their dwellings in trees, and generally on the top of the Mauritia Palms.—*Person. Narrat.*, ch. xxv.

latter are abundant in their hunting grounds. The flesh of deer and other animals they dry on stages in the sun and store away in hollow trees for future use, closing the apertures with clay. They invariably cook their meat with fire, and avow a preference for the iguana lizard and roasted monkeys above all other dainties.

The *Rock Veddahs* are divided into small clans or families associated by relationship, who agree in partitioning the forest among themselves for hunting grounds, the limits of each family's possessions being marked by streams, hills, rocks, or some well-known trees, and these conventional allotments are always honourably recognised and mutually preserved from violation. Each party has a headman, the most energetic senior of the tribe, but who exercises no sort of authority beyond distributing at a particular season the honey captured by the various members of the clan. The produce of the chase they dry and collect for barter, carrying it to the borders of the inhabited country, whither the ubiquitous Moors resort, bringing cloths, axes, arrow-heads, and other articles to be exchanged for deer flesh, elephants' tusks, and bees' wax. In these transactions the wild Veddahs are seldom seen by those with whom they come to deal.[1] They deposit in the night the articles which they are disposed to part with, indicating by some mutually understood signals the description of those they expect in return; and these being brought in the following day to the appointed place, disappear during the ensuing night. Money to them is worthless, but coco-nuts, salt, hatchets, iron, arrow-heads, and dyed clothes, or cooking chatties, are valuables much in request.

Their language, which is limited to a very few words,

---

[1] The concurrent testimonies on this curious custom of the Veddahs, from the first century to the present time, have been adverted to before. See *ante*, Vol. I. Pt. v. ch. ii. p. 568.

is a dialect of Singhalese without any admixture from the Sanskrit or Pali [1] — a circumstance indicative of their repugnance to intercourse with strangers. But so degraded are some of these wretched outcasts, that it has appeared doubtful in certain cases whether they possess any language whatever. One gentleman [2] who resided long in their vicinity has assured me that not only is their dialect incomprehensible to a Singhalese, but that even their communications with one another are made by signs, grimaces, and guttural sounds which bear little or no resemblance to distinct words or systematised language. They have no marriage rites; although they acknowledge the marital obligation and the duty of supporting their own families. Marriages, amongst them, are settled by the parents of the contracting parties; the father of the bride presents his son-in-law with a bow; his own father assigns him a right of chase in a portion of his hunting ground; he presents the lady with a cloth and some rude ornaments; and she follows him into the forest as his wife. The community is too poor to afford polygamy. A gentleman who in a hunting excursion had passed the night near a clan of Wild Veddahs, gave me a description of their mode of going to rest. The chief first stretched himself on the ground, after having placed his bow at hand and clutched his hatchet, which is always an object of much care and solicitude. The children and younger members next lay down around him in close contact for sake of the warmth — whilst the rest took up their places in a circle at some distance as if to watch for the safety of the party during the night.

They have no knowledge of a God, nor of a future

---

[1] The Dutch, in their limited intercourse with the Veddahs, found them singularly disposed to silence and to intercourse by signs, and VALENTYN dwells on the paucity of words in their dialect.—*Oud en Nieuw Oost-Indien*, ch. xv. p. 208.

[2] G. R. Mercer, Esq., of the Civil Service, who held office at Badulla.

state; no temples, no idols, no altars, prayers or charms; and, in short, no instinct of worship, except, it is reported, some addiction to ceremonies analogous to devil worship, in order to avert storms and lightning; and when sick, they send for devil dancers to drive away the evil spirit, who is believed to inflict the disease. The dance is executed in front of an offering of something eatable, placed on a tripod of sticks, the dancer having his head and girdle decorated with green leaves. At first he shuffles with his feet to a plaintive air, but by degrees he works himself into a state of great excitement and action, accompanied by moans and screams, and during this paroxysm, he professes to be inspired with instruction for the cure of the patient.

So rude are the Veddahs in all respects, that they do not even bury their dead, but cover them with leaves and brush-wood in the jungle. They have no system of caste amongst themselves; but, singular to say, this degraded race is still regarded by the Singhalese as of the most honourable extraction, and is recognised by them as belonging to one of the highest castes.[1] This belief originates in a legend to the effect that a Veddah chased by a wild animal took refuge in a tree, whence all night long he threw down flowers to drive away his pursuer. But in the morning instead of a wild beast, he found an idol under the tree, who addressed him with the announcement, that as he had passed the night in worshipping and offering flowers, the race of the Veddahs should ever after take the highest place in the caste of the Vellales or cultivators, the most exalted of all. The Veddahs smile at the story and say they know nothing of it, but nevertheless they would not touch meat dressed by a low-caste Kandyan.

---

[1] LASSEN, in his *Indische Alterthums Kunde*, vol. ii. p. 1,002, suggests that the Veddahs may be the descendants of the degraded caste of Lambakanakos alluded to in the *Mahawanso;* but the conjecture is undoubtedly erroneous.

The *Village Veddahs* are but a shade superior to the wild tribes of the jungle. They manifest no sympathy, and maintain no association with them. They occupy a position intermediate between that of the semi-civilised Kandyans of the Wanny and the coast, and the Veddahs of the rock, but evince, to the present day, their ancestral reluctance to adopt the habits of civilised life. They are probably to some extent the descendants of Kandyans who may have intermingled with the wild race, and whose offspring, from their intercourse with the natives of the adjoining districts, have acquired a smattering of Tamil, in addition to their natural dialect of Singhalese.[1] They wear a bit of cloth a little larger than that worn by the tribes of the forest, and the women ornament themselves with necklaces of brass beads, and bangles cut from the chank shell. The ears of the children when seven or eight years old, are bored with a thorn by the father, and decorated with rings. The Veddahs have no idea of time or distance, no names for hours, days, or years. They have no doctors, and no knowledge of medicine, beyond the practice of applying bark and leaves to a wound. They have no games, no amusements, no music, and as to education it is so utterly unknown, that the Wild Veddahs are unable to count beyond five on their own fingers. Even the Village Veddahs are somewhat migratory in their habits, removing their huts as facilities vary for cultivating a little Indian corn and yams, and occasionally they accept wages in kind from the Moors for watching the paddi-fields at night, in order to drive away wild elephants. The women plait mats from the palm leaf, and the men make bows, the strings of which are prepared from the tough bark of the Rittagaha or Upas

---

[1] Boyd, in his account of his Embassy to Kandy, speaks highly of the character and abilities of a Veddah who had been assigned to him as interpreter at Trincomalie, and who, in his interviews with the King of Kandy, translated Singhalese into Tamil.—*Miscell. Works,* vol. ii. p. 234.

tree, but beyond these they have no knowledge of any manufacture.

The *Coast Veddahs*, another tribe who might almost be considered a third class, have settled themselves in the jungles between Batticaloa and Trincomalie, and subsist by assisting the fishermen in their operations, or in felling timber for the Moors, to be floated down the rivers to the sea.

The Rock Veddahs, who till lately resided almost exclusively within the Bintenne forests, consisted of five clans or hunting parties, but it is obvious that no data whatever can exist to aid us in forming an approximate estimate of their numbers. The settlements of the Village Veddahs, are in the vicinity of the lagoon districts around Batticaloa, where as they have mingled by slow degrees with the inhabitants on the outskirts of that region, it is difficult now to discriminate them with precision, but they do not exceed one hundred and forty families, divided into nine little communities, distinguished by peculiarities known only to each other. The Coast Veddahs are principally in the vicinity of Eraoor, and the shores extending northwards towards Venloos Bay; where they may probably reckon four to five hundred individuals. The entire number of Veddahs of all classes in Ceylon has been estimated at eight thousand, but this is obviously a mere conjecture, and probably an exaggerated one.

Mr. Atherton, the Assistant Government Agent of the district, who exhibited a laudable energy in seconding the efforts made by the Government Officers to reclaim these outcasts, spoke to me in favourable terms of the gentleness of their disposition, apparent amidst extreme indifference to morals, although grave crimes are rarely committed. In case of theft the delinquent, if detected, is forced to make restitution, but undergoes no punishment. If a girl be carried off from her parents, she is claimed and brought home; and the husband of a faithless wife is equally contented to receive her back, his family inflicting a flogging on the seducer. Murder is almost unknown, but when discovered, it is compromised for goods, or some other consideration paid to the relatives of the deceased. Mr. Atherton described the Veddahs as in general gentle and affectionate to each other, and remarkably attached to their children and relatives. Widows are always supported by the community, and receive their share of all fruits, grain, and produce of the chase. "They appeared to him a quiet and submissive race, obeying the slightest intimation of a wish, and very grateful for attention or assistance. They are sometimes accused of plundering the fields adjacent to their haunts, but on investigation the charge has generally been shown to have been false, and brought by the Moormen with a view to defraud the Veddahs, whom they habitually impose upon, cheating them shamefully in all their transactions of barter and exchange."[1]

---

[1] Extract from a *private letter*. The following story of the death of a Veddah, told by Major Macready, formerly Military Secretary in Ceylon, appeared in one of the Ceylon newspapers in 1847. The writer and his companions were awaiting in silence the approach of a herd of elephants, when their "anticipated sport was interrupted by a wild and mournful howl, which spoke unmistakeably of some sad mischance. Those who were nearest to the cry ran down, and to their horror found a Veddah, a fine young fellow, surrounded by his people and seated, his back against a tree, with his intestines in his lap. A wild buffalo that he had passed almost without notice in the cover had rushed on him from behind, knocked him down, and gored him from the groin upwards as he fell. There never, I believe, in the world or in all the fanciful imaginations of poetic minds seeking to illustrate the dignity of our nature, was a finer picture of manly fortitude than in that noble savage. He positively never—never once, during the many hours we were with him, showed by a move or the contraction of a muscle, that he felt pain from his wound, or feared the death that seemed too sure to follow it — though the perspiration literally pouring from his cheek and shoulders showed how much he suffered. He looked up calmly in our faces poor fellow; if it was to find comfort or confidence there, I fear he found little of either. I do not believe that one of us could check the tears that involuntarily flowed to see the manly fellow and to know his fate inevitable. We did all we could — made a litter, carried him to his rock, built a shed over him, put back the bowels, and sewed up the wound, but the end of the story was that the poor fellow died the day after to our great grief."

About the year 1838, the condition of this neglected people attracted the attention of the Governor, Mr. Stewart Mackenzie, and he attempted to penetrate their country, but was turned back by an attack of jungle fever. The Assistant Government Agent, however, in conjunction with the Wesleyan Methodist missionaries at Batticaloa, were commissioned to place themselves in communication with the Veddahs, and to make them offers of land and houses, seed-grain, tools, and protection, if they would consent to abandon their forest life, and become settlers and cultivators in the low-country. Mr. Atherton and the Rev. Mr. Stott succeeded during their journey in obtaining the fullest and most accurate information possible as to their actual condition and sufferings. Their destitution they discovered to be so great, that in one community they found seven families with but a single iron mammotie (hoe) amongst them for the cultivation of the whole settlement; and such was their want of even weapons for the chase, that but one arrow was left in a family. Mr. Atherton gave them twelve, with directions to divide them with three clans; but so ignorant was the headman, that he could not even separate them into four equal parcels. Many of the Rock Veddahs willingly availed themselves of the offer of settlement and assistance, but firmly refused to remove from the immediate vicinity of their native forest. Cottages were built for them in their own district, rice-land assigned them, wells dug, coco-nuts planted, and two communities were speedily settled at Vippam-madoo, close by their ancient hunting-fields. There they were provided with seed, hoes and axes, for agriculture, and clothes and food for their immediate wants. A school-house was subsequently erected, and masters sent to instruct them through the medium of the Singhalese language; and the experiment so far succeeded, that settlements on the same plan were afterwards formed at other places, the principal being in the Bintenne District, at Oomany and Villengelavelly. The teachers, however, at the first locality misconducted themselves, the neighbouring Kandyans were unfavourable to the measure, and the settlement at Vippam-madoo was eventually broken up, and the Veddahs again dispersed. But the good effects of even this temporary experiment were apparent; not one of the Veddahs returned again to his cave and savage habits, but each built for himself a house of bark, on the plan of the one he had left, and continued to practise the cultivation he had been taught. The other colony at Oomany continues to the present day prosperous and successful; twenty-five families are resident around it; rice and other grains are produced in sufficiency, and coco-nuts are planted near the cottages. The only desertions have been the departures of those in search of employment, who have removed to other villages in quest of it. The school was closed in 1847, owing to there being no more children at the time requiring instruction; but the missionaries have been so successful, that the whole community have professed themselves Christians, and abandoned their addiction to devil dances. Their former appellation, derived from the peculiarity of their habits, can no longer apply, and it may thus be said, that the distinction of the Rock Veddahs has ceased to exist in that part of the country; all having more or less adopted the customs and habits of villagers.

Amongst the Village Veddahs also, the efforts of the Government have been even more successful; their disposition to become settled has been confirmed by permission to cultivate land, and encouraged by presents of tools and seed-grain; and upwards of eighty families were located in villages under the direction of Mr. Atherton. A few refused all offers of permanent settlement, preferring their own wild and wandering life, and casual employment, as watchers or occasional labourers, amongst the Moorish villagers ; but generally speaking, the mass are becoming gradually assimilated in their habits, and intermingled with the ordinary native population of the district.

The third class, the Coast Veddahs, to the amount of about three hundred, have in like manner been signally improved in their condition, by attention to their wants and comforts. They were the last to listen to the invitations, or to avail themselves of the assistance, of Government; at length, in 1844, they came in, expressing the utmost reluctance to abandon the sea-shore and the water, but accepting gladly patches of land, which were cleared for them in the forest, near the beach ; cottages were built, fruit-trees planted, and seed supplied; and they are now concentrated in the beautiful woody headlands around the Bay of Venloos, where they maintain themselves by fishing, or cutting ebony and satin-wood in the forests, to be floated down the river to the Bay. Education has made progress; the Wesleyan Missionaries have been active; the great majority have embraced Christianity, and there can be no reasonable doubt, that within a very few years, the habits of this singular race will be absolutely changed, and their appellation of Veddahs be retained only as a traditionary name.

Formerly the vast tract of forest between the Kandyan mountain and the sea, frequented by these people and known as the Veddah Ratta, or "Country of the Veddahs," was regarded by Europeans with apprehension; excited by the exaggerated representation made by the Kandyans as to the savage disposition of the Veddahs, and none but armed parties ventured to pass through their fastnesses. Of late years, this delusion has been entirely dispelled ; and travellers now feel themselves as safe in the vicinity of the tribes, as in that of the villages of the Singhalese. They are constantly visited by traders in search of deer's-horns and ivory; and the inhabitants of Velassy obtain from their wild neighbours supplies of dried deer's-flesh and honey. The Veddahs themselves have in a great degree cast aside their timidity, and not only come out into the open country with confidence, but even venture into the towns, for such commodities as they have the means of purchasing. The experiment has cost the Government but a few hundred pounds, and I am justified in saying that the expenditure has been well repaid by even the partial reclamation of this harmless race from a state of debasement, scarcely, if at all, elevated above that of the animals which they follow in the chase.

The morning after our arrival at Bintenne, a party of Veddahs about sixty in number, were brought in by the headman to be exhibited before us. It was a melancholy spectacle. We were assured that they were Rock Veddahs, but this I doubted; they were more probably unsettled stragglers from the Veddah villages, with perhaps a few genuine denizens of the forest. But they were miserable objects, active but timid, and athletic though deformed, with large heads and misshapen limbs. Their long black hair and beards fell down to their middle in uncombed lumps, they stood with their faces bent towards the ground, and their restless eyes twinkled upwards with an expression of uneasiness and apprehension. They wore the smallest conceivable patches of dirty cloth about their loins; and were each armed with an iron-headed axe stuck in their girdle, a rude bow about six feet long, strung with twisted bark; and a handful of clumsy arrows feathered with peacock's pinions, and with iron heads about seven inches long, unbarbed, and tapering to a point. At our request they shot at a target, but they exhibited no skill, only one arrow out of three striking the central mark. The truth is, that the

Veddahs are indifferent marksmen, and bring down their game by surprise rather than by adroitness with the bow. If it be only wounded they give chase, and hang upon its track till it falls exhausted or presents an opportunity for repeating the shot. In this way, it is said, that their mode of killing the elephant is by planting an arrow in the spongy substance which forms the sole of his foot, when the shaft breaking short off festers in the wound, and the huge creature eventually becomes their prey through exhaustion and pain. They danced for us, after the exhibition of their archery, shuffling with their feet to a low and plaintive chaunt, and shaking their long hair, till it concealed the upper part of their body; and as they excited themselves with their exercise they uttered shrill cries, jumped in the air, and clung round each other's necks. We were told that the dance generally ended in a kind of frenzy, after which they sunk exhausted on the ground; but the whole scene was so repulsive and humiliating that we could not permit the arrival of this dénouement; and dispersed the party with a present of some silver. They received it without an apparent emotion, and slunk off into the jungle, some few afterwards returning to be hired as coolies to carry our light baggage on towards Batticaloa.

On our route thither we encountered straggling parties of Veddahs at several points of the journey; but they all presented the same characteristics of wretchedness and dejection,—projecting mouths, prominent teeth, flattened noses, stunted stature, and the other evidences of the physical depravity which is the usual consequence of hunger and ignorance. The children were unsightly objects, entirely naked, with misshapen joints, huge heads, and protuberant stomachs;—the women, who were apparently reluctant to appear, were the most repulsive specimens of humanity I have ever seen in any country.

On one occasion we saw the Veddahs perform the operation more frequently read of than witnessed, of kindling a fire by the friction of two dried sticks.[1] For this purpose one of them took his arrow, broke it into two pieces, sharpened the one like a pencil, and made a hole in the other to receive its point. Then placing the latter on the ground, and holding it down firmly with his toes, he whirled the pointed one round in the hole, rolling it rapidly between the palms of his hands. In a few moments it began to smoke, a little charcoal then fell in powder, and presently a spark jumped out, kindled the charcoal dust, and the end was accomplished. The Veddah blew it gently with his breath, lighted a dry leaf by its heat, and piling up small chips and dry twigs upon the flame, raised in a few minutes a cheerful blaze, by which our servants prepared their coffee.

On leaving Bintenne our company divided;—one party, whose object was hunting, turning northward, in search of wild elephants, deer, and smaller game, in pursuit of which they had hitherto met with but indifferent success, because the country was under water, and the natives were deterred from beating the jungle through fear of crocodiles. The other, with the Commissioner of Roads, my son, and myself, kept on a course due east through the forests towards Batticaloa. The richness of the region amongst the low hills which we passed in this direction was quite astonishing; pasture, where the forests became broken, was luxuriant in the extreme; and we rode across long tracts of land adapted in the highest degree for the production of grain, and still showing traces of ancient cultivation, but now solitary and utterly neglected. Satin-wood and ebony were more and more

[1] The wood used for this purpose by the natives of Tahiti is that of *Hibiscus tiliaceus*.—DARWIN, *Nat. Voy.*, ch. xviii.

frequent as we approached the low country; and game and wild animals became abundant in these favourite and undisturbed retreats.

The only road in the direction of the sea was a wide path carried east and west from the shore of the lake at Batticaloa to Teldenia, at the foot of the Badulla Mountains; and on this we occasionally met the tavalams or little caravans of bullock drivers, bringing up commodities of all kinds to the hills of the interior, and carrying down coffee and other produce for sale on the coast. This track is speedily becoming one of great importance, as it connects the coffee districts of the central province with the extensive coco-nut plantations near Batticaloa; and not only is it used for conveying the cotton cloths, rice, salt, and fish from the coast; but in time the coffee crops of Badulla are likely to find their way by it to the sea for shipment, in preference to traversing the circuitous and much more costly route through Kandy to Colombo.

On the lower slopes of the hills where they gradually sink into the plain, the pasture in the open parks or *talawas* is of the most luxuriant description. From the vast herds of deer and wild buffaloes which frequent them, there can be little doubt that they would be well suited for rearing horses and cattle; but, unfortunately, this is a pursuit for which the Kandyans have no inclination, and of which they possess no experience, horses being seldom employed by them for any purpose; and black cattle only kept to supply bullocks for tillage and transport. Milk they never use, the calves enjoying it unstinted; and the prejudice is universal, that the cows would die were it otherwise disposed of.

Approaching Batticaloa we exchanged these luxuriant pastures and wooded park-like landscapes for swampy marshes, overgrown with brushwood and literally swarming with leeches; and finally, on coming within a few miles of the sea, we rode across a wide sandy plain only partially cultivated, which extended as far as the eye could reach. Far on its eastern verge, the long groves of coco-nut palms are discernible, which fringe the shore, and stretch thirty miles north and south of Batticaloa.

CHAP. IV.

BATTICALOA. — COCO-NUT PLANTATIONS. — STRANGE CUSTOMS. THE "MUSICAL FISH." — THE SALT LAKES.

A remarkable peculiarity characterises the division of the island in which the fort of Batticaloa is situated, and, in fact, nearly the whole eastern section of Ceylon. The coast and in-lying country, for two hundred miles from north to south, and from ten to thirty miles inland, is a flat alluvial plain, sandy but verdant, in the immediate vicinity of the shore, and covered with jungle and forest as it recedes towards the interior. Across this a number of rivers of greater or less magnitude flow into the sea, some branching from the Mahawelli-ganga, and others issuing from the tanks and broken reservoirs in the depths of the forest. Owing to the permeable and unresisting nature of the soil, these streams have repeatedly changed their course, when swollen by the tropical rains, or obstructed by the falling in of their banks; and as the level nature of the country permits their abandoned channels to retain water, these have become still lakes communicating with the original river, and thus a network of navigable canals has been spread over the entire surface of the district. Their banks are covered with mangroves, growing to the height of fifty feet, and the water ebbs and flows beneath their roots, which rise in innumerable arches above its surface. When the tide is low and the sands uncovered, quantities of shellfish peculiar to brackish water are found collected under the mangrove roots, or crawling over the damp slopes; and in particular two varieties of

Cerithium[1] are equally remarkable for their size and the activity of their motions.

With the exception of the sea-line, this part of the coast has not been minutely surveyed, nor have these singular and solitary inlets ever been thoroughly explored. Their navigation is only known to the natives, who find their way through devious passages by noting particular trees, or by other landmarks known to them, but too indistinct to serve as guides to the unpractised eye of a European. When gliding noiselessly in a canoe, nothing can be more striking than the sensation caused by turning unexpectedly into one of these quiet and unfrequented openings, where dense foliage lines each side and almost meets above the water. The trees are covered with birds of gorgeous plumage; pea-fowl sun themselves on the branches, and snowy egrets and azure kingfishers station themselves lower down to watch the fish, which frequent these undisturbed pools in prodigious numbers. The silence and stillness of these places is quite remarkable; the mournful cry of the water-fowl is heard from an incredible distance; and the plash of a crocodile as he plunges into the stream, or the surprise of a deer when, disturbed at his morning draught, he

> "Stamps with all his hoofs together,
> Listens with one foot uplifted,"

and breaks away to conceal himself in the jungle, cause an instant commotion amongst the fishing birds and cranes; they rise heavily on their unwieldy wings, and betake themselves to the highest trees, where they wait for the intruder's departure to resume their patient watch upon the mangroves.

In the immediate vicinity of Batticaloa the country is but partially wooded, and the fort and town are built on an island in one of those singular estuaries, where the confluence of several streams has formed a lake some thirty or forty miles long, though scarcely

---

[1] C. telescopium, C. palustre.

more than one or two in breadth. At its southern extremity this narrow inlet penetrates a marshy and almost submerged country, covered with bulrushes and lotus. Here water-fowl are found in astonishing numbers and of infinite variety, their haunts being seldom disturbed by a sportsman, and so unfrequented as to be entirely out of the ordinary route of travellers.

The little islet in the lake on which the fort stands is called by the natives Poeliantivoe, the "island of tamarinds;" and its approach from the land side is extremely picturesque, thick groves of coco-nut palms forming an impervious shade above the white houses of the town, each of which is surrounded by a garden of fruit trees and flowering shrubs. A few hundred yards beyond the landing place, we emerged from a green lane upon the esplanade, with the old Dutch fortress in front, beyond which we caught glimpses of the Bay of Bengal, through the forest of palms.

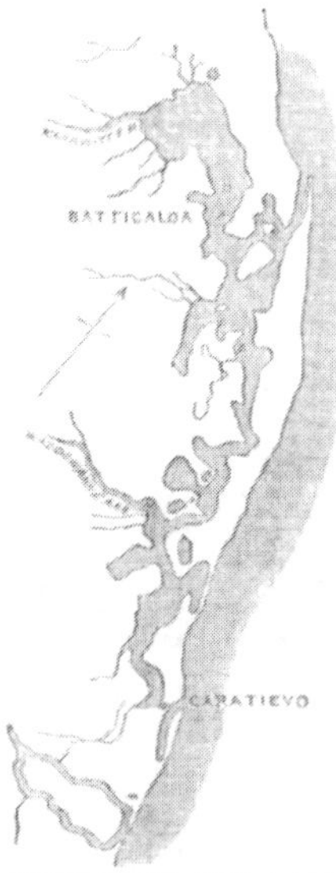

The line of coast north and south of Batticaloa presents a remarkable example of the great sandy formations elsewhere described[1], resulting from the conjoint action of the rivers and the ocean currents. It is nearly thirty miles in length with a breadth of little more than a mile and a half, and separates the sea from the still waters of the lagoon.

This natural embankment is covered from one extremity to the other with plantations of coco-nut trees, many of them of very ancient growth, the peculiar adaptation of the soil having been discovered at an early period by the Moors, whose descendants have settled

---

[1] See *ante*, Vol. I. Pt. I. ch. i. p. 45.

themselves in a dense colony at this favourite spot. The success of the cultivation, the remarkable luxuriance of the trees, and the unusual weight and richness of the fruit, attracted the attention of European speculators, and the entire line of coast for sixteen miles north of Batticaloa, and for twenty-seven miles to the south, is now one continuous garden of palms, pre-eminent for beauty and luxuriance. One unripe nut was brought to me weighing fifteen pounds, and of these a tree in full bearing produces annually from one hundred and twenty to one hundred and fifty, equal to a ton of fruit from a single coco-palm in the course of a year. Such is their excellence that the nuts of this district are sold for 3*l.* a thousand, whilst those on the south-western side of the island do not bring more than two-thirds of this price.

The natives ascribe this superiority to the combination of advantages to be found at Batticaloa,—a soil sandy and pervious, a profusion of water from the fresh lake on the one side, and the sea on the other; a saline atmosphere caused by the constant tossing of the spray on the adjacent shore, a warm and genial sun and timely rains during both monsoons; as the proximity of this district to the Kandyan mountains secures for it an equable and plenteous supply.

The peninsula of Jaffna competes with Batticaloa in this species of cultivation. Each locality has facilities peculiar to itself, but whilst Jaffna has the advantage in population and labour, I am disposed to believe that Batticaloa enjoys peculiarities of climate and position, that entitle it to the preference; but the experiment now in progress at both is so recent as to render it premature to hazard an opinion as to comparative results.

In the meantime the energy with which the enterprise has been urged forward at Batticaloa, has given a remarkable impulse to the activity and prosperity of the district;—the tonnage of the port doubled within a few years; the former postal communication by the circuitous route of Kandy and Trincomalie was found inadequate to the wants of the planters; and new roads and canals have been eagerly projected to connect their estates with the interior, and furnish the requisite facilities for the conveyance of stores and the transport of produce.

The Moors are almost the only section of the native population who divide this valuable culture with the English. They have numerous and flourishing villages throughout the district, and almost monopolise the trade of Batticaloa, exporting ebony, satin-wood and timber, and introducing cotton goods and brass-ware from the Coromandel coast. Their dhoneys ply between Ceylon and the French possessions at Pondicherry and Karical, and they export rice and Indian corn to Colombo, and deer's-horns and wax to Point de Galle, collecting the latter from the Veddahs in barter for coco-nuts and salt. They are likewise manufacturers, and employ the Tamils in the village of Arrapatoo in weaving cotton twist, imported from India, into a coarse kind of damask, which is in such demand that the supply is insufficient even for the consumption of Colombo.

Far less frequented by Singhalese and Europeans than any other portion of Ceylon, the Eastern Province has retained many ancient habits, and presents more frequent instances of curious social peculiarities than are to be noticed in the rest of the island. In the western extremity of the province adjoining Bintenne, a custom prevails, and has acquired the recognition of law, whereby nephews by the sister's side succeed to the inheritance to the exclusion of the possessor's sons. This anomalous arrangement is observed in various parts of India, in Sylhet and Kachar, in Canara, and amongst the Nairs in the south of the Dekkan.[1]

[1] "The Nairs are the military caste in Malabar; with them the custom on marriage is for a woman not to leave her mother's house, or even to consort with her husband. It is his duty to provide her with food,

The guardianship of the sacred island of Ramiseram is vested in a chief of the tribe of *Byragees*, who is always devoted to celibacy, the succession being perpetuated in the line of his sister. Traces of the same custom are to be found amongst some of the African tribes, and even among the North American Indians, the Hurons and the Natchez, preferring the female to the male line, and setting aside the claims of the direct heir in favour of the son of a sister.[1]

The Singhalese kings frequently married their sisters[2]; and the natives explain the usage by a legend to the effect that one of their kings being directed by an oracle to sacrifice a male child of the blood royal in order to thwart the malice of a demon who nightly destroyed the bund of a tank in process of construction, his queen refused to surrender one of her children; on which his sister voluntarily devoted her own boy to death, and the king, in honour of her patriotism, declared that nephews were ever after to be entitled to the succession in preference to sons.

Feudal service prevails in its amplest details in this singular district. For example, the country around Amblantorre, to the west of Batticaloa, is rich in paddi-land, the whole of which is claimed by the chief of the district "the Vanniah of Manmone." According to the custom of the country, he directs its cultivation by the villagers; they acknowledge his authority, and, so long as they live on the land, devote their whole time and labour to his service, receiving in return a di-

---

clothing, and ornaments, but he is not recognised as father of her children, and indeed usually is not so, for temporary wedlock is allowed to her with anyone, provided he be of equal or higher caste to herself. On the death of her mother the wedded Nairine lives with her brothers, and in consequence of this strange ordinance a man's heirs are not his own children, but the children of his sister. * * The family of the Zamorin of Calicut (the reigning prince of Malabar when the Portuguese arrived) belonged to the Nair caste, and among his descendants to the present day "the eldest son of the eldest sister always succeeds to the vacant musnud."—Sir E. PERRY'S *Bird's-eye-view of India*, ch. xiv. p. 84; *Asiatic Researches*, vol. v. p. 12; BUCHANAN'S *Mysore*, vol. ii. p. 412; *Asiat. Soc. Journ. Bengal*, vol. ix. p. 834.

[1] HUMBOLDT, *Personal Nar.* ch. xxvi.

[2] VALENTYN, *Oud en Nieuw Oost-Indien*, ch. iv. p. 63.

vision of the grain, a share of milk from his cattle, and the certainty of support in periods of famine and distress. Their houses, gardens, and wells, though built, planted, and dug by themselves, are the property of the chief, who alone can dispose of them. According to the report of Mr. Atherton, the government agent of the district, these serfs, whilst they live on the land, are bound to perform every service for the lord of the soil, without pay; "they fence his gardens, cover his houses, carry his baggage, perform the work of coolies in balams [1], fish for him, act as his messengers; and, when absent from his village, they must provide food for himself and his servants. They may, in fact, be called his slaves except that they are at liberty to quit his service for that of another chief when they choose. But as they seldom do change, it may safely be presumed that they are contented with the arrangement, and their healthy and pleasant faces sufficiently prove that they are well fed and happy."

The ancient organisation for rice-cultivation, known as the "*village system*," exists in undiminished vigour throughout the Eastern province;—during the unoccupied portion of the year, between the two rice harvests, the villagers enjoy an interval of absolute idleness and ease; but on the arrival of the proper season to resume their tillage, the whole community recommence labour simultaneously. The chief of the district supplies tools, hatchets, cattle, and seed grain; the people repair the dams and channels which lead the water through the rice ground; plough it, tramp the mud, sow and fence it, and complete the work by their joint labour. One portion (generally one-eighth) is cultivated exclusively for the lord of the soil. Together with a tithe of the remainder, he gets a share for the services and labour of the cattle, and deducts the seed grain advanced by him, with an increase of 50 per cent. The residue of the harvest is then divided into conventional

[1] Canoes.

shares amongst the villagers and their hereditary officers, including the doctor, schoolmaster, tomtom-beater, barber, and washerman.[1]

The two latter individuals are the most important functionaries in the little community; they operate for all, but receive no remuneration except their periodical share of the rice crop. In addition to their peculiar professional duties, the barber and the washer are the official witnesses to every legal conveyance and deed; and every marriage and important ceremony must be solemnised in their presence, in order to ensure testimony to its validity. In Ceylon, as in India generally, even the poorest natives never wash their own linen, and that duty has devolved immemorially on the washer caste of the community. But, in addition to these services, the headman of the washers has entrusted to him the duty of preparing apartments for the reception of visitors of distinction, which it is the custom to hang with white cloths. In every village where we rested during our journeys, a house was thus garnished for us, the walls and ceilings having been covered previously to our arrival with white cloths, borrowed from the villagers for the occasion. These cloths it is a part of the washer's duty to keep or collect for every ceremonial observance; such as a wedding, a feast, or the arrival in the village of strangers or persons in authority, on whose departure they are taken down by him to be bleached and returned to their respective owners.

In this oriental custom of the "honours of the white cloth" as it exists at the present day in Ceylon, may

[1] Out of the community of interest thus engendered throughout the district arose another curious practice which still prevails in some parts of the province. The care of the fences and watercourses is entrusted by sections to every field servant interested in the crop, and to secure their faithful performance of this duty it is customary for the villagers to elect one of themselves as an overseer, with power to inspect every portion of the work, and by common consent to inflict corporal punishment in case of neglect, the delinquent being compelled at the division of the harvest to pay to this functionary a proportion of his own share as *remuneration for his trouble in whipping him.*

be discerned the origin of the "hangings" of which the room-paper of modern times is but a recent imitation. The introduction of tapestry was one of the refinements which followed the return of the Crusaders (a fact indicated by the term *tapis Sarrazinois* [1]), and in Europe, as in India, its first use was to conceal the rude earth-work and stones which formed the walls of every apartment; and to impart unusual splendour on the occasion of festivities or royal receptions.[2]

Two circumstances serve to establish the identity of practice in the western hemisphere with that which still prevails in the East; the painted and embroidered pieces which in Europe adorned the walls upon occasions of ceremony were not exclusively appropriated to that purpose, but, like the πέπλος of the Greeks, were worn as shawls by their wealthy proprietors, just as the cloths which the Singhalese and Tamils suspend in honour of their guests, and spread upon the foot-paths to receive them, form portions of the ordinary apparel of their owners. Æschylus represents Agamemnon as rejecting the "garments" εἵματα, that Clytemnestra had directed to be spread on his path to welcome him on his return from Troy.[3] Plutarch mentions that when Cato left the Macedonian army, the soldiers laid down their cloths for him to walk on; and the more solemn illustration will suggest itself of the multitude, who "spread their garments on the way" to welcome the Saviour to Jerusalem. The other point of similarity is that in Europe, as in Ceylon, these highly prized articles were not fixtures on the walls [4],

---

[1] JUBINAL, *Recherches sur l'usage des Tapisseries, &c.*, p. 16.

[2] "Non seulement elles servirent alors pour tendre les appartemens et faire disparaître leur nudité, mais on les employa surtout dans les occasions solennelles; par exemple, aux entrées des princes, à donner une physionomie joyeuse aux villes et aux places publiques."—*Ibid.*, p. 20.

[3] ÆSCHYLUS, *Agam.*, v. 896.

[4] In the *Transactions of the Kilkenny Archæological Society* are documents showing that the tapestries belonging to the Ormonde family were carried from house to house as the earls removed from one of their residences to another. Vol. ii. p. 8.

but were taken down and stored away on the departure of the individual in honour of whose arrival they had been hung up.

After leaving the rice grounds in the vicinity of Bintenne, and passing through the long extent of uninhabited forest which lies to the eastward of them, where for thirty miles no human dwelling meets the eye on any side, the first symptoms of life and activity which we encountered were the "natties" or patches of what is called "Chena" cultivation[1], scattered through the woods as we drew nearer to Batticaloa. Large spaces in the forest of two and three hundred acres suddenly appeared cleared of the timber, and enclosed by rustic fences, with a few temporary huts run up in the centre, and all the surrounding area divided into patches of Indian corn, coracan, gram, and dry paddi: with plots of esculents and curry stuffs of every variety, onions, chillies, yams, cassava, and sweet potatoes; whilst cotton plants, more or less advanced to maturity, are scattered throughout the whole space which had been brought into cultivation.

The process of Chena cultivation in this province is uniform and simple. The forest being felled, burned, cleared, and fenced, each individual's share is distinguished by marks, huts are erected for the several families, and in September the land is planted with Indian corn and pumpkins; and melon seeds are sown, and cassava plants put down round the enclosure. In December, the Indian corn is pulled in the cob and carried to market; and the ground is re-sown with millet and other kinds of grain, chillies, sweet potatoes, sugar-cane, hemp, yams, and other vegetables, over which an unwearied watch is kept up till March and April, when all is gathered and carried off. But as the cotton plants, which are put in at the same time

[1] The custom of "Chena" farms is of extreme antiquity in Ceylon. It is alluded to in the *Mahawanso*, B.C. 161, ch. xxiii. p. 140.

with the small grain, and other articles that form the second crop after the Indian corn has been pulled, require two years to come to maturity; one party is left behind to tend and gather, whilst their companions move forward into the forest to commence the process of felling the trees, and forming another Chena farm.

The Chena cultivation lasts but for two years in any one locality. It is undertaken by a company of speculators under a license from the government agent of the district, and a single crop of grain having been secured and sufficient time allowed for the ripening and collection of the cotton, the whole enclosure is abandoned and permitted to return to jungle, the adventurers moving onward to clear a fresh Chena elsewhere, and take a crop off some other enclosure, to be in turn abandoned like the first; as in this province no Chena is considered worth the labour of a second cultivation until after an interval of fifteen years from the first harvest.

During the period of cultivation great numbers resort to the forests, comfortable huts are built; poultry is reared, thread spun, and chatties and other earthenware vessels are made and fired; and by this primitive mode of life, which has attractions much superior to the monotonous cultivation of a coco-nut garden or an ancestral paddi farm, numbers of the population find the means of support. It likewise suits the fancy of those who feel repugnant to labour for hire, but begrudge no toil upon any spot of earth which they can call their own; where they can choose their own hours for work and follow their own impulses to rest and idleness. It is impossible to deny that this system tends to encourage the natives in their predilection for a restless and unsettled life, and that it therefore militates against their attaching themselves to fixed pursuits, through which the interests of the whole community would eventually be advanced. It likewise leads to the destruction of large tracts of forest land, which, after conversion to Chena, are unprofitable for a long series of years; but, on the other hand, it is equally evident that the custom tends materially to augment the food of the district (especially during periods of drought); to sustain the wages of labour, and to prevent an undue increase in the market value of the first necessaries of life. Regarding it in this light, and looking to the prodigious extent of forest land in the island, of which the Chena cultivation affects only a minute and unsaleable portion, it is a prevalent and plausible supposition, in which, however, I am little disposed to acquiesce, that the advantages are sufficient to counterbalance the disadvantages of the system.

The old Dutch fort of Batticaloa is a grim little quadrangular stronghold, with a battery at each angle connected by a loop-holed wall, and surrounded by a ditch swarming with crocodiles. The interior of the square is surrounded by soldiers' quarters, and encloses a house for the commandant, a bomb-proof magazine, and, the invariable accompaniment of every Dutch fortification, a church of the most Calvinistic simplicity.

In the fifteenth century, Batticaloa (which was formerly called by the Tamils *Maticaloa*, from *Mada-kalappoo*, the "muddy lake") was a fief of the kingdom of Kandy, held by one of the chiefs of the Wanny[1]; and on a branch of the Natoor river there are still to be seen the remains of a stone bridge which led to a palace of the "Vanichee," or queen of the district.[2]

The Portuguese, whose jurisdiction at Batticaloa, did not extend beyond the island of Poeliantivoe, built the

[1] PORCACCHI, in his *Isolario*, published at Padua in 1570, gives a strange account of the inhabitants of "Batech," which from the context would appear to mean Batticaloa. He describes them as being perpetually at war with their neighbours, eating the flesh of their prisoners, and selling their scalps at high prices: "di maniera che volendo comprare alcuna mercantia, danno due ò piu teste all' incontro secondo il valore: et chi ha più teste in casa è riputato il piu ricco."—P. 188. This information he got from the Moors, but it applies with truth to no tribe in Ceylon.

[2] VALENTYN, *Oud en Nieuw Oost-Indien*, ch. xv. p. 223.

fort in 1627 in violation of their treaty with the emperor.[1] This was the first spot on which "the Hollander" secured a footing in Ceylon, when afterwards invited by the king of Kandy to assist him against the insolence and tyranny of the Portuguese. In 1638, the Dutch admiral arrived from Batavia with a flotilla of six ships of war; and, according to the historian of the defeated party, the Portuguese Fort was so ill situated for defence and the walls so unsubstantial, that in a very few days a breach was made by the artillery, two bastions were overthrown, the garrison capitulated, and not one stone was left on another.[2]

On the esplanade in front of the government house there are the remains of what had formerly been a Dutch garden, with a reservoir in the centre, abounding with tortoises[3] and small fish. Contrary to the usual habits of the kingfisher[4], which is fond of lonely places, where it can pursue its prey unmolested, large numbers of these beautiful creatures sat all day long on the branches above the water, perfectly undisturbed and indifferent to our presence, allowing us at all times to approach within a few yards of them.

The lagoon of Batticaloa, and indeed all the still waters of this district, are remarkable for the numbers and prodigious size of the crocodiles which infest them. Their teeth are sometimes so large that the natives mount them with silver lids and use them for boxes to carry the powdered chunam, which they chew with the betel leaf. On the morning after our arrival a crocodile was caught within a few yards of the government agent's residence, where a hook had been laid the night before, baited with the entrails of a goat, and made fast, in the native fashion, by a bunch of fine cords, which the

---

[1] See *ante*, Vol. I. Pt. VI. ch. ii. p. 40; RIBEYRO, lib. ii. ch. i. p. 189; VALENTYN, *Oud en Nieuw Oost-Indien*, ch. x. p. 118.

[2] RIBEYRO, lib. ii. ch. vi. p. 227.

[3] *Emys Sebæ*, and *Emyda Ceylonensis*, the "Ibba" and "Kiri-ibba" of the Singhalese.

[4] *Halcyon Capensis*.

creature cannot gnaw asunder as he would a solid rope, since they sink into the spaces between his teeth. The one taken was small, being only about ten or eleven feet in length, whereas they are frequently killed from fifteen to nineteen feet long. As long as he was in the water, he made strong resistance to being hauled on shore, carrying the canoe out into the deep channel, and occasionally raising his head above the water, and clashing his jaws together menacingly. This action has a horrid sound, as the crocodile has no fleshy lips, and he brings his teeth and the bones of his mouth together with a loud crash, like the clank of two pieces of hard wood. After playing him a little, the boatmen drew him to land, and when once fairly on the shore all his courage and energy seemed suddenly to desert him. He tried once or twice to regain the water, but at last lay motionless and perfectly helpless on the sand. It was no easy matter to kill him; a rifle ball sent diagonally through his breast had little or no effect, and even when the shot had been repeated more than once, he was as lively as ever. He feigned death and lay motionless, with his eyes closed, but, on being pricked with a spear, he suddenly regained all his activity. He was at last finished by a harpoon and then opened. His maw contained several small tortoises, and a quantity of broken bricks and gravel, taken medicinally, to promote digestion, which in these creatures is said to be so slow, that the natives assert that the crocodile, from choice, never swallows his prey when fresh, but conceals it under a bank till far advanced in putrefaction.

During our journeys we had numerous opportunities of observing the habits of these hideous creatures, and I am far from considering them so formidable as is usually supposed. They are evidently not wantonly destructive; they act only under the influence of hunger, and even then their motions on land are awkward and ungainly, their action timid, and their whole demeanour devoid of the sagacity and courage which characterise other animals of prey.

On the occasion of another visit which I made to Batticaloa, in September, 1848, I made some inquiries relative to a story which had reached me of musical sounds, said to be heard issuing from the bottom of the lake, at several places, both above and below the ferry opposite the old Dutch Fort; and which the natives suppose to proceed from some fish peculiar to the locality. The report was confirmed to me in all its particulars, and one of the spots whence the sounds proceed was pointed out between the pier and a rock which intersects the channel, two or three hundred yards to the eastward. They were said to be heard at night, and most distinctly when the moon was nearest the full, and they were described as resembling the faint sweet notes of an Æolian harp. I sent for some of the fishermen, who said they were perfectly aware of the fact, and that their fathers had always known of the existence of the musical sounds heard, they said, at the spot alluded to, but only during the dry season, and they cease when the lake is swollen by the freshes after the rain. They believed them to proceed from a shell, which is known by the Tamil name of (*oorie coolooroo cradoo*, or) the "crying shell," a name in which the sound seems to have been adopted as an echo of the sense. I sent them in search of the shell, and they returned bringing me some living specimens of different shells, chiefly *littorina* and *cerithium*.[1]

[1] *Littorina lævis. Cerithium palustre.* Of the latter the specimens brought to me were dwarfed and solid, exhibiting in this particular the usual peculiarities that distinguish (1.) shells inhabiting a rocky locality from (2.) their congeners in a sandy bottom. Their longitudinal development was less, with greater breadth, and increased strength and weight.

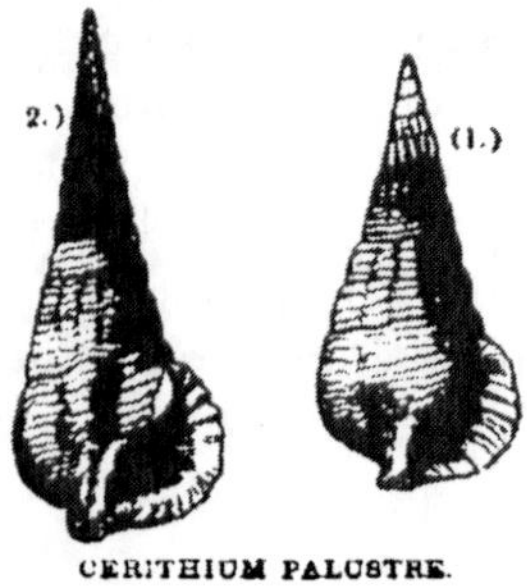

CERITHIUM PALUSTRE.

In the evening when the moon had risen, I took a boat and accompanied the fishermen to the spot. We rowed about two hundred yards north-east of the jetty by the fort gate; there was not a breath of wind, nor a ripple except that caused by the dip of our oars; and on coming to the point mentioned, I distinctly heard the sounds in question. They came up from the water like the gentle thrills of a musical chord, or the faint vibrations of a wine-glass when its rim is rubbed by a wet finger. It was not one sustained note, but a multitude of tiny sounds, each clear and distinct in itself; the sweetest treble mingling with the lowest bass. On applying the ear to the woodwork of the boat, the vibration was greatly increased in volume by conduction. The sounds varied considerably at different points, as we moved across the lake, as if the number of the animals from which they proceeded was greatest in particular spots; and occasionally we rowed out of hearing of them altogether, until on returning to the original locality the sounds were at once renewed.

This fact seems to indicate that the cause of the sounds, whatever they may be, are stationary at several points; and this agrees with the statement of the natives, that they are produced by mollusca, and not by fish. They came evidently and sensibly from the depth of the lake, and there was nothing in the surrounding circumstances to support a conjecture that they could be the reverberation of noises made by insects on the shore, conveyed along the surface of the water; for they were loudest and most distinct at those points where the nature of the land, and the intervention of the fort and its buildings, forbade the possibility of this kind of conduction.

Sounds somewhat similar are heard under water at some places on the western coast of India, especially in the harbour of Bombay. At Caldera, in Chili, musical cadences are stated to issue from the sea near the landing place; they are described as rising and falling fully four notes, resembling the tones of harp strings, and mingling like those at Batticaloa, till they produce a musical discord of great delicacy and sweetness. The animals from which they proceed have not been identified at either place, and the mystery remains unsolved, whether those at Batticaloa are given forth by fishes or by molluscs.

Certain fishes are known to utter sounds when removed from the water[1], and some are capable of making noises when under it[2]; but all the circumstances connected with the sounds which I heard at Batticaloa are unfavourable to the conjecture, that they were produced by either.

Organs of hearing have been clearly ascertained to exist, not only in fishes[3], but in mollusca. In an oyster the presence of an acoustic apparatus of the simplest possible construction has been established by the discoveries of Siebold[4], and from our knowledge of the reciprocal relations existing between the faculties of hearing and of producing sounds, the ascertained existence of the one

---

[1] The Cuckoo Gurnard (*Triglia cuculus*) and the maigre (*Sciæna aquila*) utter sounds when taken out of the water (YARRELL, vol. i. p. 44, 107); and herrings when the net has just been drawn have been observed to do the same. This effect has been attributed to the escape of air from the air bladder, but no air bladder has been found in the *Cottus*, which makes a similar noise.

[2] The fishermen assert that a fish about five inches in length, found in the lake at Colombo, and called by them "*magoora*," makes a grunt when disturbed under water. PALLEGOIX, in his account of Siam, speaks of a fish resembling a sole, but of brilliant colouring with black spots, which the natives call the "dog's tongue," that attaches itself to the bottom of a boat, "et fait entendre un bruit tres-sonore et même harmonieux."—Tom. i. p. 194. A *Silurus*, found in the Rio Parana, and called the "armado," is remarkable for a harsh grating noise when caught by hook or line, and which can be distinctly heard when the fish is beneath the water."—DARWIN, *Nat. Journ.* ch. vii. Aristotle and Ælian were aware of the existence of this faculty in some of the fishes of the Mediterranean. ARISTOTLE, *De Animal.*, lib. iv. ch. ix.; ÆLIAN, *De Nat. Anim.*, lib. x. ch. xi.; see also PLINY, lib. ix. ch. vii., lib. xi. ch.cxiii.; ATHENÆUS, lib. vii. ch. iii. vi.

[3] AGASSIZ, *Comparative Physiology*, sec. ii. 158.

[4] It consists of two round vesicles containing fluid, and crystalline or elliptical calcareous particles or otolites, remarkable for their oscillatory action in the living or recently killed animal. OWEN'S *Lectures on the Comparative Anatomy and Physiology of the Invertebrate Animals*, 1855, p. 511-552.

might afford legitimate grounds for inferring the co-existence of the other in animals of the same class.

Besides, it has been clearly established, that one at least of the gasteropoda is furnished with the power of producing sounds. Dr. Grant, in 1826, communicated to the Edinburgh Philosophical Society the fact, that on placing some specimens of the *Tritonia arborescens* in a glass vessel filled with sea water, his attention was attracted by a noise which he ascertained to proceed from these mollusca. It resembled the "clink" of a steel wire on the side of the jar, one stroke only being given at a time, and repeated at short intervals.[1]

The affinity of structure between the *Tritonia* and the mollusca inhabiting the shells brought to me at Batticaloa, might justify the belief of the natives of Ceylon, that the latter are the authors of the sounds I heard; and the description of those emitted by the former as given by Dr. Grant, so nearly resemble them that I have always regretted my inability, on the occasion of my visits to Batticaloa, to investigate the subject more narrowly. At subsequent periods I have renewed my efforts, but without success, to obtain specimens or observations of the habits of the living mollusca.

The only species afterwards sent to me were *Cerithia*; but no vigilance sufficed to catch the desired sounds, and I still hesitate to accept the dictum of the fishermen, as the same mollusc abounds in all the other brackish estuaries on the coast; and it would be singular, if true, that the phenomenon of its uttering a musical note should be confined to a single spot in the lagoon of Batticaloa.[2]

On leaving Batticaloa we had to encounter still more of the inconveniences to which travellers in Ceylon are

---

[1] *Edinburgh Philosophical Journ.*, vol. xiv. p. 188.

[2] A letter which I received from Dr. Grant on this subject, I have placed in a note to the present chapter, in the hope that it may stimulate some other inquirer in Ceylon to prosecute the investigation which I was unable to carry out successfully.

exposed. The route before us was wild and inhospitable in the extreme, traversed by innumerable inlets and rivers, and leading across long extents of salt marshes and unhealthy swamps. Our foot runners, worn out by their recent journey, deserted in numbers, regardless alike of threats of punishment and temptations of reward. We had the utmost difficulty in hiring grass-cutters and coolies to carry our provisions and baggage to Trincomalie; and we were obliged to provide and take with us from Batticaloa rice for their food, bread for ourselves, and fodder for our horses.

On the afternoon of the 18th of February we crossed the lake, and took the road northward towards the village of Eraoor, through a rich country lined the whole way with coco-nut plantations on our right hand, and on the left abounding with large tracts of rice-ground, carefully cultivated, and plentifully irrigated from an arm of the lagoon, which here forms a broad canal, connecting Batticaloa with the populous district of Eraoor. To the west, and far in the distance, were the remarkably-shaped mountains of the Friar's Hood, and Gunner's Quoin, rising abruptly above the forests of the Wanny.

Eraoor is a Moorish village, and one of the largest in the district. Its inhabitants are chiefly agriculturists, though the manufacture of cotton cloth is conducted on a small scale; but the principal occupation of the section of its population not engaged in cultivation, is as drivers of tavalams into the interior; carrying coco-nuts, salt, and brass-ware from the coast, in order to change these commodities for areca-nuts, deer's horns, and wax.

The Moors of Eraoor were celebrated for their courage and address in the capture of wild elephants, so long as these were in demand for the courts of the Indian princes. Of late years, however, the demand has almost ceased; though, at the time of our visit, a vakeel was at Jaffna in search of elephants for the Raja of Sattara.

The Panickeas, or elephant hunters of Eraoor, use no arms or apparatus of any kind, except a noosed rope, with which they steal upon the elephant when at rest ; and whilst one of the party provokes him in front till he puts himself in motion, another slips the noose over his foot as he raises it behind, and at once brings him up by taking a turn of the rope round the nearest tree. Formerly, in passing through the villages, it was customary to see two or three elephants so captured, and made fast to stakes near the houses of the panickeas, to await the arrival of purchasers. Now the only employment of hunters is the occasional search after buffaloes, that break away from the village to join the wild herds in the marshes and jungles, where they are followed and brought back by these stealthy pursuers.

The first great river which we crossed, north of Batticaloa, was the Natoor, which discharges itself into the sea, at the beautiful Bay of Venloos. We rowed down it from Chittandy in a double canoe, formed of two hollowed trees laid side by side, joined by a platform, and covered with an awning of white cloth. Its stream is wide and rapid, studded with numerous fertile islands, and is navigable for a considerable distance westward ; but its course has never been thoroughly explored by Europeans. Numbers of the Coast Veddahs have recently settled in the forests near its mouth, and are now engaged as fishermen in the bay, each of the families cultivating a little patch of rice near his own dwelling.

The scenery round Venloos Bay is charming. The sea is overhung by gentle acclivities wooded to the summit; and in an opening between two of these the river flows through a cluster of little islands covered with mangroves and acacias. A bar of rocks projects across it, at a short distance from the shore ; and these are frequented all day long by pelicans, that come at sunrise to fish, and at evening return to their solitary breeding-places remote from the sea. The strand is literally covered with beautiful shells in endless varieties; and, in the course of our very short visit, we added largely to our collections. The shell-dealers from Trincomalie derive their principal supplies from Venloos, and know the proper season to visit it for each particular variety; but the entire coast, as far north as the Elephant Pass, is indented by little rocky inlets, where shells of every description may be collected in great abundance.

This trade is exclusively in the hands of the Moors, who clean the shells with great expertness, arrange them in satin-wood boxes, and send them to Colombo and all parts of the island for sale. In general, the specimens are more prized for their beauty than valued for their rarity, though some of the "Argus" cowries [1] have been sold as high as *four guineas* a pair.

Our elephants and horses swam the river about a mile from the sea, and after a tedious and wearisome day's journey, we pitched our tents in a marsh beside the salt lake of Panetjen-Kerny. Before reaching our camp for the night, I rowed for five miles in a canoe, up one of the solitary inlets of the Natoor, between forests of mangroves, and landed near the ruins of the ancient stone bridge, called "Vanattey Palam," that tradition says led to the residence of the Wanninchee, or ancient queen of the Wanny, the ruins of which are still visible in the jungle. The bridge had been constructed of single stones; and huge squared pillars still stand in the middle of the stream, supporting transverse pieces of prodigious dimensions, evidently designed to carry a wooden platform as the roadway.

Our course towards Panetjen-Kerny had lain through one continuous marsh, frequently some inches under

---

[1] *Cypræa Argus.*

water, and poched by wild elephants into deep holes, that rendered riding dangerous. It was covered with myriads of wild fowl—flamingoes, white paddy birds, wild ducks, curlews, snipe, and a varied multitude of others.

The salt lake, or leway of Panetjen-Kerny, is a very remarkable spot. Tradition says that it was once the site of a royal residence; the district surrounding it having been submerged by irruptions of the sea, which never thoroughly retired, but left behind the present lake, and the vast saline marshes from which the whole district now derives its supply of salt. The leway itself is six miles in length by three broad, and is capable of yielding ten thousand bushels of salt in the season for collection. It is a wild and desolate spot, and exhibits apparent traces of some such calamity as the legend records.

The country retains more or less the same dreary character from the Natoor river to the Vergel, the branch of the Mahawelli-ganga before alluded to [1], which here separates the revenue district of Batticaloa from that of Trincomalie. As we approached towards the north, the forests became more frequent; but where we crossed the Vergel the river traverses a rich alluvial plain, cultivated with rice, and studded occasionally with prosperous villages. This stream is one of the deepest and most dangerous in Ceylon, and the soil through which it flows being loose and alluvial, it has hollowed out its channel to such a depth, that the banks stand high, and almost perpendicular on either side, so that we were obliged to cut a sloping pathway, down which our horses scrambled to pass the stream.

Our elephants were reluctant to cross; and our horses, equally frightened at the rapidity of its current, required some violence to force them down the bank, and as they swam with difficulty after the canoe, two

---

[1] See Vol. II. Part IX. ch. ii. p. 424.

crocodiles kept close to them all the time, and were only deterred from attacking them by some balls from a rifle.

A river so impetuous, and flowing through a level country, is subject to sudden inundations arising from the fall of the rains in the hills of the interior. Some years ago, a military officer and his lady, proceeding to Trincomalie, were detained by a rise of the Vergel river, that overflowed the adjacent village, and drove the inhabitants to take refuge on a neighbouring rock, till the waters subsided. Contrary to expectation, the rains, instead of ceasing, increased; the whole country, far and wide, was laid under water; and a fortnight elapsed ere the party were enabled to descend and pursue their journey.

The mouths of the Vergel, before it empties itself into the sea, form a delta called Arnitivoe, or the "island of elephants," on which we passed the night in a rest-house, on the northern bank. A wide and shallow tank, close by the place where we halted, is a favourite haunt of these animals, from which the place takes its name; and the ground near it showed abundant evidences of their recent resort, being poched into deep holes in every direction by their feet. A gentleman assured me that, on one occasion, at this spot, he counted two hundred elephants in one group, and that others were hidden by the jungle. We were unfortunate in seeing none; but the evening after we had passed, a herd of sixty came close beside the rest-house, and were seen by some travellers, quietly browsing there till the morning.

As yet, no public roads exist in this portion of the island; for the path frequented by the tappal runners is a mere track along the sea-coast, obliterated by every rise of a river, or overflow of a salt marsh. When the time arrives for constructing a highway, to connect the two eastern ports of Trincomalie and Batticaloa, it will be expedient to carry the road further inland, so as to cross the great rivers before they branch off into arms and deltas; rendering one bridge sufficient instead of many; whilst the streams thus avoided, and the innumerable inlets and bays, into which they diverge in all directions, will afford facilities for canal navigation at a trifling expense, such as will add to the value of local produce, by facilitating the traffic between the interior and the coast.

The night before reaching Trincomalie, we passed in tents under a tope of tamarind trees, close by the tank of Topoor. The night-scene in such a position is solemnly impressive. The sky is so "cloudless, clear, and beautiful," that the very starlight casts a shadow, and the constellation of the "Southern Cross" awakens the solemn consciousness of a new home in another hemisphere.[1] The camp-followers gather in groups round the watch-fires, the horses picketed beside them, and the elephants stand apart under the trees, lazily fanning themselves with branches to drive off the tormenting mosquitoes. Throughout these solitudes, absolute silence never reigns; the hoarse voice of the tank-frogs resounds from a distance, and close at hand is heard the incessant metallic chirp of the hyla, the shrill call and answer of the tree-cricket, and the hum of the myriad insects, which keep up their murmurs from sunset to dawn. Within, the stillness of the tent is disturbed by the flutter of the night moths, or its gloom is startled by the entrance of the fire-fly, that dashes around in circles, alternately kindling and concealing its brilliancy; and then suddenly departing, leaves all in darkness as before. At length,

> "Night wanes,
> The mists around the mountains curled
> Melt into morn; and light awakes the world."

At Cottiar, on the following morning, we halted by

---

[1] Já descoberto tinhamos diante
Lá no novo hemispherio nova estrella
Naõ vista de outra gente, etc.
CAMOENS, *Lusiada*, ch. v. s. xiv.

the identical tamarind tree, under which two centuries before Captain Robert Knox, the gentlest of historians and the meekest of captives, was betrayed by the Kandyans, and thence carried into their hills; to be detained an inoffensive prisoner from boyhood to grey hairs. But to that captivity we are indebted for the most faithful and life-like portraiture that was ever drawn of a semi-civilised, but remarkable people.

Cottiar, or Koetjar (as it is called, in the old Dutch maps of Ceylon), was a place of importance in the sixteenth and seventeenth centuries; when it carried on an active trade with the coast of India, whilst Trincomalie, notwithstanding its magnificent bay, was then comparatively insignificant. It was this circumstance, and the consequent facilities which it afforded for repairs, that in 1659 induced Knox, the father of the good old chronicler, to resort to Cottiar, in order to refit his dismasted ship, when he, and his son, and his ship's company, were seized and consigned to their long captivity, by the order of Raja Singha II.

In 1612, the Dutch, by the treaty negotiated by Buschouwer, obtained permission from the Emperor of Kandy to erect a fort at Cottiar, "provided the King of Cottiarum may enjoy his customs and other revenues;"[1] and in 1675, they had constantly from eighty to one hundred ships, bringing clothes and other wares from Coromandel, to be bartered for areca-nuts, palmyra sugar, and timber.[2] The country surrounding it was then full of villages; rich in arable and pasture lands; producing large quantities of rice for exportation, and importing merchandise annually to the value of one hundred thousand pagodas. But within less than a century, the whole aspect of the place was changed; the Dutch abandoned their fort; trade

[1] BALDÆUS, ch. x. p. 616; VALENTYN, *Oud en Nieuw Oost-Indien*, ch. ix. p. 112.

[2] VALENTYN, ch. xv. p. 221.

deserted the harbour; the town fell to ruin, and the Governor of Trincomalie, writing in 1786 (the Dutch having resumed possession of the district about twenty years before), described the region as an uncultivated solitude, and the people as savages, "with hardly anything of human nature, but its outward form;"—and strongly recommended that an effort should be made to colonise Cottiar with labourers from China or Java.[1] To the present day, the district remains thinly populated; the village itself is chiefly inhabited by fishers, and the only tolerable building is the old rest-house, apparently of the time of the Dutch.

At Cottiar I was struck with the prodigious size of the edible oysters, which were brought to us at the rest-house. The shell of one of these measured a little more than eleven inches in length, by half as many in breadth: thus unexpectedly attesting the correctness of one of the stories related by the historians of Alexander's expedition, that in India they had found oysters a foot long.[2]

We found the government barge awaiting us at the mouth of the river, and after a sail of an hour and a half across the magnificent bay of Trincomalie, we passed the batteries of Fort Ostenburg, and landed in the inner harbour on the seventeenth day from leaving Kandy.

---

[1] *Journal of* FABRICIUS VAN SENDEN, A.D. 1786.

[2] "In Indico mari Alexandri rerum auctores pedalia inveniri prodidere."—PLIN., *Nat. Hist.*, lib. xxxii. ch. 31. DARWIN says, that amongst the fossils of Patagonia, he found "a massive gigantic oyster, sometimes even a foot in diameter."—*Nat. Voy.*, ch. viii.

NOTE.

TRITONIA ARBORESCENS.

THE following is the letter of Dr. Grant, referred to at page 471: —

Sir, — I have perused with much interest, your remarkable communication received yesterday, respecting the musical sounds which you heard proceeding from under water, on the east coast of Ceylon. I cannot parallel the phenomenon you witnessed at Batticaloa, as produced by marine animals, with anything with which my past experience has made me acquainted in marine zoology. Excepting the faint clink of the *Tritonia arborescens*, repeated only once every minute or two, and apparently produced by the mouth armed with two dense horny laminæ, I am not aware of any sounds produced in the sea by branchiated invertebrata. It is to be regretted that in the memorandum you have not mentioned your observations on the living specimens brought you by the sailors as the animals which produced the sounds. Your authentication of the hitherto unknown fact, would probably lead to the discovery of the same phenomenon in other common accessible paludinæ, and other allied branchiated animals, and to the solution of a problem, which is still to me a mystery, even regarding the *tritonia*.

My two living *tritonia*, contained in a large clear colourless glass cylinder, filled with pure sea water, and placed on the central table of the Wernerian Natural History Society of Edinburgh, around which many members were sitting, continued to clink audibly within the distance of twelve feet during the whole meeting. These small animals were individually not half the size of the last joint of my little finger. What effect the mellow sounds of millions of these, covering the shallow bottom of a tranquil estuary, in the silence of night, might produce, I can scarcely conjecture.

In the absence of your authentication, and of all geological explanation of the continuous sounds, and of all source of fallacy from the hum and buzz of living creatures in the air or on the land, or swimming on the waters, I must say that I should be inclined to seek for the source of sounds so audible as those you describe rather among the pulmonated vertebrata, which swarm in the depths of these seas—as fishes, serpents (of which my friend Dr. Cantor has described about twelve species he found in the Bay of Bengal), turtles, palmated birds, pinnipedous and cetaceous mammalia, &c.

The publication of your memorandum in its present form, though not quite satisfactory, will, I think, be eminently calculated to excite useful inquiry into a neglected and curious part of the economy of nature.

I remain, Sir,

Yours most respectfully,

ROBERT E. GRANT.

Sir J. Emerson Tennent, &c. &c.

CHAP. V.

TRINCOMALIE.—THE EBONY FORESTS.—THE GREAT TANK OF PADIVIL.—CROCODILES.

THE Bay of Trincomalie presents to the eye a scene of singular beauty. Landlocked, and still as an inland lake, its broad expanse of waters, its numerous beautiful islands, and its rocky headlands, together with the

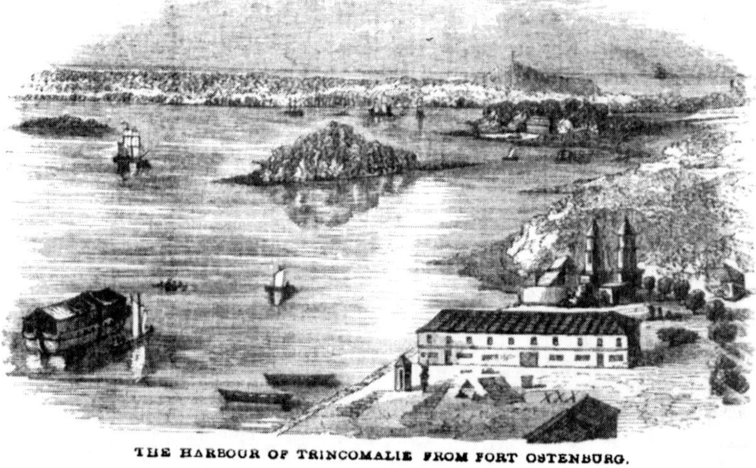

THE HARBOUR OF TRINCOMALIE FROM FORT OSTENBURG.

woody acclivities in its vicinity, and the towering mountains in the distance, combine to form an oriental Windermere.[1]

[1] The position and beauty of the Bay of Trincomalie, the overhanging rocks at its entrance, the stillness of the expanse within, and the luxuriance of the wooded acclivities surrounding all, forcibly recall VIRGIL'S imaginary description of the harbour of Carthage—

Est in secessu longo locus: insula portum
Efficit objectu laterum quibus omnis ab alto
Frangitur inque sinus scindit sese unda reductos.
Hinc atque hinc vastæ rupes geminique minantur
In cœlum scopuli; quorum sub vertice late
Æquora tuta silent:—sum sylvis scæna coruscis,
Desuper horrentique atrum nemus imminet umbra.

ÆNEID, lib. i. 95, etc.

The town is built on the neck of a bold peninsula, which stretches between the inner and outer harbours, rising, at its southern extremity, into lofty precipices covered to their summits with luxuriant forests; and is strengthened, at the narrow entrance of the inner harbour, by the batteries of Fort Ostenburg, rising one above another for the defence of the port and arsenal. A huge rock to seaward has been surmounted by the works of Fort Frederick; but it is commanded from the adjacent heights; and being situated three miles to the northward of the dock-yard and the mouth of the inner harbour, it protects only the outer anchorage, and is available solely as a *point d'appui*. Even now, and notwithstanding their extent, the military works are utterly incommensurate with the importance of the position, and would be found ineffectual for its protection in the event of attack.

Trincomalie, though a place of great antiquity, derived its ancient renown less from political than from religious associations. The Malabar invaders appear to have adopted it as the site of one of their most celebrated shrines; and a pagoda which stood upon the lofty cliff, now known as the "Saamy Rock," and included within the fortifications of Fort Frederick, was the resort of pilgrims from all parts of India. With this edifice, which is still spoken of as the "Temple of a Thousand Columns," is connected one of the most graceful of the Tamil legends. An oracle had declared, that over the dominions of one of the kings of the Dekkan impended a peril, which was only to be averted by the sacrifice of his infant daughter; who was, in consequence, committed to the sea in an ark of sandal wood. The child was wafted to the coast of Ceylon, and landed south of Trincomalie, at a place still known by the name of Pannoa[1], or the "smiling infant,"

[1] The districts at the southern extremity of Batticaloa, *Pannoa*, and *Panaham*, are so called from the two Tamil words "*palen-nagai*," the smiling babe.

where, being adopted by the king of the district, she succeeded to his dominions. Meantime, a Hindu prince, having ascertained from the Puranas that the rock of Trincomalie was a holy fragment of the golden mountain of Meru, hurled into its present site during a conflict of the gods, repaired to Ceylon, and erected upon it a temple to Siva. The princess, hearing of his arrival, sent an army to expel him, but concluded the war by accepting him as her husband; and in order to endow the pagoda which he had built, she attached to it the vast rice-fields of Tamblegam, and formed the great tank of Kandelai, or Gan-talawa [1], for the purpose of irrigating the surrounding plain. In process of time, the princess died, and the king, retiring to the Saamy Rock, shut himself up in the pagoda, and was found translated into a golden lotus on the altar of Siva.

In the earlier portion of their career in Ceylon, the Portuguese showed the utmost indifference to the possession of Trincomalie; but after the appearance of the Dutch on this coast, and the conclusion of an alliance between them and the Emperor of Kandy, Constantine de Saa, in 1622, alarmed at the possibility of these dangerous rivals forming establishments in the island, took possession of the two ports of Batticaloa and Trincomalie, and ruthlessly demolished the "Temple of a Thousand Columns," in order to employ its materials in fortifying the heights on which it stood.[2] Some of the idols were rescued from this desecration, and conveyed to the pagoda of Tamblegam [3]; but fragments of

---

[1] This, of course, is erroneous, the tank having been formed by King Maha Sen between A.D. 275–301. — *Mahawanso*, ch. xxxiii. p. 238. The *Ceylon Government Gazette*, for Nov. 1831, contains the translation of a metrical legend written by KAVI RAJA VAROTHAYEN, an ancient Tamil bard of Ceylon, who says that the temple was built by Kulak' Kotu Maharaja, son of a king of Coromandel; who also reclaimed the surrounding lands for the support of the priests.

[2] VALENTYN, *Oud en Nieuw Oost-Indien, &c.*, ch. xvi. p. 367; RIBEYRO, tom. ii. ch. i. p. 188.

[3] *Journal of* VAN SENDEN, Governor of Trincomalie, A.D. 1786.

carved stone-work and slabs bearing inscriptions[1] in ancient characters, are still to be discerned in the walls of the fort, and on the platforms for the guns.

The site of this sacrilege is still held in the profoundest veneration by the Hindus. Once in each year[2], a procession, attended by crowds of devotees, who bring offerings of fruits and flowers, repairs, at sunset, to the spot where the rock projects four hundred feet above the ocean; — a series of ceremonies is performed, including the mysterious breaking of a coco-nut against the cliff; and the officiating Brahman concludes his invocation by elevating a brazen censer above his head filled with inflammable materials, the light of which, as they burn, is reflected far over the sea.

The promontory sustains a monument of later times, with which a story of touching interest is associated. The daughter of a gentleman of rank in the civil service of Holland, was betrothed to an officer, who repudiated the engagement; and his period of foreign service having expired, he embarked for Europe. But as the ship passed the precipice, the forsaken girl flung herself from the sacred rock into the sea; and a pillar, with an inscription now nearly obliterated[3], recalls the fate of this eastern Sappho, and records the date of the catastrophe.

Shortly after the rupture between Louis XIV. and the United Provinces in 1672, the French Admiral de la Haye took possession of Trincomalie. The Dutch in their panic abandoned the fort, as well as those of Cottiar and Batticaloa; but the French, having laid waste the surrounding country, were unable to provision their fleet, and were forced to retire from their conquest.[4]

They renewed the attempt in 1782, when Admiral

---

[1] Facsimiles of three of these inscriptions will be found in the *Journ. Asiat. Soc. Bengal,* vol. v. p. 550, 556.

[2] On the 23rd January.

[3] "TOT GEDACTENIS VAN FRANCINA VAN REEDE LUF * * MYDREGT DESEN A°,1687 24 APRIL OPGEREGT."

[4] VALENTYN, *Oud en Nieuw Oost-Indien,* ch. xv. p. 256.

the Bailli de Suffrein, in the absence of the British commander, compelled the English garrison to withdraw to Madras, and took possession of the fort; but in the following year, it was restored to the Dutch, by whom it was held till the capture of Ceylon by Great Britain in 1795.[1]

The condition of neglect and insecurity which Trincomalie exhibits at the present day, is painfully irreconcilable with the terms of exultation with which its capture was originally announced to the nation. Then it was extolled, as the sole harbour of refuge to the east of Cape Comorin, Bombay being the only capacious port on the west coast of Hindustan; and projects were in contemplation, to render it the grand emporium of Oriental commerce, the Gibraltar of India, and the arsenal of the East. Remembering these exciting assurances, and contemplating the capabilities presented by the locality for their utmost realisation; an extreme feeling of disappointment is excited now by looking upon its incomplete fortifications, its neglected works, and its reduced military establishments — utterly unequal to any emergency. These render Trincomalie as insecure at the present day as it was unprepared in the last century for the assaults of Suffrein and De la Haye.[2]

With all its natural advantages the country immediately around the bay is deserted; the native population, with the exception of the Moors, are poor and unenterprising; and the town is consequently dependent on Jaffna, Batticaloa, and the coast of India for its supplies of rice, fruits, curry-stuffs and coco-nuts; which the facility of water-carriage renders cheap and abundant.

---

[1] See *ante*, Vol. II. Pt. VI. ch. iii. p. 66.

[2] The appreciation of the harbour of Trincomalie as "le meilleur port, sans contredit, de cette partie de l'Asie;" and the surprise excited by its neglect, are forcibly expressed by LAPLACE, *Circumnavigation de l'Artemise*, tom. ii. ch. viii. p. 157.

The constant residence of the civil authorities of the province, the presence of the military, and the occasional visits of the squadron under the naval commander-in-chief, are the main circumstances to which Trincomalie is indebted for whatever measure of prosperity it enjoys.

With the exception of the official buildings, the town is poorly constructed, and the bazaars the least inviting in Ceylon. There are a number of Hindu temples, with the usual paraphernalia of idols and cars, for religious festivals and processions; but these are in such barbarous taste as to stifle interest and repel curiosity.

On comparing this magnificent bay with the open and unsheltered roadstead of Colombo, and the dangerous and incommodious harbour of Galle, it excites an emotion of surprise and regret that any other than Trincomalie should ever have been selected as the seat of government and the commercial capital of Ceylon. But the adoption of Colombo by the Portuguese, and its retention by the Dutch, were not matters of deliberation or choice. Its selection was determined solely by the accident of its proximity to the only district of the island which produced the precious cinnamon, which, as Baldæus quaintly observes, has always been "the Helen or bride of contest," whose exclusive possession was disputed in turn by every European invader.

The Portuguese constructed the fort of Colombo to control the petty princes of the interior, and enable their officers to exact their annual tribute of the precious spice; in their eagerness for which the productions or capabilities of all the rest of Ceylon were disregarded. On the same principle, the policy of the Dutch was exclusively directed to secure this grand monopoly; and, as they prohibited trade from all hands other than their own, they never even dreamed of considering what port might be the most advantageous for external commerce; or best calculated to encourage industry and promote the internal prosperity of the Singhalese.[1]

For years after the occupation of Ceylon by the British, the new conquerors were influenced by the same motives as their predecessors; and their plantations of cinnamon were guarded as the only sources of income. For the security of these valuable possessions of the crown, it had become indispensable to retain the residence of the Governor in their immediate vicinity; and hence the continued retention of Colombo as the capital of the colony.

Within recent years, however, the circumstances of the island have materially altered. Cinnamon has not only ceased to be a Government monopoly, but it has ceased to be productive to the revenue, even as an article of general export. Instead of one pampered object of cultivation engrossing all care and influencing all policy, other interests, not local or exclusive, but popular and universal, have grown up in every part of the island, demanding an equal share of encouragement, and advancing an equal claim to public attention. Hence the question of the position most suitable, conventionally as well as geographically, for the seat of government, and the centre of trade and its operations, has been already mooted and warmly discussed in Ceylon.[2]

At some distance from the sea, the soil in the neighbourhood of Colombo is of the poorest and least productive description, a stiff unyielding clay, with a slight admixture of vegetable mould on the surface, capable of bearing rice, but only after frequent fallows, and with the most laborious cultivation, for the maintenance of which the supply of water is by no means abundant. On the other hand, throughout the country to the west of Trincomalie, the soil, except in the imme-

[1] See VALENTYN, *Oud en Nieuw Oost-Indien*, ch. xii. p. 149; ch. xiii. p. 165.

[2] Sir H. G. WARD'S *Minute on the Eastern Province*, 1856.

diate vicinity of the sea, is rich and productive, and the numerous rivers which flow eastward from the mountain zone afford the amplest facilities for the cultivation of every species of produce; and the forests abound with an exhaustless supply of timber available either for local consumption or for foreign export. On the western side of the island, the land has been cultivated for an indefinite period uninterruptedly, and to such an extent that it now exhibits symptoms of exhaustion. Besides which, its eager occupation and minute subdivision amongst innumerable small cultivators, and its unsuitability for the production of more than a very limited number of articles, serve to show that over population has been added to the other evils of poverty of soil and deficiency of capital. On the eastern coast, on the contrary, cultivation has been so long suspended that everything wears the aspect of a new country, presenting not only a ready outlet for the overcrowded or impoverished population of other districts, but capable of affording increased facilities and advantages for the general benefit of the island.

As a harbour, Trincomalie is renowned for its extent and security; but its peculiar superiority over every other in the Indian seas consists in its perfect accessibility to every description of craft in every variation of weather. It can be entered with equal facility and safety in the north-east as in the south-west monsoon, and the water within is so deep that vessels can lie close to the beach, and discharge or receive cargo without the intervention of boats. Its geographical position has already caused its adoption as the most favourable point for a naval rendezvous and dock-yard; whence instructions and intelligence can be most rapidly communicated to the various forces in the eastern seas. Regarding Ceylon at the present moment as the centre of all operations for postal communications with Madras and Calcutta, the Straits settlements, China, and Australia, as well as with the

French, Dutch, and Spanish possessions in the East, the insufficiency and defects of Point de Galle as a harbour, are so evident, as to render it idle to institute a comparative inquiry into the manifest advantages offered by Trincomalie. The unrivalled position of the latter for commerce, fronting the Bay of Bengal, and presenting a natural point of rendezvous and departure for all vessels trading to India and the East, marks it out as having been destined for a great emporium, to which vessels of all nations will yet find it their interest to resort.

To the natives great and lasting benefits would accrue from the adoption of Trincomalie as the commercial capital of Ceylon. Cultivation would be restored to the now deserted districts of Tamankadua and the Wanny; and an immediate impulse would be applied to increase labour and employment of every kind. Above all, such a step would secure to the planters the advantage of having their produce shipped in a commodious harbour, where vessels can lie and receive their lading alongside the wharves at all seasons of the year; instead of having it carried in boats, as at present, a distance of a mile or more in the open roadstead of Colombo, to be put on board in the offing;—an operation that can only be performed with safety during one period of the year, when the wind blows off the shore; and even then it is beset by accidents, often involving the damage of the coffee by sea-water, or its discolourment by damp.

The measure for transferring the seat of government and trade from Colombo to Trincomalie, will encounter opposition from those already in possession of commercial establishments on the western coast, who may naturally hesitate to exchange ascertained facilities for contingent advantages in another locality. A grave obstacle too is said to exist in the circumstance, that the rains are usually prevalent at Trincomalie at the particular season when coffee requires to be dried at the shipping place, preparatory to embarcation. But even were the latter objection uniformly existent, (which is far from being the case,) its inconveniences would soon be obviated by improvements in the process of drying, by the construction of more suitable buildings, and by greatly increased facilities of transport.

The project may at present be premature, and its realisation remote, but it is one which the changing circumstances of the colony is rendering year by year more obvious and imminent; and the growing conviction of its utility in the minds of the planting and agricultural community, by far the most influential in Ceylon, will eventually overcome the scruples and hesitation of the mercantile body.

The once fertile plains of Tamblegam are now a shallow lake, some twenty miles in circumference, communicating with the western side of the Bay of Trincomalie. The natives have a tradition which accords with the legend, before adverted to, that at no remote period the bottom of this lake was one broad expanse of paddi-fields, irrigated by a canal from the enormous tank at Kandelai, twenty-four miles to the westward. But the tank was permitted to fall into ruin; and the waters, escaping in a torrent, converted their ordinary outlet into an impetuous river, which speedily overflowed the plains below, and burst open an entrance for the sea, which, once admitted, ever since has continued to hold possession. An examination of the locality confirms, to some extent, the possible truth of this tradition. The remains of the great tank are still in fine preservation, and could be readily restored; but the waters issuing from the broken bund, although partially applied to cultivation, flow almost neglected through the lagoon of Tamblegam.[1]

The Tamblegam lake itself is chiefly valuable for its

---

[1] *Report of* Dr. KELAART, Oct. 1857.

fish. It produces in singular perfection the thin transparent oyster (*Placuna placenta*), whose clear white shells are used, in China and elsewhere, as a substitute for window glass. They are also collected annually for the sake of the diminutive pearls contained in them, and these are exported to the coast of India, to be burned into a species of lime, which the more luxurious princes affect to chew with their betel. So prolific are the mollusca of the *Placuna*, that the quantity taken by the licensed renter in the three years prior to 1858, could not have been less than eighteen millions.[1] They delight in brackish water, and on more than one recent occasion, an excess of either salt water or fresh has proved fatal to great numbers of them.

The forest approaches so close to the town that the vicinity of Trincomalie is often visited by wild animals. In one of my evening drives on the high road, in the direction of Nillavelli, the passage was obstructed by a herd of wild elephants, and the carriage had to halt whilst the horse-keepers drove them into the jungle. Leopards frequently approach the town[2], and monkeys[3] are so numerous, as to be a pest in the gardens. Their method of approach was described to me by a gentleman, whose grounds they frequently visited. A green sward separated his garden from the jungle, and across this a single monkey would cautiously steal about twenty paces, and halt to assure himself, by eye and ear, that all was safe. Presently a second would venture out from the trees, pass in front of the first, and squat himself, after making another reconnaissance. A third, and possibly a fourth, would thus stealthily ap-

[1] *Report of* Dr. KELAART, Oct. 1857.

[2] A belief is prevalent at Trincomalie that a Bengal tiger inhabits the jungle in its vicinity; and the story runs that it escaped from the wreck of a vessel on which it had been embarked for England. Officers of the Government state positively that they have more than once come on it whilst hunting; and one gentleman of the Royal Engineers who had seen it, assured me that he could not be mistaken as to its being a tiger of India, and one of the largest description.

[3] *Presbytes cephalopterus. P. Priamus.*

proach, always gaining an advance beyond the last vidette; and finally the whole body, having ascertained the absence of danger, advanced hastily but noiselessly to the enclosure; and having with infinite rapidity secured a sufficient supply of fruit, the troop dispersed simultaneously, with a rush and an exulting scamper, conscious that caution was no longer essential.

After a rest of a few days at Trincomalie, to recruit our foot-runners and coolies, we resumed our course towards the north. My design was to keep the line of the sea-coast as far as Lake Kokelai, and having made the circuit of it, then to turn westward into the great central forest of the Wanny, in order to reach the ruins of the tank, at Padivil, the largest as well as the most perfect of those ancient and gigantic works in Ceylon. Afterwards, returning eastward again to the coast at Moeletivoe it was my intention to proceed to the north of the island, in order to visit the Peninsula of Jaffna.

The country to be traversed in this route presents, so far as regards the sea-coast, many features similar to those which characterise the region we had passed after leaving Batticaloa; with the exception, that rivers occur less frequently and are less dangerous. The salt formations cease a few miles north of Trincomalie, and the inhospitable swamps and marshes that lie between the Mahawelli-ganga and the sea, farther to the south, are exchanged for the rich pastures and rice grounds of the Wanny, which occur at intervals in the openings of the forests. The population of the interior is so scattered and meagre, that no cultivation is carried on beyond the minimum requisite for the bare sustenance of the locality, and the only occupation which brings the dwellers in this region into contact with strangers, is the felling of timber in the forests, to be floated down the rivers to the coast.

The parties engaged in this business lead a wandering life, which is not without its attractions; less lucrative perhaps than the wild existence of the lumberers of North America, but infinitely more enjoyable and exciting. The timber-cutters of Ceylon obtain a licence from the government agent, and having formed themselves into companies, betake themselves at the proper season to those parts of the forest where ebony and cabinet woods are known to abound in sufficiently close proximity to water to ensure their easy transport when felled. In our morning and evening rides through the woods, before and after sunset, we frequently came upon these wandering parties, each with a bullock-cart to carry their axes, cooking utensils, and rice; and followed by hired assistants. They were either setting out on an excursion of two or three months into the interior, or returning after having felled the intended quantity of timber, leaving it to be floated down the rivers, and brought round by sea to Trincomalie. There was always an air of gaiety and recklessness about all the parties I met, very characteristic of their unrestrained and roving habits. The warmth of the climate renders them indifferent to clothing; they cook and eat beneath the shade of the forest; sleep under the open sky, with a watchfire to keep off the wild animals; and by sunrise their axes are echoing through the solitary woods.

Ebony is the most important of the trees which they are in the habit of felling, as well as the one involving the greatest amount of labour, from the hardness and weight of the timber, which is so dense and heavy, that, to permit of their moving it at all, they are obliged to cut it into very short logs. The densely black portion, which is an article of commerce, occupies the centre of the tree; and in order to reach it, the whiter wood that surrounds it is carefully cut away. The Arabs were so well aware of this peculiarity in ebony, that Albyrouni, in his treatise on India[1], calls it the

[1] ALBYROUNI, in REINAUD'S *Fragm. Arabes*, vol. i. p. 124. Ebony was so prized by the Romans, that PLINY says Pompey had it carried in his triumph after the defeat of Mithridates.—*Nat. Hist.* lib. xii. cap. ix.

"black marrow of a tree, divested of its outer integuments."

Besides ebony and satin-wood, one of the most valuable of the trees in these forests is the iron-wood (the *Na-gaha* of the Singhalese[1]), the name being expressive of its intense solidity and duration. It is always planted as an ornament near the temples, not only because of the loveliness of its broad, violet-perfumed flowers, the outer leaves of which are white and their centres a deep maroon, but also because of the gracefulness of its shape, the dark polished green of its foliage, and the brilliant red of its young leaves and shoots, which in their season suffuse the surface of the tree with crimson.

The only high road in the direction we were now travelling extended but four miles north of Trincomalie, where it terminated at an unbridged inlet of the sea. Having forded this on horseback, we entered the forest on the opposite side, by an unfinished bridle-path, which conducted us as far as Nillavelli, the great station for the supply of salt to the eastern provinces. Here it is collected from artificial pans, which are capable of yielding, on an exigency, 50,000 bushels in the year; but they are never employed for the preparation of more than half that quantity. The salt of Ceylon is of the purest description, and the capabilities of the island for its production are so great, that, in ordinary seasons, it could satisfy the demand of the whole continent of India. But the policy of the East India Company, and the necessity of creating a revenue from their own resources, has for the present suspended the export from Ceylon.

At Nillavelli the salt-pans extend for about a mile in length, and about one-sixteenth of a mile in breadth, along the margin of a shallow estuary. They vary in size, from forty to sixty feet square, with the depth of about twelve inches, and are formed simply by levelling

---

[1] *Messua ferrea.*

and embanking the clayey soil, which is deeply impregnated by the constant deposit of salt from the overflowing of the sea. This line of the shore is portioned off in strips, the property of different proprietors; and each of these is formed into a succession of pans, varying from five to seven in number, at the discretion of the proprietor. The process of manufacture is simple: the sea-water is raised into one of the pans by means of a wooden scoop swung from a triangle, and having been allowed to rest for a day or two to deposit its sand and earthy particles, it is run off successively into a second and a third reservoir, to complete the process of defecation. By degrees it becomes fitted for the final operation of evaporating the sea-water, which is performed in the remaining pans, in which the brine lies exposed to the intense heat of the sun. The dry crystals of salt are then cautiously collected from the surface of the clay and removed to the Government stores.

A few miles north of Nillavelli, at the village of Coomberapoote, the process is much more simple and expeditious, but the salt is less pure and of proportionately lower value. There it is prepared by merely constructing a dam to prevent the retirement of the sea, which spreads far on the level shore, to the depth of a few inches. In the course of from ten to fourteen days, according to the intensity of the sun, the evaporation is complete, and the salt may be lifted in a thick crust from the surface of the soil. In both cases the rapidity and success of the process is entirely dependent on the heat of the weather, and the collection can only be made about four times in each year, as the occurrence of rain would be fatal to the operation.

A few miles inland from Nillavelli there are two places of interest, one the hot springs, Kannea[1], and the other a nameless spot in the deep solitudes of the

---

[1] An analysis of the water will be found in the *Asiatic Annual Register* for 1800, p. 8; and in the *Account of Ceylon*, by Dr. DAVY, p. 43.

forest, where there have recently been discovered extensive ruins of temples and buildings; and remains of richly carved stone-work; but as to their age or history, the inhabitants possess not the faintest tradition. The hot wells, in addition to their medical qualities, are held sacred in the eyes of the Tamils, from their dedication to Kannea, the mother of Rawana. They are a place of constant resort for the devout, who repair to them on the thirtieth day after the death of their friends, to perform certain funeral rites, and distribute alms and rice amongst the poorer members of their families. The ruins of a temple to Ganesa are still to be traced The masonry and conduits by which the wells are enclosed and the water conducted, were probably the work of the Dutch, who were aware of the hygienic properties of the spring.

We passed the night in the rest-house of Nillavelli, built on the model of one of those substantial edifices, by which "the Hollander" has left a memento of his presence in the maritime districts of Ceylon. This old house is said to have been timbered from the wreck of a ship, stranded on the seashore within gunshot of the village. Thence by Coomberapoote, Cuchavelli, Terrai and Koombanda-mootoo, we made our way to the southern shore of the lake of Kokelai, halfway between Jaffna and Trincomalie. This line of coast is indented at frequent intervals by rocky bays, where the fishermen have established themselves in villages, less with a view to the pursuit of their ordinary calling, than for facility of communication with the smuggling boats that carry on a contraband trade with India; landing cotton, cloth, brass ware, and other articles from the Coromandel coast, which are carried through forest paths to be bartered in the Kandyan country.

The rocks, which run into the sea near these coves are deeply impregnated with iron; and at Cutchavelli in particular, the sand for some miles was as black as coal, bearing at least fifty per cent. of magnetic iron, and reduced to an almost impalpable dust by the continued action of the surf.

Here the shore abounded with shells, amongst others with a species of *Bullia*[1], the inhabitant of which has the faculty of mooring itself firmly by sending down its membraneous foot into the wet sand, where, imbibing the water, this organ expands horizontally into a broad fleshy disc, by which the animal anchors itself, and thus secured, collects its food in the ripple of the waves. On the slightest alarm, the water is discharged, the disc collapses into its original dimensions, and the shell and its inhabitant disappear together beneath the sand.

On the rocks which are washed by the surf there are quantities of the curious little fish, *Salarias alticus*[2], which possesses the faculty of darting along the surface of the water, and running up the wet stones, with the utmost ease and rapidity. By aid of its pectoral and ventral fins and gill-cases, it moves across the damp sand, ascends the roots of the mangroves, and climbs up the smooth face of the rocks in search of flies; adhering so securely as not to be detached by repeated assaults of the waves. These little creatures are so nimble, that it is almost impossible to lay hold of them, as they scramble to the edge, and plunge into the sea on the slightest attempt to molest them. They are from three to four inches in length, and of a dark brown colour, almost indistinguishable from the rocks they frequent.

In the immediate vicinity of the sea, our ride was always sufficiently cool, owing to the prevalence of the north-east monsoon; but inland, the heat was intolerable while passing over the white sandy plains which abound in this district, and are but scantily covered with verdure. To avoid this, we travelled as much as

---

[1] *B. Vittata.*

[2] CUVIER and VALENCIENNES, *Hist. Nat. des Poissons*, tom. xi. p. 249.

possible before sunrise, by far the most interesting hour in these climates for observing the habits of the animals and early birds. Sometimes our horses were frightened by the sudden plunge of a crocodile, as we disturbed him on the sands; but, more frequently, we ourselves were startled in the morning twilight by a deer bounding across our path into cover, or an elephant shuffling out of our way, and trampling down the jungle as he leisurely retired. On one occasion, an hour before sunrise, we rode suddenly into the centre of a herd of wild hogs, at least a hundred in number, that were feeding amongst some clumps of acacias, and gave battle immediately in defence of their young, which the coolies laid hold of without hesitation or pity. Our guns brought down two or three full grown ones, that proved an acceptable feast for our people.

The Lake of Kokelai is a very remarkable spot; like that of Tamblegam, it is about twenty miles in circumference; and, like it, it is believed to have been at one time a rich and fertile plain, in which the cultivation of rice was carried on by means of the enormous reservoir of Padivil, some twenty miles inland; but, by a calamity similar to that which I have before recorded, the sluices became decayed, the embankments of the tank gave way, and the overcharged channels suddenly inundated the plains below, whence the collected waters burst their way into the sea, which, once admitted to enter, has never since been excluded, and now ebbs and flows with every variation of the tide. The bottom of the lake is never wholly dry, but its deepest spots do not much exceed six or seven feet. It is so shallow at all times, that in the south-west monsoon, when the rains are light and the waters low, the surf forms a bar of sand across the entrance, and it ceases for a time to communicate with the sea. Were advantage taken of this peculiarity, the sea might be permanently and effectually kept out; but, in its present condition, the bar disappears with the change of the monsoon, the pent-up waters of the lake again burst open a passage, and the salt water returns to renew and perpetuate barrenness. The woods surrounding the lake abound with pea-fowl and game; and its shores are remarkable for the profusion of wild animals by which they are frequented; herds of buffaloes and deer, wild hogs, jackals, and hares.

On emerging from the forest, we obtained the first sight of the lake, at its south-western extremity, near the little village of Amera-Vayal [1], and rode eastward along the shore to the opening which admits the sea. It was a sultry day, and in the exhalation from the salt-encrusted sand, we witnessed one of the most beautiful instances that I had seen in Ceylon of the Fata Morgana. The water appeared, in the distance, to cover the ground over which we were to pass; and right before us, in its midst, we saw a fairy island of graceful vegetation, and the shadows of its tall trees reflected in the waves of the imaginary lake. A ride of a quarter of an hour dispelled the beautiful deception; without entirely disappearing, the lines and features became fainter as we approached, till they melted into air; but not without leaving a doubt whether a scene so perfect in all its parts could be really an illusion.

The Tamil village of Kokelai is close by the junction of the lake with the sea, and in the vast pastures around it, which are enriched by the proximity of this large sheet of fresh or nearly fresh water, numerous herds of cattle were grazing, the finest and most numerous I had seen in the province. At Kokotodawey we came up with the Government agent of the northern province, Mr. Dyke, whom we found, with five tents and a large suite of followers, encamped close to the

---

[1] Amerawayeliam, in General FRASER's Map.

village; and along with his company, the following morning, we resumed our tour round the north of the lake, completing the circuit at Amera-Vayal, whence we had started two days before.

In order to do this, we had to cross the river flowing out of the great tank of Padivil, by which the lake of Kokelai is formed. The dimensions of this tank may be inferred from the fact, that the stream issuing from its ruins is between two and three hundred feet broad, and so deep and impetuous, that it was with difficulty our horses crossed it in safety. The country along its banks is rich, and would be fertile, but the place is so neglected that herds of wild buffaloes were rolling in the marshes, and elephants are so abundant that the water was still trickling into the footmarks in the sand, which they had left a moment before, having crossed a branch of the river on our approach.

As the immediate vicinity of the great tank is so infested with malaria, as to render it dangerous to pass the night there; we arranged to halt and sleep at a Tamil village about ten miles to the south-west of it, called Liende-hitte-hamelawa. The following day, after inspecting the tank in the morning, we proposed to ride to Koolan-colom, eighteen miles beyond it, and there to rest for the night.

As this plan involved a long day's journey, we started for the tank, from our sleeping-place, by torchlight, some hours before the sun. It was tedious work; the path under the trees being used by the natives only on foot, the branches, thorns, and climbing plants closed overhead so low, that for a great part of the way it was impossible to ride in the gloom, and we were obliged to get down and lead our horses. The direction of the foot-path had nowhere been chosen with a view to the convenience of riders; it ran along the embankments of neglected tanks, and over rocks of gneiss, which occasionally diversify the mountainous level of the forest, and their sloping sides rendered it difficult for horses to retain a secure footing. So little is this country known or frequented by Europeans, that the Odear, or native headman, who acted as our guide to the great tank, told me I was the third white man who had visited it for thirty years.

Owing to the richness of the soil and the abundance of water, the trees were of extraordinary size, especially the species of *Strychnos*, which rose into vast mounds of verdure covered profusely with rich orange fruit. The *palu*, by far the most valuable timber tree of the north, here attains gigantic dimensions, and its topmost branches are the favourite resort of the Buceros, the Indian Toucan.

Before daybreak we entered on the bed of the tank of Padivil, at its south-eastern angle, and proceeded towards the main embankment, a ride which occupied us nearly two hours. The tank itself is the basin of a broad and shallow valley, formed by two lines of low hills, which gradually sink into the plain as they approach towards the sea. The extreme breadth of the enclosed space may be twelve or fourteen miles, narrowing to eleven at the spot where the retaining bund has been constructed across the valley; and when this enormous embankment was in effectual repair, and the reservoir filled by the rains, the water must have been thrown back along the basin of the valley for at least fifteen miles. It is difficult now to determine the precise distances, as the recent overgrowth of wood and jungle has obliterated all lines left by the original level of the lake at its junction with the forest. Even when we rode over it, the centre of the tank was deeply submerged, so that notwithstanding the partial escape, the water still covered an area of ten miles in diameter. Its depth when full must be very considerable, for high on the branches of the trees which grow in the area, the last flood had left quantities of driftwood and withered grass; and the rocks and banks were coated with the yeasty foam, that remains after the subsidence of an agitated flood.

The bed of the tank was difficult to ride over, being still soft and treacherous, although covered everywhere with tall and waving grass; and in every direction it was poched into deep holes by the innumerable elephants that had congregated to roll in the soft mud, to bathe in the collected water, or to luxuriate in the rich herbage, under the cool shade of the trees. The ground, too, was thrown up into hummocks like great mole-hills, which, the natives told us, were formed by a huge earth-worm, common in Ceylon, nearly two feet in length, and as thick as a small snake. Through these inequalities the water was still running off in natural drains towards the great channel in the centre, that conducts it to the broken sluice; and across these it was sometimes difficult to find a safe footing for our horses.

In a lonely spot, towards the very centre of the tank, we came unexpectedly upon an extraordinary scene. A sheet of still water, two or three hundred yards broad, and about half a mile long, was surrounded by a line of tall forest-trees, whose branches stretched above it. The sun had not yet risen, when we perceived some white objects seated in large numbers on the tops of the trees, and as we came nearer we discovered that a vast colony of pelicans had formed their settlement and breeding-place in this solitary retreat. They literally covered the trees in hundreds; and their heavy nests, like those of the swan, constructed of large sticks, formed great platforms, sustained by the horizontal branches. In each nest there were three eggs, rather larger than those of a goose, and the male bird stood patiently beside the female as she sat upon them

Nor was this all; along with the pelicans prodigious numbers of other large water birds had selected this for their dwelling-place, and covered the trees in thousands, standing on the topmost branches: tall flamingoes, herons, egrets, storks, ibises, and other waders. We had disturbed them thus early, before their habitual hour for betaking themselves to the fishing-fields. By degrees, as the light increased, we saw them beginning to move upon the trees; they looked around them on every side, stretched their awkward legs behind them, extended their broad wings, gradually rose in groups, and slowly soared away in the direction of the sea-shore.

The pelicans were apparently later in their movements; they allowed us to approach as near them as the swampy nature of the soil would permit; and even when a gun was discharged amongst them, those only moved off which the particles of shot disturbed. They were in such numbers at this favourite place, that the water over which they had taken up their residence was swarming with crocodiles, attracted by the frequent fall of the young birds; and the natives refused, from fear of them, to wade in for one of the larger pelicans which had fallen, struck by a rifle ball. It was altogether a very remarkable sight.

About seven o'clock we reached our destination, near the great breach in the embankment, having first effected a passage with difficulty over the wide stream, that was flowing towards it from the basin of the tank. The huge bank was concealed from sight by the trees with which it is overgrown, till suddenly we found ourselves at its foot. It is a prodigious work, nearly eleven miles in length, thirty feet broad at the top, about two hundred at the base, upwards of seventy high, and faced throughout its whole extent by layers of squared stone.

The fatal breach through which the waters escape is an ugly chasm, two hundred feet broad, and half as many deep, with the river running slowly below.[1] This

[1] The natives have a tradition that the destruction of the bund was effected by a foreign enemy that landed at Kokelai, and burst the embankment by heating the rock with fire, and quenching it with *acid milk.*

breach affords a good idea of the immense magnitude of the work, as it presents a perfect section of the embankment from summit to base. As we stood upon the verge of it above, we looked down upon the tops of the highest trees; and a pelican's nest, with young birds, was resting on a branch a considerable way below us.

We walked about two miles along the embankment to see one of the sluices, which remains so far entire as to permit its original construction to be clearly understood. From its position, I am of opinion that the breach in the embankment through which the water now escapes was originally the second sluice, which had been carried away by the pressure of the waters at some remote period. The existing sluice is a very remarkable work, not merely from its dimensions, but from the ingenuity and excellence of its workmanship. It is built of layers of hewn stones, varying from six to twelve feet in length, and still exhibiting a sharp edge and every mark of the chisel. These rise into a ponderous wall immediately above the vents which regulated the escape of the water; and each layer of the work is kept in its place by the frequent insertion, endwise, of long plinths of stone, whose extremities project beyond the surface, with a flange to key the several courses, and prevent them from being forced out of their places. The ends of these retaining stones are carved with elephants' heads and other devices, like the extremities of gothic corbels; and numbers of similarly sculptured blocks are lying about in every direction, though the precise nature of the original ornaments is no longer apparent.

About the centre of the great embankment, advantage has been taken of a rock, about two hundred feet high, which has been included in the bund, to give strength to the work. We climbed to the top of this rock. The sun was now high, and the heat intense; for, in addition to the warmth of the day, the stone itself was still glowing from its exposure to many previous suns. It was covered with vegetation, springing vigorously from every handful of earth that had lodged in the interstices of the stone; and, amongst a variety of curious plants, we found the screwed Euphorbia[1], the only specimen of it which I saw in the island. The view from this height was something wonderful—it was, in fact, one of the most memorable scenes I witnessed in Ceylon. Towards the west, the mountains near Anarajapoora were dimly visible in the extreme distance; but between us and the sea, and for miles on all sides, there was scarcely an eminence, and not one half as high as the rock on which we stood. To the farthest verge of the horizon there extended one vast unbroken ocean of verdure, varied only by the tints of the forest, and with no object on which the eye could rest, save here and there a tree a little loftier than the rest, that served to undulate the otherwise uniform surface.

Turning to the side next the tank, its prodigious area lay stretched below us; broken into numerous ponds, and diversified with groves of trees. About half a mile from where we stood, a herd of wild buffaloes were lumbering through the long grass, and rolling in the fresh mud. These, with the birds, and a deer, which came to drink from the watercourse, were the only living creatures to be seen in any direction; but the natives regard the tank and the surrounding jungle as the great breeding-place of most of the wild animals, elks, elephants, and bears.

As to human habitation, the nearest was in the village where we had passed the preceding night; but we were told that a troop of unsettled Veddahs had lately sown some rice on the verge of the reservoir, and taken their departure after securing their little crop. To feed a few wandering outcasts—such is the sole use to which this

---

[1] *Euphorbia tortilis.*

gigantic work is at present subservient; yet its capabilities are so prodigious, that it might be made to fertilise a district equal in extent to an English county.

The solution of the inquiry as to who was the constructor of this mighty monument remains buried in obscurity. So vast is the scale on which it is projected, that it has been conjectured to be the great lake known as "the Sea of Prakrama;"[1] but the investigations of some recent explorers appear to me to have succeeded in establishing the conjecture of Colonel FORBES[2], and in fixing the site of the latter between Dambool and the Amban-ganga.[3] Sir H. G. WARD has ascribed the formation of Padivil to Maha Sen, A.D. 66[4]; but this is erroneous, as Maha Sen did not ascend the throne till A.D. 275, and an inscription of an earlier date on the rock at Mihintala[5], records that the lake of "Pahadewila" was at that period the property of the temple.

On the top of the great embankment itself, and close by the breach, there stands a tall sculptured stone with two engraved compartments, the possible record of its history, but the Odear informed us that "the characters were Nagari, and the dialect Pali, or some other language no longer understood by the people."

The command of labour must have been extraordinary at the time when such a construction was successfully carried out, and the population enormous to whose use

---

[1] See a paper by DE SOYZA MOODLIAR, in the *Journal of the Ceylon Branch of the Asiat. Soc. for* 1856-8, p. 140, in which the author rests his supposition on a passage in the lxviiith chap. of the *Mahawanso*, which relates that Prakrama Bahu, having enlarged the Panda Wapi, or Tank of Panda, gave it the name of the "Sea of Prakrama." *Panda*, De Soyza conjectures, may be identical with Padivil; but if Upham's version be correct, there is a still more striking passage in the lxxviith chap. which states that Prakrama Bahu, among others, repaired the tank of "Padie." Both verses, however, refer only to the repair, and not to the original formation of the tank, which would appear to have taken place nearly a thousand years before.

[2] FORBES' *Eleven Years in Ceylon*, vol. ii. ch. ii. p. 33.

[3] See the *Report of Messrs.* ADAMS, CHURCHILL *and* BAILEY, *on the Ellahara Canal.*

[4] *Minute on the Eastern Province*, 1856, p. 4.

[5] See *Appendix to* TURNOUR'S *Epitome, &c.*, p. 79, 86. The *Mahawanso*, ch. xxxvii. enumerate by name the "sixteen" tanks constructed by Maha Sen, but "Padivil" is not one of them.

it was adapted. The number of cubic yards in the bund is upwards of 17,000,000; and, at the ordinary value of labour in this country, it must have cost 1,300,000*l.*, without including the stone facing on the inner side of the bank. The same sum of money that would be absorbed at the present day in making the embankment of Padivil, would be sufficient to form an English railway, one hundred and twenty miles long, and its completion would occupy 10,000 men for more than five years. Be it remembered, too, that in addition to thirty of these immense reservoirs in Ceylon, there are from five hundred to seven hundred smaller tanks distributed over the face of the country, the majority in ruins, but many still in serviceable order, and all susceptible of effectual restoration.

Having devoted the morning to visiting the several parts of this magnificent ruin, we returned to our tents, which had been pitched at the foot of the great embankment, near the breach through which the current of the waters escaped. Here we were rejoined by Captain Gallwey, and the party of hunters who had separated from us at Bintenne, and who brought us a welcome addition to our larder in the shape of a buck, which they killed on the confines of the great tank. In the afternoon we started for Koolan-colom.

The region in which Padivil is situated is conventionally known by the epithet of the "Wanny."[1] It forms the extreme northern section of the island, immediately adjoining the peninsula of Jaffna, and in the time of the Dutch its southern boundaries were the Aripo river[2] and the Kalu-aar. Of its earlier history no satisfactory record survives, beyond the ascertained fact that, after the withdrawal of the Singha-

---

[1] Two derivations are assigned to this word, one significant of the "*forest*," which covers it to a great extent; the other of the intense "*heat*" which characterises the region.

[2] In the map given by VALENTYN, the Aripo river is called by the Dutch the "Koronda Weya."

lese sovereigns from their northern capitals in the fourteenth century, and the abandonment of their deserted country to the Malabars, the latter, disorganised and distracted in turn, by the ruin they themselves had made, were broken up into small principalities under semi-independent chiefs, and of these the Wanny was one of the last that survived the general decay.

In modern times the Wanny was governed by native princes, styled *Wannyahs*, and occasionally by females with the title of *Wanninchees;* their chiefs professed allegiance and paid tribute to the Malabar rajahs of Jaffna; and later still to the kings of Kandy; but their submission to the latter was ostensible rather than real, and involved scarcely a virtual subjection.

The Portuguese, after the capture of Jaffna-patam, became the nominal sovereigns of the Wanny; but their dominion never extended beyond the sea-coast, and they exercised no actual control over its restless chieftains and their followers. The Dutch, as the successors of Portugal, affected to assert a right of supremacy; but were only enabled to enforce their annual tribute of elephants by a frequent resort to arms.[1] In 1782 these continued conflicts were brought to an apparent issue by a combined and vigorous effort of the Dutch, who routed the forces of the Wannyahs at all points, and reduced their country to at least the outward semblance of submission. It is characteristic of the spirit of this people that the Dutch met nowhere a more determined resistance than from one of the native princesses, the Wanninchee Maria Sembatte, whom they were obliged to carry away prisoner, and to detain in captivity in the fort of Colombo.

For the security of their conquests the Dutch erected a fort at Moeletivoe, on the eastern coast; but the sole

[1] VALENTYN, *Oud en Nieuw Oost-Indien*, ch. iii. p. 40; ch. xiii. p. 172; BALDÆUS, p. 717; KNOX, p. 175.

result of their policy was the impoverishment and desolation of the Wanny, without insuring its thorough subjection. The people, impatient of their presence and control, appear to have abandoned agriculture and peaceful pursuits, and to have betaken themselves to a wild and marauding life, making sudden descents on the cultivated lands on either seaborde of the island, and carrying on a predatory warfare against the Dutch in their settlements at Manaar and Trincomalie. They penetrated even into the peninsula of Jaffna, across the isthmus of which the Dutch were compelled to build a line of small forts, and to loophole the church at Elephant Pass, in order to keep the Wannyahs at bay.

After the transfer of the sovereignty of Ceylon to the British, the excesses and turbulence of this part of the country still continued. In 1803, on the occasion of our first hostilities with the king of Kandy, Pandara Wannyah, an influential chief on the borders of the Neuera-kalawa district, undertook to expel the English from his country, and succeeded in occupying Cottiar, on the bay of Trincomalie. He drove out the garrison at Moeletivoe, and sei ed the fort, which had been left in charge of a British officer and a few Sepoys; — they escaped in a fisher's boat to Jaffna, whilst the insurgents carried away some useless cannon, that still lie buried in a rice-field near the Padivil tank. The attempt was of course followed by no permanent success; the insurgents were speedily dislodged; the forts retaken, and the power of the chiefs of the Wanny was finally and effectually extinguished. Their last descendant and representative was an old lady, who, in 1848, resided near the fort of Jaffna, and enjoyed a small hereditary estate, the remnant of her ancestral possessions.

The result of these intestine wars and calamities consummated the ruin of the Wanny: the cattle, so essential to cultivation, were carried off; the tanks were injured, partly through abandonment, and partly by natural causes — amongst which was a storm, in 1802, during which the waters in the larger lakes were driven so furiously on the bunds, that many of them gave way; and there being no one to repair the damage, it spread so as almost to defy renovation by any means at the command of the local communities. In addition to these calamities, the lawless guerillas of Pandara formed themselves into troops of banditti, and after the suppression of the rebellion infested the province from sea to sea; plundering the villages and solitary hamlets, and carrying away the inhabitants, particularly the women and girls, to be sold as slaves within the territory of the Kandyan king.

Danger thus drove the remnant of the inhabitants from the richer districts of the Wanny, to the poor and sandy soil in the vicinity of the forts on the coast, where they could carry on tillage, and dwell in comparative security; — and the central forests, thus abandoned to solitude, became in a few years so infested and overrun with elephants, that the efforts of the Government were directed to their destruction, as cultivation, when the people had courage to resume it, was rendered impracticable by their ravages.

The mode of capturing elephants, by the inhabitants of the Wanny, differs from that pursued in the Singhalese districts, and is effected by sinking concealed holes in the paths frequented by the animals. On the top of each hole a running noose is placed, the other end of the rope being made fast to an adjoining tree; and the foot of the elephant, in sinking, gives play to a spring, formed by a bough cautiously bent, which, in its recoil, carries the noose high up on the leg, thus effectually securing the captive.[1]

At Koolan-colom, where we slept, after riding eighteen miles from Padivil, I was disturbed towards morning in my tent by a disagreeable incident, not of unusual

---

[1] *Report on the State of the Wanny in* 1807, by George Turnour, Esq.

occurrence with travellers in these forests. I was suddenly awakened by a violent smarting in my face and neck, and from my throat and shoulders pulled off handfuls of insects, that were biting me intolerably. On starting from my bed, my feet and ankles were instantly assailed. The tent was dark, but obtaining a light from the watch-fire, I found myself covered with large black ants, each half an inch long, and furnished with powerful mandibles, with which they inflicted the torment I had felt. In one of their migrations, a colony of these fierce creatures, called Kaddias by the Singhalese, had approached my tent in a stream four or five feet in breadth, and composed of myriads of individuals. They had made their way in under the canvas of the tent ; and, on finding my bed in the line of their march, had held on their course, as their custom is, directly across it, descending again to the floor of the tent, and streaming out at the opposite side into the jungle. My pillow and sheets were literally black with their numbers. In their onslaught, however, they use only their mandibles, and bite without infusing any venom into the wound, which does not inflame like the bite of the hill-ant at home. With one exception[1], I think that none of the numerous species of ants in Ceylon are provided with the reservoir of formic acid — the injection of which so aggravates the assault of the common English ant.

On this part of our journey, instead of deferring dinner till our arrival at the places where our tents were pitched for the night, we frequently had it laid under a tree in some open glade of the forest, and these afternoon halts were full of pleasant incidents. So plentiful was game in this part of the country, that on one occasion at Mollia-velle between Peria-itty-madoo

[1] The species alluded to is found in the northern parts of Ceylon, and appears to belong to the genus *Myrmica* of *Latreille*. It is distinguishable by its elongation, and a double knot on the peduncle. Its sting is extremely virulent. Amongst the multitude of ants in Ceylon there may be others similarly provided with venom, but this is the only one I have seen.

and Moeletivoe, when seated round our pic-nic repast at the side of a green opening in the jungle, a buck stepped out from cover within a hundred yards of us, threw up his head, gazed at the party for a few moments in surprise, and began leisurely to graze where he stood. Presently, two peacocks, one with a train of prodigious splendour, strutted out on the sward, and by and by no less than five jungle fowl, their plumage gleaming like metal, joined the party, and all fed undisturbed within pistol-shot of where we were seated. No morbid appetite for "sport" was permitted to abuse the confidence which these innocent creatures displayed.

Cultivation in this district is carried on by small tanks, one of which is attached to almost every Tamil village that we passed. These villages differ widely in every particular from those of the Kandyans or the low-country Singhalese. The latter generally consist of ill-arranged houses, seldom lighted by windows; the coco-nut garden which adjoins them is strewn with leaves and rubbish, and frequently a stagnant puddle at the door. Those of the Kandyans might be equally described by the same epithets of filth and discomfort, in addition to which, they have the fancy for being always carefully carried to a secure distance from any high road, buried in the hottest hollows, and concealed in the closest folds of the hills. The villages in the north of the Wanny, on the contrary, are always placed in the most open and airy situations that the forest will afford; often surrounded by a wide pasture for their sheep and cattle; with rice grounds, and their never-failing accompaniment, an artificial tank. Each house is built in a well-fenced enclosure, from which all grass and weeds are removed, and the white sand raked every morning, so clean that it looks almost like a flagged courtyard. In the centre of this a platform is raised, somewhat larger than the area of the intended dwelling, and the sides and top of this little terrace, so far as it is visible, are coated with chunam, and kept carefully whitened and trim. On this platform stands the house, a low cottage, with a projecting roof, covered with palm leaves, and about the door are grouped the owners of the dwelling, and their little naked children, with glossy black hair, graceful limbs decorated with armlets, anklets, and rings.

The pursuits of this people are exclusively agricultural, and their gardens are kept in the nicest order, thickly planted with jak-trees, mangoes, coco-nuts, orange, limes, and all the fruit trees of the South. Here, too, the beautiful palmyra palm ,which abounds over the north of the island, begins to appear, and its plaited stem is often wreathed with a plentiful growth of the pepper vine, from which the Tamils collect a remunerative crop. Round the dwelling-houses we saw a variety of vegetables, little if at all cultivated by the Singhalese ; amongst the rest a small but very delicious melon, which was trained on a trellis in the courtyards.

The first appearance of the Tamils and of their agricultural economy was calculated to convey a most favourable impression of their industry and capabilities, and this was fully borne out when I came to see the cultivation on a large scale which they carry on most successfully throughout the whole Peninsula of Jaffna.

About sunrise on the morning on which we approached the old fort of Moeletivoe, whilst riding over the sandy plain by which it is surrounded, we came suddenly upon a crocodile asleep under some bushes of the Buffalo-thorn, several hundred yards from the water. The terror of the poor wretch was extreme, when he awoke and found himself discovered and completely surrounded. He was a hideous creature, upwards of ten feet long, and evidently of prodigious strength, had he been in a condition to exert it, but consternation completely paralysed him. He started to his feet and turned round in a circle hissing and clanking his bony jaws, with his ugly green eye intently fixed upon us. On being struck he lay perfectly quiet and apparently dead. Presently he looked round cunningly, and made a rush towards the water, but on a second blow he lay again motionless and feigning death. We tried to rouse him, but without effect, pulled his tail, slapped his back, struck his hard scales, and teased him in every way, but all in vain; nothing would induce him to move till accidentally my son, a boy of twelve years old, tickled him gently under the arm, and in an instant he drew it close to his side and turned to avoid a repetition of the experiment. Again he was touched under the other arm, and the same emotion was exhibited, the great monster twisting about like an infant to avoid being tickled. The scene was highly amusing, but the sun was high and we pursued our journey to Moeletivoe, leaving the crocodile to make his way to the adjoining lake.

The Fort here was built by the Dutch, to keep the Wannyahs in check. It is merely a quadrangular earthwork thrown up on the wild sea beach of the Bay of Bengal, without harbour, shelter, or other advantage to recommend it. In the general insurrection which followed the massacre of Major Davie's garrison at Kandy in 1803, the fort was captured by the insurgents, but quickly recovered by the British.[1] Its remains at the present day consist of bastions at the angles on the land side, a pile of Dutch barracks, and a Commandant's quarters, which are now the residence and offices of the Assistant to the Government Agent of the northern province. It is a solitary place, no European being living on any side within fifty miles.

A formidable surf bursts upon the shore during the north-east monsoon, and has piled it high with mounds of yellow sand. The remains of shells upon the water mark show how rich the sea is in mollusca at this point. Amongst them were prodigious numbers of the ubiquitous violet-coloured *Ianthina*[2], which rises when the sea

[1] See *ante*, Vol. II. Pt. VI. ch. iii. p. 84.

[2] *Ianthina communis*, Krauss. *I. prolongata*, Blainv.

is calm, and by means of its inflated vesicles floats lightly on the surface.

The fort is surrounded by the remains of a military ditch of considerable depth, and, as usual, filled with crocodiles. The day before our arrival one of them seized a sheep within a few yards of the Residence and was dragging it through the shallow water, when the coolies gave chase, and the reptile abandoned his captive and fled. Another inlet of the sea which we crossed on leaving Moeletivoe was also swarming with these creatures: we passed it at a point called Wattor-wakall-aar on a ledge of sunken rocks almost level with the water, and at least twenty of them were resting their noses on the stones within a dozen yards of our path, the rest of their bodies being covered by the water. We did not molest them, and they took not the slightest notice of us.

CHAP. VI.

THE PENINSULA OF JAFFNA.—THE PALMYRA PALM.

From Moeletivoe we turned north-west towards the great trunk road that connects the Kandyan country with Jaffna, and joined it at Kandavelle; where we passed the night in the rest-house. The following day we rode across the shallow sandy gulf that forms the southern boundary of the peninsula, and entered it by the Elephant Pass; a ford which has acquired its name from being one of the points chosen by the wild elephants for their passage from the mainland, at the season when the fruit of the palmyra palms, which abound on the other side of the estuary, is beginning to ripen.[1]

Close beside the northern shore stands a rest-house, erected from the materials of an old Dutch fort, part of the outer wall of which is still remaining. This and two similar strongholds at short distances across the isthmus at Pass Beschuter[2] and Pass Pyl, were erected by the

---

[1] See *post*, p. 525.

[2] Professor Lee conjectures that Beschuter may be identified with "Buzna," a place which Ibn Batuta visited on his way from Gampola to Adam's Peak; and that the name may be derived from the Persian word *Buzna*, a monkey. (See note to Lee's translation of the *Travels of Ibn Batuta*, p. 187.) But independently of the fact that the "Buzna" of the traveller was on a bend of the Mahawelli-ganga, and had no identification with Jaffna, it is difficult to see how the Persian term "buzna" could have been vernacular in Ceylon. The probability is, that the modern Pass Beschuter obtained its name from the remarkable man Marcellus de Boschouwer or Boschouder, who, in the beginning of the seventeenth century, played so important a part at the Court of the Emperor of Kandy, by whom he was created Prince of Migone. See *ante*, Vol. II. Pt. vi. ch. ii. p. 38; and in the same manner Pass Pyl, according to Valentyn, was so called in honour of Lorenzo Van Pyl, Governor of Jaffnapatam, in 1679. "Pas Pyl ter gedagtenis van den Landvoogd Pyl."—*Oud en Nieuw Oost-Indien*, ch. ii. p.30.

Dutch, for the accommodation of guards stationed here to check the incursions of the Wannyahs and their predatory followers; one of whose last exploits was the seizure of the fort at Elephant Pass in 1803, at the same time that they succeeded in dislodging the garrison at Moeletivoe.

On crossing over into the peninsula of Jaffna, we immediately perceive a striking change in the soil, the climate, the productions, and the people. The country presents one uniform level; unbroken by a single hill, and scarcely varied by an undulation of more than a very few feet. So slight is its elevation above the sea that, in addition to the principal gulf which separates it from the mainland, several other inlets penetrate and intersect the district, forming extensive shallow lagoons impassable for boats, except at a considerable distance from the shore.

It has been already stated that the western coast of Ceylon has been undergoing a gradual upheaval; and, at no distant period, extensive fields of madrepore and breccia have been elevated throughout the peninsula, in close proximity to the shore. The estuaries that cover the portion still submerged, though scarcely available from their shallowness for the purpose of traffic or carriage, are not without their salutary uses. They contribute to the deposit and formation of quantities of the finest salt, which is one of the chief riches of this district; — and, in the total absence of rivers or streams, they serve to fertilise the surrounding lands by filtration; whilst the evaporation from their surface so tends to moisten and refresh the air that the climate is never so oppressive as that of adjoining portions of Ceylon; and by the Dutch as well as by the English Jaffna has always been regarded as one of the healthiest parts of the island.

Throughout this remarkable portion of Ceylon, the characteristic of the landscape is the profusion of the beautiful palmyra palm (*Borassus flabelliformis*).[1] It retains the name *Palmeira brava*, bestowed on it by the Portuguese, as if to express their appreciation of its form and qualities. These valuable trees flourish in great topes and forests, that cover miles in various parts of the peninsula and the adjacent islands. Their broad fan-like leaves, though inferior in dimensions to those of the gigantic talipat, are more gracefully arranged round the stem, which towers to the height of seventy or eighty feet, though the average is somewhat less. Unlike the coco-nut palm, whose softer and more spongy wood bends under the weight of its crown of leaves and fruit, the timber of the palmyra is compact and hard, so that the tree rises vertically to its full altitude without a curve or deviation[2], and no object in vegetable nature presents an aspect of greater luxuriance than this majestic palm when laden with its huge clusters of fruit, each the size of an ostrich's egg, of a rich brown tint, fading into bright golden at its base. It is not till the tree has attained a mature age, that its leaves begin to detach themselves from the stem, they ascend it from the ground to its summit in spiral convolutions, enveloping it so densely as to present the closest cover for the many animals, ichneumons, squirrels, and crowds of monkeys which resort to it for concealment. In these hiding places, the latter defy all the arts of the sportsman, unless

[1] The fullest and most accurate account which I have seen of the physiology, culture, and uses of the palmyra is contained in a Monograph by Mr. FERGUSON, of the Surveyor-General's Department in Ceylon, entitled *The Palmyra Palm and its Products*. Colombo, 1850.

[2] In some exceedingly rare instances, the palmyra, like the doom palm of India, is found in Ceylon, with a double crown, the trunk having separated into several distinct branches at a considerable height from the ground. FORBES, in his *Oriental Memoirs*, vol. ii. ch. vii. p. 201, mentions one of these tuft-headed palmyras at Amhedabad, which was looked on as a very uncommon variety, and a "great curiosity." So many palmyras on Diu Island, at the southern extremity of Guzerat, and at other places near Bombay, have compound heads, that it has been attempted to distinguish them as the *B. dichotomus*.

he be accompanied by a dog, in which case the monkey, as if fascinated and forgetful of its wonted caution, in its eagerness to watch the movements of the dog, invariably exposes itself and falls a victim to curiosity.

As the leaves nearest the ground begin to decay from the larger trees, a portion of their stalks still remain attached to the trunk. Grasping these, convolvuli, ipomœas, and other climbing plants, ascend in great variety, and clothe the palm with festoons of flowers and verdure. The cavities on the stem become also receptacles for epiphytic plants, which germinate and flourish there in infinite profusion.

The figs, and particularly the banyan, — their seeds being deposited by the birds in these recesses, — speedily seize upon the palmyra, enlacing it with their nimble shoots, till they reach the earth and take root. An entirely new tree is thus formed around the original palm, above which the crown of the palmyra is alone to be discerned, "issuing from the trunk of the banyan, as if it grew thence, whereas the palm being the older tree, runs down through its centre, and has its own root in the ground."[1]

The Tamils look with increased veneration on their sacred tree thus united in "marriage with the palm." Examples of this fantastic union are frequent in the topes of Jaffna, and a specimen now in the Museum of Belfast of the trunk of the Borassus thus enlaced by the banyan, as well as another in the collection at Kew, were procured by Dr. Gardner and myself in the forests I am now describing.

So multifarious are the uses of the palmyra and its products to the natives of the countries favoured by its growth, that the Hindus have dedicated it to Ganesa, and celebrate it as the "Kalpa tree," or "tree of life," of their Paradise. A Tamil poem, of which a translation

---

[1] ROXBURGH.

is given by Mr. FERGUSON[1], professes to describe the creation of the palmyra, and the "eight hundred and one" uses to which the tree is applied. It opens by describing the various productions of the earth, created by Brahma, as insufficient for the wants of mankind; one substance being still desired capable of "assuaging hunger and curing disease, feeding the people and enriching the race," and men in their distress and perplexity, "trembling like water on the leaf of the lotus," made poojahs, and prayed to Siva for relief. Siva heard their prayers, and sternly called upon Vishnu to explain the neglect of his function of preservation. Vishnu attributes the blame to the insufficient provision of Brahma for the wants of mankind, and Brahma being called to account, trembled in his turn, and "with his finger under his under lip," pleaded that he had exerted his power of creation to the utmost of his knowledge. Siva, thus baffled, directs Brahma to transplant the Kalpa tree from Paradise to earth. Brahma obeyed, and "at the injunction of Siva adorned with the crescent moon, he created in abundance the heavenly tree palmyra."

Of all the palms, the palmyra, with the exception of the date, has probably the widest geographical distribution; it extends from the confines of Arabia to the isles of Amboyna and Timor, and is found in every region of Hindustan, from the Indus to Siam. It is cultivated more or less in every district of Ceylon, but plantations on a vast scale are exclusively confined to the district of Jaffna.[2]

---

[1] *Essay on the Palmyra, &c.* Appx. p. 1. The Tamil author was ARUNACHALAM, of Combaconum, in Tanjore. In his hands the 801 uses of the palm dwindles into a very small proportion of that number.

[2] RUMPHIUS, in his account of the palmyra in the *Herbarium Amboinense*, quaintly says: "It is truly remarkable that the two nuts of India, the coconut and the palmyra, cherish such secret envy and hatred towards each other, that they will not grow in the same field, nor in one and the same region, which however must be attributed to the great wisdom of the Creator, who is unwilling that these trees, so productive and so necessary to the human race, should grow in the same locality. We see

Taking the area of the Jaffna peninsula at seven hundred square miles, Mr. FERGUSON, whose experience as a Government Surveyor entitles his authority to respect, estimates that if one-fourteenth of the land be devoted to palmyras, even at the rate of two hundred trees to an acre, which is far below the ordinary ratio, "the number of palms in this district alone must be close upon 7,000,000, the edible product of which supply one-fourth of the food of 220,000 inhabitants."

On the continent of India the œconomical value of the palmyra is equally signal, its fruits affording a compensating resource to 7,000,000 of Hindus, on every occasion of famine or failure of the rice crop. In fact, the palmyra fruit season has nearly as great an influence on the periodical immigration of the coolies from the Coromandel coast to Ceylon in search of employment on the coffee estates, as that produced by the cutting of the rice harvest. In what is emphatically called the "Palmyra regions," in the southern Dekkan, the saving of the fruit is always followed by an increased emigration, including numbers who had previously returned from Ceylon for the express purpose of assisting at this important domestic operation.

---

that in all the western parts of Hindustan and Ceylon, the coco-nut tree grows abundantly and vigorously, but there we rarely or never see a palmyra. On the other hand, in the eastern parts of Ceylon and Coromandel, the palmyra predominates, and the coco-nut is rare, and those few that do grow are always to be found in some solitary place. It is true that instances may be known where the two are growing together, but always in less numbers and sickly. I have seen an Amboina or Palmyra tree perfect and of full growth, which had been cultivated with great labour and was nevertheless always barren, because that it stood amongst many coco-nut trees." The real cause of the barrenness in the instance alluded to by Rumphius must have been that the palm grew apart from a male tree of its own species; but unfortunately for the general correctness of the piece of folk-lore thus recorded, although at the time Rumphius wrote the "two nuts" had practically divided Ceylon between them; the coco-nut monopolizing the south, and the palmyra having colonised the northern districts of the island; the fallacy of the popular belief is now conclusively demonstrated, as the plantations of coco-nuts at Jaffna have recently become so prodigious, as almost to out-number the palmyras; which have in many instances been felled to make room for their rivals.

The palmyra must attain an age, variously stated at from fifteen to thirty years, before it begins to yield fruit. The spathes of the fruit-bearing trees exhibit themselves in November and December, and the toddy-drawer forthwith commences his operations, climbing by the assistance of a loop of flexible jungle vine, sufficiently wide to admit both his ancles, and leave a space between them ; thus enabling him to grasp the trunk of the tree with his feet, and support himself as he ascends. Having pruned off the stalks of fallen leaves, and cleansed the crown from old fruit stalks, and other superfluous matter, he binds the spathes tightly with thongs to prevent them from further expansion, and descends, after having thoroughly bruised the embryo flowers within to facilitate the exit of juice. For several succeeding mornings the operation of crushing is repeated, and each day a thin slice is taken off the end of the racemes to facilitate the exit of the sap, and prevent its bursting the spathe. About the eighth morning the sap begins to exude ; an event which is notified by the immediate appearance of birds, especially of the "toddy bird," a species of shrike (*Artamus fuscus*), attracted by the flies and other insects, which come to feed on the luscious juice of the palm. The crows, ever on the alert when any unusual movement is in progress, keep up a constant chattering and wrangling ; and about this period the palmyra becomes the resort of the palm-cat and the glossy and graceful genet, which frequent the trees, and especially the crown of the coco-nuts, in quest of birds.[1]

---

[1] FERGUSON'S *Monograph on the Palmyra*, p. 30. KELAART, in his *Fauna Zeylanica*, names this cat (which the Singhalese call *oogoo-dood*, and the Tamils *Maranaya*), the Paradoxurus Typus. He says it is common at Colombo, lodging by day on the trees, where it lies rolled up in a ball, and that it lives for months in confinement solely on vegetable food, but preferring flesh, especially that of birds. He adds that the fact of its consuming the toddy of the palmyra is well established ;—but to me it appears more probable that it resorts to the palm during the time of toddy-drawing for the sake of the birds, which in turn are allured by the flies that then abound.

On ascertaining that the first flow of the sap has taken place, the toddy-drawer again trims the wounded spathe, and inserts its extremity in an earthen chatty, to collect the juice. Morning and evening these vessels are emptied, and for a period of four or five months the palmyra will continue to pour forth its sap at the rate of three quarts a day. But once in every three years the operation is omitted, and the fruit is allowed to form, without which the natives assert that the tree would pine and die.

The juice, if permitted to rest and ferment, is speedily converted into toddy, a slightly intoxicating and unpalatable drink.[1] It is not used for distillation at Jaffna; and for that purpose is said to be inferior to that of the coconut palm. If intended to be made into *sugar*, a little lime is added to the sap, and the liquor, after being boiled down to the consistency of syrup, is poured into small baskets made of the palmyra leaf, where it cools, and a partial crystallisation ensues. In this state, and without undergoing any further process to discharge the molasses, it is sold as *jaggery* in the bazaars, at about three farthings per pound.

The quantity of toddy annually produced by a male-palmyra is but one-third or one-fourth of that obtained from a female tree. Three quarts of toddy will yield one pound of jaggery. Of the produce of Jaffna, about 10,000 cwt. are annually exported to the opposite coast of India, where it undergoes the process of refining. The granulation is said to surpass that of the sugar-cane; and considerable quantities of palmyra sugar are annually exported to Europe from Cuddalore and Madras. As yet, no attempts have been made in Ceylon to perfect the manufacture by refining jaggery on a large scale, nor have the experiments hitherto

[1] The toddy is converted into vinegar by exposing it to the sun in earthen vessels, where it is permitted to ferment freely.

instituted been sufficient to remove the apprehensions that the cost of culture and treatment, added to local disadvantages, will always render it difficult for the produce of the palmyra to compete with that of the sugar-cane in European markets, or even in Ceylon.

If the fruit be permitted to form, instead of being crushed in embryo by the toddy-drawer, it ripens about July or August, and presents itself in luxuriant clusters of from ten to twenty on each flower stem, of which the tree bears seven or eight. Such is their size and weight, that a single cluster is a sufficient load for a coolie. As the period of their ripening approaches, the elephants from the main land cross over into the peninsula at points of the isthmus, to feed upon the fallen fruit, or pull down the younger plants for the sake of the tender leaves of the crown.

Almost invariably, the tough and polished case of the fruit contains within it three intensely hard seeds, embedded in a farinaceous orange pulp, mixed with fibre. The taste of this pulp in its natural state is sweet, but too oily and rank to be palatable to a European. The natives eat it, occasionally raw, more frequently roasted; but the prevailing practice is to extract it by pressure, and convert it into "poonatoo [1]," by drying it in squares in the sun; after which it is preserved in the smoke of their houses, and used in various forms, either for cakes, soup, or curry.

Another form in which food is extracted from the palmyra, is by planting the seeds or kernels of the fruit, the germs of which in their first stage of growth are of the shape and dimensions of a parsnip, but of a more firm and waxy consistency. These are dried in

[1] HUMBOLDT found the Indians on the Upper Orinoco making a preparation from the *Piritu Palm*, the fruit of which seems to resemble that of the Palmyra, being "a farinaceous substance, as yellow as the yolk of an egg slightly saccharine, and extremely nutritious."—*Narrative*, ch. xxii.

the sun, and when dressed in slices, form a palatable kind of vegetable. Under the name of *kelingoos*, these roots are exported in large quantities from Point Pedro to Colombo and other parts of Ceylon, and esteemed a delicacy in all the southern bazaars. The kelingoo is reducible to a flour, which in the time of the Dutch was so much prized for its delicacy that it was sent home as an enviable present to friends in Holland.

The shell of the seeds, after the kelingoos have been taken from them, are collected and charred, in which state they are used by the blacksmiths and workers in metal, who believe them to surpass all other fuel in the power of engendering a glowing heat.

The wood of the palmyra is so hard and durable, that a proverb of the Tamils says, "it lives for a lac of years after planting, and lasts for a lac of years when felled." It consists, like the other palms, of straight horny fibres, which confer the faculty of separation into lengths, and as these are said to resist the attacks of the white ants, they are used universally in Ceylon and India, for roofing and similar purposes. The export from Jaffna alone of palmyra rafters and reapers (laths), consumes annually between 70,000 and 80,000 palms, each of the value of from three to six shillings. The trees require to have reached a considerable age before they are fit to be cut for timber; at one hundred years they are held to be good, but the older they are the harder and blacker the wood. Rafters and pieces requiring strength and solidity are taken from the lower part of the trunk, laths and reapers from the top. The outer circumference of the tree always yields the firmest and most compact timber [1], and the Singha-

[1] The centre of the palmyra and its top are soft and spongy, containing a kind of coarse farina intermixed with woody fibre. For this reason the natives of Jaffna lay these portions in places where game are plentiful, and the wild hogs and hares, attracted to feed on them, are thus secured to the sportsman. (See FERGUSON, p. 16.)

lese have an idea that the side next the south is superior to the rest of the wood. There can be no doubt that the timber of the female palm is much harder and blacker than that of the male; inasmuch as it brings nearly triple its price: the natives are so well aware of the difference, that they resort to the device of immersing the male tree in salt water to deepen its colour as well as to add to its weight.[1]

The leaves are in almost greater request than the wood and fruit of the palmyra. Once in every two years the thatch of the native houses and the fences of their fields are renewed with this convenient and most suitable substance; the old material being carefully conveyed as manure to their rice-lands. Mats are woven for the floors and ceilings, and baskets are plaited so densely that they serve to carry water for irrigating fields and gardens. Caps, fans, and umbrellas are all provided from the same inexhaustible source, and strips of the finer leaves steeped in milk to render them elastic, and smoothed by pressure so as to enable them to be written on with a stile, serve for their books and correspondence; and are kept, duly stamped, at the cutcherries to be used instead of parchment for deeds and legal documents.[2] These are but a few of

---

[1] PLINY notices as a fact, that certain woods on being dried after immersion in the sea, acquire additional density and durability.—*Nat. Hist.*, lib. xiii. ch. 1.

[2] In the Arabian manuscript of ALBYROUNI, who wrote his account of India in the tenth century, he describes a tree in the south of the Dekkan, resembling the date or the coco-nut palm, on the leaves of which the natives wrote, and passing a cord through a hole in the centre formed books. These leaves, he says, were a cubit in length and three fingerbreadths wide, and, according to him, they were called "*târy*." By Tary, M. REINAUD, who quotes from the Arabic, supposes Albyrouni to mean *tala*, but it is clear that he meant, not the *talipat*, but the palmyra; as he specially says that the fruit of the tree he alludes to is eatable, which that of the talipat is not. Besides *Tari* is one of the native Tamil names for the palmyra. REINAUD, *Mém. sur l'Inde*, p. 305-307, says "les Européens ont donné aux feuilles de cet arbre le nom d'*olla;* mot qui a été mis en usage par les auteurs Portugais." But DE BARROS, though he uses the term "*olla*" to denote the leaves used for writing in India, says expressly that it is an Indian word: "todo o gentio da India, as cousas que quer encommodar à memoria per escritura, he em humas folhas de palma, *a que elles chamam*

the innumerable benefits derived by the natives of Ceylon from their precious palm; which supplies at once shelter, furniture, food, drink, oil, and fuel for themselves; with forage for their cattle, and utensils for their farms. No single production of nature, not even the coco-nut itself, is capable of conferring so many blessings on mankind in the early stages of civilisation; and hence that outburst of simple gratitude in which it has been exalted by the Tamils into an object of veneration, and celebrated in songs as a tree transplanted from Paradise.

At about eight miles from Elephant Pass we found our tent pitched in the forest near Palai, in the immediate vicinity of the numerous coco-nut plantations, which have been recently opened in this division of Jaffna. The cultivation of this palm on the sea-coast of Ceylon was commenced by Europeans, about the same time that plantations of coffee began to be opened in the mountain ranges of the interior. The suitability of Jaffna for its growth attracted attention about the year 1842, and between that and the present time more than ten thousand acres of government land have been purchased and partially planted, and upwards of fifty estates are now under cultivation, in the district of Pachelapalle.

For some years after the establishment of coco-nut plantations on a large scale, the high value of coco-nut oil promised to render the speculation extremely remunerative in its results; but of late years the enter-

---

olla."—Dec. i. tom. i. pt. ii. lib. ix. ch. iii. p. 322. The leaves are called *Olei* in the Tamil poem of Arunachalam on the Palmyra.

To prepare the olas for writing, the leaf of the palm is taken while tender, and the flat portions being cut into strips and freed from the ribs and woody tendons, are boiled and afterwards dried, first in the shade and afterwards in the sun. In this state they are called by the Singhalese *kara-kola*, and applied to the more ordinary purposes. But a still finer description, called *Pusk-ola*, is prepared in the temples by the Samanero priests and novices, who, after damping the karakola, draw it tightly over the sharp edge of a board, so as to remove all inequalities and render it polished and smooth.

prise has been somewhat discouraged by the non-realisation of the hopes of the first adventurers. Though luxuriant in their early growth, the young palms failed to come to maturity within the anticipated period, and the great operations of crushing and exporting the oil have scarcely yet commenced within the Jaffna peninsula.

Experience has shown that the further the coco-nut palm is removed from the shore and the influence of the sea, the more its growth is diminished, and the less abundant its fruit.[1] Hence, and also from the palms' requiring constant irrigation during the early stages of their growth, the Jaffna planters have selected for their operations those portions of the coast which are flanked by estuaries and intersected by inland lakes, where wells can be sunk at a small cost and water carried with the least expense.

The first operation in coco-nut planting is the formation of a nursery, for which purpose the ripe nuts are placed in squares containing about four hundred each; these are covered an inch deep with sand and seaweed or soft mud from the beach, and watered daily till they germinate. The nuts put down in April are sufficiently grown to be planted out before the rains of September, and they are then set out in holes three feet deep and twenty to thirty feet apart, experience having shown that the practice of the natives in crowding them into less than half that space is prejudicial to the growth of the trees, those in the centre yielding little or no fruit. Before putting in the young plant, it is customary to bed the roots with soft

---

[1] I have been told by an experienced planter at Jaffna, that of two estates, one at Tatto-van-kadoo, where the soil is grey sand, and where water is abundant at twelve feet deep, the coco-nut trees usually attained the height of twelve feet in three years; whilst similar plants tended with great care reached only one-half that height within the same period, on an estate at Aya-nan-guy-kadoo, within a short distance, where the soil was red sand and the supplies of water limited even at a depth of twenty-one feet from the surface.

mud and seaweed, and for the first two years they must be watered, and protected from the glare of the sun under shades made of the plaited fronds of the coco-nut palm or the fan-like leaves of the palmyra.

During the early stages, too, the anxieties of the planter are incessant. He must invent plans to protect the young plants from wild hogs, rats, and elephants, with all of whom the tender shoots are especial favourites, and as the stem ascends, it has to encounter the most destructive enemy of all, the "cooroominiya" beetles (*Batocera rubus*), which penetrate the trunk near the ground and deposit their eggs[1]; the grubs, when hatched, eating their way upwards through the centre of the tree to the top, where they pierce the young leaf-buds and do incredible damage. As the injuries from these united causes involve the loss of about one-fourth of the plants put down, constant renewal is required, in order to replace those destroyed. After the second year, irrigation becomes unnecessary, and all that is then required is to keep the ground ploughed and free from weeds, and each alternate year to dress the young palms with sea-weed and salt manure.

Towards the end of the fifth year, the flower-stock may be expected to appear; but the period varies, and is sometimes delayed till the seventh year and even later. Every stock will bring to maturity from five to thirty nuts, a tree on an average yielding sixty in the course of a year; and each nut requires twelve months to ripen. The fruit when collected is stripped of its outer bark, which is macerated to convert the fibre into coir, whilst the fleshy lining of the shell is dried by exposure in the sun, preparatory to expressing the oil. The ordinary estimate is, that one thousand full-grown nuts of Jaffna will yield five hundred and twenty-five pounds of *copra*

---

[1] See *ante*, Vol. I. Pt. II. ch. vi. p. 249.

when dried, which in turn will produce twenty-five gallons of coco-nut oil.

Mingled with the palm-trees, the forests of Jaffna present the usual undergrowth of jungle brushwood, mimosas, mustard-trees, and the hardier timbers which flourish in unpromising soil. In the vicinity of the villages and houses, the artificial garden mould produces mangoes, oranges, citrons, tamarinds, and all the ordinary fruit-trees of Ceylon in abundance. In spite of all the difficulties of soil and irrigation, a large quantity of rice is grown, though not enough to suffice for the actual consumption of the inhabitants. The flat surface of the ground is in many places an obstacle to the extension of rice cultivation, inasmuch as it prevents the water from flowing down over the necessary terraces; — and to obviate this difficulty, the natives of many districts are obliged to reduce the level of their fields with incredible labour and toil, hollowing them to the depth of several feet, heaping up the excavated earth in high mounds, and thus admitting the rains and collected water to flow into the cavities, where it is retained till the grain is ripe.

Black cattle are pastured in large numbers, and the finest sheep in Ceylon are reared upon the dry plains which overlie the limestone and coral rock, on the northern and western coasts. There sheep, instead of being coated with wool, are covered with long hair, resembling that of goats, and the horny callosities that defend their knees, and which arise from their habit of kneeling down to crop the short herbage, serve to distinguish the Jaffna flocks from those of the other portions of the island.[1] At the time of our visit, a sandy road from Pallai to Kodigammo ran almost continuously between the palmyra fences of the recently opened coco-nut estates, a great part of which are the property of Bengal civilians and others

[1] At Jaffna a sheep may be purchased for a shilling or eighteenpence. Their flesh being little in demand by the Tamils, they are probably kept to fold in the fields for the sake of manure.

in the service of the East India Company; but as we approached the west, the country is amply provided with metalled highways and bridges, and intersected in all directions by parish-roads. Jaffna is in fact the only part of Ceylon in which the native population seem clearly to appreciate the value of roads, and are anxious to afford every facility, and contribute every assistance for their construction.

At Kodigammo we turned northward and passed through Varany, on our way to Point Pedro, crossing the great estuary of Sirrokally, and driving through a district from which the rice crops had recently been gathered, and in which the cattle, instead of being left to forage for themselves, as is the custom in the rest of the island, were folded in shady pens and well-enclosed fields.

The prevalence of this practice, and the care with which fencing is universally attended to, is the best evidence of the value set upon land by a dense population. Their perception of the rights of property, and their desire to maintain and respect them, are amply attested by their many arrangements to restrain the trespass of cattle. On the other hand, one of the most serious annoyances with which the planters of the south have had to contend, both on their coffee and sugar estates, arises from the notorious indifference of the Kandyans and Singhalese in this particular, and their disregard of all precautions for securing their buffaloes and bullocks by day or by night.

In the immediate neighbourhood of Point Pedro (and the description applies equally to the vicinity of Jaffna and the western division of the peninsula in general), the perfection of the village cultivation is truly remarkable; it is horticulture rather than agriculture, and reminds one of the market-gardens of Fulham and Chelsea more forcibly than anything I have seen out of England. Almost every cottage has a garden attached to it, wherein are grown fruit-trees and flowers, the latter being used in great quantities for decoration and offerings in the temples. Each is situated in a well-secured enclosure, with one or more wells. From these, night and day, but chiefly during the night, labourers are employed in raising water, by means of vessels (frequently woven of palm-leaves) attached to horizontal levers; something like the sakkias used by the peasants on the Nile for a similar purpose, except that in Jaffna two persons at least are required at each well, one of whom walks back and forward along the lever, whilst the other below directs the bucket in its ascent and empties its contents into a reservoir, whence, by removing a clod of earth with the foot, it is admitted into conducting channels, and led to the several beds in succession.[1] The value of these wells is extreme in a country where rivers and even the smallest stream are unknown, and where the cultivators are entirely dependent on the rains of the two monsoons. But such has been the indefatigable industry of the people in providing them, that they may be said to have virtually added a third harvest to the year, by the extent to which they have multiplied the means of irrigation around their principal towns and villages.

The articles raised by this species of garden cultivation are of infinite variety. Every field is carefully fenced in with paling formed of the mid-ribs of the palmyra-leaf, or by rows of prickly plants, aloes, cactus, euphorbia, and others; and each is divided into small beds, each containing a different crop; but the most frequent and valuable crops are the ingredients for the preparation of curry; such as onions and chilies, which are exported to all parts of the coast and carried in large quantities into the interior. Along with these, are turmeric, ginger, pumpkins, brinjals, gourds, melons, yams,

---

[1] This feature in the irrigation of the Tamil gardens has been aptly adduced in illustration of the text, "*with the sole of my foot* have I dried up the rivers of besieged places," 2 *Kings*, ch. xix. 24.

sweet-potatoes, keere (or country cabbage), arrow-root, and gram. In these carefully tended little farms weeds are nowhere to be seen; the walks between the different beds are straight and accurately clean; and, from the profusion of water with which they are supplied, there is a freshness and cool verdure over these beautiful fields which singularly contrasts with the arid and sun-scorched plains that surround them.

But the grand staple of the district, and that on which the prosperity of its agriculture is chiefly dependent, is tobacco, for the excellence of which Jaffna has long been celebrated in the South of India; and at a former period it was in equal request in Sumatra, Java, and the Eastern Archipelago. The export is now almost confined to Travancore, the Raja of which has an agent resident at Jaffna to purchase up the produce from the growers. It is on the breadth and success of this crop that the extent and excellence of all the others are mainly dependent; for, as the ground requires to be highly prepared for tobacco, two and even three crops of a less exhausting description are afterwards taken off it in succession, without additional manuring; whilst the increasing demand for tobacco causes new land to be broken up for its growth, thus stimulating a constantly progressive improvement in the culture of all the inferior lands.

The dry grains (as contradistinguished from rice, which is grown in water), produced in Jaffna are more numerous than those cultivated in other parts of Ceylon, *varagoo*[1], *kolloo*, millet, *moondy*, and pulse of various kinds being raised in addition to *coracan*[2] and *gingele*.[3] The necessity of importing a portion of the rice consumed within the district is thus compensated to some extent, since the inhabitants are enabled to export their

---

1 *Paspalum frumentaceum.*
2 *Cynosurus corocanus.*
3 *Sesamum Orientale.*

own surplus produce of other articles to nearly an equivalent amount.

In the midst of these interesting gardens is the village of Point Pedro, a corruption of the Portuguese *Punta das Pedras*, "the rocky cape," a name descriptive of the natural features of the coast. Point Pedro is not, as generally represented, the extreme point of Ceylon, for the coast trends still farther north at Point Palmyra, a promontory some miles to the westward. Close by the beach there is still standing the "tall Tamarind-tree" commemorated by Baldæus [1], who preached under its shade to the first Protestant converts in Ceylon. This historical tree is forty-two feet in circumference at the base of the trunk.

Point Pedro is an open roadstead, which affords, however, tolerably secure anchorage within the shelter of a coral reef. Although twenty miles distant from Jaffna, it must still be regarded as its principal port; for though Jaffna appears on the map to be situated on the sea, the water shoals so, that the town is not approachable within some miles by square-rigged vessels, which consequently receive and discharge their cargoes at Point Pedro to the north, and at Kayts, in Leyden Island, twelve miles to the south-west. To a great degree, the little town of Point Pedro partakes of the care which is lavishly bestowed upon the gardens around it; its streets are trim and regular, its houses more substantial and commodious than usual, and its Hindu temple and tank are on a scale that attests the wealth and liberality of its devotees.

In the evening we drove along the shore to Valvettitorre, a village about three miles to the west of Point Pedro, containing a much larger population, and one equally industrious and enterprising. There was a vessel of considerable tonnage on the stocks, the Tamil ship-

---

[1] BALDÆUS, p. 730.

builders of this little place being amongst the most successful in Ceylon. As we entered the village, we passed by a large well under a grove of palms and tamarind-trees, around which, as it was sunset, the females of the place were collected, according to the immemorial custom of the East, "at the time of the evening, even the time that the women go out to draw water." In figure and carriage, the Tamil women are much superior to the Singhalese. This is shown to advantage in their singularly graceful and classical costume, consisting of a long fold of cloth, enveloping the body below the waist, and brought tastefully over the left shoulder, leaving the right arm and the bosom free. This, together with the custom of carrying vases of water and other burdens on their heads, gives them an erect and stately gait, and disposes their limbs in attitudes so graceful as to render them, when young and finely featured, the most unadorned models for a sculptor.

The following morning we drove before breakfast to Jaffna, a distance of twenty-one miles, by Achavelle, Potoor, and Copay. Near Potoor, at a place called Navakeeré, there is a remarkable well, elsewhere alluded to [1], which is one of the wonders of the peninsula. It occurs in a bed of stratified limestone, so hollow that in passing over it the footsteps of our horses sounded as though they were striking on an arch. The well is about thirty feet in diameter, and sinks to a depth of four-and-twenty fathoms. On the surface it is fresh, but lower down it is brackish and salt, and on plunging a bottle to the extreme depth, the water came up highly fœtid, and giving off bubbles of sulphuretted

[1] See Vol. I. Pt. I. ch. i. p. 21. BALDÆUS says, p. 723, that the well of Potoor was "opened by a thunderbolt." This probably refers to the native tradition, that the well was opened by Rama by a stroke of his arrow, to refresh his followers, when seeking to recover Sita. The similarity of this legend to the act of Moses in smiting the rock to procure water for the Israelites is another of the coincidences which occasionally strike us between the Scripture histories and the eastern chronicles.

hydrogen gas. But the most remarkable fact connected with this well is that its surface rises and falls a few inches once in every twelve hours, but it never overflows its banks, and is never reduced below a certain fixed point, even by the abstraction of large quantities of water. In 1824, the Governor, Sir Edward Barnes, conceived the idea of using this apparently inexhaustible spring for maintaining a perpetual irrigation of the surrounding districts. With this view, he caused a steam-engine with three pumps to be erected at the well of Potoor. But for some reason, which I have been unable to ascertain[1], the attempt was soon abandoned. In reporting the early progress of the experiment, the Government officer of the district represented that the pumps, though worked incessantly for forty-eight hours, and drawing off a prodigious quantity of water, had in no degree reduced the apparent contents of the well, which rose each day precisely an inch and a half between the hours of seven in the morning and one o'clock in the afternoon; and again between eight o'clock and twelve at night — falling to an equivalent extent in the intervals.[2] The natives are perfectly familiar with all these phenomena, and believe that the well communicates with the sea at the Kieremalie, near Kangesen-torre, a distance of seven miles, from which they affirm that a subterranean stream flows inwards, as

[1] I have since been told that lands irrigated by the water procured from the well were found to yield no increase, the grain reaped being scarcely equal to the quantity of seed sown in the ground.

[2] This rise of the water is very curious;— but the phenomena have been too imperfectly investigated to be susceptible of ready explanation. I can have little doubt that the Government officer reported with tolerable accuracy the fact as he found it; a fact, moreover, which is stated to have been well known to the natives, both in regard to this well, and another at a short distance from it. It is to be hoped that future exploration will disclose the causes of these mysterious oscillations: meantime we must rest content with the popular hypothesis of a communication direct from the sea to the bottom of the well, where the water is salt, by means of some irregular fissure; and refer the presence of fresher water at top to percolation through the coral rock, and perhaps to casual additions, derived at rare intervals, from surface supply.

"Alph, the sacred river, ran
Through caverns measureless to man
Down to a sunless sea."

There certainly are numerous springs in the sands along the shore at the point referred to[1], whose openings are covered by the tide at high water; but whether a connection exists between any one of them and the well of Potoor is a problem still unsolved.

At Potoor, one of the fine old churches erected by the Portuguese abuts on the high road, and has recently been restored, the Wesleyan Mission having a successful station in the vicinity. From thence into Jaffna the road passes through a succession of fields so cleanly cultivated and securely fenced, that a stranger might almost fancy a resemblance between it and a scene in England,—an illusion which is not dispelled on arriving at the residence of Mr. Dyke, the Government agent of the province: a spacious mansion in the midst of a park-like demesne, studded with forest-trees, and diversified with clumps of flowers and groups of the choicest and rarest plants and shrubs of Ceylon.

In the court-yard to the rear is a spacious garden, in which Mr. Dyke has succeeded in cultivating the black grape of Madeira, trained over a trellis,—the want of winter rest for the plants being supplied by baring the roots, and exposing them to the sun. The vines give two crops in the year,—the principal one in

[1] This legend of a subterranean river in Ceylon was carried westward by the Arabian mariners in the middle ages; and it will be remembered that Sindbad of the Sea, in his sixth voyage, wherein he narrates his arrival in Serendib, describes his shipwreck on the coast, "near a lofty mountain," underneath which a stream was flowing inland. Embarking on this, on a raft of aloes and sandal-wood, together with heaps of the pearls, jacinths, and ambergris which he collected on the beach, Sindbad "proceeded to the place where the river entered," and in the midst of profound darkness, was carried under ground by the current, though a passage so narrow and low, that "the raft rubbed against the sides, and his head against the roof." Emerging at last into light, his "eyes beheld an extensive tract, and a company of people like Abyssinians, who had come to irrigate their fields and sown lands," and who forthwith conducted him to the presence of the King of Serendib.—Lane's *Arabian Nights*, vol. iii.

March, and the second in September,—but the operation of stripping the roots is only resorted to once, about the time of pruning in July.[1] The fruit from some cuttings of white Muscat vines, obtained from Pondicherry by Mr. Dyke in 1840, proved to be identical with the Jaffna grape, the Dutch having probably brought the latter from Negapatam, whence it had been carried from Muscat. Of late years, the Tamils at Jaffna have begun to cultivate the vine; so that grapes are now not only procurable in the public market, but are also occasionally sent for sale to Colombo.

Jaffna has been peopled by Tamils for at least two thousand years, the original settlement being of date coeval with the earliest Malabar invasion of the island, B.C. 204[2], and their chiefs continued to assume the rank

---

[1] See Vol. I. Pt. I. ch. iii. p. 89.

[2] The arrival of the Tamils and the expulsion of the Nagas is commemorated in an ancient poem, called the *Kylasa Mala*, a translation of which will be found in the *Asiat. Journ.* for 1827, vol. xxiv. p. 53, and the substance of it has been embodied in a sketch of the ancient history of Jaffna, by CASIE CHITTY, in the *Journ.* of the *Asiatic Society of Colombo*, 1847, p. 69. The purport of the legend is, that a princess of Tanjore, desirous of being freed from a horse's head with which she had the misfortune to be born, was directed in a vision to bathe in the well of Keremalc, on the northern shore of Ceylon, near which a temple still exists that, commemorative of her cure, bears the name "Mahavittepuram," and an annual festival is performed in her honour. The legend runs, that one of her followers, a minstrel or "Yalpanen," having made his way to the Singhalese Court, the reigning sovereign, charmed by his powers, conferred on him the territory of the peninsula, which thereafter took the name of *Yalpannan*, or *Yalpanna nadu*, by which it is still known to the natives, though corrupted by Europeans into Jaffna and Jaffnapatam. This occurrence took place a century before the Christian era, and, in succession to the lutanist, there arose a dynasty of Rajahs of Jaffna, who held their court at Nalloor, and thence extended their conquest over the Wanny and Manaar. It is even possible that "Rachias," the ambassador who arrived at Rome in the reign of Claudius, may have represented, not the Singhalese monarch, but the Rajah of Jaffna. De Couto relates that about the year 1574, when João de Melho de Sampaio was Captain of Manaar, there were discovered, under the foundation of a building, an iron chain of curious workmanship, and coins on which the letter *C* was legible, and on the reverse the letters R. M. N. R., which were understood to mean CLAUDIUS IMPERATOR ROMANORUM, and were supposed to have been brought to Ceylon by the freedman of Annius Plocamus, who was the first Roman that landed on the island, "e cousa he possivel, que fossem estas moedas das que alli levou o Liberto de Anio."—DE COUTO, Dec. v. liv. i. ch. vii. vol. ii. pt. i. p. 71.

and title of independent princes down to the seventeenth century. The *Rajavali* recounts the occasions on which they carried on wars with the Singhalese kings of the island[1]; — and their authority and influence in the fourteenth century are attested by the protection which the Raja (whose dominions then extended as far south as Chilaw) afforded to Ibn Batuta, whom, with his companions, he permitted to visit the sacred footstep on the summit of Adam's Peak.[2]

Elsewhere, the story has been told of the persecution of the native converts who had embraced Christianity under the preaching of St. Francis Xavier, about the year 1544, and of the wars undertaken by the Portuguese to avenge them, which terminated, A.D. 1617, in the conquest of their country and its final annexation to the possessions of Portugal in Ceylon.[3] In their turn, the Portuguese were expelled by the Dutch in 1658; but although the tenure of Jaffna by the former did not much exceed forty years, the exertions which they made, during that brief period, to establish the Roman Catholic religion are attested by the number of churches they built. These remain to the present day, having served in turn for the missionaries of three nations, of Portugal, Holland, and England, and successively witnessed the celebration of the rites of three communions, the Roman Catholic, the Reformed, and the Episcopalian.[4] The Portuguese divided the peninsula into parishes, with schools and a mansion for the priests in each; and within the town they maintained a college of Jesuits, a convent of Franciscans, and a monastery of Dominican Friars.[5]

---

[1] *Rajavali*, p. 268.

[2] IBN BATUTA, *Travels, &c.*, Trans. by Lee, pp. 183-185.

[3] FARIA Y SOUZA, vol. iii. ch. xii. p. 259. See the portion of the present work relative to the Portuguese in Ceylon, Vol. II. Pt. VI. ch. i. p. 29.

[4] Views of the most important of these buildings as they were found by the Dutch, are given in the illustrations to the work of BALDÆUS on Ceylon.

[5] For an account of the missionary proceedings of the Portuguese at Jaffna, see Sir J. EMERSON TENNENT'S *History of Christianity in Ceylon*, ch. i. p. 10.

On the occupation of Ceylon by the British, the principal European inhabitants emigrated to Batavia; yet, of all the settlements of Holland in the island, none is still so thoroughly Dutch in its architecture and aspect as the town of Jaffna. The houses, like those of Colombo, consist of a single story, but they are large and commodious, with broad verandahs, lofty ceilings, and spacious apartments. Every building, inside and out, is as clean and showy as whitewash, fresh paint, bright red tiles and brick floors can make them. The majority of them are detached, and situated in enclosed gardens filled with fruit-trees and flowering shrubs; and I am told, some years ago, the finest specimens of antique carved furniture in ebony and calamander, cabinets, arm-chairs, and ponderous sofas, were still to be seen in these ancient dwellings of the former rulers of the island. The streets of the town are broad and regular, and are planted, as usual, with lines of Suria trees, for the sake of their agreeable shade and yellow flowers.

The fort, which was entirely reconstructed by the Dutch, is the most perfect little military work in Ceylon, —a pentagon, built of blocks of white coral, and surrounded by a moat. It contains several excellent buildings, a residence for the Commandant, and an old church in the form of a Greek cross. This, by the capitulation of 1795, was specially reserved for the Presbyterian Consistory, but by their courtesy is at present used for the service of the Church of England.[1]

The native town is almost exclusively occupied by Tamils and Moors, and the tradesmen and dealers exhibit in their several pursuits no less intelligence and industry than characterise the rural population. They weave a substantial cotton cloth, which is dyed and

[1] VALENTYN describes the fortress of Jaffnapatam with great particularity, its bastions, its ravelin, and water pass; and such was the importance attached to it by the Dutch, that he says the garrison maintained there was much stronger than that of Batavia.—*Oud en Nieuw Oost-Indien*, ch. ii. p. 30.

ornamented by a class of calico-painters, the descendants of a party who were invited to settle here under the Dutch Government, nearly two hundred years ago. The goldsmiths are ingenious and excellent workmen, and produce bangles, chains, and rings, whose execution is as fine as their designs are tasteful. Nothing is more interesting than to watch one of these primitive artists at his occupation, seated in the open air, with no other apparatus than a few clumsy tools, a blow-pipe, and a chatty full of sand on which to light his charcoal-fire.

The crushing of the coco-nut for the expression of the oil is another flourishing branch of trade, and for this purpose the natives erect their creaking mills under the shade of the groves of palm-trees near their houses. These consist of the trunk of a tree hollowed into a mortar, in which a heavy upright pestle is worked round by a bullock yoked to a transverse beam.

A NATIVE OIL MILL.

Jaffna is almost the only place in Ceylon of which it might be said that no one is idle or unprofitably employed. The bazaars are full of activity, and stocked with a greater variety of fruits and vegetables than is to be seen in any other town in the island. Every one appears to be more or less busy; and at the season of the year when labour is not in demand at home, numbers of the natives go off to trade in the interior;

carrying adventures of curry stuffs, betel-leaves, and other produce, to be sold in the villages of the Wanny. Large bodies of them also resort annually to the south, where they find lucrative employment in repairing the village tanks,—a species of labour in which they are peculiarly expert, and which the Singhalese are too indolent or too litigious to perform for themselves. If the deserted fields and solitudes of the Wanny are ever again to be re-peopled and re-tilled, I am inclined to believe that the movement for that purpose will come from the Tamils of Jaffna; for, looking to their increasing intelligence and wealth, their habits of industry and adaptation to an agricultural life, I can have little doubt that, as population increases, and the arable lands of the peninsula become occupied, emigration will gradually be directed towards the south, where, with the natural capabilities of the soil and the facilities for irrigation, one half of the exertion and toil bestowed on the reluctant sands of Jaffna would speedily convert the wilderness into a garden. Already there is a satisfaction, experienced in no other portion of Ceylon, in visiting their villages and farms, and in witnessing the industrious habits and improved processes of the peasantry. The whole district is covered with a net-work of roads, and at certain situations there exist what are maintained in no other part of the island (except at Matura in the south), regular markets, to which the peasantry resort from a distance, and bring their fruit, vegetables, and other produce for sale. These markets are generally held in the early morning, before the sun pours down his fiercest rays; and in driving along the roads at such an hour, the active and busy picture which they present would have strongly reminded me of some rural scenes in England, had it not been for the disproportionate share of the labour borne by the women, who always seemed to carry the heaviest burdens, and to take the most toilsome share in the business of the day.

Even amongst the more civilised portion of the Tamils, there is no characteristic which so forcibly as this demonstrates the barbarism of their customs, and the degraded nature of their domestic relations. Though the outward demeanour of men of the higher castes and of ambitious pretensions, and the nature of their public pursuits, may draw off attention from their homes and their personal habits; still their social arrangements, and the economy of their private establishments, when these can be examined, exhibit a picture of demoralisation truly deplorable.

Notwithstanding all that has been achieved by the successful labours of the Christian missions in the peninsula[1], the private life of such of the lowest classes of the people as are still uninfluenced by moral instruction, and untouched by civilisation, is, of course, still more depraved and disgusting. Their households exhibit none of those endearments and comforts which constitute the charms and attractions of a home. Sensuality and gain are the two passions of their existence, and in the pursuit of these they exhibit a licentiousness so shocking, and practices so inconceivably vile, as would scarcely obtain credence from those who are familiar only with the aspect and usages of civilised life, even in its lowest and least attractive forms.

Amongst the Tamils in Ceylon, as amongst the natives on the coast of India, the belief in sorcery is strongly and generally entertained, and its professors turn the practice of witchcraft and charms to lucrative account, pandering to the worst passions of degraded humanity by the secret exercise of pretended arts, and the performance of revolting ceremonies. In 1849, an occurrence of this kind was brought officially under my notice, involving the disclosure of practices, the existence of which amidst a dense popu-

[1] For an account of the missions in Jaffna, and especially of the American missionaries and their labours, see Sir J. EMERSON TENNENT'S *History of Christianity in Ceylon*, ch. iv. pp. 138—176, &c.

lation, and in the vicinity of the chief town of the province, is in itself an exemplification of the mass of barbarism and superstition which still exists amongst the natives of Jaffna, even after three hundred years of European government, and despite the labours and achievements of so many Christian teachers and ministers.

In December, 1848, the police vidahn of Vannarpoonne, in the suburbs of Jaffna, came to the magistrate in much mental agitation and distress, to complain that the remains of his son, a boy of about eight years of age, which had been buried the day before, had been disinterred during the night, and that the head had been severed from the body to be used for the purposes of witchcraft. Suspicion fell on a native doctor of the village, who was extensively consulted as an adept in the occult sciences; but no evidence could be produced sufficient to connect him with the transaction. The vidahn stated to the magistrate that a general belief existed amongst the Tamils in the fatal effects of a ceremony, performed with the skull of a child, with the design of producing the death of an individual against whom the incantation was directed. The skull of a male child, and particularly of a first-born, is preferred, and the effects are regarded as more certain if it be killed expressly for the occasion; but for ordinary purposes, the head of one who had died a natural death is presumed to be sufficient. The form of the ceremony is to draw certain figures and cabalistic signs upon the skull, after it has been scraped and denuded of the flesh; adding the name of the individual upon whom the charm is to take effect. A paste is then prepared, composed of sand from the footprints of the intended victim, and a portion of his hair moistened with his saliva, and this, being spread upon a leaden plate, is taken, together with the skull to the graveyard of the village, where for forty nights the evil spirits are invoked to destroy the person so denounced. The universal belief of the natives is, that as the ceremony proceeds, and the paste dries up on the leaden plate, the sufferer will waste away and decline, and that death, as an inevitable consequence, must follow.

In this instance a watch was kept upon the proceedings of the suspected doctor, and it was ascertained that he and his family were engaged in the most infamous practices. His sons were his assistants in operations similar to that which has been described, and in the preparation of philters to facilitate seduction and medicines for procuring abortion. His house was an asylum for unmarried females in pregnancy, where their accouchements were assisted by women retained for their knowledge of midwifery; and the skulls of the infants were applied as occasion required for the composition of love potions and the performance of incantations.

In the course of the following month[1], a second complaint against the same individual was brought before the magistrate at Jaffna, to the effect that on a stated morning, he had murdered an infant in order to possess himself of its head, and that at the moment of bringing the charge, a second child was concealed in his dwelling, and destined for a similar fate. On searching the house the body of one child was found as represented, with the head recently severed; and after considerable search, the other little creature was discovered, still alive, under some baskets near the roof of an inner apartment. The doctor and his sons had been seen on previous occasions to bury something in the garden at the rear of the building. On this being dug over, the remains of other children were discovered, in sufficient numbers to attest the extent of the practice. Unfortunately the criminal was himself permitted to escape; the character of his establishment, and the testimony of the women in his service

[1] 8th January, 1849.

giving some colour to his assertion, that the infants whose remains were disinterred had died a natural death; whilst he was able to offer a plausible explanation for the mutilation of the body that had been found, by declaring that it was devoured by a Pariah dog. His papers were seized by the magistrate, among which was a volume of receipts for compounding nefarious preparations and poisons;—and along with these a manuscript book containing the necessary diagrams and forms of invocation to "Siva the Destroyer," for every imaginable purpose—"to seduce the affections of a female—to effect a separation between a husband and wife—to procure abortion—to possess with a devil—to afflict with sickness,"—and innumerable directions "for procuring the death of an enemy." In this remarkable treatise on domestic medicine, there was not one single receipt for the cure of disease amongst the numerous formulas for its infliction; nor one instruction for effecting a harmless or benevolent purpose amidst diagrams and directions for gratifying the depraved passions, and encouraging the fiendish designs of the author's dupes.

Thus the same energy of character in which the Tamils of Jaffna constitutionally excel the Singhalese and Kandyans, and which is strikingly exhibited in all their ordinary pursuits, is equally perceptible in its vicious as in its moral developments. In both particulars the two races that are most nearly assimilated in Ceylon are the Hindus of the northern province, and the active-minded and vigorous Moors of the south and east;—next to these are the mountaineers of Kandy and Oovah; whilst the weakest and the most cunning are the natives of the lowlands and the maritime districts. The statistics of crime as exhibited by the calendars of the Supreme Court are demonstrative of these local peculiarities. Amongst the Singhalese of the low country, the majority of the crimes cognisable by the higher tribunals are generally of a secondary character, and the instances in which violence to the person accompanies offences against property are fewer than in other parts of the island. The proportion of cases so aggravated increases in the southern and Kandyan provinces; and crime in the north consists principally of burglary, frequently accompanied by personal violence and characterised by daring and combination.[1]

[1] From a paper on the state of crime in *Ceylon*, by the Hon. Mr. Justice STARKE, published in the *Transactions of the Ceylon Asiatic Society*, vol. i. p. 52.

CHAP. VII.

THE ISLANDS.—ADAM'S BRIDGE AND THE PEARL FISHERY.

As, owing to the shallows, the Government steamer,—the "Seaforth," on board which we were to be received at Jaffna,—was unable to approach nearer than the group of islands that lie off the western point of the peninsula, we were rowed in one of the great canoes called *ballams*, or *vallams*[1] through the channel of Kayts[2], under the miniature fort of Hammaniel[3], and embarked off the island of Analativoe or Donna Clara.[4] We brought to, an hour after starting, at the island of Delft. "The portion of Ceylon," says PLINY, "which approaches nearest to India is the promontory of *Coliacum*, and midway between it and the mainland is *the island of the Sun;*"[5]—assuming the Coliacum of Pliny

---

[1] The ballams are usually hollowed out of the trunk of the *Angely* or *Angelica* tree (*artocarpus hirsuta?*). These canoes are generally brought from the coast of India, chiefly from Mangalore and Calicut.

[2] Kayts, or Cays, was so called from the Portuguese term for a wharf, *cais* or *caes*, this being the utmost point to which a sea-going vessel could enter the shallows on approaching Jaffna.

[3] VALENTYN explains this term by saying, that as the outline of Ceylon resembled that of a ham, this little island occupied the position of its shank or heel, whence its name, "*hamman-hiel.*" — *Oud en Nieuw Oost-Indien*, ch. i. p. 18; elsewhere, ch. xv. p. 217, VALENTYN calls Hammaniel the "Water Fort:" upon this, and upon the land fort at Kangesentorre, the Dutch relied as defences against the passage of ships towards Jaffna.—*Ibid.* ch. ii. p. 31.

[4] Donna Clara, who appears to have been the chief owner of this islet in the time of the Portuguese, was renowned for her extraordinary size; her chair, according to RIBEYRO, was preserved in his time as the sole curiosity of the island; "et les deux plus gros hommes y peuvent tenir assis très à l'aise et très au large."—Lib. i. ch. xxv. p. 190.

[5] PLINY, *Nat. Hist.*, lib. xvi. ch. xxiv. The Coliacum of PLINY is identical with the Κόλχοι of the *Periplus*, the Κωλιακον of STRABO, and the "Κωλιῶος αἴης" of DIONYSIUS PERIEGETES, verse 1148; see also VINCENT's *Periplus*, &c., vol. ii. p. 488, 502.

to be *Ramancoil* or Ramiseram, Delft would appear to be "the island of the Sun." Its length does not exceed seven or eight miles, and a tiny lake, formed in a depression in its centre, so facilitates vegetation and the growth of trees, that the Portuguese, whilst in possession of Manaar, occupied it as a breeding place for cattle and horses, and hence it acquired from them its designations of the "Ilha das Vacas," and "Ilha dos Cavallos."[1] The breed of the latter, which had been originally imported from Arabia, was kept up by the Dutch, and afterwards for some time by the English, the horses being allowed the free range of the island, and when required were caught by the lasso, in the use of which the natives had probably been instructed by the Portuguese.[2] The stud was discontinued many years ago, the buildings constructed for it have since gone to ruin, and the island is now thickly inhabited and partially brought under cultivation.

As we approached the Indian side of the channel at sunrise on the following morning, we landed on the island of Ramiseram, to visit the Great Pagoda, the lofty towers of which were visible long before we were able to discern the low sandy beach on which it is built. This shrine, which, in the estimation of the Brahmans, has rendered Ramiseram one of the most sacred spots in the universe, is dedicated to Rama, whose invasion of Ceylon from this point is commemorated by so many incidents

---

[1] RIBEYRO says, it was also called by the Portuguese the "Ilha das Cabras," because of the multitude of goats which it fed, and he adds that it supplied the finest bezoar stones in the world. (Lib. i. ch. xxv. p. 188.)

[2] "The horses run wild on the island and are caught by driving them into a *korahl*, which is circular and fenced with round stones—here, one in particular being pitched on, some of the natives set after him with ropes made into a noose, eight fathom long, and the thickness of a man's finger. This they contrive to throw about one of his hind legs whilst he is in full gallop, and thus make sure of him. One cannot see this manœuvre practised without the greatest astonishment, for these horse-catchers are so trained that they never fail. They teach their children this art (by practising) on a man, and I have tried them on myself. I had only to say on which arm or foot I chose to have the rope thrown while I was running as fast as I was able, and it was done."—*Memoirs of Wolf*, p. 197.

in the surrounding region. The islet on which it stands is, and has been immemorially, exempted from cultivation; its inhabitants are interdicted from all secular pursuits and callings, and the place consecrated to devotion, solemnity, and repose. The temple or *coil*, with its majestic towers, its vast and gloomy colonnades, and its walls encrusted with carved work and statuary, exhibits a grand example of the style of such monuments in Southern India; though inferior in dimensions to those of Seringham, Madura, and Tanjore.[1]

We found the vicinity of the Pagoda surrounded by thousands of pilgrims from all parts of India; mingled with whom were fakirs of the most hideous aspect, exhibiting their limbs in inconceivably repulsive attitudes. Gaudy vehicles, covered with gilding and velvet, and drawn by cream-coloured oxen, carried ladies of distinction, who had crossed in pilgrimage from the opposite coast, and beside the grand porch stood the lofty cars of the idol, structures of richly-carved wood adorned with vermilion and gold. At the great entrance of the temple, we were received by the officers, and conducted round the immense quadrangle, supported by innumerable columns. Here we were met by the band of nautch girls, who presented us with flowers, and performed before us one of their melancholy and spiritless movements, which is less a dance than a series of postures, wherein the absence of grace is sought to be compensated by abrupt gestures, stamping the feet and wringing the arms, to extract an inharmonious accompaniment from the jingling of bangles and anklets.

On leaving the temple, we rounded the western point of the island, and entered the gulf of Manaar, by the Paumbam Passage, which here intersects Adam's Bridge.

[1] Detailed descriptions of the Temple of Ramiseram, and its establishment will be found in Lord VALENTIA'S *Travels, &c.*, vol. i. p. 339, &c.; and in CORDINER'S *Ceylon, &c.*, vol. ii. ch. xv. p. 12; PERCIVAL'S *Ceylon, &c.*, vol. i. p. 80.

The advantages of this narrow channel are so striking, and the facilities already afforded by its enlargement are so highly appreciated, that surprise is excited that a work of such imperial importance as the deepening of this channel should have been so long deferred, and so imperfectly accomplished, when at last undertaken. Such is the circuit that a vessel is obliged to make in sailing from Bombay to Madras, in order to guard against calms on the line, and to weather the Maldives and Ceylon, that practically she "performs a voyage of five thousand miles, although the real distance by sea does not exceed *fifteen hundred*."[1] The barrier that here obstructs the communication between Palk's Bay and the Gulf, — appropriately called the "dam," — is about a mile and quarter in length. The rocks, which are flat upon the upper surface, have been so curiously broken up and intersected by the action of the waves, that they present the closest possible resemblance to

PAUMBAM PASSAGE, ADAM'S BRIDGE

deliberate arrangement, and "bear every appearance of having been placed there by art."[2]

Formerly, the fissure, through which small craft alone

[1] *Minute of the* GOVERNOR OF MADRAS, November, 1828.

[2] COTTON'S *Report on the Paumbam Passage*, September, 1822.

could pass, was but thirty-five yards wide, with a maximum depth of little more than six feet of water.[1] Lately, this passage has been so enlarged and improved, that vessels drawing ten feet may venture through it in safety. On the east side, the white houses of the village of Paumbam line the beach, nestling beneath groves of coco-nut palms and arborescent mimosas, and on the west the low line of the Indian coast approaches so close, that the passage of the steamer disturbed the sea-birds which were feeding in the ripple of the waves upon the shore.

Turning eastward at Paumbam, on our way towards Manaar and Aripo, we kept as close as the shallows rendered prudent, to the long line of sandy embankments, which form the barrier of Adam's Bridge. The composition of this singular reef has been already alluded to[2], and recent examinations have shown that, instead of being a remnant of the original rock, by which Ceylon is supposed to have been once connected with the Indian continent, it is in reality a comparatively recent ridge of conglomerate and sandstone[3], covered with alluvial deposits, carried by the currents and heaped up at this particular point, whilst the gradual rising of the coast has contributed to give the reef its present altitude.[4]

---

[1] BALDÆUS relates the improbable story, that in 1657 fifteen Portuguese frigates, chased by the Dutch cruisers, escaped through the passage of Paumbam; a circumstance which he accounts for by the still more unlikely conjecture, that the natives in charge of the channel had the power of adjusting the depth of the water by "either laying in or removing certain stones from the entrance."—P. 709.

[2] See Vol. I. Pt. I. ch. i. p. 15, 20.

[3] "It appears to be sandstone of a soft description, and generally in an advanced stage of decay. It is hardest at the surface, and becomes softer and coarser towards the bottom, which last has more the appearance of indurated gravel than rock."—Major SIM'S *Report on Adam's Bridge*, 1828; see Capt. STEWART'S *Report to the Governor of Ceylon*, 1837.

[4] The Dutch, although they adopted the popular theory that Ceylon had been separated from India by a sudden convulsion, entertained doubts of the primary formation of Adam's Bridge, and VALENTYN suggests that its origin is referable to the deposit of sand at the point where the currents meet at the change of the monsoons.—*Oud en Nieuw Oost-Indien*, ch. xv. p. 218.

From its frequent disruption by the sea, and the deposit of sand-drift on its surface, the formation to the east, between Ramiseram and Manaar, presents less of the artificial appearance which is exhibited in the vicinity of Paumbam, and which no doubt sufficed in ancient times to establish the belief that it was in reality a causeway constructed by superhuman power. The Hindus ascribed its origin to Rama[1], and amongst the Mahometans, the belief that Adam had found a retreat in Ceylon on his expulsion from Paradise, led to the conjectures that he must either have alighted from the sky, or passed by this singular causeway.

[1] The legend of the building of the bridge by Rama for the passage of his army to the conquest of Lanka, forms one of the episodes in the *Ramayana*. In the *Calcutta Review*, No. x. p. 290, a translation of this passage has been given, and the mischievous character of Hanuman, the monkey-god, has been preserved in the tale which is related, to the effect that his jealousy of Nala, who was associated with him in forming the Bridge, led him to obstruct rather than to further the work. The legend is told as follows: Rama having solicited Nala (one of the monkey chiefs) to throw a bridge across the Strait, the latter relying on the power imparted to him by Brahma "of causing stones, trees, and rocks to float," undertook to complete the task within a month, although the distance from Lanka to the mainland was then eight hundred miles. "He first caused one of the huge forests which grew along the shore to be transplanted and placed upon the waters. Upon this bedding of trees he placed several strata of rocks, and made the breadth of the bridge eighty miles. The first day he completed the work to a length of eight miles, beginning from the north and proceeding southward. While the bridge was being built the deafening noises produced by the mallets, and the incessant cries of 'Victory to Rama,' rent the air."

Of all the monkeys none so exerted himself in bringing rocks as Hanuman, until becoming enraged, and regarding it as an indignity that Nala should receive them in his left hand, Hanuman lifted a mountain under which to crush him; but was appeased by the interposition of Rama, who explained that the action of Nala was the ordinary practice of masons. "When the bridge extended to 100 miles in length, hundreds of squirrels came to the sea-shore to assist in the work. On the shore they rolled their bodies among heaps of dust, then, going up to the bridge, they shook off the dust, and thus effectually filled the minute crevices. Hanuman, not appreciating the services of these little creatures, flung numbers of them into the sea. With tearful eyes they came to Rama, and said, 'O Lord, we are grievously annoyed by Hanuman.' Summoning Hanuman into his presence, Rama thus addressed him, 'Why dost thou dishonour the squirrels? Let every one contribute to the work according to his ability.' Hanuman blushed, and the benevolent and merciful Rama stroked the squirrels on their backs. Thus did Nala in the space of a month construct a bridge extending eight hundred miles in length and eighty in breadth, and when the work was finished the monkeys cried out, 'Victory to Rama, Victory to Rama.'"

VALENTYN says, that the name of Adam's Bridge was first conferred on it by the Portuguese[1]; but there is existing evidence to show that centuries before the appearance of the Portuguese in the East, the Arabs believed that Adam had passed by this way into Ceylon.[2]

In coasting along this remarkable shore, the extreme purity of the water enabled us to see, with astonishing distinctness, the coral groves which rise in the clear blue depths, and conceal the surface of the sand and rocks. Their branches, when severed, are exquisitely beautiful, so long as they retain the faint purple halo that plays around their ivory tips, but which disappears after a very short exposure to the air[3]; so rapidly does atmospheric exposure affect them, that immediately after withdrawing them from the water, we almost fail to recognise the lovely objects which a moment before were glowing in the still recesses below. The cilia and bright tentacula of the polypi are withdrawn and concealed the instant the coral is disturbed, but these, when expanded in the water, cover the surface with brilliant tints, intense crimson and emerald green. Feeding amongst them, are to be seen nudibranchiate mollusca and *aplysia* of strange forms; and through the branches dart small fishes, with scales that glisten like enamelled silver.

Manaar appears to be the island of Epiodorus, which, according to the *Periplus*, was the seat of the pearl fishery.[4] At the present day, its importance has greatly declined. The Portuguese, who wrested it from the Raja of Jaffna, in 1560[5], fortified the town

---

[1] VALENTYN, *Oud en Nieuw Oost-Indien*, ch. xv. p. 235.

[2] See a passage in KASWINI'S *Ajaib el Makhlookat*, written in the thirteenth century, and quoted by Sir W. OUSELEY.—*Travels, &c.*, vol. i. p. 37.

[3] PLINY says that the soldiers of Alexander noticed the purple halo which plays about the coral in the Indian seas when first withdrawn from the water, "in alto quasdam arbusculas colore bubuli cornus ramosas *et cacuminibus rubentes.*"—PLINY, *Nat. Hist.*, lib. xiii. ch. li.

[4] *Periplus*, ch. lix. See VINCENT, vol. ii. p. 480.

[5] DE COUTO, dec. vii. lib. iii. ch. v. vol. iv. pt. i. p. 210; VALENTYN, ch. xii. p. 147; FARIA Y SOUZA, pt. ii. ch. xv. vol. ii. p. 206.

for the protection of their own trade, and the Dutch, who seized it in 1658, were so conscious of its value, strategetical as well as commercial, that they designated it "the key of Jaffnapatam," and maintained in it at all times an effective garrison, under the apprehension that the Portuguese, if they ever attempted a re-conquest of Ceylon, would direct their first efforts to the recovery of Manaar.[1]

During the early ages, a considerable portion of the trade between the east and west of India was carried through the narrow channel which separates Manaar from Ceylon, and active establishments were formed, not only at Mantotte on the mainland, but in the little island itself, to be used for unlading and reloading such craft as it was necessary to lighten, in order to assist them over the shoals.[2] No other than commercial motives could have led to the formation of populous towns in the midst of arid wastes, around which fertile lands extended on every side, and hence the peopling of Manaar, whose barren sand-drifts, though incapable of producing a sufficient quantity of grain for the wants of its inhabitants, were adapted to the growth of the palmyra and the coco-nut palm.

Manaar also yields in abundance the choya-root[3], which was once exported to Europe for the sake of its brilliant red dye; and its shores, besides producing salt, afford favourable positions for the fishery of chanks[4],

---

[1] "De sleutel van 't Ryk van Jaffnapatam."—VALENTYN, *Oud en Nieuw Oost-Indien*, ch. xii. p. 150.

[2] See a paper by Sir ALEXANDER JOHNSTON, containing particulars of the early settlement of the Mahometans in Ceylon, collected from the traditions of the Moors at the present day.—*Trans. Roy. Asiat. Soc.*, vol. i. p. 538†; BERTOLACCI, p. 20.

[3] *Hedyotis umbellata.*

[4] COSMAS INDICOPLEUSTES evidently refers to chanks when he speaks of the port of Marallo, *βάλλουσα κοχλιους*, and ABOUZEYD calls them "*schenek*,—mot par lequel on désigne cette grande coquille qui sert de trompette et qui est très-recherché."—*Voyages Arabes, &c.*, tom. i. p. 6. Hence as early as the sixth and seventh centuries, the vicinity of Ceylon was fished for these valuable shells. See LASSEN, *Alterthumskunde*, vol. i. p. 194; REINAUD, *Mém. sur l'Inde*, p. 229. The fishery of chanks was formerly a Government royalty, and was annually farmed, but the monopoly was abandoned some years ago. BERTOLACCI, p. 263, and a writer in the *Asiatic Journal for* 1827, p. 469, both mention a curious local peculiarity observed by the

and the preparation of the holothuria, which feed on the coral polypi, and are captured to be dried in the sun, and exported to China under the name of "tripang" and *bicho de mar*.[1]

One of the most remarkable animals on the coast is the dugong[2], a phytophagous cetacean, numbers of which are attracted to the inlets, from the bay of Calpentyn to Adam's Bridge, by the still water and the abundance of marine algæ in these parts of the gulf. The rude approach to the human outline, observed in the shape of the head of this creature, and the attitude

FEMALE DUGONG OF CEYLON.

fishermen in the natural history of the chank. "All shells found to the northward of a line drawn from a point about midway from Manaar to the opposite coast (of India) are of the kind called *patty*, and are distinguished by a short flat head; and all those found to the southward of that line are of the kind called *pajel*, and are known from having a longer and more pointed head than the former. Nor is there ever an instance of deviation from this singular law of nature. The *Wallampory*, or "right hand chanks," are found of both kinds.

[1] On placing one of these curious creatures in a basin it discharged the contents of its stomach; first, streams of water, and then quantities of sand, small stones, and comminuted coral and shells until it was reduced to a flaccid mass—again inflating itself to its original size by re-imbibing the water. Mr. BRODIE, in a valuable paper on the districts of Chilaw and Putlam, printed in the *Journ. of the Ceylon Branch of the Asiatic Society*, says of the tripang that the holothurias are picked up at ebb tide, and after being embowelled are boiled for two hours till quite soft, and then dried in the sun. The price, on the spot, is about three shillings and ninepence for 1000, and "this quantity," he says, "can be easily collected by two men during one ebb tide."

[2] *Halicore Dugung*.

of the mother while suckling her young, holding it to her breast with one flipper, while swimming with the other, holding the heads of both above water, and when disturbed, suddenly diving and displaying her fish-like tail,—these, together with her habitual demonstrations of strong maternal affection, probably gave rise to the fable of the "mermaid;" and thus that earliest invention of mythical physiology may be traced to the Arab seamen and the Greeks, who had watched the movements of the dugong in the waters of Manaar.

Megasthenes records the existence of a creature in the ocean, near Taprobane, with the aspect of a woman[1]; and Ælian, adopting and enlarging on his information, peoples the seas of Ceylon with fishes having the heads of lions, panthers, and rams, and, stranger still, *cetaceans in the form of satyrs.* Statements such as these must have had their origin in the hairs, which are set round the mouth of the dugong, somewhat resembling a beard, which Ælian and Megasthenes both particularise, from their resemblance to the hair of a woman; "καὶ γυναικῶν ὄπσιν ἔχουσιν αἶσπερ ἀντι πγοκάμων ἄκανθαι προς ἤρητηνται."[2]

The Portuguese cherished the belief in the mermaid, and the annalist of the exploits of the Jesuits in India, gravely records that seven of these monsters, male and female, were captured at Manaar in 1560, and carried to Goa, where they were dissected by Demas Bosquez, physician to the Viceroy, and "their internal structure found to be in all respects conformable to the human."[3] One which was killed at Manaar and sent to me to Colombo[4] in 1847, measured upwards of seven feet in length; but specimens considerably larger have been taken at Calpentyn, and their flesh is represented to me as closely resembling veal.

---

[1] MEGASTHENES, *Indica*, fragm. lix.

[2] ÆLIAN, *Nat. Hist.*, lib. xvi. ch. xviii.

[3] *Hist. de la Compagnie de Jésus*, quoted in the *Asiat. Journ.* vol. xiv. p. 461; and in FORBES' *Orient. Memoirs*, vol. i. p. 421.

[4] The skeleton is now in the Museum of the Natural History Society of Belfast.

The fort at Manaar, built by the Portuguese and strengthened by the Dutch, is still in tolerable repair, and the village presents an aspect of industry and comfort. But the country beyond is sterile and repulsive, covered by a stunted growth of umbrella trees and buffalo thorns. The most singular objects in the landscape are a number of the monstrous baobab trees (*Adansonia digitata*), whose importation from the western coast of Africa to India and Ceylon is a mystery as yet unsolved. The popular conjecture is, that it was the work of the Portuguese; but the age of the trees, as indicated by their prodigious dimensions, is altogether inconsistent with this hypothesis, and their introduction is probably referable to the same early mariners who brought the coffee-tree to Arabia, and the cinnamon laurel to Malabar.

BAOBAB TREES AT MANAAR.

The huge and shapeless mass of wood in these singular trees resembles a bulb rather than a stem. One of the largest, at Manaar, measured upwards of thirty feet in circumference, although it was a very little more in height.

No scene in Ceylon presents so dreary an aspect as the long sweep of desolate shore to which, from time immemorial, adventurers have resorted from the utmost ends of the earth in search of the precious pearls for which this gulf is renowned. On approaching it the perceptible landmark is a building erected by Lord Guildford, as a temporary residence for the Governor, and known by the name of the "Doric," from the style of its architecture. A few coco-nut palms appear next above the low sandy beach, and presently are discovered the scattered houses which form the villages of Aripo and Condatchy.

Between these two places, or rather between the Kalaar and Arrive rivers, the shore is raised to a height of many feet, by enormous mounds of shells, the accumulations of ages, the millions of oysters [1], robbed of their pearls, having been year after year flung into heaps, that extend for a distance of many miles.

During the progress of a fishery, this singular and dreary expanse becomes suddenly enlivened by the crowds who congregate from distant parts of India; a town is improvised by the construction of temporary dwellings, huts of timber and cajans, with tents of palm leaves or canvas; and bazaars spring up, to feed the multitude on land, as well as the seamen and divers in the fleets of boats that cover the bay.

My visit to the pearl banks was made in company with Capt. Steuart, the official inspector, and my immediate object was to inquire into the causes of the suspension of the fisheries, and to ascertain the probability of reviving a source of revenue, the gross receipts from which had failed for several years to defray the cost of conservancy. In fact, as it afterwards proved, the pearl banks, between 1837 and 1854, were an annual charge, instead of producing an annual income, to the colony. The conjecture, hastily adopted, to account for the disappearance of mature shells, had reference to mechanical

---

[1] It is almost unnecessary to say that the shell fish which produces the true Oriental pearls is not an oyster, but belongs to the genus Avicula, or more correctly, Meleagrina. It is the *Meleagrina Margaritifera* of Lamarck.

causes; the received hypothesis being that the young broods had been swept off their accustomed feeding grounds owing to the establishment of unusual currents, occasioned by deepening the narrow passage at Paumbam. It was also suggested, that a previous Governor, in his eagerness to replenish the colonial treasury, had so "scraped" and impoverished the beds as to exterminate the oysters. To me, neither of these suppositions appeared worthy of acceptance; for, in the frequent disruptions of Adam's Bridge, there was ample evidence that the currents in the Gulf of Manaar had been changed at former times without destroying the pearls; and, moreover, the oysters had disappeared on many former occasions, without any imputation of improper management on the part of the conservators, and returned after much longer intervals of absence than that which fell under my own notice, and which was then creating serious apprehension in the colony.

A similar interruption had been experienced between 1820 and 1828: the Dutch had had no fishing for twenty-seven years, from 1768 till 1796, and they had been equally unsuccessful from 1732 till 1746. The Arabs were well acquainted with similar vicissitudes, and Albyrouni (a contemporary of Avicenna), who served under Mahmoud of Ghaznee, and wrote in the eleventh century, says that the pearl fishery, which formerly existed in the Gulf of Serendib, had become exhausted in his time, simultaneously with the appearance of a fishery at Sofala, in the country of the Zends, where pearls were unknown before; and says, hence arose the conjecture that the pearl oyster of Serendib had migrated to Sofala.[1]

[1] "Il y avait autrefois dans le Golfe de Serendyb, une pêcherie de perles qui s'est epuisée de notre temps. D'un autre côté il s'est formé une pêcherie à Sofala dans le pays des Zends, là où il n'en existait pas auparavant—on dit qui c'est la pêcherie de Serendyb qui s'est transportée à Sofala."—ALBYROUNI, *in* REINAUD'S *Fragmens Arabes, &c.*, p. 125; see also REINAUD'S *Mémoire sur l'Inde*, p. 228.

It appeared to me that the explanation of the phenomenon was to be sought, not merely in external causes, but also in the instincts and faculties of the animals themselves; and, on my return to Colombo, I ventured to renew a recommendation, which had been made years before, that a scientific inspector should be appointed to study the habits and the natural history of the pearl-oyster, and that his investigations should be facilitated by the means at the disposal of the Government.

Dr. Kelaart was appointed to this office, by Sir H. G. Ward, in 1857, and already his researches have developed results of great interest. In opposition to the received opinion that the pearl-oyster was incapable of voluntary movement, and unable of itself to quit the place to which it is originally attached[1], he has demonstrated, not only that it possesses locomotive powers, but also that their exercise is indispensable to its economy when obliged to search for food, or compelled to escape from local impurities. He has shown that, for this purpose, it can sever its byssus, and reform it at pleasure, so as to migrate and moor itself in favourable situations.[2] The establishment of this important fact may tend to solve the mystery of their occasional disappearances; and if coupled with the further discovery that it is susceptible of translation from place to place, and even from salt to brackish water, it seems reasonable to expect that beds may be formed with advantage in positions suitable for its growth and protection. Thus, like the edible oyster of our own shores, the pearl-oyster may be brought within the domain of pisciculture, and banks may be created in suitable places, just as the southern shores of France are now being colonised with oysters.

[1] STEUART'S *Pearl Fisheries of Ceylon*, p. 27; CORDINER'S *Ceylon, &c.*, vol. ii. p. 45.

[2] See Dr. KELAART'S Report on the Pearl Oyster in the *Ceylon Calendar for* 1858.—*Appendix*, p. 14.

under the direction of M. Coste.[1] The operation of sowing the sea with pearl, should the experiment succeed, would be as gorgeous in reality, as it is grand in conception; and the wealth of Ceylon, in her "treasures of the deep," might eclipse the renown of her gems when she merited the title of the "Island of Rubies."

On my arrival at Aripo, the pearl-divers, under the orders of their Adapanaar, put to sea, and commenced the examination of the banks.[2] The persons engaged in this calling are chiefly Tamils and Moors, who are trained for the service by diving for chanks. The pieces of apparatus employed to assist the diver in his operations are exceedingly simple in their character: they consist merely of a stone, about thirty pounds' weight, to accelerate the rapidity of his descent, this is suspended over the side of the boat, with a loop attached to it for receiving the foot; and of a net-work basket, which he takes down to the bottom and fills with the oysters as he collects them. MASSOUDI, one of the earliest Arabian geographers, describing, in the ninth century, the habits of the pearl-divers in the Persian Gulf, says that, before descending, each filled his ears with cotton steeped in oil, and compressed his nostrils by a piece of tortoise-shell.[3] This practice continues

[1] *Rapport de* M. COSTE, Professor d'Embryogénie, &c., Paris, 1858.

[2] Detailed accounts of the pearl fishery of Ceylon and the conduct of the divers, will be found in PERCIVAL'S *Ceylon*, ch. iii.; and in CORDINER'S *Ceylon*, vol. ii. ch. xvi. There is also a valuable paper on the same subject by Mr. LE BECK, in the *Asiatic Researches*, vol. v. p. 993; but by far the most able and intelligent description is contained in the *Account of the Pearl Fisheries of Ceylon*, by JAMES STEUART, Esq., Inspector of the Pearl Banks, 4to. Colombo, 1843.

[3] MASSOUDI says that the Persian divers, as they could not breathe through their nostrils, *cleft the root of the ear* for that purpose: "*Ils se fendaient la racine de l'oreille pour respirer;* en effet, ils ne peuvent se servir pour cet objet des narines, vu qu'ils se les bouchent avec des morceaux d'ecailles de tortue marine ou bien avec des morceaux de corne ayant la forme d'un fer de lance. En même temps ils se mettent dans l'oreille du coton trempé dans de l'huile." —*Moroudj-al-Dzeheb, &c.*, REINAUD, *Mémoire sur l'Inde*, p. 228.

there to the present day[1]; but the diver of Ceylon rejects all such expedients; he inserts his foot in the "sinking stone" and inhales a full breath; presses his nostrils with his left hand; raises his body as high as possible above water, to give force to his descent; and, liberating the stone from its fastenings, he sinks rapidly below the surface. As soon as he has reached the bottom, the stone is drawn up, and the diver, throwing himself on his face, commences with alacrity to fill his basket with oysters. This, on a concerted signal, is hauled rapidly to the surface; the diver assisting his own ascent by springing on the rope as it rises.

Improbable tales have been told of the capacity which these men acquire of remaining for prolonged periods under water. The divers who attended on this occasion were amongst the most expert on the coast, yet not one of them was able to complete a full minute below. Captain Steuart, who filled for many years the office of Inspector of the Pearl Banks, assured me that he had never known a diver to continue at the bottom longer than eighty-seven seconds, nor to attain a greater depth than thirteen fathoms; and on ordinary occasions they seldom exceeded fifty-five seconds in nine fathom water.[2]

The only precaution to which the Ceylon diver devotedly resorts, is the mystic ceremony of the shark-charmer, whose exorcism is an indispensable preliminary to every fishery. His power is believed to be

[1] Colonel WILSON says they compress the nose with horn, and close the ears with beeswax. See *Memorandum on the Pearl fisheries in Persian Gulf.—Journ. Geogr. Soc.* 1833, vol. iii. p. 283.

[2] RIBEYRO says that a diver could remain below whilst two *credos* were being repeated: "Il s'y tient l'espace de deux *credo*."—Lib. i. ch. xxii. p. 160. PERCIVAL says the usual time for them to be under water was two minutes, but that some divers stayed *four* or *five*, and one *six* minutes.—*Ceylon*, p. 91; LE BECK says that in 1797 he saw a Caffre boy from Karical, remain down for the space of seven minutes.—*Asiat. Res.* vol. v. p. 402.

hereditary; nor is it supposed that the value of his incantations is at all dependent upon the religious faith professed by the operator, for the present head of the family happens to be a Roman Catholic. At the time of our visit this mysterious functionary was ill and unable to attend; but he sent an accredited substitute, who assured me that although he himself was ignorant of the grand and mystic secret, the fact of his presence, as a representative of the higher authority, would be recognised and respected by the sharks.

Strange to say, though the Gulf of Manaar abounds with these hideous creatures, not more than one well authenticated accident[1] is known to have occurred from this source during any pearl fishery since the British have had possession of Ceylon. In all probability the reason is that the sharks are alarmed by the unusual number of boats, the multitude of divers, the noise of the crews, the incessant plunging of the sinking stones, and the descent and ascent of the baskets filled with shells. The dark colour of the divers themselves may also be a protection, whiter skins might not experience an equal impunity; and Massoudi relates that the divers of the Persian Gulf were so conscious of this advantage of colour, that they were accustomed to blacken their limbs, in order to baffle the sea monsters.[2]

The result of our examination of the pearl banks, on this occasion, was such as to discourage the hope of an early fishery. The oysters in point of number were abundant, but in size they were little more than "spat," the largest being barely a fourth of an inch in diameter. As at least seven years are required to furnish the growth at which pearls may be sought with advantage, the inspec-

---

[1] CORDINER'S *Ceylon*, vol. ii. p. 52.

[2] "Ils s'enduisaient les pieds et les jambes d'une substance noirâtre, afin de faire peur aux monstres marins, que, sans cela, seraient tentés de les devorer."—*Moroudj-al-Dzeheb*: REINAUD, *Mém. sur l Inde*, p. 228.

tion served only to suggest the prospect (which has since been realised) that in time the income from this source might be expected to revive;—and, forced to content ourselves with this anticipation, we weighed anchor from Condatchy, on the 30th March, and arrived on the following day at Colombo.

PART X.

THE RUINED CITIES.

CHAPTER I.

SIGIRI AND POLLANARRUA.

STRANGE as it may seem, it is nevertheless true, that Ceylon found no sufficient protection in its remoteness from the turbulent scenes of 1848, against the sporadic influence of the revolutionary miasma that overspread Europe in the spring of that year. The intelligence that monarchy had been overthrown, and a republic established in France, though received with indifference by the Tamils in the French settlement of Pondicherry, was eagerly employed to arouse the long suppressed wishes of the Kandyans for the restoration of their national independence[1]; at a time, moreover, when a variety of circumstances concurred to fan the tendency to discontent.[2] The exertions which, notwithstanding an excess of outlay over income, were successfully made by the government of Viscount Torrington to improve the financial system and relieve the commerce of the island by revising the tariff, had entailed the duty of re-distributing taxation, so as to extend some share of the burden to classes which had long been accustomed to almost total exemption from fiscal demands. In order to include the native population, who had previously contributed little to the public revenue, ordinances were passed to impose a small tax on shops, on fire-arms and dogs[3], and to require from each adult male six days' labour in the year (or three shillings

[1] *Papers relative to Ceylon,* presented to Parliament, 1849, p. 154–157.

[2] EARL GREY'S *Colonial Policy of Lord John Russell's Administration.* Vol. ii. p. 178, &c.

[3] The tax on fire-arms was intended to place some check on their possession by improper persons, and the tax on dogs was designed to diminish their numbers, and thus obviate the barbarous expedient of their annual slaughter in the streets. See Vol. I. Pt. II. ch. i. p. 145.

as its equivalent in money), to be applied exclusively to the formation of roads in the immediate locality of the contributors. The opportunity was tempting to represent the new taxes as a national grievance; and the facility was increased by the simultaneous issue of blank forms for collecting the agricultural statistics of the colony to be embodied in the Annual Report to the Secretary of State. These were represented to the Kandyans, by some of the disaffected chiefs, as a device for carrying out the intention of the Government to impose an onerous tax on the entire thirty or forty articles to be enumerated in the returns: and in the course of a few weeks the alarm became so general that tumultuous assemblages forced their way into the town of Kandy to demand explanations from the officials.

Information having been received by the Government from all quarters of the pains that had been taken to misrepresent their intentions and to disseminate discontent, it became necessary that I should visit the disquieted districts, and by personal exposition of the ordinances, disabuse the minds of the native population of the delusions by which their credulity had been imposed upon.

In the discharge of this duty, I met the people in public assemblies at Kandy and in the principal towns and villages throughout the central provinces of the island, traversing it northward from Matelle and Dambool to the ancient capitals of Pollanarrua and Anarajapoora, and returning by the west coast, through Putlam and Chilaw, to Colombo. Thence by sea I made the circuit of the island, stopping at every town on the coast, from Galle and Matura to Hambangtotte, Batticaloa, Trincomalie, and Jaffna.

As regarded its effect in removing the delusions by which the native races had been misled, my journey was signally successful. The Moors around the sea coast, the Tamils in the north, and the peaceful inhabitants of the great central forests, replied to my addresses by expressions of their entire satisfaction, and afterwards attested the sincerity of their assurances by refusing to take any share in the rebellious movements that eventually broke out;—but the Kandyan priests and those of the chiefs, by whom the obnoxious taxes had been used as a mere pretext for arousing their followers, on finding their devices exposed, abandoned all subterfuge, avowed their impatience of British rule, and took up arms to restore a national sovereignty. The means adopted by Lord Torrington to meet and stifle this dangerous movement are too recent and familiar to require recapitulation[1] here; and the circumstance is adverted to merely in explanation of the objects of the tour during which I visited the ruined capitals of Ceylon.

After an interview with the people in the great hall of the Pavilion at Kandy, on the 11th of July, 1848, I crossed the Mahawelli-ganga at the ferry of Katugastotte, near the tree which marks the scene of the massacre of Major Davie's party in 1803, and proceeded by the Trincomalie road in the direction of Matelle. The village on the opposite side of the river is inhabited by the Gahalayas, a race less degraded in blood, but more infamous in character than the Rodiyas. They acted as public executioners during the reign of the Kandyan kings, and being thus excluded from the social pale and withdrawn from the healthy influences of popular opinion, they became in later times thieves and marauders, and subsisted to a great extent by the plunder of travellers.

For seventeen miles the highway runs generally within sight of the Pinga-oya, a tributary of the Mahawelli-ganga, and as it approaches Matelle the road traverses luxuriant forests, now partially converted into flourishing plantations of coffee. The mountains over

[1] See EVIDENCE *taken by the Select Committee of the House of Commons on the Affairs of Ceylon*, 1850 *and* 1851, and PAPERS laid before Parliament, 1849, 1851, 1852.

which these are spread rise to the altitude of 5000 feet, wooded to their summits, and exhibiting noble specimens of some of the most remarkable trees in Ceylon, particularly talipat palms of towering height, and iron-wood trees, with crimson tipped foliage and mounds of delicate flowers. Nestled in a valley enclosed by these magnificent hills lies the picturesque town of Matelle, commanded by the now abandoned earthwork of Fort Mac Dowell.

Although no architectural antiquities remain to attest its former importance, Matelle, the *Maha-talawa* of the Singhalese chronicles, has been the scene of memorable events in the history of Ceylon.[1] Ninety years before the Christian era, it was one of the residences of the King Walagam-bahu, when driven from his capital by the Malabar invaders, and in the seventeenth century, A. D. 1630, it was formed into a principality, and conferred by King Senerat on the son of his predecessor, Wimala Dharma.[2] Some of the wealthiest of the Kandyan chiefs have their residences in its vicinity[3], and to the present day traces of the former luxury of the district are to be discovered in the occupations of the people. They excel in carving ivory, and in chasing the elaborately ornamented knives and swords of ceremony, which were formerly worn at the Kandyan court; they weave delicate matting for covering couches, and they paint, with a lacquer prepared by themselves, the shafts of the spears and wands which were formerly carried on occasions of ceremony.[4]

About two miles north of Matelle the road passes within sight of the Alu Wihara, the temple in which, a

---

[1] *Rajaratnacari*, p. 43, *Mahawanso* (UPHAM's Version), vol. i. ch. xxxiii. p. 210, TURNOUR's *Epitome, &c.*, p. 19.

[2] See *ante*, Vol. II. Pt. VI. ch. ii. p. 41. The fullest account of this interesting district, will be found in Major FORBES's *Eleven Years in Ceylon*, the author having held for some years an official appointment at Matelle.

[3] Among others, the patrimonial mansion and estates of the unhappy Eheylapola, the tragedy in whose family has been already related, Vol. II. Pt. VI. ch. iii. p. 87.

[4] For the preparation of this lacquer see *ante*, Vol. I. Pt. IV. ch. vii. p. 491, n.

century before the Christian era, scribes employed by the Singhalese king reduced to writing the doctrines of Buddha, which had been previously preserved by tradition alone.[1] The scene is a very extraordinary one;—huge masses of granitic rock have been precipitated from the crest of a mountain, and on these other masses have been hurled, which in their descent have splintered those beneath into gigantic fragments. In the fissures caused by these convulsions numbers of small apartments were formed at an early period, only two of which now remain. The principal one is almost concealed beneath the overhanging brow of an enormous boulder in a gloomy recess, darkened by beetling rocks, and shaded by the surrounding forest.

THE ALU WIHARA.

We passed the night at Nalandé, thirty miles north of Kandy, and slept in the small Roman Catholic church, which was prepared for our reception by screening off the altar. This was a kind of accommodation for

[1] See *ante*, Vol. I. Pt. III. ch. viii. p. 375.

which, during this and other journeys in the northern provinces, we were more than once indebted to the courtesy of the priests.

The country between Matelle and Nalande is extremely beautiful, and the road winds between wooded hills, the offsets of the Kandyan ranges, which here gradually sink into the level of the great northern plain. These are traversed by numerous streams, chiefly flowing eastward to the Amban-ganga, and in crossing, or, as too often happens, in fording them, one is forcibly impressed with the wisdom of the course recommended by Sir Howard Douglas, to be pursued in opening up an eastern country with highways,—to *build the bridges first*, and trust to the future for the formation of roads.

In Ceylon, for nine-tenths of the year, the ground is so indurated by the sun that it may be made traversable for wheel carriages simply by levelling the surface; and the real obstacle to movement is the depth of the nullahs hollowed out by the numerous rivers when swollen by the rains. Were the latter bridged over in the first instance, the traffic attracted would ensure the eventual construction of roads; but in Ceylon, where the opposite practice has prevailed, and roads have been opened in all directions, without bridges to connect them, they necessarily fall into disuse, and speedily become overgrown with jungle. Those who have visited Ceylon will admit, as an axiomatic truth, that in such a country bridges are more important than roads; whereas, roads without bridges are comparatively without value.

To the right of our line of march, between Lenadora and Dambool, stretched the low country once traversed by the celebrated canal of Ellahara, cut by Prakrama-bahu, in the 12th century[1], by which tradition asserts that an inland navigation was maintained from this

[1] FORBES'S *Eleven Years in Ceylon*, vol. ii. p. 95.

portion of Matelle to the sea; and in the bark of a tamarind-tree of patriarchal age and gigantic dimensions the peasantry point to marks said to be left by the ropes that were used in ancient times to moor boats at this point.[1] This remarkable channel served, at a later period, to conduct the waters of the Amban-ganga into the series of enormous tanks at Minery, Kowdellai, and Kandelai; and these, together with the intervening portions of low country, flooded by the intercepted waters, probably formed the submerged expanse which was known as the "*Sea of Prakrama.*"

Long before reaching Dambool, the enormous rock is descried, underneath which the temple has been hollowed out, which, from its antiquity, its magnitude, and the richness of its decorations, is by far the most renowned in Ceylon. The rock is a huge and somewhat cylindrical mound of gneiss, upwards of five hundred feet in height, and about two thousand feet in

THE ROCK AND TEMPLE OF DAMBOOL

length. It lies almost insulated on the otherwise level plain, and unconcealed by any verdure except a few

[1] *Report of* Messrs. ADAMS, CHURCHILL, and BAILEY, *on the Ellahara Canal.*

stunted plants in such crevices as retain sufficient moisture to support vegetation.

The cavern, which has been converted into a temple of Buddha, is the recess formed by the cylindric outline of the rock, enlarged by detaching with wedges further portions from the overhanging mass. No attempt has been made to impart an artificial character to the interior[1], and it retains the rude aspect of a cave, extending about one hundred and seventy feet in length and seventy feet broad, with a height of twenty feet in front, contracting as it recedes till it sinks into the level of the floor. It contains several separate apartments without any architectural arrangement, being merely irregularities in the natural recess somewhat enlarged by human labour. There is no effort at external decoration; the cliff is not scarped or cut into façades and columns, as at Karli and Ellora; and the partitions which separate the internal chambers are not pillars or colonnades, as in the caves of Elephanta and Ajunta, but rude walls of rock left untouched by the workman.

The ascent is by a steep and toilsome path across the lower mass of the great rock, and the grand gateway, profusely adorned with carvings in stone[2], and disclosing within a sedent figure of "the vanquisher," is approached on crossing a court-yard, which encloses a Bo-tree and some coco-nut palms.

The scene presented on entering is very striking,—the light being barely sufficient to display the long lines of statues of Buddha in the varied attitudes of exhortation and repose. They are arranged in unusual

[1] A detailed account of the Temple of Dambool is given in FORBES'S *Eleven Years in Ceylon*, vol. i. ch. xvi. p. 367, and one more recent by Mr. KNIGHTON, was published in the *Journal of the Asiatic Society of Bengal* for 1847, vol. xvi. pt. i. p. 340.

[2] A prominent object among the carvings at Dambool, and on other Buddhist monuments, is the *Makara*, a monster with the trunk of an elephant, the feet of a lion, the teeth of a crocodile, the eyes of a monkey, and the ears of a pig.

profusion, and some are of extraordinary magnitude, one in a reclining posture being upwards of forty feet in length.

ENTRANCE TO THE TEMPLE OF DAMBOOL.

The ceiling of this gloomy vault is concealed with painted cloths, and the walls of the principal apartment, the Maha-raja-dewale, are covered with a series of highly-coloured illustrations of scenes in the history of Buddhism, such as the landing of Wijayo, the preaching of Mahindo, and the combat of Dutugaimunu and Elala. A dagoba of graceful proportions occupies the centre of the hall, and the drops which filter through a crevice in the overhanging rock are caught in a hollow in the floor, and held to be as sacred as the waters of the Ganges. The temple contains a strange commixture of Brahmanical and Buddhist worship, and in all the apartments the statues of Hindu deities range with those of the great apostle of the Singhalese faith. Here, too, national gratitude has erected monuments to the memory of Walagam-bahu, the king by whom the temple was first endowed B.C. 86[1], and of Kirti Nissanga, whose munificence in its restoration and embellishment after its destruction by the Malabars in the twelfth century[2], is recorded in an inscription on the rock in the court-yard of the temple.[3] From the splendour which it then attained, the temple was afterwards known as *Swarna-giri-guhaaya*, "the Cave of the Golden Rock," a name from which we may infer that a *cave* among the Buddhists in Ceylon, as among their co-religionists in Ava, was not only the prototype of a temple, but also the model, the aspect and gloom of which it was the aim of such buildings in after times to emulate. In Burmah many of the pagodas are hollowed out in imitation of caverns, and are described by the word *koo*, which signifies "a cave."[4]

---

[1] *Rajaratnacari*, p. 43.

[2] The *Rajavali* says that Kirti Nissanga placed 72,000 statues of Buddha in this temple, p. 255. But this is an oriental pleonasm as the *Mahawanso*, ch. lxxix., reduces the number to *seventy-three*, and the *Rajaratnacari* to thirty-three, p. 92. The *Mahawanso*, to typify the munificence of Kirti Nissanga, says he "covered the walls of the temple with plates of silver, and roofed the buildings with tiles of gold."

[3] This remarkable inscription is translated at length in the Appendix to TURNOUR'S *Epitome*, &c., p. 95.

[4] "Amongst the Buddhist temples at Pagan, on the Irawaddi, there are several so named, such as *Shwé-koo*, "the golden cave," *Sembyo-koo*, "the elephant cave," &c. YULE'S *Ava*. p. 36.

The story has been already told[1] of the parricide king Kasyapa, who, in the fifth century, obtained the throne of Ceylon by the murder of his father Dhatu Sena, and who subsequently retired to the inaccessible fort of Sigiri. This extraordinary natural stronghold is situated in the heart of the great central forest, about fifteen miles north-east of Dambool. At Enamalua we left the highway to wind under the shade of the thick woods, by narrow tracks and jungle paths, until we reached the beautiful tank above which this gigantic cylindrical rock starts upwards to a height prodigious in comparison with the size of its section at any point, the area of its upper surface being very little more than an acre in extent. Its scarped walls are nearly perpendicular, and in some places they overhang their base. The formation of this singular cliff can only be ascribed to its upheaval by a subterranean force, so circumscribed in action that its effects were confined within a very few yards, yet so irresistible as to have shot aloft this prodigious pencil of stone to the height of nearly four hundred feet.

FORTIFIED ROCK OF SIGIRI.

The *Mahawanso* minutely describes the measures taken by Kasyapa, after the assassination of the king his father, whom he caused to be "built up in a wall, embedding

[1] See Vol. I., Pt. III. ch. ix.; *Mahawanso*, ch. xxxviii. p. 259.

him in it, with his face to the east, and plastering the aperture with clay.[1] Having repaired to Sigiri, a place difficult of access to men, and clearing it all round, *he surrounded it with a rampart.* He built there habitations which could only be reached by flights of steps, and these he ornamented with figures of lions, *Siha*, whence it obtained the name of *Siha-giri*, the 'Lions' Rock.'"[2] There are still the remains of an embankment, which, as tradition tells, once enclosed the entire area of the rock, forming a deep fosse filled with water, by which the fortress was protected. Of this the tank already alluded to was a part. It swarms with crocodiles, and at the time of my visit was thickly covered with the white and red flowers of the lotus.

To render this extraordinary retreat secure, Kasyapa carried galleries along the face of the cliff, partially hollowing them out of the rock, and protected them in front by strong curtain-walls of stone. A spring still trickles down the precipice, the existence of which has given rise to the tradition that a cistern was formed at the top, whose waters overflow after the torrents of the monsoons, but no adventurous climber has succeeded in testing the truth of the popular belief. The palace of the king stood on a triangular bastion, facing the north-west, and protected on two sides by the moat. It is now a shapeless mass of débris and fallen brickwork.

Our attempts to penetrate the ruined galleries were defeated by the insufferable heat which glowed within the walls, and the oppressive smell caused by the bats that inhabit them in thousands. Numbers of snakes

---

[1] *Mahawanso*, ch. xxxviii.

[2] A writer in the number of *Young Ceylon*, for April, 1851, p. 77, says that having succeeded in penetrating the great gallery, which must have been constructed nearly fourteen hundred years ago, he found it "covered with a thick coat of chunam, as white and as bright as if it were only a month old, with fresco paintings, chiefly of lions, whence its name Singha-giri or Sigiri." This serves to correct an error in FORBES's *Eleven Years in Ceylon*, vol. ii. p. 2, in which the existence of the lions is disputed, and *Sikhari* is said to be an ordinary term for any "*hill-fort*."

were also discerned amongst the mounds of brickwork over which we were obliged to clamber. A bear which we disturbed retreated into one of the caves, many of which are to be found amongst the ruins; and after a toilsome scramble we returned to bathe and breakfast in the cool pansela of green branches, which the corale of Enamalua, the chief of the district, had constructed for our reception.

Whilst seated here, we witnessed the extravagances of two professional devil-dancers, who were performing a ceremony in front of a little altar, for the recovery of a patient who was dying close by. It is difficult to imagine anything more demoniac than the aspect, movements, and noises of these wild creatures; their features distorted with exertion and excitement; and their hair, in tangled ropes, tossed in all directions, as they swung round in mad contortions.

DEVIL-DANCERS.

A few miles from Sigiri, we crossed a low ridge of hills,—the Hudu-Kanda, the summit of which commands a wonderful prospect over the waving expanse of verdure that clothes the apparently unbounded range of forest stretching to the verge of the horizon. Far to the east, the broad stream of the Maha-welli-ganga is discernible, with the sunbeams dancing on its waters;—here and there a single solitary peak rises abruptly above the tops of the trees, and the vast ruins of Pollanarrua, with its enormous dagobas, each a mountain of brickwork, are as conspicuous as the hills themselves in the distance.

In this part of our journey human habitations were rare; and where they existed they were so closely concealed by the trees that the whole scene appeared a leafy solitude. The only road within miles was the one we had left at Enamalua[1]; and it is characteristic of the people of this region that, on traversing the forest, they calculate their march, not by the eye or by measures of distance, but by sounds. Thus, a "*dog's cry*," indicates a quarter of a mile; a "*cock's crow*," something more; and a "*hoo*," implies the space over which a man can be heard when shouting that particular monosyllable at the pitch of his voice.[2] As all these tests are more or less conjectural, the replies of the

[1] A curious circumstance connected with the rebellion which was imminent at the moment when I was traversing this portion of Ceylon, was reported to me by the principal civil officer, in whose district it occurred. Preparatory to the march of the Pretender to Anarajapoora, the mass of the population were observed to turn out and address themselves earnestly to clear a road through the forest, to the north of Kornegalle in the direction of Dambool, and when interrogated, they replied that a great personage was expected to arrive from India to be crowned at the temple. Does not this recall the summons of the prophet, "*Prepare ye the way of the Lord, make His path straight*," Isaiah iv. 4; Matthew iii. 3;—a cry which is rendered palpably intelligible when traversing a "wilderness" such as this over-run with jungle and trees. It is remarkable that a similar expression occurs in the *Mahawanso*, ch. xxv., in describing the march of Dutugaimunu to recover the sacred city from the usurper Elala, when "*having had a road cleared through the wilderness*, he mounted his state elephant and took the field," p. 150.

[2] This seems identical with the Scotch expression of "a far *cry* to Loch Awe." It is a curious coincidence that the Singhalese concur with the most ancient people of the East, the Chaldæans, Arabs, and Egyptians, not only in counting time by periods of *seven* days, but by distinguishing the days of the week by the planets whose names have been conferred on them. Thus Saturday by the Romans and all modern European nations has been called from *Saturn;* Sunday from the *Sun;* Monday from the *Moon;* Tuesday from *Mars;* Wednesday from *Mercury;* Thursday from *Jupiter;* and Friday from *Venus*. Amongst the Singhalese the names are as follows:—Sunday "Irida," from "*iru*" the Sun, and *da* a contraction of *dawasa* a day; Monday, "Sanduda" from "*Chanduya*," the Moon; Tuesday, "Angaharuwada" from *Angaharuwa*, the planet Mars; Wednesday "Badadada," from "*Buda*," the planet Mercury; Thursday "Brahaspatinda" from "*Brahaspati*," the planet Jupiter; Friday, "Sicurada" from "*Sikura*" the planet Venus; and Saturday, "Senasurada" from "*Senasura*," the planet Saturn. For this remark I am indebted to Mr. Mercer, late of the Ceylon Civil Service.

natives as to distances in Ceylon, must always be taken with caution; for, unlike the peasantry of Scotland, whose energy leads them to disregard toil and underestimate the ground to be travelled, a Singhalese, when asked the way to the next village, generally adds to instead of diminishing its remoteness.

On the 15th we forded the Amban-ganga, in the vicinity of Cottawellé, a Singhalese village partly inhabited by Moors, where I halted for the day, in order to hold one of those interviews with the people which, as already explained, formed the special object of my journey.[1]

The following morning, recrossing the Amban-ganga, we rode through the forest to Toparé, as Pollanarrua, the mediæval capital of Ceylon, is now called, probably from a corruption of "Topa-weva," the name of the beautiful tank on the margin of which the ruined city stands. Its waters have long shrunk within a circumscribed area, and the grand embankment along which we rode for some miles now encloses a broad savannah, beyond which, towering above the highest trees, we discern the lofty dagobas and the summit of the great temple.

No scene can be conceived more impressive than this beautiful city must have been in its pristine splendour: its stately buildings stretching along the shore of the lake, their gilded cupolas[2] reflected on its still expanse and embowered in the dense foliage of the surrounding forests. At the present day it is by far the most remarkable assemblage of ruins in Ceylon, not alone from the number and dimensions, but from the architectural superiority, of its buildings.

Pollanarrua was a place of importance at a very early period, so much so that the king, Sri Sangabo III., without

[1] A detailed account of these meetings will be found in the papers laid before Parliament, on the affairs of Ceylon, A.D. 1849, p. 137.

[2] The *Mahawanso* says that the enormous dome of the Rankot Dagoba was covered with gilding, by the Queen of Prakrama Bahu, ch. lxxii.

altogether deserting the capital, made this his favourite residence, and died here A. D. 718.[1] It had similar attractions for his successors, and Mahindo I., towards the close of the eighth century, abandoned Anarajapoora for Pollanarrua, where he erected a palace and numerous temples, one of which contained a statue of Buddha in gold. Owing to the increasing power of the Malabars, the seat of government was never again permanently restored to the north. Pollanarrua itself was captured and sacked by those insatiable marauders in 1023[2], and remained in their hands till recovered by Wijayo Bahu, the ancestor of the renowned Prakrama, A.D. 1071. Here Prakrama was crowned in 1153, and here he and his ancestors held their court till fresh disasters at the hands of their intestine foes, including the plunder of Pollanarrua a second time [3], compelled the native sovereigns to retire finally from their northern dominions, and forced them in the fourteenth century to found new capitals in the mountains of Rohuna.

It was to Prakrama Bahu I. that Pollanarrua owed the magnificence which is attested by the ruins that survive to the present day, and it is questionable whether any of the existing monuments at Toparé are of a date anterior to his accession.[4]

The *Mahawanso* tells us that, in his time, the city extended nine *gows* (or about thirty miles) in length, by four in breadth.[5] He surrounded it with a wall and gates, constructed a fort within the enceinte, built a residence for the royal family, erected numerous temples for the national worship, planted gardens, founded hospitals and schools, and rendered the new capital in every essential a rival worthy of the old. The Rankot Dagoba, whose enormous mound of masonry still towers

---

[1] TURNOUR'S *Epitome*, &c., p. 33.

[2] *Rajavali*, p. 256, &c.

[3] Pollanarrua was plundered a second time by the Malabars, A.D. 1204. *Mahawanso*, ch. lxxix.

[4] For an account of the works constructed by Prakrama I. at Pollanarrua, see *ante*, Vol. I. Pt. III. ch. xi. p. 408, 409.

[5] *Mahawanso*, ch. lxxii.

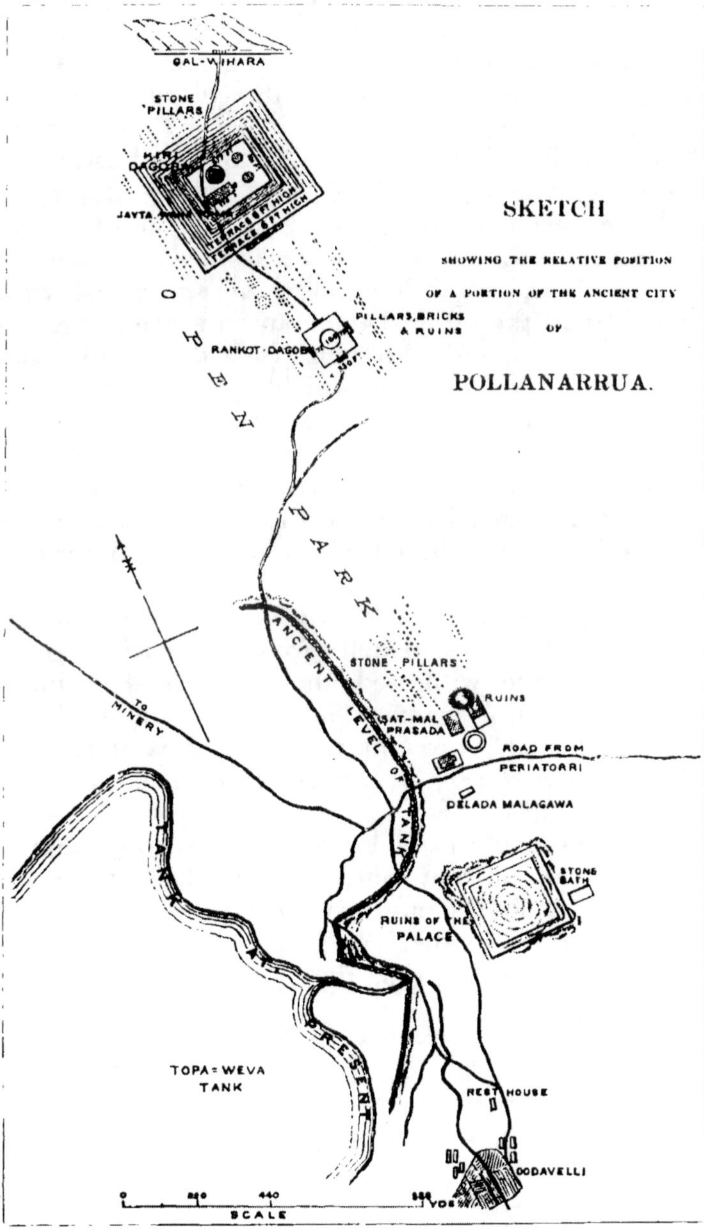
SKETCH
SHOWING THE RELATIVE POSITION
OF A PORTION OF THE ANCIENT CITY
OF
POLLANARRUA.
GAL-VIHARA
STONE PILLARS
KIRI DAGOBA
JAYTA
TERRACE 6 FT HIGH
TERRACE 6 FT HIGH
PILLARS, BRICKS & RUINS
RANKOT DAGOBA
OPEN PARK
ANCIENT LEVEL OF TANK
STONE PILLARS
RUINS
SAT-MAL PRASADA
ROAD FROM PERIATORRI
TO MINERY
DELADA MALAGAWA
STONE BATH
RUINS OF THE PALACE
TANK AT PRESENT
TOPA-WEVA TANK
REST HOUSE
DODAVELLI
0
220
440
660
YDS
SCALE

above the forest, was erected by his queen, and the beautiful lake, on whose shores these surprising edifices were raised, although formed long before his reign[1], was indebted for its enlarged dimensions to the lavish munificence of Prakrama.

The remains of Toparé appear to have been unknown to the Portuguese writers on Ceylon, although the Singhalese have a tradition that the injury done to some of the monuments was occasioned by some Portuguese soldiers, who dug there in search of treasure. Valentyn and the other Dutch authors are equally silent regarding them, and although Knox during his captivity traversed the country in which the ruins are situated, he was not aware of their existence. A British officer on his march from Bintenne to Minery, in 1817, heard of them for the first time from his Singhalese guides, and in 1820, Mr. Fagan, of the 2nd Ceylon regiment, was the first Englishman who visited and described the forgotten city.[2]

From the village of Oodoovelli, where our tents had been pitched below a patriarchal tamarind tree, old enough to have witnessed the pomp and triumphs of king Prakrama, a walk of less than a mile along the bend of the lake brought us to the ruins of the palace. This building forms a square with a large entrance hall in front, the whole raised upon a terrace of cut stone. The material is brick coated with chunam, and richly decorated, not only around the doorways and windows, but in the numerous compartments into which the exterior is divided by pilasters. The outer walls have suffered little from time, but are split in all di-

[1] It was made by Upatissa II., A.D. 400, *Rajaratnacari*, p. 74. It appears to have been repaired by King Sena, A.D. 838.—TURNOUR'S *Epitome*, p. 35.

[2] Mr. FAGAN'S account appeared in the *Ceylon Gazette*, for October, 1st, 1820, whence it was copied into the *Asiatic Journal*, vol. ix. p. 137, and vol. xvi. p. 164. Major FORBES saw and described the place in 1831, *Eleven Years in Ceylon*, vol. i. p. 391. For the ground plan which accompanies this chapter, I am indebted to Mr. Hall, of the Surveyor-General's Department, by whom it was prepared in 1840.

rections by the rending force of the fig trees, whose seeds germinating in the roof, have sent down their roots, penetrating the masonry and streaming over the walls and terraces as if the wood had been congealed from a state of fluidity. The roof, which consisted of brickwork, has partially fallen in, but several chambers

THE PALACE AT POLLANARRUA.

are still entire. From exploring these, however, we were deterred by the heat and the intolerable stench of the bats. Its superior state of preservation leads to the conjecture, that this remarkable structure is of a somewhat later date than the reign of Prakrama Bahu. But in addition to this its site and elevation do not correspond with the description in the *Mahawanso* of the palace erected by him. It stands near the southern extremity of the city, and cannot be said to consist of more than one story, whereas the royal residence of Prakrama was in the centre of Pollanarrua, and was "seven stories high, and contained four thousand rooms, with hundreds of stone columns." [1]

The present edifice was probably constructed at the close of the thirteenth century, when the city, after its destruction by the Malabars, was restored by Wijayo Bahu IV.[2], and the remains of the original palace are to be sought further north, in the direction of the Jayta-wana-rama, where groups of stone pillars and mounds of brickwork and débris serve to indicate its site. This is rendered the more likely by the presence on the spot of the *Sat-mahal-prasada*, whose name perpetuates the memory of "the seven-storied house."

THE SAT MAHAL-PRASADA

In front of this extraordinary building lies an enormous carved slab, called the *Gal-pota*, or "Stone-book," from its resemblance to a Singhalese volume of olas. It is a monolith twenty-six feet in length by more than four broad, and two feet thick, bearing an inscription, one passage of which records that

[1] *Mahawanso*, ch. lxxii.

[2] *Mahawanso*, ch. lxxxvi. lxxxviii.

"this engraved stone is the one which the strong men of the King Nissanga brought from the mountain of Mihintala at Anarajapoora," a distance of more than eighty miles.[1] The edges of the slab are richly carved with ornamental borders representing rows of the hanza, the sacred goose of the Buddhists.

A further circumstance which seems to fix the position of the palace of Prakrama at this spot is, that in connection with it the king is said, in the *Mahawanso*, to have built many "outer halls made of stone *of an oval form*, with large and small gates, glittering walls and staircases,"[2] and close by the Sat-mahal-prasada there is a building which corresponds with this description.

THE ROUND HOUSE AT TOPARÉ.

This curious edifice, which stands on a terrace and appears to have been hypæthral, is approached on four sides by staircases and gates. The walls are about

[1] A translation of the entire of this remarkable inscription, which was engraved about the year 1198 A.D., is given in the Appendix to TURNOUR'S *Epitome*, p. 94.

[2] *Mahawanso*, ch. lxxii.

twenty feet high, and are divided into compartments by pilasters. If it be not the work of Prakrama, it is probably that of Kitsen Kisdas, one of his immediate successors, who usurped the throne in 1187, and who, according to the *Rajavali*, "built the Kiri-dagoba at Pollanarrua, a house for the dalada, and a *temple of a globular form* for the same." [1]

Another remarkable building in the same group is the Dalada Malagawa, the depository of the sacred tooth during its enshrinement at Pollanarrua. The temple originally destined for this purpose was built by Prakrama Bahu [2], "at a yodun's distance from the palace;" but the ruins, as they present themselves at the present day, so closely conform to the description of the Dalada temple, as recorded in the inscription on the great stone at the Sat-makal-prasada, as to leave no doubt that this is the identical shrine formed by Kirti Nissanga about the year A.D. 1198. — "It had a covered terrace around it, and an open hall decorated with wreaths and festoons, and likewise gateways and walls." [3] How nearly this corresponds to the ground plan of the ruin may be seen from the subjoined survey.

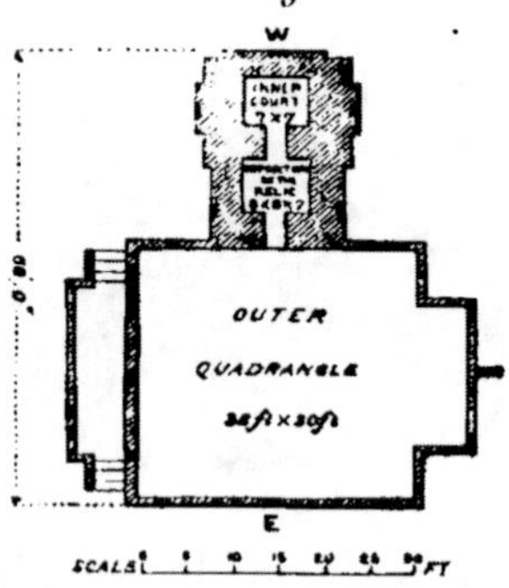

PLAN OF THE DALADA MALAGAWA.

Proceeding northward along the great street, which,

---

[1] *Rajavali*, p. 255.

[2] *Mahawanso*, ch. lxxiii.

[3] Inscription, &c. See *Appendix to* TURNOUR'S *Epitome, &c.*, p. 94; see also *Rajaratnacari*, p. 92. It was restored by Wijayo Bahu IV. A.D. 1279 (*Mahawanso*, ch. lxxxvii.), and again by Prakrama Bahu III. A.D. 1319 (*Ibid.* ch. lxxxviii.).

though grass grown is clearly discernible by the foundations of the houses that line it on either side, the path leads to the Rankot Dagoba [1], a solid mass of circular brickwork, 186 feet in diameter, and apparently about two hundred feet high.

THE RANKOT DAGOBA.

The destruction of the crust of chunam with which the monument was originally coated, has permitted the lodgment of seeds, and the trees and climbing plants with which it is now covered have fractured it in every direction, and must eventually consummate its destruction. One peculiarity which characterises this Dagoba, is the number of small structures resembling chapels, that are ranged around its base, and which, with their profusion of ornaments, add considerably to the picturesque appearance of the pile. These, from some expressions in the inscriptions on the great stone tablet, would appear to have been added by King Kirti Nissanga.

Still advancing along the main street, we come next to an immense edifice of brick, in the highest style of ornamented southern Indian architecture. This is the Jayta-wana-rama, a temple of great dimensions, built by Prakrama Bahu I., after the model, it is said, of one erected by Buddha himself at Kapili-vastu, the place of

[1] Called likewise the *Ruan-welle-saye*, or "place of golden dust."

his birth.[1] The exterior is profusely decorated with architectural devices in chunam, and the character of the whole, so unlike that of the Buddhist buildings in other parts of the island, is corroborative of the statement in the *Mahawanso*, that Prakrama the Great brought artists from the opposite coast of India to construct the buildings at Pollanarrua, and repair those of Anarajapoora.[2] The style seems to belong to the Saracenic period, and the grand entrance to the temple at the eastern end is flanked by two polygonal turrets, which forcibly recall the outline of the Kotub Minar at Delhi. The porch was originally guarded on either side by two figures in alto-relievo, only one of which remains, and at the extremity of the main aisle, is reared a gigantic statue of Buddha, formed of brickwork coated over with chunam. It is partially concealed by the débris of the fallen roof, but the portion uncovered measures fifty-eight feet in height from the knees to the crown of the head.

I had reason to regret that the destruction of the roof of this extraordinary temple, and my want of preparation for a special examination of that portion of the ruins, rendered it impossible for me to determine a highly interesting point in reference to this colossal statue. Allusion has already been made to the identity in certain particulars observable between the Buddhist temples of Ava and those of Ceylon.[3] Amongst the buildings at Pagamnyo, on the Irawaddi, is a pagoda known as the "cave of Ananda," and in it a gilded figure of Buddha, similar in attitude to that in the Jayta-wana-rama, stands in a vaulted cell, situated at the further extremity of a darkened aisle. Into the alcove in which it is placed the only light that is admitted streams through an opening so situated as to

[1] *Rajaratnacari*, p. 18; *Mahawanso*, ch. lxxvii.; *Rajavali*, p. 252. A side-view of the elevation of this temple will be found in Sir J. EMERSON TENNENT'S *History of Cristianity in Ceylon*, p. 33.

[2] *Mahawanso*, ch. lxxv., lxxvii.

[3] See *ante*, p. 578.

THE JAYTA WANA RAMA.

be unseen by the spectator in front, and thence it is poured like a halo over the head of the glorified object below.[1]

STATUE AND SECTION OF A BUDDHIST TEMPLE IN AVA.

This mode of illuminating an interior is common in the rock-cut Basilicas of India, in which "one undivided volume of light, coming through a single opening over head, falls directly on the altar or other principal object, leaving the rest of the structure in comparative obscurity."[2] The similarity of position and the identity of attitude between the two statues in Ava and Ceylon, suggest the conjecture that the figure at Pollanarrua, like that at Pagan-myo, may have been placed in the recess which it occupies, so as to admit of being lighted in a similar manner from an aperture concealed in the

---

[1] Yule's *Embassy to Ava*, p. 38.
[2] Fergusson's *Handbook of Architecture*, vol. i. p. 27, 313.

roof; and it will be an interesting inquiry, for some future explorer provided with the necessary facilities, to determine, by a minute examination of the walls, whether they may not have been so constructed as to cast a mysterious light on the gilded idol below.

Standing on the same terrace with the Jayta-wana-rama, is another dagoba somewhat smaller than the Rankot. From the snowy whiteness of the chunam with which the latter was covered, it acquired the epithet of "Kiri," which signifies milk. In its original purity this enormous dome, as fair as marble and surmounted by a gilded spire, must have been an object of beauty amidst the scenery which surrounds it. It was built A.D. 1187[1], and after a lapse of nearly seven hundred years, the *tee* by which it is crowned remains almost uninjured, and the outline of the dagoba is still clearly defined, withstanding the disruptions caused by the trees which have rooted themselves in its fissures.

In close proximity to these sacred monuments, a group of stone pillars marks the spot at which the *gam-sabawa*, or council of the municipality, held its meetings to administer justice in disputes between the citizens. This ancient institution, identical in its objects with the village *punchayets* of Hindustan, the γερουσία of the Greeks, and the assembly of "the elders in the gate" among the Jews and the Romans, still exists in Ceylon, and throughout the more secluded districts arbitrates in all matters affecting property and morals, excepting only the graver offences and crimes, of which cognisance is taken by the constituted tribunals.[2]

But the most remarkable of all the antiquities at Toparé, is the Gal-wihara, a rock temple hollowed in the face of a cliff of granitic stone which overhangs the level plain at the north of the city. So far as I am aware, it is the only example in Ceylon of an attempt to fashion an architectural design out of the rock after the

---

[1] *Rajavali*, p. 254.

[2] KNOX'S *Ceylon*, pt. ii. ch. v. p. 52.

THE GAL WIHARA AT POLLANARRUA

manner of the cave temples of Ajunta and Ellora. The temple itself is a little cell, with entrances between columns; and an altar at the rear on which is a sedent statue of Buddha, admirably carved, all forming undetached parts of the living rock. Outside, to the left, is a second sedent figure, of more colossal dimensions, and still more richly decorated; and to the right are two statues likewise of Buddha, in the usual attitudes of exhortation and repose. The length of the reclining figure to the right is forty-five feet, the upright one is twenty-three, and the sitting statue to the left sixteen feet from the pedestal to the crown of the head.

Between the little temple and the upright statue the face of the rock has been sloped and levelled to receive a verbose inscription, no doubt commemorative of the virtues and munificence of the founder. The *Mahawanso* records the formation of this rock temple by Prakrama Bahu, at the close of the twelfth century, and describes the attitude of the statues "in a sitting and a lying posture, which he caused to be hewn in the same stone."[1] With the date thus authenticated, one cannot avoid being struck by the fact that the art exhibited in the execution of these singular monuments of Ceylon was far in advance of that which was prevalent in Europe at the period when they were erected.

The objects here described are only those which lie in one direct line, and in the comparatively open ground along the embankment of the lake; these, however, form but a limited portion of the ruins existing at Toparé; the jungle for a considerable distance around is filled with similar remains, mounds of brickwork, carved stones, broken statues, fallen columns, inscribed slabs, and the walls and foundations of overthrown buildings. Nothing so lofty as the great dagobas, or so grand as the

---

[1] *Mahawanso*, ch. lxxvii.

Jayta-wana-rama is likely to have escaped observation, but the natives declare that the forest abounds with other monuments; and one offered to conduct me to a fort a few miles distant, with a statue of a king on the rampart. Of the domestic edifices and the houses of the people, not a vestige remains, except a few wells, and some baths fed by conduits from the lake.

We rode back to the village of Oodoovelli by the grass-grown street of the ancient capital, the same along which the Singhalese chroniclers relate that the Great Prakrama, "arraying himself with royal apparel, and mounted on an elephant, with a golden umbrella over his head," passed in the pomp of his military triumphs to return thanks for his victories at the shrine of the dalada.[1]

Close by the great tamarind tree, under which our tents were pitched, was a tope of coco-nut palms, that proved to be the resort of an innumerable colony of plumb-headed paroquets.[2] Our arrival having taken place in the forenoon, whilst the birds were all away, we were not at first aware of their habits; but about sunset as we were preparing for dinner, they began to come back in great numbers, chattering, screaming, and romping with delight, as they reunited after their day's excursion. Every minute the din increased as the stragglers came in, till at length their noise fairly drowned our voices in the tents. By degrees the racket subsided, and as soon as it was dark the whole multitude sank into silence and repose. But at dawning a similar scene was re-enacted, one sleepless individual awoke its mate and commenced a rapid patter of felicitations, another and another succeeded, until the whole tribe were in excitement, moving along the fronds of the palms, shaking the dew from their plumage, bowing, clamouring, coquetting, and preening their feathers.

---

[1] *Mahawanso*, ch. lxxiii.

[2] *Palæornis Alexandri*, Linn.

At length the first detachment took its departure for the forest, others followed in rapid succession, and by the time the sun was risen, the whole of the noisy community had dispersed, and we were free to turn again to sleep.

CHAP. II.

MINERY — ANARAJAPOORA — AND THE WEST COAST.

A DAY'S ride under the shade of the forest brought us from Toparé to the beautiful artificial Lake of Minery, passing on our way the tank of Girentalla, which, but for the vicinity of the "inland sea," by which it is eclipsed, would be regarded as one of the wonders of the island. Universal acclaim pronounces Minery, and the surrounding scenery, to be the most charming sylvan spot in Ceylon. The reservoir is upwards of twenty miles in circumference; but, as it lies embayed at the confluence of numerous valleys, separated by low and wooded steeps, no point upon its margin commands a view of its entire expanse. The whole scene, the hills, the hanging woods, and the glassy waters of the lake, seemed to my mind like visions of Killarney, warmed and illumined by an eastern sun. The level land, where it approached the lake, waved with luxuriant grass, so high that it almost hid the horsemen; and the shallows were so profusely covered by the leaves and flowers of the lotus as to conceal the still water.

We rode for a mile along the great embankment, which, although overgrown with lofty trees, remains nearly perfect, and the ancient conduit still gives issue to the pent-up flood that, after fertilising a considerable area, flows in a broad stream to the Mahawelli-ganga. We halted for the night in a rest-house, near the residence of the headman of the village, close by a little temple consecrated to the memory of the individual by whom the tank was constructed.

This national benefactor was no other than the apostate king, Maha Sen, who, in the third century before Christ [1], temporarily abjured the religion of Buddha, persecuted its priests, and overthrew its temples and statues. But having subsequently recanted his errors, he sought to atone for his sacrilege by restoring the monuments of "the Vanquisher," and conciliated his outraged subjects by the construction of works of utility.[2] Amongst the latter was the Lake of Minery, or *Minihiri*, which, as the native chronicles say, was formed by the conjoint labour of "men and demons;" the demons (or Yakkos) being the aborigines of the district.[3] It is a striking illustration of the grateful remembrance in which the people still hold the memory of the king by whom these enormous reservoirs were formed, that they not only forgot his apostacy, but, by a grateful apotheosis, have exalted him to the rank of a god. The small chapel near which we rested was dedicated to the *Mineria Sawmy*, "the God of the lake," and contains, as its sole relic, a bow that belonged to the deified monarch.

Till within the last few years, Minery abounded in wild animals to such an extent, that it became one of the favourite resorts of elephant hunters and of sportsmen in search of buffaloes and deer; but the increased number of guns in the hands of the natives, the annual burning of the tall grass by the peasantry, and, above all, the slaughter committed by the Moors, who dry the deer flesh on stages in the sun, preparatory to carrying it to the Kandyan hills, have reduced the quantities of game to such an extent that the spot is now rarely traversed by Europeans.

As the object of my journey rendered it essential that I should visit the numerous villages in the heart of the island before proceeding north to Anarajapoora, I turned westward on leaving Minery, crossed the great

---

[1] See *ante*, Vol. I. Pt. III. ch. vi. p. 365; and ch. viii. *Ib.* p. 381, &c.

[2] *Mahawanso*, ch. xxxv. p. 234.

[3] *Rajaratnacari*, p. 69; *Rajavali*, p. 237.

eastern road at Haboorenna, skirted the mysterious mountain of Rittagalla, which, from its having been in ancient times a retreat of the aboriginal *Yakkos*, is still believed by the peasantry to be the abode of "demons,"[1] and reached the ruins of the ancient city of Vigitapoora, near the vast Kalaweva tank, the most stupendous work of the kind in Ceylon.

The tank of Kalaweva, or Kalawapi, was formed by King Dhatu Sena about the year 460, by drawing an embankment across the Kala-oya, which, flowing from the vicinity of the great temple of Dambool, reaches the sea at Calpentyn.

Dhatu Sena was the monarch before alluded to, whose son, Mogallana, caused him to be bound "in chains and built up in a wall" — a retributive fate which, according to the *Mahawanso*, the king drew down upon himself because, when forming the Kalawapi tank, he buried a priest under the embankment, who was too profoundly absorbed in meditation to provide for his own safety.[2]

The work was conceived on the grandest imaginable scale. The area submerged was more than forty miles in circumference, the waters of the river being thrown back by the embankment, till they overflowed the low lands round the rock, which overhangs the temple of Dambool, at a distance of twenty miles from Kalaweva. In the opposite direction a canal more than sixty miles in length communicated with Anarajapoora.

The retaining bund of the tank is twelve miles long, and the spill-water, formed of hammered granite, is aptly described by Turnour as "one of the most stupendous monuments of misapplied human labour in the island."[3] This misapplication was exhibited by the inefficiency of the work, for the superfluous waters, instead

---

[1] For an explanation of these *convertible* terms, see Vol. I. Pt. III. ch. ii. p. 330.

[2] *Mahawanso*, ch. xxxviii. p. 262. See *ante*, Vol. I. Pt. III. ch. ix. p. 391.

[3] Note to the *Mahawanso*, p. 11.

of escaping by the intended overfall, burst the enormous embankment, and the tank was destroyed. This took place at a period so remote, that the area of the original lake now forms part of the forest, and venerable trees, whose dimensions attest their age, cover the long ridge of the embankment.

Vigita-poora having been the residence of a king five hundred years before the Christian era, was a fortress and a city when Anarajapoora was still a village.[1] One of the episodes in the *Mahawanso* describes its siege by Dutugaimunu, B.C. 204, when it was surrounded by a "triple battlement, and entered by a gate of iron."[2] So late as the twelfth century, the city was rebuilt and its monuments restored by Prakrama Bahu I.; but such has been the rapid decay, incident to the climate, and consequent on the desertion of the place, through fear of the malaria diffused by the bursting of the great tank, that hardly a vestige now remains except the foundations of the fort, a dagoba evidently built of bricks taken from the city wall, a few stone troughs and chiseled pillars, and the mounds of earth that serve to mark the site of the ancient buildings.

Whilst riding near the fort, our attention was suddenly attracted by an intolerable stench proceeding from the timber of a tree which was being felled by a party of natives. These, equally with ourselves, seemed overcome by the abominable smell emitted by the tree, which is known by the Singhalese as the *gooræenda* — a name expressive of this offensive quality of its wood. A gentleman long engaged in the department of the Surveyor-general, assures me, that such is the loathing and sickness produced by its fœtid odour, that when woodmen are engaged in felling a boundary, the simple word *gooræenda!* passed along the line to indicate that one of these odious trees requires to be removed,

---

[1] It was the capital of Panduwaasa, B.C. 504.—*Mahawanso*, ch. viii. p. 55.

[2] *Mahawanso*, ch. xxv. p. 152.

suffices to place the party on the alert ; — and all who can, effect their escape from the vicinity.[1]

A few years prior to my tour through this part of Ceylon, a gentleman who accompanied me on the present journey chanced to follow the track of a herd of

COLOSSAL STATUE AT THE AUKANA WIHARA

wild elephants near the tank of Kalaweva, when he suddenly found himself in front of a gigantic statue in

---

[1] The Gooroenda did not escape the keen observation of Thunberg, when he visited Ceylon in A.D. 1776, but the specimens brought to him contained neither flowers nor fruit, and hence he could only decide that it was not the *Sterculia fœtida*, nor the *Anagyris fœtida*.—THUNBERG'S *Travels*, vol. iv. pp. 234-5. The Gooroenda is not the only tree so shunned; Dr. GARDNER described in the *Calcutta Journal of Natural Hist.*, (vol. vii. p. 2) a new genus of plants which he found in Ceylon, and called *Dysodidendron*, from the offensive smell of all the species comprised in it.

the forest, whose existence had been previously unknown to Europeans. He led us to the spot, and our surprise was extreme on beholding a figure of Buddha, nearly fifty feet in height, carved from the face of a granite cliff, and so detached that only two slender ties had been left unhewn at the back to support the colossus by maintaining its attachment with living stone.

The scene was most remarkable. As usual, advantage had been taken of a group of enormous rocks, to form temples and panselas in the fissures between, and prodigious labour had been expended in hewing steps, hollowing niches, and excavating baths. There had formerly been a pandal to shelter the statue, and holes still remain in the rock which had served for the insertion of the columns that supported it. The place was deserted and silent. Close by dwelt one solitary priest, with no attendant save a neophyte, his pupil; he told us that the statue had been made by order of Prakrama Bahu [1], and that the temple in its prosperity was called *Nægampaha Estane*, but since it fell into ruins, it has been known as the Aukana Wihara.

Turning northward from the temple, a long ride through the forest brought us to the foot of the sacred hill of Mihintala, which overlooks the ancient capital Anarajapoora.

Mihintala is undoubtedly the most ancient scene of mountain worship in Ceylon. Venerated by the Singhalese ere Gotama impressed his foot-print on the summit of Adam's Peak [2], its highest point was known in the sacred legends as the Cliff of Ambatthalo, on which

[1] At Sessaeroowe Kande Wihara, on the southern verge of the Seven Corles, there is a statue which, in size, attitude, and other particulars, bears a close resemblance to that described above. Some of equally colossal dimensions are described by BUCHANAN, in his *Account of Mysore*, one in the open air at a Jain temple in Canara, and one of Gotama Raja, at Carculla, 38 feet high. Vol. iii. p. 83, 410.

[2] *Mahawanso*, ch. xiii. p. 77; FORBES' *Eleven Years in Ceylon*, vol. i. p. 384.

Mahindo alighted when arriving in Ceylon to establish the religion of Buddha. It was to a spot near the summit that the king was allured, while following a *devo* under the form of an elk, when he encountered the great apostle and became his first convert[1]; here it was that Mahindo died[2], and on this holy hill, his disciples, in remembrance of his virtues, bestowed the name of their divine teacher.[3]

The mountain is one of a few insulated elevations, which here rise suddenly from the plain; its height is upwards of a thousand feet, its slopes are densely covered with wood, and its summit is crowned by huge rocks of riven granite. Sigiri is a hill scarped into a fortress; Mihintala, a mountain carved into a temple. The ascent is on the northern side, and the southern face, which is almost precipitous, commands a magnificent view which reaches across the island from sea to sea. A flight of steps, more than a thousand in number[4], partly hewn out of the rock, but generally formed of slabs of granite fifteen feet wide, leads from the base to the highest peak of the mountain.

On a small plateau near the top, the dwellings of the priests and the principal buildings are grouped round the Ambustella dagoba, which marks the spot whereon occurred the interview between Mahindo and his royal convert Devenipiatissa. Unlike the generality of such monuments, the Ambustella is built of stone instead of brick; on a terrace encircled by octagonal pillars,

[1] *Mahawanso*, ch. xiv. p. 79.

[2] B.C. 206, *Mahawanso*, ch. xx. p. 124.

[3] It had previously been called "Missa" (*Mahawanso*, ch. xii. p. 77), and "*Missako*" (*Ibid.* ch. xvii. p. 106); and after Mahindo had deposited there the numerous relics of Buddha sent to Ceylon by Asoca, until buildings could be erected to receive them at the capital, he changed its name to *Chetiyo* (*Ibid.*); Chetiya-giri, being the capital of a kingdom, the sovereign of which was a kinsman of his own (*Ibid.* ch. xiii. p. 76). It was afterwards called "*Solomastane*," or the Place of the Sixteen Relics; and finally, Mihintala. FA HIAN, the Chinese Buddhist, calls it Po-thi,—*Foë Kouë Ki*, ch. xxxviii. p. 335, and HIOUEN THSANG, *Mo-hi-in-to-lo*. (See *Pélerins Buddhistes*, tom. ii. p. 140.)

[4] The priests told me the steps numbered *eighteen hundred and forty*, and that they had been formed by King Maha Dailiya Mana, who reigned A.D. 8.—See TURNOUR'S *Epitome*, p. 19.

the capitals of which are ornamented by carvings of the sacred goose.[1] Close beside it is a broken statue

MIHINTALA.

of the pious monarch. The cells are still remaining which, according to the *Mahawanso*, Devenipiatissa caused to be hollowed in the rock[2], and near them is the Nagasandhi tank made for the priesthood by King Aggrabodhi, A. D. 589.[3] Thence the last flight of steps leads to the summit of Ambatthalo crowned by the Etwihara dagoba, a semicircular pile of brick work one hundred feet high, which enshrines a single hair from the forehead of Buddha. This remarkable structure has stood for upwards of eighteen centuries. It was built by Baatiya Raja about the first year of the

---

[1] For the honours paid to the goose, see Vol. I. Pt. IV. ch. vii. p. 485.

[2] *Mahawanso*, ch. xii. p. 103; *Rajavali*, p. 184.

[3] *Mahawanso*, ch. xlii.

THE AMBUSTELLA DAGOBA, MIHINTALA.

Christian era, and the *Mahawanso* relates that, on its completion, the king caused it to be enveloped in a jewelled covering ornamented with pearls, and spread a foot carpet from Mihintala to Anarajapoora, that pilgrims might proceed all the way with *unwashed* feet.[1] The rock in many places bears inscriptions recording the munificence of the sovereigns of Ceylon, and the ground is strewn with the fragments of broken carved-work and the débris of ruined buildings. On the face of the cliff a ledge of granite artificially levelled is pointed out as "the bed of Mahindo," from which a view of extraordinary beauty extends over an expanse of foliage that stretches to the verge of the horizon. Towering above this ocean of verdure are the gigantic dagobas of Anarajapoora, whose artificial lakes lie glittering in the sunbeams below; and, dim in the distance, can be descried the sacred rock of Dambool, and the mysterious summit of the Ritta-galla mountain.

The road leading from the base of Mihintala to Anarajapoora, a distance of nearly eight miles, is marked by as many traces of antiquity as the Appian Way between Aricia and Rome. It passes between mouldering walls, by mounds where the grass imperfectly conceals the ruins beneath, and by fragments of fallen columns that mark the sites of perished monuments. It was the *Via Sacra* of the Buddhist hierarchy, along which they conducted processions led by their sovereigns from the temple at the capitol to the peak of Ambatthalo.[2] Though now overgrown with jungle and forest trees, it was traversed by chariots two thousand years ago, when the pious king Devenipiatissa sent his carriage to bring Mahindo to the sacred city.[3]

Passing by the noble tank of Neuera-weva, and having forded the Malwatte-oya (the Kadamba of the *Maha-*

[1] *Mahawanso,* ch. xxxiv. p. 213.

[2] *Mahawanso,* ch. xxxvii. p. 240. These processions are minutely described by FA HIAN, *Foë Koué Ki,* ch. xxxviii. p. 335.

[3] *Mahawanso,* ch. xiv. p. 80.

PLAN OF A PORTION OF THE SACRED CITY OF

ANARAJAPOORA,

FROM A SURVEY MADE BY MAJOR SKINNER, DEPUTY-ASSISTANT QUARTERMASTER-GENERAL, 1832.

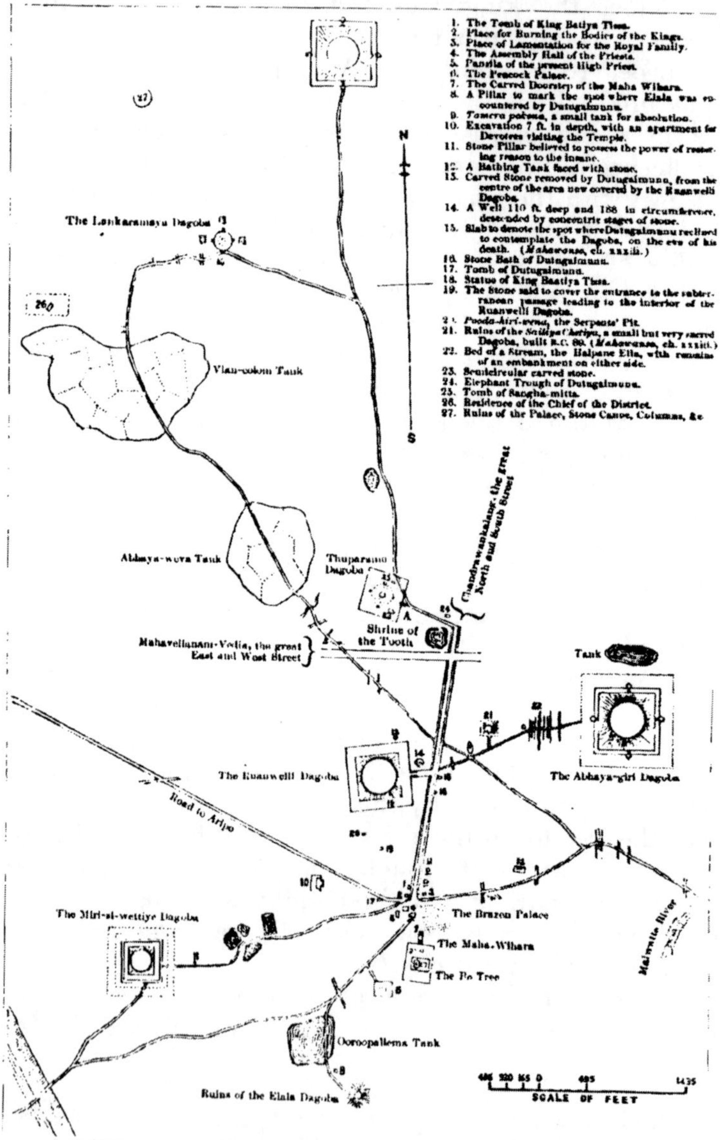

wanso), we rode through the thick forest, which covers everything with an impervious shade, except where the piety of pilgrims and devotees has caused a space to be cleared round the principal monuments. Here the air is heavy and unwholesome, vegetation is rank, and malaria broods over the waters, as they escape from the broken tanks; one of which, the Abhaya-weva, is the oldest in Ceylon.[1] The solitary city has shrunk into a few scattered huts that scarcely merit the designation of a village.[2] The humble dwelling of a government officer, the pansila of the officiating priests, a wretched bazaar, and the houses of the native headmen, are all that now remains of the metropolis of Anuradha, the "Anurogrammum Regium" of Ptolemy, the sacred capital of "the kingdom of Lions," on whose splendours the Chinese travellers of the early ages expatiated with religious fervour.[3] The present aspect of the place furnishes proofs that these encomiums were not unmerited, and shows that the whole area, extending for some miles in every direction, must have been covered with buildings of singular magnificence, surrounded by groves of odoriferous trees. It recalls the description of the palace of Kubla Khan,

> "Where twice five miles of fertile ground,
> With walls and towers, were girded round;

[1] This tank, called also the Jaya-weva, was constructed B.C. 505. *Mahawanso*, ch. x. p. 65. See *ante*, Pt. III. ch. ii. p. 328.

[2] For an account of the ancient city, as described in the Singhalese Chronicles, see Vol. I. Pt. IV. ch. vii. p. 493. Capt. CHAPMAN, Roy. Art. F.R.S., published in 1832, *Some Remarks on the Ancient City of Anarajapoora* in the *Transact. of the Roy. Asiat. Soc.* vol. iii. p. 463, and in 1852 he communicated a further paper on the same subject, which has been printed in the *Asiat. Soc. Journal*, vol. xiii. p. 164. There is also an interesting account of the Ruins, by Mr. KNIGHTON, in the *Journ. of the Asiat. Soc. of Bengal for* 1847, vol. xvi. pt. i. p. 213.

[3] FA HIAN, *Foë Kouë Ki*, ch. xxxviii. p. 333. The antiquity claimed for Anarajapoora by the *Rajaratnacari*, exceeds that assigned to it by the *Mahawanso*, the former asserting that it existed as a city before the advent of the first Buddha to Ceylon (p. 2). FORBES infers, from the absence of anything in the site and the soil to recommend it for selection as a town, that the place must have been chosen on superstitious grounds at a time when Mihintala was the scene of hill-worship, prior to the introduction of Buddhism.—*Eleven Years in Ceylon*, vol. i. ch. x. p. 207.

And there were gardens, bright with sinuous rills,
  Where blossomed many an incense-bearing tree,
And forests, ancient as the hills,
  Enfolding sunny spots of greenery."[1]

On reaching the grass-grown street which intersected the city from north to south, the first object that strikes the eye is the vast collection of stone columns, each twelve feet in height, that mark the site of the *Maha-*

RUINS OF THE BRAZEN PALACE.

lowa-paya, the "Brazen Palace" of Dutugaimunu[2]; which, according to the *Mahawanso*, was supported by "sixteen hundred pillars of rock."[3]

These pillars retain the marks of the wedges by which they were split off in the quarry, and are so rough and undressed, that they suggest the idea of having been formerly coated with chunam; a conjecture which is supported by those passages in the *Mahawanso* which describe the beauty and decorations of the original buildings.[4]

---

[1] COLERIDGE.

[2] See an account of this building, Vol. I. Pt. III. ch. v. p. 356.

[3] *Mahawanso*, ch. xxxvi.

[4] *Mahawanso*, ch. xxvii. p. 163. The *Rajavali*, p. 222, implies that they were covered with copper.—See *ante*, Vol. I. Pt. IV. ch. vii. p. 482.

In close proximity to the Brazen Palace are numerous places of interest; such as the tomb of King Batiya Tissa, the only person permitted by the priests to enter the subterranean chamber beneath the Ruanwelli dagoba[1];—the spot on which the bodies of the kings were consumed;—the "Place of Lamentation" for the royal family;—the "Rangse-malle-chetiya," an assembly-hall for the priests; and the "Palace of the Peacock," built in the first century of the Christian era.[2]

But that which renders the fallen city illustrious even in ruins, is the possession of the *Jaya Sri Maha Bodin-Wohanse*, "the Victorious, Illustrious, Supreme Lord, the Sacred Bo-Tree," the planting of which forms the grandest episode in the sacred annals of Ceylon.[3]

The Bo-tree of Anarajapoora is, in all probability, *the oldest historical tree in the world.* It was planted 288 years before Christ, and hence it is now 2147 years old. Ages varying from one to five thousand years have been assigned to the *baobabs* of Senegal, the *eucalyptus* of Tasmania, the dragon-tree of Orotava, the *Wellingtonia* of California, and the chesnut of Mount Etna.[4] But all these estimates are matters of conjecture, and such calculations, however ingenious, must be purely inferential; whereas the age of the Bo-tree is *matter of record*, its conservancy has been an object of solicitude to successive dynasties,

---

[1] *Mahawanso*, ch. xxxiv. p. 212.

[2] *Rajaratnacari*, p. 73.

[3] *Mahawanso*, ch. xviii. xix.; *Rajaratnacari*, p. 34; *Rajavali*, p. 184. For an account of the arrival of the Bo-tree from Magadha, and its planting at Anarajapoora, see *ante*, Vol. I. Pt. III. ch. iii. p. 341.

[4] DE CANDOLLE has propounded the theory that trees *do not die of old age* in the proper sense of the term, and that if uninjured externally there is no necessary limit to the duration of tree life. "On doit d'ailleurs envisager un arbre comme un être multiple, composé d'autant d'individus qu'il y a des bourgeons; à peu près comme une masse de polypes est formée par une infinité d'individus agglomérés. D'après ces considérations on a conclu avec raison, que l'âge auquel peuvent parvenir les arbres est *illimité*, et qu'ils ne périssent que par la rupture des branches qui entraîne la carie du tronc, ou par d'autres causes tout à fait accidentelles. L'observation," &c.—*Bibl. Univ. de Genève*, tom. xlvi. p. 394.

and the story of its vicissitudes has been preserved in a series of continuous chronicles amongst the most authentic that have been handed down by mankind.[1]

THE SACRED BO-TREE.

Compared with it the Oak of Ellerslie is but a sapling: and the Conqueror's Oak in Windsor Forest, barely numbers half its years. The yew-trees of Fountains Abbey are

[1] A chronological series of historical passages in which the prolonged existence of the sacred tree has been recorded, will be found in a note appended to this chapter.

believed to have flourished there twelve hundred years ago; the olives in the Garden of Gethsemane were full grown when the Saracens were expelled from Jerusalem; and the cypress of Soma, in Lombardy, is said to have been a tree in the time of Julius Cæsar; yet, the Bo-tree is older than the oldest of these by a century, and would almost seem to verify the prophecy pronounced when it was planted, that it would "flourish and be green for ever."

The degree of sanctity with which this extraordinary tree has been invested in the imagination of the Buddhists, may be compared to the feeling of veneration with which Christians would regard the attested wood of the cross. To it [1], kings have even dedicated their dominions, in testimony of their belief that it is a branch of the identical fig-tree under which Gotama Buddha reclined at Uruwelaya [2], when he underwent his apotheosis. When the king of Magadha, in compliance with the request of the sovereign of Ceylon, was willing to send him a portion of that sanctified tree to be planted at Anarajapoora, he was deterred by the reflection that "*it cannot be meet to lop it with any weapon;*" but, under the instruction of the high priest, using vermilion in a golden pencil, he made a streak on the branch, which, "*severing itself*, hovered over the mouth of a vase filled with scented soil," into which it struck its roots and descended.[3] Taking the legend as a sacred law, the Buddhist priests to the present day object religiously to "lop it with any weapon," and are contented to collect any leaves which, *severing themselves*, may chance to fall to the ground. These are regarded as treasures by the pilgrims, who carry them away to the remotest parts of the island. It is even suspected, that rather than strip the branches, the importunities of an impatient devotee are sometimes

[1] *Mahawanso*, ch. xvii. xix.

[2] *Ibid.* ch. i. (B.C. 536.)

[3] *Ibid.* ch. xviii. p. 113.

silenced by the pious fraud of substituting the foliage of some other fig for that of the exalted Bo-tree. I expressed a wish to have a few leaves of the genuine plant, and the native officer undertook to bring them to me *at night.* The other bo-trees which are found in the vicinity of every temple in Ceylon, are said to be all derived from the parent tree at Anarajapoora, but they have been propagated by seeds; the priesthood adhering in this respect to the precedent recorded in the *Mahawanso*, when Mahindo himself, "taking up a fruit as it fell, gave it to the king to plant."[1]

Nor is this superstitious anxiety a feeling of recent growth. It can be traced to the remotest periods of Buddhism; and the same homage which is paid to the tree at the present day was wont to be manifested two thousand years ago. Age after age the sacred annals record the works which successive sovereigns erected for the preservation of the Bo-tree: the walls which they built around it, the carvings with which they adorned them, and the stone steps which they constructed to lead to the sacred enclosure. The latter were raised by a king, A. D. 182[2]; and in 223, a stone ledge was added to the enclosing wall.[3] Century after century, repairs or additions to the buildings are recorded in the Singhalese annals. King Abhaya, A. D. 240, placed "a cornice on the parapet, a porch at the southern entrance, four hexagonal pillars of stone at the corners, and a statue of Buddha at each entrance."[4] His successor, Mahassen, caused "two statues of bronze to be cast and erected in the hall of the great Bo-tree;"[5] and mention is made in the sacred annals, nearly two thousand years later, of the celebration of a festival, which, "from the period when the supreme Bo-tree was planted, the rulers of Lanka held every twelfth year, for the purpose of watering it."[6]

---

1 *Mahawanso*, ch. xix.
2 *Ibid.* ch. xxxvi.
3 *Ibid.* ch. xxxvi.
4 *Ibid.* ch. xxxvi.
5 *Ibid.* ch. xxxvii.
6 *Ibid.* ch. xxxviii.

In the fifth century, Fa Hian found the Bo-tree in vigorous health, and its guardians displaying towards it the same vigilant tenderness which they exhibit at the present day: " quand l'arbre fut haut d'environ vingt *tchang* il pencha du côté du sud-est. Le roi, craignant qu'il ne tombât, le fit étayer par huit ou neuf piliers, qui formèrent une enceinte en le soutenant . . . Les religieux de la Raison (Buddhists), ont l'habitude de l'honorer sans relâche." [1]

The author of the *Mahawanso*, who wrote between the years 459 and 478 A.D., after relating the ceremonial which had been observed nearly eight hundred years before at the planting of the venerated tree by Mahindo, concludes by saying: "Thus this monarch of the forest, endowed with miraculous powers, *has stood for ages* in the delightful Maha-mego garden in Lanka, promoting the spiritual welfare of its inhabitants and the propagation of true religion." [2]

In A.D. 804, the reigning king "caused a hall to be built in honour of and near to the Bo-tree, at Anuradhapoora-neuera;" [3] and in A.D. 1153, Prakrama-Bahu "made a house around Jaya-maha Bodhin-Wohanse, *i.e.* the Bo-tree." [4] It will be observed that throughout these notices (and they are but a few out of a multitude) the object of veneration is always alluded to as "*the*" Bo-tree, no doubt having ever been suggested as to its identity; and the *Rajavali*, a still later authority than those already quoted, speaking of Wijayo-Bahu (who recovered the southern division of Ceylon from the Malabars, A.D. 1240), says he was a "descendant of the family who had brought the Bo-tree *yet existing* to Ceylon." [5]

Regarded with so much idolatry, tended with attention so unremitting, resorted to from all lands in which the name of Buddha is held in veneration, and

[1] Fa Hian, *Foë Koue Ki*, ch. xxxviii.

[2] *Mahawanso*, ch. xix.

[3] *Rajaratnacari*, p. 79.

[4] *Ibid.* p. 89.

[5] *Rajavali*, p. 257.

its vicissitudes recorded in the sacred history of an island the inhabitants of which considered themselves blessed by the possession of so heavenly a treasure; the conjecture (had it ever been hazarded) that the original tree might have died and its place been supplied by one secretly substituted, may fairly be regarded as an hypothetical impossibility. Such an event as the death of the great Bo-tree of Anarajapoora would have spread consternation, not only throughout Ceylon, but over Siam and China. It would have been regarded as a visitation too portentous to be contemplated with equanimity, and recorded with a becoming sense of the calamity, in the annals of every Buddhist nation in Asia.

It is strange, too, that amidst the intestine convulsions which so often expelled the native Singhalese sovereigns and seated the Malabar conquerors in their capital, when dagobas and temples of Buddha-worship suffered spoliation, and the most precious relics were carried away as warlike trophies, the Bo-tree was uniformly spared by the conquerors and permitted to flourish unmolested. Had it been otherwise, the Singhalese chroniclers would not have failed to arouse the indignation of the faithful by denouncing an insult offered by Brahmanical rivals to the most sacred adjunct of the Buddhist religion. But so far from this being the case not a single instance is on record of indignity offered to the tree; whilst the sacred historians recount with befitting emotion the spoliation of wiharas and the overthrow of temples.

At the present day the aspect of the tree suggests the idea of extreme antiquity; the branches, which have rambled at their will far beyond the outline of its enclosure, the rude pillars of masonry that have been carried out to support them, the retaining walls which shore up the parent stem, the time-worn steps by which the place is approached, and the grotesque carvings that decorate the stonework and friezes; all impart the conviction that the tree which they encompass has been watched over with abiding solicitude and regarded with an excess of veneration that could never attach to an object of dubious authenticity.

The marvellous tree is situated in an enclosure approached through the porch of the temple, the priests of which are charged with its preservation. The principal building is modern and plain, but amongst the materials of which it is built are some antique carvings of singular excellence. The most remarkable of these is a semicir-

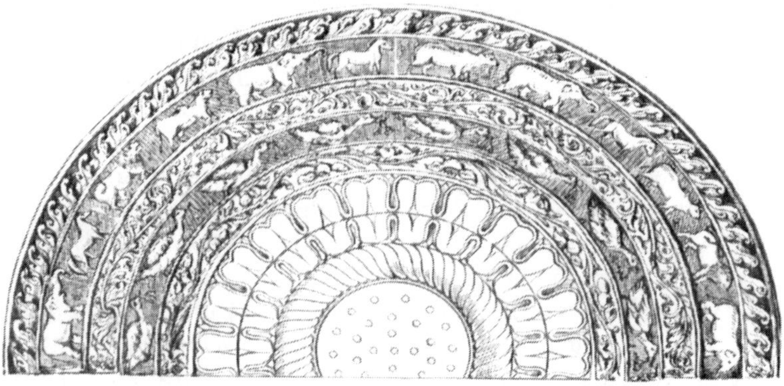

CARVED STONE AT ANARAJAPOORA.

cular slab, which now forms a doorstep to the principal entrance, and surpasses, both in the design and execution of the devices by which it is decorated, any similar relic that I have seen in Ceylon.

Its ornaments consist of concentric fillets, the three innermost of which represent the lotus in its various stages of bud, leaf, and flower; that in the centre is a row of the *hanza* or sacred goose[1], and on the outer one is a procession of the horse, the elephant, the lion, and Brahmanee ox.

In the vicinity of the Bo-tree is the spot rendered memorable by the death-struggle and tomb of the chival-

---

[1] See *ante*, Vol. I. Pt. IV. ch. vii.

rous Elala, whose defeat by Dutugaimunu has been elsewhere described.[1] A solitary column stands on the scene of the conflict, a grassy mound covers the remnants of a dagoba erected by the conqueror to commemorate his victory, and in the shade of the adjoining forest is concealed the tomb of the fallen chief, from respect for whom it was the custom of the kings "on reaching this quarter of the city to silence their musical bands;"[2] and so profound is the veneration of the Singhalese for the memory of Elala, that even to the present day the place is regarded with awe, and shown to strangers with mysterious reluctance.

Close by are the remains of one of the most ancient dagobas, the Mirisiwettye, or as it is called in the *Mahawanso*, the "*Marichawatti*," built by Dutugaimunu to commemorate the recovery of his kingdom B.C. 161.[3] It is now a mere barrow of earth overrun with jungle.

Returning by the Brazen Palace, and passing along the great northern street, the Ruanwelli, the Dagoba of the "Golden Dust," by far the most celebrated in Ceylon, is descried above the trees to the left. This enormous pile, the descriptions of which occupy so large a space in the *Mahawanso*, was begun by Dutugaimunu one hundred and sixty years before the Christian era, and completed by his successor, after having occupied almost twenty years in its erection.[4] Its original outline was destroyed by the Malabars A.D. 1214[5], but it is still a little mountain of masonry, upwards of one hundred and fifty feet high[6], overgrown with jungle and trees. The terrace which sustains it is comparatively perfect, and from its sides protrude the

[1] See *ante*, Vol. I. Pt. III. ch. V. p. 353.

[2] *Mahawanso*, ch. xxv. p. 155; see also *ante*, Vol. I. Pt. III. ch. V. p. 353.

[3] *Mahawanso*, ch. xxvi. p. 159; *Rajavali*, p. 222.

[4] *Mahawanso*, ch. xxxiii. p. 200.

[5] *Ibid.* ch. lxxix.

[6] In 1830 the height was 189 feet, but it is now less than 150 feet. A comparative view of the dimensions of the principal dagobas at Anarajapoora, may be obtained from the following diagram:—

heads of elephants, whose concealed bodies appear to be supporting the structure. Around it the pious care of the Buddhists has preserved numerous memorials of its founder; an octagonal inscribed column, which the legends say once stood in the centre of the space now occupied by the great dagoba[1]; a slab which marks the spot where Dutugaimunu died[2], and a stone with carved pilasters which covers his tomb. On the south side of the terrace is a statue of King Batiya Tissa, who reigned at the dawning of the Christian era; and in front is the entrance to the subterranean passage by which it is pretended that the priest conducted him privately to view the interior of the dagoba.[3]

Eastward from the Ruanwelli dagoba is that known as the Abhayagiri, erected by Walagam Bahu to commemorate the recovery of his throne after the expulsion of the Malabars, B.C. 87.[4] When entire, it was the most stupendous in Ceylon, having been originally four hundred and five feet high from the ground to the summit

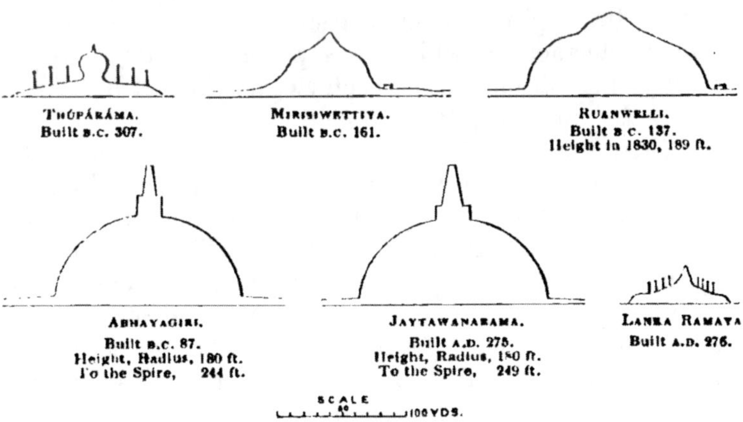

COMPARATIVE DIMENSIONS OF THE SEVERAL DAGOBAS AT ANARAJAPOORA.

[1] *Mahawanso*, ch. xxix. p. 169.

[2] *Ibid.* ch. xxxii.

[3] *Ibid.* ch. xxiv. See a notice of this tradition in the chapter on Singhalese literature, Vol. I. Pt. IV. ch. x.

[4] *Mahawanso*, ch. xxxiii. p. 206; *Rajaratnacari*, p. 41; see *ante*, Vol. I. Pt. III. ch. iv. p. 346.

of the spire. After a lapse of nearly two thousand years, and after undergoing frequent reductions and restorations, it is still upwards of two hundred and forty feet in height. Like the Ruanwelli, it too is densely covered with trees which have taken root in the clefts of the masonry, and huge heaps of displaced bricks lie in decay around its base.

Near the intersection of the two great streets of the city stands the Thuparama, the most venerated of all the dagobas in Ceylon, having been constructed by King Devenipiatissa to enshrine the collar-bone of Buddha[1], three centuries before the Christian era. So sacred was this dagoba held to be, that Upatissa, A.D. 400, caused a case to be made for it of "metal ornamented with gold;"[2] and within this last twenty years a pious priest at Anarajapoora collected funds from the devout for clearing it of the plants by which it had been previously overrun and covering it with a coating of chunam. Its outline is peculiar, being flattened at the top and so hollowed at the sides as to give it the configuration of a bell.[3] Its height is about seventy feet from the ground, and the terrace on which it is placed is surrounded by rows of monolithic pillars, each twenty-six feet high, with richly decorated capitals.

When the *dalada* was brought from India, in the fourth century[4], it was placed for security in a building at the foot of the Thuparama dagoba, and here it was shortly afterwards seen by FA HIAN.[5] The ruins of this edifice still remain, and in front of them is a semicircular stone, similar in design to that at the entrance to the great Wihara, but inferior in execution. Another remarkable object in the same vicinity is a block of granite, upwards of ten feet in length, hollowed into a cistern,

---

[1] *Mahawanso*, ch. xvii. p. 108.

[2] *Ibid.* ch. xxxvii. p. 250.

[3] See diagram, p. 621, note. A view of this dagoba, from an unpublished lithograph, by Prinsep, is given in the *Handbook of Architecture*, by FERGUSSON, who pronounces it to be "older than any monument now existing on the continent of India," vol. i. p. 41.

[4] *Mahawanso*, ch. xxxvii. p. 241.

[5] *Foĕ Kouĕ Ki*, ch. xxxviii.

which tradition has described as the trough of Dutugaimunu's elephant.

Beyond the Thuparama stands the Lanka-ramaya, a dagoba of the third century, which is still in tolerable preservation; and further to the north is the Jayta-wanarama[1], erected by Maha Sen, A.D. 330. It still rises to the height of two hundred and forty-nine feet, and is clothed to the summit with trees of the largest size.

THE JAYTA-WANA-RAMA DAGOBA.

The solid mass of masonry in this vast mound is prodigious. Its *diameter* is three hundred and sixty feet, and its present height (including the pedestal and spire) two hundred and forty-nine feet; so that the contents of the semicircular dome of brickwork and the platform of stone, seven hundred and twenty feet square and fifteen feet high, exceed *twenty millions of cubical feet.*

Even with the facilities which modern invention supplies for economising labour, the building of such a mass would at present occupy five hundred bricklayers

[1] Called *Jeta-wanno*, in the *Mahawanso.*

from six to seven years, and would involve an expenditure of at least a million sterling. The materials are sufficient to raise eight thousand houses each with twenty feet frontage, and these would form thirty streets half-a-mile in length. They would construct a town the size of Ipswich or Coventry; they would line an ordinary railway tunnel twenty miles long, or form a wall one foot in thickness and ten feet in height, reaching from London to Edinburgh.

Such are the dagobas of Anarajapoora, structures whose stupendous dimensions and the waste and misapplication of labour lavished on them are hardly outdone even in the instance of the Pyramids of Egypt. In the infancy of art, the origin of these "high places" may possibly have been the ambition to expand the earthen mound which covered the ashes of the dead into the dimensions of the eternal hills, the earliest altars for adoration and sacrifice. And in their present condition, alike defiant of decay and triumphant over time, they are invested with singular interest as monuments of an age before the people of the East had learned to hollow caves in rocks, or elevate temples on the solid earth.

For miles round Anarajapoora the surface of the country is covered with remnants and fragments of the ancient city; in some places the soil is red with the dust of crumbling bricks; broken statues of bulls and elephants, stone sarcophagi and pedestals, ornamented with grotesque human figures, lie hidden in the jungle; but the most surprising of all is the multitude of columns, "the world of hewn stone pillars," which excited the astonishment of Knox when effecting his escape from captivity.

The number of wild animals in the surrounding district is quite extraordinary. Elephants are seen close to the ruins, buffaloes luxuriate in the damp sedge, crocodiles abound in the tanks, herds of deer

---

[1] *Relation, &c.*, pt. iv. ch. ii. p. 165.

browse in the glades, bears and jackals[1] skulk amongst fallen columns, and innumerable birds, especially peafowl, jungle-cocks, and paroquets break the still solitude by their incessant calls.

Before leaving for Aripo, the priests of the great temple waited upon me bringing with them a youth, the lineal representative of an ancestor who accompanied the Bo-tree in its voyage from Magadha to Ceylon B.C. 289. The chiefship of the district has been ever since in the same family, and the boy, who bears the title of Suriya-Kumara-Singha, "Prince of the Lion and the Sun," can boast an unbroken descent, compared with whose antiquity the most renowned peerages of Europe are but creations of yesterday.

From Anarajapoora, I returned to the west coast, following the line of the Malwatte-oya[2], the ancient Kadamba, which flows into the Gulf of Manaar, north of Aripo. Within a few miles of the coast our party passed, at Taikum, the immense causeway of cut granite, two hundred and fifty yards in length, and upwards of fifteen feet high, by which it was attempted to divert the waters of the river into the canal, that was designed to supply the Giants' Tank.[3] None of the great reservoirs of Ceylon have attracted so much attention as this stupendous work. The retaining bund of the reservoir, which is three hundred feet broad at the base, can be traced for more than fifteen miles, and,

[1] It is a curious coincidence that the belief in the alleged alliance between the lion and the jackal, which seems to prevail in every country where the former exists, has extended to Ceylon, where the lion is not found; and is to be traced in one of their sacred books of the greatest antiquity. In the *Guna Jataka*, one of those legendary records which describes the transmigrations of Buddha, and which probably is coeval with the Christian era, he is introduced under the form of a lion, which having failed in seizing a deer, is carried by the force of the spring into a marsh, from which he is unable to escape till the arrival of a jackal, which "making a channel for the water to come from the lake to the feet of the lion, thus softened the mud and relieved the former from his confinement."—HARDY's *Buddhism*, ch. v. p. 113.

[2] Literally the "River of the Garden of Flowers."

[3] The modern name of the tank is "*Ka'ucarré.*"

as the country is level, the area which its waters were intended to cover would have been nearly equal to that of the lake of Geneva. At the present day the bed of the tank is the site of ten populous villages, and of eight which are now deserted.[1] Its restoration was successively an object of solicitude to the Dutch and British Governments, and surveys were ordered at various times to determine the expediency of reconstructing it.[2] Its history has always been a subject of unsatisfied inquiry, as the national chronicles contain no record of its founder. A recent discovery has, however, served to damp alike historical and utilitarian speculations; for it has been ascertained that, owing to an error in the original levels, the canal from the river, instead of feeding the tank, returned its unavailing waters to the channel of the Malwatte river. Hence the costly embankment was an utter waste of labour, and the Singhalese historians, disheartened by the failure of the attempt, appeared to have made no record of the persons or the period at which the abortive enterprise was undertaken.[3]

Along this shore of the island, the country is sultry in climate and dreary in aspect. The trees are chiefly stunted acacias, the "mustard tree" of Scripture, (*Salvadora Persica*), and the wood-apple (*Feronia elephantum*), with a copious undergrowth of the buffalo thorn[4], whose formidable spines exceed in diameter the branches from which they spring. Deer are abundant near the open glades, and the rivers and tanks literally swarm

---

[1] When the tank was surveyed by the Dutch in 1791, there were *twenty-four* villages within the area of the bed.

[2] BURNAND'S *Memoir on Ceylon*, *Asiat. Journ.*, vol. xi. p. 557. The Dutch had the tank surveyed in 1739 and in 1791. The British Government caused it to be examined with a view to restoration in 1807, and again in 1812.

[3] See *ante*, Vol. I. Pt. IV. ch. vi. p. 468. The people of the district told the Dutch Governor, Imhoff, who visited the Giant's Tank in 1739, that it had been commenced *four hundred* years before by a king who died before completing it. (*Ceylon Miscellany*. Cotta, 1843, p. 4.)

[4] *Acacia latronum.*

with crocodiles. The country around Aripo is still cultivated by industrious Tamils, descendants of a race who had established themselves there at a time when the Dutch had a garrison at Aripo for the protection of the pearl banks. Such was the abundance of provisions at that time, that Valentyn says an ox could be purchased for half a rix-dollar.[1]

For coolness as well as convenience, the road from Aripo to Putlam keeps close to the sea as far as Kudramalie, a head-land whose name, "the mountain of the horse," assists to identify it with the Hippurus or Hipporos at which (according to Pliny), the freedman of Annius Plocamus landed, whose visit to Ceylon led to the embassy despatched from the sovereign to the Emperor Claudius.[2]

The most interesting object in Putlam at the time of my visit was a Baobab tree[3] that stood near the Moorish burying-ground, and although but seventy feet high, was then forty-six feet in circumference. A very few years afterwards it was overthrown and destroyed, during the deepening of a well situated close to its roots.

Putlam[4] was probably the place at which Wijayo disembarked with his followers to undertake the conquest of Ceylon; and in 1839, the ruins of Tamana-Neuera, the city where he established his residence[5], were discovered in the forest about ten miles from the sea. It was the "*Battala*" at which Ibn Batuta landed in 1327.[6]

---

[1] *Oud en Nieuw Oost-Indien*, ch. i. p. 28.

[2] PLINY, lib. vi. c. xxii. Kudramalé still retains traces of its having been a place of importance at a very remote period. Its association with the *horse* may possibly be referable to a Hindu origin, the horse being the emblem of one of the great rivers fabled to flow from the sacred lake of Anotattho, in the mythical region of the Himalaya. The horse figures amongst the ancient stone carvings at Anarajapoora, along with the elephant and the cow, and the legend of the horse is associated with Mahavitta-puram in the peninsula of Jaffna.

[3] *Adansonia digitata.*

[4] Putlam was called by the Portuguese, *Portaloon.*

[5] *Rajaratnacari*, p. 27; *Rajavali*, p. 168; *Mahawanso*, ch. vii. p. 47. An account of the ruins of Tamana Neuera was communicated by CASIE CHITTY to the Royal Asiatic Society in 1841, and published in their *Journal*, vol. vi. p. 242.

[6] See *ante*, Vol. I. Pt. v. ch. ii. p. 330.

Then, as now, the main source of employment for the population was derived from the salt-works, which still constitute the principal wealth of the place.[1]

A great estuary, or "*gobb*," separates Putlam from the peninsula of Calpentyn, the population of which, chiefly Tamils and Moors, are amongst the most industrious in Ceylon. The soil is admirably suited for the growth of the coco-nut palm, of which large plantations have been formed in recent years, and considerable quantities are annually exported of a lichen (*Rocella fuciformis* of Acharius), which yields the red orchil dye. Though too shallow for shipping, the bay is actively traversed by dhoneys and ballams; and a canal formed by the Dutch, maintains the communication with Colombo.

The bay of Calpentyn has always been remarkable for an extraordinary abundance of fish[2]; and there is a considerable trade in that article salt and dried; as well as in sharks' fins and trepang for exportation to China. The shore also produces an esculent fucus, nearly allied to *Chondrus crispus;* and known as "Calpentyn moss." The turtle, which are caught here in staked enclosures called *sars*, are the finest in Ceylon; but the fishermen express their dread of the sea-snakes[3] which infest the

[1] An interesting paper on the *Manufacture of Salt at Putlam*, by A. O. Brodie, Esq., will be found in the *Journ. of the Ceylon Branch of the Asiat. Soc. for* 1847, vol. ii. p. 99.

[2] Valentyn says, "If there is any place on the surface of the globe in which fish is more abundant than another, it is Calpentyn."—*Oud en Nieuw Oost-Indien*, ch. xv. p. 222.

[3] *Hydrus Major?* Shaw. In the course of an attempt which was recently made to place a lighthouse on the great rocks off the southern coast of Ceylon, known by seamen as the Basses, or *Baros*, the workmen who first landed found that portion of the surface liable to be covered by the tides, honey-combed, and sunk into deep holes filled with water, in which were abundance of fishes and molluscs. Some of these cavities contained also sea snakes from four to five feet long, which were described as having the head "hooded like the Cobra de Capello, and of a light grey colour, slightly speckled. They coiled themselves like serpents on land, and darted at poles thrust in among them. The Singhalese who accompanied the party, said that they not only bit venomously, but crushed the limb of any intruder in their coils." The Basses are believed to be the remnants of the island of Giri, swallowed up by the sea.—*Mahawanso*, ch. i. p. 4; see *ante*, Vol. I. Pt. i. ch. i. p. 7. They may possibly be the *Bassæ* of Ptolemy's map.

shallows, and whose bite they believe to be fatal. Shells[1] are so abundant on the shore of the bay that they serve to supply the district with lime. The capabilities of Calpentyn were so highly appreciated by the Dutch that, on wresting the peninsula from the Portuguese, they constructed a fort, the buildings of which are in tolerable repair, and introduced the vine, which still flourishes in the peninsula.[2]

Calpentyn has of late years attained celebrity from a statue of St. Ann, which is said to work miracles, and to whose shrine pilgrims resort in thousands, not Roman Catholics alone but Mahometans and Hindus, who, without absolute faith in St. Ann, think it polite to be respectful to her representative, whom they address as *Hanna Bibi.*

Chilaw, the *Salabham* of the Tamils and the *Salawat* through which Ibn Batuta passed on his way to Adam's Peak, is a place of no great antiquity. It was wrested from the king of Ceylon by the Tamils in the fourteenth century[3], and though nominally recovered, it was never virtually restored, having been occupied in turn by the Moors, the Portuguese, and Dutch, from the last of whom it was taken by the English in 1796.[4]

From Chilaw to Negombo the road passes through almost continuous coco-nut plantations; and in the

---

[1] Owing to the profusion of dead shells, the shore at Calpentyn is so frequented by hermit-crabs, that on approaching their haunts the beach seems all in motion as they hasten to conceal themselves, hurrying to and fro, and clashing their shells together in their precipitancy and confusion.

[2] VALENTYN, *Oud en Nieuw Oost-Indien*, ch. xv. p. 223.

[3] *Rajavali*, p. 264.

[4] The forest to the east of Chilaw contains, within a radius of twenty or thirty miles, the ruins of a number of ancient cities; amongst others, Dambedenia, near the Kaymel river, which was the capital of Wijayo Bahu III., A.D. 1235; and Yapahoo, north of the Dedroo Oya, where the Court was held from A.D. 1301, till its removal to Kornegalle a few years later. The only remains of the former are some finely chiselled columns amongst mounds of grass-grown rubbish and hidden brickwork. At Yapahoo there are extensive ruins, a doorway fourteen feet high, supported by granite pillars carrying an ornamental frieze, and a window admitting the light through apertures perforated in a richly carved entablature, the tracery on which contains figures of the lion and the sacred goose.

shade of the palms one hears the creaking of the primitive mills, which, from time immemorial, have been used by the natives for expressing the oil. Under a large banyan-tree on the side of the highway, near the village of Madampé, is an altar to Tannavilla Abhaya, a chief who, in the fourteenth century, ruled over the district, under the title of king of Madampé. He died by his own hand; but, in gratitude for his services, his subjects celebrated his apotheosis, and the people now worship him as the tutelary deity of the place.

Negombo, although, according to Burnouf, its name, *Naga-bouh*, would imply that it was the "land of the serpent worshippers" (*Nagas*)[1], was a place of no importance till the Portuguese took possession of it as a sanitary station, and erected a small enclosure defended by five guns, under the command of a captain, with a few soldiers and a chaplain.[2] The Dutch, struck with the commercial value of the district, and its adaptability for the growth of cinnamon, converted the stockade into a fortress with four batteries, for the protection of the Chalias in their employment.[3] The result justified their foresight, and Valentyn pronounces that the cinnamon grown at Negombo was "the best in the known world, as well as the most abundant."[4]

The encomium was not misplaced; and, so long as the finest qualities of the spice were in demand, the specimens grown at Kaderani commanded the highest prices. Of late years, however, the enterprise has been less remunerative, and the cultivation of coco-nuts has superseded that of cinnamon. The town still retains its external aspect of importance; the fort, though no longer garrisoned, is in effective repair, and the white

---

[1] *Journal Asiatique*, tom. viii. p. 134. The ordinary derivation of Negombo is, however, *Mi-gamoa*, the "village of bees."

[2] HAAFNER, *Voyages, &c.*, tom. i. p. 368; RIBEYRO, p. i. ch. xii.

[3] VALENTYN, *Oud en Nieuw Oost-Indien*, ch. xiii. p. 26.

[4] *Ibid.*, p. 166. See *ante*, Vol. I. Pt. v. ch. ii.

villas of the Dutch burghers give it an aspect of cheerfulness and prosperity.

At Negombo I was met by an orderly from the Governor, with an express, to apprise me that a rebellion had broken out in the central provinces, and that a king having been crowned in the temple of Dambool was then on his march towards Kandy, with an armed force of adherents. My horses were instantly ordered, and early in the morning of the 30th of July, 1848, I returned to Colombo.

NOTE TO CHAPTER II.

THE SACRED BO-TREE.

THE following passages serving to indicate the prolonged existence of the Bo-tree planted by Devenipiatissa, B.C. 288, and to identify it with the tree still existing at Anarajapoora, are extracted from the several historical works which treat of Ceylon.

B.C. 288. The tree was planted by Devenipiatissa. (*Mahawanso*, ch. xix. p. 121.)

B.C. 161. The King Dutugaimunu "caused a splendid and magnificent festival of offerings to the Bo-tree to be celebrated." (*Mahawanso*, ch. xxvi. p. 165.)

B.C. 136. The King Batiyatissa I., "in honour of the pre-eminent Bo-tree, celebrated annually, without intermission, the solemn festival of watering it." (*Mahawanso*, ch. xxxiv. p. 212.

A.D. 62. "The King Waahsaba kept up an illumination of one thousand lamps at the Chetiyo mountain at the Thuparama, at the Mahathupo, and at the Bo-tree." (*Mahawanso*, ch. xxxv. p. 221.) "He also caused exquisite statues to be formed of the four Buddhas of their exact stature, and built an edifice to contain them near the delightful Bo-tree." (*Ibid.*)

A.D. 179. "The next king was called Koohoona Raja, who caused a stone stair to be erected on the four sides of the consecrated Bo-gaha tree." *Rajaratnacari*, p. 60; *Mahawanso*, ch. xxxvi. p. 226.)

A.D. 201. King Waira Tissa "caused to be formed two halls, one at the Maha wihara, and another on the south-east side of the Bo-tree, and two metallic images, for them." (*Mahawanso*, ch. xxxvi. p. 226; *Rajaratnacari*, p. 60.)

A.D. 223. King Abha Sen "built a stone ledge around the Bo-tree." (*Mahawanso*, ch. xxxvi. p. 228.) "Such was his zeal for the true religion, that he caused a pavement of marble to be made around the Bo-gaha-tree." (*Rajaratnacari*, p. 61.)

A.D. 231. "On the demise of Abha Sri Naaga, the son of his brother reigned two years in Lanka. This monarch repaired the wall around the great Bo-tree." (*Mahawanso*, ch. xxxvi. p. 228.)

A.D. 240. King Gothaabhaya, "at the place of the Bo-gaha, caused to be erected three houses of stone, in each of which he placed a figure of Buddha sitting." (*Rajaratnacari*, p. 65.) "At the great Bo-tree he added a stone ledge or cornice to its parapet wall, a porch at its southern entrance, and at its four corners he placed hexagonal stone pillars. Having had three stone images of Buddha made, he placed them at the three entrances, as well as a stone altar at the southern entrance." (*Mahawanso*, ch. xxxvi. p. 232.)

A.D. 253. "On the demise of his father, Detoo Tissa succeeded to the monarchy. He built three portal arches at the great Bo-tree." (*Mahawanso*, ch. xxxvi. p. 233.)

A.D. 275. Even the schismatic Maha Sen respected the sanctity of the Bo-tree, and during his period of hostility to the priesthood, he "built a hall for the reception of an image of Buddha at the Bo-tree, and a delightful edifice for relics, as well as a quadrangular hall." (*Mahawanso*, ch. xxxvii. p. 235.) And at a subsequent period, after his reconciliation to the church, "the Raja, having had two brazen images cast, placed them in the hall of the great Bo-tree." (*Ibid.*, p. 236.)

A.D. 301. His son Sri Meghawarna, having prepared a statue of Mahindo to be placed on Mihintala, conveyed it in a solemn procession through the city of Anarajapoora, "and kept it for three months in the precincts of the Bo-tree." (*Mahawanso*, ch. xxxvii. p. 241.)

A.D. 329. The same king "celebrated a festival at the Bo-tree in the twenty-eighth year of his reign." (*Ibid.*, p. 242.)

A.D. 414. FA HIAN, the Chinese traveller, saw the Bo-tree at Anarajapoora, and calls it "l'arbre *Pei-to*." His narrative leaves little doubt as to its being identical with the tree whose planting is commemorated in the *Mahawanso*. FA HIAN describes its inclination to one side, and the erection of pillars to support its branches:—"Les anciens rois de ce pays envoyèrent dans 'le royaume du Milieu' chercher des graines de l'arbre *Pei-to*. On les planta à côté de la salle de Foë. Quand l'arbre fut haut d'environ vingt tchang, il pencha du côté du sud-est. Le roi craignant qu'il ne tombât, le fit étayer par huit ou neuf piliers qui formèrent une enceinte en le soutenant. L'arbre au milieu de la place où il s'appuyait, poussa une branche qui perça un pilier, descendit à terre et prit racine. Sa grandeur est environ de quatre *wei*. Ces piliers, quoiqu'ils soient fendus par le milieu, et tout déjectés, ne sont cependant pas enlevés par les hommes. Au-dessous de l'arbre on a élevé une chapelle dans laquelle est une statue assise. Les religieux de la Raison ont l'habitude de l'honorer sans relâche."—(FA HIAN, *Foë kouë ki*, cxxxviii. p. 332.)

A.D. 459. The King Dhaatu Sena, "employing his army therein, restored the Maha-wihara as well as the edifice of the Bo-tree." (*Mahawanso*, ch. xxxviii. p. 256.) "He celebrated a festival for the purpose of watering the supreme Bo-tree: from the period the tree had been planted, the rulers in Lanka had held such a festival every twelfth year." (*Ibid.*, p. 257.)

A.D. 459—478. Mahanamo, the author of this portion of the *Mahawanso*, who wrote between the years 459 A.D. and 478 A.D., says, after describing the ceremony of planting it: "Thus this monarch of the forest endowed with miraculous powers has stood for ages in the delightful Mahamego garden in Lanka, promoting the spiritual welfare of the inhabitants, and the propagation of true religion." (*Mahawanso*, ch. xix. p. 121.)

A.D. 534. Silaakaali Raja "made daily offerings to the Bo-tree, and placed an altar before it." (*Mahawanso*, ch. xli. TURNOUR's MS. Transl.)

A.D. 567. The King Kitsri-Magha "covered the edifice of the Bo-tree with sheets of lead." (*Mahawanso*, ch. xli. TURNOUR's MS. Transl.)

A.D. 586. Maha-Naga "constructed a parapet wall round the Bo-tree, and covered it with a golden edifice." (*Mahawanso*, ch. xli. TURNOUR's MS. Transl.)

A.D. 815. King Kuda Daapula Raja "caused to be built a house in honour of and near to the Bo-tree at Anuradhe-pura-Nuwara; he caused to be made a figure of Buddha in gold, and was a favourable king to the religion of Buddha." (*Rajaratnacari*, p. 79, TURNOUR's *Epitome*, p. 33; *Mahawanso*, ch. xlix.)

A.D. 1153. King Prakrama Bahu "repaired all the decayed palaces of the city, cleared away the jungle, and made a house around the Jaya maha Bodin wohanse, *i. e.* the Bo-tree." (*Rajaratnacari*, p. 89; *Rajavali*, p. 253; *Mahawanso*, ch. lxiv.)

A.D. 1240. The author of the portion of the *Rajavali* which records the reign of Wijayo Bahu, speaking of the exhaustion of the solar race and the accession of those kings of mingled blood who followed them, describes them as the "descendants of the family who had brought to Ceylon *the Bo-tree still existing*." (*Rajavali*, p. 257.)

A.D. 1675. According to a pretended prophecy, the city of Sitawacca, destroyed by the Portuguese in the wars with Maaya Dunnai, was to be rebuilt "whenever the Bo-tree of Anarajapoora should lose one of its branches;" and in 1674, when it was learned that a branch of the famous tree had been struck by lightning, the Dutch took advantage of the popular feeling to restore some of the buildings. (VALENTYN, ch. xv. p. 230.)

A.D. 1724. VALENTYN, who wrote his great work on Ceylon about the close of the 17th century (he went to India in A.D. 1686), says, in speaking of the Bo-tree, "which tree is still to be seen at the Great Pagoda," at Anarajapoora. (VALENTYN, ch. iv.)

A.D. 1739. King Raja Singha, who built his palace at Hanguranketti near Kandy, caused it to be inscribed on a rock, that he had "dedicated lands in the Wanny to the sacred Bo-tree." (FORBES's *Eleven Years in Ceylon*, vol. ii. p. 119.)

INDEX.

THE END.